THE COMPLETE
GOSPELS

Translation Panel

The Scholars Version

Editor in Chief: † Robert W. Funk, Westar Institute

Harold W. Attridge, Yale University
† Edward F. Beutner, Westar Institute
Ron Cameron, Wesleyan University
John Dominic Crossan, DePaul University
Jon B. Daniels, Defiance College
Arthur J. Dewey, Xavier University
Joanna Dewey, Episcopal Divinity School
Robert T. Fortna, Vassar College
Charles W. Hedrick, Southwest Missouri State University
Julian V. Hills, Marquette University
Ronald F. Hock, University of Southern California
Roy W. Hoover, Whitman College
Eduard Iricinschi, Van Leer Institute
Arland D. Jacobson, Concordia College
Lance Jenott, Princeton University
Perry V. Kea, University of Indianapolis
Karen L. King, Harvard Divinity School
John S. Kloppenborg, University of Toronto
Helmut Koester, Harvard Divinity School
Lane C. McGaughy, Willamette University
Marvin W. Meyer, Chapman University
Robert J. Miller, Juniata College
Stephen J. Patterson, Willamette University
† Daryl D. Schmidt, Texas Christian University
Bernard Brandon Scott, Phillips Theological Seminary
Philip Sellew, University of Minnesota
Christine R. Shea, Ball State University
Mahlon H. Smith, Rutgers University
Philippa Townsend, Ursinus College

THE COMPLETE
GOSPELS

The Scholars Version

FOURTH EDITION

Robert J. Miller, editor

POLEBRIDGE PRESS
Salem, Oregon

in memory of

Bob Funk

Daryl Schmidt

Ed Beutner

Cover and interior design by Robaire Ream

Library of Congress Cataloging-in-Publication Data

Bible. N.T. Gospels. English. Scholars. 2010.
 The complete Gospels : the scholars version / Robert J. Miller, editor. --
4th ed.
    p. cm.
ISBN 978-1-59815-018-6 (alk. paper)
I. Miller, Robert J. (Robert Joseph), 1954- II. Title.
BS2553.S24 2010
226'.05208--dc22

                                    2010031832

Mixed Sources
Product group from well-managed
forests and other controlled sources
www.fsc.org Cert no. SW-COC-002283
© 1996 Forest Stewardship Council

Contents

Acknowledgments

Robert Funk, founder of the Westar Institute and Polebridge Press, conceived the original idea of the Scholars Version translation and *The Complete Gospels*. He was the driving force behind the project. He recruited the original team of scholars, refereed their debates, and lent his prodigious knowledge of Greek to our deliberations. SV is the collective product of all the participants, yet Bob Funk is the one person without whom it would not have come to be. His death deprived us of one of the twentieth century's most eminent grammarians of the Greek language, a visionary leader, and a genuine friend.

Daryl Schmidt worked tirelessly and selflessly on the SV panel. Though every page of SV was shaped by his contributions, he steadfastly deflected the personal credit he so richly deserved. Daryl exemplified for us all the highest ideals of collegiality. His broad and deep expertise in Greek was surpassed only by the generosity of his spirit.

Edward Beutner, poet and wordsmith extraordinaire, also labored enthusiastically throughout the translation project. His infectious delight in the artful play of language inspired many of the felicitous turns of phrase in SV. Ed served the gospels both as a priest and a scholar, and sought for himself only the quiet satisfactions of contributing to a project in which he deeply believed. His genuine humanity was a gift to all who were privileged to know him.

This book is dedicated to the memory of our three departed friends and colleagues.

Joanna Dewey, Perry Kea, and Arthur Dewey worked with skill and dedication for over two years to revise the SV translation.

Char Matejovsky managed the production of the volume and devised the book's design, arranging the mass of information on the page in a way both friendly to the user and pleasing to the eye. Her endless patience, cheerful perseverance, and prevenient good sense have made the book more than the sum of its parts.

Contributors

Harold Attridge is the Reverend Henry L. Slack Dean of Yale Divinity School & Lillian Claus Professor of New Testament at Yale University, New Haven, Connecticut.

Infancy Gospel of Thomas: draft translation, introduction, notes

Ron Cameron is Professor of Religion at Wesleyan University, Middletown, Connecticut.

Secret Book of James: draft translation

John Dominic Crossan is Professor Emeritus of Biblical Studies at DePaul University, Chicago.

Oxyrhynchus Gospel 1224: draft translation, introduction, notes

Jon B. Daniels was Assistant Professor of Religious Studies at Defiance College, Defiance, Ohio.

Egerton Gospel: draft translation, introduction, notes

Arthur J. Dewey is Professor of Theology at Xavier University, Cincinnati, Ohio.

Gospel of Peter: draft translation, introduction, notes
Scholars Version Revision Committee

Joanna Dewey is the Harvey H. Guthrie, Jr. Professor Emerita of Biblical Studies at Episcopal Divinity School, Cambridge, Massachusetts.

Gospel of Mark: introduction
Scholars Version Revision Committee

Robert T. Fortna is Professor Emeritus of Religion at Vassar College, Poughkeepsie, New York.

Signs Gospel, Gospel of John: draft translation, introduction, notes

† **Robert W. Funk** was director of the Westar Institute and publisher of Polebridge Press.

Oxyrhynchus Gospel 840: draft translation
Editor-in-Chief, The Scholars Version

Charles W. Hedrick is Distinguished Professor Emeritus of Religious Studies at Southwest Missouri State University, Springfield, Missouri.

Gospel of the Savior: draft translation, introduction, notes

Julian V. Hills is Associate Professor of Theology at Marquette University, Milwaukee, Wisconsin.

> *Dialogue of the Savior: draft translation, introduction, notes*
> *Gospel of John: draft translation*

Ronald F. Hock is Professor of Religion at the University of Southern California, Los Angeles.

> *Infancy Gospel of James: draft translation, introduction, notes*
> *Infancy Gospel of Thomas: draft translation, introduction, notes*

Eduard Iricinschi is Polonsky Postdoctoral Fellow at the Van Leer Institute in Jerusalem.

> *Gospel of Judas: draft translation, introduction, notes*

Arland D. Jacobson is the retired Director of the CHARIS Ecumenical Center at Concordia College, Moorhead, Minnesota.

> *Sayings Gospel Q: introduction, notes*

Lance Jenott is a Ph.D. Candidate in Religion at Princeton University, Princeton, New Jersey.

> *Gospel of Judas: draft translation, introduction, notes*

Perry Kea is Associate Professor of Religion and Philosophy at the University of Indianapolis in Indiana.

> *Scholars Version Revision Committee*

Karen L. King is Hollis Professor of Divinity at Harvard Divinity School, Cambridge, Massachusetts.

> *Gospel of Mary: draft translation, introduction, notes*

John S. Kloppenborg is Professor of Religion at the Department and Centre for the Study of Religion at the University of Toronto.

> *Gospel of the Hebrews, Nazoreans, and Ebionites: draft translations, introductions, notes*

Helmut Koester is John H. Morison Research Professor of Divinity and Winn Research Professor of Ecclesiastical History at Harvard Divinity School, Cambridge, Massachusetts.

> *Mystical Gospel of Mark: draft translation, introduction, notes*

Marvin W. Meyer is Griset Professor of Bible and Christian Studies at Chapman University, Orange, California.

> *Gospel of Thomas: draft translation*

Robert J. Miller is Rosenberger Professor of Religious Studies and Christian Thought at Juniata College, Huntingdon, Pennsylvania.
Gospel of Luke: draft translation, introduction, notes
Gospel of John: notes
Gospels of the Hebrews, Nazoreans, and Ebionites: introductions, notes
Oxyrhynchus Gospel 1224: introduction, notes
Scholars Version Revision Committee

Stephen J. Patterson is George H. Atkinson Professor of Religious and Ethical Studies at Willamette University, Salem, Oregon.
Gospel of Thomas: draft translation, introduction, notes
Orphan Sayings & Stories: draft translations, introduction, notes
Mystical Gospel of Mark: draft translation, introduction, notes

Donald Rappé is Associate Professor of Theology at Mount Mary College, Milwaukee, Wisconsin.
Secret Book of James: introduction, notes

† **Daryl D. Schmidt** was Professor of Religion at Texas Christian University, Fort Worth, Texas
Editor, Greek text of the gospels
General Editor, The Scholars Version

Bernard Brandon Scott is Darbeth Distinguished Professor of New Testament at Phillips Theological Seminary, Tulsa, Oklahoma.
Gospel of Matthew: draft translation, introduction, notes

Philip Sellew is Associate Professor of Classical Studies at the University of Minnesota, Minneapolis.
Gospel of Mark: draft translation, introduction, notes
Oxyrhynchus Gospel 840: introduction, notes

Philippa Townsend is Assistant Professor of Philosophy and Religion at Ursinus College, Collegeville, Pennsylvania.
Gospel of Judas: draft translation, introduction, notes

Sigla

Used in the translation

⟨ ⟩   Pointed brackets indicate a subject, object, or other element implied by the original language and supplied by the translator.

[ ]   Square brackets indicate words which have been restored from a lacuna or emended from a scribal error. (See the essay on *Emendation and restoration,* pp. 331–32.)

[. . .]   A lacuna or gap in the manuscript that cannot be satisfactorily restored.

( )   Parentheses are used in the usual sense, to indicate parenthetical remarks and narrative asides in the original text.

Used in cross references

Cross references are to passages in the canonical books of the Old and New Testaments and in the extracanonical works included in this volume. Occasionally, the notes refer to especially significant parallel passages in extracanonical texts not included in *The Complete Gospels.* In these cases, the passages referred to are quoted in the notes.

//   Primary parallel: a pericope or saying with a significant degree of verbal similarity

Cf.   Secondary parallel: a similar or comparable passage with a low degree of verbal similarity

◊   Old Testament reference: an Old Testament passage quoted or alluded to, or Old Testament laws or customs presupposed in a gospel passage

Ⓓ   A doublet: a duplicate version of a story or saying within the same gospel

Ⓘ   Narrative index: a reference to an earlier or later event narrated in the same gospel

Q   The Sayings Gospel Q (found only in Matthew and Luke): a passage in Matthew or Luke also found in Q

Ⓢ   Source reference (only in the Infancy Gospel of James): an Old Testament or New Testament passage whose wording or substance is used to create a new passage

Ⓣ   Thematic parallel: a passage with a comparable theme or motif

How to Use this Book

Birth of Jesus

Astrologers from the East

Titles of narrative segments, indicated in bold print

¹⁷In sum, the generations from Abraham to David come to fourteen, those from David to the Babylonian Exile come to fourteen, and those from the Babylonian Exile to the Anointed also come to fourteen.

¹⁸**The genesis of Jesus** the Anointed was as follows. While his mother Mary was betrothed to Joseph, but before she moved in with him, she was found to be pregnant by the holy spirit. ¹⁹Although Joseph her husband was a virtuous man, he didn't want to expose her publicly; so he planned to break off their betrothal quietly.

²⁰While he was thinking about these things, a messenger of the Lord appeared to him in a dream with these words: "Joseph, son of David, don't hesitate to take Mary as your wife, since the holy spirit is responsible for her pregnancy. ²¹She will give birth to a son and you will name him Jesus, because he will save his people from their sins." ²²All of this happened in order to fulfill the prediction of the Lord spoken through the prophet:

> ²³Look, a young woman will conceive her first child
>> and she will give birth to a son,
>> and they will name him Emmanuel.

(The name means "God is with us").

²⁴Joseph got up and did what the messenger of the Lord told him: he took Mary as his wife. ²⁵He did not sleep with her until she had given birth to a son. Joseph named him Jesus.

2 **Jesus was born** in Bethlehem, Judea, when Herod was king. Astrologers from the East showed up in Jerusalem just then. ²"Tell us," they said, "where

Cross references to parallels, quotations, and allusions

1:18–25
//Lk 2:1–7
1:20
⊕ Mt 2:12, 19, 22; 27:19
1:23
◊ Is 7:14 (LXX), Is 8:8, 10 (LXX); ⊕ Mt 18:20, 28:20
2:1–6
//Lk 2:8–14

Notes on the original text

1:18 A few mss omit *Jesus*.
1:25 Some mss read "her firstborn" son.

Comments

1:17 Matthew has arranged this genealogy around the number 14, which is the numerical value of David's name in Hebrew. There are only thirteen generations in the last group from the Babylonian exile to the Anointed One.
1:19 Because Joseph was *virtuous*, he was committed to obeying the Jewish law which prohibited a man from marrying a woman who was carrying someone else's child (see Deut 22:28–29). His reverence for the law is balanced by his compassion, which is evident in his desire not to humiliate Mary by a public divorce, a divorce being necessary to undo a betrothal.
1:20 *Dreams* are often occasions for revelations; e.g., Jacob's dreams (Gen 20:12), Joseph's dreams (Genesis 37), or Daniel's interpretations of dreams (Daniel 2).
1:21 The Greek name *Jesus* is derived from the Hebrew "Joshua" which according to popular etymology means "Yahweh is salvation." This multilingual wordplay is echoed in this verse.
1:23 This is the first of a number of distinctive quotations of the Old Testament introduced by a nearly identical formula. (See the cameo essay for an explanation of the translation of Isaiah's prophecy.)
1:25 The act of naming the child is tantamount to adoption, claiming the child as his own. Thus Jesus is a legal son of Joseph.
2:1 *Bethlehem*, a few miles south of Jerusalem, was the ancestral home of David (1 Sam 16:1), as well as the burial place of Rachel (Gen 35:19), whose lament is mentioned in 2:18. The city also figures prominently in the story of Ruth, who is mentioned in the genealogy.

Abbreviations

Acts	Acts of the Apostles	Judg, Jgs	Judges
Amos, Am	Amos	1–2 Kgs	1–2 Kings
Bar	Baruch	Lam	Lamentations
BCE	before the Common Era	Lev, Lv	Leviticus
CE	of the Common Era	Luke, Lk	Gospel of Luke
1–2 Chr	1–2 Chronicles	LXX	the Septuagint, the Greek translation of the OT
Col	Colossians		
1–2 Cor	1–2 Corinthians	1–2 Macc, Mc	1–2 Maccabees
Dan, Dn	Daniel	Mal	Malachi
Deut, Dt	Deuteronomy	Mark, Mk	Gospel of Mark
DialSav, DSav	Dialogue of the Savior	Mary	Gospel of Mary
Eccl	Ecclesiastes	Matt, Mt	Gospel of Matthew
EgerG	Egerton Gospel	Mic, Mi	Micah
Eph	Ephesians	ms(s)	manuscript(s)
2 Esd	2 Esdras	MysMk	Mystical Gospel of Mark
Esth, Est	Esther	Nah	Nahum
Exod, Ex	Exodus	Neh	Nehemiah
Ezek, Ez	Ezekiel	NT	New Testament
Ezra, Ezr	Ezra	Num, Nm	Numbers
Gal	Galatians	Obad, Ob	Obadiah
GEbi	Gospel of the Ebionites	OT	Old Testament
Gen, Gn	Genesis	Pet	Gospel of Peter
GHeb	Gospel of the Hebrews	1–2 Pet	1–2 Peter
GNaz	Gospel of the Nazoreans	Phil	Philippians
GOxy 840	Gospel Oxyrhynchus 840	Phlm	Philemon
GOxy 1224	Gospel Oxyrhynchus 1224	POxy	Papyrus Oxyrhynchus
GSav	Gospel of the Savior	Prov, Prv	Proverbs
Hab	Habakkuk	Ps(s)	Psalms
Hag	Haggai	Rev, Rv	Revelation
Heb	Hebrews	Rom	Romans
Hos	Hosea	Ruth, Ru	Ruth
InJas	Infancy Gospel of James	1–2 Sam, Sm	1–2 Samuel
InThom	Infancy Gospel of Thomas	SecJas, SJas	Secret Book of James
IQP	the International Q Project	SG	Signs Gospel
Isa, Is	Isaiah	Sir	Sirach
Jas	James	Sus	Susanna
Jdt	Judith	SV	the Scholars Version translation
Jer	Jeremiah		
Job	Job	1–2 Thess, Thes	1–2 Thessalonians
Joel	Joel	Thom, Th	Gospel of Thomas
John, Jn	Gospel of John	1–2 Tim, Tm	1–2 Timothy
1–2–3 John, Jn	1–2–3 John	Titus, Ti	Titus
Jonah, Jon	Jonah	Tob	Tobit
Josh, Jos	Joshua	Wis	Wisdom
Judas	Gospel of Judas	Zech, Zec	Zechariah
Jude	Letter of Jude	Zeph	Zephaniah

ΠΟΥΧΣΕΙΣΤΟΜΝΗ
ΜΕΙΟΝΚΑΙΒΛΕΠΕΙ
ΤΟΝΛΙΘΟΝΗΡΜΕΝ
ΛΠΟΤΗΣΘΥΡΑΣΕΚΤ
ΜΝΗΜΙΟΥΤΡΕΧΕΙ
ΚΑΙΕΡΧΕΤΑΙΠΡΟΣ
ΣΙΜΩΝΑΠΕΤΡΟΝ
ΚΑΙΠΡΟΣΤΟΝΑΛΛ
ΜΑΘΗΤΗΝΟΝΕΦΙ
ΛΕΙΟΙΣΚΑΙΛΕΓΕΙ
ΤΟΙΣΗΡΑΝΤΟΝΚΝ
ΕΚΤΟΥΜΝΗΜΙΟΥΚΑΙ
ΟΥΚΟΙΔΑΜΕΝΠΟΥ
ΕΘΗΚΑΝΑΥΤΟΝΕΞΗΛ
ΘΕΝΟΥΝΟΠΕΤΡΟ
ΚΑΙΟΑΛΛΟΣΜΑΘΗ
ΤΗΣΚΑΙΕΤΡΕΧΟΝ
ΔΥΟΟΜΟΥΠΡΟΕ
ΔΡΑΜΕΝΔΕΤΑΧΙΟΝ
ΤΟΥΠΕΤΡΟΥΚΑΙΗΛ
ΘΕΝΕΙΣΤΟΜΝΗΜ
ΠΡΩΤΟΣΚΑΙΠΑΡΑΚ
ΤΑΣΒΛΕΠΕΙΤΑΟΘΟ
ΝΙΑΚΕΙΜΕΝΑΚΑΙ
ΤΟΣΟΥΔΑΡΙΟΝΟΗΝ
ΕΠΙΤΗΣΚΕΦΑΛΗ
ΑΥΤΟΥΟΥΜΕΤΑΤΩ
ΟΘΟΝΙΩΝΚΕΙΜ
ΑΛΛΑΧΩΡΙΣΕΝΤ
ΛΙΓΜΕΝΟΝΕΙΣΕΝΑ
ΤΟΠΟΝΤΟΤΕΟΥΝ
ΕΙΣΗΛΘΕΝΚΑΙΟΑ
ΛΟΣΜΑΘΗΤΗΣΟ
ΘΩΝΠΡΩΤΟΣΕΙ
ΤΟΜΝΗΜΙΟΝΚΑΙ
ΕΙΔΕΝΚΑΙΕΠΙΣΤ
ΣΕΝΟΥΔΕΠΩΙΔΑ
ΗΔΕΙΤΗΝΓΡΑΦΗΝ
ΟΤΙΔΕΙΑΥΤΟΝΕΚ
ΚΡΩΝΑΝΑΣΤΗΝ
ΑΠΗΛΘΟΝΟΥΝΠΑ
ΛΙΝΠΡΟΣΑΥΤΟΥ
ΜΑΘΗΤΑΙΜΑΡΙΑΜ
ΔΕΙΣΤΗΚΕΙΕΝΤΩ
ΜΝΗΜΙΩΚΛΑΙΟΥ
ΣΑΩΣΟΥΝΕΚΛΑΙ
ΠΑΡΕΚΥΨΕΝΕΙΣΤ
ΜΝΗΜΙΟΝΚΑΙ

Codex Sinaiticus was discovered at St. Catherine's monastery in the Sinai peninsula in 1844. Shown here is a column of New Testament folio 60 containing John 20:1–11. The Greek is written in all capital letters without word breaks or punctuation, and contains numerous marginal corrections. See page 2 (over) for an English representation of the passage. *Photograph courtesy of the British Library. Used by permission.*

~&THEYMAKETHEIR
WAYTOTHETOMB

~BUTHEDIDNTGOINTHEN
SIMONPETERCOMESALONG
BEHINDHIMANDWENTINHE
TOOSEESTHESTRIPSOF
BURIALCLOTHTHERE

COMESTOTHETOMBANDSE
ESTHATTHESTONEHASBEE
NMOVEDAWAYSOSHERUNS
ANDCOMESTOSIMONPETER
ANDTHEOTHERDISCIPLETHE
ONETHATJESUSLOVEDAND
TELLSTHEMTHEYVETAKEN
THEMASTERFROMTHETOM
BANDWEDON'TKNOWWHE
RETHEYVEPUTHIMSOPETER
ANDTHEOTHERDISCIPLEWE
NTOUT̃ANDTHETWOOFTHE
MWERERUNNINGALONGTO
GETHER̃FASTERTHANPETER
ANDWASTHEFIRSTTOREACH
THETOMBSTOOPINGDOWNH
ECOULDSEETHESTRIPSOFBUR
IALCLOTHLYINGTHERẼANDA
LSOTHECLOTHTHEYHADUSE
DTOCOVERHISHEADLYINGN
OTWITHTHESTRIPSOFBURIAL
CLOTHBUTROLLEDUPBYITSE
LFTHENTHEOTHERDISCIPLE
WHOHADBEENTHEFIRSTTOR
EACHTHETOMBCAMEINHESA
WALLTHISANDHEBELIEVED
BUTSINCENEITHEROFTHEM
YETUNDERSTOODTHEPROPH
ECYTHATHEWASDESTINEDTO
RISEFROMTHEDEADTHESEDIS
CIPLESWENTBACKHOMEMAR
YHOWEVERSTOODCRYINGOU
TSIDEANDINHERTEARSSHEST
OOPEDTOLOOKINTOTHETOMB

~&BUTTHEOTHER
DISCIPLERAN

Introduction

The Complete Gospels offers its readers several distinctive features.

First, it is the premier publication of the Scholars Version translation of the gospels, and represents the efforts of a group of independent scholars to capture the meaning of the original documents in living American English and in a text that is entirely free of ecclesiastical control.

The Complete Gospels is also the first publication to include both the canonical gospels and their principal extracanonical counterparts under one cover. Within this anthology can be found:

- the lost *Q Gospel*, in a reconstructed text that is the fruit of years of critical scholarly work. The Q Gospel is a crucial literary source for the Gospels of Matthew and Luke.
- the first publication for the general reader of the *Signs Gospel*, which many believe underlies the canonical Gospel of John, and is thus older than the Fourth Gospel.
- the first publication for the general reader of the fragmentary *Gospel of the Savior*, which was discovered in the 1990s, as well as the *Gospel of Judas*, which came to light in 2006.
- the first publication of the miscellaneous collection we call "Orphan Sayings and Stories"—anecdotes and sayings that never found a firm place in the manuscript tradition of any particular gospel, but which nevertheless survived as notes in one or more manuscripts.

The Complete Gospels offers introductions to each gospel together with notes and cross references in order to provide readers with information necessary for the critical study of the texts. The *introductions* set each text in its ancient historical and religious contexts, and discuss the overall structure and central themes. The *cross references* point out the numerous parallel passages, intratextual indicators, and thematic parallels in order to help the reader see how the individual passages of a gospel fit into the rich tapestry of Jewish and early Christian texts. The *notes* explain important translation issues, supply necessary background information, offer guidance in understanding difficult passages, and honestly indicate problems in the texts or in our understanding of them. Our contributors drop the pretense that scholars have all the answers. We strive to avoid both talking down to readers and talking over their heads. Our goal is to make these fascinating ancient texts intelligible and inviting to all who are willing to devote the necessary time and effort to study them.

What is a gospel?

The word "gospel" translates the Greek *euangelion,* which literally means "good news." The term first appears in Christian literature in the letters of Paul, where it already has a technical sense, referring to the message about the death, resurrection, and return of Jesus Christ (e.g., 1 Cor 15:1–5). While two of the four New Testament narratives about Jesus contain the word "gospel" (it is missing in Luke and John), they use it to indicate not the written works themselves, but rather the message preached either by Jesus (Matthew) or about him (Mark). Not until the middle of the second century are documents recounting the words and deeds of Jesus called gospels.

The New Testament gospels are complex works of literature that draw on a variety of oral and written sources—some claiming to come from the lips of Jesus and some telling about him—that include miracle stories, collections of his parables and sayings, traditions about his birth and childhood, and stories about his death and resurrection. To be sure, these different formats for preserving and transmitting Jesus traditions influenced the shape of the New Testament narrative gospels; in addition, however, they often became crystallized into distinctive literary works that were also called gospels, but not all of which took the form of narratives.

The Complete Gospels presents examples of these different gospel forms. Besides the four New Testament gospels, we find what may be called a miracle gospel (the Signs Gospel), infancy gospels (the Infancy Gospels of James and Thomas), and a passion gospel (the Gospel of Peter). In addition are sayings and discourse gospels: the Q Gospel; the Gospels of Thomas, Mary, and Judas; the Secret Book of James; and the Dialogue of the Savior. Also included are fragments of gospels whose full character and ancient titles are unknown (the Gospel of the Savior, the Gospels of the Hebrews, Nazoreans, and Ebionites, the Egerton Gospel, and the Oxyrhynchus Gospels 840 and 1224), an esoteric edition of a New Testament gospel (the Mystical Gospel of Mark), and some free-floating Jesus traditions (our so-called orphan sayings and stories).

What records have survived?

No manuscripts from the hands of the original authors of the gospels survive. All of our gospels, then, come to us at several removes from their authors. Mark, Matthew, Luke, and John are preserved in about 3, 500 manuscripts. Best represented among these manuscripts is the Gospel of John, which was as much a favorite in the ancient Christian community as it is in modern times. The Greek texts behind our English translation are reconstructions produced by patient and exacting comparison of thousands of differences in wording among the numerous copies. Most of the other gospels, however, come to us from the ancient world on the most meager of surviving records.

Of the eighteen other gospels in this volume, only two are amply represented by surviving manuscripts: the infancy gospels, James and Thomas. The large number of extant copies of these witnesses to the popularity of stories about the births of Mary and Jesus, and the wondrous activities of the young Jesus.

Nine of our gospels are so rare that each is known to us on the basis of a single precious manuscript: the Gospels of Peter and Judas, the Secret Book of James, the Dialogue of the Savior, the Gospel of the Savior, the Egerton Gospel, the Mystical Gospel of Mark, and the Oxyrhynchus Gospels 840 and 1224. The Gospel of Thomas is preserved in full form only in Coptic, but it has also survived in three important Greek fragments, which attest to the fact that it was originally written in Greek. The incomplete Gospel of Mary appears in Coptic and several Greek fragments.

Several of our gospels are not even preserved in their original language. All but one of the gospels in this anthology were originally written in Greek, but the Gospel of Thomas (except for the Greek fragments), the Secret Book of James, the Dialogue of the Savior, the Gospel of Judas, and the Gospel of the Savior are known to us only in Coptic translations. Five gospels exist only in fragmentary form: the Gospel of Peter, the Gospel of the Savior, the Egerton Gospel, and the Oxyrhynchus Gospels 840 and 1224. One gospel (Dialogue of the Savior) has numerous gaps in the manuscript, one (Gospel of Judas) is missing a considerable portion of its text, and another one (Gospel of Mary) is missing about half of its pages. The Gospels of the Hebrews, Ebionites, and Nazoreans are preserved only in fragments, in the writings of the early Christian authors who quoted from them. The Mystical Gospel of Mark is available only in a transcription made by an eighteenth-century scholar.

The other two gospels in this volume (the Signs Gospel and the Q Gospel) are not even "texts" in the strict sense, since we have no manuscript copies of them at all. They have been reconstructed by being isolated from the larger texts in which they are embedded: the Signs Gospel from John, and Q from Matthew and Luke.

Beyond the holy four

Most who have sought to understand the words and deeds of Jesus and the traditions about him have confined their attention to the New Testament gospels. Those texts are readily available and have been intensively studied. Many interested in Jesus were not even aware of the existence of other gospels, or if they knew of them, did not know where to find them. While scholars had access to these documents—they are called "extracanonical" gospels because they were not included in the scriptural canon—and could study them in the original languages, the vast majority of scholars tended to dismiss these other gospels as unimportant, on the hasty assumption that all of them were fanciful elaborations based on the New Testament gospels, or at least came from a much later period. However, research in the last several decades has significantly broadened our understanding of the diversity and complexity of the early Jesus traditions. Many scholars now find it necessary to turn to the extracanonical gospels to learn about the development of even the earliest Jesus traditions. These texts disclose to us how Christian communities gathered, arranged, modified, embellished, interpreted, and created traditions about the teachings and deeds of Jesus. All of the canonical and extracanonical texts in this volume are witnesses to early Jesus traditions. And all of them contain traditions independent of the New Testament gospels.

Authorized and canonical

During the first few centuries after Jesus, most Christian communities, if they were fortunate enough to possess written gospels at all, contented themselves with one or more of the four major gospels. These predominant narratives eventually gained formal ecclesiastical approval in the fourth century with a ruling by the Greek-speaking hierarchy that the only gospels authorized for official use—that is, those belonging to the rule or norm of the church and therefore canonical—were the texts attributed to Matthew, Mark, Luke, and John. However, in earlier centuries many Christians had cherished other gospels that they sincerely believed to embody revealed truths about Jesus. It is only from the perspective of later centuries that these texts, which nourished the faith of generations of Christians, can be called non-canonical. The distinction between the canonical and the non-canonical gospels did not exist in the period of Christian origins, and therefore is not helpful for understanding the earliest centuries of Christianity in their rich diversity. In short, texts excluded from the canon of the New Testament nevertheless disclose valuable historical information—and may still offer spiritual inspiration.

The Complete Gospels

The Complete Gospels makes available to the general reader all the principal texts required for the critical study of the early gospel tradition. In addition to the four New Testament gospels, other gospels were selected with three considerations in mind. The extracanonical gospels selected are those which

1. date from the first and second centuries;
2. are more or less independent of the canonical gospels and contain significant material that is not derived from them; and
3. significantly contribute to our understanding of the developments in the Jesus traditions leading up to and surrounding the New Testament gospels.

The list of the gospels in this volume was determined after lengthy discussions by a panel of scholars who teach college and seminary courses on the New Testament. The canonical gospels are sufficiently well known not to require an introduction here. But it may be helpful to summarize the nature and value of the remaining texts.

The *Signs Gospel is* a source for most of the narrative in the Gospel of John, and may well be the earliest written account of the deeds of Jesus.

The *Q Gospel*, source for much of Jesus' teaching recorded in the Gospels of Matthew and Luke, witnesses to a very early stage of theological reflection in the Jesus tradition.

Core elements of the *Gospel of Thomas* are as old as the synoptic gospels, and have proven a valuable source for the teachings of the historical Jesus. In its later layer, Thomas is the record of a Christian community creatively accommodating influences from the philosophical-religious tradition known as Middle Platonism.

The *Secret Book of James* and the *Dialogue of the Savior* show the modulation in the form of the sayings gospel from the simple collection of sayings we see in Thomas to their amalgamation into extended discourses and dialogues, a development in the use and interpretation of Jesus' sayings that is paralleled in the Gospel of John.

The *Gospel of Mary* is an historical window into both the interpretation of the teaching of Jesus from the perspectives of ancient philosophy and the heated debate among early Christians about the role of women in the churches.

The *Gospel of Judas* takes the familiar story of the betrayal and sacrifice of Jesus and explores its ethical and theological implications. It also strongly criticizes Christian leaders who glorified martyrdom.

The *Infancy Gospels of James and Thomas* testify to the popular, if theologically unsophisticated, interest among early Christians in elaborating and embellishing the edifying biographical circumstances of Jesus' birth, childhood, and family background.

The *Gospel of Peter,* in the partial form in which we have it, is an early passion gospel with important differences from the other passion narratives. It may contain, in an embedded source document, the primary material for the passion and resurrection stories in the canonical gospels.

The *Gospel of the Savior*, which shares a common tradition with the Gospels of Matthew, John, and Thomas, reflects many of the early stages of the Jesus tradition: individual sayings, collections of loosely associated sayings, brief dialogues between Jesus and his disciples, and a creative retelling of the passion story. Some sayings in this gospel may reflect the earliest level of the Jesus tradition.

The *Egerton Gospel* and the *Oxyrhynchus Gospels 840* and *1224* are fragmentary remnants of early, independent, and otherwise unknown gospels that display parallels to the canonical gospels.

The *Mystical Gospel of Mark* consists of excerpts from a variant edition of the Gospel of Mark, and might represent an earlier version of Mark than the one in the New Testament.

The fragments of the *Gospels of the Hebrews, Nazoreans, and Ebionites* represent distinctive ways in which Jewish Christians interpreted the Jesus tradition.

The twenty-two gospels and gospel fragments in this volume, not including the orphan sayings and stories, are the principal texts needed for understanding the early Jesus traditions. While other orthodox and heretical gospels are required for tracing later developments, *The Complete Gospels* is designed to serve the needs of the teacher, student, and lay reader at all but the most advanced level.

In keeping with the attempt to present a "complete" collection of gospels for the general reader, three selections have been added in this new edition: two newly discovered gospels (the Gospel of Judas and the Gospel of the Savior) and a critically reconstructed text of the Q Gospel.

The Translation

The primary aim of the Scholars Version (SV) is to recreate for the contemporary reader an approximation of the experience of the original audiences of the gospels. In striving to achieve this ideal, the translators of SV have been guided by three convictions about the original texts of the gospels: they were written in the language of everyday life, they were intended to be read aloud, and they often used ordinary words to express religious meanings. Much of SV's distinctiveness is the result of its translators' commitment to enable these qualities of the ancient language to shine through in SV's contemporary English.

Principle One: Plain talk

The Greek of the gospels was the Greek of the marketplace, not the Greek of high literature. However, most English translations, especially those sponsored by church bodies or Bible societies, render the gospels into an elevated and formal English appropriate to communal worship and private devotion. SV, by contrast, attempts to translate the gospels into the living language used by speakers of American English. Some comparisons between SV and NRSV (the New Revised Standard Version) can illustrate the difference between the two levels of language. (NRSV is an appropriate contrast because of its descent from the iconic King James Version, its very wide acceptance, and its attempt to mirror the phrasing of the original Greek.) In the exchange between a leper and Jesus in Mark 1:40–41, the NRSV's leper says, "If you choose, you can make me clean," and Jesus replies, "I do choose. Be made clean." In SV the leper says, "If you want to, you can make me clean;" Jesus replies, "Okay—you're clean." In another example, Jesus yells at a shouting demon to "Shut up" (Mark 1:25), using the same command as he does when rebuking a fierce storm in Mark 4:39: "Be quiet; shut up!" Contrast that with NRSV's "Be silent" to the demon and "Peace! Be Still!" to the storm. In SV Mark 2:17, people wonder about Jesus, asking themselves, "Why does this guy talk like this?" That question in NRSV comes out, "Why does this fellow speak in this way?"

No doubt some readers will be surprised that Jesus would say "Okay" and "Shut up" or that he would be referred to as a "guy." Such surprise only shows how accustomed today's readers are to expect that biblical characters should speak more formally than the readers themselves do.

Principle Two: Sounds like us

The gospels, like all ancient writings, were written to be *heard*, not read silently. SV therefore aims at English that sounds natural to American ears. To this end SV uses contractions when they sound natural in spoken English. For example,

Jesus says, "Don't pass judgment, so you won't be judged" (Matt 7:1), "Ask—it'll be given to you; seek—you'll find" (Matt 7:7), and frequently emphasizes his pronouncements by opening them with "I'm telling you."

In the process of preparing SV, draft translations were read aloud by many people and repeatedly adjusted until the language "sounded right." One particular goal of this effort was that proverbial sayings should sound like proverbs. Here are three examples, paired with their NRSV counterparts for contrast.

Matt 6:21

SV: What you treasure is your heart's true measure.
NRSV: Where your treasure is, there your heart will be also.

Mark 2:17

SV: Since when do the able-bodied need a doctor? It's the sick who do.
NRSV: Those who are well have no need of a physician, but those who are sick.

Mark 4:9

SV: Anyone here with two good ears, use 'em.
NRSV: Let anyone with ears to hear listen.

The oral quality of the gospels is especially evident in the Gospel of Mark. A distinctive feature of Mark's narrative style is the way he tells his story as a series of events that follow each other in rapid succession. Mark often strings sentences together with conjunctions (frequently a simple "and") and fast paced adverbs (he is fond of the Greek word that means "right away"). The scene in which Jesus heals Peter's mother-in-law (Mark 1:29–31) provides a good illustration of Mark's pacing:

> And right away they left the meeting place and entered the house of Simon and Andrew along with James and John. Simon's mother-in-law was in bed with a fever, and they told him about her right away. He went up to her, took hold of her hand, raised her up, and the fever disappeared. Then she started looking after them.

An unusual aspect of Mark's oral style is his preference for telling his story in the present tense, as if the events are happening right as he narrates them. In many passages Mark abruptly switches back and forth between present and past tenses. Observe, for example, Mark 1:40–41.

> Then a leper comes up to him, pleads with him, falls down on his knees, and says to him, "If you want to, you can make me clean."
> Although Jesus was indignant, he stretched out his hand, touched him, and says to him, "Okay—you're clean!"

It is noteworthy that Luke changed over 150 of Mark's present tenses into the past tense, reflecting Luke's more cultivated—though less vivid—literary style. Luke's version of the above scene reads as follows:

There was this man covered with leprosy. Seeing Jesus, he knelt with his face to the ground and begged him, "Master, if you want to, you can make me clean."

Jesus stretched out his hand, touched him, saying, "Okay—you're clean!" (Luke 5:12–13)

Other English translations follow Luke's practice of correcting Mark by translating his present tenses as past, thereby losing some of the liveliness and oral quality of his narration. SV lets Mark's present tenses come through in English.

Another characteristic of Mark's narrative style in his use of the Greek imperfect tense, which is often used to describe repeated or typical past actions (as in "the birds would sing every morning"). Observe how the verbs function in Mark 4:1–2 as SV faithfully reproduces Mark's present and imperfect tenses.

¹Once again he started to teach beside the sea. An enormous crowd gathers around him, so he climbs into a boat and sits there on the water facing the huge crowd on the shore.

²He would then teach them many things in parables. In the course of his teaching he would tell them . . .

The present tenses in verse 1 make for vivid narration, while the imperfect tenses ("would teach" and "would tell") in verse 2 signal that this kind of thing happened more than once, that Jesus typically told parables on occasions like this. Among the parables he told was the parable of the sower (Mark 4:2–8), at the end of which Mark reports, "And he would say, 'Anyone here with two good ears, use 'em'" (4:9). The imperfect form "would say" gives the impression that it was Jesus' habit to conclude his parables by challenging his listeners to search out their meanings. Contrast that with the NRSV translation of Mark 4:1–2, 9.

¹Again he began to teach beside the sea. Such a very large crowd gathered around him that he got into a boat on the sea and sat there, while the whole crowd was beside the sea on the land.

²He began to teach them many things in parables, and in his teaching he said to them . . .

⁹And he said, "Let anyone with ears to hear listen."

Not only does NRSV bleach out Mark's present tenses, but as English translations customarily do, it renders Mark's imperfects as simple pasts, thereby making what Mark describes as a typical practice seem like a one-time event.

Principle Three: Pre-theological

The gospels borrowed a number of terms and expressions from the ordinary language of the day to refer to religious concepts emerging within the early Jesus movements. Over time those terms acquired specialized theological or sacred connotations, but for the gospels' first audiences such words were embedded in their ordinary speech. SV seeks to recover these nuances by "de-theologizing" some key gospel terms, that is, translating ancient terms with words that restore their original secular connotations. The Greek word *pistis*, for example, traditionally translated "faith," usually appears in SV as "trust." In SV Jesus assures those whom he heals, "Your trust has made you well," in contrast to the standard English translation, "Your faith has saved you." This example also shows how SV chooses "made well" to convey the original sense of recovery from a physical ailment, rather than the theologically loaded "saved." In the same spirit, SV opts for "congregation" over "church" and "meeting place" over "synagogue." In another example, when the gospels apply to Jesus the Greek word *kyrios* in its usual sense of a boss or owner of a slave, SV translates "master" rather than "lord," an English word rooted in the British class system. SV reserves "Lord" for instances when *kyrios* refers to God, since Greek-speaking Jews had long used the word that way by the time the gospels were written.

In some cases, SV achieves a measure of de-theologizing simply by using lower case letters for some words that are traditionally capitalized. (Ancient Greek was originally written entirely in capital letters, as the picture of Codex Sinaiticus on p. 1 illustrates. Capitalized English nouns therefore reflect the interpretive decisions of translators.) SV thus uses "son" even when it refers to Jesus and chooses not to capitalize "holy spirit" (see the cameo essay on pp. 441–42). Nor does it capitalize "temple," even when referring to the grand temple in Jerusalem. SV also uses lower case pronouns when referring to God. SV reserves capitals for titles that function as proper names: for example, "the Human One," "the Anointed One," "the Baptizer," "the Sabbath," "Law" when it refers to Torah, "Father" when it is a title for God, and "Heaven" when, in Matthew's gospel, it serves as a circumlocution for God (see the note to Matt 3:2). Similarly, the introductions, notes, and essays in this volume capitalize "gospel" only when it is part of a title—thus, "the Gospel of John," but "John's gospel."

Although SV aims to render the gospels in the language of twenty-first-century Americans, its readers are reminded that the setting of the gospels was an ancient world, and foreign to us in significant ways. For example, in passages that mention money, SV uses the ancient names for currencies rather than converting them into approximate dollar amounts. The exceptions are two passages where SV uses colloquial English to convey the hyperbolically high and pitifully low monetary values in play: in the parable in which a debtor owes a "gazillion dollars" (Matt 18:24) and when Jesus poignantly asks, "What do two sparrows cost? A couple of bucks?" (Matt 10:29).

SV does not downplay the harsh realities of the ancient world that might be repugnant to most contemporary readers. For example, slavery was a mainstay of ancient economies and therefore a ubiquitous feature of everyday life. Some English translations soften that brutal reality by often referring to slaves as "servants." SV uses "slaves" whenever the original language does. A second example may be even more disturbing. In the ancient Jewish communities where the Christian movements got started, differences over religious issues were often argued with a fierceness that can be offensive to modern sensitivities shaped by religious tolerance. SV aims to convey the intensity of such polemics by, for example, allowing Jesus to "damn" his religious opponents, rather than resort to the euphemistic and archaic "woe" that appears in most English translations. And SV has Jesus bluntly tell the unrepentant city of Capernaum, "You'll go to hell" rather than using the less direct and somewhat quaint "You will be brought down to Hades" of the NRSV (Luke 10:15).

SV avoids sexist language for humanity whenever possible, using gender inclusive terms except when the passage refers to a specific man or woman. When Greek masculine singular pronouns refer to people and not solely to males, SV typically converts them into genderless plurals or "you" or "he and she." However, SV generally maintains the masculine pronoun for God, preserving the male-centered bias of the ancient texts.

History of the Scholars Version

The SV project began in the fall of 1988, when Robert W. Funk set four translators to work drafting renditions of the canonical gospels. During the 1989 New Year's holiday those four gathered and compared what they had produced. It was the first step in a three-year process of crafting the distinctive tone and style of the Scholars Version.

As work on the translations continued, other members of the growing SV team checked the accuracy of the drafts, compared parallel passages, and labored to make the English truly contemporary. Several revisions were circulated and further suggestions were exchanged. Adjustments to one passage would often ricochet into other passages where the wording was similar. Numerous passages were reworked repeatedly.

Gradually a common vision emerged. We refined the principles of translation that enabled us to progress toward the dual goals of being scrupulously faithful to the ancient texts while echoing the speech of ordinary people in our communities. Yet when we began few of us anticipated how difficult the task would become.

Several important problems defied easy solution. Especially troublesome were a handful of phrases that are central to the gospels, such as the terms traditionally translated "Son of Man," "Kingdom of God," and "Lord." While we insisted that those misleading and anachronistic renderings must be abandoned, it was not easy to arrive at fresh translations. Other issues, less central but no less thorny, also had to be resolved: for example, whether to translate the name *Petros* as "Peter" (its English equivalent) or as "Rock" (its literal meaning); how to handle the sexist bias inherent in English pronouns; and what to do with references to "the Jews," a term with modern ethnic and religious resonances quite foreign to our ancient texts.

Different solutions were proposed, and honest and vigorous disagreements arose. Several people changed their minds on certain issues, some more than once. Consensus emerged as compromises were achieved, though in some cases team members privately demurred. Such is the nature of collaboration. Individuals work together to produce something bigger and better than any could achieve alone. They submit their work to the collective judgment of the group. They support the outcome of the process even if they must concede a point in honest debate along the way. And the translations in the SV represent the work of some two dozen scholars who undertook the task of producing working drafts. In some cases, those drafts were adopted with only modest changes; in others virtually nothing remains of the original proposals. Thus the entire SV panel bears collective responsibility for the work as a whole.

The SV first appeared in the initial edition of *The Complete Gospels* in 1992. For the book's third edition in 1994, numerous miscellaneous improvements were made in the translation. Over the years that SV has been used in college, university, and seminary courses, as well as in individual and group study, the editor received many thoughtful suggestions for further improvements. When plans were made in 2007 for a fourth edition of *The Complete Gospels*, a systematic revision of SV was undertaken, a project that took over two years to complete. A revision committee scrutinized the gospels verse by verse, and hundreds of verses have been revised, some slightly and some completely. Some of those changes were made for the sake of clarity or style, but most aimed at bringing the English closer to the American language as commonly spoken in the twenty-first century. Every proposed revision was considered by the full committee. On a number of difficult questions the committee revisited its earlier decisions as alternate solutions emerged in the process of ongoing discussion. On particularly important revisions, the committee brought its proposals to the Jesus Seminar for deliberation, debate, and decision. All of the revisions noted below were approved by solid majority votes in the Seminar.

Notable Changes in the New Edition

The present edition features new translations of two crucial phrases that occur nearly two hundred times in the canonical gospels. *Ho huios tou anthrōpou*, traditionally translated "the Son of Man" and formerly in SV "the son of Adam," is now "the Human One" (see p. 208). *Hē basileia tou theou*, traditionally "the kingdom of God" and formerly in SV either "God's imperial rule" or "God's domain," is now "the empire of God" (see p. 22).

Another crucial and frequent problem arises from the term *Ioudaios*. After much discussion of whether it is better rendered "Judean" or "Jew," the revision committee and the Jesus Seminar decided that its meaning differs depending on context. Thus both translations appear in the new edition (see pp. 203–204).

Several revisions affect a very few but highly significant passages. Three of the more important among these are the following.

- "The empire of God is arriving" conveys the delicate nuance of the tense of the verb in Mark 1:15 and elsewhere.
- "The empire of God is among you" affirms that the preposition in Luke 17:21 means "among" rather than "within."
- In perhaps the most controversial innovation in SV, the "virgin" in the Immanuel prophecy quoted in Matthew 1:23 is now "young woman" (see p. 64).

Revisions like those above help to communicate the theological import of some gospels passages. The present edition of SV contains numerous other revisions that affect the more subtle qualities of the gospels, what we might call their "feel." The following are some representative examples.

- In the Gospel of John, Jesus now emphasizes his solemn affirmations with "Let me tell you" instead of "I swear."
- Also in John, Jesus now addresses his mother as "Lady" instead of "Woman."
- People now "kneel" before Jesus instead of "falling down" before him.
- Luke's ubiquitous phrase *kai egeneto*, which he borrowed from the Greek Old Testament deliberately to make his story sound old-fashioned, is now "and it came to pass," a recognizably "biblical" expression in English (see p. 124).
- "Synagogues" are now mostly "meeting places," restoring the original secular meaning of the Greek word *synagōgē*.
- Barabbas and the two men crucified with Jesus, traditionally called "thieves," were formerly "rebels" in SV; they are now "insurgents."

Finally, a specific aim of this revision of SV is to use consistent English for the same Greek and different English where the original varies, whenever that practice is compatible with SV's primary aim of producing English that is fluent, accurate, and familiar. The translation of every gospel passage was checked against its parallel passages and if need be adjusted so that the similarities and differences in the Greek would, when feasible, be reflected in the English. This fine-tuning of SV is intended to facilitate the careful comparison of passages, a practice indispensable to the academic study of the gospels. All the SV translators are teachers, and SV has been designed and revised to serve as a versatile resource for the classroom as well as for the serious individual seeker.

The synoptic puzzle

The similarities between and among the three synoptic gospels (Matthew, Mark, and Luke) are striking. The three are called "synoptic," in fact, because they present a "common view" of Jesus. Most scholars believe that Matthew and Luke employed Mark as the basis of their gospels, to which they add other materials. There are powerful arguments to support this conclusion:

1. Agreement between Matthew and Luke begins where Mark begins and ends where Mark ends.
2. Matthew reproduces about 90% of Mark, Luke about 50%. They often reproduce Mark in the same order. When they disagree, either Matthew or Luke supports the sequence in Mark.
3. In segments that the three gospels have in common, verbal agreement averages about 50%. The extent of the agreement may be observed in the sample of the triple tradition reproduced below: the lines are matched for easy comparison.
4. In the triple tradition—segments all three gospels have in common— Matthew and Mark often agree against Luke, and Luke and Mark often agree against Matthew, but Matthew and Luke rarely agree against Mark.

These facts and the close examination of agreements and disagreements in minute detail have led scholars to conclude that Mark is the adopted basis of Matthew and Luke.

This conclusion implies two further findings:

5. Mark is responsible for the chronological outline of the life of Jesus represented by the synoptics; Matthew and Luke do not have independent evidence for the order of events.
6. Mark is the earliest of the three.

Mark 2:16–17	Matt 9:11–12	Luke 5:30–31
[16]And whenever the Pharisees' scholars saw him eating with sinners and toll collectors, they	[11]And whenever the Pharisees saw this, they	[30]The Pharisees and their scholars
would question his disciples, "What's he doing eating with toll collectors and sinners?"	would question his disciples, "Why does your teacher eat with toll collectors and sinners?"	would complain to his disciples, "Why do you people eat and drink with toll collectors and sinners?"
[17] When Jesus overhears, he says to them, "Since when do the able-bodied need a doctor? It's the sick who do."	[12]When Jesus overheard, he said, "Since when do the able-bodied need a doctor? It's the sick who do."	[31]In response Jesus said to them, "Since when do the healthy need a doctor? It's the sick who do."

Narrative Gospels

P⁵², the earliest fragment of the gospels, dates to about 125 CE. It contains a few words from John 18:31–33 and 18:37–38. *Reprinted with the permission of The John Rylands University Library of Manchester, England.*

The Gospel of Mark

Introduction

Story, structure, and narrative themes

In the Gospel of Mark we encounter a vivid and powerful telling of the story of Jesus. Through a rapid tumble of arresting scenes we watch Jesus emerge on the public stage, newly baptized and victorious over Satan, masterful yet oddly mysterious (chapter 1). A reluctant champion of the diseased and demon possessed, Jesus does spiritual battle against the "unclean spirits" arrayed against him and his cause, "the empire of God." Larger and larger crowds of onlookers are soon drawn to Jesus' doings, crowds who form a chorus that is always curious, often sympathetic, but also frequently rather menacing (chapters 2-3). What attracts these crowds is Jesus' quick success as faith healer and exorcist extraordinaire; soon Jesus turns to confront these crowds with strange yet telling speech (4:1–34).

As Jesus and his small band of disciples move through the little towns, barren countryside, and stormy lake that make up of the gospel's controlling landscape, the sense of inevitable confrontation and foreboding grows stronger and stronger. Opposition to his practices and his disciples' habits comes from social, religious, and political leaders, both those in Galilee and others summoned from Jerusalem (e.g., 3:19–22 and 7:1–21). Eventually Jesus himself will lead his group to the capital city for the final confrontation that leads to his arrest and execution by the Roman authorities.

The story presents three interlocking plot levels of conflict: (1) the background cosmic struggle of God and Satan, (2) the middle level struggle of conflict between Jesus and the authorities and (3) the foreground struggle of Jesus and the disciples. Two dominant themes throughout the gospel are the question of Jesus' identity and the nature of discipleship, which Mark calls "following Jesus." At the midpoint of the narrative Jesus asks his followers, "What are people saying about me? . . . What about you, who do you say I am?" (8:27–30). This scene serves as the story's fulcrum, as Peter's statement "You are the Anointed One!" leads to Jesus' puzzling and terrifying predictions about the divine necessity for "the Human One" to be persecuted and killed and yet to rise again (8:31; 9:31; 10:33–34). Those who want to "follow" Jesus are told to "pick up your cross" (8:34) and to serve those with less power and status than themselves (9:35, 10:42–44). The disciples, already mystified about Jesus and his actions,

19

are now left even more troubled and confused as they move on to Jerusalem. There Jesus engages in dramatic and dangerous debate with various authority figures and disrupts the commerce of the temple, acting out its coming destruction (chapters 11–12).

While contemplating the glory and beauty of the temple buildings, Jesus gives a second long speech, addressed within the story to his most intimate circle, but also to Mark's Christian audience, about the troubles and distress in which they were caught up (chapter 13). After an unnamed woman signals Jesus' approaching death with a symbolic anointing, come a final meal and a wrenching scene of foreboding in Gethsemane (chapter 14). At Jesus' arrest, the disciples all flee. Jesus silently accepts flogging and torturous death on the cross (chapter 15). The story ends when three named faithful women go to minister to his body but instead encounter a mysterious, shining youth who tells them that Jesus has risen from the dead. Rather than report this astonishing news, the women in their turn flee (chapter 16), leaving to Mark's audience the task of being faithful followers.

Origins of the Gospel

Mark is generally thought to be the oldest surviving written gospel. The document itself never mentions its author, nor the place, time, or circumstances of its origin, but scholars have inferred that the gospel was composed at about the time of the Roman-Judean War (66–70 CE), probably in Greek-speaking Syria. Most scholars use the traditional name "Mark" as a convenient way to refer to the anonymous composer. Sometime in the second century the tradition grew up of connecting the unnamed author with the name "Mark," perhaps the John Mark mentioned in Luke's Acts of the Apostles (Acts 12:12, 25; 15:37–39). Another common tradition of the ancient church connected the gospel in various ways with the apostle Peter, probably because a Mark is mentioned as a devoted follower of Peter in 1 Peter 5:13. This very indirect association may have helped lead to the further tradition that the book was written at Rome, the scene of Peter's martyrdom.

If Mark's is the first gospel, its predecessors would not have been evangelists in a literary sense, but instead storytellers, prophets, teachers, missionaries, or community organizers, who passed along memories and stories of Jesus in their own particular social and church situations. When composing his text, Mark drew on many sorts of existing material for his own new purposes of narration, probably building on a growing oral narrative. Identifying Mark's sources, and judging whether they were available in written or oral form, is a difficult enterprise. Confidence varies about our ability to isolate other sorts of pre-Markan sources, such as a passion narrative, a series of miracle stories, or cycles of controversy dialogues, or collections of mysterious sayings coupled with explanations. Throughout, Mark has made the material his own.

Notes on Mark's narrative style

The Gospel of Mark is composed in a lively and direct oral story style. The Greek prose employed is the informal language of ordinary men and women of the eastern Mediterranean culture in the first century. Instead of the polished literary style of an accomplished artistic writer, in this gospel we find an immediacy and simplicity of description, a certain harshness and awkwardness in expression, repetition of favored words and constructions, but nonetheless a tight narrative structure. Those features have led scholars to believe that Mark's story is still close to the oral preaching environment and may have been composed and transmitted primarily orally.

Most translations of the gospels flatten all their individual "voices" into one. The Scholars Version of Mark attempts to represent the composer's rushed, folksy, and vivid style in reasonably good English prose, while still leaving room for stylistic comparison with the translations of other documents. For example, in Mark's story everything seems to happen "right away" or "right then and there," two of the phrases we use to translate the very frequent *euthus* (traditionally translated "immediately"). Matthew and Luke reduce the use of *euthus* considerably. Mark likes to use the present tense even when describing past events, something that gives his story a vivid but uncultivated tone. Luke changes about 150 of these "historic presents" into past tense verbs. Very many of Mark's sentences begin with the word "and." Matthew and Luke, in the interest of more polished style, frequently replace Mark's parataxis ("and . . . and . . . and") with subordinate clauses.

Mark frequently postpones providing some important details until well into the story when he tells his various episodes, which is characteristic of oral style. Then, mostly using the Greek conjunction *gar* (meaning "for" or "since"), Mark will supply this sometimes crucial tidbit by way of a parenthetical aside, usually translated "You see, . . ." The most famous example is the very last phrase of the Gospel story, when the women have turned and run in terror from the tomb and failed to inform others of Jesus' reported resurrection. Mark explains: "Talk about terrified . . . !" (16:8). Other instances are found at 2:15; 3:10, 21, 30; 5:28, 42; 6:14, 31, 52; 7:3–4; 9:6; 11:13; and the first mention of the "faithful women" only at 15:40–41.

Expansions in Mark's text

During the process of copying and recopying Mark's gospel, Christian scribes introduced some major expansions into the text, most famously at the end of the story. Unsatisfied with the conclusion showing the terrified disciples running away from the tomb (at 16:8), early copyists preferred to continue with additions of various length to portray the risen Jesus appearing to his disciples and commanding them to begin the work of evangelization. These additions are traditionally called the "Shorter Ending" and "Longer Ending" of Mark, though it would be more appropriate to term them shorter and longer "supplements." Most of this material is closely patterned on other post-resurrection appearance stories, especially those in Luke's gospel. For details see "The Endings of the Gospel of Mark," pp. 461–62.

A twentieth-century discovery in the correspondence of Clement of Alexandria, a late second-century Christian theologian, has uncovered the existence of an alternative version of Mark, which Clement calls "More Spiritual Mark" or "Mystical Mark." At two places Clement quotes additional material from this otherwise unknown edition of Mark (for details see the textual notes at 10:34–35 and 10:46).

The empire of God

The traditional translation of the Greek phrase *basileia tou theou* as "kingdom of God" has lost its bite over the centuries. In modern English, the overtly political meaning of "kingdom" is overshadowed by associations with the fantasy worlds of King Arthur, *The Lord of the Rings*, and even Disney. But in the ancient world the word *basileia* had ominous overtones. A *basileia* was ruled by a *basileus*, an autocrat who was an absolute ruler, a figure whom we today would describe as a dictator or tyrant. Ancient audiences would not be surprised that kings in the gospels reflexively slaughter those whom they perceive as threats to their power (see Matt 2:16, 22:7; Luke 19:27).

In the first century the word *basileia* would invariably call to mind the Roman *basileia*, under whose oppressive and seemingly omnipotent power the audiences of the gospels were forced to live. An effective translation of *basileia* should make the association with Roman tyranny explicit and restore the word's political sense and menacing overtones. The SV translators thus chose "empire."

This translation also makes it easy to recognize that Jesus used this term (or its Aramaic equivalent, *malkut*) with irony. God's *basileia* is an upside-down version of Rome's: the poor are congratulated, debts are canceled, slaves are in authority, etc. The ironic quality of God's *basileia* does not cancel out the ominous overtones of *basileia*. On the contrary, those ominous overtones have to ring loud for the irony to work.

The Gospel of Mark

[handwritten: mediator between humans & God, credibility]

1 **The good news** of Jesus the Anointed begins ²with something Isaiah the prophet wrote:

> Here is my messenger,
> whom I send on ahead of you
> > to prepare your way!
> ³A voice of someone shouting in the desert,
> > "Make ready the way of the Lord,
> > make his paths straight."

⁴So, John the Baptizer appeared in the desert calling for baptism and a change of heart that lead to forgiveness of sins. ⁵And everyone from the Judean countryside and all the residents of Jerusalem streamed out to him and got baptized by him in the Jordan River, admitting their sins. ⁶And John wore a mantle made of camel hair and had a leather belt around his waist and lived on grasshoppers and wild honey. ⁷And he began his proclamation by saying, "Someone more powerful than I will succeed me, whose sandal straps I am not fit to bend down and untie. ⁸I've been baptizing you with water, but he will baptize you with holy spirit."

⁹**During that same period** Jesus came from Nazareth, Galilee, and was baptized in the Jordan by John. ¹⁰And right away as he got up out of the water, he saw the skies torn open and the spirit coming down toward him like a dove. ¹¹There was also a voice from the skies: "You are my son, the one I love—I fully approve of you."

[handwritten left margin: talking about Jesus]

[sidebar notes:]

A voice in the desert

Jesus baptized

[handwritten: Mark believes the end is coming any minute]

1:2–6
//Mt 3:1–6,
Lk 3:1–6,
Jn 1:19–23,
GEbi 3;
cf. GEbi 1

1:2–3
◊Mal 3:1,
Is 40:3 (LXX),
Ex 23:20

1:4
Ⓣ GHeb 2: 1,
GNaz 2:1

1:6
◊2 Kgs 1:8 (LXX)

1:7–8
Cf. Q 3:16b–17;
Mt 3:7, 11–12;
Lk 3:16; Jn 1:26–27

1:9–11
Cf. Mt 3:13–17,
Lk 3:21–22,
Jn 1:29–34,
GHeb 3, GEbi 4

1:11
//GEbi 4:3;
◊Is 42:1, 44:2;
Ps 2:7

1:1 Many mss add "son of God" after *Anointed*.

1:1 The opening line of the *good news* (or "gospel") announces Jesus' identity to the reader, although the secret of his true identity will be hidden from most of the individuals that Jesus encounters as the story unfolds.

The Greek word *christos* is traditionally left untranslated and rendered as though part of Jesus' name ("Christ"), but this practice does not correspond with the use of the word within Mark's story. Its translation here as *the Anointed* reflects the meaning it would convey to a reader of Mark's time and also suggests its use as a title.

1:4–6 John's unusual dress characterizes him as a prophet at work in the *desert* (see Zech 13:4; 2 Kgs 1:8; Heb 11:37; compare Q 7:24–25), linking him to the promise quoted in v. 3.

A time in the *desert* is a key event in many biblical heroes' careers (see, e.g., 1 Kings 19; Acts 21:38) and also reflects an Exodus typology prominent in the OT prophets (Hos 2:14; 12:9; and esp. Isaiah chaps. 40–51).

1:9 Jesus appears with even less biographical explanation than did John: the reader is expected to already know who these figures are. This verse seems to imply that *Nazareth* is Jesus' hometown, a place mentioned without name in 6:1–6.

1:10–11 Mark relates the *tearing open* of the skies and the *voice* from above as Jesus' own experience, something apparently not seen and heard by anyone else. Contrast Luke 3:21–22, John 1:31, and the transfiguration scene in Mark 9:7. The *voice from the skies* was a traditional Jewish way to describe public communication from God.

*Jesus tested in
the desert*

A voice in Galilee

*Jesus calls his
first disciples*

A day's work

¹²**And right away** the spirit drives him out into the desert. ¹³And he was in the desert for forty days, being put to the test by Satan. And he was among the wild animals, and the heavenly messengers looked after him.

¹⁴**After John was turned in**, Jesus came to Galilee proclaiming God's good news. ¹⁵His message went: "The time is up: the empire of God is arriving! Change your ways, and put your trust in the good news."

¹⁶**As he was walking** along by the Sea of Galilee, he spotted Simon and Andrew, Simon's brother, casting ⟨their nets⟩ into the sea—since they were fishermen—¹⁷and Jesus said to them, "Follow me and I'll have you fishing for people!"

¹⁸And right then and there they abandoned their nets and followed him.

¹⁹When he had gone a little farther, he caught sight of James, son of Zebedee, and his brother John mending their nets in the boat. ²⁰And right away he called out to them as well, and they left their father Zebedee behind in the boat with the hired hands and accompanied him.

²¹**Then they come to Capernaum**, and right away on the Sabbath he went to the meeting place and started teaching. ²²They were astonished at his teaching, since he would teach them on his own authority, unlike the scholars.

²³Now right then and there in their meeting place was a person possessed by an unclean spirit, which shouted, ²⁴"Jesus! What do you want with us, you Nazarene? Have you come to destroy us? I know who you are: God's holy man!"

²⁵But Jesus yelled at it, "Shut up and get out of him!"

²⁶Then the unclean spirit threw the man into convulsions, and it came out of him with a loud shriek. ²⁷And they were all so amazed that they asked them-

1:12–13
Cf. Q 4:1–13,
Mt 4:1–11,
Lk 4:1–13, GHeb 4

1:14–15
//Mt 4:12, 17;
Lk 4:14–15;
cf. Jn 4:1–3, 43–46a

1:16–20
//Mt 4:18–22;
cf. Lk 5:1–11,
Jn 21:1–14,
GEbi 2:3

1:21–28
//Mt 7:28–29,
Lk 4:31–37

1:12–13 A period of *forty days* was traditional in biblical stories to mark significant transitions (e.g., Noah's rain in Genesis 7, Elijah's flight in 1 Kings 19; compare the forty years of Israel's wanderings in the Exodus).

1:14–15 A vivid summary of the main themes of Jesus' ministry. Mark uses summary statements to report Jesus' activities and their effect (as in 1:32–34; 3:7–12; 6:56).

1:16 Mark usually begins a new episode with a brief mention of place or time, as here with *As he was walking along by the Sea of Galilee*. Other examples in this chapter include 1:14; 1:21; 1:29; 1:32; and 1:35. With brief comments such as these, the narrator skillfully moves from one individual scene to another, which suggests that the author used the technique as a way to combine stories that earlier had been told separately.

1:16–20 Here Jesus calls as his first followers two pairs of brothers who will remain his closest companions (though Andrew plays a less prominent role). Their immediate response to Jesus' summons, apparently with no previous contact, emphasizes Jesus' spellbinding authority. (Contrast John 1:35–42 and Luke 5:1–11.) We will see the close connection of these men with Jesus in the healing of the little girl in 5:37ff.; the scene of Jesus' transfiguration in 9:2–8; in the temple dialogue in 13:3ff; the Gethsemane scene in 14:32ff.; the ambitions of James and John in 10:35–40; and note also the sequence of the list of the twelve at 3:16–19.

1:21–28 Jesus performs his first exorcism at *Capernaum*, a town in Galilee that seems to be his main base of operations (see also 2:1; 3:19; 9:33). Here too we see a strong emphasis laid on Jesus' role as *teacher* (vv. 21, 22, 27). Jesus' actions on the sabbath and in meeting places quickly arouse hostile notice (2:23–28 and 3:1–6).

Stories of exorcisms display certain stock elements, including here a confrontation between Jesus and the demon (v. 24); Jesus' rebuke, silencing, and word of command for the unclean spirit to depart (v. 25); the performance of the cure (v. 26); the wonder of the bystanders (v. 27); and the effect of increasing Jesus' fame (v. 28). A similar pattern is followed in the two other exorcisms that Mark will describe in full (5:1–20, esp. vv. 7–14; and 9:25–27).

1:23–24 The *unclean spirit* (Mark's favorite term for demons) knows who Jesus is and what his mission entails, though most onlookers remain confused.

selves, "What's this? A new kind of teaching backed by authority! He gives orders even to unclean spirits and they obey him!"

²⁸And right away his reputation spread everywhere throughout the whole area of Galilee.

²⁹And right away they left the meeting place and entered the house of Simon and Andrew along with James and John. ³⁰Simon's mother-in-law was in bed with a fever, and they told him about her right away. ³¹He went up to her, took hold of her hand, raised her up, and the fever disappeared. Then she started looking after them.

³²In the evening, at sundown, they would bring all the sick and demon possessed to him. ³³And the whole town would crowd around the door. ³⁴On such occasions he cured many people afflicted with various diseases and drove out many demons. He would never let the demons speak, because they realized who he was.

³⁵**And rising early**, while it was still very dark, he went outside and stole away to an isolated place, where he started praying. ³⁶Then Simon and those with him hunted him down. ³⁷When they had found him they say to him, "They're all looking for you."

³⁸But he replies, "Let's go somewhere else, to the neighboring villages, so I can speak there too, since that's what I came for."

³⁹So he went all around Galilee speaking in their meeting places and driving out demons.

⁴⁰**Then a leper comes up** to him, pleads with him, falls down on his knees, and says to him, "If you want to, you can make me clean."

⁴¹Although Jesus was indignant, he stretched out his hand, touched him, and says to him, "Okay—you're clean!"

1:29–31
//Mt 8:14–15,
Lk 4:38–39
1:32–34
//Mt 8:16–17,
Lk 4:40–41
1:35–38
//Lk 4:42–43
1:39
//Mt 4:23;
cf. Mt 9:35, Lk 4:44
1:40–44
//Mt 8:2–4,
Lk 5:12–16,
EgerG 2:1–4

1:41 Most mss read "And Jesus was moved" in place of *Although Jesus was indignant.*

1:29–31 This is the first of many miraculous healings by Jesus described in Mark, and it unfolds in a conventional three-part structure: first a *description* of the ailment (v. 30); then Jesus' *performance* of a cure (v. 31a); finally a *demonstration* of the cure, through either an act of the healed person or the reaction of onlookers (v. 31b). The cure's effectiveness in this case is shown by Simon's mother-in-law being able to perform her socially prescribed duty of serving guests food. The same basic pattern is followed, though rarely so compactly, in several other healing stories (1:40–45; 2:3, 11–12; 3:1–6; 5:25–34, 35–42; 7:32–35; 8:22–25; 10:46–52).

1:32–34 This summary statement from Mark displays many aspects of his characteristic style: redundancy (*In the evening, at sundown, . . .*), hyperbole (*all the sick and demon possessed, the whole town*), and secrecy (*He would never let the demons speak*).

1:35–38 The first clear indication of the pressing effects of the crowds who are being drawn to Jesus by his great deeds. The overwhelming presence of crowds is a narrative theme repeatedly emphasized as the story develops (see also 1:45; 2:13; 3:7–10, 19b–20; 4:1; 5:21, 24; 6:54–56; 7:14; 8:1, 34; 9:14; 10:1, 46; 12:12). Jesus is often shown trying to avoid the presence of the crowds, sometimes seeking privacy in order to perform miracles or impart special instruction (e.g., 1:45; 5:37; 6:31; 7:17, 24, 33; 8:23; 9:28, 30; 10:10, 32b).

1:40 *Lepers* were considered ritually impure. This sort of uncleanliness endangered the purity required of the people for proper worship of God. For the social and religious context see esp. Leviticus 13–14 and the note below at 2:15–17.

Jesus cures a paralytic

[42] And right away the leprosy disappeared, and he was made clean. [43] And Jesus snapped at him, and right away threw him out [44] with this warning: "Don't tell anyone anything, but go, have a priest examine you. Then offer for your cleansing what Moses commanded, as evidence ⟨of your cure⟩."

[45] But after he left, he started telling everyone and spreading the story, so that Jesus could no longer enter a town openly, but had to stay out in isolated places. Yet they continued to come to him from everywhere.

insertion & framing device

2 **Some days later** he went back to Capernaum and was rumored to be at home. [2] And many people crowded around so there was no longer any room, even outside the door. Then he started speaking to them. [3] Some people then show up with a paralytic being carried by four of them. [4] And when they couldn't get near him because of the crowd, they removed the roof above him. After digging it out, they lowered the mat on which the paralytic was lying. [5] When Jesus noticed their trust, he says to the paralytic, "Child, your sins are forgiven."

[6] Some of the scholars were sitting there and silently objecting: [7] "Why does this guy talk like this? He's blaspheming! Who can forgive sins except the one God?"

[8] And right away, because Jesus could sense that they were objecting to what he had said, he says to them: "Why are you objecting to all this? [9] Which is easier: to say to the paralytic, 'Your sins are forgiven,' or to say, 'Get up, pick up your mat and walk'? [10] But just so that you realize that on earth the Human One has authority to forgive sins"—he says to the paralytic—[11] "You there, get up, pick up your mat and go home!"

[12] And he got up, picked his mat right up, and walked out as everyone looked on. So they all became ecstatic, extolled God, and exclaimed, "We've never seen the likes of this!"

2:1–12
//Mt 9:1–8,
Lk 5:17–26;
cf. Jn 5:2–9

2:11
//Jn 5:8–9

1:43–45 Jesus' anger (v. 41) and stern warning not to make him known, conveyed by *snapping* (literally "snorting") at the cured leper, is connected to a key narrative theme in Mark's gospel, the mandated "secret" of Jesus' true identity. Jesus repeatedly attempts to hide his actions, at least until he reaches Jerusalem, but usually without much apparent success (see also 1:25–28, 34; 3:12; 5:43; 7:36; 8:26).

It is an irony characteristic of Mark's story that while the demon possessed and the sick and even his opponents seem to recognize who Jesus is, his own followers display constant confusion or ignorance.

2:4 The paralytic's friends *dig* through a flat mud roof, the typical construction for ordinary houses in ancient Palestine.

2:5 Jesus pronounces divine forgiveness for the paralyzed person and only heals him as a demonstration of his warrant to do so as the Human One (for this title see note at 2:10).

People frequently interpreted illness as punishment for sin (see, e.g., John 9 or the Book of Job).

2:6–9 The confrontation between Jesus and *some of the scholars* opens a new theme in Mark's narrative, that of opposition from the Jewish elite over questions of religious practice. This warning note sounds louder and louder as the story develops and helps to explain the rationale for the leadership's actions later in Jerusalem. Jesus' difficulties with the "scholars," the "Pharisees," or the aristocratic priestly establishment are featured throughout the story.

2:10 Here for the first time Jesus refers to the enigmatic figure of *the Human One* (more literally, "the son of the human being"). See the cameo essay on p. 208. In the gospels the figure of *the Human One* is mentioned only by Jesus himself, and he often seems to use it as an indirect reference to himself in the third person.

¹³**Again he went out** by the sea. And, with a huge crowd gathered around him, he started teaching.

¹⁴As he was walking along, he caught sight of Levi, the son of Alphaeus, sitting at the toll booth, and he says to him, "Follow me."

And Levi got up and followed him.

¹⁵**It so happened** that Jesus was reclining ⟨for dinner⟩ in his house, along with many toll collectors and sinners and Jesus' disciples. (You see, there were many of these people and they were all following him.)

¹⁶And whenever the Pharisees' scholars saw him eating with sinners and toll collectors, they would question his disciples, "What's he doing eating with toll collectors and sinners?"

¹⁷When Jesus overhears, he says to them, "Since when do the able-bodied need a doctor? It's the sick who do. I did not come to enlist the upright but sinners!"

¹⁸**John's disciples and the Pharisees** had the custom of fasting, and they come and ask him, "Why do the disciples of John fast, and the disciples of the Pharisees, but your disciples don't?"

¹⁹And Jesus said to them, "The groom's friends can't fast while the groom is around, can they? So long as the groom is around, you can't expect them to fast. ²⁰But the days will come when the groom is taken away from them, and then they will fast, on that day.

Levi becomes a follower

Jesus dines with sinners

Fasting & feasting

2:13–14
//Mt 9:9,
Lk 5:27–28

2:14
Cf. GEbi 2:4

2:15–17
//Mt 9:10–13,
Lk 5:29–32,
GOxy 1224 5:1–2;
cf. Lk 19:1–10

2:18–20
//Mt 9:14–15,
Lk 5:33–35,
Th 104;
cf. Jn 3:25–30

2:14 Levi represents the class of *toll collectors* employed by big businessmen or "tax farmers," who were contracted by the Roman authorities to raise government revenues in subjected territories through small tariffs and excise charges. Verse 15 equates toll collectors with *sinners*, meaning those who do not follow God's law.

2:15–17 Jesus' meals and his dinner companions are an important gospel theme, since questions of food and its preparation are a central concern in traditional Judaism. Some people, such as the Pharisees, considered it dangerous to eat with others who did not follow the same dietary customs. Often Jesus attracts notice and controversy by eating with those whom other Jews (here the oddly named *the Pharisees' scholars*) considered "unclean" (see note at 1:40–45). In Mark's story, Jesus is portrayed as being less than fastidious in his dealings with people that more circumspect Jews considered suspect in terms of religious purity. Here in chapter 2 we see Jesus consorting with the sick, "sinners," and toll collectors, as well as leading a group that didn't fast and was rather careless about sabbath observance.

In passing Mark mentions that the group around Jesus includes his *disciples*, the conventional translation of a word meaning "student" or "trainee." In Mark's story Jesus teaches and his followers struggle to learn, not in a conventional school setting, but instead mostly in reaction to particular situations arising in their travels from place to place.

The customary Greek phrasing for "sitting down to a meal" was *to recline*, as Jesus does here, that is, to lie down on dining couches to be served.

2:17 Jesus' statement uses a well-known proverb to compare his actions to the work of a doctor. This is Mark's first example of how Jesus closes off debate with a striking word or pithy statement. His opponents are given no further chance to respond. Indeed the whole scene (perhaps v. 14 too) seems to function primarily to set up the punch line featuring Jesus' memorable words. The next two episodes (2:18–22, 23–28) are further instances of this formal type, which scholars have labelled variously the pronouncement story, chreia, or apophthegm.

2:18–20 This is the first of only two references in Mark to *John's disciples* (see 6:29; Q 7:18, 31–35; John 3:25–30). *Fasting* (usually accompanied by prayer) was a regular practice of pious Jews as a sign of mourning, contrition, or penitence. (For other comments in the gospel tradition see Matt 6:16; Luke 18:12; Thom 14:1; 27; 104.) Wedding imagery was favored in the gospels as a way to picture Jesus and his role (see Matt 22:1–14; 25:1–13; John 3:29; Thom 75; DialSav 50). In the OT Israel is often portrayed as God's bride (e.g., Hosea 1–3; Isa 54:4; Jer 2:2).

*The Human One
over the Sabbath*

*Man with a
crippled hand*

By the sea

²¹"Nobody sews a piece of unshrunk cloth on an old garment, otherwise the new, unshrunk patch pulls away from the old and creates a worse tear.

²²"And nobody pours new wine into old wineskins, otherwise the wine will burst the skins, and destroy both the wine and the skins. Instead, ⟨put⟩ new wine into new wineskins." *one-liner*

²³**It so happened** that he was making his way through the grainfields on the Sabbath, and his disciples began to strip heads of grain as they made their way. ²⁴And the Pharisees started to argue with him: "See here, why are they doing what's not permitted on the Sabbath?"

²⁵And he says to them: "I guess you don't recall what David did when he found it necessary, when both he and his companions were hungry. ²⁶He went into the house of God, when Abiathar was chief priest, and ate the consecrated bread, and even gave some to his men to eat. No one is permitted to eat this bread, except the priests."

²⁷And he continued, *one-liner*

> The Sabbath was created for human beings,
>   not human beings for the Sabbath.

²⁸So, the Human One is master even of the Sabbath.

insertion & framing device

3 **Then he went back** to the meeting place, and a man with a crippled hand was there. ²So they kept an eye on him, to see whether he would heal the man on the Sabbath, so they could denounce him. ³And he says to the man with the crippled hand, "Get up here in front of everybody." ⁴Then he says to them, "On the Sabbath is it permitted to do good or to do evil, to save life or to kill?"

But they remained silent. ⁵And looking right at them with outrage, exasperated at their closed mindedness, he says to the man, "Hold out your hand."

He held it out and his hand was restored. ⁶Then the Pharisees left immediately with the Herodians and hatched a plot against him, to destroy him.

⁷**Then Jesus withdrew** with his disciples to the sea, and a huge crowd from

2:21–22
//Mt 9:16–17,
Lk 5:36–39,
Th 47:3–5

2:23–28
//Mt 12:1–8,
Lk 6:1–5;
◊1 Sm 21:1–7;
Dt 5:14, 23:25–26;
Ex 20:10

2:26
◊Lv 24:5–9

2:27–28
Cf. Th 27

3:1–6
//Mt 12:9–14,
Lk 6:6–11;
cf. GNaz 4

3:7–12
//Lk 6:17–19;
cf. Mt 4:23–25,
12:15–16

2:26 Some mss omit *when Abiathar was chief priest* (see 1 Sam 21:1–7).

2:21–22 The contrast and even incompatibility between what is *old* and what is *new* is used to highlight the great significance found in Jesus.

2:23–28 Jesus' followers are shown violating the observance of the Sabbath rest, one of the central commandments of Judaism (featured in the Ten Commandments in Exod 20:8–11 and Deut 5:12–15). In their defense, Jesus appeals to the example of how King David also violated a religious prohibition, though in his case because of real want. The story alluded to (found in 1 Samuel 21) mentions Ahimelech instead of his son *Abiathar* as the high priest (compare Matt 12:4; Luke 6:4). The point for Mark, how-ever, is that Jesus, acting as the Human One, has authority comparable to David's to establish guidelines for proper religious behavior for his followers (vv. 27–28). Jesus as representative of true humanity has precedence over Sabbath and its observance.

3:1–6 This is the first clear statement in Mark's story of the malevolent intentions of Jesus' opponents. His fate had already been intimated in Jesus' picture of the groom being "taken away" (2:20).

3:7–8 Mark pictures Jesus as attracting huge multitudes who virtually empty out most of biblical Israel as well as the neighboring regions of Idumea, the Trans-Jordan, and even

Galilee followed. When they heard what he was doing, a huge crowd from Judea, ⁸and from Jerusalem and Idumea and across the Jordan, and from around Tyre and Sidon, collected around him. ⁹And he told his disciples to have a small boat ready for him on account of the crowd, so they wouldn't mob him. (¹⁰You see, he had healed so many that all who had diseases were pushing forward to touch him.) ¹¹The unclean spirits also, whenever they faced him, would kneel before him and shout out, "You son of God, you!" ¹²But he always warned them not to tell who he was.

¹³**Then he goes up** on the mountain and summons those he wanted, and they came to him. ¹⁴He formed a group of twelve to be his companions, and to be sent out to preach, ¹⁵and to have authority to drive out demons.

¹⁶And to Simon he gave the nickname Rock ⟨(Peter)⟩, ¹⁷and to James, the son of Zebedee, and to John, his brother, he also gave a nickname, Boanerges (which means "Sons of Thunder"); ¹⁸and Andrew and Philip and Bartholomew and Matthew and Thomas and James, the son of Alphaeus; and Thaddeus and Simon the Zealot; ¹⁹and Judas Iscariot, who, in the end, turned him in.

²⁰**Then he goes home**, and once again a crowd gathers, so they couldn't even have a meal. ²¹When his relatives heard about it, they came to take him away. (You see, they thought he was out of his mind.) ²²And the scholars who had come down from Jerusalem would say, "He is possessed by Beelzebul" and "He drives out demons with the power of the head demon."

²³And after calling them over, he would speak to them in riddles: "How can Satan drive out Satan? ²⁴After all, if an empire is divided against itself, that empire cannot survive. ²⁵And if a household is divided against itself, that household won't be able to survive. ²⁶So if Satan rebels against himself and is divided, he cannot endure but is doomed. *one-liner*

²⁷"No one can enter a strong man's house to plunder his belongings unless he first ties him up. Only then does he plunder his house. *one-liner*

[margin notes: The Twelve / Beelzebul controversy / insertion & framing device]

3:9
① Mk 4:1

3:13–19
//Mt 10:1–4,
Lk 6:12–16;
cf. GEbi 2:3

3:22–26
//Q 11:14–18;
Mt 9:35–38,
12:22–26;
Lk 11:14–18

3:27
//Mt 12:19,
Lk 11:21–22, Th 35

3:14 Some mss insert "whom he also named apostles" after *twelve*.

---

the regions surrounding the great port cities of Tyre and Sidon, which lay to the north in what today is Lebanon.

3:13–19 Jesus leads his group up an unnamed mountain. Mark creates an evocative landscape at will (empty places, a mountain, the seaside, "his home" or "the house"), without regard to narrative connection or plausibility. Simon is nicknamed *Peter*, meaning "Rock," a name that will eventually prove sadly ironic when even Simon "the Rock" wavers at the end.

3:21 The note on Jesus' relatives is interrupted by a new controversy over Jesus and the source of his power, with the topic of Jesus' true family relations then resumed in 3:31–

35 (a case of Mark's interpolation or "sandwiching" technique; see 5:21–24a [24b–34], 35–43; 6:7–13 [14–29], 30; 14:1–2 [3–9], 10–11).

Mark often provides explanations in parenthetical asides inserted somewhere in the middle of an episode, as here (v. 21: *You see, they thought he was out of his mind*). See also 3:10; 6:14, 31, 52; 7:3; 9:6; 11:13; 16:8.

3:22 *Beelzebul* is an obscure divine or spirit figure equated with Satan in v. 24.

3:23 Mark frequently portrays Jesus speaking in *riddles* or analogies or figurative speech, all of which Mark calls "parables."

one-liner

3:28–29
//Mt 12:31–32,
Lk 12:10, Th 44

3:31–35
//Mt 12:46–50,
Lk 8:19–21, Th 99,
GEbi 5

3:35
//GHeb 4a

4:1–2
//Mt 13:1–3a,
Lk 8:4

4:3–8
//Mt 13:3b–8,
Lk 8:5–8a, Th 9;
cf. SJas 8:3

4:5
Ⓣ Judas 3:7

4:9
//Mt 11:15, 13:9,
43b; Lk 8:8b,
14:35b; Mary 2:5,
3:14; Rev 2:7a, 11a,
17a, 3:6, 13, 22,
13:9a; Th 8:4, 21:10,
24:2, 63:4, 65:8,
96:3;
Ⓓ Mk 4:23 [7:16]

4:10–12
//Mt 13:10–15,
Lk 8:9–10;
◊ Is 6:9–10, Jer 5:21,
Ez 12:2

[28]"Let me tell you: all offenses and whatever blasphemies humankind might blaspheme will be forgiven them. [29]But whoever blasphemes against the holy spirit is never forgiven, but is guilty of an eternal sin"—[30]because they were saying, "He is possessed by an unclean spirit."

[31]**Then his mother** and his brothers arrive. While still outside, they send in and ask for him. [32]A crowd was sitting around him, and they say to him, "Look, your mother and your brothers are outside looking for you."

[33]In response he says to them, "Who are my mother and brothers?"

[34]And looking right at those seated around him in a circle, he says, "Here are my mother and my brothers. [35]Whoever does God's will, that's my brother and sister and mother."

4 **Once again he started to teach** beside the sea. An enormous crowd gathers around him, so he climbs into a boat and sits there on the water facing the huge crowd on the shore.

[2]He would then teach them many things in parables. In the course of his teaching he would tell them:

[3]Listen to this! This sower went out to sow. [4]While he was sowing, some seed fell along the path, and the birds came and devoured it. [5]Other seed fell on rocky ground where there wasn't much soil, and it came up right away because the soil had no depth. [6]But when the sun came up it was scorched, and because it had no root it withered. [7]Still other seed fell among thorns, and the thorns came up and choked it, so that it produced no fruit. [8]Finally, some seed fell on good soil and started producing fruit. The seed sprouted and grew: one part had a yield of thirty, another part sixty, and a third part one hundred.

[9]And he would say, "Anyone here with two good ears, use 'em!"

[10]**Whenever he went off by himself**, those close to him, together with the Twelve, would ask him about the parables. [11]And he would say to them: "You

---

3:31–35 Jesus' mother and other relations play only a minor and not very positive role in Mark's story (see also 6:3). Jesus' words about his true family strike a discordant note within the ancient value system that gave primacy to kinship relations. See also 10:28–31.

4:1–2 The crowd forces Jesus into the boat, from which he speaks his first of two major addresses in Mark's story. The parables here convey Jesus' commentary on the events of his own time as well as the time leading up to the crisis facing Mark's community. Jesus' other major address is the "apocalyptic discourse" spoken to a few chosen followers in chapter 13.

4:3–8 The parable of the Sower is actually concerned less with the actions of the human farmer than with the drama of natural processes: the fate of a series of seeds cast on various soils. The harvest obtained from the seed cast on good earth contrasts vividly with the losses experienced when other seeds fail to produce fruit.

Jesus introduces the story with a call to *listen*. The need for effective "listening" is stressed throughout this section (4:3, 9, 33–34).

4:8 Many scholars believe that the return of *thirty, sixty, or one hundred* seeds is intended to portray an extravagant harvest, though the point may simply be that though many seeds are lost in the process of sowing and growth, those that do bear fruit do so in great numbers.

4:10–12 Several times Mark shows Jesus moving into a private setting to explain his public speech or deeds to his chosen group (see also 7:17; 9:28; 10:10).

have been given the secret of the empire of God; but to those outside everything is presented in parables, [12]so that

> They may look with eyes wide open
>> but never quite see,
> and may listen with ears attuned
>> but never quite understand,
> otherwise they might turn around and find forgiveness.

[13]**Then he says to them**: "You don't get this parable, so how are you going to understand other parables? [14]The 'sower' is 'sowing' the message. [15]The first group are the ones 'along the path': here the message 'is sown,' but when they hear, right away Satan comes and steals the message that has been 'sown' into them. [16]The second group are the ones sown 'on rocky ground.' Whenever they listen to the message, right away they receive it happily. [17]Yet they do not have their own 'root' and so are short-lived. When tribulation or persecution comes because of the message, right away they are brought down. [18]And the third group are those sown 'among the thorns.' These are the ones who have listened to the message, [19]but the worries of the age and the seductiveness of wealth and the yearning for everything else come and 'choke' the message and they become 'fruitless.' [20]And the final group are the ones sown 'on good soil.' They are the ones who listen to the message and take it in and 'bear fruit, here thirty, there sixty, and there one hundred.'"

[21]**And he was saying** to them, "Since when is the lamp brought in to be put under the bushel basket or under the bed? It's put on the lampstand, isn't it?

[22]"After all, there is nothing hidden except to be brought to light, nor anything kept secret that won't be exposed.

[23]"If anyone here has two good ears, use 'em!"

[24]**And he went on to say** to them, "Pay attention to what you hear! The standard you apply will be the standard applied to you, and then some.

[25]"In fact, to those who have, more will be given, and from those who don't have, even what they do have will be taken away!"   one-liner

4:13–20
//Mt 13:18–23,
Lk 8:11–15;
cf. SJas 6:17

4:13
Cf. SJas 5:5

4:21
//Q 11:33;
Mt 5:15; Lk 8:16,
11:33; Th 33:2–3

4:22
//Q 12:2;
Mt 10:26b; Lk 8:17,
12:2; Th 5:2, 6:5–6

4:23
//Mt 11:15, 13:9,
43b; Lk 8:8b,
14:35b; Mary 2:5,
3:14; Rev 2:7a,11a,
17a, 3:6, 13, 22,
13:9a; Th 8:4, 21:10,
24:2, 63:4, 65:8,
96:3;
Ⓓ Mk 4:9 [7:16]

4:24
//Q 6:38c, Mt 7:2b,
Lk 6:38c

4:25
//Q 19:26;
Mt 13:12, 25:29;
Lk 8:18b, 19:26;
Th 41

Here *the secret of the empire of God* is said to be given only to the insiders, while to others Jesus' meaning is obscured (see also vv. 33–34).

The prophetic words quoted from Isaiah 6 were a favorite passage for Christians as they tried to explain the lack of a positive response to Jesus and his followers from their fellow Jews (see, e.g., Acts 28:25–28 and John 12:40).

4:13–20 After a characteristic rebuke for their lack of understanding, Jesus proceeds to explain his symbolic story

to his followers (see 7:14–23; 8:14–21). The key words of the parable are picked up and interpreted allegorically to explain the various failures and successes of the group's efforts at mission. The symbols shift from a focus on the soils and seeds to the fate of the plants that shoot up, and then are devoured, scorched, choked, or in some cases flourish in the difficult conditions of Jesus' work and Mark's community history.

²⁶**And he was saying**:

The empire of God is like this: suppose someone sows seed on the ground, ²⁷and sleeps and rises night and day, and the seed sprouts and matures, although the sower is unaware of it. ²⁸The earth produces fruit on its own, first a shoot, then a head, then mature grain on the head. ²⁹But when the grain ripens, right away he sends for the sickle, because it's harvest time.

³⁰**And he was saying**:

To what should we compare the empire of God, or what parable should we use for it? ³¹Think about the mustard seed: when it is sown on the ground, though it is the smallest of all the seeds on the earth, ³²—yet when it is sown, it comes up, and becomes the biggest of all garden plants, and produces branches, so that the birds of the sky can nest in its shade.

³³**And with the help of many such parables** he would speak his message to them according to their ability to comprehend. ³⁴Yet he would not say anything to them except by way of parable, but would explain everything in private to his own disciples.

³⁵**Later in the day**, when evening had come, he says to them, "Let's go across to the other side." ³⁶After sending the crowd away, they took him along since he was in the boat, and other boats accompanied him. ³⁷Then a great squall comes up and the waves begin to pound against the boat, so that the boat suddenly began to fill up. ³⁸He was in the stern, sleeping on a cushion. And they wake him up and say to him, "Teacher, don't you care? We're sinking!"

³⁹Then he got up and rebuked the wind and said to the sea, "Be quiet, shut up!"

The wind then died down and there was a great calm.

⁴⁰He said to them, "Why are you such cowards? You still don't trust, do you?"

⁴¹And they were completely terrified and would say to one another, "Who in the world is this? Even the wind and the sea obey him."

4:26–29
Cf. Th 21:9

4:30–32
//Q 13:18–19, Mt 13:31–32, Lk 13:18–19, Th 20;
◊ Ez 17:22–24; Dn 4:10–12, 21; Ⓣ DSav 36:1

4:33–34
//Mt 13:34

4:35–41
//Mt 8:18, 23–27, Lk 8:22–25;
◊ Ps 89:8–9, 93:3–4, 106:8–9; Is 59:9–10; Jon 1:4–5

4:26–32 In these brief symbolic pictures we have Jesus' continued prediction of the difficulties and apparent uncertainties at hand and to come. The workings of *the empire of God* are again likened to the inexplicable processes of nature, with the emphasis still lying on the contrast between unpromising beginnings and great endings.

4:35–41 Here Mark describes the first of several boat trips across the Galilean lake. Mark calls this lake the *sea*, using a word (*thalassa*) that most Greek writers reserve for the much larger Mediterranean (Luke uses the more proper term for a lake, *limnē*, in Luke 5:1; 8:22–23, 33).

The squall on the sea and Jesus' masterful silencing of the elements resonate powerfully within the biblical tradition of God's creative and redemptive control of the waters (e.g., Genesis 1; Exodus 14; Psalms 69; 89; 93; 104–7; Isaiah 43; 51:9–10). The story also helps Mark develop his theme of the faltering trust and faulty comprehension of Jesus' band of followers. Unwittingly they awaken Jesus with words elsewhere addressed to God (e.g., Ps 44:23). Jesus stills the storm with the formula for silencing a demon (see 1:25).

5 **And they came** to the other side of the sea, to the region of the Gerasenes. [2]And when he got out of the boat, right away a man possessed by an unclean spirit came from the tombs to meet him. [3]This man made his home in the tombs, and nobody was able to bind him, not even with a chain, [4]because, though he had often been bound with shackles and chains, he would break the shackles and pull the chains apart, and nobody could subdue him. [5]And day and night he would howl among the tombs and across the hills and keep bruising himself on the stones. [6]And when he saw Jesus from a distance, he ran up and knelt before him [7]and, screaming at the top of his voice, he says, "What do you want with me, Jesus, you son of the most high God? For God's sake, don't torment me!" [8]—because he had been saying to it, "Come out of this man, you filthy spirit!"

[9]And Jesus started questioning him, "What's your name?"

"My name is Legion," it says, "because there are many of us."

[10]And it kept begging him over and over again not to expel them from their territory.

[11]Now over there by the mountain a large herd of pigs was feeding. [12]And so they bargained with him, "Send us over to the pigs so we may enter them!"

[13]And he agreed. And then the unclean spirits came out and entered the pigs, and the herd stampeded down the bluff into the sea, about two thousand of them, and drowned in the sea. [14]And the herdsmen ran off and reported it in town and out in the country.

And they went out to see what had happened. [15]And they come to Jesus and notice the demon possessed man sitting there with his clothes on and with his wits about him, the one who had harbored Legion, and they got scared. [16]And those who had seen told them what had happened to the possessed man, and all about the pigs. [17]And they started begging him to leave their region. [18]And as Jesus was getting into the boat, the man who had been possessed kept pleading with him to let him come along. [19]And he would not let him, but says to him, "Go home to your people and tell them what the Lord has done for you—how he has shown mercy to you."

[20]And he went away and started spreading the news in the Ten Cities about what Jesus had done for him, and everybody would marvel.

5:1 Some mss read *Gerasenes,* others "Gadarenes" or "Gergesenes."

5:1–20
//Mt 8:28–34,
Lk 8:26–39

5:1–20 The placing of this episode in Gerasa, thirty miles from the lake, led to several "corrections" in the manuscript tradition. The story is one of Mark's longest and provides a good example of his rambling descriptive style (Matthew and Luke retell the story just as effectively with many fewer words).

5:9 For Mark's audience the Latin name of the demon, *Legion,* likely functioned as code language, making the story also refer to the desired expulsion of the Roman armies from the land.

5:20 The *Ten Cities* was a league of ten cities mostly east of the Jordan, a predominantly gentile region.

Jairus' daughter

*Jesus cures
a woman*

*Jairus' daughter
revived*

²¹**When Jesus had again crossed** over to the other side, a large crowd gathered around him, and he was beside the sea. ²²And one of the synagogue officials comes, Jairus by name, and as soon as he sees him, he kneels at his feet ²³and pleads with him and begs, "My little daughter is on the verge of death, so come and put your hands on her so she may be cured and live."

²⁴And Jesus set out with him.

And a large crowd started following and shoving against him. ²⁵And there was a woman who had experienced a chronic flow of blood for twelve years, ²⁶who had endured much under many doctors, and who had spent everything she had, but hadn't been helped at all, but instead had gotten worse. ²⁷When she heard about Jesus, she came up from behind in the crowd and touched his cloak. (²⁸You see, she was saying, "If I could just touch his clothes, I'll be cured.") ²⁹And right away her flow of blood stopped, and she sensed in her body that she was cured of her illness.

³⁰And right away, because Jesus realized that power had drained out of him, he turned around and started asking the crowd, "Who touched my clothes?"

³¹And his disciples said to him, "You see the crowd jostling you around and you're asking, 'Who touched me?'"

³²And he started looking around to see who had done this. ³³Although the woman got scared and started trembling, realizing what had happened to her, she came and knelt before him and told him the whole truth.

³⁴He said to her, "Daughter, your trust has cured you. Go in peace, and be healed of your affliction."

³⁵**While he was still speaking**, the synagogue official's people approach and say, "Your daughter has died; why keep bothering the teacher?"

³⁶When Jesus overheard this conversation, he says to the official, "Don't be afraid, just have trust!"

³⁷And he wouldn't let anyone follow along with him except Peter and James and John, James' brother. ³⁸When they come to the official's house, he notices a lot of clamor and people crying and wailing, ³⁹and he goes in and says to them, "Why are you carrying on like this? The child hasn't died; she's sleeping."

⁴⁰And they started laughing at him. But he throws everyone out and takes the child's father and her mother and his companions and goes in where the child is. ⁴¹And he takes the child by the hand and says to her, *"talitha kum"*

5:21–43
//Mt 9:18–26,
Lk 8:40–56

5:21–43 Here we find Mark relating two miraculous healings, one of which (vv. 24b–34) has been enclosed or "sandwiched" within the other (vv. 22–24a, 35–43; see note at 3:21). The interposing of the second story provides some dramatic suspense while Jairus' daughter lies on the verge of death.

5:22 Jairus (one of the few people given a name among the many who encounter Jesus in Mark's story) is a *synagogue official*, a wealthy patron of the local house of meeting and prayer.

5:27–29 The woman's method of self-cure, by touching Jesus' garments, is reminiscent of the magical healing powers thought to be alive in the personal articles of holy people. See the effects of Paul's handkerchiefs in Acts 19:11–12.

(which means, "Little girl—I'm talking to you—get up!"). ⁴²And right away the little girl got up and started walking around. (You see, she was twelve years old.)

And they were downright ecstatic. ⁴³And he gave them strict orders that no one should learn about this, and he told them to give her something to eat.

6 **Then he left that place**, and he comes to his hometown, and his disciples follow him. ²When the Sabbath arrived, he started teaching in the meeting place; and many who heard him were astounded and said so: "Where's he getting all this?" and "Where'd he get all this wisdom?" and "Where'd he get the power to perform such miracles? ³This is the carpenter, isn't it? Isn't he the son of Mary? And aren't his brothers James, Joses, Judas, and Simon? And aren't his sisters our neighbors?" And they took offense at him.

⁴Jesus used to tell them, "No prophet is disrespected, except on his home turf and among his relatives and at home."

⁵He was unable to perform a single miracle there, except that he did cure a few by laying hands on them, ⁶though he was always shocked at their lack of trust. And he used to go around the villages, teaching in a circuit.

⁷**Then he summoned the Twelve** and started sending them out in pairs and giving them authority over unclean spirits. ⁸And he instructed them not to take anything on the way, except a staff: no bread, no knapsack, no spending money, ⁹but to wear sandals, and to wear no more than one shirt. ¹⁰And he went on to say to them, "Wherever you enter someone's house, stay there until you leave town. ¹¹And whatever place does not welcome you or listen to you, get out of there and shake the dust off your feet in witness against them."

¹²So they set out and announced that people should turn their lives around, ¹³and they were driving out demons and anointing many sick people with oil and healing them.

¹⁴**King Herod heard** about it—by now, Jesus' fame had spread—and people kept saying that John the Baptizer had been raised from the dead and that's why miraculous powers were at work in him. ¹⁵But others were saying that he was Elijah, and others that he was a prophet like one of the ⟨old time⟩ prophets.

insertion & framing device

Marginal cross-references:

No respect at home

Instructions for the road

Herod beheads John

6:1–6a
//Mt 13:53–58,
Lk 4:16–30
6:4
//Mt 13:57,
Lk 4:24, Jn 4:44,
Th 31
6:6b–13
//Mt 9:35;
10:1, 7–11;
Lk 9:1–6;
cf. Q 10:2–12;
Mt 9:37–38,
10:7–15;
Lk 10:1–12
6:10–11
//Q 10:5–12;
Mt 10:11–15;
Lk 9:4, 10:5–12;
1 Cor 10:27;
Th 14:4
6:14–29
//Mt 14:3–13;
cf. Lk 3:19–20,
9:7–9;
◊ Est 5:3, 7:2

6:1–6 This episode enacts the typical theme that one is not a hero to one's own family or neighbors. The *hometown* (literally, "native district") is unnamed but clearly lies somewhere in Galilee. If the note in 1:9 is meant to refer to Jesus' place of origin then the scene is located in Nazareth.
6:7–13 The disciples' journey of warning, exorcism, and faith healing is the only time in Mark's story where Jesus' followers have any success in carrying out his instructions (see their report at 6:30). The strange rules about the messengers' travel equipment emphasize the special meaning of their trip as a summons to heed Jesus' words about God's empire.

6:11 *Shaking off a town's dust* is a gesture both of contempt and of warning.
6:14–29 Mark's narrative about the Baptizer and King Herod (a son of Herod "the Great") is one of the Gospel's most gripping and effective stories. The scene is punctuated with the typical motifs of folktale (the seductive dancing girl, the extravagant oath, the scheming wife). We get a rare example of the "flashback" technique as Herod wonders whether the stir aroused by the disciples' journey could be John's doing. We learn of John's fate just as the followers of Jesus are enjoying their first success, a combination which casts a troubling shadow on their future work.

[16]When Herod got wind of it, he started declaring, "John, the one I beheaded, has been raised!"

[17]Earlier Herod himself had sent someone to arrest John and put him in chains in a dungeon, on account of Herodias, his brother Philip's wife, because he had married her. ([18]You see, John had said to Herod, "It is not right for you to have your brother's wife.")

[19]So Herodias nursed a grudge against him and wanted to eliminate him, but she couldn't manage it, [20]because Herod was afraid of John. He knew that he was an upright and holy man, and so protected him, and, although he listened to him frequently, he was very confused, yet he listened to him eagerly.

[21]Now a festival day came, when Herod gave a banquet on his birthday for his courtiers, and his commanders, and the leading citizens of Galilee. [22]And the daughter of Herodias came in and captivated Herod and his dinner guests by dancing. The king said to the girl, "Ask me for whatever you wish and I'll grant it to you!" [23]Then he swore an oath to her: "I'll grant you whatever you ask for, up to half my domain!"

[24]She went out and said to her mother, "What should I ask for?"

And she replied, "The head of John the Baptizer!"

[25]Right away she hurried back and made her request: "I want you to give me the head of John the Baptizer on a platter, right now!"

[26]The king grew regretful, but because of his oaths and the dinner guests, he didn't want to refuse her. [27]So right away the king sent for the executioner and commanded him to bring his head. And he went away and beheaded ⟨John⟩ in prison. [28]He brought his head on a platter and presented it to the girl, and the girl gave it to her mother. [29]When his disciples heard about it, they came and got his body and put it in a tomb.

[30]**Then the apostles regroup** around Jesus and they reported to him everything that they had done and taught.

[31]And he says to them, "You come by yourselves to an isolated place and rest a little."

(You see, many were coming and going and they didn't even have a chance to eat.)

[32]So they went away in the boat privately to an isolated place. [33]But many noticed them leaving and figured it out and raced there on foot from all the towns and got there ahead of them. [34]When he came ashore, he saw a huge crowd and was moved by them, because they resembled sheep without a shepherd, and he started teaching them at length.

6:30
//Lk 9:10a

6:32–44
//Mt 14:13–21,
Lk 9:10b–17,
Jn 6:1–13

6:34
◊Nm 27:16–17,
1 Kgs 22:17;
Jdt 11:19

6:30–44 Jesus' miracle of feeding evokes God's care for the starving Israelites during the Exodus. The allusion is strengthened by Jesus' command to have the people arranged in groups of *hundreds and fifties* (v. 40), reminiscent of the groupings of the wandering people of God (Exod 18:25).

*Loaves & fish
for 5,000*

Jesus departs

*Jesus walks
on the sea*

A cloak that cures

[35]**And as the hour** had already grown late, his disciples were approaching him and saying, "This is a desert place and it's late. [36]Send them away so that they can go to the farms and villages around here to buy something to eat."

[37]But in response he said to them, "Give them something to eat yourselves."

And they say to him, "Are we supposed to go out and buy two hundred denarii worth of bread and donate it for their meal?"

[38]So he says to them, "How many loaves do you have? Go look."

And when they find out, they say, "Five, and two fish."

[39]Next he instructed them all to recline to eat, some over here, some over there, on the green grass. [40]So they sat down group by group, in hundreds and in fifties. [41]And he took the five loaves and the two fish, looked up to the sky, gave a blessing, and broke the bread apart, and started giving it to his disciples to pass around to them; and even the two fish they shared with everybody. [42]Everybody had more than enough to eat. [43]Then they picked up twelve baskets full of leftovers, including some fish. [44]And the number of men who had some bread came to five thousand.

[45]**And right away** he made his disciples embark in the boat and go ahead to the opposite shore toward Bethsaida, while he himself dispersed the crowd. [46]And once he got away from them, he went off to the mountain to pray.

[47]**When evening came**, the boat was in the middle of the sea, and he was alone on the land. [48]When he saw they were having a rough time making headway, because the wind was against them, at about three o'clock in the morning he comes toward them walking on the sea and intending to go past them. [49]But when they saw him walking on the sea, they thought he was a ghost and they cried out, [50]because they all saw him and were terrified. But right away he spoke with them and says to them, "Take heart, it's me! Don't be afraid." [51]And he climbed into the boat with them, and the wind died down. By this time they were completely dumbfounded. ([52]You see, they hadn't understood about the loaves; their minds were closed.)

[53]**Once they had crossed** over to land, they landed at Gennesaret and moored. [54]As soon as they had gotten out of the boat, people immediately recognized him, [55]and they ran around over the whole area and started bringing those who were ill on mats to wherever he was rumored to be. [56]And wherever he would go, into villages, or towns, or onto farms, they would lay out the sick in the marketplaces and beg him to let them touch the fringe of his cloak. And all those who managed to touch it were cured.

6:35–44
Ⓓ Mk 8:1–9

6:38–42
◊2 Kgs 4:42–44

6:45–52
//Mt 14:22–33,
Jn 6:16–21

6:53–56
//Mt 14:34–36;
cf. Jn 6:22–24

6:45–52 This brief tale confirms Jesus' mastery over the elements of nature as well as his followers' continued mystification.

6:52 The multiplication of the loaves should have disclosed Jesus' identity and divine authority to the disciples, but *their minds were closed* (literally, "their hearts were hardened"), a biblical phrase suggesting a deliberate veiling on God's part for some larger purpose (e.g., Exod 4:21; 7:13; 14:17).

7 **The Pharisees gather** around him, along with some of the scholars, who had come from Jerusalem. ²When they notice some of his disciples eating their meal with defiled hands, that is to say, without washing their hands (³you see, the Pharisees and the Jews never eat without first washing their hands in a particular way, always observing the tradition of the elders, ⁴and they won't eat when they get back from the marketplace without washing again, and there are many other traditions they cherish, such as the washing of cups and jugs and kettles), ⁵the Pharisees and the scholars start questioning him: "Why don't your disciples live up to the tradition of the elders, instead of eating bread with defiled hands?"

⁶And he answered them, "How accurately Isaiah foretold you phonies when he wrote,

> This people honors me with their lips,
>> but their heart stays far away from me.
> ⁷Their worship of me is empty,
>> because they insist on teachings that are human regulations.

⁸You have set aside God's commandment and hold fast to human tradition."

⁹Or he would say to them, "How expert you've become at putting aside God's commandment to establish your own tradition. ¹⁰For example, Moses said, 'Honor your father and your mother' and 'Those who curse their fathers or mothers absolutely must die.' ¹¹But you say, 'If people say to their fathers or mothers, "Whatever I might have spent to support you is *korban*"' (which means "consecrated to God"), ¹²you no longer let those persons do anything for their fathers or mothers. ¹³So you end up invalidating God's word with your own tradition, which you then perpetuate. And you do all kinds of other things like that."

¹⁴**Once again** he summoned the crowd and would say to them, "Listen to me, all of you, and try to understand. ¹⁵What goes into you can't defile you; what comes out of you can. ¹⁶If anyone here has two good ears, use 'em!"

¹⁷When he entered a house away from the crowd, his disciples started questioning him about the riddle. ¹⁸And he says to them, "Are you as dim-witted as

7:1–13
//Mt 15:1–9

7:6–7
//EgerG 3:6;
◊Is 29:13

7:10
◊Ex 20:12, 21:17;
Lv 20:9; Dt 5:16

7:14–15
//Mt 15:10–11,
Th 14:5

7:17–23
//Mt 15:15–20;
Ⓣ Mk 4:10–20,
8:14–21, 9:28–30,
10:10–12

7:16 This entire verse is missing in some early mss.

7:3–4 Mark addresses his audience directly, presuming that his readers will not understand or follow these ordinary Jewish rules of food preparation any more than the disciples did.

7:6 The word we translate as *phonies* (traditionally simply transliterated as "hypocrites") means someone who acts a part in an insincere manner.

7:11–13 *Korban* is the Hebrew word for offerings made to God (see Lev 1:2; Num 7:13). The suggestion that dedications could be made to avoid one's obligation to care for needy parents is not known from other sources; rabbinic Jewish texts suggest that vows may be broken in such circumstances.

7:14–23 Mark counterposes the crowd with both Jesus' antagonists and followers. In chapter 4 the crowd is deliberately left confused while the disciples are given the secret to

one-liner

the rest? Don't you realize that nothing from outside can defile by going into a person, [19]because it doesn't get to the heart but passes into the stomach, and comes out in the outhouse?" (This is how everything we eat is purified.)

[20]And he went on to say, "It's what comes out of a person that defiles. [21]For from out of the human heart issue wicked intentions: sexual immorality, thefts, murders, [22]adulteries, greed, wickedness, deceit, promiscuity, an evil eye, blasphemy, arrogance, lack of good sense. [23]All these evil things come from the inside out and defile you."

[24]**From there he got up** and went away to the regions of Tyre. Whenever he visited a house he wanted no one to know, but he could not escape notice. [25]But right away a woman whose daughter had an unclean spirit heard about him, and came and knelt at his feet. [26]The woman was a Greek, by race a Phoenician from Syria, and she started asking him to drive the demon out of her daughter. [27]He was saying to her, "Let the children be fed first, since it isn't good to take bread out of children's mouths and throw it to the dogs!"

[28]But she answered him, "Sir, even the dogs under the table get to eat scraps ⟨dropped by⟩ children!"

[29]Then he said to her, "For that insightful answer, be on your way, the demon has come out of your daughter."

[30]She returned home and found the child lying on the bed and the demon gone.

[31]**Then he left** the regions of Tyre and traveled through Sidon to the Sea of Galilee, through the middle of the region known as the Ten Cities.

[32]And they bring him a deaf-mute and plead with him to lay his hand on him. [33]Taking him aside from the crowd in private, he stuck his fingers into the man's ears and spat and touched his tongue. [34]And looking up to the sky, he groaned and says to him, *"ephphatha"* (which means, "Be opened"). [35]And right away his ears opened up and his speech impediment was removed and he started speaking properly. [36]Then he ordered them to tell no one. But the more he ordered them not to, they more they spread it around.

[37]And they were completely dumbfounded. "He's done everything and done it well," they said; "He even makes the deaf hear and the mute speak!"

A Greek woman's daughter healed

A deaf mute healed

7:24–30
//Mt 15:21–28

7:31–37
Cf. Mt 15:29–31

---

understanding (4:10–12, 33–34). Here in v. 18, and again after a second miracle of feeding (8:1–10, 14–21), Jesus reproaches the confused disciples in the same terms he had used earlier for the uncomprehending crowds.

7:28–30 The gentile woman wins Jesus over with a swift retort. This is Jesus' only miracle from a distance in Mark's story.

7:31 Mark's geographical sense seems confused here, since Tyre is *south* of Sidon: to *return* to the Sea of Galilee from

Tyre would not normally mean a journey *north* to Sidon, nor to the *southeast* through the gentile region of the Ten Cities (see 5:20). What seems to be intended is a general indication of a trip through non-Israelite areas to the north and east of Galilee.

7:32–37 Jesus' cure of the deaf and mute man uses the techniques of magical healing: touching the ailing part, use of spittle, command in an exotic language (exotic to Mark's readers, that is).

Loaves & fish
for 4,000

Demand for a sign

Bread & leaven

8 **And in those days**, there was again a huge crowd without anything to eat, so he calls the disciples aside and says to them, ²"I feel sorry for the crowd, because they have already spent three days with me and now they've run out of food. ³If I send these people home hungry, they will collapse on the way and some of them have come from quite a distance."

⁴And his disciples answered him, "How can anyone feed these people bread out here in this desert place?"

⁵And he started asking them, "How many loaves do you have?"

They replied, "Seven."

⁶Then he orders the crowd to sit down on the ground. And he took the seven loaves, gave thanks, and broke them into pieces, and started giving them to his disciples to hand out; and they passed them around to the crowd. ⁷They also had a few small fish. When he had blessed them, he told them to hand those out as well. ⁸They had more than enough to eat. Then they picked up seven big baskets of leftover scraps. ⁹There were about four thousand people there. Then he started sending them away.

¹⁰**And right away** he got into the boat with his disciples and went to the Dalmanutha district.

¹¹The Pharisees came out and started to argue with him. To put him to the test, they demanded a sign from heaven. ¹²He groaned under his breath and says, "Why does this generation demand a sign? Let me tell you, this generation won't get any sign!" ¹³And turning his back on them, he got back in the boat and crossed over to the other side.

¹⁴**They forgot to bring** any bread and had nothing with them in the boat except one loaf. ¹⁵Then he started warning them, "Look, watch out for the leaven of the Pharisees and the leaven of Herod."

¹⁶They began discussing with one another that they had no bread. ¹⁷And because he was aware of this, he says to them, "Why are you talking about bread you don't have? You still don't get it, do you? You still haven't got the point, have you? Are you just closed-minded? ¹⁸You have eyes, but you still don't see, and you have ears, but you still don't hear. Don't you even remember ¹⁹how many baskets full of scraps you picked up when I broke up the five loaves for the five thousand?"

"Twelve," they reply to him.

8:1–10
//Mt 15:32–39;
Ⓓ Mk 6:35–44;
◊2 Kgs 4:42–44

8:11–12
//Mt 12:38–39;
cf. Q 11:29–30;
Mt 12:38–39,
16:1–4;
Lk 11:14–16, 29–30

8:14–21
//Mt 16:5–12;
Ⓘ Mk 6:35–44,
51–52; 7:14–21;
8:1–10

8:15
//Mt 16:6, Lk 12:1

8:18
◊Jer 5:21, Ez 12:2

8:15 Some mss read "the Herodians" in place of *Herod*.

8:1–9 This story is a doublet of the feeding of five thousand men (6:35–44) with a few circumstantial details changed (seven loaves instead of five, big baskets in place of the ordinary baskets found in the first story).
8:13–21 Another scene of the disciples unable to under-

stand Jesus' meaning. Direct references are made to the two feeding miracles related in 6:30–44 and 8:1–10; the disciples are rebuked in terms reminiscent of 4:10–12 and 7:17.

²⁰"When I broke up the seven loaves for the four thousand, how many big baskets full of scraps did you pick up?"

And they say, "Seven."

²¹And he repeats, "You still don't understand, do you?"

²²**They come to Bethsaida**, and they bring him a blind man, and plead with him to touch him. ²³He took the blind man by the hand and led him out of the village. And he spat into his eyes, and placed his hands on him, and started questioning him, "Do you see anything?"

²⁴And he looked up and began to say, "I see human figures, as though they were trees walking around."

²⁵Then he put his hands on his eyes a second time. And he opened his eyes, and his sight was restored, and he saw everything clearly. ²⁶And he sent him home, saying, "Don't even go into the village."

²⁷**Jesus and his disciples** set out for the villages of Caesarea Philippi. On the way he started questioning his disciples, asking them, "What are people saying about me?"

²⁸And they told him, "⟨Some say,⟩ 'John the Baptizer,' and others, 'Elijah,' but others, 'One of the prophets.'"

²⁹But he kept pressing them, "What about you, who do you say I am?"

Peter responds to him, "You are the Anointed One!" ³⁰And he warned them not to tell anyone about him.

³¹**He started teaching** them that the Human One was destined to endure much, and be rejected by the elders and the chief priests and the scholars, and be killed, and after three days rise. ³²And he was putting this in plain language. And Peter took him aside and began to lecture him. ³³But he turned, noticed his disciples, and reprimanded Peter verbally: "Get out of my sight, you Satan, you, because you're not thinking in God's terms, but in human terms." ᵒⁿᵉ⁻ˡⁱⁿᵉʳ

³⁴**After he called the crowd** together with his disciples, he said to them, "If any of you wants to come after me, you should deny yourself, pick up your cross, and follow after me. ³⁵Remember, if you try to save your life, you'll lose it, but if you lose your life for the sake of the good news, you'll save it. ³⁶After all, what good does it do to acquire the whole world and forfeit your life? ³⁷Or, what would you give in exchange for life?

³⁸"Moreover, if any of you are ashamed of me and my message in this adulterous and sinful generation, of you the Human One will likewise be ashamed

8:27–30
//Mt 16:13–20,
Lk 9:18–21;
cf. Jn 6:67–69,
Th 13

8:31–33
//Mt 16:21–23,
Lk 9:22;
Ⓣ Mk 9:30–32,
10:32–34

8:31
Ⓣ GSav 18:2

8:34–35
Ⓣ SJas 4:10–5:3

8:34–9:1
//Mt 16:24–28,
Lk 9:23–27

8:34
Cf. Q 14:27,
Mt 10:38, Th 55:2;
Ⓣ DSav 11:4

8:35
cf. Mt 10:39,
Lk 17:33, Jn 12:25

8:22–26 Mark concludes the first half of his story with this healing of a blind man. The cure's initial failure and the magical aspects of the healing may explain why the other gospel writers fail to record this story.

8:27–33 A key juncture in Mark's story. Peter steps forward to assert Jesus' identity as God's *Anointed One*. Jesus meets this confession not with relief or approval but instead with a warning of impending suffering for "the Human

One." Peter's disapproval of this prediction represents our own confusion as readers; he and we are rebuked for not seeing things from God's point of view.

8:38 Rebuking God's people as *adulterous and sinful* is a theme of biblical prophets going back to Hosea, who charged that Israel's "going after other gods" was tantamount to committing adultery against their lawful spouse Yahweh.

Jesus transformed

Elijah must come

*A mute spirit
expelled*

when he comes in his Father's glory accompanied by the holy heavenly messengers." 9 ¹And he was telling them, "Let me tell you, some of those standing here won't ever taste death before they see the empire of God arriving in force."

9

one-liner

²**Six days later**, Jesus takes Peter and James and John along and leads them off by themselves to a lofty mountain. He was transformed in front of them, ³and his clothes became an intensely brilliant white, whiter than any laundry on earth could make them. ⁴Elijah appeared to them, with Moses, and they were conversing with Jesus. ⁵Peter responds by saying to Jesus, "Rabbi, it's a good thing we're here. How about we set up three tents, one for you and one for Moses and one for Elijah?" (⁶You see, he didn't know what else to say, since they were terrified.)

⁷And a cloud moved in and cast a shadow over them, and a voice came out of the cloud: "This is my son, the one I love, listen to him!" ⁸Suddenly, as they looked around, they saw no one, but were alone with Jesus.

⁹**And as they were walking** down the mountain he instructed them not to describe what they had seen to anyone, until the Human One rises from among the dead.

¹⁰And they kept it to themselves, puzzling over what this could mean, this 'rising from the dead.' ¹¹And they started questioning him, "The scholars claim, don't they, that Elijah must come first?"

¹²He was responding to them, "Of course Elijah comes first to restore everything. So, how does scripture claim that the Human One will endure much and be treated with contempt? ¹³But take my word for it: Elijah did in fact arrive, just as the scriptures said he would, and they did to him whatever they pleased."

¹⁴**When they rejoined the disciples**, they saw a huge crowd surrounding them and scholars arguing with them. ¹⁵And right away, when the whole crowd caught sight of him, they were amazed and rushed up to meet him. ¹⁶He asked them, "Why are you bothering to argue with them?"

9:2–8
//Mt 17:1–8,
Lk 9:28–36

9:7
//Mk 1:11;
Ⓣ Judas 6:10;
◊ Is 42:1, 44:2

9:9–13
//Mt 17:9–13;
◊ 1 Kgs 19:2, 10

9:14–27
//Mt 17:14–18,
Lk 9:37–43a

9:1 This prediction suggests that Mark's story arose at a time when some people from Jesus' time were still known to be alive, and God's empire rule was expected *to arrive in force* at any moment.

9:2–8 The select group of three inner disciples privately see Jesus *transformed* on *a lofty mountain*. Again Mark provides his characters with a symbolic landscape appropriate to the moment, without having to get too specific about the geographical details.

Two significant heroes of faith also appear. *Moses'* burial place was never found (see Deut 34:6); *Elijah* was said to have been taken to heaven before death (2 Kings 2). Some people expected one or both to return in the last days.

This time God's voice is addressed to those around Jesus. The scene confirms for them (and for the reader) that Jesus

has divine warrant for his work.

9:11–13 The Israelite prophet Elijah was seen in Mal 4:5–6 as a forerunner of the "coming of the day of the Lord," a time when peoples' hearts would be redirected to love of family and neighbor. Here Jesus explains that Elijah has come in the person of John the Baptizer. (Matthew makes the identification crystal clear to his readers at 17:13).

9:14–29 This episode combines elements of both an exorcism and a healing story. Jesus makes the cure depend on *trust* (v. 23). His disciples (though without their leaders Peter, James, and John) had been unable to cure the boy. In a private scene at home at the end of the story (vv. 28–29) Jesus chooses not to rebuke them for failure but instead to give them some practical advice for the next time.

¹⁷And someone from the crowd answered him, "Teacher, I brought my son to you, because he has a mute spirit. ¹⁸Whenever it takes him over, it knocks him down, and he foams at the mouth and grinds his teeth and stiffens up. I asked your disciples to drive it out, but they couldn't."

¹⁹In response he says, "You distrustful generation, how much longer do I have to be around you? How much longer do I have to put up with you? Bring him over here!"

²⁰And they brought him over to him. And when the spirit noticed him, right away it threw him into convulsions, and he fell to the ground, and kept rolling around, foaming at the mouth. ²¹And Jesus asked his father, "How long has he been like this?"

He replied, "Ever since he was a child. ²²It has frequently tried to destroy him by throwing him into fire and into water. So if you can do anything, take pity on us and help us!"

²³Jesus said to him, "What do you mean, 'If you can'? Anything is possible for those who trust."

²⁴Right away the father of the child cried out and said, "I do trust! Help my lack of trust!"

²⁵When Jesus saw that the crowd was about to mob them, he rebuked the unclean spirit, commanding it, "Deaf and mute spirit, I command you, get out of him and don't ever go back inside him!"

²⁶And after he shrieked and went into a series of convulsions, it came out. And he took on the appearance of a corpse, so that the rumor went around that he had died. ²⁷But Jesus took hold of his hand and raised him, and there he stood.

²⁸And when he had gone home, his disciples started questioning him privately, "Why couldn't we drive it out?"

²⁹He said to them, "The only thing that can drive this kind out is prayer."

³⁰**They left there** and started going through Galilee, and he did not want anyone to know. ³¹You see, he was instructing his disciples and telling them, "The Human One will be turned over to his enemies, and they will kill him. And three days after he is killed he will rise." ³²They didn't understand this instruction and they dreaded asking him about it.

³³**And they came to Capernaum**. When he got home, he started questioning them, "What were you arguing about on the way?" ³⁴And they fell silent, because on the way they had been bickering about who was greatest.

³⁵He sat down and called the Twelve and says to them, "If any of you wants to be 'number one,' you have to be last of all and servant of all."

one-liner

Second passion prediction

Number one is last

9:28–30
//Mt 17:19–20;
Ⓣ Mk 7:17–23,
10:10–12

9:30–32
//Mt 17:22–23;
Lk 9:43b–45;
Ⓣ Mk 8:31–33,
10:32–24

9:33–37
//Mt 18:1–2, 5;
Lk 9:46–48

9:30–32 Jesus repeats his prediction about the approaching suffering, death, and rising of the Human One, again arousing fear and consternation in his followers.

[36]And he took a child and had her stand in front of them, and he put his arm around her, and he said to them, [37]"Whoever welcomes a child like this in my name is welcoming me. And whoever welcomes me is not so much welcoming me as the one who sent me."

[38]**John said to him**, "Teacher, we saw someone driving out demons in your name, so we tried to stop him, because he wasn't one of our followers."

[39]Jesus responded, "Don't stop him. You see, no one who performs a miracle in my name will then turn around and curse me. [40]For whoever is not against us is on our side. [41]You see, whoever gives you a cup of water to drink because you carry the name of the Anointed One, let me tell you: such a person certainly won't go unrewarded!

[42]"**And any of you who entraps** and exploits one of these little trusting souls would be better off if you had a millstone tied around your neck and were thrown into the sea!

[43]"And if your hand gets you into trouble, cut it off! It's better for you to enter life maimed than to wind up in Gehenna, in the unquenchable fire, with both hands! [45]And if your foot gets you into trouble, cut it off! It's better for you to enter life lame than to be thrown into Gehenna with both feet! [47]And if your eye gets you into trouble, rip it out! It's better for you to enter God's empire one-eyed than to be thrown into Gehenna with both eyes, [48]where the worm never dies and the fire never goes out!

[49]"You see, everyone will be salted with fire. [50]Salt is good, but if salt becomes tasteless, how will you renew it? Maintain 'salt' among yourselves and be at peace with one another."

10 **And from there he gets up** and goes to the territory of Judea and across the Jordan, and again crowds gather around him. And again, as usual, he started teaching them.

[2]And Pharisees approach him and, to test him, they ask whether a husband is permitted to divorce his wife. [3]In response he said to them, "What did Moses command you?"

9:37
Cf. Q 10:16;
Mt 10:40; Lk 10:16;
Jn 5:24, 12:43b–
44,13:20

9:38–40
//Lk 9:49–50

9:40
Cf. Q 11:23,
Mt 12:30, Lk 11:23,
GOxy 1224 6:1

9:41
Cf. Mt 10:42

9:42–48
//Mt 18:6–9

9:42
//Lk 17:1–2

9:48
◊Is 66:24

9:50
//Q 14:34–35,
Mt 5:13,
Lk 14:34–35;
◊Lv 2:13

10:1–12
//Mt 19:1–12

9:43, 45 Many mss repeat v. 48 at the end of vv. 43 and 45.

9:38–41 Jesus declares that in his fight "the foe of my foe is my friend." Elsewhere in the gospel tradition we find the more exclusive version of the saying, that "those who aren't with me are against me" (Q 11:23).

9:43 The word *Gehenna* derives from the name of the valley of Hinnom, adjacent to ancient Jerusalem. By Jesus' day the name had become synonymous with a place of fiery punishment after death, due perhaps to associations with stories of forbidden human sacrifices by fire in the valley (see 2 Chron 28:3; 33:6; Jer 7:31–32; 19:6; 32:35).

10:1 Jesus begins his journey southward from Galilee towards his fate in Jerusalem. Again he is surrounded by crowds, religious antagonists, and disciples.

10:2–12 We are told that the Pharisees' question arises not from ignorance but from malice. Jesus engages in some scriptural jousting, trumping the Mosaic commandment (found in the fifth book of the Bible) with his own proof-texts from the opening chapters of Genesis. In v. 9 Jesus forbids divorce despite Moses' provisions. This leads to another private scene at home where Jesus forbids not divorce but remarriage.

⁴They replied, "Moses allowed a man to get a divorce by preparing a certificate of separation."

⁵Jesus said to them, "He gave you this injunction because you are headstrong. ⁶But in the beginning, at the creation, 'God made them male and female.' ⁷'For this reason, a man will leave his father and mother and be united with his wife, ⁸and the two will become one body.' That's why they are no longer two, but 'one body.' ⁹Therefore those God has coupled together, no one else should separate."

¹⁰And once again, as usual, when they got home, the disciples questioned him about this. ¹¹And he says to them, "Whoever divorces his wife and marries another commits adultery against her; ¹²and if she divorces her husband and marries another, she commits adultery."

¹³**And they would bring children** to him so he could lay hands on them, but the disciples scolded them. ¹⁴Then Jesus grew indignant when he saw this and said to them, "Let the children come up to me; don't try to stop them. After all, God's empire belongs to people like these. ¹⁵Let me tell you, whoever doesn't welcome the empire of God the way a child would, will never set foot in ⟨his empire⟩." ¹⁶After he put his arms around them, he blesses them, laying his hands on them.

¹⁷**As he was traveling** along the way, someone ran up, knelt before him, and started questioning him, "Good teacher, what do I have to do to inherit everlasting life?"

¹⁸Jesus said to him, "Why do you call me good? No one is good except God alone. ¹⁹You know the commandments: 'You shall not murder, you shall not commit adultery, you shall not steal, you shall not give false testimony, you shall not defraud, and you shall honor your father and mother.'"

²⁰He said to him, "Teacher, I have observed all these things since I was a child."

²¹Jesus looked at him and loved him and said to him, "You are missing one thing: make your move, sell whatever you have, and give ⟨the money⟩ to the poor, and you will have treasure in heaven. And then come on, follow me!"

²²But stunned by this advice, he went away dejected, since he had a fortune.

²³**After looking around**, Jesus says to his disciples, "How difficult it is for those with money to enter God's empire!" ²⁴The disciples were amazed at his words.

In response Jesus says again, "Children, how difficult it is to enter God's empire! ²⁵It's easier for a camel to squeeze through the eye of a needle than for the wealthy to get into God's empire!"

Children in God's empire

Man with money

Needle's eye

10:4
◊ Dt 24:1

10:6–8
◊ Gn 1:27, 2:24

10:10–12
Ⓣ Mk 7:17–23, 9:28–20

10:11–12
//Mt 5:31–32, 19:9; Lk 16:18; 1 Cor 7:10

10:13–16
//Mt 19:13–15, Lk 18:15–17

10:15
//Mt 18:3; cf. Jn 3:1–10, Th 22

10:17–31
//Mt 19:16–30, Lk 18:18–30, GNaz 6

10:19
◊ Ex 20:12–16, Dt 5:16–20

10:17–22 Jesus is wary of accepting the eager praise of this man who runs up and kneels before him: *Why do you call me good?*. Throughout Mark's story the motives of those who approach Jesus are carefully scrutinized, with Jesus remaining indifferent to or suspicious of various ways in which people characterize him.

10:23–27 The rich man's sorrow leads to one of Jesus' most memorable pronouncements, about *the camel and the eye of a needle*. The image is both exaggerated and shocking, since most people presume that the wealthy already have God's favor and thus have *inheriting everlasting life* (v. 17) all taken care of.

²⁶And they were totally amazed, saying to each other, "Well then, who can be saved?"

²⁷Jesus looks them in the eye and says, "For humans it's impossible, but not for God; you see, everything's possible for God."

²⁸Peter began telling him, "Look at us, we left everything to follow you!"

²⁹Jesus said, "Let me tell you, there is no one who has left home or brothers or sisters or mother or father or children or farms on my account and on account of the good news, ³⁰who won't receive a hundred times as much now, in the present time: homes and brothers and sisters and mothers and children and farms—including persecutions—and in the age to come, eternal life.

³¹"Many of the first will be last, and many of the last will be first."

³²**On the way up** to Jerusalem, Jesus was leading the way; they were anxious, and those following were afraid. Once again he took the Twelve aside and started telling them what was going to happen to him. ³³"Listen, we're going up to Jerusalem, and the Human One will be turned over to the chief priests and the scholars, and they will sentence him to death, and turn him over to foreigners, ³⁴and they will make fun of him, and spit on him, and flog him, and kill ⟨him⟩. But after three days he will rise."

³⁵**Then James and John**, the sons of Zebedee, come up to him, and say to him, "Teacher, we want you to do for us whatever we ask."

³⁶He said to them, "What do you want me to do for you?"

³⁷They reply to him, "In your glory, let one of us sit at your right hand, and the other at your left."

10:28
Cf. SJas 4:1

10:31
Cf. Mt 20:l6,
Lk 13:30, Th 4:2

10:32–34
//Mt 20:17–19,
Lk 18:31–34;
Ⓣ Mk 8:31–32,
9:30–32

10:35–40
//Mt 20:20–23

10:34, 35 Between these verses the Mystical Gospel of Mark continues: "And they come to Bethany, and a woman was there whose brother had died. She knelt down in front of Jesus and says to him, 'Son of David, have mercy on me.' But the disciples rebuked her. And Jesus got angry and went with her into the garden where the tomb was. Just then a loud voice was heard from inside the tomb. Then Jesus went up and rolled the stone away from the entrance to the tomb. He went right in where the young man was, stuck out his hand, grabbed him by the hand, and raised him up. The young man looked at Jesus, loved him, and began to beg him to be with him. Then they left the tomb and went into the young man's house. (Incidentally, he was rich.)

"Six days later Jesus gave him an order; and when evening had come, the young man went to him, dressed only in a linen cloth. He spent that night with him, because Jesus taught him the mystery of the empire of God. From there ⟨Jesus⟩ got up and returned to the other side of the Jordan."

10:28–31 In response to Peter's outburst (*We left everything to follow you!*) Jesus promises a replacement family made up of the group itself, though this transfer of affections will also involve harassment and pain. Jesus had made the same move himself in 3:31–35.

10:32–34 Jesus' third prediction of the approaching sufferings of the Human One is the most detailed yet. We will see

precisely these items acted out in chapters 14–15.

10:35–45 Jesus responds to James and John's request for preferential treatment with a promise of suffering and death, expressed in the church's sacramental language of *cup* and *baptism* (v. 38). For the first time (v. 45) Jesus' own approaching death is explained in terms of its benefit for others: *as a ransom for many.*

*Number one
is slave*

Blind Bartimaeus

*Jesus enters
Jerusalem*

³⁸Jesus said to them, "You have no idea what you're asking for. Can you drink the cup that I'm drinking, or go through the baptism I'm going through?"

³⁹They said to him, "We can!"

Jesus said to them, "The cup I'm drinking you'll be drinking, and the baptism I'm going through you'll go through, ⁴⁰but as for sitting at my right or my left, that's not mine to grant, but belongs to those for whom it has been reserved."

⁴¹**When the other ten heard** of it, they were incensed with James and John. ⁴²Calling them aside, Jesus says to them, "You know how those who supposedly rule over foreigners lord it over them, and how their strong men tyrannize them. ⁴³But it's not going to be like that with you. With you, whoever wants to become great must be your servant, ⁴⁴and whoever among you wants to be 'number one' must be everybody's slave. ⁴⁵You see, the Human One didn't come to be served, but to serve and to give his life as a ransom for many."

⁴⁶**Then they come to Jericho**. As he was leaving Jericho with his disciples and a good-sized crowd, Bartimaeus, a blind beggar, the son of Timaeus, was sitting by the wayside. ⁴⁷When he heard that it was Jesus the Nazarene, he began to shout, "Son of David, Jesus, have mercy on me!"

⁴⁸And many kept yelling at him to shut up, but he shouted all the louder, "Son of David, have mercy on me!"

⁴⁹Jesus paused and said, "Call him over here!"

They called to the blind man, "Be brave, get up, he's calling you!" ⁵⁰So he threw off his cloak, and jumped to his feet, and went over to Jesus.

⁵¹In response Jesus said, "What do you want me to do for you?"

The blind man said to him, "Rabbi, I want to see again."

⁵²And Jesus said to him, "Get going; your trust has cured you." And right away he regained his sight, and he started following him on the way.

11 When they get close to Jerusalem, near Bethphage and Bethany at the Mount of Olives, he sends off two of his disciples ²with these instructions: "Go into the village across the way, and after you enter it, right away you'll find a colt

10:41–45
//Mt 20:24–28,
Lk 22:24–26;
cf. Mt 23:11,
Jn 13:1–20,
Mk 9:35

10:46–52
//Mt 20:29–34,
Lk 18:35–43

11:1–10
//Mt 21:1–9,
Lk 19:28–38;
◊ Zec 9:9

10:46 After *they come to Jericho* the Mystical Gospel of Mark continues: "The sister of the young man whom Jesus loved was there, along with his mother and Salome, but Jesus refused to see them."

10:46–52 Jesus' journey is framed with two healings of blind men, here and in 8:22–26. Instead of being sent home silent, this time the cured man follows Jesus on his way.
10:46 Jesus' odd entry and immediate exit from Jericho are supplemented in the shorter fragment from Mystical Mark.
10:47 Bartimaeus shouts out that Jesus is *son of David*, a

messianic title from which Jesus seems to distance himself in 12:34–37.
11:1–10 Entry into the great city is made with careful planning, with a scouting mission and even a staged reception. Within the world of Mark story, this is Jesus' first visit to Jerusalem.

Fig tree without figs

*Jesus disrupts
the temple*

tied up, one that has never been ridden. Untie it and bring it here. ³If anyone says, 'Why are you doing this?' just say, 'The master needs it and he will send it back here right away.'"

⁴They set out and found a colt tied up at the door out on the street, and they untie it. ⁵Some of the people standing around started saying to them, "What do you think you're doing, untying that colt?" ⁶But they said just what Jesus had told them to say, so they left them alone.

⁷So they bring the colt to Jesus, and they throw their cloaks over it; then he got on it. ⁸And many people spread their cloaks on the road, while others cut leafy branches from the fields. ⁹Those leading the way and those following kept shouting,

> Hosanna! Blessed is the one who comes in the name of the Lord!
>
> ¹⁰Blessed is the coming kingdom of our father David!
>
> Hosanna in the highest ⟨heaven⟩!

¹¹**And he went into Jerusalem** to the temple area and took stock of everything, but, since the hour was already late, he returned to Bethany with the Twelve.

¹²On the next day, as they were leaving Bethany, he was hungry. ¹³So when he spotted a fig tree in the distance with leaves on it, he went up to it hoping to find something on it. But when he got up next to it, he found nothing on it but leaves. (You see, it wasn't 'time' for figs.) ¹⁴And he reacted by saying to it, "May no one so much as taste your fruit again!" And his disciples were listening.

¹⁵**They come to Jerusalem.** And he went into the temple and began throwing the vendors and the customers out of the temple area, and he knocked over the currency exchange tables, along with the chairs of the dove merchants, ¹⁶and he wouldn't even let anyone carry a container through the temple area. ¹⁷Then he started teaching and saying to them, "Don't the scriptures say,

> My house shall be designated a house of prayer for all peoples?

But you have turned it into 'a hideout for bandits'!"

*insertion &
framing
device*

11:9–10
◊Ps 118:25–26

11:11
//Mt 21:10, 17

11:12–14
//Mt 21:18–19

11:15–17
//Mt 21:12–13,
Lk 19:45–46;
cf. Jn 2:14–16

11:17
◊Is 56:7, Jer 7:11

11:3–6 The mysterious instructions about the colt, and their immediate fulfillment in the narrative, increase the disciples' (and reader's) confidence about Jesus' mastery of the situation.

11:8–9 The disciples shout words from Ps 118:25–26: *Hosanna* is a Greek transliteration of Hebrew words meaning "Save, we pray!" Waving of branches (called palm fronds only in John 12:13) is known in the ancient Festival of Tabernacles, but this was an autumn event.

Exactly how many people are involved in the entry scene is left rather vague—perhaps it is only Jesus' group that have stage managed the event. (Luke, Matthew, and especially John get larger crowds of bystanders involved.)

11:11 Jesus himself now scouts out the territory around

the temple, but rather than spend the night in the city, he slips back out of town after dark with his inner circle back to the neighboring village of *Bethany*. They will not spend the night in Jerusalem until Jesus' betrayal and arrest in Gethsemane.

11:13–25 Jesus creates havoc in the temple precincts. The critique of sales practices is both effective and provocative.

The story is framed by Jesus' curse of the unfortunate *fig tree*. The disciples and readers see a demonstration of Jesus' power and predictive abilities. The fig tree episode then becomes a memorable example for Jesus' instructions about confident prayer technique, and perhaps also, in view of Mark's "sandwiching" technique, a symbolic sign about the fate of the temple.

Mountains into the sea

On whose authority?

Leased vineyard

[18]And the chief priests and the scholars heard this and kept looking for a way to destroy him. (You see, they were afraid of him because the whole crowd was astonished at his teaching.) [19]And when it grew dark, they were leaving the city.

[20]**As they were walking** along early in the morning, they saw the fig tree withered from the roots up. [21]And Peter remembered and says to him, "Rabbi, look, the fig tree you cursed has withered!"

[22]In response Jesus says to them, "Have trust in God. [23]Let me tell you, those who say to this mountain, 'Up with you and into the sea!' and do not waver in their conviction, but trust that what they say will happen, that's the way it will be. [24]This is why I keep telling you, trust that you will receive everything you pray and ask for, and that's the way it will turn out. [25]And when you stand up to pray, if you are holding anything against anyone, forgive them, so your Father in heaven may forgive your transgressions." one-liner

[27]**Again they come to Jerusalem.** As he walks around in the temple area, the chief priests and scholars and elders come up to him [28]and start questioning him: "Where'd you get the authority to do these things?" or, "Who gave you the authority to do these things?"

[29]But Jesus said to them, "I have one question for you. If you answer me, then I will tell you by what authority I do these things. [30]Tell me, was the baptism of John from Heaven or was it of from humans? Answer me that."

[31]And they conferred among themselves, saying, "If we say 'from Heaven,' he'll say, 'Then why didn't you trust him?' [32]But if we say 'From humans! . . .'" They were afraid of the crowd. (You see, everybody considered John a genuine prophet.) [33]So they answered Jesus by saying, "We can't tell."

And Jesus says to them, "Then I'm not going to tell you by what authority I do these things!"

12 **And he began to speak** to them in parables.

> A man planted a vineyard, put a hedge around it, dug a winepress, built a tower, leased it out to some farmers, and went abroad. [2]In due time he sent a slave to the farmers to collect his share of the vineyard's crop from them. [3]But they grabbed him, beat him, and sent him away empty-handed. [4]And again he sent

11:18–19
//Lk 19:47–48

11:20–25
//Mt 21:20–22

11:23
Cf. Th 48,106

11:24
Cf. Q 11:9–10;
Mt 7:7–8, 21:22;
Lk 11:9–10;
Jn 14:13–14;
15:7, 16; 16:23

11:25
Cf. Q 6:37,
Mt 6:14–15,
Lk 6:37c

11:27–33
//Mt 21:23–27,
Lk 20:1–8

12:1–11
//Mt 21:33–43,
Lk 20:9–18,
Th 65–66;
◊Is 5:1–2

11:25 Many mss include a v. 26: "But if you do not forgive, neither will your Father in heaven forgive your misdeeds."

11:27–33 Jesus returns to the city for a day of deadly serious banter and confrontation with religious authority figures. First Jesus silences his antagonists with a clever trick question, again linking his work with that of John. Verse 30 is a good example of the typical Jewish reticence in making direct mention of God: Jesus is asking: Did John's baptism have divine warrant?

12:1–12 Jesus addresses his symbolic story to his opponents. The imagery is taken from the picture of God's vineyard in Isaiah 5. The story's meaning is crystal clear to Jesus' opponents: they are plotting to do away with God's son (v. 6).

another slave to them, but they attacked him and abused him. ⁵Then he sent another, and this one they killed; many others followed, some of whom they beat, others of whom they killed.

⁶Finally he sent his son, whom he loved. He said to himself, "They will show this son of mine some respect."

⁷But those farmers said to one another, "This guy's the heir! Come on, let's kill him and the inheritance will be ours!" ⁸So they grabbed him, and killed him, and threw him outside the vineyard.

⁹What will the owner of the vineyard do? He will come in person, and massacre those farmers, and give the vineyard to others.

¹⁰It seems you haven't read in scripture:

> A stone that the builders threw away
>> has ended up as the keystone.
> ¹¹It was the Lord's doing,
>> something we find amazing.

¹²They kept looking for some opportunity to seize him, but they were afraid of the crowd because they understood that he had aimed the parable at them. So they left him there and went away.

¹³**And they send some of the Pharisees** and the Herodians to him to trap him with a riddle. ¹⁴They come and say to him, "Teacher, we know that you are honest and impartial, because you pay no attention to appearances, but instead you teach God's way forthrightly. Is it permissible to pay the poll tax to Caesar or not? Should we pay or should we not pay?"

¹⁵But he saw through their trap, and said to them, "Why do you provoke me like this? Let me have a look at a denarius."

¹⁶They handed him one, and he says to them, "Whose image is this? Whose name is on it?"

They replied, "Caesar's."

¹⁷Jesus said to them, "Pay to Caesar what belongs to Caesar, and to God what belongs to God."

And they were dumbfounded at him.

¹⁸**And some Sadducees**—those who maintain there is no resurrection—come up to him and they start questioning him. ¹⁹"Teacher," they said, "Moses wrote for our benefit, 'If someone's brother dies and leaves his widow childless,

12:10
◊Ps 118:22–23

12:12
//Mt 21:45–46,
Lk 20:19

12:13–17
//Mt 22:15–22,
Lk 20:20–26,
Th 100,
EgerG 3:1–6

12:18–27
//Mt 22:23–32,
Lk 20:27–38

12:19
◊Gn 38:8,
Dt 25:5–6

12:13–17 Again Jesus outsmarts those setting out to trap him. Jesus *dumbfounds* them when he avoids sounding like a dangerous revolutionary, by not refusing to pay taxes to the Romans, but also avoids looking like a collaborator, when he points out the coin (which Mark calls by its Latin name, *denarius*), comes from the Roman emperor anyway.

12:18–27 The *Sadducees* argued against the Pharisees (and the Jesus movement) that there was no scriptural basis for belief in the resurrection of the dead. Their question to

Jesus is the sort of logical dilemma they thought should confound those who held this "modern" or "unbiblical" belief. Jesus disposes of their exaggerated problem with sarcasm (*you ignore both the scriptures and the power of God*), explanation of the angelic status of the resurrected, and an ingenious prooftext from the Torah: when God mentions the long-dead *Abraham, Isaac, and Jacob*, he must mean people who in some sense are still alive.

his brother shall take the widow as his wife and produce offspring for his brother.' ²⁰There were seven brothers; now the first took a wife but left no children when he died. ²¹So the second married her but died without leaving offspring, and the third likewise. ²²In fact, all seven ⟨married her but⟩ left no offspring. Finally, the wife died too. ²³In the resurrection, after they rise, whose wife will she be, since all seven had her as a wife?"

²⁴Jesus said to them, "Isn't this the reason you've missed the point: that you ignore both the scriptures and the power of God? ²⁵You see, when men and women rise from the dead, they do not marry, but resemble heaven's messengers. ²⁶As for whether or not the dead are raised, I guess you haven't read in the book of Moses in the passage about the bush, how God spoke to him: 'I am the God of Abraham and the God of Isaac and the God of Jacob.' ²⁷This is not the God of the dead, but of the living—you're constantly missing the point."

²⁸**And one of the scholars** approached when he heard them arguing, and because he saw how skillfully Jesus answered them, he asked him, "Of all the commandments, which is the most important?"

²⁹Jesus answered, "The first is, 'Hear, Israel, the Lord your God is one Lord, ³⁰and you shall love the Lord your God with all your heart and all your soul and all your mind and with all your strength.' ³¹The second is this: 'You shall love your neighbor as yourself.' There is no other commandment greater than these."

³²And the scholar said to him, "That's a fine answer, Teacher. You have correctly said that God is one and there is no other beside him. ³³And 'to love him with all one's heart and with all one's mind and with all one's strength' and 'to love one's neighbor as oneself' is greater than all the burnt offerings and sacrifices put together."

³⁴And when Jesus saw that he answered him sensibly, he said to him, "You are not far from God's empire."

And from then on no one dared question him.

³⁵**And while Jesus was teaching** in the temple area, he was asking this question: "How can the scholars claim that the Anointed One is the son of David? ³⁶David himself said under the influence of the holy spirit,

> The Lord said to my lord,
>> "Sit here at my right,
>> until I make your enemies grovel at your feet."

³⁷David himself calls him 'lord,' so how can he be his son?"

12:26
◊Ex 3:6

12:28–34
//Mt 22:34–40,
46; Lk 10:25–28,
20:39–40;
◊Dt 6:4–5,
Lv 19:18,
1 Sm 15:22

12:35–37
//Mt 22:41–46,
Lk 20:41–44;
◊Ps 110:1

12:28–34 Jesus answers the scholar by reciting *Hear, Israel*, the *Shema*, the central confession and self-definition of Israelite belief. Pious Jews would often wear amulets containing these and similar phrases deriving from the opening words of the Decalogue.

12:35–37 With the crowds now properly impressed, Jesus poses his own riddle. He quotes the opening lines of Psalm 110, used in the coronation rituals of ancient Israelite and Judean kings. The (anointed) king referred to is taken by Jesus to mean the Messiah (the Hebrew word meaning "anointed"). This little story suggests that Mark does not agree with the tradition that Jesus was a *son of David* (a descendant of David's line), since otherwise Jesus' words mean that he is denying his own legitimacy to be considered God's Anointed.

Scholars' privileges

Widow's pittance

Monumental buildings destroyed

Apocalyptic signs

And a huge crowd was listening to him with delight.

[³⁸**In his teaching** he was saying, "Look out for the scholars who like to parade around in long robes, and ⟨insist on⟩ respectful greetings in the marketplaces ³⁹and the prominent seats in the synagogues and the best couches at banquets. ⁴⁰They are the ones who prey on widows and their families, and then recite long prayers just to look good. These people will get what's coming to them, and more!" ᴏɴᴇ-ʟɪɴᴇʀ]

⁴¹**And he sat across** from the temple treasury and was observing the crowd dropping money into the collection box. And many wealthy people would drop large amounts in. ⁴²Then one poor widow came and put in two quarters, which is a pittance. ⁴³And he motioned his disciples over and said to them, "Let me tell you, this poor widow has contributed more than all those who dropped something into the collection box. ⁴⁴You see, they were all donating out of their surplus, whereas she, out of her poverty, was contributing all she had, her whole livelihood."

13 **And as he was going** out of the temple area, one of his disciples remarks to him, "Teacher, look, what magnificent masonry! What wonderful buildings!"

²And Jesus replied to him, "Take a good look at these monumental buildings! Not a single stone will be left on top of another! Every last one will certainly be knocked down!"

³**And as he was sitting** on the Mount of Olives across from the temple, Peter was asking him privately, as would James and John and Andrew, ⁴"Tell us, when are these things going to happen, and what will be the sign to show when all these things are about to culminate?"

⁵And Jesus began to say to them, "Stay alert, or else someone might deceive you. ⁶You know, many will come using my name and claim, 'I'm the one!' and they will deceive many people. ⁷When you hear of wars and rumors of wars, don't be afraid. These are inevitable, but it is not yet the End. ⁸For nation will rise up against nation and empire against empire; there will be earthquakes everywhere; there will be famines. These things mark the beginning of the birth pangs.

⁹"But you look out for yourselves. They'll turn you over to Jewish councils, and beat you in synagogues, and haul you up before governors and kings on my account, so you can make your case to them. ¹⁰Yet the good news must first be

12:38–40
//Mt 23:6,
Lk 20:45–47

12:41–44
//Lk 21:1–4

13:1–2
//Mt 24:1–2,
Lk 21:5–6

13:3–8
//Mt 24:3–8,
Lk 21:7–11

13:5
//Mary 4:3

13:9–13
//Mt 24:9,
10:17–22;
Lk 21:12–17

13:1–2 Jesus gives an apocalyptic edge to his followers' admiration of the temple area, which had been greatly enlarged and adorned by Herod the Great. Many of his subjects resented paying the heavy taxes that Herod exacted for this and other large-scale building projects.

13:3–37 In another private scene, this time set on a ridge facing the temple mount across the Kidron valley, Jesus' inner circle asks him to explain his outburst about the temple's

impending destruction. In response, Jesus delivers his second long speech in Mark's story, this time addressing the turbulent experiences to come.

In good apocalyptic style, Jesus' predictions are in effect a summary of the Markan audience's recent history. Picking their way through the confusion and disorder to come will be a dangerous task.

announced to all peoples. [11]And when they take you away to turn you in, don't be worried about what you should say. Instead, whatever occurs to you at the moment, say that. For it's not you who are speaking but the holy spirit. [12]And one brother will turn in another to be put to death, and a father his child, and children will turn against their parents and kill them. [13]And you'll be universally hated because of me. Those who hold out to the End will be saved.

[14]**"When you see the 'devastating desecration'** standing where it should not—the lector had better figure out what this means—then the people in Judea should head for the hills. [15]No one on the roof should go downstairs, no one should enter the house to retrieve anything, [16]and no one in the field should turn back to get a coat. [17]It'll be too bad for pregnant women and nursing mothers in those days! [18]Pray that none of this happens in winter! [19]For those days will see tribulation the likes of which has not occurred since God created the world until now, and will never occur again. [20]And if the Lord had not cut short the days, no human being would have survived. But he did shorten the days for the sake of the chosen people whom he selected. [21]And then if someone says to you, 'Look, here's the Anointed One,' or 'Look, there he is!' don't count on it! [22]After all, phony messiahs and phony prophets will show up, and they'll provide signs and omens in an attempt to deceive, if possible, the chosen people. [23]But you be on your guard. I have warned you about everything in advance.

[24]**But in those days**, after that tribulation,

> the sun will be darkened,
>   and the moon will not give off her glow;
> [25]the stars will fall from the sky,
>   and the heavenly forces will be shaken.

[26]"And then they will see the Human One coming on the clouds with great power and splendor. [27]And then he will send out messengers and will gather the chosen people from the four winds, from the ends of the earth to the edge of the sky.

[28]"Take a cue from the fig tree. When its branch is already in bud and leaves come out, you know that summer is near. [29]So, when you see these things hap-

Days of distress

The Human One comes on clouds

13:14–20
//Mt 24:15–22,
Lk 21:20–24;
cf. Lk 17:31
13:14
◊Dn 9:27, 11:31,
12:11; 1 Mc 1:54
13:21–23
//Mt 24:23–25,
Th 113;
◊Dt 13:2–4
13:21
//Mary 4:4
13:24
◊Is 13:10, 34:4
13:24–27
//Mt 24:29–31,
Lk 21:25–28,
Rev 1:7
13:26
◊Dn 7:13–14,
4 Ezr 13:1–3
13:28–32
//Mt 24:32–36,
Lk 21:29–33

13:14 Here is the most obvious instance of Mark breaking through his narrative conventions to speak directly to the reader—even though in the story Jesus is apparently still speaking to his inner group. (See also 7:3–4.)

The *devastating desecration* alludes to the apocalyptic Book of Daniel (Dan 9:27; 11:31; 12:11), where attempts by Hellenistic rulers to convert the Jerusalem temple into a shrine of Zeus in the early second century BCE were interpreted as a sign of the near approach of the end (1 Macc 1:54). Mark's readers are meant to connect this "prophecy" with a desecration or the threat of one sometime closer to their own day, perhaps the emperor Caligula's attempt to

place his own statue in the temple (in 40/41 CE), or perhaps the disturbances surrounding the great revolt against the Romans in 66–70.

13:21–23 The warning about *phony messiahs* and *phony prophets* evokes Moses' warnings in Deut 13:2–4, but probably also describes the confusion of Mark's own day.

13:24–32 The heavenly disturbances that usher in the arrival of *the Human One on the clouds* resonate with the imagery of cosmic catastrophe found in biblical prophecy and apocalyptic (compare, e.g., Isa 13:10; 34:4; Dan 7:13–14; also 2 Esdras 13:1–3).

No one knows the
day or hour

Woman anoints
Jesus

Priests promise
to pay

pen, you should realize that he is near, just outside your door. ³⁰Let me tell you, this generation certainly won't pass away before all these things happen! ³¹The earth will pass away and so will the sky, but my words will never pass away.

³²**"As for that exact day** or hour—no one knows, not even heaven's messengers, nor even the son, no one, except the Father.

³³"Be on guard! Stay alert! For you never know what time it is. ³⁴It's like a person who takes a trip and puts slaves in charge, each with a task, and orders the doorkeeper to be alert. ³⁵Therefore, stay alert! For you never know when the landlord returns, maybe at dusk, or at midnight, or when the rooster crows, or maybe early in the morning. ³⁶He may return suddenly and find you asleep. ³⁷What I'm telling you, I say to everyone: stay alert!"

14 **Now it was two days** until Passover and the festival of Unleavened Bread. And the chief priests and the scholars were looking for some way to seize him by trickery and kill him. ²For they kept saying, "Not during the festival, otherwise the people will riot."

³When he was in Bethany at the house of Simon the leper, he was just reclining there, and a woman came in carrying an alabaster jar of aromatic ointment made from pure and expensive nard. She broke the jar and poured ⟨the ointment⟩ on his head.

⁴Now some were annoyed ⟨and thought⟩ to themselves, "What good does it do to waste this ointment? ⁵She could have sold the ointment for more than three hundred denarii and given ⟨the money⟩ to the poor." And they were angry with her.

⁶Then Jesus said, "Let her alone! Why are you giving her a hard time? She has done a good deed for me. ⁷Remember, the poor will always be around, and whenever you want you can do good for them, but I won't always be around. ⁸She did what she could; she has planned ahead by anointing my body for burial. ⁹Let me tell you, wherever the good news is announced in all the world, the story of what she's done will be told in her memory."

¹⁰**And Judas Iscariot**, one of the Twelve, went off to the chief priests to turn him over to them. ¹¹When they heard, they were delighted, and promised to pay him in silver. And he started looking for a good opportunity to turn him in.

13:33–37
//Mt 24:42;
cf. Mt 25:13–15,
Lk 19:12–13

14:1–2
//Mt 26:2–5,
Lk 22:1–2;
cf. Jn 11:55–57;
Ⓣ Judas 6:12

14:3–9
//Mt 26:6–13;
cf. Lk 7:36–50,
Jn 12:1–8

14:10–11
//Mt 26:17–19,
Lk 22:3–6

13:33–37 Jesus ends his apocalyptic speech with a brief similitude about the return of one's *landlord* or master at an unexpected time. At the end Jesus turns once again from his inner group to address Mark's readers directly: *What I'm telling you, I say to everyone: stay alert!*

14:1–2 With the approach of the *Passover* festival the threat of violence to Jesus becomes even stronger. Major feast days attracted huge crowds of pilgrims to the holy city. Mark's crowds again play a shifting role, here shielding Jesus from the malevolent intentions of the city aristocracy, perhaps unwittingly; soon their mood will turn ugly (15:8).

14:3–9 Mark "sandwiches" a story about a private meal in Bethany into his larger theme about the Jewish leaders looking for a way to get rid of Jesus (resumed in vv. 10–11). Here an unnamed woman pours out a vessel of expensive ointment on Jesus' head. The disciples miss the point, which Jesus makes clear: the woman has signalled his impending death and burial.

14:9 It must be unintentional irony when Mark has Jesus predict that this story will always be *told in memory* of a woman whose very name escapes him.

¹²**On the first day of Unleavened Bread**, when they would sacrifice the Passover lamb, his disciples say to him, "Where do you want us to go and get things ready for you to celebrate Passover?"

¹³He sends two of his disciples and says to them, "Go into the city, and a man carrying a water pot will meet you. Follow him, ¹⁴and whatever place he enters say to the head of the house, 'The teacher asks, "Where is my guest room where I can celebrate Passover with my disciples?"' ¹⁵And he'll show you a large upstairs room that has been arranged. That's the place where you should get ready for us."

¹⁶And the disciples left, went into the city, and found it exactly as he had told them; and they got things ready for Passover. ¹⁷When evening comes, he arrives with the Twelve. ¹⁸And as they reclined ⟨for dinner⟩ and were eating, Jesus said, "Let me tell you, one of you eating with me is going to turn me in!"

¹⁹They got very upset and said to him one after another, "I'm not the one, am I?"

²⁰But he said to them, "It's one of the Twelve, the one who is dipping into the bowl with me. ²¹The Human One departs just as the scriptures predict, but damn the one responsible for turning the Human One in! That man would be better off if he'd never been born!"

²²And as they were eating, he took a loaf, gave a blessing, broke it into pieces, and offered it to them. And he said, "Take some; this is my body!" ²³He also took a cup, gave thanks, and offered it to them, and they all drank from it. ²⁴And he said to them, "This is my blood of the covenant, which has been poured out for many. ²⁵Let me tell you, I'll never touch a drop of the fruit of the vine until that day when I drink it for the first time in God's empire."

²⁶And they sang a hymn and left for the Mount of Olives.

²⁷**And Jesus says to them**, "You will all be shaken and fall away. Remember, scripture says,

> I will strike the shepherd and the sheep will be scattered.

²⁸But after I'm raised I'll go ahead of you to Galilee."

²⁹Peter said to him, "Even if everyone else is shaken and falls away, I won't!"

³⁰And Jesus says to him, "Let me tell you, tonight before the rooster crows twice you will disown me three times."

Jesus celebrates Passover

Peter takes an oath

14:12–16
//Mt 26:17–19,
Lk 22:7–13

14:12
//GEbi 7:1

14:17–21
//Mt 26:20–25;
Lk 22:14, 21–23;
cf. Jn 13:21–26

14:21b
Ⓣ Job 3:2,11;
Jer 20:14–18

14:22–25
//Mt 26:26–29,
Lk 22:15–20;
cf. Jn 6:48–58,
1 Cor 11:23–25

14:22
Cf. GHeb 9:4

14:24
//GSav 14:18
◊Ex 24:8, Jer 31:31,
Zec 9:11

14:25
Cf. GHeb 9:2

14:26–31
//Mt 26:30–35;
cf. Lk 22:31–34,
Jn 13:36–38

14:27
//GSav 4:7;
◊Zec 13:7

14:28
Ⓘ Mk 16:7

14:12–16 The story of the Passover feast resumes as Jesus sends two disciples to make preparations for the only meal he will eat in Jerusalem. Jesus' detailed instructions are followed exactly; his control and foreknowledge give the readers confidence that Jesus is master of his destiny.

14:22–25 The scene narrating the passing of bread and wine is told simply, with little or no explanation of Jesus' surprising words. Presumably Mark's readers knew all about this last meal and what it signified from their own customary remembrances (see 1 Cor 11:23–26 and Luke 22:196).

14:24 The *blood of the covenant* alludes to the sacrifice on Mount Sinai that sealed the covenant between Yahweh and Israel (Exod 24:8), language redirected by Israelite prophecy in a spiritual or moralizing fashion (e.g., Jer 31:31). The terminology is that of the church celebrating its sacrament: Jesus says his blood *has been poured out for many*, to seal a new redemptive covenant, though in Mark's story the death is still a day ahead.

14:28 Jesus predicts his resurrection and appearance *in Galilee*, something the reader is meant to remember when hearing the young man's words from the tomb in 16:7.

[31]But he repeated it with more bluster: "Even if they condemn me to die with you, I will never disown you!" And so said they all.

[32]**And they go to a place** named Gethsemane, and he says to his disciples, "Sit down here while I pray."

[33]And he takes Peter and James and John along with him, and he grew apprehensive and full of anguish. [34]He says to them, "I'm so sad I could die. You stay here and be alert."

[35]And he would move on a little, lay facedown on the ground, and pray that he might avoid the crisis, if possible. [36]And he was saying, "*Abba* (Father), all things are possible for you. Take this cup away from me. But it's your will that matters, not mine."

[37]And he returns and finds them sleeping, and says to Peter, "Simon, are you sleeping? Couldn't you stay awake for one hour? [38]Be alert and pray that you won't be put to the test. The spirit is willing, but the flesh is weak."

[39]And once again he went away and prayed, saying the same thing. [40]And once again he came and found them sleeping, since their eyes had grown very heavy, and they didn't know what to say to him.

[41]And he comes a third time and says to them, "You may as well sleep on now and get your rest. It's all over! The time has come! Look, the Human One is being turned over to sinners. [42]Get up, let's go! See for yourselves! Here comes the one who is going to turn me in."

[43]**And right away**, while he was still speaking, Judas, one of the Twelve, shows up, and with him a crowd, dispatched by the chief priests and the scholars and the elders, wielding swords and clubs. [44]Now the one who was to turn him in had arranged a signal with them, saying, "The one I'm going to kiss is the one you want. Arrest him and escort him safely away." [45]And right away he arrives, comes up to him, and says, "Rabbi," and kissed him.

[46]And they laid hands on him and seized him. [47]One of those standing around drew his sword and swung at the chief priest's slave and cut off his ear. [48]In response Jesus said to them, "Have you come to arrest me with swords and clubs as you would an insurgent? [49]I was with you in the temple area day after day teaching and you didn't seize me. But the scriptures must be fulfilled!"

[50]And they all deserted him and ran away. [51]And a young man was following him, wearing a shroud over his nude body, and they grab him. [52]But he dropped the shroud and ran away naked.

14:32–42
//Mt 26:36–46,
Lk 22:39–46

14:34
Cf. Jn 12:27;
◊Ps 42:5–6,11–12;
43:5

14:35–36
//GSav 14:14

14:38
Ⓣ GSav 4:1

14:41
Cf. GSav 15:1;
Ⓣ EgerG 1:9

14:42
//GSav 4:2

14:43–50
//Mt 26:47–56;
cf. Lk 22:47–53,
Jn 18:2–12

14:51–52
Ⓣ MysMk

14:32–42 Mark gives us a rare glimpse of Jesus' inner thoughts when we overhear his prayer to his father while his closest followers sleep. The contrast between Jesus' resolve and the disciples' weakness is powerfully drawn.

14:51–52 The nameless *young man* who watches Jesus' arrest from afar has long puzzled interpreters. One suggestion is that for Mark the youth symbolizes all of Jesus' followers, both in Jesus' "then" and in Mark's "now," *running away* in terror from the prospect of Jesus' (and their) fate. A young man with a robe also appears in 16:5–7 and in the longer Mystical Mark fragment.

⁵³**And they brought Jesus** before the chief priest, and all the chief priests and elders and scholars assemble.

⁵⁴Peter followed him at a distance until he was inside the courtyard of the chief priest, and was sitting with the attendants and keeping warm by the fire.

⁵⁵The chief priests and the whole Council were looking for evidence against Jesus in order to issue a death sentence, but they couldn't find any. ⁵⁶Although many gave false evidence against him, their stories didn't agree. ⁵⁷And some people stood up and testified falsely against him, ⁵⁸"We have heard him saying, 'I'll destroy this temple made with hands and in three days I'll build another, not made with hands!'" ⁵⁹Yet even then their stories did not agree.

⁶⁰And the chief priest got up and questioned Jesus, "Don't you have anything to say? Why do these people testify against you?"

⁶¹But he was silent and refused to answer.

Once again the chief priest questioned him and says to him, "Are you the Anointed One, the son of the Blessed One?"

⁶²Jesus replied, "I am! And you will see the Human One sitting at the right hand of Power and coming with the clouds of the sky!"

⁶³Then the chief priest tore his vestments and says, "Why do we still need witnesses? ⁶⁴You have heard the blasphemy! What do you think?" And they all concurred in the death penalty.

⁶⁵And some began to spit on him, and to put a blindfold on him, and beat him, and say to him, "Prophesy!" And the guards slapped him around as they took him into custody.

⁶⁶**And while Peter was below** in the courtyard, one of the chief priest's slave women comes over, ⁶⁷and sees Peter warming himself; she looks at him closely and says, "You too were with that Nazarene, Jesus."

⁶⁸But he denied it, saying, "I haven't the slightest idea what you're talking about." And he went outside into the forecourt.

⁶⁹And when the slave woman saw him, she once again began to say to those standing nearby, "This guy is one of them."

⁷⁰But once again he denied it.

And a little later, those standing nearby were saying to Peter, "You really are one of them, since you also are a Galilean."

⁷¹But he began to curse and swear, "I don't know this man you're talking about!" ⁷²And just then a rooster crowed a second time, and Peter remembered what Jesus had told him: "Before a rooster crows twice you will disown me three times." And he broke down and started to cry.

Trial before the Council

A rooster crows

insertion & framing device

14:53–54
//Mt 26:57–58,
Lk 22:54–55,
Jn 18:13–15

14:55–65
//Mt 26:59–68;
cf. Lk 22:67–71,
63–65; Jn 18:19–24

14:58
Cf. Th 71, Jn 2:19

14:62
Ⓣ Mk 13:26;
◊ Dn 7:13,
4 Ezr 13:1–3

14:63–64
◊ Lv 24:16

14:65
Cf. Pet 3:4

14:66–72
//Mt 26:69–75;
Lk 22:56–62;
Jn 18:17, 25–27

14:53–72 The trial before the Jewish Council is artfully portrayed, with an especially poignant Markan "sandwich" showing Peter skulking in the courtyard all the while (vv. 54, 66–72).

Mark tells a frightening story of official malevolence. It is difficult to reconcile much of Mark's picture with known Jewish judicial procedures: a secret court session, at night, with trumped-up and contradictory evidence. Jesus' initial refusal to speak is no defense. Finally Jesus' avowal of his messiahship (14:62) provokes the desired verdict.

15 **And right away**, at daybreak, the chief priests, after consulting with the elders and scholars and the whole Council, bound Jesus and led him away and turned him over to Pilate. [2]And Pilate questioned him: *"You* are 'the King of the Judeans'?"

And in response he says to him, "If you say so."

[3]And the chief priests started a long list of accusations against him. [4]Again Pilate tried questioning him: "Don't you have some answer to give? Look at the long list of charges they bring against you!"

[5]But Jesus still did not respond, so Pilate was astonished.

[6]At each festival it was the custom for ⟨the Roman governor⟩ to set one prisoner free for them, whichever one they requested. [7]And one called Barabbas was being held with the insurgents who had committed murder during the insurrection. [8]And when the crowd arrived, they began to demand that he do what he usually did for them.

[9]And in response Pilate said to them, "Do you want me to set 'the King of the Judeans' free for you?" ([10]You see, he realized that the chief priests had turned him over out of envy.)

[11]But the chief priests incited the crowd to get Barabbas set free for them instead.

[12]But in response Pilate again said to them, "What do you want me to do with the man you call 'the King of the Judeans'?"

[13]And they in turn shouted, "Crucify him!"

[14]Pilate kept saying to them, "Why? What has he done wrong?"

But they shouted all the louder, "Crucify him!" [15]And because Pilate was always looking to satisfy the crowd, he set Barabbas free for them, had Jesus flogged, and then turned him over to be crucified.

[16]**And the ⟨Roman⟩ soldiers** led him away to the courtyard of the governor's residence, and they summoned the whole company ⟨of troops⟩. [17]And they dressed him in purple and crowned him with a garland woven of thorns. [18]And they began to salute him: "Greetings, 'King of the Judeans'!" [19]And they kept striking him on the head with a stick, and spitting on him; and they were getting down on their knees and bowing down to him. [20]And when they had

15:1
//Mt 27:1–2,
Lk 22:66–23:1;
cf. Jn 18:28

15:2–5
//Mt 27:11–14,
Lk 23:3;
cf. Jn 18:33–37

15:2–3
Ⓣ GSav 13:8

15:6–14
//Mt 27:15–23,
Lk 23:17–23,
Jn 18:39–40

15:7
Cf. GNaz 9

15:15
//Mt 27:26,
Lk 23:24–25;
cf. Jn 19:16a

15:16–20a
//Mt 27:27–31a,
Jn 19:2–3;
cf. Pet 2:36–3:4

15:1–15 The portrayal of Jesus' trial before *Pilate* is more in keeping with what we know of ancient judicial procedure than his nighttime Council appearance, though the supposed custom of freeing a dangerous criminal at the festival (v. 6) is unknown outside the gospels and would in fact be highly unlikely in such a volatile situation.

Roman governors had enormous discretion in matters of public order. Their power is difficult to reconcile with Mark's portrait of Pilate as a helpless tool of the Jewish leaders, submissive to the demands of a bloodthirsty mob. Nonetheless a Roman magistrate would not shrink from

using summary punishment to preserve order in such an uncertain situation.

15:15 Roman *flogging* was a brutal torture reserved for those condemned to death. Metal bits on the ends of whips could inflict horrible wounds.

15:16–39 Jesus' maltreatment and execution by the soldiers highlight the ironies in describing the death of a submissive and suffering *king*. The Roman legionnaires have unwittingly furthered God's secret purposes by dressing Jesus up as a king (vv. 17–20) and labelling his cross with his royal title (v. 26).

made fun of him, they stripped off the purple and put his own clothes back on him. And they lead him out to crucify him.

²¹**And they conscript someone** named Simon of Cyrene, who was coming in from the country, the father of Alexander and Rufus, to carry his cross.

²²And they bring him to the place Golgotha (which means "Place of the Skull"). ²³And they tried to give him wine mixed with myrrh, but he didn't take it. ²⁴And they crucify him, and they divide up his clothes, casting lots to see who would get what. ²⁵It was nine o'clock in the morning when they crucified him. ²⁶And the placard, on which the charge against him was inscribed, read, 'The King of the Judeans.' ²⁷And with him they crucify two insurgents, one on his right and one on his left.

²⁹Those passing by kept taunting him, wagging their heads, and saying, "Well, well, well! *You're* the one who was going to destroy the temple and rebuild it in three days! ³⁰Save yourself and come down from that cross."

³¹Likewise the chief priests had made fun of him to one another, along with the scholars; they were saying, "He saved others, but he can't even save himself! ³²'The Anointed One,' 'the King of Israel,' should come down from the cross here and now, so that we can see for ourselves and believe!"

Even those being crucified along with him were insulting him.

³³**And when noon came**, darkness blanketed the whole land until midafternoon. ³⁴And at three o'clock in the afternoon Jesus shouted at the top of his voice, *"Eloi, Eloi, lema sabachthani"* (which means "My God, my God, why have you abandoned me?").

³⁵And when some of those standing nearby heard, they were saying, "Listen, he's calling Elijah!" ³⁶And someone ran and filled a sponge with sour wine, stuck it on a stick, and offered him a drink, saying, "Let's see if Elijah comes to rescue him!"

³⁷But Jesus let out a great shout and breathed his last.

³⁸And the curtain of the temple was torn in two from top to bottom! ³⁹When the Roman officer in charge saw that he had died like this, he said, "This man really was God's son!"

⁴⁰Now some women were observing from a distance, among whom were Mary of Magdala, and Mary the mother of James the younger and Joses, and

15:28 Some mss add a verse here, traditionally numbered 15:28: "And the scripture that says, 'And he was considered a criminal was fulfilled.'"

15:20b–21
//Mt 27:31b–32,
Lk 23:26;
cf. Jn 19:16b–17a

15:22–26
//Mt 27:33–37;
Lk 23:33–34;
Jn 19:17b–19, 24;
Pet 4:1–2

15:23
◊ Ps 69:22

15:24
◊ Ps 22:18

15:27–32a
//Mt 27:38–42;
Lk 23:33b, 35, 17

15:27
//Pet 4:1

15:29–31
Ⓣ GSav 11:1

15:29
◊ Ps 22:8

15:32b
//Mt 27:44;
cf. Lk 23:39–43,
Pet 4:4

15:33–39
//Mt 27:45–54,
Lk 23:44–48,
Jn 19:28–30;
cf. Pet 5:1–6

15:33
◊ Am 8:9

15:34
◊ Ps 22:2

15:36
◊ Ps 69:22

15:38
Cf. GNaz 10a

15:40–41
//Mt 27:55–56,
Lk 23:49;
cf. Jn 19:25b–27;
◊ Ps 37:12

15:22–32 The scene of Jesus' crucifixion is studded with scriptural allusions and quotations, chiefly from the Psalms (see the cross references).

15:39 Mark's theme of Jesus' hidden identity reaches its ironic climax when the *Roman officer* offers as Jesus' epitaph a remark that was presumably meant as sarcasm, not an indication of a sudden change of heart: *This man really was God's son*. We readers are privileged to realize that those

soldiers knew even more than they thought they did.

15:40–41 The sudden and unprepared mention of these three women, *Mary of Magdala, Mary the mother of James and Joses, and Salome*, who Mark now tells us *had regularly followed and assisted* Jesus during his public work in Galilee, is an extreme example of the narrator's tendency to withhold apparently important information until we are far into a story (on this see the Introduction to Mark).

Salome. ⁴¹These women had regularly followed and assisted him when he was in Galilee, along with many other women who had come up to Jerusalem in his company.

⁴²**And since it was the preparation day** (the day before the Sabbath), and already getting dark, ⁴³Joseph of Arimathea, a respected Council member, who himself was anticipating the empire of God, came forward and dared to go to Pilate to request the body of Jesus. ⁴⁴And Pilate was surprised that he had died so soon. He summoned the Roman officer and asked him whether he had been dead for long. ⁴⁵And when he had been briefed by the officer, he granted the body to Joseph. ⁴⁶And he bought a shroud and took him down and wrapped him in the shroud, and placed him in a tomb that had been hewn out of rock, and rolled a stone up against the opening of the tomb. ⁴⁷And Mary of Magdala and Mary the mother of Joses noted where he had been laid to rest.

16 **And when the Sabbath was over**, Mary of Magdala and Mary the mother of James and Salome bought spices so they could go and anoint him. ²And very early on Sunday they got to the tomb just as the sun was coming up. ³And they had been asking themselves, "Who will help us roll the stone away from the opening of the tomb?" ⁴Then they look up and discover that the stone has been rolled away. (You see, the stone was very large.)

⁵And when they went into the tomb, they saw a young man sitting on the right, wearing a white robe, and they grew apprehensive.

⁶He says to them, "Don't be alarmed. You are looking for Jesus the Nazarene who was crucified. He was raised, he is not here. Look at the spot where they put him. ⁷But go and tell his disciples, including 'Rock,' 'He is going ahead of you to Galilee. There you will see him, just as he told you.'"

⁸And once they got outside, they ran away from the tomb, because great fear and excitement got the better of them. And they didn't breathe a word of it to anyone: talk about terrified . . .

15:42–47
//Mt 27:57–61,
Lk 23:50–55,
Jn 19:38–42;
cf. Pet 2:1–3a, 6:1–4;
◊Dt 21:22–23,
Jos 10:26–27

16:1–8
Cf. Mt 28:1–8,
Lk 24:1–9,
Pet 12:1–13:3,
Jn 20:1–10

16:7
① Mk 14:28

16:8 The best ancient mss conclude the Gospel of Mark with this verse. Other mss supply lengthier narrative endings. See "The endings of the Gospel of Mark," pp. 461–62.

15:42–47 In this scene about Joseph and Pilate, Mark skillfully establishes that Jesus really died and that the women really knew where he was buried. Jesus' quick death and burial provide a motivation for the women to visit Jesus' tomb as soon as would be proper. All these points could otherwise be questioned by those doubting reports of Jesus' resurrection.

Joseph of Arimathea has not previously been mentioned and his care and concern here are quite unexpected. Affluent families would purchase *tombs hewn out of rock* (v. 46) large enough for the eventual burial of several generations. Is Joseph in effect bringing Jesus into his family? Jesus' own relatives seem to be far out of the picture.

16:1–8 When the women so recently introduced (15:40,

47) approach Jesus' tomb, their worry as to *who will roll away the stone* is unexplained until Mark adds, again a bit late, that *the stone was very large* (v. 4).

The women's fear does not necessarily remain the readers' final thought: *the young man* in the dazzling clothes, while terrifying the women into silence, confirms the readers' expectations, based on Jesus' frequent predictions of his fate (esp. 10:33–34; 14:28).

16:8 *talk about terrified* . . . With daring narrative skill, Mark ends his story in mid sentence. Later copyists of this gospel added what they believed to be more appropriate endings; see "The endings of the Gospel of Mark," pp. 461–62.

The Gospel of Matthew

Introduction

The most quoted and influential of the synoptic gospels until modern times was the Gospel of Matthew. The earliest commentaries were on this gospel, and the large number of surviving fragments suggest that it was copied more frequently than the other synoptic gospels. The popularity of Matthew can be explained by three factors: (1) the author was allegedly Matthew, one of the first followers of Jesus; (2) it came first in the New Testament canon; (3) it contained virtually all of Mark, making Mark all but superfluous.

Sources and plot

The Gospel of Matthew is based on the Gospel of Mark and the Q Gospel.

The outline of Mark is evident in Matthew. Matthew employs the same basic plot as Mark:

1. Jesus' baptism and initial ministry in Galilee
2. Peter's confession at Caesarea Philippi and the transfiguration
3. journey to Jerusalem and debates in the temple
4. concluding tragic death and resurrection.

However, Matthew does not simply repeat Mark's story. While Mark begins with John the Baptizer's preaching, Matthew launches his gospel with a genealogy and birth narrative that shows Jesus to be the son of David and thus both king and the Anointed One. At the gospel's conclusion the author appends a commissioning scene in which the risen Jesus sends the eleven disciples out to baptize the whole world.

Five sermons

By far the most notable additions to Mark's outline are the five sermons. Each has a distinctive theme and concludes with the formula, "when Jesus had finished . . ." (7:28; 11:1; 13:53; 19:1; 26:1). Much of the material in these sermons is derived from the Q Gospel.

The famous Sermon on the Mount (chaps. 5–7) sets forth a Christian interpretation of the Jewish Law. The second sermon (chap. 10) deals with the sending out of the disciples and by implication with the practice of Christian missionaries. The third sermon (chap. 13) derives its core from Mark 4, but Matthew's version is composed of parables and interpretations that expose the mixed nature of the congregation: it is made up of wheat and weeds, the good and the bad. The next sermon (chap. 18) also advances the theme of the congregation by addressing those responsible for the community's order. Yet the guiding principle is not authority but forgiveness. The final sermon (chaps. 24–25) deals with events to occur at the end of history (eschatology). The first part copies Jesus' preaching about the end from Mark 13; the second part focuses on the last judgment in which the standard to be applied is how each person has treated the least of his or her fellow humans.

Author

The early church tradition held that the author of this gospel was the apostle Matthew. Papias, one of the early authorities of the church (about 150 CE), claimed that "Matthew organized the sayings in the Hebrew language, but everyone has translated them as best he could." Papias knew the Gospel of Matthew only in its current form and had not seen a version in a Semitic language. Even though later church authorities accepted Papias' assertions, modern scholars have rejected them for a variety of reasons. First, there is no evidence that the gospel was originally composed in Hebrew. It is written in good Koine Greek of the period. Moreover, it is dependent on Q and Mark, both of which existed only in Greek. Finally, this gospel is not a collection of sayings, like Q, but a narrative with an ordered plot. To refer to the author as Matthew is only a convention.

Date & community

Since the Gospel of Matthew refers to the destruction of Jerusalem in the parable of the banquet, when the king sends his troops to destroy "their city" (22:7), it must have been composed after 70 CE. It is generally thought to have been written before the end of the first century.

The picture of the Matthean community that emerges from a study of this gospel is that of a community engaged in intense debate with rabbinic Judaism and creating new institutions to replace the destroyed temple. Both groups are trying to define themselves. This is the only gospel in which the Greek word *ekklēsia*, meaning church or congregation, appears. Prior to the destruction of the temple in Jerusalem there were many different competing interpretations of what it meant to be an Israelite. But the destruction of Jerusalem set in motion for Judaism and Christianity a long process of consolidation and self-definition that reached its first definitive form around the beginning of the third century. In Judaism this process received a powerful impetus with the triumph of Pharisaism and rabbinic Judaism. In Christianity this process eventuated in what was to become the orthodoxy reflected in the early creeds and institutions.

The Matthean group, recently expelled from the synagogue (5:11), is contesting with the synagogue over who is the true Israel. The Christians and Jesus stand in the line of John the Baptizer and the prophets. For this reason the summary of Jesus' message is the same as John the Baptizer's (3:2; 4:17), and John, the last of the prophets, baptizes Jesus. The Pharisees erected the tombs of the prophets (23:29) and they persecute the Christians who follow the prophets (5:12). The line of true Israel is, then, the prophets, John the Baptizer, Jesus, and the Matthean community.

This forging of a self-definition over and against emerging rabbinic Judaism is important to remember in reading Matthew's gospel. The debate is not between Judaism and Christianity, nor between Jew and Gentile, but between two parties within Judaism. Both groups are withdrawing and consolidating into antagonistic camps.

The rejection of the Pharisees in Matthew implies neither the rejection of Judaism nor the Jewish Law. This gospel emphasizes that the Pharisees sit in the chair of Moses (23:2), yet the standard epithet for them is "phonies" or "impostors." Both Jesus and John the Baptizer address them as "spawn of Satan" (3:7; 12:34; 23:33) and John prophesies that their end is near. As "phonies" they practice their religion in public (6:1–2); they cleanse the outside of the cup, but inside they are "full of greed and self-indulgence" (23:25).

As for the Law, not even the smallest part will pass away (5:18). Matthew portrays Jesus as the true and authoritative interpreter of the Law. He restores it to its original meaning: "As you know, our ancestors were told . . . But I tell you" (5:21).

Use of scripture

At important moments in the story, the narrator quotes from the scriptures, using the standard formula: "All this happened in order to fulfill the prediction of the Lord spoken through the prophet" (1:22; 2:15, 18, 23, 25; 4:14–16; 5:17; 8:17; 12:17–21; 13:14–15, 35; 21:4–5; 26:56; 27:9). Normally such citations are employed to resolve conflict in the story or buttress especially important positions. Matthew even changes several items in Mark's stories to make the narrative fit the quotations. For example, he has Jesus ride into Jerusalem on both a donkey and a colt (21:7), an odd and confusing picture when compared with the simple colt in Mark's version of the scene (Mark 11:7). But the prophecy from Zechariah 9:9, which is composed in Semitic parallelism, reads:

> Look, your king is coming to you;
> > he is triumphant, victorious,
> yet humble, riding on a donkey,
> > on a colt foaled by a donkey.

Matthew takes the two lines quite literally and has Jesus ride two animals, rather than understanding the second line as a poetic repetition of the first. Beyond that, Matthew has blended Zechariah 9:9 with Isaiah 62:11 and created a unique version (see Matt 21:5). Close attention to Matthew's use of quotations from scripture is a sure guide to distinctive features of the Matthean gospel.

Self-portrait

The author has left what seems to be self-portrait in 13:52: "every scholar who is schooled in the empire of Heaven is like some proprietor who produces from his storeroom treasures old and new." This suggests how the Matthean community understands itself: it pores over the records of the past (the scriptures) but it produces something new and original—a new understanding of the Law.

The scholar evidently plays an important role in this community. Jesus is regularly pictured as teaching. Yet as important as scholarship and teaching is to this community, Jesus is addressed as "teacher" or "Rabbi" only by outsiders. The disciples and believers refer to him as "Master" or "Lord."

"Virgin" or "young woman"?

SV features a unique translation of the prophecy from Isaiah quoted in Matthew 1:23: "a young woman will conceive her first child." Virtually all English translations render this prophecy "a virgin will conceive," on the assumption that the Greek word *parthenos* means "virgin." However, the word more precisely refers to a young woman who has not yet borne her first child—as, for example, in LXX Joel 1:8, which refers to a *parthenos* who is a widow: "Lament like a *parthenos* dressed in sackcloth for the husband of her youth." It is instructive that the only other passage in Matthew besides 1:23 containing the word *parthenos* is the parable about the ten "maidens" (Matt 25:1–12), which has nothing to do with virginity.

Parthenos could be used to denote a virgin, but in such cases that meaning had to be clarified by the context, usually by means of an adjectival phrase, as in "a *parthenos* who had not known a man." (In biblical usage, to "know" another person can be a euphemism for sexual intercourse.) An attentive reader will note how carefully Luke, who surely believed in the virgin birth, constructed the dialogue between Mary and the angel Gabriel (Luke 1:34–35) in such a way as help his audience understand that Mary was a virgin. Apparently, he thought that describing Mary simply as a *parthenos* ("girl") in 1:27 would not by itself convey that meaning unambiguously.

Matthew's annunciation scene, however, does not presuppose a virgin birth, or at least shows no interest in the matter. Matthew says only that God's holy spirit is responsible for Mary's pregnancy (1:20). In a Jewish context like Matthew's, that does not exclude the possibility that a human male was involved. It means that Mary's condition is under God's protection and will serve God's will.

In any case, Matthew's interest in the Isaiah prophecy does not have to do with a miraculous conception—which is not in view in Isaiah's original context either—but in the rich symbolism of the name Emmanuel: God will be with his people through the life, teaching, miracles, death, and resurrection of Jesus.

The Gospel of Matthew

1 **This is the Book of Genesis** of Jesus the Anointed, son of David, son of Abraham.

Jesus' family tree

²Abraham was the father of Isaac, Isaac of Jacob, Jacob of Judah and his brothers, ³and Judah and Tamar were the parents of Perez and Zerah. Perez was the father of Hezron, Hezron of Aram, ⁴Aram of Amminadab, Amminadab of Nahshon, Nahshon of Salmon, ⁵and Salmon and Rahab were the parents of Boaz. Boaz and Ruth were the parents of Obed. Obed was the father of Jesse, ⁶and Jesse of David the king.

David and Uriah's wife were the parents of Solomon. ⁷Solomon was the father of Rehoboam, Rehoboam of Abijah, Abijah of Asaph, ⁸Asaph of Jehoshaphat, Jehoshaphat of Joram, Joram of Uzziah, ⁹Uzziah of Jotham, Jotham of Ahaz, Ahaz of Hezekiah, ¹⁰Hezekiah of Manasseh, Manasseh of Amos, Amos of Josiah, ¹¹and Josiah was the father of Jeconiah and his brothers at the time of the exile to Babylon.

¹²After the Babylonian exile, Jeconiah was the father of Shealtiel, Shealtiel of Zerubbabel, ¹³Zerubbabel of Abiud, Abiud of Eliakim, Eliakim of Azor, ¹⁴Azor of Zadok, Zadok of Achim, Achim of Eliud, ¹⁵Eliud of Eleazar, Eleazar of Matthan, Matthan of Jacob. ¹⁶And Jacob was the father of Joseph, the husband of Mary, who was the mother of Jesus. Jesus is known as the Anointed.

1:1–17
//Lk 3:23–38
1:2–6
◊ 1 Chr 2:1–15
1:3–6
◊ Ru 4:18–22
1:3
◊ Gn 38
1:5
◊ Jos 2, Ru 4:13–17
1:7–12
◊ 1 Chr 3:10–19

1:1–11 The first two sections of genealogy are based on the genealogies of 1 Chronicles 1–3 and Ruth 4:18–22. It is impossible to reconcile the genealogy in Matthew with the one in Luke (3:23–38).

1:1 *The Book of Genesis*: The opening words of the gospel (*biblos geneseōs,* literally, "the book of origins") are also the name of the first book of the Bible.

Anointed is the literal meaning of the Greek title often transliterated in English as "Christ." David establishes the royal line and Abraham the line of Israel.

1:3 *Judah* was *Tamar's* father-in-law (Genesis 38).

1:5 *Rahab* was the prostitute of Jericho who helped the Israelites overtake Jericho (Joshua 2). She is nowhere mentioned as the mother of Boaz. *Ruth*, a gentile, was the great-grandmother of David (Ruth 4:18–22).

1:6 *Uriah's wife* was Bathsheba. After David raped her, he engineered her husband's death (2 Samuel 11).

1:7 *Asaph* is probably a confusion for Asa, the fifth king in David's line. Asaph was psalm singer appointed by David (I Chr 6:39). A number of psalms are also attributed to him (e.g., Psalm 50).

1:8 According to 1 Chr 3:11–12, *Joram* was the great-great-grandfather of *Uzziah* (called Azariah in 1 Chronicles).

1:10 The actual successor of Manasseh was Amon, not *Amos*. Some manuscripts make the correction.

1:11 According to 1 Chr 3:15–16, *Josiah* was the grandfather of *Jeconiah*.

1:13 *Abiud* is not mentioned among the sons of Zerubbabel (1 Chr 3:19).

1:15 With *Matthan*, Joseph's grandfather, the genealogy no longer follows 1 Chronicles.

1:16 The fact that this is Joseph's genealogy and not Mary's looks forward to his adoption of Jesus in the birth story (vv. 21, 25).

[17]In sum, the generations from Abraham to David come to fourteen, those from David to the Babylonian Exile come to fourteen, and those from the Babylonian Exile to the Anointed also come to fourteen.

[18]**The genesis of Jesus** the Anointed was as follows. While his mother Mary was betrothed to Joseph, but before she moved in with him, she was found to be pregnant by the holy spirit. [19]Although Joseph her husband was a virtuous man, he didn't want to expose her publicly; so he planned to break off their betrothal quietly.

[20]While he was thinking about these things, a messenger of the Lord appeared to him in a dream with these words: "Joseph, son of David, don't hesitate to take Mary as your wife, since the holy spirit is responsible for her pregnancy. [21]She will give birth to a son and you will name him Jesus, because he will save his people from their sins." [22]All of this happened in order to fulfill the prediction of the Lord spoken through the prophet:

[23]Look, a young woman will conceive her first child
> and she will give birth to a son,
and they will name him Emmanuel.

(The name means "God is with us").
[24]Joseph got up and did what the messenger of the Lord told him: he took Mary as his wife. [25]He did not sleep with her until she had given birth to a son. Joseph named him Jesus.

2 **Jesus was born** in Bethlehem, Judea, when Herod was king. Astrologers from the East showed up in Jerusalem just then. [2]"Tell us," they said, "where

1:18–25
//Lk 2:1–7

1:20
Ⓣ Mt 2:12, 19, 22; 27:19

1:23
◊Is 7:14 (LXX), Is 8:8, 10 (LXX); Ⓣ Mt 18:20, 28:20

2:1–6
//Lk 2:8–14

1:18 A few mss omit *Jesus*.
1:25 Some mss read "her firstborn" son.

1:17 Matthew has arranged this genealogy around the number 14, which is the numerical value of David's name in Hebrew. There are only thirteen generations in the last group from the Babylonian exile to the Anointed One.
1:19 Because Joseph was *virtuous*, he was committed to obeying the Jewish law which prohibited a man from marrying a woman who was carrying someone else's child (see Deut 22:28–29). His reverence for the law is balanced by his compassion, which is evident in his desire not to humiliate Mary by a public divorce, a divorce being necessary to undo a betrothal.
1:20 *Dreams* are often occasions for revelations; e.g., Jacob's dreams (Gen 20:12), Joseph's dreams (Genesis 37), or Daniel's interpretations of dreams (Daniel 2).
1:21 The Greek name *Jesus* is derived from the Hebrew

"Joshua" which according to popular etymology means "Yahweh is salvation." This multilingual wordplay is echoed in this verse.
1:23 This is the first of a number of distinctive quotations of the Old Testament introduced by a nearly identical formula. (See the cameo essay for an explanation of the translation of Isaiah's prophecy.)
1:25 The act of naming the child is tantamount to adoption, claiming the child as his own. Thus Jesus is a legal son of Joseph.
2:1 *Bethlehem*, a few miles south of Jerusalem, was the ancestral home of David (1 Sam 16:1), as well as the burial place of Rachel (Gen 35:19), whose lament is mentioned in 2:18. The city also figures prominently in the story of Ruth, who is mentioned in the genealogy.

to find the one born to be king of the Judeans. We have observed his star at its rising and have come to pay him homage."

³When this news reached King Herod, he was visibly shaken, and all Jerusalem along with him. ⁴He called together all the chief priests and local experts, and pressed them for information: "Where is the Anointed One supposed to be born?"

⁵They replied, "In Bethlehem, Judea. This is how it is put by the prophet:

> ⁶And you, Bethlehem, in the land of Judah,
>> in no way are you least among the leaders of Judah.
>
> Out of you will come a leader
>> who will shepherd my people, Israel."

⁷Then Herod called the astrologers together secretly and ascertained from them the precise time the star became visible. ⁸Then he sent them to Bethlehem with these instructions: "Go make a careful search for the child. When you find him, report back to me, so I can also go and pay him homage."

⁹They listened to what the king had to say and continued on their way.

And there guiding them on was the star that they had observed in the East. It led them on until it came to a standstill above where the child lay. ¹⁰Once they saw the star, they were beside themselves with joy. ¹¹And they arrived at the house and saw the child with his mother Mary. They knelt down and paid him homage. Then they opened their treasure chests and presented him with gifts—gold, pure incense, and aromatic ointment. ¹²And because they had been advised in a dream not to return to Herod, they journeyed back to their own country by a different route.

¹³**After the astrologers** had departed, a messenger of the Lord appeared in a dream to Joseph, saying, "Get up, take the child and his mother and flee to Egypt. Stay there until I give you instructions. You see, Herod is determined to hunt the child down and destroy him."

¹⁴So Joseph got up and took the child and his mother under cover of night and set out for Egypt. ¹⁵There they remained until Herod's death. This happened in order to fulfill the prediction of the Lord spoken through the prophet:

> I called my son out of Egypt.

2:3
Ⓣ Mt 21:10

2:6
Cf. Jn 7:42;
◊ Mi 5:2, 2 Sm 5:2

2:9b–12
//Lk 2:15–20

2:11
◊ Ps 72:10–11,
Is 60:6

2:12
Ⓣ Mt 1:20; 2:19, 22; 27:19

2:13
◊ Ex 2:15

2:15
Cf. GNaz 1;
◊ Hos 11:1

Herod the king is Herod the Great who ruled both Judea and Galilee from 37 to 4 BCE.

Astrologers were also involved in magic, the observation of the stars, and wisdom.

2:2 *star*: Despite numerous attempts to identify a specific astronomical event as the Bethlehem star, no effort has proven successful.

2:4 The *chief priests* were those who held positions of authority in the temple hierarchy.

The *local experts* were usually employed in the bureaucracy. In the gospels they are frequently linked with the Pharisees.

2:11 The *gifts* were most likely picked for their expensiveness.

2:13 The flight into *Egypt* and the eventual return recalls the captivity and exodus themes so prominent in Israel's history.

[16]**When Herod realized** he had been duped by the astrologers, he was outraged. He then issued orders to kill all the children two years old and younger in Bethlehem and the surrounding region. This corresponded to the time ⟨of the star⟩ that he had learned from the astrologers. [17]Then the prediction spoken through Jeremiah the prophet was fulfilled:

> [18]In Ramah the sound of mourning
>> and bitter grieving was heard:
>
> Rachel weeping for her children.
>
> She refused to be consoled
>> because they were no more.

[19]**After Herod's death**, a messenger of the Lord appeared in a dream to Joseph in Egypt: [20]"Get up, take the child and his mother, and go to the land of Israel; those who were seeking the child's life are dead."

[21]So he got up, took the child and his mother, and went to the land of Israel. [22]He heard that Archelaus was the king of Judea in the place of his father Herod; as a consequence, he was afraid to go there. He was instructed in a dream to go to Galilee. [23]So he went there and settled in a town called Nazareth, in order to fulfill the prediction of the prophets that he will be called a Nazorean.

3 **In due course** John the Baptizer appears in the Judean desert, [2]calling out, "change your ways because the empire of Heaven is arriving."

[3]No doubt this is the person described by Isaiah the prophet:

> A voice of someone shouting in the desert,
> "Make ready the way of the Lord;
>> make his paths straight."

2:18
◊Jer 31:15

2:19
Ⓣ Mt 1:20; 2:12, 22; 27:19

2:22
Ⓣ Mt 1:20; 2:12, 19; 27:19

2:23
Cf. GNaz 1;
◊Jgs 13:5

3:1–12
//Mk 1:2–8,
Lk 3:1–20;
cf. Jn 1:19–28

3:2
//Mk 1:15;
Ⓣ Mt 4:17, 10:7

3:3
◊Is 40:3

2:18 Some mss read *the sound of* "dirges and" *mourning*. This appears to be an effort of early scribes to bring the quote into conformity with Jer 31:15 LXX.

2:16 Historians are unable to find any evidence of the murder of the children.

2:18 *Ramah* of Benjamin is about five miles north of Jerusalem. It was the place from which the Israelites were sent into exile in Babylon.

Rachel was the wife of Jacob whose name was also "Israel" (Gen 32:28).

2:22 *Archelaus*, the son of Herod the Great, ruled as ethnarch of Judea, Samaria, and Idumea from 4 BCE until 6 CE, when Rome banished him and made Judea a Roman province.

2:23 In this story Jesus is a Judean who, after the sojourn in Egypt, moves to *Nazareth* in Galilee, while in Luke Jesus is a Galilean whose parents must travel to Bethlehem in Judea (Luke 2:4).

he will be called a Nazorean: There is no such prophecy in the OT. The statement might be a free paraphrase of LXX Judg 13:5 or 16:17. Matthew's *Nazorean* is spelled differently than Mark's "Nazarene" (e.g., in Mark 1:24).

3:2 *the empire of Heaven*: Pious Jews often substituted alternate expressions for the word "God." In keeping with this Jewish custom, Matthew often uses "Heaven" as a circumlocution for "God." Thus, *the empire of Heaven* is simply Matthew's adaptation of what other gospels call "the empire of God." Matthew's expression does not by itself mean that God's empire is in heaven.

[4]Now this same John wore clothes made of camel hair and had a leather belt around his waist; he lived on grasshoppers and wild honey. [5]Then Jerusalem, and all Judea, and all the region around the Jordan streamed out to him, [6]and got baptized in the Jordan River by him, admitting their sins.

[7]When he saw that many of the Pharisees and Sadducees were coming for baptism, John said to them, "You spawn of Satan! Who warned you to flee from the impending doom? [8]Well then, start producing fruit suitable for a change of heart, [9]and don't even think of saying to yourselves, 'We have Abraham for our father.' Let me tell you, God can raise up children for Abraham right out of these rocks! [10]Even now the axe is aimed at the root of the trees. So every tree not producing choice fruit gets cut down and tossed into the fire.

[11]"I baptize you with water for a change of heart, but someone more powerful than I will succeed me. I'm not fit to take off his sandals. He'll baptize you with holy spirit and fire. [12]His pitchfork is in his hand, and he'll make a clean sweep of his threshing floor, and gather the wheat into his granary, but the chaff he'll burn in a fire that can't be put out."

[13]**Then Jesus comes** from Galilee to John at the Jordan to get baptized by him. [14]And John tried to stop him with these words: "I'm the one who needs to get baptized by you, yet you come to me?"

[15]In response, Jesus said to him, "Let it go for now. This is the right thing for us to do." Then John gave into to him.

[16]Right after Jesus had been baptized, he got up out of the water, and—amazingly—the skies opened up and he saw God's spirit coming down on him like a dove, perching on him, [17]and—listen!—there was a voice from the skies, which said, "This is my son, the one I love—I fully approve of him."

4 **Then Jesus was guided** into the desert by the spirit to be put to the test by the devil. [2]And after he had fasted forty days and forty nights, he was famished.

John baptizes Jesus

Jesus is tested

3:4–7
//GEbi 3;
cf. GEbi 1

3:4
◊2 Kgs 1:8

Q3:7–10
//Lk 3:7–9

3:7
① Mt 12:24, 23:33

3:10
① Mt 7:19

3:11
//Acts 1:5, 11:16,
13:24–25

3:13–17
//Mk 1:9–11,
Lk 3:21–22,
Jn 1:29–34,
GHeb 3, GEbi 4

3:14–15
//GEbi 4:7–8;
cf. GHeb 2:2,
GNaz 2:2

3:15
① Mt 5:17

3:17
//GEbi 4:6;
① Mt 12:18, 17:5;
◊Ps 2:7, Is 42:1,
44:2

Q4:1–11
//Mk 1:12–13,
Lk 4:1–13

4:1
① Heb 4:15;
cf. GHeb 4

4:2
◊Ex 34:28,
Dt 9:9, 1 Kgs 19:8

3:7 *Sadducees* were one of the main groups of Jewish society. They were mostly priests and belonged to the upper class. Many of their members served in the Council. Theologically they were very conservative, accepting only the Torah as scripture and rejecting belief in the resurrection. While in the gospels they are frequently allied with the Pharisees, in rabbinic literature they are the Pharisees' opponents.

Pharisees were likewise one of the principal groups of first-century Judaism and were generally popular among the ordinary people. They were interpreters of the Law and made an effort to apply it to all aspects of life. In the post-70 period they became the principal Jewish opponents of Christianity, which accounts for the strident opposition to them in the gospels.

3:15 John the Baptizer's dilemma parallels Joseph's. To do

the right thing here he should not baptize Jesus, just as Joseph should not marry Mary.

3:16 Unlike Mark (Mark 1:10) Matthew seems to envision the coming of the spirit as a physical event (see likewise Luke 3:22).

4:1 *Devil* is a translation of the Greek word *diabolos* meaning "accuser" or "slanderer." In the LXX it is used to translate the Hebrew word *satan*, which means "adversary." In the New Testament, Devil and Satan mean the same thing. In the Hebrew Bible, Satan is a member of God's court (Job 1:1; Zech 3:1–2; 1 Chr 21:1) and is not the embodiment of evil. That notion develops after 200 BCE.

4:2 *Forty days and forty nights* recalls Moses' time with God on Mount Sinai (Exod 24:18) and Elijah's period of fasting (1 Kgs 19:8).

A voice in Galilee

³And the tester confronted him and said, "To prove you're God's son, order these stones to turn into bread."

⁴He responded, "It is written,

> Human beings shall not live on bread alone, but on every word that comes from God's mouth."

⁵Then the devil conducts him to the holy city, sets him on the high point of the temple, ⁶and says to him, "To prove you're God's son, jump off; remember, it is written,

> To his heavenly messengers he will give orders about you,

and

> With their hands they will catch you,
> so you won't even stub your toe on a stone."

⁷Jesus said to him, "Elsewhere it is written,

> You shall not put the Lord your God to the test."

⁸Again the devil takes him to a very high mountain and shows him all the empires of the world and their splendor, ⁹and says to him, "I'll give you all these, if you will kneel down and pay homage to me."

¹⁰Finally Jesus says to him, "Get out of here, Satan! Remember, it is written,

> You shall pay homage to the Lord your God, and him alone shall you revere."

¹¹Then the devil leaves him, and heavenly messengers arrive out of nowhere and look after him.

¹²**When Jesus heard** that John had been locked up, he headed for Galilee. ¹³He took leave of Nazareth to go and settle down in Capernaum-by-the-sea, in the territory of Zebulun and Naphtali, ¹⁴in order to fulfill the prediction spoken through Isaiah the prophet:

> ¹⁵Land of Zebulun and of Naphtali,
>> the way to the sea,
>> across the Jordan,
>> Galilee of the pagans.
> ¹⁶The people who languished in darkness
>> have seen a great light,
> those who have wasted away in the shadow of death,
>> for them a light has risen.

4:4
◊Dt 8:3

4:6
◊Ps 91:11–12

4:7
◊Dt 6:16

4:8–10
Cf. GHeb 4

4:10
◊Dt 6:13

4:11
①Jn 1:51

4:12–17
//Mk 1:14–15,
Lk 4:14–15

4:12
①Mt 14:3

4:15–16
◊Is 9:1–2

4:10 Some mss conform Jesus' dismissal of Satan to his dismissal of Peter in 16:23: "Get out of my sight."

4:13 *Capernaum* is a town on the northwest shore of the Sea of Galilee.

¹⁷From that time on Jesus began to proclaim: "Change your ways because the empire of Heaven is arriving."

¹⁸**As he was walking** by the Sea of Galilee, he spotted two brothers, Simon, also known as Peter, and Andrew his brother, throwing their net in the sea, since they were fishermen. ¹⁹And Jesus says to them, "Follow me and I'll have you fishing for people!" ²⁰So right then and there they abandoned their nets and followed him.

²¹When he had gone on a little farther, he caught sight of two other brothers, James, son of Zebedee, and his brother John, in the boat with Zebedee their father, mending their nets, and he also called out to them. ²²Right then and there they abandoned their boat and their father and followed him.

²³**And he toured** all over Galilee, teaching in their meeting places, proclaiming the good news of the empire ⟨of Heaven⟩, and healing every disease and every ailment the people had. ²⁴And his reputation spread through the whole of Syria. They brought him everyone who was ill, who suffered from any kind of disease or was in intense pain, who was possessed, who was epileptic, or paralyzed, and he cured them. ²⁵And huge crowds followed him from Galilee and the Ten Cities and Jerusalem and Judea and from across the Jordan.

5 First Discourse: What Heaven's Empire Demands
Seeing the crowds, he climbed up the mountain, and when he had sat down, his disciples came to him. ²He then began to speak, and this is what he would teach them:

> ³Congratulations to the poor in spirit!
>> The empire of Heaven belongs to them.
> ⁴Congratulations to those who grieve!
>> They will be consoled.
> ⁵Congratulations to the gentle!
>> They will inherit the earth.
> ⁶Congratulations to those who hunger and thirst for justice!
>> They will have a feast.
> ⁷Congratulations to the merciful!
>> They will receive mercy.
> ⁸Congratulations to those whose motives are pure!
>> They will see God.

4:17 A few mss omit *Change your ways.*

Jesus calls his first disciples

A teaching tour in Galilee

Congratulations

4:17
//Mt 3:2, 10:7

4:18–20
//Mk 1:16–18,
Lk 5:1–3,
Jn 1:40–42;
cf. GEbi 2:3

4:21–22
//Mk 1:19–20,
Lk 5:4–11

4:23–25
//Mk 1:35–39,
Lk 4:42–44

4:23
ⓣ Mt 9:35,
Mary 4:8

5:1–12
//Lk 6:17–26

5:1
ⓣ Mk 3:13,
Lk 6:12–14, Jn 6:3

Q5:3
//Lk 6:20, Th 54;
ⓣ Mt 11:5;
ⓣ Jas 2:5

Q5:4
//Lk 6:21;
◊ Is 61:2

5:5
◊ Ps 37:11

Q5:6
//Lk 6:21, Th 69:2

5:8
◊ Ps 24:3–4

4:23 Matthew generally refers to *their meeting places* (traditionally translated "synagogues"), which indicates that this gospel was written after the followers of Jesus had separated from official Judaism.

4:24 *Syria* is the major Roman province in the East which includes Galilee, Judea, Samaria. Its capital was Antioch. Here it may refer to the area around Damascus.

4:25 *The Ten Cities* was a confederation of Hellenistic cities in the area east of Samaria and Galilee.

5:1 *The mountain* may be an allusion to Moses ascending Mount Sinai. This gospel ends with Jesus on the mountain with his disciples.

Salt & light

Law & prophets

On anger

⁹Congratulations to those who work for peace!
　They will be called God's children.
¹⁰Congratulations to those who have suffered persecution for the sake of justice!
　The empire of Heaven belongs to them.

¹¹"Congratulations to you when they denounce you and persecute you and spread malicious gossip about you because of me. ¹²Rejoice and be glad! In heaven you'll be more than rewarded. Remember, that is how they persecuted the prophets who preceded you.

¹³"**You are the salt** of the earth. But if salt loses its zing, how will it be made salty? It's then good for nothing, except to be thrown out and stomped on. ¹⁴You are the light of the world. A city sitting on top of a mountain can't be concealed. ¹⁵Nor do people light a lamp and put it under a bushel basket, but instead on a lampstand, where it sheds light for everyone in the house. ¹⁶That's how your light should shine in public, so others can see your good deeds and praise your Father in the heavens.

¹⁷"**Don't imagine** that I have come to annul the Law or the Prophets. I have come not to annul but to fulfill. ¹⁸Let me tell you, before earth and sky pass away, not one iota, not one serif, will disappear from the Law, until it all happens. ¹⁹Whoever ignores one of the least ⟨important⟩ of these commandments, and teaches others to do so, will be called least ⟨important⟩ in the empire of Heaven. But whoever acts on ⟨these commandments⟩ and teaches ⟨others to do so⟩ will be called great in the empire of Heaven. ²⁰Let me tell you, unless you live your religion more fully than the scholars and Pharisees, you won't set foot in the empire of Heaven.

²¹"**As you know**, our ancestors were told, 'You shall not kill' and 'Whoever kills will be subject to judgment.' ²²But I tell you, those who are angry with a companion will be brought before a tribunal. And those who say to a companion, 'You moron,' will be subject to the sentence of the court. And whoever says, 'You idiot,' deserves the fires of Gehenna. ²³So, even if you happen to be offering your gift at the altar and recall that your friend has some claim against you, ²⁴leave your gift there at the altar. First go and be reconciled with your friend, and only then return and offer your gift. ²⁵You should settle quickly with your

5:10
//Th 69:1

Q5:11
//Lk 6:22, Th 68:1

Q5:13
//Mk 9:50,
Lk 14:34–35,
GSav 1:4

5:14
//GSav 1:4;
Ⓣ Th 32

Q5:15
//Mk 4:21, Lk 8:16,
Lk 11:33, Th 33:2–3

5:17
Cf. GEbi 6

Q5:18
//Lk 16:17

5:21
◊Ex 20:13, Dt 5:17

5:23–24
Cf. Mk 11:25

Q5:25–26
//Lk 12:58–59

5:11 A few mss add "tell lies" to the triad of *denounce and persecute and spread malicious gossip.*
5:22 To mitigate the rigor of the statement, some mss add "without cause" after *a companion.*

5:16 *Father in the heavens* or "heavenly Father" is a distinctive Matthean phrase.
5:17 *Law* and *Prophets* refer to the first two parts of the Hebrew Bible: Law, Prophets, and Writings. "The Law" can stand for the whole of the Hebrew Bible as well as for the first five books (the Torah or Pentateuch).
5:18 *Iota* is the smallest Greek letter and a *serif* is the "hook" on a Hebrew letter.
5:22 For *moron* the text uses an Aramaic word *raka*, a term of mild abuse.
　Gehenna is derived from the Hebrew meaning "valley of Hinnon," which ran southwest of Jerusalem. At one time human sacrifice was practiced there (2 Chr 28:3; Jer 7:32). In the NT it is a metaphor for hell.

accuser while you are both on the way ⟨to court⟩, or else your accuser will turn you over to the judge, and the judge to the bailiff, and you are thrown in jail. 26Let me tell you, you'll never get out of there until you've paid the last dime.

27"**As you know**, we once were told, 'You shall not commit adultery.' 28But I tell you, those who leer at a woman with lust have already committed adultery with her in their minds. 29And if your right eye gets you into trouble, rip it out and throw it away! You'd be better off losing a part of your body, than having your whole body thrown into Gehenna. 30And if your right hand gets you into trouble, cut it off and throw it away! You'd be better off losing a part of your body, than having your whole body wind up in Gehenna.

31"**We once were told**, 'Whoever divorces his wife must give her a certificate of divorce.' 32But I tell you, anyone who divorces his wife (except in the case of immorality) forces her into adultery; and whoever marries a divorced woman commits adultery.

33"**Again, as you know**, our ancestors were told, 'You shall not break an oath,' and 'Oaths sworn in the name of God shall be kept.' 34But I tell you, don't swear at all. Don't invoke heaven, because it is the throne of God, 35and don't invoke earth, because it is God's footstool, and don't invoke Jerusalem, because it is the city of the great king. 36You shouldn't swear by your head either, since you aren't able to turn a single hair either white or black. 37Rather, your responses should be simply 'Yes' and 'No.' Anything beyond that is inspired by the evil one.

38"**As you know**, we once were told, 'An eye for an eye' and 'A tooth for a tooth.' 39But I tell you, don't react violently against the one who is evil; when someone slaps you on the right cheek, turn the other as well. 40If someone is determined to sue you for your shirt, let him have your coat along with it. 41Further, when anyone conscripts you for one mile, go along an extra mile. 42Give to those who beg from you; and don't turn away those who want to borrow from you.

43"**As you know**, we once were told, 'You shall love your neighbor' and 'You shall hate your enemy.' 44But I tell you, love your enemies and pray for your persecutors. 45You'll then become children of your Father in the heavens, for God makes the sun rise on both the bad and the good, and sends rain on both the just and the unjust. 46Tell me, if you love those who love you, why should you be rewarded for that? Even the toll collectors do as much, don't they? 47And if you greet only your friends, what have you done that is exceptional? Even the

On lust

On divorce

On oaths

Eye for an eye

Love for enemies

5:27
◊ Ex 20:13, Dt 5:17

5:29–30
① Mt 18:8–9

Q5:31–32
//Mk 10:10–12,
Lk 16:18;
① Mt 19:7–9

5:31
◊ Dt 24:1–4

5:32
① 1 Cor 7:10–11

5:33
◊ Lv 19:12

5:34
① Mt 23:16–22

5:34–35
◊ Is 66:1

5:35
◊ Ps 48:2

5:38
◊ Ex 21:23–25,
Lv 24:19–20,
Dt 19:21

Q5:39–42
//Lk 6:27–31

Q5:43–48
//Lk 6:27–36

5:43
◊ Lv 19:18

5:32 The exception clause is similar to the one in 19:9.
5:41 *Conscription* was a common and oppressive way of raising troops.
5:43 *"You shall hate your enemy"* does not occur in the He-

brew Bible. It may be a reference to a verse in the Community Rule of the Dead Sea Scrolls: "They may love all that He has chosen and hate all that he has rejected."

pagans do as much, don't they? ⁴⁸To sum up, you shall be perfect, in the same way your heavenly Father is perfect.

6 "**Take care** that you don't flaunt your religion in public to be noticed by others. Otherwise, you'll have no reward from your Father in the heavens. ²For example, when you give to charity, don't bother to toot your own horn as some phonies do in synagogues and on the street. They are seeking human recognition. Let me tell you, they've already received their reward. ³Instead, when you give to charity, don't let your left hand in on what your right hand is up to, ⁴so your acts of charity will stay secret. And your Father, who sees what happens in secret, will reward you.

⁵"**And when you pray**, don't act like phonies. They love to stand up and pray in synagogues and on street corners, so they can show off in public. Let me tell you, they've already received their reward. ⁶When you pray, go into a room by yourself and shut the door behind you. Then pray to your Father, the hidden one. And your Father, who sees what happens in secret, will reward you. ⁷And when you pray, you should not babble on as the pagans do. They imagine that the more they say, the more attention they get. ⁸So don't imitate them. After all, your Father knows what you need before you ask. ⁹Instead, you should pray like this:

> Our Father in the heavens,
>   your name be revered.
> ¹⁰Your empire be established,
>   your will be done on earth as it is in heaven.
> ¹¹Provide us with the bread we need for the day.
> ¹²Forgive our debts
>   to the extent that we have forgiven those in debt to us.
> ¹³And don't make us face the test,
>   but rescue us from the evil one.

5:48
◊Dt 18:13, Lv 19:2;
Ⓣ 1 Cor 14:20

6:1–4
//Th 14:1–3

6:3
//Th 62:2

Q6:5–15
//Lk 11:1–4

6:6
◊Is 26:20

6:11
//GNaz 3

5:47 Many mss read "toll collectors" instead of *pagans*.
6:12 Many mss read "we forgive" instead of *we have forgiven*.
6:13 At the end of the verse, many mss insert "for yours is the kingdom, the power, and the glory. Amen." This reflects an adaptation of the prayer for liturgical use (see 1 Chr 29:10–11).

5:48 To *be perfect* means to follow all the demands of the Torah without any reduction. See 1 Cor 14:20 where Christians are urged by Paul not to be babies but mature. The same Greek word is used to translate "mature."
6:2 The Greek word transliterated into English as "hypocrite" and here translated *phony* means an actor in a play. Only in Hellenistic Judaism and early Christianity does the word have an exclusively negative sense. Thirteen times in Matthew it refers to the Pharisees.

6:7 Gentile prayers were noted for their piling up of epithets.
6:11 The meaning of the Greek translated *we need for the day* is very debated. Origen, a church author of the third century and one of the greatest early Christian scholars, thought that the word was coined by the evangelists. Its only certain occurrence in the Greek language is in the Lord's prayer.

On fasting

On possessions

Eye & light

Two masters

On anxieties

On judging

¹⁴"For if you forgive the offenses of others, your heavenly Father will also forgive yours, ¹⁵and if you don't forgive others, neither will your heavenly Father forgive your offenses.

¹⁶"**When you fast**, don't make a spectacle of your remorse as the phonies do. As you know, they make their faces unrecognizable so their fasting may be publicly recognized. Let me tell you, they've already received their reward. ¹⁷When you fast, brush your hair and wash your face, ¹⁸so your fasting will not be noticed by others, but by your Father, the hidden one, and your Father, who sees what happens in secret, will reward you.

¹⁹"**Don't pile up possessions** here on earth, where moths and insects eat away and where burglars break in and steal. ²⁰Instead, gather your nest egg in heaven, where neither moths nor insects eat away and where no burglars break in or steal. ²¹As you know, what you treasure is your heart's true measure.

²²"**The eye** is the body's lamp. It follows that if your eye is clear, your whole body will be flooded with light. ²³If your eye is clouded, your whole body will be shrouded in darkness. If, then, the light within you is darkness, how dark that can be!

²⁴"**No one can** be a slave to two masters. That slave will either hate one and love the other, or be devoted to one and disdain the other. You can't be enslaved to both God and Mammon.

²⁵"**That's why I'm telling you**, don't fret about your life—what you're going to eat and drink, or about your body—what you're going to wear. There's more to living than food and clothing, isn't there? ²⁶Take a look at the birds of the sky: they don't plant or harvest or gather into barns. Yet your heavenly Father feeds them. You're worth more than they, aren't you? ²⁷Can any of you add one hour to life by fretting about it? ²⁸Why worry about clothes? Notice how the wild lilies grow: they don't toil and they never spin. ²⁹But let me tell you, even Solomon at the height of his glory was never decked out like one of them. ³⁰If God dresses up the grass in the field, which is here today and is thrown into an oven tomorrow, won't ⟨God care for⟩ you even more, you with your meager trust? ³¹So don't fret. Don't say, 'What are we going to eat?' or 'What are we going to drink?' or 'What are we going to wear?' ³²These are all things pagans seek. After all, your heavenly Father is aware that you need them all. ³³Seek God's empire and his justice first, and all these things will come to you as a bonus. ³⁴So don't fret about tomorrow. Let tomorrow fret about itself. The troubles that the day brings are enough.

7 "**Don't pass judgment**, so you won't be judged. ²Don't forget, the judgment you hand out will be the judgment you get back. And the standard you

6:15
Cf. Mk 11:25

6:16–18
Ⓣ Th 6; 14:1–3

6:16
◊Is 58:5

Q6:19–21
//Lk 12:33–34

6:19
//Th 76:3;
◊Is 51:8

6:21
//Mary 7:4

Q6:22–23
//Lk 11:34–36,
Th 24:3, DSav 6

Q6:24
//Lk 16:13, Th 47:2

Q6:25–34
//Lk 12:22–34

6:25
//Th 36

6:26
◊Job 38:41

6:30
Ⓣ Mt 8:26, 14:31,
16:8, 17:20

6:31
//Th 36

6:34
//DSav 20:1

Q7:1–5
//Lk 6:37–42

7:1
//Mary 9:12

7:2
//Mk 4:24–25

6:24 *Mammon* is an Aramaic word meaning "wealth." Here Matthew seems to use it as the name of a false god.

7:3–5
//Th 26
7:6
//Th 93
Q7:7–11
//Lk 11:9–13
7:7
//Th 92:1; 94;
cf. Th 2
7:7–8
Ⓣ Mt 21:22
7:8
//Mary 4:7,
GHeb 6b
Q7:12
//Lk 6:31
Q7:13–14
//Lk 13:22–30
Q7:15–20
//Lk 6:43–45
7:15
Ⓣ Mk 13:22,
Mt 24:24
7:16
//Th 45:1
7:17
//Mt 12:33–37
7:19
//Mt 3:10
7:21–23
Ⓣ Mt 25:31–46
Q7:21
//Lk 6:46;
cf. EgerG 3:5
Q7:22–23
//Lk 13:26–27
7:22
Ⓣ Mk 9:38–40
7:23
◊Ps 6:8
Q7:24–27
//Lk 6:47–49

apply will be the standard applied to you. ³Why do you notice the sliver in your friend's eye, but overlook the timber in your own? ⁴How can you say to your friend, 'Let me get the sliver out of your eye,' when there is that timber in your own? ⁵You phony, first take the timber out of your own eye and then you'll see well enough to remove the sliver from your friend's eye.

⁶"**Don't offer to dogs** what is sacred, and don't throw your pearls to pigs, or they'll trample them underfoot and turn and tear you to shreds.

⁷"**Ask—it'll be given** to you; seek—you'll find; knock—it'll be opened for you. ⁸Everyone who asks receives; everyone who seeks finds; and for the one who knocks it is opened. ⁹Who among you would hand a son a stone when he's asking for bread? ¹⁰Again, who would hand him a snake when he's asking for fish? Of course no one would! ¹¹So if you, worthless as you are, know how to give your children good gifts, isn't it much more likely that your Father in the heavens will give good things to those who ask him?

¹²"**Always treat people** the way you want them to treat you. This sums up the Law and the Prophets.

¹³"**Try to get in** through the narrow gate. Wide and smooth is the road that leads to destruction. The majority are taking that route. ¹⁴Narrow and rough is the road that leads to life. Only a minority discover it.

¹⁵"**Be on the lookout** for phony prophets, who make their pitch disguised as sheep; inside they are really voracious wolves. ¹⁶You'll know who they are by what they produce. Since when do people pick grapes from thorns or figs from thistles? ¹⁷Every healthy tree produces choice fruit, but the rotten tree produces spoiled fruit. ¹⁸A healthy tree cannot produce spoiled fruit, any more than a rotten tree can produce choice fruit. ¹⁹Every tree that does not produce choice fruit gets cut down and tossed on the fire. ²⁰Remember, you'll know who they are by what they produce.

²¹"**Not everyone** who addresses me as 'Master, master,' will get into the empire of Heaven—only those who carry out the will of my Father in heaven. ²²On that day many will say to me, 'Master, master, didn't we use your name when we prophesied? Didn't we use your name when we exorcised demons? Didn't we use your name when we performed all those miracles?' ²³Then I will tell them honestly, 'I never knew you; get away from me, you subverters of the Law!'

²⁴"**Everyone who listens** to these words of mine and acts on them will be like a prudent man who built a house on bedrock. ²⁵Later the rain fell, and the torrents came, and the winds blew and pounded that house, yet it did not collapse, since its foundation rested on bedrock. ²⁶Everyone who listens to these words of mine and doesn't act on them will be like a stupid man, who built a house on sand. ²⁷When the rain fell, and the torrents came, and the winds blew and pounded that house, it collapsed—it totally collapsed."

7:15 *Phony prophets* is a reference to Christian prophets.

7:21 *Master* can also be translated "Lord." A double meaning is surely intended here.

²⁸And so it happened that, when Jesus had finished this discourse, the crowds were astonished at his teaching, ²⁹since he had been teaching them on his own authority, unlike their own scholars. (End of first discourse)

8 **When he came down** from the mountain, huge crowds followed him. ²Just then a leper appeared, bowed down to him, and said, "Master, if you want to, you can make me clean."

³And he stretched out his hand, touched him, and says, "Okay—you're clean!" And right away his leprosy was cleansed. ⁴Then Jesus warns him, "Don't tell anyone, but go, have a priest examine you. Then offer the gift that Moses commanded, as evidence ⟨of your cure⟩."

⁵**When he had entered** Capernaum, a Roman officer approached him and pleaded with him, ⁶"Sir, my servant boy was struck down with paralysis and is in terrible pain."

⁷And he said to him, "I'll come and cure him."

⁸And the officer replied, "Sir, I don't deserve to have you in my house, but only say the word and my boy will be cured. ⁹After all, I myself am under orders, and I have soldiers under me. I order one to go, and he goes; I order another to come, and he comes; and I order my slave to do something, and he does it."

¹⁰As Jesus listened he was amazed and said to those who followed, "Let me tell you, I have not found such trust in a single Israelite! ¹¹I predict that many will come from east and west and dine with Abraham and Isaac and Jacob in the empire of Heaven, ¹²but those who think the empire of Heaven belongs to them will be thrown out into the utter darkness. There'll be weeping and grinding of teeth out there."

¹³And Jesus said to the Roman officer, "Be on your way. Let it happen for you according to your trust." And the boy was cured at that precise moment.

¹⁴**And when Jesus came** to Peter's house, he noticed his mother-in-law lying sick with a fever. ¹⁵He touched her hand and the fever disappeared. Then she got up and started looking after him.

¹⁶**In the evening**, they brought him many who were demon possessed. He drove out the spirits with a command, and all those who were ill he cured, ¹⁷in order to fulfill the prediction spoken through Isaiah the prophet:

> He took away our illnesses
> and carried off our diseases.

8:13 Several mss add: "The officer returned to his house and found at that very moment that the boy was in good health."

7:28 *And so it happened that, when Jesus had finished . . .* This formulaic phrase occurs at the end of each of the five major speeches in Matthew (7:28, 11:1, 13:53, 19:1, 26:1).

Jesus cures a leper

Jesus cures an officer's servant

Jesus heals Peter's mother-in-law

At day's end

7:28
Ⓘ Mt 11:1 13:53, 19:1, 26:1

7:29
Ⓣ Mk 1:21–22, Mt 13:54, Lk 4:32

8:1–4
//Mk 1:40–45, Lk 5:12–16;
Ⓣ EgerG 2:1–4

8:4
◊ Lv 14:2–20

Q8:5–13
//Lk 7:1–10, Jn 4:45–54

Q8:11–12
//Lk 13:28–30

8:11
Ⓣ GSav 1:3

8:12
Cf. Mt 13:42, 50, 22:13, 24:51, 25:30; Lk 13:28

8:14–15
//Mk 1:29–31, Lk 4:38–39

8:16–17
//Mk 1:32–34, Lk 4:40–41

8:17
◊ Is 53:4

Foxes have dens

Rebuking wind & wave

Demons of Gadara

¹⁸**When Jesus saw** the crowds around him, he gave orders to cross over to the other side. ¹⁹And one scholar came forward and said to him, "Teacher, I'll follow you wherever you go."

²⁰And Jesus says to him, "Foxes have dens, and birds of the sky have nests, but the Human One has nowhere to rest his head."

²¹Another of his disciples said to him, "Master, first let me go and bury my father."

²²But Jesus says to him, "Follow me, and leave it to the dead to bury their own dead."

²³**When he got into a boat**, his disciples followed him. ²⁴And just then a powerful earthquake hit the sea, so that the boat was swamped by the waves; but he was asleep. ²⁵And they went and woke him up, and said to him, "Master, save us! We're sinking!"

²⁶He says to them, "Why are you such cowards, you with your meager trust?" Then he got up and rebuked the winds and the sea, and there was a great calm.

²⁷And everyone was astounded, saying, "What kind of person is this? Even the winds and the sea obey him."

²⁸**And when he came** to the other side, to the region of the Gadarenes, he was met by two people possessed by demons who came out from the tombs. They were so hard to deal with that no one could pass that way. ²⁹And just then they screamed, "What do you want with us, you son of God? Did you come here ahead of time to torment us?" ³⁰And a large herd of pigs was feeding off in the distance. ³¹And the demons kept bargaining with him: "If you drive us out, send us into the herd of pigs."

³²And he said to them, "Get out ⟨of him⟩!"

And they came out and went into the pigs, and suddenly the whole herd stampeded down the bluff into the sea and drowned in the water. ³³The herdsmen ran off and went into town and reported everything, especially about the possessed pair. ³⁴And what do you know, the whole town came out to meet Jesus. And when they saw him, they begged him to move on from their district.

Q8:18–22
//Lk 9:57–62

8:20
//Th 86

8:23–27
//Mk 4:35–41,
Lk 8:22–25

8:24
◊ Jon 1:4

8:26
Ⓣ Mt 6:30, 14:31,
16:8, 17:20

8:28–34
//Mk 5:1–20,
Lk 8:26–39

8:18 Most mss report that "huge" *crowds* surrounded Jesus. While only several very early mss have the simple crowds, it is most likely that the scribes elaborated the size.
8:28 Some mss spell the name of people in the region "Gerasenes," while other mss spell it "Gergesenes."

8:18 To *cross over to the other side* is a generic note indicating narrative motion, not a specific place.
8:20 This is the first occurrence of the title *Human One* in Matthew's gospel. It is only used in the speech of Jesus; never in reference to him (see the cameo essay on p. 208). Matthew uses the title in three ways: Jesus refers to (1) his present activity, as in this verse; (2) his passion and resurrection (17:22); (3) coming activity of the Human One as judge (16:27).

8:21 *To bury* the dead is one of the most important tasks of the living towards the dead. To bury one's parents is the highest duty of a son.
8:28 Gadara is the city of the *Gadarenes*. It is one of the Ten Cities and is situated southeast of the Sea of Galilee (see note at 4:25).
8:31 *Pigs* were unclean for Jews (Lev 11:7; Deut 14:8).

9 **After he got on board** the boat, he crossed over and came to his own town. [2]The next thing you know, some people were bringing him a paralytic lying on a bed. When Jesus noticed their trust, he said to the paralytic, "Be brave, child, your sins are forgiven."

[3]At that some of the scholars said to themselves, "This guy is blaspheming!"

[4]Because he understood the way they thought, Jesus said, "Why do you harbor evil thoughts? [5]Which is easier: to say, 'Your sins are forgiven,' or to say, 'Get up and walk'? [6]But just so that you realize that on earth the Human One has authority to forgive sins"—he then says to the paralytic—"Get up, pick up your bed and go home."

[7]And he got up and went home. [8]When the crowds saw this, they became fearful, and praised God for giving such authority to humans.

[9]**As Jesus was walking** along there, he caught sight of a man sitting at the toll booth, one named Matthew, and he says to him, "Follow me!" And he got up and followed him.

[10]**And it so happened**, while he was dining in his house, that many toll collectors and sinners showed up just then and dined with Jesus and his disciples.

[11]And whenever the Pharisees saw this, they would question his disciples, "Why does your teacher eat with toll collectors and sinners?"

[12]When Jesus overheard, he said, "Since when do the able-bodied need a doctor? It's the sick who do. [13]Go and learn what this means, 'It's mercy I desire instead of sacrifice.' After all, I did not come to enlist the upright but sinners!"

[14]**Then the disciples of John** come up to him, and ask, "Why do we fast, and the Pharisees fast, but not your disciples?"

[15]And Jesus said to them, "The groom's friends can't mourn as long as the groom is around, can they? But the days will come when the groom is taken away from them, and then they will fast. [16]Nobody patches an old garment with a piece of unshrunken cloth, since the patch pulls away from the garment and creates a worse tear. [17]Nor do they pour new wine into old wineskins, otherwise the wineskins burst, the wine gushes out, and the wineskins are destroyed. Instead, they put new wine in new wineskins and both are preserved."

[18]**Just as he was saying** these things to them, one of the officials came, kept bowing down to him, and said, "My daughter has just died. But come and put your hand on her and she will live." [19]And Jesus got up and followed him, along with his disciples.

[20]**And just then** a woman who had experienced a chronic flow of blood for twelve years came up from behind and touched the hem of his cloak. ([21]You see, she was saying to herself, "If I only touch his cloak, I'll be cured.") [22]When Jesus

---

Jesus cures a paralytic

Matthew becomes a follower

Jesus dines with sinners

Fasting & feating

Official's daughter

Jesus cures a woman

9:1–8
//Mk 2:1–12,
Lk 5:17–26

9:6
Ⓣ Jn 5:8

9:9–13
//Mk 2:14–17,
Lk 5:27–32,
GOxy 1224 5:1–2

9:9
Cf. GEbi 2:4

9:13
Ⓣ Mt 12:7;
cf. GEbi 6;
◊ Hos 6:6

9:14–17
//Mk 2:18–22,
Lk 5:33–39

9:14
Ⓣ Mt 11: 18–19

9:15
Cf. Th 27, 104

9:16–17
//Th 47:3–5

9:18–26
//Mk 5:21–43,
Lk 8:40–56

9:20
◊ Lv 15:25, Dt 22:29

9:1 *His own town* refers to Capernaum.

turned around and saw her, he said, "Be brave, daughter, your trust has cured you." And the woman was cured right then and there.

²³**And when Jesus came** into the home of the official and saw the mourners with their flutes, and the crowd making a disturbance, ²⁴he said, "Go away; the girl hasn't died; she's sleeping." And they started laughing at him. ²⁵When the crowd had been thrown out, he came in and took the little girl by the hand and raised her up. ²⁶And news of this spread all around that region.

²⁷**And when Jesus left** there, two blind men followed him, shouting, "Have mercy on us, son of David."

²⁸When Jesus arrived home, the blind men came to him. Jesus says to them, "Do you trust that I can do this?"

They reply to him, "Yes, master."

²⁹Then he touched their eyes, saying, "Let it happen to you according to your trust."³⁰And their eyes were opened. Then Jesus snapped at them, saying, "See that no one finds out about it."³¹But they went out and spread the news of him throughout that whole territory.

³²**Just as they were leaving**, they brought to him a mute who was demon-possessed. ³³And after the demon had been driven out, the mute started to speak. And the crowd was amazed and said, "Nothing like this has ever been seen in Israel."

³⁴But the Pharisees would say, "He drives out demons with the power of the head demon."

³⁵**And Jesus went** about all the towns and villages, teaching in their meeting places and proclaiming the gospel of the empire ⟨of Heaven⟩ and healing every disease and ailment. ³⁶When he saw the crowd, he was moved by them because they were beaten down and helpless, like sheep without a shepherd. ³⁷Then he said to his disciples, "The crop is good, but there are few to harvest it. ³⁸So beg the harvest boss to dispatch workers to the fields."

10 Second Discourse: Instructions for the Disciples' Mission
And summoning his twelve disciples he gave them authority to drive out unclean spirits and to heal every disease and every ailment. ²The names of the twelve apostles were these: first, Simon, also known as Rock ⟨(Peter)⟩, and Andrew his brother, and James the son of Zebedee and John his brother, ³Philip and Bartholomew, Thomas, and Matthew the toll collector, James the son of Alphaeus, and Thaddaeus, ⁴Simon the Zealot, and Judas of Iscariot, the one who, in the end, turned him in.

9:27–31
Ⓓ Mt 20:29–34;
//Mk 10:46–52,
Lk 18:35–43

Q9:32–34
Ⓓ Mt 12:22–24;
//Mk 3:22,
Lk 11:14–15

9:35
Cf. Mk 1:39, 6:6b;
Lk 8:1;
Ⓣ Mary 4:8;
Ⓘ Mt 4:23

9:36
Ⓣ Mk 6:34;
◊Nm 27:16–17,
1 Kgs 22:17,
Jdt 11:19

Q9:37–38
//Lk 10:2, Th 73

9:37
Ⓣ Jn 4:35

10:1–4
//Mk 3:13–19,
Lk 6:12–16;
cf. GEbi 2:3

10:1
//Mk 6:7, Lk 9:1

9:34 A few mss omit this verse.
10:3 A few mss have "Lebbaeus" instead of *Thaddaeus*. Many mss have "Lebbaeus who is called Thaddaeus."

9:23 *Flutes* were used by professional mourners.
10:2 *Rock* is a translation of Greek *Petros*, which was a nickname (4:18) but was taken as a proper name by later Christians.

⁵**Jesus sent out these twelve** after he had given them these instructions: "Don't travel foreign roads and don't enter a Samaritan town, ⁶but go instead to the lost sheep of the house of Israel.

⁷"Go and announce: 'The empire of Heaven has arrived.'

⁸"Heal the sick, raise the dead, cleanse the lepers, drive out demons. You have received freely, so freely give. ⁹Don't get gold or silver or copper coins for spending money, ¹⁰don't take a knapsack for the road, or two shirts, or sandals, or a staff; for 'the worker deserves to be fed.'

¹¹"Whichever town or village you enter, find out who is deserving; stay there until you leave. ¹²When you enter a house, greet it. ¹³And if the house is deserving, give it your peace blessing, but if it is unworthy, withdraw your peace blessing. ¹⁴And if anyone will not welcome you, or listen to your words, as you are going out of that house or town shake the dust off your feet. ¹⁵Let me tell you, the land of Sodom and Gomorrah will be better off on judgment day than that town. ⎯ *End*

¹⁶"**Look, I'm sending you** out like sheep to a pack of wolves. Therefore you must be as sly as snakes and as simple as pigeons. ¹⁷And beware of people, for they'll turn you over to Jewish councils and flog you in synagogues. ¹⁸And you'll be hauled up before governors and even kings on my account so you can make your case to them and to the gentiles. ¹⁹And when they lock you up, don't worry about how you should speak or what you should say. It will occur to you at that moment what to say. ²⁰For it's not you who are speaking but your Father's spirit speaking through you. ²¹One brother will turn in another to be put to death, and a father his child, and children will turn against their parents and kill them. ²²And you'll be universally hated because of me. But those who hold out to the end will be saved. ²³When they persecute you in this town, flee to another. Let me tell you, you certainly won't have gone through the towns of Israel before the Human One comes.

²⁴"**Students are not above** their teachers, nor slaves above their masters. ²⁵It's enough for students to become like their teachers and slaves to be like their masters. If they have dubbed the master of the house 'Beelzebul,' aren't they even more likely to malign the members of his household?

²⁶"**So don't be afraid** of them. After all, there is nothing covered up that won't be exposed, or hidden that won't be made known. ²⁷What I say to you in

Instructions for the Twelve

Fate of the disciples

Student & teacher

Have no fear

Q10:5–15
//Mk 6:6–13;
Lk 9:1–6, 10:1–15

10:6
//Mt 15:24

10:7
//Mt 3:2, 4:17

10:10
//1 Tm 5:18;
Ⓣ 1 Cor 9:14

10:15
◊Gn 19:24

10:16–23
//Mk 13:9–13,
Lk 21:12–19

10:16
//Lk 10:3, Th 39:3

10:17
Ⓓ Mt 24:9

Q10:19–20
//Lk 12:11–12;
cf. Jn 14:26

10:21
◊Mi 7:6

10:22
Ⓓ Mt 24:13;
cf. Jn 15:18

Q10:24
//Lk 6:40;
cf. Jn 13:16, 15:20

10:25
Cf. Mt 9:34, 12:24;
Lk 11:15

Q10:26–33
//Lk 12:1–12

10:26
//Mk 4:22; Th 5:2,
6:5–6; Lk 8:17

10:27
Cf. Th 33:1

10:23 In the middle of the verse, a few mss add: "And when they persecute you in another, flee to yet another one."

10:5 This is the beginning of the second of five major sermons in Matthew (see 7:28).
10:25 In 2 Kgs 1:2–16 *Beelzebul* is a god of the Philistines.

By the time of the New Testament the name was used as one of several names for the Devil.

Way of the cross

Welcoming Jesus'
followers

John queries Jesus

the dark, say in the light, and what you hear whispered in your ear, announce from the rooftops.

²⁸"Don't fear those who kill the body but cannot kill the soul; instead, you ought to fear the one who can destroy both the soul and the body in Gehenna. ²⁹What do two sparrows cost? A couple of bucks? Yet not one of them will fall to the ground without your Father's consent. ³⁰As for you, even the hairs on your head have all been counted. ³¹So, don't be so timid; you're worth more than a flock of sparrows. ³²Everyone who acknowledges me in public, I too will acknowledge before my Father in the heavens. ³³But the one who disowns me in public, I too will disown in front of my Father in the heavens.

³⁴"**Don't get the idea** that I came to bring peace on earth. I didn't come to bring peace, but a sword! ³⁵After all, I've come to pit a man against his father, a daughter against her mother, and a daughter-in-law against her mother-in-law. ³⁶Your enemies live under your own roof.

³⁷"If you love your father and mother more than me, you're not worthy of me, and if you love your son or daughter more than me, you're not worthy of me. ³⁸Unless you take your cross and come along with me, you're not worthy of me. ³⁹By finding your life, you'll lose it, but by losing your life for my sake, you'll find it.

⁴⁰"**The one who welcomes** you is welcoming me, and the one who welcomes me is welcoming the one who sent me. ⁴¹The one who welcomes a prophet as a prophet will be treated like a prophet; and the one who welcomes a just person as a just person will be treated like a just person. ⁴²And whoever gives so much as a cup of cool water to one of these little ones, because the little one is a follower of mine, let me tell you, such a person certainly won't go unrewarded."

11 And so it happened that, when Jesus had finished instructing his twelve disciples, he moved on from there to teach and proclaim in their towns.

²**While John was in prison** he heard about what the Anointed One had been doing and he sent his disciples ³to ask, "Are you the one who is to come or do we have to wait for another?"

⁴And so Jesus answered them, "Go report to John what you have heard and seen:

> ⁵The blind see again
>   and the lame walk;
> lepers are cleansed
>   and the deaf hear;
> the dead are raised,
>   and the poor have the good news preached to them.

⁶Congratulations to those who don't take offense at me."

10:30
//Lk 21:18;
◊1 Sm 14:45,
2 Sm 14:11

10:33
//Mk 8:38, Lk 9:26

Q10:34–36
//Lk 12:49–53,
Th 16;
cf. GNaz 11

10:35–36
◊Mi 7:5–6

Q10:37–39
//Lk 14:25–27

10:37–38
//Th 55;
cf. Th 101:1–2

10:38–39
//Mk 8:34–35,
Mt 16:24–25,
Lk 9:23–24;
cf. Jn 12:25

10:39
//Lk 17:33

Q10:40
//Lk 10:16

10:42
//Mk 9:41

Q11:1–6
//Lk 7:18–23

11:1
① Mt 7:28, 13:53,
19:1, 26:1

11:5
◊Is 35:6, 29:18

⁷**After ⟨John's disciples⟩** had departed, Jesus began to talk to the crowds about John. "What did you go out to the desert to gawk at? A reed shaking in the wind? ⁸What did you really go out to see? A man dressed in fancy clothes? But wait! Those who wear fancy clothes are found in royal houses. ⁹Come on, what did you go out to see? A prophet? Yes, that's what you went out to see, and even more than a prophet.

¹⁰"This is the one about whom it was written:

> Here is my messenger,
> whom I send on ahead of you
> to prepare your way before you.

¹¹"Let me tell you, among those born of women no one has arisen who is greater than John the Baptizer; yet the least ⟨important⟩ in the empire of Heaven is greater than he is.

¹²"From the time of John the Baptizer until now the empire of Heaven has been breaking in violently, and violent men are trying to seize it. ¹³You see, the Prophets and the Law predicted everything up to John's time. ¹⁴And if you are willing to admit it, John is the Elijah who was to come. ¹⁵Anyone here with ears, use 'em!

¹⁶"**What does this generation** remind me of? It is like children sitting in marketplaces who call out to others,

> ¹⁷We played the flute for you,
> but you wouldn't dance;
> we sang a dirge
> but you wouldn't mourn.

¹⁸Just remember, John appeared on the scene neither eating nor drinking, and they say, 'He's possessed.' ¹⁹The Human One appeared on the scene both eating and drinking, and they say, 'There's a glutton and a drunk, a crony of toll collectors and sinners!' Indeed, Wisdom is vindicated by her deeds."

²⁰**Then he began to insult** the towns where he had performed most of his miracles, because they had not changed their ways. ²¹"Damn you, Chorazin! Damn you, Bethsaida! If the miracles done in you had been done in Tyre and

Jesus praises John

Children in marketplaces

Damn you Chorazin

Q11:7–15
//Lk 7:24–30

11:7–8
//Th 78

11:10
Cf. Mk 1:2;
◊Mal 3:1

11:11
//Th 46

Q11:12–13
//Lk 16:16

11:14
Cf. Mk 9:13,
Jn 1:21;
◊Mal 4:5

Q11:16–19
//Lk 7:31–35

11:18
Ⓣ Mt 9:14

Q11:20–24
//Lk 10:12–15

11:9 Ancient manuscripts have no punctuation, so Jesus' question could also be translated, "Why did you go out? To see a prophet?" (see Thom 78).

11:12 The Greek grammar here is very difficult. In more traditional translations the empire of Heaven "is suffering violence." Such a translation has been justified by the notion that Heaven's empire must be peaceful. However, the normal use of the verb in Greek is not passive but active:

Heaven's empire *has been breaking in violently.*

11:16 The *marketplace* was the normal place where children recited their lessons for their tutors.

11:21 *Chorazin* was a Jewish town just north of Capernaum. *Bethsaida* was most probably situated at the mouth of the Jordan river as it entered the north end of the Sea of Galilee. *Tyre* and *Sidon* were the two leading cities of ancient Phoenicia.

Father & son

*The Human One
over the Sabbath*

*Jesus heals a man
with a crippled
hand*

Sidon, they would have ⟨sat⟩ in sackcloth and ashes and changed their ways long ago. ²²So I'm telling you, Tyre and Sidon will be better off on judgment day than you. ²³And you, Capernaum, you don't think you'll be exalted to heaven, do you? No, you'll go to hell. Because if the miracles done within your boundaries had been done in Sodom, Sodom would still be around. ²⁴So I'm telling you, the land of Sodom will be better off on judgment day than you."

²⁵**At that point**, Jesus responded, "I praise you, Father, master of earth and sky, because you have hidden these things from the wise and the learned but revealed them to the unsophisticated; ²⁶yes indeed, Father, because that is the way you want it.

²⁷"My Father has turned everything over to me. No one knows the son except the Father, nor does anyone know the Father except the son—and anyone to whom the son wishes to reveal him. ²⁸All you who toil and are overloaded come to me, and I will refresh you. ²⁹Take my yoke upon you and learn from me, because I am gentle and modest and your lives will find rest. ³⁰For my yoke is comfortable and my load is light."

12 **On that occasion** Jesus walked through the grainfields on the Sabbath. His disciples were hungry and began to strip heads of grain and chew them. ²When the Pharisees saw this, they argued with him, "See here, your disciples are doing what's not permitted on the Sabbath."

³He said to them, "I guess you don't recall what David did when he and his companions were hungry. ⁴He went into the house of God, and ate the consecrated bread, which no one is permitted to eat—not even David or his companions—except the priests alone! ⁵Or haven't you read in the Law that during the Sabbath the priests violate the Sabbath in the temple and are held blameless? ⁶Yet I say to you, someone greater than the temple is here. ⁷And if you had known what this means, 'It's mercy I desire instead of sacrifice,' you would not have condemned those who are blameless. ⁸Remember, the Human One is master of the Sabbath."

⁹**And when he had moved on**, he went into their meeting place. ¹⁰Just then a man with a crippled hand appeared, and they asked him, "Is it permitted to heal on the Sabbath?" so they could discredit him.

¹¹He asked them, "If you had only a single sheep, and it fell into a ditch on the Sabbath, wouldn't you grab it and pull it out? ¹²A person is worth way more than a sheep. So, it is permitted to do good on the Sabbath!"

¹³Then he says to the man, "Hold out your hand!"

He held it out and it was restored to health like the other. ¹⁴The Pharisees went out and hatched a plot against him to destroy him.

11:23
◊ Is 14:13–15

11:24
Ⓓ Mt 10:15

Q11:25–30
//Lk 10:21–22

11:27
Cf. Jn 3:35, 7:29

11:28–29
◊ Sir 51:23–27

11:28–30
//Th 90

11:29
◊ Jer 6:16

12:1–8
//Mk 2:23–28,
Lk 6:1–5

12:1
◊ Dt 23:25

12:3–4
◊ 1 Sm 21:1–6

12:4
◊ Lv 24:5–9

12:7
Ⓘ Mt 9:13;
cf. GEbi 6;
◊ Hos 6:6

12:9–14
//Mk 3:1–6,
Lk 6:6–11;
cf. GNaz 4

12:11–12
//Lk 14:5;
cf. Lk 13:15

11:29 The symbolism of a *yoke* was not viewed negatively in the ancient world, but is a beneficent symbol of the disci- pline and resulting good life produced by following the Law or the teaching of Jesus.

¹⁵**Aware of this**, Jesus withdrew from there, and huge crowds followed him, and he healed all of them. ¹⁶And he warned them not to disclose his identity, ¹⁷in order to fulfill the prediction spoken through Isaiah the prophet:

> ¹⁸Here is my servant whom I have selected,
> > the one I love, of whom I fully approve.
> I will put my spirit upon him,
> > and he will announce judgment for gentiles.
> ¹⁹He will not be contentious,
> > nor loud-mouthed,
> > nor will anyone hear his voice on the streets.
> ²⁰He is not about to break a crushed reed,
> > and he's not one to snuff out a smoldering wick,
> until he brings forth a decisive victory,
> > ²¹and gentiles put their hope in his name.

²²**Then they brought** to him a blind and mute person who was demon possessed, and he cured him so the mute could both speak and to see. ²³And the entire crowd was beside itself and was saying, "This man can't be the son of David, can he?"

²⁴But when the Pharisees heard of it, they said, "This guy drives out demons only with the power of Beelzebul, the head demon."

²⁵But he knew how they thought, and said to them, "Every empire divided against itself is devastated, and no town or household divided against itself can survive. ²⁶So if Satan drives out Satan, he is divided against himself. In that case, how can his empire survive?

²⁷"Suppose I do drive out demons with the power of Beelzebul, then with whose power do your own people drive ⟨them⟩ out? That's why they will be your judges. ²⁸But if I drive out demons with the spirit of God, then God's empire has come for you.

²⁹"Or how can anyone enter a strong man's house and plunder his belongings, unless he first ties him up? Only then does he plunder his house.

³⁰"Those who aren't with me are against me, and those one who don't gather with me scatter. ³¹That's why I tell you: every offense and blasphemy will be forgiven humankind, but the blasphemy of the spirit won't be forgiven. ³²And the one who speaks a word against the Human One will be forgiven; but the one who speaks a word against the holy spirit won't be forgiven, neither in this age nor in the age to come.

³³"If you make the tree choice, its fruit will be choice; if you make the tree rotten, its fruit will be rotten. After all, the tree is known by its fruit. ³⁴You spawn of Satan, how can your speech be good when you are evil? As you know, the mouth gives voice to what the heart is full of. ³⁵The good person produces good things out of a fund of good; and the evil person produces evil things out

Jesus withdraws

Beelzebul controversy

12:15–21
//Mk 3:7–12,
Lk 6:17–19

12:18–21
◊ Is 42:1–4

Q12:22–37
//Mk 3:20–30,
Lk 11:14–23

12:22–24
Ⓓ Mt 9:32–34

12:29
//Th 35

12:30
Cf. Mk 9:40,
Lk 9:50

12:31–32
//Th 44

Q12:32
//Lk 12:10

12:33–35
//Th 45

Q12:33
//Lk 6:43–44;
cf. Mt 7:20

Q12:34–35
//Lk 6:45

12:34
Cf. Mt 15:18;
Ⓘ Mt 3:7, 23:33

of a fund of evil. [36]Let me tell you, on judgment day people will have to account for every thoughtless word they utter. [37]Your own words will vindicate you, and your own words will condemn you."

[38]**Then some of the scholars** and Pharisees responded to him, "Teacher, we would like to see a sign from you."

[39]In response he said to them, "An evil and adulterous generation demands a sign, and no sign will be given it—except the sign of Jonah the prophet! [40]You see, just as 'Jonah was in the belly of a sea monster for three days and three nights,' so the Human One will be in the heart of the earth for three days and three nights.

[41]"On judgment day, the citizens of Nineveh will come back to life along with this generation and condemn it, because they had a change of heart in response to Jonah's message. Yet take note: what is right here is greater than Jonah.

[42]"On judgment day, the queen of the south will be brought back to life along with this generation, and she will condemn it, because she came from the ends of the earth to listen to Solomon's wisdom. Yet take note: what is right here is greater than Solomon.

[43]"**When an unclean spirit** leaves a person, it wanders through waterless places in search of a place to rest. When it doesn't find one, [44]it then says, 'I will return to the home I left.' It then returns and finds the place empty, swept, and put in order. [45]Next, it goes out and brings back with it seven other spirits more vile than itself, who enter and settle in there. So that person ends up worse off than when he or she started. That's how it will be for this evil generation."

[46]**While he was still speaking** to the crowds, his mother and brothers showed up outside; they had come to speak to him. [47]Someone said to him, "Look, your mother and your brothers are outside and they want to speak to you."

[48]In response he said to the one speaking to him, "Who is my mother and who are my brothers?" [49]And he pointed to his disciples and said, "Here are my mother and my brothers. [50]For whoever does the will of my Father in heaven, that's my brother and sister and mother."

13 Third Discourse: Most of the Parables
[1]**That same day**, Jesus left the house and sat beside the sea. [2]Huge crowds gathered around him, so he climbed into a boat and sat down, while the entire crowd stood on the sea shore. [3]He told them many things in parables:

> This sower went out to sow. [4]While he was sowing, some seed fell along the path, and the birds came and devoured it. [5]Other seed fell on rocky ground where

---

12:47 In Greek both vv. 46 and 47 end with the same word. This led many mss to skip over and omit v. 47.

13:3 This marks the beginning of the third sermon (see 7:28).

there wasn't much soil, and it came up right away because the soil had no depth. ⁶When the sun came up it was scorched, and because it had no roots it withered. ⁷Still other seed fell among thorns, and the thorns came up and choked them. ⁸Other seed fell on good soil and started producing fruit: one part had a yield of one hundred, another a yield of sixty, and a third a yield of thirty.

⌐⁹"Anyone here with ears, use 'em!"⌐

¹⁰**And his disciples came** up and said to him, "Why do you instruct them only in parables?"

¹¹In response he said to them, "You've been given the privilege of knowing the secrets of the empire of Heaven, but that privilege has not been granted to anyone else. ¹²In fact, to those who have, more will be given, and then some; and from those who don't have, even what they do have will be taken away. ¹³That is why I tell them parables, because

When they look they don't really see
and when they listen they don't really hear
    or understand.

¹⁴Moreover, in them the prophecy of Isaiah is fulfilled, the one which says,

You listen closely, yet you won't ever understand,
    and you look intently but won't ever see.
¹⁵For the mind of this people has grown dull,
    and their ears are hard of hearing,
    and they have shut their eyes,
otherwise they might actually see with their eyes,
    and hear with their ears,
    and understand with their minds,
and turn around
    and I would heal them.

¹⁶How privileged are your eyes because they see, and your ears because they hear. ¹⁷Let me tell you, many prophets and just persons have longed to see what you see and never saw it, and to hear what you hear and never heard it.

¹⁸"**You there**, pay attention to the interpretation of the sower. ¹⁹When anyone listens to the message of the empire of ⟨Heaven⟩ and does not understand it, the evil one comes and steals away what was sown in the heart: this is the one who is sown 'along the path.' ²⁰The one who is sown 'on rocky ground' is the one who listens to the message and right away receives it happily. ²¹However, this one lacks its own 'root' and so is short-lived. When tribulation or persecution comes because of the message, right away that person is brought down. ²²And the one sown 'into the thorns' is the one who listens to the message, but the worries of the age and the seductiveness of wealth 'choke' the message and it becomes 'fruitless.' ²³The one who is sown 'on the good soil' is the one who

In parables

Understanding the sower

13:10–17
//Mk 4:10–12,
Lk 9:9–10

13:12
Ⓓ Mt 25:29;
//Mk 4:25; Lk 8:18,
19:26; Th 41

13:13–15
◊Is 6:9–10

Q13:16–17
//Lk 10:23–24

13:18–23
//Mk 4:13–20,
Lk 8:11–15

Weeds in the field

*Mustard seed
& leaven*

Only in parables

*Understanding the
weeds in the field*

listens to the message and understands, who really 'bears fruit and yields here a hundred, there sixty, and there thirty.'"

[24]**He spun out another parable** for them:

> The empire of Heaven is like someone who sowed good seed in his field. [25]And while everyone was asleep, his enemy came and scattered weed seed around in his wheat and stole away. [26]And when the crop sprouted and produced grain, then the weeds also appeared. [27]The owner's slaves came and asked him, "Master, didn't you sow good seed in your field? Then why are there weeds everywhere?" [28]He replied to them, "Some enemy has done this." The slaves said to him, "So do you want us to go and pull the weeds?" [29]He replied, "No, otherwise you'll uproot the wheat at the same time as you pull the weeds. [30]Let them grow up together until the harvest, and at harvest time I'll say to the harvesters, 'Gather the weeds first and bind them in bundles for burning, but gather the wheat into my granary.'"

[31]**He put another parable** before them with these words:

> The empire of Heaven is like a mustard seed that a man took and sowed in his field. [32]Though it is the smallest of all seeds, when it grows up, it is the largest of garden plants, and becomes a tree, so that the birds of the sky come and roost in its branches.

[33]He told them another parable:

> The empire of Heaven is like leaven that a woman took and concealed in fifty pounds of flour until it was all leavened.

[34]**Jesus spoke all these things** to the crowds in parables. And he would not say anything to them except by way of parable, [35]in order to fulfill the prediction spoken through the prophet:

> I will open my mouth in parables,
> I will utter secrets kept since the foundation of the world.

[36]**Then he left** the crowds and went into the house. His disciples came to him with this request: "Explain the parable about the weeds in the field to us." [37]This was his response: "The one who 'sows the good seed' is the Human One. [38]'The field' is the world and 'the good seed' are children of the empire ⟨of Heaven⟩, but 'the weeds' represent children of the evil one. [39]'The enemy' who

13:24–30
//Th 57

Q13:31–32
//Mk 4:30–32,
Lk 13:18–19, Th 20

13:32
◊Ez 17:23, 31:69;
Dn 4:20–22

Q13:33
//Lk 13:20, Th 96;
◊Ex 12:15;
Ⓣ Mt 16:6,
1 Cor 5:6, Gal 5:9

13:34
//Mk 4:33–34

13:35
◊Ps 78:2–3;
cf. SJas 6:15

13:35 A few mss have supplied the prophet Isaiah's name. Some mss do not have *of the world.* Scribes may have copied it here from the parallel in 25:34. *Foundation* then means "beginning."

13:31 *The mustard seed's* smallness was proverbial, but it is botanically impossible for it to become a *tree.*
13:33 The ancients viewed the process of leaven as corrupting the loaf, like a corpse, causing it to swell up. Therefore leaven is unclean, something to be avoided (16:11). Leaven is the symbol of the unholy (Exod 12:15).

sows ⟨the weeds⟩ is the devil, and 'the harvest' is the end of the present age; 'the harvesters' are the heavenly messengers. ⁴⁰Just as the weeds are gathered and destroyed by fire—that's how it will be at the end of the age. ⁴¹The Human One will send his messengers and they will gather all the traps and the subverters of the Law out of his empire ⁴²and throw them into the fiery furnace. People in that place will weep and grind their teeth. ⁴³Then the virtuous will shine like the sun in my Father's empire. Anyone here with ears, use 'em!

⁴⁴**The empire of Heaven** is like treasure hidden in a field. When someone finds it, that person covers it up again, and out of sheer joy goes and sells every last possession and buys that field.

⁴⁵Again, the empire of Heaven is like some merchant looking for beautiful pearls. ⁴⁶When he finds one priceless pearl, he sells everything he owns and buys it.

⁴⁷Once more: the empire of Heaven is like a net that is cast into the sea and catches all kinds of fish. ⁴⁸When the net is full, they haul it ashore. Then they sit down and collect the good fish into baskets, but the worthless fish they throw away. ⁴⁹This is how the present age will end. God's messengers will go out and separate the evil from the just ⁵⁰and throw the evil into the fiery furnace. People in that place will weep and grind their teeth.

⁵¹"Do you understand all these things?"

"Of course," they replied.

⁵²He said to them, "That's why every scholar who is schooled in the empire of Heaven is like some proprietor who produces from his storeroom treasures old and new."

⁵³And so it happened that, when Jesus had finished these parables, he moved on from there.

⁵⁴**And he came to his hometown** and resumed teaching them in their meeting place, so they were astounded and said so: "Where did this wisdom and these miracles come from? ⁵⁵This is the carpenter's son, isn't it? Isn't his mother called Mary? And aren't his brothers James and Joseph and Simon and Judas? ⁵⁶And aren't all his sisters neighbors of ours? So where did he get all this?" ⁵⁷And they took offense at him.

Jesus said to them, "No prophet is disrespected, except on his home turf and at home!" ⁵⁸And he did not perform many miracles there because of their lack of trust.

14 **On that occasion** Herod the tetrarch heard the rumor about Jesus ²and said to his servants, "This is John the Baptizer. He's been raised from the dead; that's why miraculous powers are at work in him."

13:41
Cf. Mt 24:31

13:42
Cf. Mt 8:12, 13:50, 22:13, 24:51, 25:30; ◊Dn 3:6

13:44
//Th 109

13:45–46
//Th 76

13:47–50
//Th 8

13:50
◊Dn 3:6

13:53–58
//Mk 6:1–6, Lk 4:16–30

13:53
① Mt 7:28, 11:1, 19:1, 26:1

13:57
//Jn 4:44, Th 31

14:1–12
//Mk 6:14–29, Lk 9:7–9

14:1 *Herod the Tetrach* is Herod Antipas, a son of Herod of the Great, the monster in Matthew 2. Antipas ruled Galilee and Perea from 4 BCE to 39 CE.

*Loaves & fish
for 5,000*

Jesus departs

*Jesus walks on
the sea*

³Herod, remember, had arrested John, put him in chains, and thrown him in prison on account of Herodias, his brother Philip's wife. ⁴John, for his part, had said to him, "It is not right for you to have her."

⁵And while Herod wanted to kill him, he was afraid of the crowd because they regarded John as a prophet. ⁶On Herod's birthday, the daughter of Herodias danced for them and captivated Herod, ⁷so he swore an oath and promised to give her whatever she asked.

⁸Prompted by her mother, she said, "Give me the head of John the Baptizer right here on a platter."

⁹The king was sad, but because of his oath and his dinner guests, he ordered that it be done. ¹⁰And he sent and had John beheaded in prison. ¹¹⟨John's⟩ head was brought on a platter and presented to the girl, and she gave it to her mother. ¹²Then his disciples came and got his body and buried him. Then they went and told Jesus.

¹³**When Jesus got word** of ⟨John's death⟩, he sailed away quietly to an isolated place. The crowds got wind of ⟨his departure⟩ and followed him on foot from the towns. ¹⁴As he stepped ashore and saw this huge crowd, he was moved by them, and healed their sick.

¹⁵When it was evening the disciples approached him and said, "This is a desert place and it's already late. Send the crowd away so that they can go to the villages and buy food for themselves."

¹⁶Jesus said to them, "They don't need to leave; give them something to eat yourselves!"

¹⁷But they say to him, "We have nothing here except five loaves and two fish."

¹⁸He said, "Bring them here to me." ¹⁹And he told the crowd to recline on the grass, and he took the five loaves and two fish, and looking up to the sky he gave a blessing, and breaking it apart he gave the bread to the disciples, and the disciples gave it to the crowd.

²⁰And everybody had more than enough to eat. Then they picked up twelve baskets full of leftovers. ²¹The number of people who had eaten came to about five thousand, not counting women and children.

²²**And right away** he made the disciples get in a boat and go ahead of him to the other side, while he dispersed the crowds. ²³After he had dispersed the crowds, he went up to the mountain privately to pray. He remained there alone well into the evening.

²⁴**By this time** the boat was already some distance from land and was being pounded by waves because the wind was against them. ²⁵About three o'clock in the morning he came toward them walking on the sea. ²⁶But when the disciples

14:3
Cf. Lk 3:19–20

14:4
◊Lv 18:16, 20:21

14:13–14
//Mk 6:30–34,
Lk 9:10–11

14:15–21
//Mk 6:35–44,
Lk 9:12–17,
Jn 6:1–15;
Ⓓ Mt 15:32–39,
Mk 8:1–10;
◊1 Kgs 4:42–44

14:19
Cf. Mt 26:26

14:22–23
//Mk 6:45–46,
Jn 6:15

14:24–33
//Mk 6:47–52,
Jn 6:16–21

14:26
Ⓣ 24:37

14:3 *Herodias* was the niece of Herod Antipas and was married to Herod *Philip,* Antipas's half brother. In order to marry Herodias Antipas had to divorce the daughter of Aretas, the powerful king of the Nabateans.

saw him walking on the sea, they were terrified. "It's a ghost," they said, and cried out in fear.

²⁷Right away Jesus spoke to them, saying, "Be brave; it's me! Don't be afraid."

²⁸In response Peter said, "Master, if it's really you, order me to come across the water to you."

²⁹He said, "Come on."

And Peter got out of the boat and walked on the water and came toward Jesus. ³⁰But with the strong wind in his face, he started to panic. And when he began to sink, he cried out, "Master, save me."

³¹Jesus immediately held out his hand and took hold of him and says to him, "You with your meager trust! Why did you hesitate?"³²And by the time they had climbed into the boat, the wind had died down.

³³Then those in the boat paid homage to him, saying, "You really are God's son."

³⁴**Once they had crossed** over they landed at Gennesaret. ³⁵And the local people recognized him and sent word into the whole surrounding area and brought him all who were ill. ³⁶And they begged him just to let them touch the fringe of his cloak. And all those who managed to touch it were cured.

15 Then the Pharisees and scholars from Jerusalem come to Jesus, and say,
²"Why do your disciples deviate from the traditions of the elders? For instance, they don't wash their hands before they eat bread."

³In response he asked them, "Why do you also break God's commandment because of your tradition? ⁴For example, God said, 'Honor your father and mother' and 'Those who curse their father or mother absolutely must die.' ⁵But you say, 'If people say to their father or mother, "Whatever I might have spent to support you has been consecrated to God," ⁶they need not honor their father.' So you end up invalidating God's word because of your tradition. ⁷How accurately Isaiah prophesied about you phonies when he said,

> ⁸This people honors me with their lips,
>   but their heart stays far away from me.
> ⁹Their worship of me is empty,
>   because they insist on teachings that are human regulations."

¹⁰**And he summoned** the crowd and said to them, "Listen and try to understand. ¹¹What goes into your mouth doesn't defile you; what comes out of your mouth does."

¹²The disciples came and said to him, "Don't you realize that the Pharisees who heard this remark were offended by it?"

A cloak that cures

Rules for handwashing

What comes out defiles

14:31
Ⓣ Mt 6:30, 8:26, 16:8, 17:20

14:34–36
//Mk 6:53–56; Ⓣ Mt 4:23, 8:16–17

15:1–9
//Mk 7:1–13

15:4
◊Ex 20:12, 21:17; Lv 20:9, Dt 5:16

15:7–9
Ⓣ EgerG 3:6

15:8–9
◊Is 29:13

15:10–20
//Mk 7:14–23

15:11
//Th 14:5

14:30 There is perhaps a double meaning in Peter's reply. It could be translated "Master, rescue me," or, in a religious sense, "Lord, save me."

15:5 *If people say* . . . is an example of case law reasoning.

¹³He responded, "Every plant which my heavenly Father does not plant will be rooted out. ¹⁴Never mind them. They are blind guides of blind people! If one blind person guides another, both will end up in some ditch."

¹⁵Then Peter replied, "Explain the riddle to us."

¹⁶He said, "Are you still as dim-witted as the rest? ¹⁷Don't you realize that everything that goes into the mouth passes into the stomach and comes out in the outhouse? ¹⁸But the things that come out of the mouth come from the heart, and those things defile a person. ¹⁹For out of the heart emerge evil intentions: murders, adulteries, sexual immorality, thefts, false testimonies, blasphemies. ²⁰These are what defile you. Eating with unwashed hands doesn't defile anybody."

²¹**So Jesus left there**, and withdrew to the district of Tyre and Sidon.

²²Just then this Canaanite woman from those parts showed up and started shouting, "Have mercy on me, sir, you son of David. My daughter is severely possessed."

²³But he did not respond at all. And his disciples came and began to complain, "Get rid of her; she's badgering us."

²⁴But in response he said, "I was sent only to the lost sheep of the house of Israel."

²⁵She came and bowed down to him, saying, "Sir, please help me."

²⁶In response he said, "It's not right to take bread out of children's mouths and throw it to the dogs."

²⁷But she said, "Of course, sir, but even the dogs eat the scraps that fall from their master's table."

²⁸Then in response Jesus said to her, "My good woman, your trust is enormous! Your wish is as good as fulfilled." And her daughter was cured at that moment.

²⁹**Then Jesus left there** and went to the sea of Galilee. And he climbed up the mountain and sat there. ³⁰And huge crowds came to him and brought with them the lame, the blind, the maimed, the mute, and many others, and they crowded around his feet and he healed them. ³¹As a result, the crowd was astonished when they saw the mute now speaking, the maimed made whole, the lame walking, and the blind seeing. And they gave all the credit to the God of Israel.

³²Then Jesus called his disciples aside and said, "I feel sorry for the crowd because they have already spent three days with me and now they've run out of food. And I don't want to send these people away hungry, for fear they'll collapse on the way."

15:13
//Th 40

Q15:14
//Lk 6:39, Th 34

15:21–28
//Mk 7:24–30

15:24
//Mt 10:6

15:29–31
//Mk 7:31–37

15:32–39
//Mk 8:1–10,
Lk 9:12–27,
Jn 6:1–15;
Ⓣ Mt 14:15–21,
Mk 6:35–44;
◊2 Kgs 4:42–44

15:14 Some mss omit *of blind people.*

15:21 For *Tyre* and *Sidon* see the note to 11:21.
15:22 A *Canaanite* is a gentile, and the Canaanites were ancient enemies of Israel.

15:25 *Sir, please help me* can also be understood as "Lord, help me."

³³And the disciples say to him, "How can we get enough bread here in this desert place to feed so many people?"

³⁴Jesus says to them, "How many loaves do you have?"

They replied, "Seven, plus a few fish."

³⁵And he ordered the crowd to sit down on the ground. ³⁶And he took the seven loaves and the fish and gave thanks and broke them into pieces, and started giving them to the disciples, and the disciples ⟨started giving them⟩ to the crowds. ³⁷And everyone had more than enough to eat. Then they picked up seven baskets full of leftovers. ³⁸Those who had eaten numbered four thousand, not counting women and children. ³⁹And after he sent the crowds away, he got into the boat and went to the Magadan region.

16 **And the Pharisees** and Sadducees came, and they put him to the test by asking him to show them a sign from heaven.

²In response he said to them, "When it's evening, you say, 'It'll be fair weather because the sky looks red.' ³Early in the morning you say, 'The day will bring winter weather because the sky looks red and dark.' You know how to read the face of the sky, but you can't discern the signs of the times. ⁴An evil and adulterous generation demands a sign, yet no sign will be given it except the sign of Jonah." And he turned his back on them and walked away.

⁵**And the disciples came** to the opposite shore, but they forgot to bring any bread. ⁶Jesus said to them, "Look, be careful: guard against the leaven of the Pharisees and Sadducees."

⁷Now they began arguing among themselves, saying, "We didn't bring any bread."

⁸Because Jesus was aware of this, he said, "Why are you puzzled that you don't have any bread, you with your meager trust? ⁹You still don't get it, do you? You don't remember the five loaves for the five thousand and how many baskets you carried away, do you? ¹⁰Nor the seven loaves for four thousand and how many big baskets you filled? ¹¹How can you possibly think I was talking to you about bread? Just be on guard against the leaven of the Pharisees and Sadducees."

¹²Then they understood that he was not talking about guarding against the leaven in bread but against the teaching of the Pharisees and Sadducees.

¹³**When Jesus came** to the region of Caesarea Philippi, he started questioning his disciples, asking, "What are people saying about the Human One?"

Request for a sign

Bread & leaven

What are people saying?

15:36
Cf. Mt 26:26

Q16:1–4
//Mk 8:11–13,
Lk 11:29–32;
Ⓓ Mt 12:38–39

16:1
Cf. Jn 6:30

16:1–2
Cf. Th 91

Q16:2–3
//Lk 12:54–56

16:5–12
//Mk 8:14–21

16:6
//Lk 12:1;
Ⓣ 1 Cor 5:6,
Gal 5:9

16:8
Ⓣ Mt 6:30, 8:26,
14:31, 17:20

16:9
Ⓓ Mt 14:15–21

16:10
Ⓓ Mt 15:32–39

16:13–20
//Mk 8:27–30,
Lk 9:18–22;
Ⓣ Th 13

16:2b–3 Some mss do not have these verses. They could have been based on Luke 12:54–56, or omitted, first in Egypt, where the description does not fit.

15:39 *Magadan* or Magdala, a small town on the western shore of the Sea of Galilee between Capernaum and Tiberias.

16:4 *The sign of Jonah* is not specified. It could be his call to

repentance or his days in the belly of the fish.

16:13 *Caesarea Philippi* was a gentile city in upper Galilee that was rebuilt by Philip (see above 14:3), who named it for Caesar and himself.

Jesus destined
to suffer

Saving & losing life

Jesus transformed

¹⁴They said, "Some ⟨say, 'He is⟩ John the Baptizer,' but others, 'Elijah,' and others, 'Jeremiah or one of the prophets.'"

¹⁵He says to them, "What about you, who do you say I am?"

¹⁶And Simon Peter responded, "You are the Anointed One, the son of the living God!"

¹⁷And in response Jesus said to him, "You are to be congratulated, Simon bar Jonah, because flesh and blood did not reveal this to you but my Father who is in heaven. ¹⁸Let me tell you, you are Peter, ⟨'the Rock,'⟩ and on this very rock I will build my congregation, and the gates of Hades will not be able to overpower it. ¹⁹I will give you the keys of the empire of Heaven, and whatever you uphold on earth will be upheld in heaven, and whatever you dismiss on earth will be dismissed in heaven."

²⁰Then he ordered the disciples to tell no one that he was the Anointed One.

²¹**From that time on** Jesus started to make it clear to his disciples that he was destined to go to Jerusalem, and endure much at the hands of the elders and chief priests and scholars, and be killed and, on the third day, be raised.

²²And Peter took him aside and began to lecture him, saying, "God forbid, master; there's no way that can happen to you."

²³But he turned and said to Peter, "Get out of my sight, you Satan, you. You're getting in my way because you're not thinking in God's terms, but in human terms."

²⁴**Then Jesus said** to his disciples, "If any of you wants to come after me you should deny yourself, pick up your cross, and follow me!

²⁵"Remember, if you try to save your life you'll lose it, but if you lose your life for my sake, you'll find it. ²⁶After all, what good will it do if you acquire the whole world but forfeit your life? Or what will you give in exchange for your life?

²⁷"Remember, the Human One is going to come in the glory of his Father with his messengers, and then he will reward everyone according to their deeds. ²⁸Let me tell you, some of those standing here won't ever taste death before they see the Human One arriving with full imperial power."

17 **Six days later,** Jesus takes Peter and James and his brother John along and he leads them off by themselves to a lofty mountain. ²He was transformed

16:16
Ⓣ Jn 6:68–69

16:19
Ⓓ Mt 18:18;
Ⓣ Jn 20:22–23

16:21–23
//Mk 8:31–33,
Lk 9:18–22

16:21
Ⓘ Mt 4:17, 26:16;
Ⓣ Mt 17:22–23,
20:17–19

16:24–28
//Mk 8:34–9:1,
Lk 9:23–27

16:24–25
Ⓓ Mt 10:38–39

16:24
//Th 55

16:25
//Jn 12:25

16:31
Ⓣ Mt 24:30, 25:31

17:1–13
//Mk 9:2–13,
Lk 9:28–36

16:21 A few mss have *Jesus* "the Anointed."

16:17 *Bar Jonah* is Aramaic for "son of Jonah." John 1:42 calls Simon the son of John.

16:18 *Peter* is an Aramaic nickname meaning "Rock," thus producing the word play.

Here and Matt 18:17 are the only two verses in which the word *congregation* (frequently translated "church") appear in the gospels. It is a term of Greek-speaking Chris-

tianity. In secular Greek it refers to a popular assembly. Early Greek-speaking Christians borrowed the term from their Bible, the Septuagint, where it frequently is used to translate the Hebrew term for the community of God (e.g., Deut 23:2).

16:19 To *uphold* and to *dismiss* refers to the power to announce a command as binding at present or not binding.

in front of them and his face shone like the sun, and his clothes turned as white as light. [3]The next thing you know, Moses and Elijah appeared to them and were conversing with Jesus.

[4]Peter said to Jesus, "Master, it's a good thing we're here. If you want, I'll set up three tents here, one for you, one for Moses, and one for Elijah."

[5]While he was still speaking, there was a bright cloud that cast a shadow over them. And just then a voice spoke from the cloud: "This is my son, the one I love—I fully approve of him. Listen to him!"

[6]And as the disciples listened, they knelt with their faces on the ground, and were frightened out of their wits.

[7]And Jesus came and touched them and said, "Get up; don't be afraid." [8]Looking up they saw no one except Jesus by himself.

[9]And as they came down from the mountain, Jesus ordered them, "Don't tell anyone about this vision until the Human One has been raised from the dead."

[10]And the disciples questioned him, "So why do the scholars claim that Elijah must come first?"

[11]In response he said, "Elijah does come and will restore everything. [12]But I'm telling you, Elijah has already come, and they did not recognize him but they did to him whatever they wanted. So the Human One is also going to suffer at their hands."

[13]Then the disciples understood that he had been talking to them about John the Baptizer.

[14]**And when they rejoined** the crowd, a person approached and knelt before him [15]and said, "Master, have mercy on my son, because he suffers terribly from epilepsy. For example, he often falls into the fire and just as often into the water. [16]So I brought him to your disciples, but they couldn't heal him."

[17]In response Jesus said, "You distrustful and perverted lot, how much longer do I have to be around you? How longer do I have to put up with you? Bring him here." [18]And Jesus rebuked the demon it and came out of him and the child was healed at that precise moment.

[19]Later the disciples came to Jesus privately and asked, "Why couldn't we drive it out?"

[20]So he says to them, "Because of your meager trust. Let me tell you, even if you have trust no bigger than a mustard seed, you will say to this mountain, 'Move from here to there,' and it will move. And nothing will be impossible for you."

17:20 Some mss add a v. 21, "This kind does not come out except with prayer and fasting." It was copied here from Mark 9:29.

17:3 *Moses* represents the Law and *Elijah* the Prophets, the first two divisions of the Hebrew Bible (see 5:17).

17:5
① Mt 3:16–17;
① Judas 6:10;
◊ Ps 2:7

17:10–11
◊ Mal 4:5–6

17:14–20
//Mk 9:14–27,
Lk 9:37–43

Q17:20
//Lk 17:6;
① Mt 6:30, 8:26,
14:31, 16:8

[22]**And when they had been reunited** in Galilee, Jesus said to them, "The Human One is destined to be turned over to his enemies, [23]and they will kill him, and on the third day he'll be raised." And they were very upset.

[24]**And when they came** to Capernaum, those who collect the temple tax came to Peter and said, "Your teacher pays his temple tax, doesn't he?" [25]He said, "That's right."

And when he got home, Jesus anticipated what was on Peter's mind. "What are you thinking, Simon? On whom do earthly kings levy taxes and tolls? Do they levy them on their own people or on foreigners?"

[26]Peter said, "On foreigners."

Jesus responded to him, "Then their own people are exempt. [27]Still, we don't want to get in trouble with them, so go down to the sea, cast your line in, and take the first fish you catch. Open its mouth and you'll find a coin. Take it and pay them for both of us."

18 *Discourse 4: Instructions for the church*
At that moment the disciples approached Jesus with the question: "Who is greatest in the empire of Heaven?"

[2]And he called a child over, had her stand in front of them, [3]and said, "Let me tell you, if you don't turn yourself around and become like children, you'll never enter the empire of Heaven. [4]Therefore, those who lower themselves to this child's level are greatest in the empire of Heaven. [5]And whoever welcomes one such child in my name is welcoming me. [6]Any of you who entraps and exploits one of these little ones who trusts me would be better off having a mill-stone hung around your neck and being drowned in the deepest part of the sea!

[7]**Damn the world** for the snares it sets! It's inevitable that traps will be set; but still, damn those who set them! [8]If your hand or your foot gets you into trouble, cut it off and throw it away! It's better for you to enter life maimed or lame than to be thrown into the eternal fire with both hands and both feet. [9]And if your eye gets you into trouble, rip it out and throw it away! After all, it's better for you to enter life one-eyed than to be thrown into Gehenna's fire with both eyes. [10]See that you don't disdain one of these little ones. For I'm telling you, their guardian angels constantly gaze on the face of my Father in heaven.

[12]**What do you think** about this? If someone has a hundred sheep and one of them wanders off, won't he leave the ninety-nine in the hills and go look for

17:22–23
//Mk 9:30–32,
Lk 9:43–45;
Ⓣ Mt 16:21,
20:17–19

17:24
◊Ex 30:13

18:1–10
//Mk 9:33–37,
9:42–50;
Lk 9:46–50

18:3–4
Cf. Mk 10:13–16,
Lk 18:15–17

18:3
Cf. Th 22;
Ⓣ Jn 3:3–5

Q18:6–7
//Lk 17:1–2

18:8–9
Ⓓ Mt 5:29–30

Q18:12–14
//Lk 15:3–7, Th 107;
◊Ez 34:6–12,
Ps 119:176

18:10 Some mss add a v. 11, "The Human One came to save the lost." This was copied from Luke 19:10.

17:24 At this time custom required that the *temple tax* be paid with two drachmas from Tyre, which is why money changers were required at the temple. Two drachmas was the equivalent of two day's labor for a peasant of the period. **17:27** The coin here is a *stater*, worth about four drachmas. **18:1** This is the beginning of the fourth sermon.

*Discipline &
forgiveness*

*The unforgiving
slave*

the one that wandered off? [13]And if he should find it, let me tell you, he'll rejoice over it more than over the ninety-nine that didn't wander off. [14]And so it is the intention of your Father in heaven that not one of these little ones be lost.

[15]"**And if some companion** does wrong, go have it out between the two of you privately. If that person listens to you, you have won your companion over. [16]And if he or she doesn't listen, take one or two people with you so that 'every fact may be supported by two or three witnesses.' [17]Then if he or she refuses to listen to them, report it to the congregation. If he or she refuses to listen even to the congregation, treat that companion like you would a pagan or toll collector. [18]Let me tell you, whatever you uphold on earth will be upheld in heaven, and whatever you dismiss on earth will be dismissed in heaven. [19]Again I assure you, if two of you on earth agree on anything you ask for, it will be done for you by my Father in heaven. [20]In fact, wherever two or three are gathered together in my name, I will be there among them."

[21]Then Peter came up and asked him, "Master, how many times can a companion wrong me and still expect my forgiveness? As many as seven times?"

[22]Jesus replies to him, "My advice to you is not seven times, but seventy-seven times.

[23]**This is why** the empire of Heaven should be compared to a human ruler who decided to settle accounts with his slaves. [24]When the process began, this debtor was brought to him who owed a gazillion dollars. [25]Since he couldn't pay it back, the ruler ordered him sold, along with his wife and children and everything he had, so he could recover his money.

[26]At this prospect, the slave knelt down and groveled before him: 'Be patient with me and I'll pay you back in full.' [27]Because he was compassionate, the master of that slave let him go and canceled the debt.

[28]As soon as he got out, that same slave collared one of his fellow slaves who owed him five thousand dollars, and grabbed him by the neck and demanded, 'Pay back what you owe!'

[29]His fellow slave knelt down and begged him, 'Be patient with me and I'll pay you back.'

[30]But he wasn't interested; instead, he went out and threw him in prison until he paid the debt.

Q18:15
//Lk 17:3

18:16
◊Dt 19:15

18:18
Ⓓ Mt 16:19;
cf. Jn 20:23

18:20
Ⓘ Mt 1:23, 28:20;
cf. Th 30:2

Q18:21–22
//Lk 17:4, GNaz 5:1;
◊Gen 4:24

18:15 Some mss made the condition more specific by inserting a "you:" *if some companion does* "you" *wrong.*

18:22 *Seventy-seven times* can also be understood as seventy times seven.
18:24 *A gazillion dollars* translates "ten thousand talents," a surreal sum, equivalent to 200,000 years' wages. By comparison, the total yearly taxation for Judea during this period was 600 talents. Some have suggested that the story involves the taxation practices of the Roman Empire.

[31]When his fellow slaves realized what had happened, they were terribly upset and went and reported to their master everything that had happened.

[32]At that point, his master summoned him. 'You wicked slave,' he says to him, 'I canceled your entire debt because you begged me. [33]Wasn't it only fair for you to treat your fellow slave with the same consideration as I treated you?' [34]And the master was so angry he turned him over to the torturers until he paid back everything he owed. [35]That's what my heavenly Father will do to you, unless you find it in your heart to forgive each one of your brothers and sisters."

19 **And so it happened** that, when Jesus had finished this instruction, he took leave of Galilee and went to the territory of Judea across the Jordan. [2]And large crowds followed him and he healed them there.

[3]**And the Pharisees** approached him and, to test him, they ask, "Is ⟨a man⟩ permitted to divorce his wife for any reason?"

[4]In response he said to them, "Haven't you read that in the beginning the Creator 'made them male and female,' [5]and that further on it says, 'for this reason, a man will leave his father and mother and be united with his wife, and the two will be one body'? [6]That's why they are longer two but 'one body.' Therefore, those whom God has coupled together, no one else should separate."

[7]They say to him, "Then why did Moses order 'a certificate of separation and divorce'?"

[8]He says to them, "Because you are obstinate Moses permitted you to divorce your wives, but it wasn't like that originally. [9]Now I say to you, whoever divorces his wife, except for immorality, and marries another commits adultery."

[10]**The disciples say** to him, "If that's the way a man has to treat wife, it's better not to marry."

[11]Then he said to them, "Not everyone can accept this teaching, only those for whom it was intended. [12]After all, there are castrated men who were born that way, and there are castrated men who were castrated by others, and there are castrated men who castrated themselves because of the empire of Heaven. If you can accept this ⟨teaching⟩, do so."

[13]**Then children were brought** to him so he could lay his hands on them and pray, but the disciples scolded them.

[14]Now Jesus said, "Let the children alone. Don't try to stop them from coming up to me. After all, the empire of Heaven belongs to people like these." [15]And he laid his hands on them and left that place.

[16]**And just then** someone came and asked him, "Teacher, what good do I have to do to have eternal life?"

19:9 Only Matthew modifies the absolute prohibition against divorce otherwise attributed to Jesus. The Greek term is not very specific but means sexual immorality of any kind, although it is frequently associated with prostitution.

[17]He said to him, "Why ask me about the good? There is only One who is good. If you want to enter life, observe the commandments."

[18]He says to him, "Which ones?"

Jesus replied, "'You shall not murder, you shall not commit adultery, you shall not steal, you shall not give false testimony, [19]you shall honor your father and mother, and you shall love your neighbor as yourself.'"

[20]The young man says to him, "I have observed all these; what am I missing?"

[21]Jesus said to him, "If you want to be perfect, make your move, sell your belongings, and give ⟨the money⟩ to the poor and you will have treasure in heaven. And then come on, follow me!"

[22]When the young man heard this advice, he went away dejected since he had a fortune.

[23]**Jesus said** to his disciples, "Let me tell you, it's difficult for the wealthy to enter the empire of Heaven. [24]I'm telling you again, it's easier for a camel to squeeze through they eye of a needle than for the wealthy to get into the empire of God."

[25]When the disciples heard this, they were very amazed and said, "Well then, who can be saved?"

[26]Jesus looked them in the eye, and said to them, "For humans this is impossible; for God everything's possible."

[27]In response Peter said to him, "Look at us, we left everything to follow you! What do we get out of it?"

[28]Jesus told them, "Let me tell you, you who have followed me, when the Human One is seated on his throne of glory in the renewal ⟨of creation⟩, you also will be seated on twelve thrones and sit in judgment on the twelve tribes of Israel. [29]And everyone who for my sake has left homes or brothers or sisters or father or mother or children or farms, will receive a hundred times as much and inherit eternal life. [30]Many of the first will be last, and many of the last will be first."

20

The empire of Heaven is like a landowner who went out first thing in the morning to hire workers for his vineyard. [2]After agreeing with the workers for a denarius a day he sent them into his vineyard.

[3]And coming out around 9 a.m. he saw others loitering in the marketplace [4]and he said to them, "You go into the vineyard too, and I'll pay you whatever is fair." [5]So they went.

Around noon he went out again, and at 3 p.m. he repeated the process. [6]About 5 p.m. he went out and found others loitering about and says to them,

19:18–19
◊Ex 20:12–16, Dt 5:16–20

19:19
Cf. Th 25;
◊Lv 19:18

19:23–30
//Mk 10:23–31,
Lk 18:26–30

19:24
//GNaz 6:5

Q19:28
Cf. Lk 22:28–30

19:30
Ⓓ Mt 20:16;
//Mk 10:31,
Lk 13:30, Th 4:2

19:23–30
//Mk 10:23–31,
Lk 18:26–30

19:24
//GNaz 6:5

Q19:28
Cf. Lk 22:28–30

19:30
Ⓓ Mt 20:16;
//Mk 10:31,
Lk 13:30, Th 4:2

19:24 The *eye of a needle* refers to a sewing needle, not, as some have maintained, a twisting gate in the city walls. The aphorism is a paradox.

20:2 The *denarius* was a subsistence wage for a laborer.

The Human One will die & rise

Jesus' cup

Number one is slave

"Why did you stand around here idle the whole day?"

⁷They reply, "Because no one hired us."

He tells them, "You go into the vineyard as well."

⁸When evening came the owner of the vineyard tells his foreman, "Call the workers and pay them their wages starting with those hired last and ending with those hired first."

⁹Those hired at 5 p.m. came up and received a denarius each. ¹⁰Those hired first approached thinking they would receive more. But they also got a demarius apiece. ¹¹They took it and began to grumble against the owner: ¹²"These guys hired last worked only an hour but you have made them equal to us who did most of the work during the heat of the day."

¹³In response he said to one of them, "Friend, did I wrong you? You did agree with me for a denarius, didn't you? ¹⁴Take what's yours and go! I choose to treat the man hired last the same as you. ¹⁵Is there some law against my doing what I please with my own money? Or are you envious because I am generous?"

¹⁶"The last will be first and the first last."

¹⁷**As he was going up** to Jerusalem, Jesus took the Twelve aside privately and said to them as they walked along, ¹⁸"Listen, we're going up to Jerusalem, and the Human One will be turned over to the chief priests and scholars, and they will sentence him to death, ¹⁹and turn him over to foreigners to be made fun of and flogged and crucified. But on the third day he will be raised."

²⁰**Then the mother** of the sons of Zebedee came up to him with her sons, bowed down before him, and asked him for a favor.

²¹He said to her, "What do you want?"

She said to him, "Give me your word that these two sons of mine may sit, one at your right hand and one at your left, in your empire."

²²In response Jesus said, "You have no idea what you're asking for. Can you drink the cup that I'm about to drink?"

They said to him, "We can!"

²³He says to them, "You'll be drinking my cup, but as for sitting at my right or my left, that's not up to me; it's for those for whom it's been reserved by my Father."

²⁴**And when the other ten** heard of it, they were incensed with the two brothers. ²⁵And calling them aside, Jesus said, "You know how foreign rulers lord it over their subjects, and how their strong men tyrannize them. ²⁶It's not going to be like that with you! With you, whoever wants to become great will be your slave, ²⁷and whoever among you wants to be 'number one' is to be your slave. ²⁸After all, the Human One didn't come to be served, but to serve and to give his life as a ransom for many."

Q20:16
Ⓓ Mt 19:30;
//Mk 10:31,
Lk 13:30, Th 4:2

20:17–19
//Mk 10:32–34,
Lk 18:31–34;
Ⓣ Mt 16:21,
17:22–23

20:20–28
//Mk 10:35–45,
Lk 22:24–47

20:24–28
Ⓣ Mt 18:1–4,
Mk 9:33–37,
Lk 9:46–50

20:26–27
Cf. Mt 23:11–12

20:15 *envious*: The master accuses the laborers of giving him the "evil eye," an expression for putting a curse on someone, still common in the Mediterranean world.

20:28 *Ransom* usually had to do with the manumission of slaves.

²⁹**And as they were leaving** Jericho, a huge crowd followed him. ³⁰There were two blind men sitting along the wayside. When they heard that Jesus was going by, they shouted, "Have mercy on us, Master, son of David."

³¹The crowd yelled at them to shut up, but they shouted all the louder, "Have mercy on us, Master, son of David."

³²Jesus paused and called out to them, "What do you want me to do for you?"

³³They said to him, "Master, open our eyes!"

³⁴Then Jesus took pity on them, touched their eyes, and right away they regained their sight and followed him.

21

When they got close to Jerusalem, and came to Bethphage at the Mount of Olives, then Jesus sent two disciples ahead ²with these instructions: "Go into the village across the way, and right away you will find a donkey tied up, and a colt alongside her. Untie them and bring them to me. ³And if anyone says anything to you, just say, 'The Master needs them and he'll send them back right away.'" ⁴This happened in order to fulfill the prediction spoken through the prophet:

> ⁵Tell the daughter of Zion,
> "Look, your king comes to you gently,
>> mounted on a donkey
>> and on a colt, the foal of a pack animal."

⁶Then the disciples went and did as Jesus instructed them, ⁷and brought the donkey and colt and they placed their cloaks on them, and he sat on top of them. ⁸The enormous crowd spread their cloaks on the road, and others cut branches from the trees and spread them on the road. ⁹The crowds leading the way and those following kept shouting,

> Hosanna to the son of David!
> Blessed is the one who comes in the name of the Lord!
> Hosanna in the highest ⟨heaven⟩.

Two blind men see

*Jesus enters
Jerusalem*

20:29–34
//Mk 10:46–52,
Lk 18:35–43;
Ⓓ Mt 9:27–31

21:1–11
//Mk 11:1–11,
Lk 19:28–40,
Jn 12:12–19

21:5
◊Zec 9:9, Is 62:11

21:9
◊Ps 118:26

20:30 Some mss omit *Master* from the blind men's shout, while a few mss substitute "Jesus."

20:29 *Jericho* was one of the more important cities of the Jordan Valley. It was an extremely ancient city, on a major ford of the Jordan river and thus important in both trade and agriculture. The valley was fertile in contrast to the surrounding barren mountains.

20:33 *Master* can also mean "Lord." This double meaning occurs a number of times in Matthew.

21:1 *Bethphage's* exact location has never been determined.

It was apparently on the side of the Mount of Olives.

21:7 Jesus is here pictured as astride both animals in literal fulfillment of the prophecy in Zechariah.

21:9 *Hosanna* is a Hebrew expression from Psalm 118 meaning "Help, I pray!" The psalm was part of Passover celebration, and pilgrims coming to Jerusalem for the festival would have shouted this like "Hurrah!" Later it was used in early Christian liturgies as an expression of joy.

Jesus disrupts
the temple

Children cheer
Jesus

Fig tree without figs

On whose
authority?

[10]And when he entered Jerusalem the whole city was shaken, saying, "Who is this?" [11]The crowds said, "This is the prophet Jesus from Nazareth in Galilee!"

[12]**And Jesus went into** God's temple and threw all the vendors and customers out of the temple area; and he knocked over the currency exchange tables, along with the chairs of the dove merchants.

[13]Then he says to them, "It is written,

My house shall be designated a house of prayer,

But you're turning it into 'a hideout for bandits'!"

[14]**And some blind and lame** people came to him in the temple area, and he healed them. [15]Then the chief priests and scholars saw the remarkable feats he performed, and the children who kept cheering in the temple area, shouting, "Hosanna to the son of David," and they were infuriated. [16]And they said to him, "Do you hear what these people are saying?"

Jesus says to them, "Of course. Have you never read the verse,

Out of the mouths of babies and nursing infants
      you brought forth praise for yourself?"

[17]And leaving them behind, he went outside the city to Bethany and spent the night there.

[18]**Early in the morning**, as he was returning to the city, he was hungry. [19]And so when he spotted a single fig tree on the way, he went up to it, and found nothing on it, only leaves, and he says to it, "You'll never bear fruit again!" And the fig tree withered right then and there.

[20]And when the disciples saw this, they expressed amazement: "How could the fig tree wither so quickly?"

[21]In response Jesus said to them, "Let me tell you, if you have trust and do not doubt, not only can you do this to a fig tree but you can even say to this mountain, 'Up with you and into the sea!' and that's what will happen; [22]and everything you ask for in prayer you'll get if you trust."

[23]**And when he came** to the temple area, the chief priests and elders of the people approached him while he was teaching, and asked, "Where'd you get the authority to do these things?" and "Who gave you this authority?"

[24]In response Jesus said to them, "I also have one question for you. If you answer me, I'll tell you by what authority I do these things. [25]The baptism of John, where did it come from? From Heaven or from humans?"

21:12–17
//Mk 11:15–19,
Lk 19:45–48,
Jn 2:13–22

21:13
◊Is 56:7, Jer 7:11

21:16
◊Ps 8:1–2

21:18–22
//Mk 11:12–25

21:21
① Mt 18:19;
//Th 48, 106;
Lk 17:5–7

21:23–27
//Mk 11:27–33,
Lk 20:1–8

21:12 Some mss omit *God's* as a modifier of *temple,* removing a rare expression not found elsewhere.

21:17 *Bethany* is a village on the side of the Mount of Olives, about two miles east of Jerusalem.

And they conferred among themselves, saying, "If we say 'from Heaven,' he'll say to us, 'Then why didn't you believe him?' [26]And if we say 'From humans! . . .' We're afraid of the crowd." (Remember, everybody considered John a prophet.) [27]So they answered Jesus by saying, "We can't tell."

He replied to them in kind: "Then I'm not going to tell you by what authority I do these things.

[28]**"Now what do you think?**

A man had two sons. He went to the first, and said, "Son, go and work in the vineyard today."

[29]He answered, "I'm on it, master," but he didn't move.

[30]Then he went to the second and said the same thing.

He responded, "I don't want to," but later on he thought better of it and went ⟨to work⟩.

[31]"Which of the two did what the father wanted?"

They said, "The second."

Jesus said to them, "Let me tell you, toll collectors and prostitutes will get into God's empire, but you will not. [32]After all, John came to you walking in the way of God, but you didn't believe him; yet toll collectors and prostitutes believed him. Even after you observed ⟨this⟩, you didn't think better of it later and believe him.

[33]**"Listen to another parable**:

There once was a landlord who "planted a vineyard, put a hedge around it, dug a winepress in it, built a tower," leased it out to some farmers, and went abroad. [34]Now when harvest time arrived, he sent his slaves to the farmers to collect his crop. [35]And the farmers grabbed his slaves, and one they beat and another they killed, and another they stoned.

[36]Again he sent other slaves, more than the first group, and they did the same thing to them.

[37]Then finally he sent his son to them, with the thought, "They'll show my son some respect."

[38]But when the farmers recognized the son they said to one another, "This guy's the heir! Come on, let's kill him and we'll have his inheritance!" [39]And they grabbed him, dragged him outside the vineyard, and killed him.

[40]"When the owner of the vineyard comes, what will he do to those farmers then?"

21:29–31 The textual transmission of the parable is very confusing. Some mss adopt the version printed above; many mss had the first son say "no," but then change his mind, while the second son says "yes," and then doesn't go. In this case the audience responds "the first." A few mss even have the first son say "no," but change his mind; the second say "yes," but not go; and the audience answer the "the second."

21:32
Ⓣ Lk 7:29–30

21:33–46
//Mk 12:1–12,
Lk 20:9–19,
Th 65–66

21:33
◊ Is 5:1–2

[41]They say to him, "He'll massacre those scum and lease the vineyard out to other farmers who will deliver their produce to him at the proper time."

[42]Jesus says to them, "It seems you haven't read in scripture:

A stone that the builders threw away

has ended up as the keystone.

It was the Lord's doing,

something we find amazing.

[43]So take my word for it: God's empire will be taken away from you and given to a people that bears its fruit."

[45]And when the chief priests and Pharisees heard his parable, they understood that he was talking about them. [46]They wanted to seize him, but were afraid of the crowds, because everyone thought he was a prophet.

22 Jesus again responded to them and told them parables.

[2]The empire of Heaven is like a king who gave a wedding celebration for his son. [3]Then he sent his slaves to summon those who had been invited to the wedding, but they declined to attend.

[4]He sent additional slaves with the instructions: "Tell those invited, 'Look, the feast is ready, the oxen and fat calves have been slaughtered, and everything is set. Come to the wedding.'"

[5]But they couldn't be bothered and went off, one to his own farm, one to his business, [6]while the rest seized his slaves, attacked and killed them.

[7]Now the king was outraged and sent his armies to destroy those murderers and burn their city. [8]Then he tells his slaves, "The wedding celebration is ready, but those we've invited didn't deserve it. [9]So go to the city gates and invite anybody you find to the wedding."

[10]Those slaves then went out into the streets and collected everybody they could find, the good and bad alike. And the wedding hall was full of guests.

[11]The king came in to see the guests for himself and noticed this one man without proper attire. [12]And he says to him, "Look pal, how'd you get in here without dressing for the occasion?"

And he was speechless.

[13]Then the king ordered his waiters, "Bind him hand and foot and throw him out into the utter darkness. They'll weep and grind their teeth out there. [14]After all, many are called but few are chosen."

21:42
◊ Ps 118:22–23

21:46
Ⓣ Judas 6:12

Q22:1–14
//Lk 14:15–24,
Th 64

22:6
Ⓣ Mt 21:35, 23:37

22:13
Cf. Mt 8:12, 13:42,
13:50, 24:51, 25:30

21:43 Many mss add a v. 44: "The one who falls over this stone will be smashed to pieces, and anyone on whom it falls will be crushed." It is most probably an interpolation from Luke 20:18.

22:7 *Burn their city* may be a reference to the destruction of Jerusalem by Titus in 70 CE. The arch celebrating his victory still stands in Rome.

¹⁵**Then the Pharisees** went and conferred on how to trap him with a riddle. ¹⁶And they send their disciples to him along with the Herodians to say, "Teacher, we know that you are honest and that you teach God's way forthrightly, and that you are impartial, because you pay no attention to appearances. ¹⁷So tell us what you think: is it permissible to pay the poll tax to Caesar or not?"

¹⁸Jesus knew how devious they were, and said, "Why do you provoke me, you phonies? ¹⁹Show me the money used to pay the poll tax."

And they handed him a denarius.

²⁰And he says to them, "Whose image is this? Whose name is on it?"

²¹They say to him, "Caesar's."

Then he says to them, "Pay to Caesar what belongs to Caesar, and to God what belongs to God!"

²²When they heard his reply, they were dumbfounded. And they withdrew from him and went away.

²³**That same day**, some Sadducees, who maintain there is no resurrection, came up to him and questioned him. ²⁴"Teacher," they said, "Moses said, 'If someone dies without children, his brother shall marry the widow and produce offspring for his brother.' ²⁵We knew these seven brothers. Now the first married and died, and since he left no children, he left his widow to his brother. ²⁶The second brother did the same thing, and the third, and so on, through the seventh brother. ²⁷Finally the wife died. ²⁸So then, in the resurrection, whose wife, of the seven, will she be, since they had all married her?"

²⁹In response Jesus said to them, "You've missed the point; you ignore both the scriptures and the power of God. ³⁰You see, at the resurrection people do not marry but resemble heaven's messengers. ³¹As for the resurrection of the dead, I guess you haven't read God's word to you: ³²'I am the God of Abraham and the God of Isaac and the God of Jacob.' This is not the God of the dead, but of the living."

³³And when the crowd heard, they were stunned by his teaching.

³⁴**When the Pharisees** learned that he had silenced the Sadducees, they conspired against him. ³⁵And one of them, a legal expert, put him to the test: ³⁶"Teacher, which commandment in the Law is the greatest?"

³⁷He replied to him, "'You shall love the Lord your God with all your heart and all your soul and all your mind.' ³⁸This commandment is first and foremost. ³⁹And the second is like it: 'You shall love your neighbor as yourself.' ⁴⁰Everything in the Law and the Prophets hangs on these two commandments."

⁴¹**When the Pharisees** gathered around, Jesus asked them, ⁴²"What do you think about the Anointed One? Whose son is he?"

God and Caesar

Wife of seven brothers

The greatest commandment

David's lord & son

22:15–22
//Mk 12:13–17, Lk 20:20–26, Th 100; cf. EgerG 3:1–6
22:22–33
//Mk 12:18–27, Lk 20:27–40
22:24
◊Dt 25:5–6
22:32
◊Ex 3:6
22:34–40
//Mk 12:28–31, Lk 10:25–28
22:37
◊Dt 6:5
22:39
◊Lv 19:18; cf. Th 25; Ⓓ Mt 19:19; Ⓣ Rom 13:8–10, Gal 5:13–15
22:41–46
//Mk 12:35–37, Lk 20:41–44

22:24 This debate involves the so-called levirate law in which a brother was obliged to take his brother's wife if she had not borne a son. This was to ensure the family line. See Deut 25:5–6.

They said to him, "David's."

[43]He said to them, "Then how can David call him 'lord,' while speaking under the influence of the spirit:

[44]The Lord said to my lord,
  "Sit here at my right,
    until I make your enemies grovel at your feet"?

[45]If David actually called him 'lord,' how can he be his son?"

[46]And no one could come up with an answer to his riddle. And from that day on no one dared ask him a question.

23 Discourse 5: The Time of the end

Then Jesus said to the crowds and to his disciples, [2]"The scholars and Pharisees occupy the chair of Moses. [3]So do everything they tell you, but don't do what they do; they don't practice what they preach. [4]They invent heavy burdens and lay them on folks' shoulders, but they themselves won't lift a finger to move them. [5]Everything they do, they do for show. So they widen their phylacteries and enlarge their tassels. [6]They love the best couches at banquets and the prominent seats in synagogues [7]and respectful greetings in marketplaces and having everyone call them 'Rabbi.' [8]But none of you are to be called 'Rabbi'; after all, you only have one teacher, and all of you belong to the same family. [9]And don't call anyone on earth 'father,' since you have only one Father, and he is in heaven. [10]You are not to be called 'instructors,' because you have only one instructor, the Anointed One. [11]Now whoever is greater than you will be your slave. [12]Those who promote themselves will be demoted and those who demote themselves will be promoted.

[13]"**You scholars and Pharisees**, you impostors! Damn you! You slam the door of the empire of Heaven in people's faces. You yourselves don't go in, and you block the way of those trying to go in.

22:44
◊Ps 110:1

22:46
Cf. Mk 12:34,
Lk 20:40

Q23:4
//Lk 11:46

23:5
◊Nm 15:37–39

23:6–7
//Mk 12:38–40,
Lk 20:45–47

Q23:6
//Lk 11:43

23:11
//Mk 9:35, 10:43;
Lk 22:26; Mt 20:26

Q23:13
//Lk 11:52;
cf. Th 39, 102

23:4 Some mss add "that are hard to bear" after *heavy burdens*. This is part of an effort of early scribes to intensify Jesus' sayings. The interpolation is based on 11:47.
23:13 Some mss add a v. 14: "Damn you, you scholars and Pharisees, impostors! You prey on widows and their families, and recite long prayers for appearance sake. Therefore, you will get a stiff sentence." This verse is clearly derived from Mark 12:40 and Luke 20:47.

23:2 *The chair of Moses* probably refers to the seat next to the ark in the synagogue where the scroll of the Law was kept. Sometimes the scroll was apparently enthroned on the seat and teachers also would teach from the seat. It represents the teaching authority of the scholars.

23:5 *Phylacteries* are amulets worn on the forehead and arm during prayer. The amulet was a little box in which there was a small piece of paper containing a verse from scripture. The amulet with its scripture verse was probably used for protection against demons.

¹⁵"You scholars and Pharisees, you impostors! Damn you! You scour land and sea to make one convert, and when you do, you make that person twice as much a child of Gehenna than you.

¹⁶"Damn you, you blind guides who claim, 'When you swear by the temple, it doesn't matter, but when you swear by the treasure in the temple, it is binding.' ¹⁷You blind fools, which is greater, the treasure or the temple that makes the gold sacred? ¹⁸You go on, 'When you swear by the altar, it doesn't matter, but when you swear by the offering that lies on the altar, it is binding.' ¹⁹You are so blind! Which is greater, the offering or the altar that makes the offering sacred? ²⁰So when you swear by the altar, you swear by the altar and everything on it. ²¹And anyone who swears by the temple, swears by the temple and the one who makes it home, ²²and anyone who swears by heaven swears by the throne of God and the one who occupies it.

²³"You scholars and Pharisees, you impostors! Damn you! You pay tithes on mint and dill and cumin too, but ignore the really important matters of the Law, such as justice and mercy and trust. It's these you should have practiced without ignoring the others. ²⁴You blind leaders! You strain out a gnat and gulp down a camel!

²⁵"You scholars and Pharisees, you impostors! Damn you! You wash the outside of cups and plates, but inside they are full of greed and self-indulgence. ²⁶You blind Pharisee, first clean the inside of the cup and then the outside will be clean too.

²⁷"You scholars and Pharisees, you impostors! Damn you! You're like whitewashed tombs: on the outside they look beautiful, but inside they are full of dead bones and every kind of decay. ²⁸So you too look like upright people on the outside, but on the inside you are doing nothing but posturing and subverting the Law.

²⁹"You scholars and Pharisees, you impostors! Damn you! You build the tombs of the prophets and decorate the graves of the just ³⁰and claim, 'If we had lived in the days of our ancestors, we wouldn't have joined them in spilling the prophets' blood.' ³¹So, you witness against yourselves: you are descendants of those who murdered the prophets, ³²and you're the spitting image of your ancestors. ³³You serpents! You spawn of Satan! How are you going to escape Gehenna's judgment? ³⁴Look, that is why I send you prophets and sages and

Q23:23
//Lk 11:42

Q23:25–26
//Lk 11:39–41,
Th 89;
cf. GOxy 840 2:8

Q23:27
//Lk 11:44

Q23:29–31
//Lk 11:47–48

23:33
Ⓣ Mt 3:17

Q23:34–36
//Lk 11:49–51

23:15 From about the second century BCE until the reign of Constantine, it appears that Judaism engaged in a strong program of conversion. Monotheism, strict sexual morality, and Sabbath observance were very attractive to pagans. The "God Fearers" mentioned in Acts (10:2, 13:26) suggests a group of pagans attracted to Judaism but who have not officially joined, perhaps because of circumcision. However,

there is no other evidence of such a group.

23:30 *Spilling the prophets' blood* is an accusation that is not borne out historically. Actually very few of the prophets were murdered.

23:34 *Prophets and sages and scholars* appears to be a description of the Christian community.

Lament over
Jerusalem

Monumental
buildings destroyed

Apocalyptic signs

scholars. Some you're going to kill and crucify, and some you're going to flog in your synagogues and hound from town to town. ³⁵And so all the innocent blood that has ever been shed on the earth will be on you, from the blood of innocent Abel to the blood of Zechariah, son of Baruch, whom you murdered between the temple and the altar. ³⁶Let me tell you, all these things are going to rain down on this generation.

³⁷"**Jerusalem, Jerusalem**, you murder the prophets and stone those sent to you! How often I wanted to gather your children as a hen gathers her chicks under her wings, but you wouldn't let me. ³⁸Can't you see, your house is being abandoned as a ruin? ³⁹I'm telling you, you certainly won't see me again until you say, 'Blessed is the one who comes in the name of the Lord.'"

24 **Jesus was leaving** the temple area on his way out, when his disciples came to him and called his attention to the sacred buildings.

²In response he said to them, "Yes, take a good look at all this! Let me tell you, not one single stone will be left on top of another! Every last one will be knocked down!"

³**As he was sitting** on the Mount of Olives, the disciples came to him privately, and said, "Tell us, when are these things going to happen, and what will be the sign of your coming and of the culmination of the age?"

⁴And in response Jesus said to them, "Stay alert, or else someone might deceive you. ⁵You know, many will come using my name, and claim, 'I'm the Anointed One!' and they will deceive many people. ⁶You're going to hear about wars and rumors of wars. See that you are not afraid. For these are inevitable, but it is not yet the End. ⁷For nation will rise up against nation and empire against empire; and there will be famines and earthquakes everywhere. ⁸Now all these things mark the beginning of the birth pangs.

⁹"At that time they will turn you in to be tortured, and will kill you, and you'll be universally hated because of me. ¹⁰And then many will fall away, and they will turn one another in and hate each other. ¹¹And many phony prophets will appear and will deceive many. ¹²And as lawlessness spreads, many people's love will grow cold. ¹³Those who hold out to the End will be saved. ¹⁴And this good news of the empire of Heaven will have been proclaimed in the whole inhabited world, so you can make your case to all peoples. And then the End will come.

23:35
Cf. GNaz 7;
◊Gn 4:8, Zec 1:1,
2 Chr 24:20–21

Q23:37–39
//Lk 13:34–35

23:37
◊Is 31:5

23:39
◊Ps 118:26

24:1–2
//Mk 13:1–2,
Lk 21:5–6

24:3–14
//Mk 13:3–13,
Lk 21:5–19

24:4
//Mary 4:3

24:5
cf. Mt 24:23–26, Mk
13:21–23,
Lk 17:23

24:7
◊Is 19:2

24:13
Ⓓ Mt 10:22

24:14
Ⓘ Mt 28:19

23:35 *Abel* to *Zechariah, son of Baruch* would seem to be a reference from the first of the prophets to the last. Abel was killed by his brother Cain (Gen 4:8); Zechariah, the last of the prophets, was killed for prophesying that God had abandoned his people. But according to 2 Chr 24:20 he was not the son of Baruch but of Jehoiada. Matthew may have confused this Zechariah with that of Zech 1:1.

¹⁵"**So when you see** the 'devastating desecration' (as described by Daniel the prophet) standing 'in the holy place'—the lector had better figure out what this means— ¹⁶then the people in Judea should head for the hills; ¹⁷no one on the roof should go downstairs to retrieve anything; ¹⁸and no one in the field should turn back to get a coat. ¹⁹It'll be too bad for pregnant women and nursing mothers in those days! ²⁰Pray that you don't have to flee during the winter or on the Sabbath. ²¹For there will be great tribulation, the likes of which has not occurred since the world began until now, and will never occur again. ²²And if those days had not been cut short, no human being would have survived. But for the sake of the chosen people, those days will be cut short.

²³"Then if someone says to you, 'Look, here's the Anointed One' or 'over here,' don't count on it! ²⁴After all, phony messiahs and phony prophets will show up, and they'll provide spectacular signs and omens in an attempt to deceive, if possible, even the chosen people. ²⁵Look, I have warned you in advance. ²⁶In fact, if they should say to you, 'Look, he's in the desert,' don't go out there; or 'Look, he's in one of the inner rooms,' don't count on it. ²⁷For just as lightning comes out of the east and is visible all the way to the west, that's what the coming of the Human One will be like. ²⁸For wherever there's a corpse, that's where vultures gather.

²⁹"**Right after the tribulation** of those days

> the sun will be darkened,
>> and the moon will not give off her glow;
> the stars will fall from the sky,
>> and the heavenly forces will be shaken.

³⁰And then the sign of the Human One will appear in the sky, and every tribe of the earth will lament, and they'll see the Human One coming on the clouds of the sky with great power and splendor. ³¹And he'll send out his messengers with a blast on the trumpet, and they'll gather his chosen people from the four winds, from one end of the sky to the other. ³²"Take a cue from the fig tree. When its branch is already in bud and leaves come out, you know that summer is near. ³³So, when you see all these things, you should realize that he is near, just outside your door. ³⁴Let me tell you, this generation certainly won't pass away before all these things happen! ³⁵The earth will pass away and so will the sky, but my words will never pass away.

24:15–28
//Mk 13:14–23,
Lk 21:20–24

24:15
◊Dn 11:31, 12:11;
1 Mc 1:54

24:17–18
//Lk 17:31

24:19
Cf.Th 79:3

24:21
◊Joel 2:2, Dn 12:1

24:23–25
Cf. Mt 24:5

24:23
//Lk 17:23,
Mary 4:4;
cf. Th 113, Lk 17:21

Q24:26–27
//Lk 17:23–24

Q24:28
//Lk 17:37;
◊Job 39:30b

24:29–36
//Mk 13:24–32,
Lk 21:25–33

24:29
◊Is 13:10

24:30–31
Ⓣ 1 Thes 4:15–16

24:30
Ⓓ Mt 26:64;
Ⓘ Mt 25:31–46;
◊Dn 7:13–14;
Ⓣ Rv 1:7

24:34
Cf. Mt 16:28,
Mk 9:1, Lk 9:27

24:15 *Devastating desecration*, as Matthew makes evident, is a reference to Dan 9:27 in which the prophet in veiled language refers to the desecration of the temple by the Syrian king Antiochus Epiphanes in 167 BCE. 1 Macc 1:54 refers to this same event in a direct fashion. In the style of apocalyptic literature, the author of the gospel is referring to some recent event in the original audience's experience. It may be either Titus's setting up of the Roman shields in the temple area after the conquest of Jerusalem in 70 CE or the Zealots' activity in the temple area during the preceding two years.

³⁶"**As for that exact day** and hour, no one knows, not even Heaven's messengers, nor even the son—no one, except the Father alone.

³⁷"The Human One's coming will be just like the days of Noah. ³⁸That's how people behaved then before the flood came: they ate and drank, married and were given in marriage, until the day Noah boarded the ark, ³⁹and they were oblivious until the flood came and swept them all away. That's how it will be when the Human One comes. ⁴⁰Then two men will be in the field; one will be taken and one will be left. ⁴¹Two women will be grinding at the mill; one will be taken and one left. ⁴²So stay alert! You never know on what day your master returns.

⁴³"Mark this well: if the homeowner had known when the burglar was coming, he would have been on guard and not have allowed anyone to break into his house. ⁴⁴Therefore, you too should be prepared. Remember, the Human One is coming when you least expect it.

⁴⁵"Who then is the trustworthy and prudent slave to whom the master assigns responsibility for his household, to provide them with food at the right time? ⁴⁶Congratulations to the slave who's on the job when his master arrives. ⁴⁷Let me tell you, he'll put him in charge of all his property. ⁴⁸But suppose that worthless slave says to himself, 'My master is taking his time,' ⁴⁹and begins to beat his fellow slaves, and starts eating and drinking with drunks, ⁵⁰that slave's master will show up on the day he least expects and at an hour he doesn't suspect. ⁵¹He'll cut him to pieces, and assign him a fate among the impostors, where they'll weep and grind their teeth.

25 **When the time comes**, the empire of Heaven will be like ten maidens who took their lamps and went out to meet the bridegroom. ²Five of them were foolish and five were prudent. ³You see, the foolish maidens took their lamps but failed to take oil with them, ⁴while the prudent ones took flasks of oil along with their lamps. ⁵When the bridegroom was delayed, they all dozed off and fell asleep.

⁶Then in the middle of the night there was a shout: "Look, the bridegroom is coming! Let's go out to meet him." ⁷Then the maidens all got up and trimmed their lamps.

⁸The foolish said to the prudent ones, "Let us have some of your oil because our lamps are going out."

Q24:37–39
//Lk 17:26–30

Q24:40–41
//Lk 17:34–35

24:42–43
Ⓣ 1 Thes 5:2,
Rv 16:15

24:42
//Mk 13:35

Q24:43–44
//Lk 12:39–40,
Th21;
cf. Th 103

Q24:45–51
//Lk 12:42–46;
cf. GNaz 8

24:51
Cf. Mt 8:12, 13:42,
13:50, 22:13, 25:30

25:1–13
Ⓣ Lk 12:35–36

24:36 *Nor even the son* is omitted by many mss, but it is present in the best early mss. The doctrinal difficulty caused by the phrase indicates why later copyists would drop the phrase.

24:46 The return of the *master* is a reference to the coming of the Human One and his judgment of the nations (see also 25:5).

25:1 This parable describes a custom not otherwise attested in Jewish practice.

25:5 *When the bridegroom was delayed* is probably a reference to the delay of the coming of the Human One.

The money in trust

⁹But the prudent maidens responded, "We can't do that in case there isn't enough for both of us. You'd better go to the merchants and buy some for yourselves."

¹⁰While they were gone to get some, the bridegroom arrived and those who had come prepared accompanied him to the wedding; then the door was closed.

¹¹The other maidens finally come and say, "Master, master, open the door for us."

¹²He responded, "Let me tell you, I don't recognize you."

¹³"So stay alert because you don't know either the day or the hour.

¹⁴**You know**, it's like a man going on a trip who called his slaves and turned his property over to them. ¹⁵To the first he gave five talents' worth of silver, to the second two talents' worth, and to the third one talent's worth, to each in proportion to his ability. Then he left.

¹⁶The one who had received five talents' worth of silver went right out and put the money to work; he doubled his investment.

¹⁷The second also doubled his money.

¹⁸But the third, who had received the smallest amount, went out, dug a hole, and hid his master's silver.

¹⁹After a long absence, the master of those slaves returned to settle accounts with them. ²⁰The first, who had received five talents' worth of silver, came and produced an additional five, with this report: "Master, you handed me five talents of silver; as you can see, I've made you five more."

²¹His master commended him: "Well done, you competent and trustworthy slave. You've been trustworthy in a little, so I'll put you in charge of a lot. Come celebrate with your master."

²²The one with two talents of silver also came and reported, "Master, you handed me two talents of silver; as you can see, I've made you two more."

²³His master commended him: "Well done, you competent and trustworthy slave. You've been trustworthy in a little, so I'll put you in charge of a lot. Come celebrate with your master."

²⁴The one who had received one talent's worth of silver also came and reported, "Master, I know that you are ruthless, reaping where you didn't sow and gathering where you didn't scatter. ²⁵Since I was afraid, I went out and buried your money in the ground. Look, here it is!"

²⁶But his master replied to him, "You incompetent and timid slave! So you knew that I reap where I didn't sow and gather where I didn't scatter, did you? ²⁷Then you should have taken my money to the bankers. Then when I returned I would have recovered what's mine, plus interest. ²⁸So take the talent away from

Q25:14–30
//Lk 19:11–27;
cf. GNaz 8

25:15 These amounts are astronomical. The smallest, *one talent's worth of silver* (a talent was a unit of weight, approxi-mately 75 pounds), represents nearly twenty years' wages for a laborer.

Sheep & goats

this guy and give it to the one who has ten. [29]In fact, to everyone who has, more will be given and then some; and from those who don't have, even what they do have will be taken away. [30]And throw this worthless slave out into the utter darkness, where they'll weep and grind their teeth."

[31]**When the Human One** comes in his glory, accompanied by all his messengers, he'll be seated on his glorious throne. [32]Then all peoples will be assembled before him, and he will separate them into groups, much as a shepherd separates sheep from goats. [33]He'll place the sheep to his right and the goats to his left. [34]Then the king will say to those at his right, "Come, you who have the blessing of my Father, inherit the empire prepared for you from the foundation of the world. [35]For I was hungry and you gave me something to eat; I was thirsty and you gave me something to drink; I was a foreigner and you offered me hospitality; [36]I was naked and you clothed me; I was ill and you visited me; I was in prison and you came to see me."

[37]Then the righteous will say to him, "Master, when did we see you hungry and feed you or thirsty and give you a drink? [38]When did we notice that you were a foreigner and offer you hospitality? Or naked and clothe you? [39]When did we find you ill or in prison and come to visit you?"

[40]And the king will respond to them, "Let me tell you, whatever you did for the least of my brothers and sisters, you did for me."

[41]Next, he will say to those at his left, "You, condemned to the everlasting fire prepared for the devil and his messengers, get away from me! [42]For I was hungry and you didn't give me anything to eat; I was thirsty and you refused me a drink; [43]I was a foreigner and you failed to offer me hospitality; naked and you didn't clothe me; ill and in prison and you didn't visit me."

[44]Then they will give him a similar reply, "Master, when did we notice that you were hungry or thirsty or a foreigner or naked or ill or in prison and not take care of you?"

[45]He will then respond, "Let me tell you, whatever you didn't do for the least of my brothers and sisters, you didn't do for me."

[46]The second group will then head for everlasting punishment, but the righteous for everlasting life."

(End of Discourse 5)

26 And so it happened that, when Jesus had concluded his discourse, he told his disciples, [2]"You know that Passover comes in two days, and the Human One will be turned over to be crucified."

25:29
//Mt 13:12, Lk 8:18, Th 41

25:30
Cf. Mt 8:12, 13:42, 13:50, 22:13, 24:51

25:31–33
Ⓣ GSav 14:20

25:31
Ⓣ Mt 16:27, 24:30; ◊ Dn 7:13–14

25:34
Ⓣ Mt 13:35, GSav 13:8

26:1
Ⓘ Mt 7:28, 11:1, 13:53, 19:1

26:2
//Mk 14:1–2, Lk 22:1–2

25:40 Some scholars think that *my brothers and sisters* refers only to the Christian community. But it should also be noted that since by the time of judgment the gospel is to be preached to all the nations, there is a correlation between the church and the world. See the interpretation of the parable of the Wheat and Weeds where the field is the world (13:38) and in the parable stands for the church (13:24).

³**Then the chief priests** and elders of the people gathered in the courtyard of the chief priest, whose name was Caiaphas, ⁴and they conspired to seize Jesus by trickery and kill him. ⁵They were saying, "Not during the festival or else the people will riot."

⁶**While Jesus was in Bethany** at the house of Simon the leper, ⁷a woman who had an alabaster jar of very expensive aromatic ointment came up to him and poured it over his head while he was reclining ⟨at table⟩. ⁸When they saw this, the disciples were annoyed, and said, "What good is this waste? ⁹She could have sold it for a good price and given ⟨the money⟩ to the poor."

¹⁰But Jesus knew what was going on and said to them, "Why are you giving this woman a hard time? After all, she has done a good deed for me. ¹¹Remember, the poor will always be around; but I won't always be around. ¹²After all, by pouring this ointment on my body she has prepared me for burial. ¹³Let me tell you, wherever this good news is announced in all the world, the story of what she's done will be told in her memory."

¹⁴**Then one of the Twelve**, Judas Iscariot by name, went to the chief priests ¹⁵and said, "What are you willing to pay me if I turn him over to you?" They agreed on thirty silver coins. ¹⁶And from that moment he started looking for a good opportunity to turn him in.

¹⁷**On the first ⟨day⟩** of Unleavened Bread the disciples came to Jesus and said, "Where do you want us to get things ready for you to celebrate Passover?"

¹⁸He said, "Go into the city to a certain guy and tell him, 'The teacher says, "My time is near; I will observe Passover at your place with my disciples."'" ¹⁹And the disciples did as Jesus instructed them and they got things ready for Passover.

²⁰When it was evening, he was reclining ⟨for the meal⟩ with his twelve disciples. ²¹And as they were eating, he said, "Let me tell you, one of you is going to turn me in."

²²And they were very upset and each one said to him in turn, "I'm not the one, am I, Master?"

²³In response he said, "The one who dips his hand in the bowl with me—that's who's going to turn me in. ²⁴The Human One departs just as the scriptures predict, but damn the one responsible for turning the Human One in! That man would be better off if he'd never been born!"

²⁵Judas, the one who was going to turn him in, responded, "You can't mean me, can you, Rabbi?"

He says to him, "You said it."

Conspiracy against Jesus

Woman anoints Jesus

Priests promise to pay

Jesus celebrates Passover

26:3–5
//Jn 11:47–53, 55–57;
Ⓣ Mk 11:18, 12:12; Lk 19:47–48, 20:19; Judas 6:12

26:6–13
//Mk 14:3–9;
cf. Lk 7:36–50,
Jn 12:1–8

26:11
◊Dt 15:11

26:14–16
//Mk 14:10–11,
Lk 23:3–6

26:15
Ⓣ Mt 4:17, 16:21,
27:3, 27:9;
◊Zec 11:12

26:17–30
//Mk 14:12–26,
Lk 22:7–23

26:17
//GEbi 7:1;
◊Ex 12:14–20

26:24b
Ⓣ Job 3:2, 11;
Jer 20:14–18

26:20–25
//Jn 13:21–30

26:3 *Caiaphas* was the high priest from 18 CE until he was deposed by Vitellius, Pontius Pilate's successor, in 36 or 37 CE. He was the successor of Annas, his father-in-law. But see Luke 3:2 and Acts 4:6 for a somewhat different assumption.

26:7 The *aromatic ointment* is myrrh, a fragrant gum with a slightly bitter taste that comes from Arabia and parts of Africa. It is used for anointing the body much like a perfume, but is also used in the preparation of a corpse for burial.

26:26–28
//1 Cor 11:23–25;
cf. Jn 6:48–58

26:26
Cf. GHeb 9:4

26:28
//GSav 14:18;
◊ Ex 24:8, Zec 9:11

26:29
Cf. GHeb 9:2

26:30
//Lk 22:39

26:31–35
//Mk 14:27–31

26:31
//GSav 4:7;
cf. Jn 16:32;
◊ Zec 13:7

26:33–34
//Lk 22:31–34,
Jn 13:36–38

26:34
① Mt 26:75

26:35
Cf. Jn 11:16

26:36–46
//Mk 14:32–42,
Lk 22:39–46

26:36
Cf. Jn 18:1

26:38–39
Cf. Jn 12:27

26:39
//GSav 14:14;
cf. Jn 18:11

26:42
① Mt 6:10

26:44
Cf. GSav 15:1

²⁶As they were eating, Jesus took a loaf, gave a blessing, and broke it into pieces. And he offered it to the disciples, and said, "Take some and eat; this is my body."

²⁷He also took a cup and gave thanks and offered it to them, saying, "Drink from it, all of you, ²⁸for this is my blood of the covenant, which has been poured out for many for the forgiveness of sins. ²⁹Now I'm telling you, from now on I won't touch a drop of this fruit of the vine, until that day when I drink it for the first time with you in my Father's empire!"

³⁰And they sang a hymn and left for the Mount of Olives.

³¹**Then Jesus says** to them, "All of you will be shaken and fall away this night because of me. Remember, it is written,

> I will strike the shepherd and the sheep of the flock will be scattered.

³²But after I'm raised, I'll go ahead of you to Galilee."

³³In response Peter said to him, "Even if everyone else is shaken and falls away because of you, I never will."

³⁴Jesus said to him, "Let me tell you, tonight before the rooster crows you will disown me three times."

³⁵Peter says to him, "Even if they condemn me to die with you, I will never disown you!" And all the disciples said the same thing.

³⁶**Then Jesus goes** with them to a place called Gethsemane, and he says to the disciples, "Sit down here while I go over there and pray."

³⁷And taking Peter and the two sons of Zebedee, he began to feel dejected and full of anguish. ³⁸He says to them, "I'm so sad I could die. You stay here with me and be alert!"

³⁹And he went a little farther, knelt with his face to the ground, and prayed, "My Father, if it's possible, take this cup away from me. But it's your will that matters, not mine."

⁴⁰And he returns to the disciples and finds them sleeping, and says to Peter, "Couldn't you stay awake with me for one hour? ⁴¹Be alert, and pray that you won't be put to the test. The spirit is willing, but the flesh is weak."

⁴²Again for a second time he went away and prayed, "My Father, if it's not possible for me to avoid drinking from this cup, then your will be done."

⁴³And once again he came and found them sleeping, since their eyes had grown heavy. ⁴⁴And leaving them again, he went away and prayed, repeating the same words for a third time.

⁴⁵Then he comes to the disciples and says to them, "Are you still sleeping and taking a rest? Look, the time has arrived! The Human One is being turned

---

26:36 *Gethsemane* means "oil press" and its exact location is unknown.

26:39 *Cup* is frequently used in the Hebrew Bible as a metaphor for suffering (e.g., Ps 11:6; 75:9).

over to sinners. ⁴⁶Get up, let's go! See for yourselves! Here comes the one who is going to turn me in."

⁴⁷**And while he was still speaking**, suddenly Judas, one of the Twelve, arrived and with him a great crowd wielding swords and clubs, dispatched by the chief priests and elders of the people.

⁴⁸Now the one who was to turn him in had arranged a sign with them, saying, "The one I'm going to kiss is the one you want. Arrest him!"

⁴⁹And right away he came up to Jesus and said, "Hello, Rabbi," and kissed him.

⁵⁰But Jesus said to him, "Friend, do what you came to do."

Then they came and laid hands on Jesus and seized him. ⁵¹All of a sudden one of those with Jesus lifted his hand, drew his sword, struck the chief priest's slave, and cut off his ear.

⁵²Then Jesus says to him, "Put your sword back where it belongs. For everyone who takes up the sword will be destroyed by the sword. ⁵³Or don't you think I can call on my Father, who would put more than twelve legions of heavenly messengers at my disposal? ⁵⁴But then how would the scriptures that say these things are inevitable be fulfilled?"

⁵⁵At that moment Jesus said to the crowds, "Have you come to arrest me with swords and clubs as you would an insurgent? I used to sit there in the temple area day after day teaching, and you didn't seize me."

⁵⁶All of this happened so the writings of the prophets would be fulfilled. Then all the disciples deserted him and ran away.

⁵⁷**Those who had arrested** Jesus brought him before Caiaphas the chief priest, where the scholars and elders had assembled. ⁵⁸But Peter followed him at a distance as far as the courtyard of the chief priest. He went inside and sat with the attendants to see how things would turn out.

⁵⁹The chief priests and the whole Council were looking for false testimony against Jesus so they might issue a death sentence; ⁶⁰but they couldn't find many perjurers to come forward. Finally, two men came forward ⁶¹and said, "This man said, 'I can destroy the temple of God and rebuild it within three days.'"

⁶²Then the chief priest got up and questioned him, "Don't you have something to say? Why do these people testify against you?"

⁶³But Jesus was silent.

And the chief priest said to him, "I ask you under oath before the living God: tell us if you are the Anointed One, the son of God!"

Judas turns Judas in

Trial before the Council

26:46
//GSav 4:2

26:47–56
//Mk 14:43–52,
Lk 22:47–54,
Jn 18:1–12

26:50
Cf. EgerG 1:8

26:52
◊Gn 9:6

26:57–58
//Mk 14:53–54,
Lk 22:54–55

26:59–68
//Mk 14:55–65;
Lk 22:63–71;
Jn 18:13–14, 19–24

26:60
◊Dt 17:6

26:61
//Jn 2:19, Th 71

26:48 The fact that Judas needs to use a *sign* indicates that Jesus was not known by face in Jerusalem.

Kissing is the equivalent of a handshake in our culture.
26:56 It is not clear which *writings of the prophets* are being fulfilled.

26:60 In Jewish legal practice *two* witnesses are required for a conviction.
26:61 Nowhere in Matthew's gospel is it reported that Jesus is going to *destroy the temple*.

Peter denies Jesus

Trial before Pilate

**Judas commits
suicide**

⁶⁴Jesus says to him, "If you say so. But I'm telling you, from now on you will see the Human One sitting at the right hand of Power and coming on the clouds of the sky."

⁶⁵Then the chief priest tore his vestment and said, "He has blasphemed! Why do we still need witnesses? See, now you have heard the blasphemy. ⁶⁶What do you think?"

In response they said, "He deserves to die!" ⁶⁷Then they spit in his face, and beat him and slapped him, ⁶⁸saying, "Prophesy for us, you Anointed One, you! Guess who hit you!"

⁶⁹**Meanwhile Peter** was sitting outside in the courtyard, and one slave woman came up to him, and said, "You too were with Jesus the Galilean."

⁷⁰But he denied it in front of everyone, saying, "I don't know what you're talking about."

⁷¹After Peter went out to the entrance, another slave woman saw him and says to those there, "This guy was with that Nazarean, Jesus."

⁷²And again he denied it with an oath: "I don't know the man!"

⁷³A little later those standing around came and said to Peter, "You really are one of them; even the way you talk gives you away!"

⁷⁴Then he began to curse and swear: "I don't know the man!"

And just then a rooster crowed. ⁷⁵And Peter remembered what Jesus had said: "Before the rooster crows you will disown me three times." And he went outside and wept bitterly.

27

When morning came, all the chief priests and elders of the people plotted against Jesus to put him to death. ²And they bound him and led him away and turned him over to Pilate the ⟨Roman⟩ governor.

³**Then Judas,** who had turned him in, realizing that Jesus had been condemned, was overcome with remorse and returned the thirty silver coins to the chief priests and elders. ⁴He said, "I've made a serious mistake in turning in this blameless man."

But they said, "What do we care? That's your business."

⁵And hurling the silver into the temple he slunk off, and went out and hanged himself.

26:64
Ⓓ Mt 24:30;
◊Dn 7:13–14,
Ps 110:1

26:65–66
◊Lv 24:16

26:65
Ⓘ Mt 9:3

26:67
//Pet 3:4

26:69–75
//Mk 14:66–72;
Lk 22:54–62;
Jn 18:15–18, 25–27

26:75
Ⓘ Mt 26:34

27:1–2
//Mk 15:1, Lk 23:1,
Jn 18:28

27:2
Cf. GHeb 1:6

27:3–10
Cf. Acts 1:15–20

27:3
Ⓘ Mt 26:15–16

27:4 A few mss have "righteous" *man.* This phrase is synonymous with *blameless man* which translates an unusual expression derived from the Greek Bible. It is associated with the violent death of God's agents (Deut 27:25 LXX, Jer 19:14). Righteousness is a favorite word of Matthew's, so it is difficult to decide what the reading should be.

26:65 It is not clear why what Jesus said is *blasphemy.*
27:2 *Pilate* was the fifth governor of Judea and his term was the second longest (26–36 CE). He was a very controversial governor, according to the contemporary Jewish historian Josephus.

⁶The chief priests took the silver and said, "It wouldn't be right to put this into the temple treasury, since it's blood money."

⁷So they devised a plan and bought the potter's field as a burial ground for foreigners. ⁸As a result, that field has been called Bloody Field even to this day. ⁹Then the prediction spoken through Jeremiah the prophet was fulfilled:

> And they took the thirty silver coins, the price put on a man's head (this is the price they put on him among the Israelites), ¹⁰and they donated it for the potter's field, as my Lord commanded me.

¹¹**Jesus stood before** the ⟨Roman⟩ governor, and the governor questioned him: "*You* are 'the King of the Judeans'?"

Jesus said, "If you say so."

¹²And while he was being accused by the chief priests and elders, he said absolutely nothing.

¹³Then Pilate says to him, "Don't you have anything to say to the long list of charges they bring against you?" ¹⁴But he did not respond to him, not to a single charge, so the governor was very astonished.

¹⁵At each festival it was the custom for the governor to set one prisoner free for the crowd, whichever one they wanted. ¹⁶⟨The Romans⟩ were then holding a notorious prisoner named Jesus Barabbas. ¹⁷When the crowd had gathered, Pilate said to them, "Do you want me to set Jesus Barabbas free for you or Jesus who is known as 'the Anointed One'?" (¹⁸You see, he knew that they had turned him in out of envy.)

¹⁹While he was sitting on the judgment seat, his wife sent a message to him: "Don't have anything to do with that innocent man, because I have agonized a great deal today over a dream about him."

²⁰The chief priests and the elders induced the crowds to ask for Barabbas but to have Jesus executed. ²¹In response ⟨to their request⟩ the governor said to them, "Which of the two do you want me to set free for you?"

They said, "Barabbas!"

²²Pilate says to them, "What should I do with Jesus, known as 'the Anointed One'?"

Everyone responded, "Have him crucified!"

Trial before Pilate continues

27:6
◊ Dt 23:19
27:9–10
◊ Zec 11:12–13
27:11–14
//Mk 15:2–5,
Lk 23:1–7,
Jn 18:29–38a
27:11
Ⓣ GSav 13:8
27:15–26
//Mk 15:6–15,
Lk 23:13–25,
Jn 18:38–19:16
27:16
Cf. GNaz 9
27:19
Ⓣ Mt 1:20; 2:12,
19, 22

27:16, 17 Many texts omit *Jesus,* but it is probably the original reading of Matthew and was omitted because of the reverence shown to the name of Jesus. The early church authority Origen (early third century) knows of mss with and without the double name, but thinks it cannot be original because "in all of the scriptures we know of no one who is a sinner called Jesus."

27:9 The quote is not from *Jeremiah* but Zechariah.
27:15 This exchange practice is otherwise unattested for the period.
27:16 *Barabbas* means in Aramaic "Son of the father."

27:19 The word translated *innocent* also means "righteous." Matthew has Pilate's wife join Judas (see 27:4 textual note) and Pilate (27:24) in declaring Jesus guiltless.

²³But he said, "Why? What has he done wrong?"

But they would shout all the louder, "Have him crucified!"

²⁴Now when Pilate could see that he was getting nowhere, but that a riot was starting instead, he took water and washed his hands in full view of the crowd and said, "I'm not responsible for this man's blood. That's your business!"

²⁵In response all the people said, "So, smear his blood on us and on our children."

²⁶Then he set Barabbas free for them, but had Jesus flogged, and then turned him over to be crucified.

²⁷**Then the governor's soldiers** took Jesus into the governor's residence and surrounded him with the whole cohort ⟨of Roman troops⟩. ²⁸They stripped him and dressed him in a crimson cloak, ²⁹and they wove a crown out of thorns and put it on his head. They placed a stick in his right hand, and bowing down before him, they made fun of him, saying, "Greetings, 'King of the Judeans'!" ³⁰And spitting on him, they took the stick and hit him on the head. ³¹And when they had made fun of him, they stripped off the cloak and put his own clothes back on him and led him out to crucify him.

³²**As they were going out**, they came across a Cyrenian named Simon. This man they conscripted to carry his cross.

³³And when they reached the place known as Golgotha (which means "Place of the Skull"), ³⁴they gave him a drink of wine mixed with gall, but once he tasted it, he didn't want to drink it. ³⁵After crucifying him, they divided up his clothes by casting lots. ³⁶And they sat down there and kept guard over him. ³⁷And over his head they put an inscription that identified his crime: "This is Jesus, the King of the Judeans."

³⁸Then they crucified two insurgents with him, one on his right and one on his left.

³⁹Those passing by kept taunting him, wagging their heads, and saying, ⁴⁰"You were going to destroy the temple and rebuild it in three days? Save yourself! If you're God's son, come down from the cross!"

⁴¹Likewise the chief priests made fun of him along with the scholars and elders; they were saying, ⁴²"He saved others, but he can't even save himself! He's the King of Israel; he should come down from the cross here and now and then

27:24
◊ Dt 21:6–9

27:25
◊ 2 Sm 1:16

27:27–31
//Mk 15:16–20,
Jn 19:1–3,
Pet 2:36–3:4

27:32
//Mk 15:21,
Lk 23:26

27:33–44
//Mk 15:22–32,
Lk 23:33–43,
Jn 19:17–24,
Pet 4:1–5

27:34
◊ Ps 69:21

27:35
◊ Ps 22:18

27:39–41
Ⓣ GSav 11:1

27:39
◊ Ps 22:7

27:40
Ⓣ Mt 26:61;
//Jn 2:19, Th 71

27:25 This cry by the crowd has been used to justify the pogroms against the Jews. But it should be noted that it only occurs in this gospel and so its historicity is highly doubtful. Moreover, if the original readers of Matthew's gospel were Jewish, they would also be implicating themselves in the death of Jesus.

27:26 Roman *flogging* was a brutal torture reserved for those condemned to death. Metal bits on the ends of whips could inflict horrible wounds.

27:28 *Crimson* is the color worn by a Roman soldier. Jesus, who entered Jerusalem as a king of peace and gentleness (21:5), is now clothed as a warrior.

27:32 *Cyrene* was a city in north Africa (modern Libya) that had a large Jewish population. They had a synagogue in Jerusalem.

27:34 *Gall* was a drug used to deaden the senses.

27:35 *Casting lots* involves either pebbles or sticks or straw.

we'll believe him. ⁴³He trusted God, so God should rescue him now if he cares about him. After all, he said, 'I'm God's son.'"

⁴⁴In the same way, the insurgents who were crucified with him were also insulting him.

⁴⁵**Beginning at noon** darkness blanketed the entire land until mid-afternoon. ⁴⁶And about three o'clock in the afternoon Jesus shouted at the top of his voice, "*Eli, Eli, lema sabachthani*" (which means, "My God, my God, why have you abandoned me?")

⁴⁷When some of those standing there heard this, they said, "This guy's calling Elijah!" ⁴⁸And right then one of them ran and took a sponge filled with sour wine and stuck it on a stick and offered him a drink.

⁴⁹But the rest were saying, "Wait! Let's see if Elijah comes to rescue him."

⁵⁰Jesus again shouted at the top of his voice and surrendered the spirit.

⁵¹**And suddenly the curtain** of the temple was torn in two from top to bottom, and the earth quaked, rocks were split apart, ⁵²and tombs were opened and many bodies of sleeping saints came back to life. ⁵³And they came out of the tombs after his resurrection and went into the holy city, where they appeared to many. ⁵⁴The Roman officer and those with him keeping watch over Jesus witnessed the sign and what had happened, and were terrified, and said, "This man really was God's son."

⁵⁵Many women were there observing from a distance—those who had followed Jesus from Galilee to minister to him, ⁵⁶among whom were Mary of Magdala, and Mary the mother of James and Joseph, and the mother of the sons of Zebedee.

⁵⁷**It was dark** when a rich man from Arimathea, by the name of Joseph, who himself was a follower of Jesus, showed up ⁵⁸and went to Pilate and requested the body of Jesus. Then Pilate ordered it to be turned over to him. ⁵⁹And taking the body, Joseph wrapped it in a clean linen shroud ⁶⁰and put it in his new tomb, which had been cut in the rock. He rolled a huge stone across the opening of the tomb and left. ⁶¹But Mary of Magdala and the other Mary stayed there, sitting across from the tomb.

⁶²**On the next day**, which is the day after preparation, the chief priests and the Pharisees met with Pilate. ⁶³"Your Excellency, we remember what that deceiver said while he was still alive: 'After three days I'm going to be raised up.' ⁶⁴So order the tomb sealed for three days so his disciples won't come and steal his body and tell everyone, 'He has been raised from the dead.' If that were to happen, the last deception will be worse than the first."

Jesus dies

Resurrection of Jewish saints

Joseph buries Jesus

The tomb is secured

27:43
◊ Ps 22:8

27:45–56
//Mk 15:33–41,
Lk 13:44–49,
Jn 19:25–37,
Pet 5:1–6

27:46
◊ Ps 22:1

27:48
◊ Ps 69:21

27:51
Cf. GNaz 10a;
◊ Ex 26:31

27:55–56
◊ Ps 38:11

27:57–61
//Mk 15:42–47,
Lk 23:50–56,
Jn 19:38–42

27:57–58
//Pet 2:1–3a

27:58
◊ Dt 21:22–23

27:59–60
//Pet 6:1–4

27:62–66
Cf. Pet 8:1–9:1

27:46 *Eli, Eli* is Hebrew; in Mark's version of this scene Jesus cries out in Aramaic (*Eloi, Eloi*). Matthew's alteration makes the word play on Elijah's name (*Elias*) easier in Greek.

27:51–52 *Earthquakes* and *the opening of tombs* are probably apocalyptic signs of the End Times.

[65]Pilate replied to them, "You have guards; go and secure it as you think best."

[66]They went and secured the tomb by sealing ⟨it with a⟩ stone and posting a guard.

28

After the sabbath, at first light on Sunday, Mary of Magdala and the other Mary came to inspect the tomb. [2]And just then there was a strong earthquake. You see, a messenger of the Lord had come down from the sky, arrived ⟨at the tomb⟩, rolled away the stone, and was sitting on it. [3]The messenger gave off a dazzling light and wore clothes as white as snow. [4]Now those who kept watch were quaking with fear and looked like corpses themselves.

[5]In response the messenger said to the women, "Don't be afraid! I know you are looking for Jesus who was crucified. [6]He is not here. You see, he was raised, just as he said. Come here; look at the spot where he was lying. [7]Go quickly and tell his disciples that he has been raised from the dead. Don't forget, he is going ahead of you to Galilee. There you will see him. That's what I came to tell you."

[8]**And they hurried away** from the tomb, afraid and filled with joy, and ran to tell his disciples.

[9]Just then Jesus met them and said, "Hello!"

They came up and grabbed his feet and paid him homage.

[10]Then Jesus says to them, "Don't be afraid. Go tell my friends so they can leave for Galilee, where they will see me."

[11]**While they were on their way**, some of the guards returned to the city and reported to the chief priests everything that had happened. [12]They met with the elders and hatched a plan. They bribed the soldiers with an adequate amount of money [13]and ordered them, "Tell everybody, 'His disciples came at night and stole his body while we were asleep.' [14]If the governor should hear about this, don't worry; we'll deal with him." [15]They took the money and did as they had been instructed. And this story has been passed around in the Jewish community until this very day.

[16]**The eleven disciples** went to the mountain in Galilee where Jesus had told them to go. [17]And when they saw him, they paid him homage; but some were dubious.

[18]And Jesus approached them and spoke these words: "All authority has been given to me in heaven and on earth. [19]You shall go and make disciples of all peoples, baptizing them in the name of the Father and the son and the holy spirit. [20]Teach them to observe everything I commanded you. I'll be with you day in and day out, as you'll see, until the culmination of the age."

27:66
◊Dn 6:17

28:1–8
//Mk 16:1–8,
Lk 24:1–11,
Jn 20:1–10,
Pet 12:1–13:3

28:18
ⓘ Mt 9:6, 11:27

28:19
ⓘ Mt 10:5–6

28:20
ⓘ Mt 1:23, 18:20

28:16 The disciples had been instructed by the messengers to go to Galilee but no *mountain* was mentioned.

28:19 *The Father and the son and the holy spirit* is the earliest Trinitarian formula in the New Testament.

The Gospel of Luke

Introduction

Introduction

Luke opens his two-volume narrative with a statement of his motive and purpose (1:1–4). Luke tactfully expresses dissatisfaction with previous narratives about Jesus and implies that his gospel will set the record straight and assure readers (addressed through Theophilus) of the integrity of their tradition. The Acts of the Apostles also begins with an address to Theophilus which refers to the gospel as "the first book." The author therefore intends both of his books to be read together (scholars usually refer to Luke's work as "Luke-Acts.")

The narrative

Luke-Acts comprises over one-fourth of the total text of the New Testament. Its sprawling narrative begins in Jerusalem before the birth of Jesus and ends with Paul preaching the gospel in Rome. It is nothing less than a story of the working out of God's plan to offer salvation to humankind. This salvation was anticipated by Israel, definitively announced by Jesus, and continues to be offered through the church. Luke-Acts carefully connects what God does in Jesus and through the church to the promises made to Israel through its prophets (examples are found at Luke 4:16–21; 18:31–34; 24:44–49; Acts 13:32–41; 26:22–23).

Luke sets the story of Jesus within this larger story. In Luke, unlike the other gospels, Jesus is not the prime mover of the narrative, though he is, of course, its central figure. Rather, it is God himself who determines the course of events in the story. Luke expresses this by describing certain events as predetermined (e.g., 2:25; 22:22; Acts 2:23; 4:27–28) or directed by the holy spirit (e.g., 3:22; 4:1, 14, 18; 12:12). Although God directs the story, he does so from "off-stage." God speaks directly only twice to certify the divine mandate of Jesus' mission (3:22 and 9:35).

Luke's portrait of Jesus

Those two divine interventions in the story underline the fundamental aspect of Luke's portrayal of Jesus: he is a prophet, a divinely commissioned agent who announces and promotes God's will for Israel. In Jesus' first public speech (4:16–30), he predicts that his mission will fulfill the words of the prophets and will meet the same reception as the prophets before him met.

Another central aspect of Luke's Jesus is his solicitude for the poor and the outcast. Jesus claims that his outreach to them constitutes his messianic credentials (7:18–22). Jesus congratulates them for belonging to God's empire (6:20–21), which he envisions as a great banquet full of the poor and the outcast (14:12–24). Conversely, Jesus warns often about the spiritual dangers of wealth (6:24–25; 8:11–15; 12:13–21; 16:13–15, 19–31; 18:18–25). Among the outcasts are sinners, to whom Jesus' mission is especially directed (5:32, 19:10). Jesus befriends "toll collectors and sinners" (5:30; 7:34; 15:1–2). He uses the despised toll collectors and Samaritans as examples of positive religious behavior (10:29–37; 17:11–19; 18:10–14; 19:2–10). Some of the more memorable passages in this gospel feature Jesus' compassion for sinners or his teaching about God's compassion for them (7:36–50; 15:1–7, 8–10, 11–32; 23:34, 39–43).

Tradition and sources

In his preface (1:1–4), Luke acknowledges that there already was a tradition of gospel writing before he began his project. Among the works to which he alludes, at least two served as his literary sources: the Gospel of Mark, from which Luke takes his narrative framework, and the Q Gospel, an important fund of teachings ascribed to Jesus. In addition, about one-third of the material in Luke's gospel has no known literary source (and so is called special Lukan material). Some of it is traditional (indeed a portion of it may well have originated with Jesus himself) and some of it is composed by Luke. Within the special Lukan material are some of the most famous teachings in the gospel tradition: the stories about Martha and Mary (10:38–39), the ten lepers (17:11–19), and Zacchaeus (19:1–10); and the parables: the Two Debtors (7:41–43), the Good Samaritan (10:29–37), the Prodigal Son (15:11–32), the Dishonest Manager (16:1–13), Lazarus and the Rich Man (16:19–31), and the Unjust Judge (18:1–8).

Structure

The gospel is not a tightly structured narrative. Luke derives his basic story outline from Mark:

1. John the Baptizer setting the stage for Jesus
2. Jesus' baptism, temptation, announcement of his message, and gathering of disciples
3. teaching and healing in Galilee
4. journey to Jerusalem, culminating in a symbolic action in the temple
5. preaching in the temple, culminating in an eschatological discourse

6. arrest, trial, and crucifixion

7. discovery of the empty tomb

Luke extends the Markan outline in both directions, adding stories of the birth and infancy of John and Jesus (chapters 1 and 2) and accounts of Jesus' resurrection appearances (chapter 24). Luke also greatly expands the journey to Jerusalem, making it a major vehicle for his exposition of Jesus' teachings. Often called the "Travel Narrative" (9:51–19:46), it contains most of the special Lukan material. It has minimal narrative structure and is almost entirely taken up with teaching.

Eschatology

In contrast to Mark, Luke downplays the belief in the imminence of the return of Jesus and the end of history. The first words of Mark's Jesus are, "The time is up: God's empire is arriving" (Mark 1: 15). The parallel verse in Luke merely reports that Jesus "taught in their meeting places" (4:15). Luke's Jesus corrects the idea that the empire of God is coming soon (19:11), pointing instead to its presence among believers (17:20–21). In 21:8 Jesus explicitly warns against those who declare that the End is near (contrast the parallel Mark 13:6).

Luke's audience

Luke shows a strong interest in the universalism of the Christian message. Jesus' offer of salvation comes first to Israel, but is meant for the whole world (2:30–32; 3:6; 13:28–29). Acts tells how and why the gospel spread beyond Israel to all peoples.

Luke's writing shows sensitivity for a gentile audience. He regularly translates or omits Aramaic terms in his sources, and often substitutes Greek names for Semitic ones. He omits Mark's story about the Syro-Phoenician woman (Mark 7:24–30), the one story most likely to offend gentiles. He depicts Jesus freely interacting with non-Jews and using them as positive examples in his teaching (4:25, 27; 7:1–10; 10:29–37; 17:11–19).

Luke presents Jesus so as to be intelligible to Greco-Roman readers. He sets Jesus' birth in the context of world history (2:1) and traces his genealogy (3:23–38) all the way to Adam (not simply to the Jewish progenitor Abraham, as in the genealogy offered by Matthew). Although Luke affirms that Jesus is the Jewish Messiah foretold in the scriptures (e.g., 4:21), Luke is the only synoptic writer to present Jesus also as a "savior" (2:11; Acts 3:13–15), a Hellenistic title for divine deliverers.

Luke's doubts about the imminence of Jesus' return and his emphasis on universalism point to his concept of the Christian movement (which is called "the Way" in Acts) as both international in membership and indefinite in duration. In this light, Luke-Acts can be seen as a charter document for a church taking stock for the long haul: showing it how to understand its past (its Jewish roots) and how to live in an open-ended present, by following the teachings of Jesus (presented in the gospel) as modeled by the earliest disciples (in Acts), and by a continual openness to the guidance of God's holy spirit.

"And behold, it came to pass"

The Greek phrase *kai egeneto* (or its equivalent *egeneto de*) is a distinctive feature of Luke's storytelling style. It occurs nearly fifty times in his gospel, but only eight times in the other three gospels combined. *Kai egeneto / egeneto de* means something like "and it happened." Luke picked up the expression from the Septuagint (the Greek translation of the Old Testament), where it is ubiquitous. By generously salting his own narrative with this phrase, Luke was deliberately using an old-fashioned expression that would sound "biblical," so as to offer his audience frequent reminders that what they were hearing from him was a sacred story like those in their Bible.

The King James Version consistently renders *kai egeneto* with "And it came to pass." Most modern English translations, by contrast, either translate the phrase in a number of different ways or simply omit it. But neither of those strategies allows modern readers to hear Luke's imitation of Old Testament style. "It came to pass" might have been ordinary spoken English in King James's time, but today people no longer use that expression unless they are trying to imitate King James English. And it is precisely this archaic, and recognizably "biblical," quality that makes "it came to pass" an apt usage in a contemporary translation. SV's reaching back to the King James Version is deliberately analogous to Luke's reaching back to the Septuagint for language that was recognizably biblical to the audience of his day.

SV's "and behold" is another reversion to King James English. The Greek phrase *kai idou*, like its Lukan cousin *kai egeneto*, is a stylistic element of the Greek Old Testament that Luke sprinkles into his story to give it a scriptural sound. *Kai idou* occurs ten times in Luke's infancy narrative (Luke 1–2), a set piece designed to evoke the sound and atmosphere of the Greek Bible in use among Jews of his day. The action begins and ends in the temple, the characters are personifications of Israel's faith and piety, and the lyrical canticles would be at home in the Book of Psalms. In these two chapters SV translates *kai idou* with "and behold," a recognizably "biblical" piece of archaic English, so as to enhance the Old Testament atmosphere of Luke's infancy narrative.

The Gospel of Luke

1 **Since so many** have undertaken to compile an orderly narrative of the events that have run their course among us, ²just as the original eyewitnesses and ministers of the word transmitted them to us, ³it seemed good that I too, after thoroughly researching everything from the beginning, should set them systematically in writing for you, Theophilus, ⁴so that Your Excellency may realize the reliability of the teachings in which you have been instructed.

⁵**In the days of Herod**, king of Judea, there was this priest named Zechariah, who belonged to the priestly clan of Abijah. His wife, a descendant of Aaron, was named Elizabeth. ⁶They were both virtuous in the sight of God, obediently following all the commandments and ordinances of the Lord. ⁷But they had no children because Elizabeth was infertile, and both were well along in years. ⁸While he was serving as priest before God when his priestly clan was on temple duty, it came to pass ⁹that he was chosen by lot, according to the custom of the priesthood, to enter the sanctuary of the Lord and offer incense.

¹⁰At the hour of incense, while the whole congregation of the people was praying outside, ¹¹there appeared to him a messenger of the Lord standing to the right of the altar of incense. ¹²When he saw him, Zechariah was shaken and overcome by fear. ¹³But the heavenly messenger said to him, "Don't be afraid, Zechariah, for your prayer has been heard, and your wife Elizabeth will bear you a son, and you shall name him John. ¹⁴And you will be joyful and elated, and many will rejoice at his birth, ¹⁵because he will be great in the sight of the Lord. He will drink no wine or beer, and he will be filled with holy spirit from the very day of his birth. ¹⁶And he will cause many of the children of Israel to turn to the Lord their God. ¹⁷He will precede him in the spirit and power of Elijah. He will turn the hearts of the parents back towards their children, and the disobedient back towards the wisdom of the just, and will make people ready for their Lord."

¹⁸But Zechariah said to the heavenly messenger, "How can I be sure of this? For I'm an old man and my wife is well along in years."

Prologue

John's birth predicted

1:1–4
① Acts 1:1–2
1:5
Cf. GEbi 1:1–2
1:13
◊Gn 17:19, Jgs 13:2–5
1:15
◊Nm 6:1–4
1:16–17
◊Mal 4:5–6, Sir 48:10
1:18
◊Gn 15:8, 18:11

1:1–4 Luke prefaces his gospel in the style of an ancient historian, referring to previous narratives on the subject and asserting how his will be better. The gospel is dedicated to *Theophilus*, of whom we have no historical information. He was probably Luke's patron.

1:5 *Herod* the Great ruled 37–4 BCE.

1:8 Priests were divided into 24 *clans*, each clan serving in the temple twice a year for one week.

1:8 *It came to pass* (*kai egeneto*) is a deliberate imitation of the style of the LXX. Its frequent use is meant to make the Gospel sound like the Jewish Bible (see the essay on p. 124). Most modern English translations omit this phrase.

1:15 Abstention from alcohol was a mark of special consecration to God practiced by Nazirites (Num 6:14). The LXX describes Samuel as "drinking no wine or liquor" (1 Sam 1:11).

[19]And the messenger answered him, "I am Gabriel, the one who stands in the presence of God. I was sent to speak to you and bring you this good news. [20]And behold, you will be struck silent and speechless until the day these things happen, because you did not trust my words, which will be fulfilled at the appropriate time."

[21]Meanwhile, the people were waiting for Zechariah, wondering why he was taking so long in the sanctuary. [22]And when he did come out and was unable to speak to them, they realized that he had seen a vision inside. And he kept making signs to them, since he could not speak. [23]And it came to pass, when his time of official service was completed, that he went back home.

[24]Afterwards, his wife Elizabeth conceived, and went into seclusion for five months, telling herself, [25]"This is how the Lord has seen fit to deal with me in his good time in taking away my disgrace."

[26]**In the sixth month** the heavenly messenger Gabriel was sent from God to a town in Galilee called Nazareth, [27]to a girl betrothed to a man named Joseph, of the house of David. The girl's name was Mary. [28]He entered and said to her, "Greetings, highly favored one! The Lord is with you."

[29]But she was shaken by these words and wondered what this greeting could mean.

[30]The heavenly messenger said to her, "Don't be afraid, Mary. You see, you have found favor with God. [31]And behold, you will conceive in your womb and give birth to a son, and you will name him Jesus. [32]He will be great and will be called son of the Most High. And the Lord God will give him the throne of David, his father. [33]He will rule over the house of Jacob forever, and his dominion will have no end."

[34]And Mary said to the messenger, "How can this be, since I'm still a virgin?"

[35]The messenger replied, "The holy spirit will hover over you, and the power of the Most High will cast its shadow on you. This is why the child to be born will be holy, and be called son of God. [36]And behold, your relative Elizabeth has also conceived a son in her old age. She who was said to be infertile is already six months along, [37]since nothing is impossible for God."

1:25
◊ Gn 30:23

1:28
◊ Jdt 13:18

1:31
Cf. Mt 1:21–23;
◊ Is 7:14

1:32–33
Ⓣ Acts 2:30, 13:23;
◊ 2 Sm 7:12–16,
Is 9:6–7

1:37
◊ Gn 18:14 (LXX)

1:28 Some mss add "Blessed are you among women" to the end of the verse.

1:25 *my disgrace*: Infertility was interpreted as a sign of God's disapproval.
1:26 *In the sixth month*: of Elizabeth's pregnancy.
1:32 It is unclear how Jesus can be descended from David if Joseph is not his father. The only information on Mary's lineage is that she is a relative of Elizabeth, a descendant of Aaron (1:5, 36).

1:34–35 Mary's question is a strange one: nothing Gabriel said (v. 31) hints that the conception will occur out of wedlock. Luke adds this artificial dialogue to ensure that his audience grasps the miraculous quality of Mary's conception.

³⁸And Mary said, "Behold the Lord's slave. I pray that all you've told me comes true." Then the heavenly messenger left her.

³⁹**At that time** Mary set out in haste for a town in the hill country of Judea, ⁴⁰where she entered Zechariah's house and greeted Elizabeth. ⁴¹And it came to pass, when Elizabeth heard Mary's greeting, that the baby jumped in her womb. Elizabeth was filled with holy spirit ⁴²and proclaimed at the top of her voice, "Blessed are you among women, and blessed is the fruit of your womb! ⁴³Who am I that the mother of my master should visit me? ⁴⁴For behold, when the sound of your greeting reached my ears, the baby jumped for joy in my womb. ⁴⁵Congratulations to her who trusted that what the Lord promised her would come true."

⁴⁶And Mary said,

> My soul extols the Lord,
>   ⁴⁷and my spirit rejoices in God my savior,
> ⁴⁸for he has taken notice of the low status of his slave girl.
>   So behold, from now on every generation will congratulate me.
> ⁴⁹The Mighty One has done great things for me,
>   and holy is his name,
> ⁵⁰and his mercy will come to generation after generation
>   of those who fear him.
> ⁵¹He has shown the strength of his arm,
>   he has routed the arrogant, along with their private schemes;
> ⁵²he has pulled the mighty down from their thrones,
>   and exalted the lowly;
> ⁵³he has filled the hungry with good things,
>   and sent the rich away empty.
> ⁵⁴He has come to the aid of his servant Israel,
>   remembering his mercy,
> ⁵⁵as he spoke to our ancestors,
>   to Abraham and to his descendants forever.

⁵⁶And Mary stayed with her about three months, and then returned home.

⁵⁷**The time came** for Elizabeth to give birth and she had a son. ⁵⁸Her neighbors and relatives heard that the Lord had shown her great mercy, and they rejoiced with her. ⁵⁹And so it came to pass on the eighth day that they came to circumcise the child; and they were going to name him Zechariah after his father. ⁶⁰His mother spoke up and said, "No; he is to be called John."

1:46–55
◊1 Sm 2:1–10
1:47
◊Hab 3:18
1:48
◊1 Sm 1:11
1:49
◊Dt 10:21, Ps 111:9
1:50
◊Ps 103:17
1:51–52
◊2 Sm 22:28
1:52
◊1 Sm 2:4, 7;
Sir 10:14; Job 5:11,
12:19
1:53
◊Ps 107:9, 2 Sm 2:5,
Job 22:9
1:54
◊Is 41:8–9, Ps 98:3
1:55
◊Mi 7:20, 2
Sm 22:51
1:59
◊Lv 12:3

1:43–44 Elizabeth's possession of holy spirit enables her, and even her unborn son, to recognize the spiritual status of Mary's child.

Birth of Jesus

⁶¹But they said to her, "No one in your family has this name." ⁶²So they made signs to his father, asking what he would like him to be called.

⁶³He asked for a writing tablet and to everyone's astonishment he wrote, "His name is John." ⁶⁴And immediately his mouth was opened and his tongue loosened, and he began to speak, blessing God.

⁶⁵All their neighbors became fearful, and all these things were talked about throughout the entire hill country of Judea. ⁶⁶And all who heard about these things took them to heart and wondered, "Now what is this child going to be?" (You see, the hand of the Lord was with him.)

⁶⁷Then his father Zechariah was filled with holy spirit and prophesied:

⁶⁸Blessed be the Lord, the God of Israel,
    for he has visited and ransomed his people.
⁶⁹He has raised up for us a horn of salvation
    in the house of David his servant.
⁷⁰This is what he promised in the words of his holy prophets of old:
    ⁷¹deliverance from our enemies,
    and from the hands of all who hate us;
    ⁷²mercy to our ancestors,
    and the remembrance of his holy covenant.
⁷³This is the oath he swore to Abraham our ancestor:
    ⁷⁴to grant that we be rescued from the hands of our enemies,
    to serve him without fear,
    ⁷⁵in holiness and righteousness before him all our days.
⁷⁶And you, child, will be called a prophet of the Most High;
    for you will go before the Lord to prepare his way,
⁷⁷to give his people knowledge of salvation
    through the forgiveness of their sins.
⁷⁸In the heartfelt mercy of our God,
    the dawn from on high will visit us,
⁷⁹to shine on those sitting in darkness,
    in the shadow of death,
    to guide our feet to the way of peace.

1:68
◊ Ps 41:13

1:69
◊ Ps 18:2

1:71
◊ Ps 106:10

1:72
◊ Ps 105:8, 106:45

1:73
◊ Mi 7:20, Gn 26:3

1:75
◊ Jos 24:14, Is 38:20

1:76
◊ Is 40:3, Mal 3:1

1:78
◊ Is 9:2

1:79
◊ Ps 107:10, Is 59:8

⁸⁰And the child grew up and became strong in spirit. He was in the desert until the day of his public appearance to Israel.

2 **In those days** it came to pass that a decree was issued by Caesar Augustus that a census be taken of the whole civilized world. (²This first census was taken

---

1:69 *horn*: a symbol of strength (see, e.g., Ps 89:17 and 92:10).
2:1 This census is attested nowhere else in ancient sources.

2:2 *Quirinius* was governor of Syria in 6–7 CE. The problem of how to reconcile the chronology of 2:2 with 1:5 (Herod died in 4 BCE) has defied solution.

while Quirinius was governor of Syria.) ³Everybody had to travel to his own town to be counted in the census. ⁴So Joseph too went up from Galilee, from the town of Nazareth, to Judea, to the town of David called Bethlehem, because he was a descendant of David, ⁵to be counted in the census with Mary, to whom he was betrothed. (Mary was pregnant.) ⁶It came to pass while they were there that the time came for her to give birth, ⁷and she gave birth to a son, her firstborn. She wrapped him in strips of cloth and laid him in a feeding trough, because the travelers' shelter had no place for them.

⁸**Now in the same area** there were shepherds living outdoors. They were keeping watch over their sheep at night, ⁹when a messenger of the Lord stood near them and the glory of the Lord shone around them. They became terrified, ¹⁰but the messenger said to them, "Don't be afraid; for behold, I bring you good news of a great joy, which is to benefit the whole nation. ¹¹Today in the city of David, the Savior was born to you—he is the Anointed One, the Lord. ¹²And this will be a sign for you: you will find a baby wrapped in strips of cloth and lying in a feeding trough."

¹³And suddenly there appeared with the messenger a whole troop of the heavenly army praising God:

> ¹⁴Glory to God in the highest ⟨heaven⟩,
> and on earth peace among those God favors!

¹⁵And it came to pass, when the messengers left and returned to heaven, that the shepherds said to one another, "Come on! Let's go over to Bethlehem and see what's happened, the event the Lord has told us about." ¹⁶And they hurried away, and found Mary and Joseph, and the baby lying in a feeding trough. ¹⁷And when they saw it they reported what they had been told about this child. ¹⁸Everyone who listened was astonished at what the shepherds told them. ¹⁹But Mary took all this in and reflected on it. ²⁰And the shepherds returned, glorifying and praising God for all they had heard and seen; everything turned out just as they had been told.

²¹**Now eight days later**, when the time came to circumcise him, they gave him the name Jesus, the name assigned him by the heavenly messenger before he was conceived in the womb.

2:14 Some mss read "peace, good will among people."

2:10
//GSav 13:12

2:11
◊2 Sm 5:7, 9 (LXX)

2:15–20
Cf. Mt 2:1–12

2:19
Ⓓ Lk 2:51

2:3–4 This procedure for a census is unattested in ancient sources and would have been an administrative and logistical nightmare.

2:7 The *travelers' shelter* was an inn surrounding a courtyard where caravans rested at night.

2:11 In the ancient world the term *Savior* was primarily a political title and was frequently applied to Roman emperors. The title is surprisingly rare in the gospels (only here, Luke 1:47, and John 4:42).

2:13 *heavenly army*: OT terminology for the supernatural beings who serve in Yahweh's heavenly court and who wage war against his enemies.

Presentation of
Jesus

²²**Now when the time came** for their purification according to the Law of Moses, they brought him up to Jerusalem to present him to the Lord—²³as it is written in the Law of the Lord, "Every male that opens the womb is to be considered holy to the Lord"—²⁴and to offer sacrifice according to what is dictated in the Law of the Lord: "A pair of turtledoves or two fledgling doves."

²⁵And behold, there was a man in Jerusalem, named Simeon, a virtuous and devout man who was waiting for the consolation of Israel, and the holy spirit was with him. ²⁶It had been disclosed to him by the holy spirit that he would not see death before he had laid eyes on the Lord's Anointed One. ²⁷And so he was guided by the spirit to the temple area. When the parents brought in the child Jesus, to perform for him what was customary according to the Law, ²⁸he took him in his arms and blessed God:

> ²⁹Now, Master, now is the time to dismiss your slave in peace,
>> since you have honored your word.
> ³⁰For my eyes have seen your salvation,
>> ³¹which you have prepared in the sight of all the peoples,
> ³²enlightenment for the gentiles
>> and splendor for your people Israel.

³³His father and mother were astonished at what was being said about him. ³⁴Then Simeon blessed them and said to Mary his mother,

> Behold, this child is linked to the fall and rise of many in Israel,
>> and is destined to be a sign that is rejected.
> ³⁵You too will have your heart broken,
>> and the schemes of many minds will be exposed.

³⁶A prophetess was also there, Anna, daughter of Phanuel, of the tribe of Asher. She was well along in years, since she had married as a young girl and lived with her husband for seven years, ³⁷and then alone as a widow until she was eighty-four. She never left the temple area, and she worshiped day and night with fasting and prayer. ³⁸Coming on the scene at that very moment, she gave thanks to God, and began to speak about the child to all who were waiting for the liberation of Jerusalem.

³⁹And when they had carried out everything required by the Law of the Lord, they returned to Galilee, to Nazareth, their hometown. ⁴⁰And the boy

2:22
◊ Lv 12:6

2:23
◊ Ex 13:2, 12, 15

2:24
◊ Lv 12:8

2:30
◊ Is 40:5

2:31
◊ Is 52:10

2:32
Ⓣ Acts 13:47, 26:23;
◊ Is 49:6

2:40
Ⓣ Lk 1:80
Ⓓ Lk 2:52

2:22 *Their* refers grammatically to Mary and Joseph. Lev 12:2–8 prescribes a ritual purification for a mother forty days after childbirth. There is no known ritual which involved the purification of both parents.
2:22–23 Such a custom of presenting a firstborn to God in the temple is unknown in Jewish tradition.

2:23 The Law (Num 3:47–48) required a firstborn son to be redeemed by payment of a fee, about which Luke is silent.
2:24 This is part of the maternal purification ritual.
2:39 *everything required by the law:* Luke emphasizes the Jewish piety of Jesus' parents.

grew up and became strong, and was filled with wisdom; and God regarded him favorably.

Jesus in the temple at twelve

A voice in the desert

⁴¹**Now his parents** used to go to Jerusalem every year for the Passover festival. ⁴²And when he was twelve years old, they went up for the festival as usual. ⁴³When the festival was over and they were returning home, the young Jesus stayed behind in Jerusalem, without his parents knowing about it. ⁴⁴Assuming that he was in the traveling party, they went a day's journey, and then began to look for him among their relatives and acquaintances. ⁴⁵When they did not find him, they returned to Jerusalem to search for him.

⁴⁶And after three days it came to pass that they found him in the temple area, sitting among the teachers, listening to them and asking them questions. ⁴⁷Everyone who listened to him was astounded at his understanding and his responses.

⁴⁸And when ⟨his parents⟩ saw him they were overwhelmed. "Child," his mother said to him, "why have you done this to us? Behold, your father and I have been worried sick looking for you."

⁴⁹"Why were you looking for me?" he said to them. "Don't you know that I'm destined to do my Father's business?"

⁵⁰But they did not understand what he was talking about. ⁵¹Then he returned with them to Nazareth, and was obedient to them. His mother took careful note of all these things. ⁵²And Jesus, precocious as he was, continued to excel in wisdom and to gain respect in the eyes of God and the people.

3 **In the fifteenth year** of the rule of Tiberius Caesar, when Pontius Pilate was governor of Judea, Herod tetrarch of Galilee, his brother Philip tetrarch of the district of Iturea and Trachonitis, and Lysanias tetrarch of Abilene, ²while Annas and Caiaphas were chief priests, the word of God came to John, son of Zechariah, in the desert. ³And he went into the whole region around the Jordan, calling for baptism and a change of heart that lead to forgiveness of sins. ⁴As is written in the book of the sayings of Isaiah the prophet,

> The voice of someone shouting in the desert:
> "Make ready the way of the Lord,
>   make his paths straight.

2:51
Ⓓ Lk 2:19
2:52
Ⓓ Lk 2:40;
◊ 1 Sm 2:26
3:1–17
//Mk 1:2–8,
Mt 3:1–12,
Jn 1:19–28
3:1–3
cf. GEbi 1
3:3
Ⓣ Acts 2:38, 13:24;
GHeb 2:1; GNaz 2:1
3:4–6
◊ Is 40:3–5
3:4
Ⓘ Lk 1:76

2:41–49 Luke follows the convention of Hellenistic biographies by including an incident from the boy's childhood that portends his future greatness.
2:49 *destined*: this term signals that Jesus' whole life is guided by divine Providence.
3:1 *The fifteenth year of Tiberius* probably points to 28 or 29 CE. This synchronizes with the reign of the other rulers, though nothing is known about *Lysanius*.

Herod: Antipas, son of Herod the Great (1:5).
3:2 There was only one *chief priest* at a time. Perhaps it was customary for former chief priests (Annas was deposed in 15 CE) to retain their title.
The word of God came to . . . is an OT phrase denoting a divine call to prophecy (see Isa 38:4; Jer 1:1; 13:3). Luke identifies John as a prophet in 1:76 and 7:26.

Jesus is baptized

⁵Every valley will be filled,
>   and every mountain and hill leveled.
What is crooked will be made straight,
>   and the rough ways smooth.
⁶Then the whole human race will see the salvation of God."

⁷So John would say to the crowds that came out to get baptized by him, "You spawn of Satan! Who warned you to flee from the impending doom? ⁸Well then, start producing fruits suitable for a change of heart, and don't even start saying to yourselves, 'We have Abraham for our father.' Let me tell you, God can raise up children for Abraham right out of these rocks! ⁹Even now the axe is aimed at the root of the trees. So every tree not producing choice fruit gets cut down and tossed into the fire."

¹⁰The crowds would ask him, "So what should we do?"

¹¹And he would answer them, "Whoever has two shirts should share with someone who has none; whoever has food should do the same." ¹²Toll collectors also came to get baptized, and they would ask him, "Teacher, what should we do?" ¹³He told them, "Charge nothing above the official rates." ¹⁴Soldiers also asked him, "And what about us?" And he said to them, "No more shakedowns! No more frame-ups either! And be satisfied with your pay."

¹⁵The people were filled with expectation and everyone was trying to figure out whether John might be the Anointed One.

¹⁶John's answer was the same to everyone: "I baptize you with water; but someone more powerful than I is coming. I'm not fit to untie his sandal straps. He'll baptize you with holy spirit and fire. ¹⁷His pitchfork is in his hand, to make a clean sweep of his threshing floor and to gather the wheat into his granary, but the chaff he'll burn in a fire that can't be put out."

¹⁸And so, with many other exhortations he preached to the people. ¹⁹But Herod the tetrarch, who had been denounced by John over the matter of Herodias, his brother's wife, ²⁰topped off all his other crimes by shutting John up in prison.

²¹**And it came to pass** when all the people were baptized, and after Jesus had been baptized and while he was praying, that the sky opened up, ²²and the holy

---

Q3:7–9
//Mt 3:7–10;
Ⓣ SJas 6:28–30

3:7
//Mt 23:33

3:8
Cf. Jn 8:39

3:9
//Mt 7:19

Q3:16–17
//Mt 3:11–12

3:16
Ⓣ Acts 1:5, 11:16, 13:25, 19:1–7

3:19–20
//Mk 6:17–18, Mt 14:3–4

Q3:21–22
//Mk 1:9–11, Mt3:13–17, Jn 1:32–34, GHeb 3, GEbi 4

3:16 Untying sandal straps was the task of a slave.

3:19 A *tetrarch* was a client ruler of a minor state in the Roman Empire.

Herod left his first wife to marry the wife of his half-brother. Such a marriage violates the Law (Lev 18:16).

3:20–21 Luke puts John's imprisonment before Jesus' baptism, reversing the Markan order of events. Thus Jesus is baptized, but apparently not by John. This contradicts

not only the other gospels, but Luke's own resumé of Jesus' career in Acts 1:21–22. Luke's probable motive for this unusual sequencing of events is to remove John from the scene before Jesus appears in public, thus clearly demarcating their careers. (See also Luke 16:16 and Acts 13:25.)

3:21 Luke often portrays Jesus *praying* at significant moments in his life (6:12; 9:18, 28; 11:2; 22:32, 41; 23:46).

spirit came down on him in bodily form like a dove, and a voice came from the sky, "You are my son; today I have fathered you."

²³**Jesus was about thirty** years old when he began his work. He was (supposedly) the son of Joseph, son of Eli, ²⁴son of Maththat, son of Levi, son of Melchi, son of Jannai, son of Joseph, ²⁵son of Mattathiah, son of Amos, son of Nahum, son of Hesli, son of Naggai, ²⁶son of Maath, son of Mattathiah, son of Semein, son of Josech, son of Joda, ²⁷son of Johanan, son of Rhesa, son of Zerubbabel, son of Shealtiel, son of Neri, ²⁸son of Melchi, son of Addi, son of Kosam, son of Elmadam, son of Er, ²⁹son of Jesus, son of Eliezer, son of Jorim, son of Maththat, son of Levi, ³⁰son of Simeon, son of Judah, son of Joseph, son of Jonam, son of Eliakim, ³¹son of Melea, son of Menna, son of Mattatha, son of Nathan, son of David, ³²son of Jesse, son of Obed, son of Boaz, son of Sala, son of Nahshon, ³³son of Amminadab, son of Admin, son of Arni, son of Hezron, son of Perez, son of Judah, ³⁴son of Jacob, son of Isaac, son of Abraham, son of Terah, son of Nahor, ³⁵son of Serug, son of Reu, son of Peleg, son of Eber, son of Shelah, ³⁶son of Kenan, son of Arphachshad, son of Shem, son of Noah, son of Lamech, ³⁷son of Methuselah, son of Enoch, son of Jared, son of Mahalalel, son of Kenan, ³⁸son of Enos, son of Seth, son of Adam, son of God.

4 **Jesus departed** from the Jordan full of holy spirit and was guided by the spirit into the desert, ²where he was put to the test by the devil for 'forty days.' He ate nothing that whole time; and when it was all over, he was famished.

³The devil said to him, "To prove you're God's son, order this stone to turn into bread."

⁴Jesus responded to him, "It is written,

> Human beings shall not live on bread alone."

⁵Then he took Jesus up, and in an instant of time showed him all the empires of the civilized world. ⁶The devil said to him, "I'll give you authority over all this and the glory that comes with it; it has been turned over to me, and I can give it to anyone I want. ⁷So, if you will pay homage to me, it will all be yours."

⁸Jesus responded, "It is written,

> You shall pay homage to the Lord your God, and him alone shall you revere."

3:22
//GEbi 4:3–4;
Ⓣ Lk 9:35;
◊Ps 2:7, Is 42:1

3:23–38
//Mt 1:1–17

3:23
Cf. GEbi 2:1

3:27–34
◊1 Chr 1–3

3:34–38
◊Gn 5:1–32,
11:10–26

Q4:1–13
//Mt 4:1–11;
cf. GHeb 4

4:1–2
//Mk 1:12–13

4:4
◊Dt 8:3

4:8
◊Dt 6:13

3:22 Most mss read "You are my son, the one I love—I fully approve of you" (as in Mark 1:11).

3:24–38 This genealogy lists 77 names from Adam to Jesus and cannot be reconciled with the genealogy in Matthew 1. The names between Joseph (v. 23) and Zerubbabel (v. 27) are otherwise unknown.

4:2 *Forty days and forty nights* recalls Moses' time with God on Mount Sinai (Exod 24:18) and Elijah's period of fasting

(1 Kgs 19:8).

4:3–13 Jesus refutes the devil's temptations by quoting scripture, refusing to fall for the devil's ability to twist its meaning (vv. 10–11). The passages Jesus quotes in v. 8 and v. 12 show that he submits to God, validating the status conferred on him at his baptism (3:21–22).

⁹Then he took him to Jerusalem, set him on the high point of the temple, and said to him, "To prove you're God's son, jump off from here; ¹⁰remember, it is written,

> To his heavenly messengers he will give orders about you,
>> to protect you,

¹¹and

> With their hands they will catch you,
>> so you won't even stub your toe on a stone."

¹²And in response Jesus said to him, "It is said,

> You shall not put the Lord your God to the test."

¹³So when the devil had tried every kind of test, he let him alone, for the time being.

¹⁴**Then Jesus returned** in the power of the spirit to Galilee. News about him spread throughout all the surrounding area. ¹⁵He used to teach in their meeting places and was acclaimed by everyone.

¹⁶**When he came to Nazareth**, where he had been brought up, he went to the meeting place on the Sabbath, as was his custom. He stood up to do the reading ¹⁷and was handed the scroll of the prophet Isaiah. He unrolled the scroll and found the place where it was written:

> ¹⁸The spirit of the Lord is upon me,
>> because he has anointed me
>> to bring good news to the poor.
> He has sent me to announce pardon for prisoners
>> and recovery of sight to the blind;
>> to set free the oppressed,
> ¹⁹to proclaim the year of the Lord's amnesty.

²⁰After rolling up the scroll, he gave it back to the attendant, and sat down; and the attention of everyone in the meeting place was riveted on him.

²¹He began by saying to them, "Today this scripture has been fulfilled as you listen."

²²And they all were responding favorably to him, and marveling at the pleasing speech that he delivered; and they were saying, "Isn't this the son of Joseph?"

²³And he said to them, "No doubt you will quote me that proverb, 'Doctor, cure yourself,' and you'll tell me, 'Do here in your hometown what we've heard you've done in Capernaum.'"

4:10–11
◊Ps 91:11–12

4:12
◊Dt 6:16

4:14–15
//Mk 1:14–15,
Mt 4:12–17

4:16–30
Cf. Mk 6:1–6,
Mt 13:53–58

4:18–19
◊Is 61:1–2

4:18
Ⓣ Lk 7:22

4:13 *for the time being* (*kairos*): until 22:3, 31–32.
4:23–24 Jesus' confrontational response is odd in light of his audience's approving reception of his message (v. 22).
  In Mark this scene (6:1–6) occurs after the miracles at Capernaum. By relocating this scene to the beginning of Jesus' public ministry, Luke creates an inconsistency in his narrative, for Jesus has not yet been to Capernaum. Luke narrates his feats there at 4:31–34 and 7:1–10.

²⁴Then he said, "Let me tell you, no prophet is welcome on his home turf. ²⁵I can assure you, there were many widows in Israel in Elijah's time, when the sky was dammed up for three and a half years, and a severe famine swept through the land. ²⁶Yet Elijah was not sent to any of them, but instead to a widow in Zarephath near Sidon. ²⁷There were also many lepers in Israel in the prophet Elisha's time; but none of them was made clean, except Naaman the Syrian."

²⁸Everyone in the meeting place was filled with rage when they heard this. ²⁹They rose up, ran him out of town, and led him to the brow of the hill on which their town was built, intending to hurl him over the cliff. ³⁰But he slipped through their fingers and got away.

³¹**He went down** to Capernaum, a town in Galilee, and he would teach them on the Sabbath. ³²They were astonished at his teaching because his message carried authority.

³³Now in the meeting place there was a man who was possessed by the spirit of an unclean demon, which screamed at the top of its voice, ³⁴"Hey Jesus! What do you want with us, you Nazarene? Have you come to destroy us? I know who you are: God's holy man."

³⁵But Jesus yelled at it, "Shut up and get out of him!"

Then the demon threw the man down in full view of everyone and came out of him without doing him any harm. ³⁶And so amazement came over them all and they were saying to one another, "What kind of message is this? With authority and power he gives orders to unclean spirits, and they leave." ³⁷So rumors about him began to spread to every corner of the surrounding region.

³⁸**He got up** from the meeting place and entered the house of Simon. Simon's mother-in-law was suffering from a high fever, and they made an appeal to him on her behalf. ³⁹He stood over her, rebuked the fever, and it disappeared. She immediately got up and started looking after them.

⁴⁰**As the sun was setting**, all those who had people sick with various diseases brought them to him. He would lay his hands on each one of them and cure them. ⁴¹Demons would also come out of many of them screaming, and saying, "You son of God, you!" But he would rebuke them and not allow them to speak, because they knew that he was the Anointed One.

⁴²The next morning he went outside and withdrew to an isolated place. Then the crowds came looking for him, and when they got to him they tried to keep him from leaving them. ⁴³He said to them, "I have to tell the good news of the

An unclean spirit expelled

Jesus heals Peter's mother-in-law

At day's end

4:24
//Jn 4:44, Th 31

4:25–26
◊ 1 Kgs 17:1–16

4:27
◊ 2 Kgs 5:1–14

4:31–37
//Mk 1:21–28

4:32
Cf. Mt 7:28–29

4:38–39
//Mk 1:29–31, Mt 8:14–15

4:40–41
//Mk 1:32–34, Mt 8:16–17

4:42–44
//Mk 1:35–39, Mt 4:23–25; cf. Acts 10:36–38

4:28–29 Their murderous rage seems highly contrived. Luke surely intends this unrealistic scene to anticipate Jesus' rejection by his own people and his death at their hands. That Luke holds the Jewish people responsible for Jesus' death is clear, for example, in Acts 3:15 (see how Peter iden- tifies his audience in Acts 3:12).

Nazareth is not built on or near a cliff face. Luke generally seems poorly informed about Palestinian geography. Aspects of his geography may therefore be fictive.

Fishing for people

Jesus cures a leper

Paralyzed person forgiven

empire of God to the other towns as well; after all, that's why I was sent." [44]And he continued to preach in the meeting places of Judea.

5 **It came to pass**, when the crowd pressed him to hear the word of God, that he was standing by Lake Gennesaret. [2]He noticed two boats moored there at the shore; the fishermen had left them and were washing their nets. [3]He got into one of the boats, the one belonging to Simon, and asked him to put out a little from the shore. Then he sat down and began to teach the crowds from the boat.

[4]When he had finished speaking, he said to Simon, "Put out into deep water and lower your nets for a catch."

[5]But Simon replied, "Master, we've been hard at it all night and haven't caught a thing. But if you insist, I'll lower the nets."

[6]So they did and netted such a huge number of fish that their nets began to tear apart. [7]They signaled to their partners in the other boat to come and lend a hand. They came and loaded both boats until they nearly sank.

[8]At the sight of this, Simon Peter fell to his knees in front of Jesus and said, "Get away from me, Master; I'm a sinful man." [9](You see, he and his companions were stunned at the catch of fish they had taken, [10]as were James and John, sons of Zebedee and partners of Simon.)

Jesus said to Simon, "Don't be afraid; from now on you'll be catching people." [11]They then brought their boats to shore, abandoned everything, and followed him.

[12]**And it came to pass**, while he was in one of the towns, that there was this man covered with leprosy. Seeing Jesus, he knelt with his face to the ground and begged him, "Master, if you want to, you can make me clean."

[13]Jesus stretched out his hand, touched him, saying, "Okay—you're clean!"

And right away the leprosy disappeared. [14]He ordered him to tell no one. "But go, have a priest examine you. Then make an offering, as Moses commanded, for your cleansing, as evidence ⟨of your cure⟩."

[15]Yet the story about him spread around all the more. Great crowds would gather to hear him and to be healed of their diseases. [16]But he would withdraw to isolated places and pray.

[17]**And it came to pass** one day, as he was teaching, that the Lord's healing power was with him. Now Pharisees and teachers of the Law, who had come from every village of Galilee and Judea and from Jerusalem, were sitting around.

5:1–11
//Mk 1:16–20,
Mt 4:18–22;
cf. GEbi 2:3

5:4–10
Cf. Jn 21:1–14

5:12–16
//Mk 1:40–45,
Mt 8:1–4;
cf. EgerG 2:1–4

5:14
◊Lv 14:2–32

5:17–26
//Mk 2:1–12,
Mt 9:1–8

4:44 Instead of *Judea*, some mss read "Galilee," which makes more sense, since 4:42–43 and 5:1 occur there.

5:1 *Lake of Gennesaret*: usually called the Sea of Galilee.
5:10–11 In Luke's storyline, unlike in Mark's, James, John, and Simon enlist as disciples *after* witnessing Jesus' miraculous powers.
5:12 Prostration was a gesture of submission and respect.

clean: recovered from leprosy, which rendered one ritually unclean.
5:16 Only Luke tells that Jesus made a habit of spending time in prayer in *isolated places*; see (presumably) 4:42, as well as 6:12, 9:18, 9:28, and (probably) 22:39.

[18]The next thing you know, some men showed up, carrying a paralyzed man on a bed. They attempted to bring him in and lay him in front of Jesus. [19]But finding no way to get him in because of the crowd, they went up onto the roof and lowered him on his pallet through the tiles into the middle of the crowd in front of Jesus.

[20]When Jesus noticed their trust, he said, "Mister, your sins have been forgiven."

[21]And the scholars and the Pharisees began to object: "Who is this guy who utters blasphemies? Who can forgive sins except God alone?"

[22]Because Jesus was aware of their objections, he responded to them, "Why are you objecting? [23]Which is easier: to say, 'Your sins have been forgiven,' or to say, 'Get up and walk'? [24]But just so you realize that on earth the Human One has authority to forgive sins"—he said to the paralyzed man—"You there, get up, pick up your pallet and go home."

[25]And immediately he stood up in front of them, picked up what he had been lying on, and went home praising God. [26]They all became ecstatic, and they began to praise God, but they were also filled with fear and exclaimed, "We saw some incredible things today!"

[27]**After these events** he went out and observed a toll collector named Levi sitting at the toll booth. He said to him, "Follow me." [28]Leaving everything behind, he got up, and followed him. [29]And Levi gave him a great banquet in his house, and a large group of toll collectors and others were dining with them.

[30]The Pharisees and their scholars would complain to his disciples, "Why do you people eat and drink with toll collectors and sinners?"

[31]In response Jesus said to them: "Since when do the healthy need a doctor? It's the sick who do. [32]I have not come to enlist the upright to change their hearts, but sinners."

[33]**They said to him,** "The disciples of John are always fasting and offering prayers, and so are those of the Pharisees, but yours just eat and drink."

[34]And Jesus said to them, "You can't make the groom's friends fast as long as the groom is around, can you? [35]But the days will come when the groom is taken away from them, and then they will fast, in those days."

[36]He then gave them a proverb: "Nobody tears a piece from a new garment and puts it on an old one, since the new one will tear and the piece from the new will not match the old. [37]And nobody pours new wine into old wineskins, otherwise the new wine will burst the wineskins, it will gush out, and the wineskins will be destroyed. [38]Instead, new wine must be put into new wineskins. [39]Besides, nobody wants new wine after drinking aged wine. As they say, 'Aged wine is just fine!'"

5:20–21
⊤ Lk 7:48–49

5:27–32
//Mk 2:14–17,
Mt 9:9–13

5:27–28
Cf. GHeb 5,
GEbi 2:4

5:29–30
//GOxy 1224 5;
⊤ Lk 7:34, 15:2,
19:7

5:33–39
//Mk 2:18–22,
Mt 9:14–17

5:35
Cf. Th 104

5:36–39
//Th 47:3–5

5:30 To eat with someone implied social approval and established a bond of friendship.

5:37 New wine produces gas bubbles as it ferments, which will burst an old wineskin.

The Human One over the Sabbath

Jesus heals a man with a crippled hand

The Twelve

Congratulations!

6 **It came to pass** that he was walking through grainfields on a Sabbath, and his disciples would strip some heads of grain, husk them in their hands, and chew them. ²Some of the Pharisees said, "Why are you doing what's not permitted on the Sabbath?"

³And Jesus answered them, "I guess you don't recall what David did when he and his companions were hungry. ⁴He went into the house of God, took and ate the consecrated bread himself, and gave some to his men to eat. No one is permitted to eat this bread except the priests alone."

⁵And he used to say to them, "The Human One is master of the Sabbath."

⁶**On another Sabbath** it came to pass that he entered the meeting place and taught. A man was there whose right hand was crippled. ⁷And the scholars and the Pharisees watched him carefully, to see if he would heal on the Sabbath, so they could find some excuse to denounce him. ⁸However, he knew their motives, and he said to the man with the crippled hand, "Get up and stand here in front of everybody." And he got to his feet and stood there.

⁹Then Jesus said to them, "Let me ask you: on the Sabbath is it permitted to do good or to do evil, to save life or to destroy it?" ¹⁰And he looked right at all of them, and said to him, "Hold out your hand!" He did and his hand was restored.

¹¹But they were filled with rage and discussed among themselves what to do with Jesus.

¹²**During that time** it came to pass that he went out to the mountain to pray, and spent the night in prayer to God. ¹³The next day, he called his disciples and selected twelve of them, whom he named apostles: ¹⁴Simon, whom he nicknamed Rock (⟨Peter⟩), and Andrew his brother, and James and John, and Philip, and Bartholomew, ¹⁵and Matthew, and Thomas, and James the son of Alphaeus, and Simon who was called the Zealot, ¹⁶and Judas the son of James, and Judas Iscariot, who turned traitor.

¹⁷**On the way down** with them, Jesus stopped at a level place. There was a huge crowd of his disciples and a great throng of people from all Judea and Jerusalem and the coast of Tyre and Sidon. ¹⁸They came to hear him and to be healed of their diseases. Those who were tormented by unclean spirits were cured. ¹⁹And everyone in the crowd tried to touch him, since power would flow out from him and heal them all.

6:1–5
//Mk 2:23–28,
Mt 12:1–8

6:4
◊Lv 24:5–9,
1 Sm 21:1–6

6:6–11
//Mk 3:1–6,
Mt 12:9–14;
cf. GNaz 4

6:9
Ⓣ Lk 14:3

6:12–16
//Mk 3:13–19,
Mt 10:1–4;
cf. GEbi 2:3

6:17–19
//Mk 3:7–12,
Mt 12:15–21

6:2 The Law permits taking grain from someone else's field (Deut 23:25). What is unlawful is working (i.e., picking grain) on the Sabbath.

6:7 Sabbath regulations forbad a physician to treat patients on the Sabbath, except in emergencies.

6:14 The nickname *Petros* literally means "Rock."

6:15 The *Zealots* were a militaristic Jewish independence movement that precipitated the war against Roman occupation in 66–70 CE. However, their existence during Jesus' lifetime is highly doubtful.

6:17 A *level place* contrasts with the setting for the parallel Sermon on the Mount in Matt 5:1. Luke's version of this speech is often called the Sermon on the Plain.

Tyre and Sidon are gentile areas outside Palestine.

²⁰Then he would look squarely at his disciples and say:

> Congratulations, you poor!
>> God's empire belongs to you.
> ²¹Congratulations, you hungry!
>> You will have a feast.
> Congratulations, you who weep now!
>> You will laugh.

Love for enemies

The Golden Rule

²²"Congratulations to you when people hate you, and when they ostracize you and spread malicious gossip about you and scorn your name as evil, because of the Human One! ²³Rejoice on that day and jump for joy! Because look: your reward is great in heaven. Bear in mind that their ancestors treated the prophets the same way.

> ²⁴Damn you rich!
>> You already have your consolation.
> ²⁵Damn you who are well-fed now!
>> You will know hunger.
> Damn you who laugh now!
>> You will learn to weep and grieve.

Q6:20–26
//Mt 5:3–12

6:20
//Th 54

6:21
//Th 69:2;
Ⓣ DSav 8:1

²⁶"Damn you when everybody speaks well of you! Bear in mind that their ancestors treated the phony prophets the same way.

²⁷"**But to you who listen** I say: love your enemies, do good to those who hate you, ²⁸bless those who curse you, pray for your abusers.

²⁹"When someone strikes you on the cheek, offer the other as well. If someone takes away your coat, don't prevent him from taking your shirt along with it.

³⁰"Give to everyone who begs from you; and when someone takes your things, don't ask for them back.

³¹"**Treat people** the same way you want them to treat you.

³²"If you love those who love you, what merit is there in that? After all, even sinners love those who love them. ³³And if you do good to those who do good to you, what merit is there in that? After all, even sinners do as much. ³⁴If you lend to those from whom you hope to gain, what merit is there in that? Even sinners lend to sinners, in order to get as much in return. ³⁵But love your enemies, and

6:22
//Th 68:1;
cf. Th 69:1;
1 Pet 3:14,
4:13–14

6:23
Acts 7:52

6:24
Cf. Jas 5:1

Q6:27–36
//Mt 5:38–48

6:27
//GOxy 1224 6:1

6:28
Ⓣ Rom 12:14,
1 Pet 3:9

6:31
//Mt 7:12;
cf. Tob 4:15

6:34–35
Cf. Th 95

6:20 *Congratulations* (*makarios*): traditionally translated "blessed." "Congratulations" better expresses the performative language of the Beatitudes, which grant the recipient recognition of good fortune. (See the essay on p. 416).

6:22 *your name*: not one's personal name, but the name of "Christian," a title attested in the NT only by Acts 11:26; 26:28; 1 Pet 4:16.

6:24 *Damn you*: traditionally translated as "Woe to you." (See the essay on p. 416.)

6:29 The *coat* and *shirt* are the full-length outer and under garments worn in the ancient world. One who lacked both garments would be nearly nude.

On judging

By their fruits

Foundations

Jesus heals an officer's slave

do good, and lend, expecting nothing in return. Your reward will be great, and you'll be children of the Most High. As you know, the Most High is generous to the ungrateful and the evil. [36]Be as compassionate as your Father is.

[37]**"Don't pass judgment**, and you won't be judged; don't condemn, and you won't be condemned; forgive, and you'll be forgiven. [38]Give, and it'll be given to you: they'll put in your lap a full measure, packed down, sifted, and overflowing. For the standard you apply will be the standard applied to you."

[39]And he posed a riddle for them: "Can one blind person guide another? Won't they both end up in some ditch?

[40]"Students are not above their teachers. But those who are fully taught will be like their teachers. [41]Why do you notice the sliver in your friend's eye, but overlook the timber in your own? [42]How can you say to your friend, 'Friend, let me get the sliver in your eye,' when you don't notice the timber in your own? You phony, first take the timber out of your own eye, and then you'll see well enough to remove the sliver in your friend's eye.

[43]"**A choice tree** does not produce rotten fruit, any more than a rotten tree produces choice fruit; [44]for each tree is known by its fruit. Figs are not gathered from thorns, nor are grapes picked from brambles. [45]The good person produces good from the fund of good in the heart, and the evil person produces evil from the evil within. As you know, the mouth gives voice to what the heart is full of.

[46]"**Why do you call me** 'Master, master,' and not do what I tell you? [47]Everyone who comes to me and pays attention to my words and acts on them— I'll show you what such a person is like: [48]That one is like a person building a house, who dug deep and laid the foundation on bedrock; when a flood came, the torrent slammed against that house, but could not shake it, because it was well built. [49]But the one who listens ⟨to my words⟩ and doesn't act ⟨on them⟩ is like a person who built a house on the ground without a foundation; when the torrent slammed against it, it immediately collapsed. And so the ruin of that house was total."

7 **After he had completed** all he had to say to his audience, he went into Capernaum.

[2]A Roman officer had a slave he was very fond of but who was sick and about to die. [3]So when he heard about Jesus, the officer sent some elders of the Jewish community to him, and asked him to come and cure his slave. [4]When they came to Jesus, they pleaded with him urgently, saying, "He deserves to have you do this for him [5]because he loves our people, and even built a meeting place for us."

[6]So Jesus went with them.

Q6:37–42
//Mt 7:1–5

6:37
//Mary 9:12

6:38
//Mk 4:24

Q6:39
//Mt 15:14, Th 34

Q6:40
//Mt 10:24–25;
Jn 13:16, 15:20;
cf. DSav 20

6:41–42
//Th 26

Q6:43–45
//Mt 7:15–20,
12:33–35; Th 45

6:44
Cf. Jas 3:12

Q6:46–49
//Mt 7:21, 24–27;
SJas 6:15c

6:46
//Mt 7:21,
EgerG 3:5

Q7:1–10
//Mt 8:5–13,
Jn 4:46–54

7:2 The *Roman officer* is a "centurion," a Latin term for an officer in command of a hundred men. However, Roman military units were not stationed in Galilee during the time of Jesus.

7:6 Entering the home of a gentile would render a Jew unclean (see Acts 10:28).

When he got close to the house, the officer dispatched friends to say to him, "Don't trouble yourself, sir, for I don't deserve to have you in my house; ⁷that's why I didn't presume to come to you in person. Just say the word, and let my boy be cured. ⁸After all, I myself am under orders and I have soldiers under me. I order one to go, and he goes; I order another to come, and he comes; and I order my slave to do something, and he does it."

⁹As Jesus listened to this he was amazed at him. He turned and said to the crowd that followed, "I'm telling you, not even in Israel have I found such trust."

¹⁰And when the emissaries returned to the house, they found the slave in good health.

¹¹**And it came to pass** soon afterward that he went to a town called Nain, accompanied by his disciples and a large crowd. ¹²As he neared the town gate, just then a dead man was being carried out, the only son of his mother, who was herself a widow. And a considerable crowd from the town was with her.

¹³When the Master saw her, his heart went out to her and he said to her, "Don't cry." ¹⁴And he went up and touched the bier. The bearers paused, and he said, "Young man—I'm talking to you—get up."

¹⁵And the dead man sat up and began to speak; then Jesus gave him back to his mother.

¹⁶Fear gripped them all and they praised God, saying, "A great prophet has been raised up among us!" and "God has visited his people!"

¹⁷And this story about him spread throughout Judea and all the surrounding area.

¹⁸**John's disciples** reported all these things to him. ¹⁹John summoned a couple of his disciples and sent them to the Master to ask, "Are you the one who is to come, or do we have to wait for someone else?"

²⁰And when the men came to Jesus, they said, "John the Baptizer sent us to you to ask: 'Are you the one who is to come, or do we have to wait for someone else?'"

²¹Jesus had just cured many of their diseases and plagues and evil spirits, and restored sight to many who were blind. ²²And so he answered them, "Go report to John what you have seen and heard:

> the blind see again,
>> the lame walk,
> lepers are cleansed,

Jesus raises a widow's son

John queries Jesus

7:11–17
◊ 1 Kgs 17:17–24
7:15
◊ 1 Kgs 17:23
7:16
Ⓣ Lk 1:68, 19:44
Q7:18–23
//Mt 11:2–6
7:22
Lk 4:18;
Ⓘ Is 35:5–6, 61:1

7:11 Some mss read "on the next day" in place of *soon afterward*.

7:7 *boy*: The Greek word *pais* can refer either to a child or to a servant.
7:11–16 This miracle closely resembles that of Elijah's in 1 Kgs 17:17–24. *Gave him back to his mother* in v. 15 is taken verbatim from 1 Kgs 17:23.

the deaf hear,

the dead are raised,

and the poor have the good news preached to them.

²³Congratulations to those who don't take offense at me.'"

²⁴**After John's messengers** had left, Jesus began to talk to the crowds about John. "What did you go out to the desert to gawk at? A reed shaking in the wind? ²⁵What did you really go out to see? A man dressed in fancy clothes? But wait! Those who dress fashionably and live in luxury are found in palaces. ²⁶Come on, what did you go out to see? A prophet? Yes, that's what you went out to see, and even more than a prophet. ²⁷This is the one about whom it was written:

Here is my messenger,

whom I send on ahead of you

to prepare your way before you.

²⁸I'm telling you, among those born of women none is greater than John; yet the least ⟨important⟩ in God's empire is greater than he is." (²⁹All the people, even the toll collectors, who were listening and had been baptized by John, vindicated God's plan; ³⁰but the Pharisees and the legal experts, who had not been baptized by him, subverted God's plan for themselves.)

³¹"**What do the people** of this generation remind me of? What are they like? ³²They are like children sitting in the marketplace and calling out to one another,

We played the flute for you,

but you wouldn't dance;

we sang a dirge,

but you wouldn't weep.

³³"Just remember, John the Baptizer appeared on the scene, eating no bread and drinking no wine, and you say, 'He's possessed.' ³⁴The Human One appeared on the scene both eating and drinking, and you say, 'There's a glutton and a drunk, a crony of toll collectors and sinners!' ³⁵Indeed, Wisdom is vindicated by all her children."

³⁶**One of the Pharisees** invited him to dinner; he entered the Pharisee's house, and reclined ⟨for the meal⟩. ³⁷A local woman, who was a sinner, found out that he was having dinner at the Pharisee's house. She suddenly showed up

---

Q7:24–28
//Mt 11:7–14

7:24–25
//Th 78

7:27
Cf. Mk 1:2;
① Lk 3:4;
◊ Mal 3:1, Ex 23:20

7:28
//Th 46

7:29–30
① Lk 20:46,
Mt 21:32

7:29
① Lk 3:12

7:30
Cf. EgerG 1:10

Q7:31–35
//Mt 11:16–19

7:34
① Lk 5:30, 15:2,
19:7;
◊ Dt 21:20

7:36–38
//Mk 14:3–9,
Mt 26:6–13,
Jn 12:1–8

7:36
① Lk 11:37, 14:1

7:36 Inviting Jesus to dinner implies that this Pharisee accepts Jesus and thus his teaching. See also 14:1.

7:37 The woman's sin is not described. The traditional as-

sumption that her sin was sexual is groundless and usually reflects gender prejudice—such an assumption is seldom applied to Peter when he calls himself a sinner in 5:8.

with an alabaster jar of aromatic ointment, [38]and stood there behind him weeping at his feet. Her tears wet his feet, and she wiped them dry with her hair; she kissed his feet, and anointed them with the ointment.

[39]The Pharisee who had invited him saw this and said to himself, "If this man were a prophet, he would know who this is and what kind of woman is touching him, since she is a sinner."

[40]And Jesus answered him, "Simon, I have something to tell you."

"Teacher," he said, "speak up."

[41]"This moneylender had two debtors; one owed five hundred denarii, and the other fifty. [42]Since neither one of them could pay, he wrote off both debts. Now which of them will love him more?" [43]Simon answered, "I would imagine, the one for whom he wrote off the larger debt."

And he said to him, "You're right." [44]Then turning to the woman, he said to Simon, "Do you see this woman? I walked into your house and you didn't offer me water for my feet; yet she has washed my feet with her tears and dried them with her hair. [45]You didn't offer me a kiss, but she hasn't stopped kissing my feet since I arrived. [46]You didn't anoint my head with oil, but she has anointed my feet with ointment. [47]For this reason, I'm telling you, her many sins have been forgiven, as this outpouring of her love shows. But the one who is forgiven little shows little love."

[48]And he said to her, "Your sins have been forgiven."

[49]Then those having dinner with him began to mutter to themselves, "Who is this who even forgives sins?"

[50]And he said to the woman, "Your trust has saved you; go in peace."

8 **And it came to pass** soon afterward that he traveled through towns and villages, preaching and announcing the good news of the empire of God. The Twelve were with him, [2]and also some women whom he had cured of evil spirits and diseases: Mary, the one from Magdala, from whom seven demons had departed, [3]and Joanna, the wife of Chuza, Herod's steward, and Susanna, and many other women, who provided for them out of their resources.

[4]**Since a huge crowd** was now gathering, and people were making their way to him from town after town, he told them some such parable as this:

> [5]A sower went out to sow his seed; and while he was sowing, some seed fell along the path, and was trampled under foot, and the birds of the sky devoured it. [6]Other seed fell on the rock; when it grew, it withered because it lacked moisture. [7]Still other seed fell among thorns; the thorns grew with it and choked it. [8]Other seed fell on fertile soil; and when it matured, it produced fruit a hundredfold.

7:48–49
Ⓣ Lk 5:20–21

7:50
Ⓣ Lk 8:48, 17:19, 18:42

8:4–8
//Mk 4:1–9, Mt 13:3–9, Th 9; cf. SJas 8:3

8:6
Ⓣ Judas 3:7

7:38 *stood behind him weeping at his feet*: Jesus was reclining to eat and so his feet would be behind him.

8:2 Mary of Magdala's *seven demons* represent physical or psychological afflictions from which Jesus delivered her.

In parables

Understanding the sower

Lamp & bed

Jesus' true family

Rebuking wind & wave

During his discourse, he would call out, "Anyone here with two good ears, use 'em!"

[9]**His disciples asked** him what this parable was all about. [10]He replied, "You have been given the privilege of knowing the secrets of the empire of God; but the rest get only parables, so that

> They may look but not see,
> listen but not understand.

[11]"**Now this is the interpretation** of the parable. The 'seed' is God's message. [12]Those 'along the path' are those who have listened to it, but then the devil comes and steals the message from their hearts, so they won't trust and be saved. [13]Those 'on the rock' are those who, when they listen to the message, receive it happily. But they 'have no root', they trust for the moment but fall away when they are tested. [14]What 'fell into the thorns' represents those who listen, but as they continue on, they are 'choked' by the worries and wealth and pleasures of life, and they do not come to maturity. [15]But the seed 'in good soil' stands for those who listen to the message and hold on to it with a good and fertile heart, and 'bear fruit' through perseverance.

[16]"**No one lights** a lamp and covers it with a pot or puts it under a bed; instead, one puts it on a lampstand, so that those who come in can see the light. [17]After all, there is nothing hidden that won't be brought to light, nor kept secret that won't be made known and exposed.

[18]"So pay attention to how you're listening; in fact, to those who have, more will be given, and from those who don't have, even what they seem to have will be taken away."

[19]**Then his mother** and his brothers came to see him, but they could not reach him because of the crowd. [20]When he was told, "Your mother and your brothers are outside and want to see you," [21]he replied to them, "My mother and my brothers are those who listen to God's message and do it."

[22]**It came to pass** that Jesus and his disciples got into a boat, and he said to them, "Let's cross to the other side of the lake."

So they shoved off, [23]and as they sailed he fell asleep. A squall descended on the lake; they were being swamped and were in serious danger. [24]And they went and woke him up, saying, "Master, master, we're sinking!"

He got up and rebuked the wind and the rough water; and they settled down, and there was a calm. [25]Then he said to them, "Where is your trust?"

8:9–10
//Mk 4:10–12,
Mt 13:10–15;
cf. SJas 6:5–6

8:10
Ⓣ Acts 28:26–27;
◊ Is 6:9–10

8:11–15
//Mk 4:13–20,
Mt 13:18–23;
cf. SJas 6:17

8:16–17
//Mk 4:21–23

8:16
//Mt 5:15,
Th 33:2–3;
Ⓓ Lk 11:33

8:17
//Mt 10:26,
Th 5:2, 6:5–6;
Ⓓ Lk 12:2

8:18
//Mk 4:25;
Mt 13:12, 25:29;
Th 41;
Ⓓ Lk 19:26

8:19–21
//Mk 3:31–35,
Mt 12:46–50,
Th 99, GEbi 5

8:21
//GHeb 4a;
cf. DSav 41:4,
Lk 11:27–28

8:22–25
//Mk 4:35–41,
Mt 8:23–27

8:19–21 Luke gently edits this scene from Mark so that Jesus does not disown his family, as he does in Mark 3:31–35.

Although they were terrified, they were astounded, saying to one another, "Who in the world is this? He commands even winds and water and they obey him?"

[26]**They sailed** to the region of the Gerasenes, which lies directly across from Galilee. [27]As he stepped out on land, this man from the town who was possessed by demons met him. For quite some time he had been going without clothes and hadn't lived in a house but stayed in the tombs instead.

[28]When he saw Jesus, he screamed and knelt before him, and said at the top of his voice, "What do you want with me, Jesus, you son of the most high God? I beg you, don't torment me." ([29]You see, he had ordered the unclean spirit to get out of the man. The demon had taken control of him many times; the man had been kept under guard, bound with chains and shackles, but he would break the bonds and be driven by the demon into the desert.)

[30]Jesus questioned him: "What is your name?"

"Legion," he said, because many demons had entered him. [31]They kept begging him not to order them to depart into the abyss.

[32]Now over there a large herd of pigs was feeding on the mountain; and they bargained with him to let them enter those pigs. And he agreed. [33]Then the demons came out of the man and entered the pigs, and the herd stampeded down the bluff into the lake and was drowned.

[34]When the herdsmen saw what had happened, they ran off and reported it in town and out in the country. [35]And people came out to see what had happened. They came to Jesus and found the man from whom the demons had gone, sitting at Jesus' feet, with his clothes on and his wits about him; and they got scared. [36]Those who had seen it explained to them how the possessed man had been cured. [37]Then the entire populace of the Gerasene region asked him to leave them; for they were gripped by a great fear.

So he got into a boat and went back. [38]The man from whom the demons had departed begged to go with him; but he dismissed him, saying, [39]"Return home and tell the story of what God has done for you." And he went his way, spreading the news throughout the whole town about what Jesus had done for him.

[40]**Now when Jesus returned**, the crowd welcomed him, for they were all waiting for him. [41]Just then a man named Jairus, a synagogue official, came up to Jesus. He knelt at Jesus' feet and begged him to come to his house, [42]because his only child, a twelve-year-old daughter, was dying.

8:26–39
//Mk 5:1–20,
Mt 8:28–34

8:40–56
//Mk 5:21–43,
Mt 9:18–26

8:26 Some mss read either "Gergesenes" or "Gadarenes."

8:26 The *Gerasenes* were probably gentiles.
8:30 *Legion* is a Latin word. There were 6,000 soldiers in a Roman legion.
8:31 *abyss*: the final prison of Satan and his demons (see

Rev 20:3). In popular belief, demons prowled the earth seeking dwelling places, usually in tombs, deserted places, or human souls (see Luke 11:24–26).

Jesus cures a woman

Jairus' daughter revived

Instructions for the road

As Jesus was walking along, the crowd milled around him. ⁴³A woman who had experienced a chronic flow of blood for twelve years, and had found no one able to heal her, ⁴⁴came up behind him, and touched the hem of his cloak. Immediately her flow of blood stopped.

⁴⁵Then Jesus said, "Who touched me?"

When everyone denied it, Peter said, "Master, the crowds are pressing in and jostling you!"

⁴⁶But Jesus insisted, "Someone touched me; I can tell that power has drained out of me."

⁴⁷And when the woman saw that she had not escaped notice, she came forward trembling, and knelt before him. In front of all the people she explained why she had touched him, and how she had been immediately healed.

⁴⁸Jesus said to her, "Daughter, your trust has cured you; go in peace."

⁴⁹**While he is still speaking**, someone from the synagogue official's house comes and says, "Your daughter is dead; don't bother the teacher further."

⁵⁰When Jesus heard this, he answered him, "Don't be afraid; just have trust, and she'll be cured."

⁵¹When he arrived at the house, he wouldn't allow anyone to go in with him except Peter and John and James, and the child's father and mother. ⁵²Everyone was crying and grieving over her, but he said, "Don't cry; she hasn't died; she's sleeping."

⁵³But they started laughing at him, certain that she had died. ⁵⁴He took her by the hand and called out, "Child, get up!" ⁵⁵Her breathing returned and she immediately got up. He ordered them to give her something to eat.

⁵⁶Her parents were quite ecstatic; but he commanded them not to tell anyone what had happened.

9 **He called the Twelve** together and gave them power and authority over all demons and to heal diseases. ²He sent them out to announce the empire of God and to heal the sick. ³He said to them, "Don't carry anything on the way: neither staff nor knapsack, neither bread nor money; no one is to take two shirts. ⁴And whichever house you enter, stay there and leave from there. ⁵And wherever they do not welcome you, leave the town and shake the dust from your feet in witness against them."

⁶And they set out and went from village to village, bringing good news and healing everywhere.

8:48
ⓣ Lk 7:50, 17:19, 18:42

9:1–6
//Mk 6:7–13, Mt 10:1, 9–14

9:1
//Mk 3:14–15

9:5
ⓣ Lk 10:11; Acts 13:51, 18:6

8:43 Many mss add "and had spent her life savings on physicians" after *twelve years*.

8:43 The woman's *chronic flow of blood* was a menstrual disorder, which would have rendered her permanently ritually unclean and have cut her off from social interaction (Lev 15:25–27).

[7]**Now Herod** the tetrarch heard about everything that was happening. He was perplexed because some were saying that John had been raised from the dead, [8]some that Elijah had appeared, and others that one of the ancient prophets had come back to life. [9]Herod said, "John I beheaded; but this one about whom I hear such things—who is he?" And he was curious to see him.

[10]**On their return** the apostles reported to him what they had done. Taking them along, Jesus withdrew privately to a town called Bethsaida. [11]But the crowds found this out and followed him. He welcomed them, spoke to them about the empire of God, and cured those in need of treatment.

[12]**As the day began** to draw to a close, the Twelve approached him and said, "Send the crowd away, so that they can go to the villages and farms around here and find food and lodging; for we are in a deserted place here."

[13]But he said to them, "Give them something to eat yourselves."

They said, "All we have are five loaves and two fish—unless we go ourselves and buy food for all these people." ([14]There were about five thousand men.)

He said to his disciples, "Have them recline in groups of about fifty." [15]They did so and got them reclined. [16]Then he took the five loaves and two fish, looked up to the sky, gave a blessing, and broke them, and started handing them out to the disciples to pass around to the crowd.

[17]And everybody had more than enough to eat. Then the leftovers were collected, twelve baskets full.

[18]**And it came to pass**, when Jesus was praying alone, that the disciples were with him; and he questioned them asking, "What are the crowds saying about me?"

[19]They said in response, "⟨Some say, 'You are⟩ John the Baptizer,' while others, 'Elijah,' and still others, 'One of the ancient prophets has come back to life.'"

[20]Then he said to them, "What about you, who do you say I am?"

And Peter responded, "God's Anointed One!"

[21]**Then he warned** them, and forbade them to tell this to anyone, [22]adding, "The Human One is destined to endure much, be rejected by the elders and chief priests and scholars, and be killed and, on the third day, be raised."

[23]**He would say** to everyone, "If any of you wants to come after me, you should deny yourself, pick up your cross every day, and follow me! [24]Remember, if you try to save your life, you'll lose it, but if you lose your life for my sake, you'll save it. [25]After all, what good does it do to acquire the whole world and

---

Margin notes

Herod is curious about Jesus

The apostles report

Loaves & fish for 5,000

What are the crowds saying?

The Human One destined to suffer

Saving & losing life

9:7–9
//Mk 6:14–16,
Mt 14:1–2

9:7–8
① Lk 9:19

9:9
① Lk 23:8

9:10–11
//Mk 6:30–34,
Mt 14:13–14

9:12–17
//Mk 6:35–44,
Mt 14:15–21,
Jn 6:1–14;
◊2 Kgs 4:42–44

9:16
① Lk 22:19, 24:30

9:18–22
//Mk 8:27–33,
Mt 16:13–23

9:22
① Lk 17:25; 22:22;
24:6–8, 26, 46

9:23–27
//Mk 8:34–9:1,
Mt 16:24–28

9:23
Cf. Th 55,
SJas 4:10–5:3;
① Lk 14:27

9:24
//Jn 12:25;
① Lk 17:33

9:7 *tetrarch*: see the note to 3:19.

9:8 It was believed that Elijah would return before the Day of the Lord (Mal 3:1; 4:5).

9:11 A typical narrative summary by which Luke sets up the following scene. Other examples are 4:14–15, 5:15,

5:17, and 6:17–19.

9:18 Jesus was *alone*, yet *the disciples were with him*: a baffling anomaly.

9:23 The *every day* in Luke's version of this saying (compare Mark 8:34–35) makes *your cross* metaphorical.

Jesus transformed

Unclean spirit expelled

lose or forfeit yourself? ²⁶Moreover, if any of you are ashamed of me and of my message, the Human One will be ashamed of you when he comes in his glory and the glory of the Father and of the holy messengers. ²⁷I'm telling you the truth: some of those standing here won't ever taste death before they see the empire of God."

²⁸**About eight days** after these sayings it came to pass that Jesus took Peter and John and James along with him and climbed up the mountain to pray. ²⁹And it came to pass as he was praying that his face took on a strange appearance, and his clothing turned dazzling white. ³⁰The next thing you know, two men were talking with him, Moses and Elijah, ³¹who appeared in glory and were discussing his departure, which he was destined to accomplish in Jerusalem.

³²Now Peter and those with him were half asleep at the time. But they came wide awake when they saw his glory and the two men standing next to him. ³³And it came to pass as the men were leaving him that Peter said to Jesus, "Master, it's a good thing we're here. How about we set up three tents, one for you, one for Moses, and one for Elijah?" (He didn't know what he was saying.)

³⁴While he was still speaking, a cloud moved in and cast a shadow over them. And their fear increased as they entered the cloud. ³⁵And out of the cloud a voice spoke: "This is my son, my chosen one. Listen to him!" ³⁶When the voice had spoken, Jesus was perceived to be alone. And they were speechless and told no one back then anything of what they had seen.

³⁷**It came to pass** on the next day, when they came down from the mountain, that a huge crowd met him. ³⁸Suddenly a man from the crowd shouted, "Teacher, I beg you to take a look at my son, for he is my only child. ³⁹Without warning a spirit gets hold of him, and all of a sudden he screams; it throws him into convulsions, causing him to foam at the mouth; and it leaves him only after abusing him. ⁴⁰I begged your disciples to drive it out, but they couldn't."

⁴¹In response Jesus said, "You distrustful and perverted generation, how much longer do I have to be around you and put up with you? Bring your son here."

⁴²But as the boy approached, the demon knocked him down and threw him into convulsions. Jesus rebuked the unclean spirit, healed the boy, and gave him back to his father.

⁴³And everybody was astounded at the majesty of God.

9:26
Ⓣ 2 Tim 2:11–13;
Ⓓ Lk 12:9

9:27
Ⓣ Lk 21:32

9:28–36
//Mk 9:2–8,
Mt 27:1–8

9:34–35
Ⓣ Judas 6:10

9:35
Ⓣ Lk 3:22;
◊ Ps 2:7, Is 42:1

9:37–43a
//Mk 9:14–27,
Mt 17:14–18

9:43b–45
//Mk 9:30–32,
Mt 17:22–23

9:35 Many mss read "the one I love" in place of *my chosen one*.

9:31 *Departure* translates the Greek word *exodos* (which is also the title of the second book of the LXX), thus associating Jesus with Moses.
9:34 Clouds are OT symbols of the presence of God (e.g.,

in Exodus 19).
9:41 Jesus' strangely abrasive response seems out of context.

While they all were marveling at everything he was doing, he said to his disciples, ⁴⁴"Mark well these words: the Human One is destined to be turned over to his enemies."

⁴⁵But they didn't understand this instruction. It was couched in veiled language, so they would not get its meaning. And they always dreaded to ask him about this remark.

⁴⁶**Now an argument** broke out among them over which of them was greatest. ⁴⁷But Jesus, knowing what was on their minds, took a child and had her stand next to him. ⁴⁸He said to them, "Whoever welcomes this child in my name is welcoming me. And whoever welcomes me is welcoming the one who sent me. Don't forget, the one who is least among you is the one who is great."

⁴⁹John said in response, "Master, we saw someone driving out demons in your name, and we tried to stop him because he isn't one of your followers."

⁵⁰But he said to him, "Don't stop him; for whoever is not against you is on your side."

⁵¹**It came to pass**, as the deadline for him to be taken up was fast approaching, that he set his sights on Jerusalem. ⁵²He sent messengers on ahead of him. They entered a Samaritan village, to get things ready for him. ⁵³But the Samaritans would not welcome him, because he had made up his mind to go on to Jerusalem. ⁵⁴When his disciples James and John realized this, they said, "Master, do you want us to call down fire from heaven and annihilate them?" ⁵⁵But he turned and reprimanded them. ⁵⁶Then they continued on to another village.

⁵⁷**As they were going** along the road, someone said to him, "I'll follow you wherever you go."

⁵⁸And Jesus said to him, "Foxes have dens, and birds of the sky have nests, but the Human One has nowhere to rest his head."

⁵⁹To another he said, "Follow me."

But he said, "First, let me go and bury my father."

⁶⁰Jesus said to him, "Leave it to the dead to bury their own dead; but you, go out and announce the empire of God."

⁶¹Another said, "I'll follow you, sir; but let me first say good-bye to my people at home."

⁶²Jesus said to him, "No one who puts his hand to the plow and looks back is qualified for the empire of God."

The Human One to be turned in

Dispute about greatness

Jesus leaves for Jerusalem

Foxes have dens

9:44
Ⓣ Lk 17:25; 18:31–33; 22:22; 24:6–8, 26, 46

9:45
Ⓣ Lk 18:34

9:46–48
//Mk 9:33–37, Mt 18:1–5; Ⓣ Lk 22:24–27

9:48a
Ⓓ Lk 10:16

9:48b
//Mt 23:11

9:49–50
//Mk 9:38–40

9:50
//Lk 11:23, GOxy 1224 6:1

9:54
◊2 Kgs 1:9–12

Q9:57–62
//Mt 8:18–22

9:58
//Th 86

9:61–62
◊1 Kgs 19:19–21

9:54 Many mss add "as Elijah did" to the end of the verse.

9:44–45 Jesus' meaning is perfectly clear to Luke's audience but is deliberately, and for no apparent reason, concealed from the disciples. See also 18:34.

9:51 *taken up*: the Greek word *analēmpsis* also means "ascension" (see Luke 24:51).

9:53 Samaritans would not offer hospitality to those travelling to the temple in Jerusalem, which the Samaritans regarded as an illegitimate rival to their own temple on Mount Gerasim (see John 4:20).

9:59–60 Burying one's parent was a son's most sacred duty.

Instructions for the seventy-two

The seventy-two report

Q10:1–12
//Mt 10:5–15,
Mk 6:7–13;
Ⓓ Lk 9:2–6

10:1
Ⓣ Lk 9:52

Q10:2
//Mt 9:37, Th 73;
cf. Jn 4:35

Q10:3
//Mt 10:16

10:7
Cf. 1 Cor 9:14,
1 Tm 5:18, DSav 20

10:8
//Th 14:4;
cf. 1 Cor 10:27

10:11
Ⓣ Acts 13:51, 18:6

10:12
Ⓣ Jude 7;
◊Gn 19:24–28

Q10:13–15
//Mt 11:20–24

10:15
◊Is 14:13–15

Q10:16
//Mt 10:40;
Jn 12:44–45, 13:20;
Ⓓ Lk 9:48

10:19
Cf. Mk 16:17–18;
◊Ps 91:13

10:20
Ⓣ Phil 4:3,
Heb 12:23,
Rv 3:5, 13:8

10 **After this** the Master appointed seventy-two others and sent them on ahead of him in pairs to every town and place that he himself intended to visit. ²He would say to them, "The crop is good, but there are few to harvest it. So beg the harvest boss to dispatch workers to the fields. ³Get going; look, I'm sending you out like lambs into a pack of wolves. ⁴Carry no purse, no knapsack, no sandals. Don't greet anyone on the road. ⁵Whenever you enter a house, first say, 'Peace to this house.' ⁶If peaceful people live there, your peace will rest on them. But if not, it will return to you. ⁷Stay at that one house, eating and drinking whatever they provide, for workers deserve their wages. Do not move from house to house. ⁸Whenever you enter a town and they welcome you, eat whatever they offer you. ⁹Cure the sick there and tell them, 'For you, God's empire has arrived.' ¹⁰But whenever you enter a town and they don't welcome you, go out into its streets and say, ¹¹'Even the dust of your town that sticks to our feet, we wipe off against you. But know this: the empire of God is arriving.' ¹²I'm telling you, on that day Sodom will be better off than that town.

¹³"Damn you, Chorazin! Damn you, Bethsaida! If the miracles done in you had been done in Tyre and Sidon, they would have sat in sackcloth and ashes and changed their ways long ago. ¹⁴But Tyre and Sidon will be better off at the judgment than you. ¹⁵And you, Capernaum, you don't think you'll be exalted to heaven, do you? No; you'll go to hell.

¹⁶"Whoever hears you hears me, and whoever rejects you rejects me, and whoever rejects me rejects the one who sent me."

¹⁷**The seventy-two** returned joyfully, saying, "Master, even the demons submit to us when we invoke your name!"

¹⁸And he said to them, "I was watching Satan fall like lightning from heaven. ¹⁹Look, I have given you authority to trample on snakes and scorpions, and over the full force of the enemy; nothing will ever harm you. ²⁰However, don't

---

10:1 Many mss read "seventy" rather than *seventy-two.*
10:17 Many mss read "seventy" rather than *seventy-two.*

10:2 The *harvest* is usually a symbol of divine judgment (Matt 13:30, 39), but here represents the gathering in of God's people (as in Isa 27:12).

10:12 *Sodom* was a city that God obliterated for its legendary wickedness (Gen 19:24–28).

10:13 *Bethsaida* is a town in Galilee. The location of *Chorazin* is unknown, but it was presumably also in Galilee. *Tyre and Sidon* were two gentile cities in what is now Lebanon. There was a history of enmity between them and Israel (e.g., Joel 3:4–8).

10:15 Jesus had performed healings in Capernaum (4:23;

7:1–10), but Luke does not report that the city rejected Jesus or his disciples.

hell: literally, *Hades*, the realm of the dead.

10:18 This vision, signifying the defeat of evil, presupposes the same symbolism as Rev 12:7–9.

10:19 The *snake* and the *scorpion* are symbols of evil in the OT (e.g., Deut 8:15).

10:20 *Inscribed in heaven* reflects an OT idea that a book in heaven contains the names of all who belong to God's people (see Exod 32:32–33 and Dan 12:1).

rejoice that the spirits submit to you; rejoice instead that your names have been inscribed in heaven."

²¹**At that moment** Jesus was overjoyed by the holy spirit and said, "I praise you, Father, master of earth and sky, because you have hidden these things from the wise and the learned but revealed them to the unsophisticated; yes indeed, Father, because that's the way you want it. ²²My Father has turned everything over to me. No one knows who the son is except the Father, or who the Father is except the son—and anyone to whom the son wishes to reveal him."

²³**Turning to the disciples** he said privately, "How privileged are the eyes that see what you see! ²⁴I'm telling you, many prophets and kings wanted to see what you see, and never saw it, and to hear what you hear, and never heard it."

²⁵**On one occasion**, a legal expert stood up to put him to the test with a question: "Teacher, what do I have to do to inherit eternal life?"

²⁶He said to him, "How do you read what is written in the Law?"

²⁷And he answered, "You shall love the Lord your God with all your heart, with all your soul, with all your strength, and with all your mind; and your neighbor as yourself."

²⁸Jesus said to him, "You're right; do this and you will have life."

²⁹But trying to justify himself, he said to Jesus, "But who is my neighbor?"

³⁰Jesus replied,

> This man was on his way from Jerusalem down to Jericho when he fell into the hands of bandits. They stripped him, beat him, and went off, leaving him half dead. ³¹Now by coincidence a priest was going down that road; when he caught sight of him, he went out of his way to avoid him. ³²In the same way, when a Levite came to the place, he took one look at him and crossed the road to avoid him. ³³But this Samaritan was traveling that way. When he came to where he was and caught sight of him, his heart went out to him. ³⁴He went up to him and bandaged his wounds, pouring olive oil and wine on them. He hoisted him onto his own animal, brought him to an inn, and looked after him. ³⁵The next day he took out two denarii, which he gave to the innkeeper, and said, "Look after him, and on my way back I'll reimburse you for any extra expense you've had."

³⁶"Which of these three, in your opinion, acted like a neighbor to the man who fell into the hands of the bandits?"

³⁷He said, "The one who showed him compassion." Jesus said to him, "Then go and do the same yourself."

Q10:21–22
//Mt 11:25–27

10:21
Cf. Th 4:1

10:22
//Jn 3:35, 10:15, 17:25–26;
ⓣ SJas 6:24–26

Q10:23–24
//Mt 13:16–17

10:24
Cf. Th 38

10:25–28
//Mk 12:28–34, Mt 22:35–40

10:25
ⓓ Lk 18:18

10:27
Cf. Th 25;
ⓣ Rom 13:8–10, Gal 5:14, Jas 2:8;
◊ Dt 6:5, Lv 19:18

10:23 The Greek word *makarios*, elsewhere translated "congratulations", is here rendered *privileged* because it is addressed to parts of the body.

10:32 *Levite*: a layman with special religious duties and privileges in teaching and worship.

10:35 A *denarius* was worth a day's wage for a laborer.

Mary & Martha

The Lord's Prayer

Friend at midnight

Ask, seek, knock

³⁸**Now as they went** along, he came to this village where a woman named Martha welcomed him into her home. ³⁹And she had a sister named Mary, who sat at the Master's feet and listened to his words. ⁴⁰But Martha kept getting distracted because she was doing all the serving. So she went up to Jesus and said, "Master, doesn't it matter to you that my sister has left me with all the serving? Tell her to give me a hand."

⁴¹But the Master answered her, "Martha, Martha, you are worried and upset about a lot of things. ⁴²But only one thing is necessary. Mary has made the better choice and it's something she will never lose."

11 **And it came to pass** when he was praying somewhere that, when he had finished, one of his disciples said to him, "Master, teach us how to pray, just as John taught his disciples."

²He said to them, "When you pray, you should say:

> Father, your name be revered.
> Your empire be established.
> ³Provide us with the bread we need day by day.
> ⁴Forgive our sins, since we too forgive everyone in debt to us.
> And don't make us face the test.

⁵**Jesus said** to them,

> Suppose you have a friend who comes to you in the middle of the night and says to you, "Friend, lend me three loaves, ⁶for a friend of mine on a trip has just shown up and I have nothing to offer him." ⁷And suppose you reply, "Stop bothering me. The door is already locked and my children and I are in bed. I can't get up to give you anything."

⁸"I'm telling you, even though you won't get up and give him anything out of friendship, you will get up and give him whatever he needs because of his shameless behavior.

⁹**And I'm telling you**, ask—it'll be given to you; seek—you'll find; knock—it'll be opened for you. ¹⁰For everyone who asks receives; everyone who seeks finds; and for the one who knocks it is opened. ¹¹Which of you fathers would hand his son a snake instead of a fish when he's asking for fish? ¹²Or a scorpion when he's asking for an egg? ¹³So if you, worthless as you are, know how to give

Q11:2–4
//Mt 6:9–15

11:3
//GNaz 3

11:4
//Mk 11:25;
cf. SJas 4:2

11:5–8
Ⓣ Lk 18:1–5

Q11:9–13
//Mt 7:7–11

11:9
//Th 94;
cf. Th 2:1, 92:1;
DSav 7:2, 11:5

11:10
//Mary 4:7,
GHeb 6b

10:42 Some mss read "few things are necessary, or only one."
11:11 Some mss insert "stone, if he asks for bread, or give him a" before *snake*.

11:3 *Day by day* translates the Greek word *epiousios*, whose meaning is disputed. Other possible translations are "daily," "for subsistence," and "for the future." Its only certain oc-currence in the Greek language is in the Lord's Prayer.
11:8 By the standards of the time, it was considered shameful to refuse a friend's request for help in offering hospitality.

your children good gifts, isn't it much more likely that the heavenly Father will give holy spirit to those who ask him?"

[14]**Jesus was driving out** a demon that was mute, and when the demon had departed the mute man spoke. And the crowds were amazed. [15]But some of them said, "He drives out demons with the power of Beelzebul, the head demon."

[16]Others were putting him to the test by demanding a sign from heaven.

[17]But he knew what they were thinking, and said to them, "Every empire divided against itself is devastated, and a house divided against a house falls. [18]If Satan is divided against himself—since you claim I drive out demons with Beelzebul's power—how will his empire endure? [19]Suppose I do drive out demons with the power of Beelzebul, then with whose power do your own people drive ⟨them⟩ out? That's why they will be your judges. [20]But if I drive out demons with the finger of God, then the empire of God has come for you.

[21]"When a strong man is fully armed and guards his courtyard, his possessions are safe. [22]But when a stronger man attacks and overpowers him, he takes away the weapons on which he was relying and divides up his loot.

[23]"Those who aren't with me are against me, and those who don't gather with me scatter.

[24]"**When an unclean spirit** leaves a person, it wanders through waterless places in search of a place to rest. When it doesn't find one, it says, 'I will go back to the home I left.' [25]It then returns, and finds the place swept and put in order. [26]Next, it goes out and brings back seven other spirits more vile than itself, who enter and settle in there. So that person ends up worse off than when he or she started."

[27]**And it came to pass**, as he was making these remarks, that a woman from the crowd raised her voice and said to him, "Congratulations to the womb that carried you and the breasts that nursed you!"

[28]"Rather," he replied, "congratulations to those who hear the word of God and keep it."

[29]**As more and more people** were crowding around him, he began to say, "This generation is an evil generation. It demands a sign, but it will be given no sign—except the sign of Jonah! [30]You see, just as Jonah became a sign for the Ninevites, so the Human One will be a sign for this generation."

[31]"On judgment day, the queen of the south will be brought back to life along with members of this generation, and she will condemn them, because she came from the ends of the earth to listen to Solomon's wisdom. Yet take note:

Beelzebul controversy

Return of an unclean spirit

Congratulations to the womb

Sign of Jonah

Q11:14–23
//Mt 12:22–30, Mk 3:22–27

Q11:15
//Mt 9:34

11:20
◊Ex 8:19

11:21–22
Cf. Th 35

11:23
//Lk 9:50, GOxy 1224 6:2

11:24–26
//Mt 12:43–45

11:27–28
//Th 79:1–2

11:28
Cf. Lk 8:21

Q11:29–32
//Mt 12:38–42

Q11:29
//Mt 16:4, Mk 8:11–12; cf. Jn 6:30; ⓣ 1 Cor 1:22

11:31
◊1 Kgs 10:1–10

11:15 The name *Beelzebul* is derived from an old Canaanite god (Baalzebul), used here presumably as another name for Satan (see v. 18).

11:23 This saying seem inconsistent with the spirit of 9:50.
11:29–30 *sign of Jonah*: a prophet preaching repentance.
11:31 *queen of the south*: see 1 Kgs 10:1–29.

Lamp & bushel

*Damn you
Pharisees & legal
experts*

what is right here is greater than Solomon. [32]On judgment day, the citizens of Nineveh will come back to life along with this generation and condemn it, because they had a change of heart in response to Jonah's message. Yet take note: what is right here is greater than Jonah.

[33]"**No one lights** a lamp and then puts it in a cellar or under a bushel basket, but instead on a lampstand so that those who come in can see the light. [34]Your eye is the body's lamp. When your eye is clear, your whole body is flooded with light. When your eye is clouded, your body is shrouded in darkness. [35]Take care, then, that the light within you is not darkness. [36]So if your whole body is flooded with light, and no corner of it is darkness, it will be completely illuminated as when a lamp's rays engulf you."

[37]**While he was speaking**, a Pharisee invites him to dinner at his house. So he came and reclined ⟨at the table⟩. [38]The Pharisee was astonished to see that he did not first wash his hands before the meal.

[39]But the Master said to him, "You Pharisees clean the outside of cups and dishes, but inside you are full of greed and evil. [40]You fools! Did not the one who made the outside also make the inside? [41]Still, donate what is inside to charity, and then you'll see how everything comes clean for you.

[42]"Damn you, Pharisees! You pay tithes on mint and rue and every herb, but neglect justice and the love of God. It's these you should have practiced without neglecting the others.

[43]"Damn you, Pharisees! You love the prominent seat in synagogues and respectful greetings in marketplaces. [44]Damn you! You're like unmarked graves that people walk on without realizing it."

[45]One of the legal experts says to him in reply, "Teacher, when you say these things you're insulting us, too."

[46]And he said, "Damn you legal experts too! You load people down with crushing burdens, but you yourselves don't lift a finger to help carry them. [47]Damn you! You build monuments to the prophets whom your ancestors murdered. [48]You are therefore witnesses to and approve of the deeds of your ancestors: they killed ⟨the prophets⟩ and you build ⟨monuments⟩ to them. [49]That's why the Wisdom of God has said, 'I will send them prophets and apostles, and some of them they are always going to kill and persecute.' [50]So, this generation will have to answer for the blood of all the prophets that has been shed since the world was founded, [51]from the blood of Abel to the blood of Zechariah, who

11:32
◊Jon 3:5

Q11:33
//Mt 5:15, Mk 4:21,
Th 33:2–3;
Ⓓ Lk 8:16

Q11:34–36
//Mt 6:22–23;
cf. Th 24:3, DSav 6

11:37–52
//Mt 23:1–36

11:37
Ⓣ Lk 7:36, 14:1

Q11:39–41
//Mt 23:25–26,
Th 89;
cf. GOxy 840 2:8

Q11:42
//Mt 23:23;
◊Mi 6:8

Q11:43
//Mt 23:6–7,
Mk 12:38–39;
Ⓓ Lk 20:46–47

Q11:44
//Mt 23:27–28

Q11:46
//Mt 23:4

Q11:47–51
//Mt 23:29–36;
Ⓣ Lk 13:33–34,
Acts 7:51–52,
Neh 9:26

11:33 A few mss omit *or under a bushel basket.*

11:32 *Nineveh* was the capital of Assyria, a bitter and brutal enemy of the Israelites in the eighth century BCE.
11:38 See the explanation in Mark 7:3.
11:44 Contact with a grave renders one unclean (see Num 19:16).

11:51 Abel was a son of Adam and Eve who was murdered by his brother (Gen 4:8–10). Zechariah was a priest who was murdered in the temple (2 Chr 24:20–22). Neither of these men are identified in the OT as prophets.

perished between the altar and the sanctuary. Yes, I'm telling you, this generation will have to answer for it.

⁵²"You legal experts, damn you! You've taken away the key of knowledge. You yourselves haven't gone in and you have blocked the way of those trying to go in."

⁵³By the time he had left there, the scholars and Pharisees began to resent him bitterly and to harass him with all kinds of questions, ⁵⁴conspiring to trap him with his own words.

12 Meanwhile, a crowd of many thousands had thronged together and were trampling each other.

He began to speak first to his disciples: "Be on guard against the leaven of the Pharisees" (that is, their hypocrisy).

²"There is nothing covered up that won't be exposed, or hidden that won't be made known. ³And so whatever you've said in the dark will be heard in the light, and what you've whispered behind closed doors will be announced from the rooftops.

⁴"**I'm telling you**, my friends, don't fear those who kill the body, and after that can do no more. ⁵I'll show you whom you ought to fear: fear the one who can kill and then has authority to cast into Gehenna. Believe me, that's the one you should fear! ⁶What do five sparrows cost? Five bucks? Yet not one of them is overlooked by God. ⁷In fact, even the hairs of your head have all been counted. Don't be so timid; you're worth more than a flock of sparrows.

⁸"**I'm telling you**, everyone who acknowledges me in public, the Human One will acknowledge in front of God's messengers. ⁹But whoever disowns me in public will be disowned in front of God's messengers. ¹⁰And everyone who utters a word against the Human One will be forgiven; but whoever blasphemes against the holy spirit won't be forgiven. ¹¹And when they make you appear in front of synagogues and haul you up before rulers and authorities, don't worry about how or in what way you should defend yourself or what you should say. ¹²The holy spirit will teach you at that very moment what you ought to say."

¹³**Someone in the crowd** said to him, "Teacher, tell my brother to divide the inheritance with me."

¹⁴But Jesus said to him, "Mister, who appointed me your judge or arbiter?"

¹⁵Then he said to them, "Watch out! Be on guard against greed in all its forms; after all, possessions, even in abundance, don't guarantee you life."

Leaven of the Pharisees

Have no fear

Acknowledgment & defense

Rich fool

Q11:52
//Mt 23:13,
Th 39:1–2;
cf. Th 102

Q12:1–10
//Mt 10:26–33

12:1
//Mk 8:15, Mt 16:6

12:2
//Mk 4:22; Th 5:2,
6:5–6;
Ⓓ Lk 8:17

12:3
//Th 33:1

12:7
//Lk 21:18,
Acts 27:34

12:8–9
Ⓣ 2 Tm 2:11–13;
Ⓓ Lk 9:26

Q12:10
//Mt 12:32,
Mk 3:28–29, Th 44

Q12:11–12
//Mt 10:19–20,
Lk 21:14–15,
Mk 13:9–11

12:13–14
//Th 72

12:14
◊ Ex 2:4

12:1 *Leaven* was a Jewish metaphor for a pervasive evil influence. See Paul's use of it in 1 Cor 5:6–7 and Gal 5:9.
12:5 *Gehenna*: the valley of Hinnom, a place outside Jerusalem associated with idolatry and fire in the OT and later used as a garbage dump. In the first century, it symbolized the place of punishment for sinners after the final judgment.
12:6 *Sparrows* were sold for food.

On anxieties

Heart's true measure

Unexpected return

[16]Then he told them a parable:

> There was a rich man whose fields produced a bumper crop. [17]"What do I do now?" he asked himself, "since I don't have any place to store my crops. [18]I know!" he said, "I'll tear down my barns and build larger ones so I can store all my grain and my goods. [19]Then I'll say to myself, 'You have plenty put away for years to come. Take it easy; eat, drink, and enjoy yourself.'" [20]But God said to him, "You fool! This very night your life will be demanded back from you. All this stuff you've collected—whose will it be now?"

[21]"That's the way it is with those who save up for themselves, but aren't rich where God is concerned."

[22]**He said to his disciples**, "That's why I'm telling you: don't fret about life, what you're going to eat—or about your body, what you're going to wear. [23]Remember, there is more to living than food and clothing. [24]Think about the crows: they don't plant or harvest, they don't have storerooms or barns. Yet God feeds them. You're worth a lot more than the birds! [25]Can any of you add an hour to life by fretting about it? [26]So if you can't do a little thing like that, why worry about the rest? [27]Think about how the lilies grow: they don't toil and they never spin. But let me tell you, even Solomon at the height of his glory was never decked out like one of them. [28]If God dresses up the grass in the field, which is here today and is tossed into the oven tomorrow, how much more will ⟨God take care of⟩ you, you with your meager trust. [29]And don't be constantly on the lookout for what you're going to eat and what you're going to drink. Don't give it a thought. [30]These are all things the world's pagans seek, and your Father is aware that you need them. [31]Instead, seek his empire and these things will come to you as a bonus.

[32]**Don't be afraid**, little flock, for it has delighted your Father to give you his empire. [33]Sell your belongings, and donate to charity; make yourselves purses that don't wear out, with inexhaustible wealth in heaven, where no burglar can get to it and no moth can destroy it. [34]As you know, what you treasure is your heart's true measure.

[35]**Keep your belts fastened** and your lamps lit. [36]Imitate those who are waiting for their master to come home from a wedding, ready to open the door for him as soon as he arrives and knocks. [37]Those slaves the master finds alert when he arrives are to be congratulated. Let me tell you, he will put on an apron, have them recline at the table, and proceed to wait on them. [38]If he gets

12:16–21
//Th 63

12:19–20
◊Sir 11:19

12:19
Cf. 1 Cor 15:32;
◊Is 22:13, Eccl 8:15

Q12:22–31
//Mt 6:25–33

12:22
//Th 36

12:24
Ⓣ Job 38:41

Q12:33–34
//Mt 6:19–21

12:33
//Th 76:3;
Ⓓ Lk 18:22

12:34
//Mary 7:4

12:35–40
//Mk 13:33–37

12:20, 22, 23 *Psychē* is the principle of life and can mean both "life" and "soul." Here the contexts require "life." *Psychē* is to be distinguished from *zōē*, which refers to the mere state of being alive, as in v. 15.

12:25 *hour*: The Greek can mean either "life span/age" or

"stature" (see 2:52 and 19:3, where it means stature or maturity). The present context favors taking it metaphorically as a reference to increasing one's length of life, rather than literally as increasing one's height.

home around midnight, or even around 3 a.m., and finds them so, they are to be congratulated! ³⁹Mark this well: if the homeowner had known what time the burglar was coming, he would not have let anyone break into his house. ⁴⁰You too should be prepared. Remember, the Human One is coming when you least expect it."

⁴¹Peter said, "Master, are you telling this parable just for us or for the benefit of everyone?"

⁴²The Master said, "Who then is the trustworthy and prudent manager to whom the master assigns responsibility for his household staff, to dole out their food allowance at the right time? ⁴³Congratulations to the slave who's on the job when his master arrives. ⁴⁴I'm telling you the truth: he'll put him in charge of all his property. ⁴⁵But suppose that slave says to himself, 'My master is taking his time getting here,' and begins to beat the servants and the maids, and to eat and drink and get drunk, ⁴⁶that slave's master will show up on the day he least expects and at an hour he doesn't suspect. He'll cut him to pieces and assign him a fate among the disloyal. ⁴⁷And the slave who knew what his master wanted, but didn't get things ready or act properly, will be flogged severely. ⁴⁸On the other hand, the slave who didn't know what his master wanted, yet did things that deserve punishment, will be flogged lightly. A great deal will be required of everyone to whom much is given; yet even more will be demanded from the one to whom a great deal has been entrusted.

⁴⁹"**I came to set** the earth on fire, and how I wish it were already ablaze! ⁵⁰I have a baptism to be baptized with, and what pressure I'm under until it's over! ⁵¹Do you think I came here to bring peace on earth? No, I'm telling you, on the contrary: conflict. ⁵²As a result, from now on in any given house there will be five in conflict, three against two and two against three. ⁵³Father will be pitted against son and son against father, mother against daughter and daughter against mother, mother-in-law against daughter-in-law and daughter-in-law against mother-in-law."

⁵⁴**He would also say** to the crowds, "When you see a cloud rising in the west, right away you say that it's going to rain; and so it does. ⁵⁵And when the wind blows from the south, you say we're in for scorching heat; and we are. ⁵⁶You phonies! You know the lay of the land and can read the face of the sky, so why don't you know how to interpret the present time?

Not peace, but conflict

Signs of the times

Q12:39–48
//Mt 24:43–51

12:39
//Th 21:5;
cf. Th 103

12:40
Ⓣ 1 Thes 5:2,
2 Pet 3:10, Rv 16:15

Q12:49–53
//Mt 10:34–36

12:49
//Th 10;
Ⓣ GSav 12:9,
Th 16:1–2

12:51–53
//Th 16;
cf. GNaz 11

12:53
◊Mi 7:6

Q12:54–56
//Mt 16:2–3, Th 91

12:39 Many mss insert "he would have watched and" after *coming*.

12:42 A *manager* (*oikonomos*) is one who administers the affairs of a wealthy household, which includes the extended family and the slaves and their families.
12:45 *My master is taking his time getting here* probably re-

flects the recognition by late first-century Christians that Jesus was not going to return (at his second coming) any time soon.
12:50 *baptism*: a figurative reference to his death.

[57]"**Why can't you decide** for yourselves what is right? [58]When you're about to appear with your accuser before the magistrate, do your best to settle with him on the way, or else he might drag you up before the judge, and the judge turn you over to the jailer, and the jailer throw you in prison. [59]I'm telling you, you'll never get out of there until you've paid every last cent."

13 **Some who were there** at the time told him about the Galileans, about how Pilate had mixed their own blood with their sacrifices. [2]He answered them, "Do you suppose that these Galileans were the worst sinners in Galilee, because they suffered this? [3]Hardly. However, let me tell you, if you don't have a change of heart, you'll all meet your doom in the same way. [4]Or how about those eighteen in Siloam, who were killed when that tower fell on them—do you suppose that they were any guiltier than the whole population of Jerusalem? [5]Hardly. However, let me tell you, if you don't have a change of heart, all of you will meet your doom in a similar fashion."

[6]**Then he told this parable**:

A man had a fig tree growing in his vineyard; he came looking for fruit on it but didn't find any.

[7]So he said to the vinekeeper, "See here, for three years in a row I've come looking for fruit on this tree, and haven't found any. Cut it down. Why should it suck the nutrients out of the soil?"

[8]In response he says to him, "Let it stand, sir, one more year, until I get a chance to dig around it and work in some manure. [9]Maybe it will produce next year; but if it doesn't, we can go ahead and cut it down."

[10]**Now he was teaching** in one of the meeting places on the Sabbath. [11]A woman showed up who for eighteen years had been afflicted by a spirit; she was bent over and unable to straighten up even a little. [12]When Jesus noticed her, he called her over and said, "Woman, you are freed from your affliction." [13]He laid hands on her, and immediately she stood up straight and began to praise God.

[14]The leader of the meeting place was indignant, however, because Jesus had healed on the Sabbath. He said to the crowd, "There are six days which we devote to work; so come on one of those days and be healed, but not on the Sabbath."

[15]But the Master answered him, "You phonies! Every last one of you unties your ox or your donkey from the feeding trough on the Sabbath and leads it

Q12:57–59
//Mt 5:25–26

13:14
◊ Ex 20:9

12:59 *Cent* translates the Greek *lepton*, a coin worth less than 1% of a denarius, the usual wage for a day of labor.
13:1 Pilate, the Roman governor, was notorious for his brutality, but this atrocity is nowhere else attested in ancient sources.

13:11 Physical abnormalities were often attributed to demons. As in this case, there was considerable overlap between the notions of healing and exorcism. Even though Jesus heals her without casting out the spirit, in v. 16 he refers to the healing as releasing her from Satan's bonds.

off to water, don't you? ¹⁶This woman, a daughter of Abraham whom Satan has kept in bondage for eighteen long years—should she not be released from these bonds just because it is the Sabbath?" ¹⁷As he said this, all his adversaries were put to shame, but most folks rejoiced at all the wonderful things he was doing.

¹⁸**Then he was saying**,

> What is the empire of God like? What does it remind me of? ¹⁹It's like a mustard seed that a man took and tossed into his garden. It grew and became a tree, and the birds of the sky roosted in its branches.

²⁰He continued,

> What does the empire of God remind me of? ²¹It's like leaven that a woman took and concealed in fifty pounds of flour until it was all leavened.

²²**On his journey** he passed through towns and villages, teaching and making his way toward Jerusalem.

²³And someone asked him, "Sir, is it true that only a few are going to be saved?"

He said to them, ²⁴"Struggle to get in through the narrow door; I'm telling you, many will try to get in, but won't be able. ²⁵Once the master of the house gets up and bars the door, you'll be left standing outside and knocking at the door: 'Master, open up for us.' But he'll answer you, 'I don't know where you come from.' ²⁶Then you'll start saying, 'We ate and drank with you, and you taught in our streets.' ²⁷But he'll reply, 'I don't know where you come from; get away from me, all you evildoers!' ²⁸There'll be weeping and grinding of teeth out there when you see Abraham and Isaac and Jacob and all the prophets in God's empire and yourselves thrown out. ²⁹And people will come from east and west, from north and south, and dine in God's empire. ³⁰And remember, those who will be first are last, and those who will be last are first."

³¹**About that time** some Pharisees approached and warned him, "Get out of here! Herod wants to kill you."

³²He replied to them, "Go tell that fox, 'Look here, today and tomorrow I'll be driving out demons and healing people, and the third day I'll be finished. ³³Still, today and tomorrow and the day after, I have to move on, because it's impossible for a prophet to die outside of Jerusalem.' ³⁴Jerusalem, Jerusalem, you murder the prophets and stone those sent to you! How often I wanted to gather your children as a hen ⟨gathers⟩ her own chicks under her wings, but you wouldn't let me. ³⁵Can't you see, your house is being abandoned? I'm telling

Mustard seed & leaven

Narrow door

Warning & lament

Q13:18–19
//Mt 13:31–32,
Th 20, Mk 4:30–32;
Ⓣ DSav 36:1
13:19
◊Dn 4:20–21
Q13:20–21
//Mt 13:33, Th 96,
SJas 6:15g
Q13:24
Cf. Mt 7:13–14
13:25
Cf. Mt 25:10–12
Q13:26–27
Cf. Mt 7:21–23;
◊Ps 6:8
Q13:28–29
//Mt 8:11–12;
Ⓣ DSav 8:8;
◊Ps 107:3
13:29
Ⓣ GSav 1:3
Q13:30
//Mt 19:30, 20:16;
Th 4:2, Mk 10:31
13:33–34
Cf. Lk 11:49,
Acts 7:51–52
Q13:34–35
//Mt 23:37–39
13:34
◊Is 31:5
13:35
Ⓣ Lk 19:37–38;
◊Ps 118:26, Jer 22:5

13:19 Jewish religious law prohibited the growing of mustard seed in a garden with other plants. Mustard is a shrub, not a tree.

13:21 *leaven*: See the note on 12:1.

13:32 *Fox* is a metaphor for a devious and deceitful person; see Ezek 13:4, where false prophets are called foxes.

13:35 *House* is most likely a reference to the temple.

Man with dropsy healed

Places of honor

Choice of guests

Dinner party

you, you certainly won't see me until the time comes when you say, 'Blessed is the one who comes in the name of the Lord.'"

14 **And it came to pass** one Sabbath, when Jesus was having dinner at the house of a prominent Pharisee, that they were keeping an eye on him. [2]This man who had dropsy suddenly showed up.

[3]Jesus addressed the legal experts and Pharisees: "Is it permitted to heal on the Sabbath, or not?"

[4]But they were silent.

So he took the man, healed him, and sent him on his way.

[5]Then he said to them, "Suppose your son or your ox falls down a well, would any of you hesitate for a second to pull him out on the Sabbath?"

[6]And they had no response to this.

[7]**He would tell a parable** for the guests, when he noticed how they were choosing the places of honor.

He said to them, [8]"When someone invites you to a wedding banquet, don't take the place of honor, in case someone more important than you has been invited. [9]Then the one who invited you both will come and say to you, 'Make room for this person,' and you'll be embarrassed to have to take the lowest place. [10]Instead, when you're invited, go take the lowest place, so when the host comes he'll say to you, 'Friend, come up higher.' Then you'll be honored in front of all those reclining ⟨around the table⟩ with you.

[11]"Those who promote themselves will be demoted, and those who demote themselves will be promoted."

[12]**Then he said** also to his host, "When you give a lunch or a dinner, don't invite your friends, or your brothers and sisters, or relatives, or rich neighbors. They might invite you in return and so you would be repaid. [13]Instead, when you throw a dinner party, invite the poor, the crippled, the lame, and the blind. [14]In that case, you are to be congratulated, since they cannot repay you. You will be repaid at the resurrection of the just."

[15]**When one of his fellow guests** heard this, he said to him, "Congratulations to those who will eat bread in the empire of God!"

[16]Jesus told him,

Someone was giving a big dinner and invited many guests. [17]At the dinner hour the host sent his slave to tell the guests, "Come, it's ready now." [18]But one by one they all began to make excuses. The first said to him, "I just bought a farm and I have to go and inspect it; please excuse me." [19]And another said, "I just bought five pairs of oxen and I'm on my way to check them out; please excuse me." [20]And another said, "I just got married and so I cannot attend." [21]So the slave

14:1–6
//Lk 6:6–11

14:5
//Mt 12:11–12

14:8–10
◊ Prv 25:6–7

Q14:11
//Mt 23:12;
Ⓓ Lk 18:14

14:15
//GSav 1:3

Q14:16–24
//Mt 22:1–10, Th 64

14:5 Some mss read "donkey" in place of *son*.

came back and reported these ⟨excuses⟩ to his master. Then the master of the house was outraged and instructed his slave, "Quick! Go out into the streets and alleys of the town, and usher in the poor, and crippled, the blind, and the lame."

²²And the slave said, "Master, your orders have been carried out, and there's still room."

²³And the master said to the slave, "Then go out into the roads and the country lanes, and force people to come in so my house will be filled. ²⁴For I'm telling you, not one of those who were invited will taste my dinner."

²⁵**Once when hordes** of people were traveling with him, he turned and addressed them: ²⁶"If any of you comes to me and does not hate your own father and mother and wife and children and brothers and sisters—yes, even your own life—you cannot be my disciple. ²⁷Unless you carry your own cross and come along with me, you cannot be my disciple.

²⁸"Think about it: if you plan to build a tower, don't you first sit down and calculate whether you can afford to complete it? ²⁹Otherwise you might lay the foundation and not be able to finish, and all the onlookers would begin to make fun of you: ³⁰'That guy started to build but couldn't finish.'

³¹"Or if a king was going to war against another king, wouldn't he first sit down and figure out whether he would be able with ten thousand men to engage an enemy coming against him with twenty thousand? ³²If he decided he couldn't, he would send an envoy to ask for terms of peace while the enemy was still a long way off.

³³"It's just like that: if you don't say good-bye to everything that belongs to you, you cannot be my disciple.

³⁴"Salt is good, but if it loses its zing, how will it be renewed? ³⁵It's no good for either earth or manure. It just gets thrown away. Anyone here with two good ears, use 'em!"

15 **Now the toll collectors** and sinners kept crowding around Jesus so they could hear him. ²But the Pharisees and the scholars would complain to each other, "This guy welcomes sinners and eats with them."

³So he told them this parable:

> ⁴Is there any one of you who owns a hundred sheep and one of them gets lost, who wouldn't leave the ninety-nine in the wild and go after the one that got lost until he finds it? ⁵And when he finds it, he is happy and hoists it onto his shoulders. ⁶Once he gets home, he invites his friends and his neighbors over, and says to them, "Celebrate with me, because I've found my lost sheep."

Q14:26–27
//Mt 10:37–38,
Th 55, 101

14:27
//Mk 8:34,
Mt 16:24;
Ⓣ Lk 9:23

Q14:34–35
//Mt 5:13, Mk 9:50

15:2
Ⓣ Lk 5:30, 7:34,
19:7;
GOxy 1224 5:1

Q15:3–7
//Mt 18:12–14,
Th 107, SJas 6:15a

14:24 The *you* is plural in the Greek; the moral of the story is thus addressed to readers, not to the slave in the story.

Lost coin

Prodigal son

[7]"I'm telling you, it'll be just like that in heaven: there'll be more celebrating over one sinner who has a change of heart than over ninety-nine virtuous people who have no need to change their hearts.

[8]**Or again**, is there any woman with ten drachmas, who if she loses one, wouldn't light a lamp and sweep the house and search high and low until she finds it? [9]When she finds it, she invites her friends and neighbors over and says, 'Celebrate with me, because I've found the drachma I lost.'

[10]"I'm telling you, it's just like that among God's messengers: they celebrate when one sinner has a change of heart."

[11]**Then he said**:

Once there was this man who had two sons. [12]The younger of them said to his father, "Father, give me the share of the property that's coming to me." So he divided his resources between them.

[13]Not too many days later, the younger son got all his things together and left home for a faraway country, where he squandered his resources by living recklessly. [14]Just when he had spent it all, a serious famine swept through that country, and he began to do without. [15]So he went and hired himself out to one of the citizens of that country, who sent him out to his farm to feed the pigs. [16]He longed to satisfy his hunger with the carob pods, which the pigs usually ate; but no one offered him anything. [17]Coming to his senses he said, "Lots of my father's hired hands have more than enough to eat, while here I am starving to death! [18]I'll get up and go to my father and I'll say to him, 'Father, I have sinned against Heaven and against you. [19]I no longer deserve to be called your son; treat me like one of your hired hands.'" [20]And he got up and returned to his father.

But while he was still a long way off, his father caught sight of him and was moved to compassion. He went running out to him, threw his arms around his neck, and kissed him. [21]And the son said to him, "Father, I have sinned against Heaven and against you. I no longer deserve to be called your son."

[22]But the father said to his slaves, "Hurry up! Bring out the finest robe and put it on him; put a ring on his finger and sandals on his feet. [23]Fetch the fat calf and slaughter it; let's have a feast and celebrate, [24]because this son of mine was dead and has come back to life; he was lost and now is found." And they started celebrating.

15:8–10
//SJas 6:15f

15:21 Some mss add "Treat me like one of your hired hands" to the end of the verse.

15:8 A *drachma*, like a denarius, was approximately a day's wage for a laborer.
15:12 In asking for his share of the inheritance, the son treats his father as if he were dead. Jewish wisdom warned

fathers against distributing an inheritance while still alive (Sir 33:20–24).
15:15 To work with pigs would be the ultimate degradation for a Jew.

²⁵Now his elder son was out in the field; and as he got closer to the house, he heard music and dancing. ²⁶He called one of the servant boys over and asked what was going on.

²⁷He told him, "Your brother has come home and your father has slaughtered the fat calf, because he has him back safe and sound."

²⁸But he was angry and refused to go in. So his father came out and began to plead with him. ²⁹But he answered his father, "See here, all these years I have slaved for you. I never once disobeyed any of your orders; but you never once let me have a kid goat so I could celebrate with my friends. ³⁰But when this son of yours shows up, the one who has devoured your assets with whores—for him you slaughter the fat calf."

³¹But ⟨the father⟩ said to him, "My child, you are always at my side. Everything that's mine is yours. ³²But we just had to celebrate and rejoice, because this brother of yours was dead and has come back to life; he was lost and now is found."

16 Or Jesus would say to the disciples:

There was this rich man whose manager had been maliciously accused of squandering his master's property. ²He called him in and said, "What's this I hear about you? Turn in your record books; you're no longer working here."

³Then the manager said to himself, "What am I going to do? My master is firing me. I'm not able to dig ditches and I'm ashamed to beg. ⁴I've got it! I know what I'll do so doors will open for me when I'm removed from management."

⁵So he called in each of his master's debtors. He said to the first, "How much do you owe my master?"

⁶He said, "Five hundred gallons of olive oil."

And he said to him, "Here is your invoice; sit down right now and make it two hundred and fifty."

⁷Then he said to another, "And how much do you owe?"

He said, "A thousand bushels of wheat."

He says to him, "Here is your invoice; make it eight hundred."

⁸The master praised the dishonest manager because he had acted prudently.

"For the children of this world are more prudent in dealing with their own kind than are the children of light.

15:30 *this son of yours*: The elder son tries to disassociate himself from his brother, a rhetorical move the father rebuts with *this brother of yours* (v. 32).

16:1 *Maliciously accused* translates a Greek word can also mean "slandered." The choice of vocabulary hints that the accusation is false.

16:6–7 The manager is probably defrauding his master.

However, the discounts may represent kickbacks to the customers of his own exorbitant commissions.

16:8 *The master* probably refers to the rich man of v. 1. The manager calls him "master" in vv. 3 and 5. The second half of this verse is probably an explanation for the master's praise, not part of the parable itself.

Slave with two masters

Law & Prophets

On divorce

Rich man & Lazarus

[9]"And I'm telling you, make use of your ill-gotten mammon to make friends for yourselves, so that when the bottom falls out they are there to welcome you into eternal dwelling places.

[10]"**Those who can be trusted** in trivial matters can also be trusted with large amounts; and those who cheat in trivial matters will also cheat where large amounts are concerned. [11]So if you can't be trusted with ill-gotten mammon, who will trust you with real wealth? [12]And if you can't be trusted with something that belongs to somebody else, who will give you property of your own? [13]No servant can be a slave to two masters. That slave will either hate one and love the other, or be devoted to one and disdain the other. You can't be enslaved to both God and mammon."

[14]The Pharisees, who were money grubbers, heard all this and sneered at him. [15]But he said to them, "You're the type who justify yourselves to others, but God reads your hearts. What people rank highest is detestable in God's estimation.

[16]"**Right up to John's time** you have the Law and the Prophets; since then God's empire has been proclaimed as good news and everyone is breaking into it violently. [17]But it's easier for earth and sky to pass away than for one serif of the Law to drop out.

[18]"**Everyone who divorces** his wife and marries another commits adultery; and the one who marries a woman divorced from her husband commits adultery.

[19]**There was this rich man**, who wore clothing fit for a king and who dined lavishly every day. [20]This poor man, named Lazarus, languished at his gate, all covered with sores. [21]He longed to eat what fell from the rich man's table. Dogs even used to come and lick his sores. [22] It came to pass that the poor man died and was carried by the heavenly messengers to be with Abraham. The rich man died too, and was buried.

[23]From Hades, where he was being tortured, he looked up and saw Abraham a long way off and Lazarus with him. [24]He called out, "Father Abraham, have pity on me! Send Lazarus to dip the tip of his finger in water and cool my tongue, for I am in torment in these flames."

[25]But Abraham said, "My child, remember that you had good fortune in your lifetime, while Lazarus had it bad. Now he is being comforted here, and you are in torment. [26]And besides all this, a great chasm has been set between us and you, so that even those who want to cross over from here to you cannot, and no one can cross over from that side to ours."

Q16:13
//Mt 6:24,
Th 47:1–2

Q16:16
//Mt 11:12–13;
cf. SJas 6:2–4

Q16:17
//Mt 5:18

Q16:18
//Mt 5:31–32, 19:9;
Mk 10:11–12;
cf. 1 Cor 7:10–11

16:9, 13 *mammon*: an Aramaic word for wealth.
16:15 *Detestable* (traditionally translated "abomination") is a term from the Law which designates ritual and moral practices incompatible with membership in the covenant community (see e.g., Lev 11:10–23; 18:22; Deut 12:31;

27:15).
16:16 *John*: the Baptizer.
16:20 *Lazarus* is not to be identified with the character in John 11.

Better off drowned

*Trust like a
mustard seed*

Worthless slaves

*Jesus heals
ten lepers*

²⁷But he said, "Father, I beg you then, send him to my father's house ²⁸—after all, I have five brothers—so he can warn them not to wind up in this place of torture."

²⁹But Abraham says, "They have Moses and the prophets; why don't they listen to them?"

³⁰"But they won't do that, father Abraham," he said. "But, if someone appears to them from the dead, they'll have a change of heart."

³¹Abraham said to him, "If they won't listen to Moses and the prophets, they won't be convinced even if someone were to rise from the dead."

17 **He said to his disciples**, "There's no way that traps won't be set; but still, damn those who set them! ²You'd be better off if you had a millstone tied around your neck and were dumped into the sea than to entrap and exploit one of these little ones. ³So be on your guard. If your companion does wrong, scold that person; if there is a change of heart, forgive the person. ⁴If someone wrongs you seven times a day, and seven times turns around and says to you, 'I'm sorry,' you must forgive that person."

⁵**The apostles said** to the Master, "Make our trust grow!"

⁶And the Master said, "If you had trust no bigger than a mustard seed, you could tell this mulberry tree, 'Uproot yourself and plant yourself in the sea,' and it would obey you.

⁷**If you had a slave** plowing or herding sheep and he came in from the fields, would any of you tell him, "Come right in and recline ⟨at the table⟩"? ⁸Wouldn't you say to him instead, "Get my dinner ready, put on your apron, and serve me while I eat and drink. You can eat and drink later"? ⁹He wouldn't thank the slave because he did what he was told to do, would he? ¹⁰The same goes for you: when you've done everything you've been told to do, say, "We're worthless slaves; we've only done our job."

¹¹**And it came to pass** on the way to Jerusalem that he was passing between Samaria and Galilee. ¹²As he was coming into this village, he was met by ten lepers, who kept their distance. ¹³They shouted, "Jesus, Master, have mercy on us!"

¹⁴When he saw them, he told them, "Go show yourselves to the priests." And it came to pass as they departed that they were made clean.

¹⁵Then one of them, realizing that he had been healed, came back. He praised God out loud, ¹⁶knelt with his face to the ground at Jesus' feet, and thanked him. (Incidentally, this man was a Samaritan.)

Q17:1–2
//Mt 18:6–7,
Mk 9:42

Q17:3
//Mt 18:15

Q17:4
//Mt 18:21–22,
GNaz 5:1

Q17:5–6
//Mt 17:20, 21:21;
Mk 11:22–23

17:6
Cf. Th 48, 106

17:14
Cf. EgerG 2:4

17:7–10 *worthless slaves*: For all his compassion for the poor and the lowly, the Jesus portrayed by Luke seems untroubled by the inequalities of slavery.

17:14 *show yourselves to the priests*: in accord with the Law in Leviticus 13–14.

Empire of God among you

Days of the Human One

Judge & widow

¹⁷But Jesus said, "Ten were cured, weren't they? What became of the other nine? ¹⁸Didn't any of them return to praise God besides this foreigner?"

¹⁹And he said to him, "Get up and be on your way; your trust has cured you."

²⁰**When asked by the Pharisees** when the empire of God would come, he answered them, "You won't be able to observe the coming of the empire of God. ²¹People won't be able to say, 'Look, here it is!' or 'Over there!' On the contrary, the empire of God is among you."

²²**And he said to the disciples**, "There'll come a time when you will yearn to see one of the days of the Human One, and you won't see it. ²³And they'll be telling you, 'Look, there it is!' or 'Look, here it is!' Don't rush off; don't pursue it. ²⁴For just as lightning flashes and lights up the sky from one end to the other, that's what the Human One will be like in his day. ²⁵But first he is destined to endure much and be rejected by this present generation. ²⁶And just as it was in the days of Noah, that's how it will be in the days of the Human One. ²⁷They ate, drank, got married, and were given in marriage, until the day Noah boarded the ark. Then the flood came and destroyed them all. ²⁸That's also the way it was in the days of Lot. Everyone ate, drank, bought, sold, planted, and built. ²⁹But on the day Lot left Sodom, fire and sulfur rained down from the sky and destroyed them all. ³⁰It will be like that on the day the Human One is revealed. ³¹On that day, if any are on the roof and their things are in the house, they had better not go down to fetch them. The same goes for those in the field: they had better not turn back for anything left behind. ³²Remember Lot's wife. ³³Whoever tries to hang on to life will lose it, but whoever loses it will preserve it. ³⁴I'm telling you, on that night there will be two on one couch; one will be taken and the other left. ³⁵There will be two women grinding together; one will be taken and the other left." ³⁷Then they asked him, "Taken where, Master?" And he said to them, "Vultures collect wherever there's a carcass."

18 **He told them a parable** about the need to pray at all times and never to lose heart. ²This is what he said:

17:19
Ⓣ Lk 7:50, 8:48, 18:42

Q17:20–21
//Th 3:1–3; 113; cf. DSav 9:3, Mary 4:4–5

Q17:23–24
//Mt 24:26–27

17:23
//Mk 13:21, Mt 24:23, Mary 4:4

Q17:26–30
//Mt 24:37–39

17:27
◊Gn 7:7

17:29
◊Gn 19:24

17:31
//Mk 13:15–16, Mt 24:17–18

17:32
◊Gn 19:26

Q17:33
//Mt 10:39, 16:25; Mk 8:35; cf. SJas 4:10–5:3; Ⓓ Lk 9:24

Q17:34–35
//Mt 24:40–41, Th 61:1

Q17:37
//Mt 24:28; Job 39:30b

18:1–8
Ⓣ Lk 11:5–8

18:1
Ⓣ Rom 12:12

17:24 Some mss omit *in his day*.

17:35 Some mss add another verse, traditionally numbered 17:36: "Two will be in the fields; one will be taken, the other left."

17:21 *Among you* translates the Greek *entos humōn. Entos* is an unusual word that can mean either "within" or "among." The traditional translation "within you" suggests within each individual. However, Greek distinguishes singular from plural "you," and this "you" is plural. "Among you" is thus the appropriate translation.

17:24 The Human One's arrival will be both sudden and obvious to all.

17:31 Most houses in this part of the world had flat roofs, where people would go in the course of daily activities.

17:37 Greek uses the same word (*aetos*) to refer to vultures and eagles.

Once there was a judge in this town who neither feared God nor had any respect for people. [3]In that same town was a widow who kept coming to him and demanding, "Give me a ruling against my opponent."

[4]For a while he refused; but eventually he said to himself, "I don't fear God and I have no respect for people, [5]but this widow keeps pestering me. So I'm going to rule in her favor, or else she'll keep coming back until she wears me down."

[6]And the Master said, "Don't you hear what this corrupt judge is saying? [7]Do you really think God won't hand out justice to his chosen ones—those who call on him day and night? Do you really think he'll put them off? [8]I'm telling you, he'll give them justice and give it quickly. Still, when the Human One comes, will he find any trust on the earth?"

[9]**Then for those who were confident** of their own moral superiority and who held everyone else in contempt, he had this parable:

[10]Two men went up to the temple to pray, one a Pharisee and the other a toll collector.

[11]The Pharisee stood up and prayed silently as follows: "I thank you, God, that I'm not like everybody else, thieving, unjust, adulterous, and especially not like that toll collector over there. [12]I fast twice a week; I donate ten percent of everything that I acquire."

[13]But the toll collector stood off by himself and didn't even dare to look up, but struck his chest, saying, "God, have mercy on me, sinner that I am."

[14]Let me tell you, the second man went back home vindicated but the first one did not. For those who promote themselves will be demoted, but those who demote themselves will be promoted.

[15]**They would even bring** him their babies so he could lay hands on them. But when the disciples noticed it, they scolded them. [16]Jesus called for the babies and said, "Let the children come up to me, and don't try to stop them. God's empire belongs to people like these.

[17]"Let me tell you, whoever doesn't welcome the empire of God the way a child would, will never enter it."

[18]**Someone from the ruling class** asked him, "Good teacher, what do I have to do to inherit eternal life?"

18:11 Some mss read "the Pharisee stood and prayed thus to himself;" a few mss read "the Pharisee stood and prayed thus."

Pharisee & toll collector

Children in God's empire

Man with money

Q18:14
//Mt 23:12;
Ⓓ Lk 14:11

18:15–17
//Mk 10:13–16,
Mt 19:13–15

18:16
Cf. Th 22:1–2

18:17
Cf. Mt 18:3;
Ⓣ SJas 2:6

18:18–30
//Mk 10:17–31,
Mt 19:16–30,
GNaz 6

18:18
Ⓓ Lk 10:25

18:3 Although a *widow*'s legal rights were protected by the Law (e.g., Deut 10:17–18 and 27:19), the parable does not say that her case was just.

18:5 The Greek word *hypopiazō* (literally, "to hit under the eye") was a boxing term, also used figuratively in the sense of "to wear down."

18:13 Striking one's chest was a ritual gesture of repentance.

[19]Jesus said to him, "Why do you call me good? No one is good except God alone. [20]You know the commandments: 'You shall not commit adultery, you shall not murder, you shall not steal, you shall not give false testimony, and you shall honor your father and mother.'"

[21]And he said, "I have observed all these since I was a child."

[22]When Jesus heard this, he said to him, "You are still short one thing. Sell everything you have and distribute ⟨the money⟩ among the poor, and you will have treasure in heaven. And then come on, follow me!"

[23]But when he heard this, he became very sad, for he was extremely rich.

[24]**When Jesus observed** that he had become very sad, he said, "How difficult it is for those with money to enter God's empire! [25]It's easier for a camel to squeeze through the eye of a needle than for the wealthy to get into God's empire."

[26]Those who heard this said, "Well then, who can be saved?"

[27]But he said, "What's impossible for humans is possible for God."

[28]Then Peter said, "Look at us! We have left what we had to follow you."

[29]And he told them, "Let me tell you, there is no one who has left home or wife or brothers or parents or children for the sake of the empire of God, [30]who won't receive many times as much in the present age, and in the age to come, eternal life."

[31]**Jesus took the Twelve** aside and said to them, "Listen, we're going up to Jerusalem, and everything written by the prophets about the Human One will come true. [32]For he will be turned over to the gentiles, and will be made fun of and insulted. They will spit on him [33]and flog him and kill him, and on the third day he will rise." [34]But they did not understand any of this; this remark was obscure to them, and they never did figure out what it meant.

[35]**It came to pass**, as he was coming into Jericho, that this blind man was sitting by the wayside begging. [36]Hearing a crowd passing through, he asked what was going on.

[37]They told him, "Jesus the Nazarene is going by."

[38]Then he shouted, "Jesus, son of David, have mercy on me!"

[39]Those in the lead kept yelling at him to shut up, but he kept shouting all the louder, "Son of David, have mercy on me!"

[40]Jesus paused and ordered them to guide the man over. When he came near, Jesus asked him, [41]"What do you want me to do for you?"

He said, "Master, I want to see again."

[42]Jesus said to him, "Then see again; your trust has cured you."

18:20
◊Ex 20:12–16

18:22
Ⓣ Lk 12:33

18:28
Ⓣ Lk 5:11, 28;
cf. SJas 4:1

18:31–34
//Mk 10:32–34,
Mt 20:17–19

18:31–33
Ⓣ Lk 9:44, 17:25,
22:22, 24:6–8

18:34
Ⓣ Lk 9:45,
24:25–27, 44–45

18:35–43
//Mk 10:46–52,
Mt 9:27–31,
20:29–34

18:42
Ⓣ Lk 7:50, 8:48,
17:19

18:25 The *camel* was the largest animal in Palestine; the *eye of a needle* was the smallest known opening.

18:34 *They did not understand any of this*, even though

this is the sixth time Jesus predicts his Passion (9:22, 9:24, 12:50, 13:32–34, 17:25).

This remark was obscure: See 9:44–45.

⁴³And immediately he regained his sight, and began to follow him, praising God all the while. And everyone who saw it gave God the praise.

19 **Then he entered Jericho** and was making his way through it. ²Now a man named Zacchaeus lived there who was a chief toll collector and a rich man. ³He was trying to see who Jesus was, but couldn't, because of the crowd, since he was short. ⁴So he ran on ahead to a point Jesus was to pass and climbed a sycamore tree to get a view of him.

⁵When Jesus reached that spot, he looked up at him and said, "Zacchaeus, hurry up and climb down; I have to stay at your house today."

⁶So he scurried down and welcomed him warmly.

⁷Everyone who saw this complained, "He's going to spend the day with some sinner!"

⁸But Zacchaeus stood his ground and said to the Master, "Look, sir, I'll give half of what I own to the poor, and if I have extorted anything from anyone, I'll pay back four times as much."

⁹Jesus said to him, "Today salvation has come to this house. This man is a real son of Abraham. ¹⁰Remember, the Human One came to seek out and to save what was lost."

¹¹**While they were still** paying attention to this exchange, he proceeded to tell a parable, because he was near Jerusalem and it seemed to them that God's empire was about to appear at any moment. ¹²So he said,

> A nobleman went off to a distant land intending to acquire a kingship for himself and then return. ¹³Calling ten of his slaves, he gave them ten minas and told them, "Do business with this while I'm away."
>
> ¹⁴His fellow citizens, however, hated him and sent a delegation right on his heels, with the petition: "We don't want this man to rule us."
>
> ¹⁵And it came to pass that he got the kingship and returned. He had those slaves summoned to whom he had given the money, in order to find out what profit they had made.
>
> ¹⁶The first came in and reported, "Master, your mina has increased ten times over."
>
> ¹⁷He said to him, "Well done, you competent slave! Because you've been trustworthy in this small matter, you are to be in charge of ten towns."
>
> ¹⁸The second came in and reported, "Master, your mina has increased five times over."

19:7
Ⓣ Lk 5:30, 7:34, 15:2
19:8
◊ Ex 22:1
19:10
◊ Ez 34:16
Q19:11–27
//Mt 25:14–30

19:1 *a chief toll collector*: one who collaborated with the Romans in administering the hated system of oppressive taxation.
19:8 Since chief toll collectors acquired their wealth through extortion, following through on this pledge would reduce Zacchaeus to poverty.
19:13 A *mina* was worth 100 denarii, about four months wages for a laborer. Compare Luke's amount to that of Matt 25:15.

¹⁹And he said to him, "And you are to be in charge of five towns."

²⁰Then the other ⟨slave⟩ came in and said, "Master, here is your money. I kept it tucked away safe in a handkerchief. ²¹You see, I was afraid of you, because you're a ruthless man: you withdraw what you didn't deposit and reap what you didn't sow."

²²He said to him, "You incompetent slave! Your own words convict you. So you knew I was ruthless, did you? That I withdraw what I didn't deposit and reap what I didn't sow? ²³So why didn't you put my money in the bank? Then I could have collected it with interest when I got back."

²⁴Then he said to his attendants, "Take the mina away from this guy and give it to the one who has ten."

²⁵"But master," they said to him, "he already has ten minas."

²⁶He replied, "I'm telling you, to everyone who has, more will be given; and from those who don't have, even what they do have will be taken away. ²⁷But now, about those enemies of mine, the ones who didn't want me to rule them: bring them here and slaughter them in front of me."

²⁸**When he had finished** the parable, he walked on ahead, on his way up to Jerusalem. ²⁹And it came to pass as he got close to Bethphage and Bethany, at the mountain called Olives, that he sent off two of the disciples ³⁰with these instructions: "Go into the village across the way. As you enter, you will find a colt tied there, one that has never been ridden. Untie it and bring it here. ³¹If anyone asks you, 'Why are you untying it?' just say, 'The Master needs it.'" ³²So those who were sent went off and found it exactly as he had described.

³³Just as they were untying the colt, its owners said to them, "What are you doing untying that colt?"

³⁴So they said, "The Master needs it."

³⁵So they brought it to Jesus. They threw their cloaks on the colt and helped Jesus mount it. ³⁶And as he rode along, people would spread their cloaks on the road. ³⁷As he approached the slope of the Mount of Olives, the entire throng of his disciples began to cheer and shout praise to God for all the miracles they had seen. ³⁸They kept repeating,

> Blessed is the king who comes in the name of the Lord!
> Peace in heaven and glory in the highest ⟨heaven⟩!

³⁹But some of the Pharisees, also in the crowd, said to him, "Teacher, restrain your disciples."

⁴⁰But he responded, "Take my word for it: if these folks were to keep quiet, these stones would shout."

19:26
//Mk 4:25,
Mt 13:12, Th 41;
Ⓓ Lk 8:18

19:28–40
//Mk 11:1–10,
Mt 21:1–9,
Jn 12:12–19

19:38
Ⓘ Lk 13:35;
◊Ps 118:26

19:30–31 This seems to be a pre-arranged password. Alternatively, the story may intend to emphasize Jesus' foreknowledge.
19:31 *Master* here translates *kyrios*. Some confusion is cre-

ated by the use of this term in v. 33 (in the plural, *owners*) and again in v. 34.
19:36 The *cloaks on the road* may be an allusion to the honor shown the new king Jehu in 2 Kgs 9:13.

[41]**When he got close** enough to catch sight of the city, he wept over it. [42]"If you—yes, you—had only recognized the path to peace even today! But as it is, it is hidden from your eyes. [43]The time will come down on you when your enemies will throw up a rampart against you and surround you, and hem you in on every side, [44]and then smash you to the ground, you and your children with you. They will not leave one stone on top of another within you, because you failed to recognize the time of your visitation."

[45]**Then he entered** the temple area and began throwing the vendors out. [46]He says to them, "It is written,

> My house shall be a house of prayer.

But you have turned it into 'a hideout for bandits'!"

[47]Every day he would teach in the temple area. The chief priests and the scholars, along with the leaders of the people, kept looking for some way to destroy him. [48]But they never figured out how to do it, because all the people hung on his every word.

20 **And it came to pass** one day, as he was teaching the people in the temple area and speaking of the good news, that the chief priests and the scholars approached him along with the elders, [2]and put this question to him: "Tell us where you got the authority to do these things? Who's the one who gave you this authority?"

[3]In response Jesus said to them, "I also have a question for you: tell me, [4]was John's baptism from Heaven or from humans?"

[5]And they started conferring among themselves, reasoning as follows: "If we say, 'From Heaven,' he'll say, 'Then why didn't you trust him?' [6]But if we say, 'From humans,' the people will all stone us." (Remember, ⟨the people⟩ were convinced John was a prophet.) [7]So they answered that they couldn't tell where it came from.

[8]And Jesus said to them, "Then I'm not going to tell you by what authority I do these things."

[9]**Then he began** to tell the people this parable:

> A man planted a vineyard, leased it out to some farmers, and went abroad for an extended time. [10]In due course he sent a slave to the farmers, so they could pay him his share of the vineyard's crop. But the farmers beat him and sent him away empty-handed. [11]He repeated his action by sending another slave; but they beat him up too, and humiliated him, and sent him away empty-handed. [12]And he sent yet a third slave; but they injured him and threw him out.
>
> [13]Then the owner of the vineyard asked himself, "What should I do now? I'll send my son, the one I love. They'll probably show him some respect."

Lament over Jerusalem

Jesus disrupts the temple

On whose authority?

Leased vineyard

19:44
ⓣ Lk 21:6

19:45–48
//Mk 11:15–19,
Mt 21:12–13,
Jn 2:13–22

19:46
◊ Is 56:7, Jer 7:11

20:1–8
//Mk 11:27–33,
Mt 21:23–27

20:2
Cf. Jn 2:18

20:4
Cf. DSav 36:1–2

20:5–6
ⓣ Lk 7:29–30

20:9–19
//Mk 12:1–12,
Mt 21:33–46, Th 65

20:9
◊ Is 5:1–2

20:10–12
◊ 2 Chr 36:15–16,
Neh 9:25–26

20:13
ⓣ Lk 3:22

19:43 This describes siege tactics used by ancient armies.   **20:9** The *farmers* here are sharecroppers.

God & Caesar

*Wife of seven
brothers*

[14]But when the farmers recognized him, they talked it over, and concluded, "This guy's the heir. Let's kill him so the inheritance will be ours." [15]So they dragged him outside the vineyard and killed him.

So what will the owner of the vineyard do to them? [16]He will come in person, massacre those farmers, and give the vineyard to others.

When they heard this, they said, "God forbid!"

[17]But Jesus looked them straight in the eye and said, "What can this scripture possibly mean: 'A stone that the builders threw away has ended up as the keystone'? [18]Everyone who falls over that stone will be smashed to bits, and anyone on whom it falls will be crushed."

[19]The scholars and the chief priests wanted to lay hands on him then and there, but they were afraid of the people because they understood he had aimed this parable at them. [20]So they kept him under surveillance, and sent spies, who feigned sincerity, so they could twist something he said and turn him over to the authority and jurisdiction of the governor.

[21]**They asked him**, "Teacher, we know that what you speak and teach is correct, that you show no favoritism, but instead teach God's way forthrightly. [22]Is it permissible for us to pay taxes to Caesar or not?"

[23]But he saw through their duplicity, and said to them, [24]"Show me a denarius. Whose image and inscription is on it?"

They said, "Caesar's."

[25]So he said to them, "Then pay to Caesar what belongs to Caesar, and to God what belongs to God!"

[26]And so they were unable to catch him in anything he said in front of the people; they were dumbfounded at his answer and fell silent.

[27]**Some of the Sadducees**—those who argue there is no resurrection—came up to him [28]and put a question to him. "Teacher," they said, "Moses wrote for our benefit, 'If someone's brother dies, leaving behind a wife but no children, his brother shall take the widow as his wife and produce offspring for his brother.' [29]Now let's say there were seven brothers; the first took a wife, and died childless. [30]Then the second [31]and the third married her, and so on. All seven ⟨married her but⟩ left no children when they died. [32]Finally, the wife died too. [33]So then, in the 'resurrection' whose wife will the woman be, since all seven had her as a wife?"

[34]And Jesus said to them, "The children of this age marry and are given in marriage; [35]but those who are considered worthy of participating in the age to come, which means 'in the resurrection from the dead,' do not marry.

20:17
Ⓣ Acts 20:17,
Th 66;
◊ Ps 118:22

20:19
Ⓣ Lk 19:47–48,
22:2; Judas 6:12

20:20–26
//Mk 12:13–17,
Mt 22:15–22,
Th 100,
EgerG 3:1–6

20:21
Cf. Jn 3:2

20:25
Ⓣ Rom 13:7

20:27–40
//Mk 12:18–27,
Mt 22:23–33

20:28
◊ Dt 25:5–10,
Gn 38:8

20:21 His enemies' compliments, couched in scriptural terminology (e.g., Deut 1:17), are blatantly sarcastic.
20:28 The allusion here is to the custom of levirate marriage (see Deut 25:5). This was a strategy to produce an heir for the dead man, in order to continue his lineage and keep his property within the family. Legally, children born of such a marriage are children of the dead man, not of the brother who physically fathered them.

³⁶They can no longer die, since they are the equivalent of heavenly messengers; they are children of God and children of the resurrection. ³⁷Moses proved that the dead are raised in the passage about the bush: he calls the Lord 'the God of Abraham, the God of Isaac, and the God of Jacob.' ³⁸So this is not the God of the dead, but of the living, since to him they are all alive."

³⁹And some of the scholars answered, "Well put, Teacher." (⁴⁰You see, they no longer dared to ask him about anything else.)

⁴¹**Then he asked them**, "How can they say that the Anointed One is the son of David? ⁴²Remember, David himself says in the book of Psalms,

> The Lord said to my lord,
>> "Sit here at my right,
>> ⁴³until I make your enemies grovel at your feet."

⁴⁴Since David calls him 'lord,' how can he be his son?"

⁴⁵**Within earshot** of the people Jesus said to the disciples, ⁴⁶"Be on guard against the scholars who like to parade around in long robes, and who love respectful greetings in the marketplaces and the prominent seats in the synagogues and the best couches at banquets. ⁴⁷They are the ones who prey on widows and their families, and then recite long prayers just to look good. These people will get what's coming to them, and more!"

21 **He looked up** and observed the rich dropping their donations into the collection box. ²Then he noticed that a needy widow put in two quarters, ³and he observed, "I'm telling you the truth: this poor widow has contributed more than all of them. ⁴You see, they all made donations out of their surplus, whereas she, out of her poverty, was contributing everything she had to live on."

⁵**When some were remarking** about how the temple was adorned with fine masonry and ornamentation, he said, ⁶"As for these things that you now admire, the time will come when not one stone will be left on top of another! Every last one will be knocked down!"

⁷**And they asked him**, "Teacher, when are these things going to happen? What will be the sign to show when these things are about to occur?"

⁸He said, "Stay alert! Don't be deceived. You know, many will come using my name and claim, 'I'm the one!' and 'The time has arrived!' Don't go running after them! ⁹And when you hear of wars and insurrections, don't panic. It's inevitable that these things happen first, but that doesn't mean the End is imminent."

20:36
Ⓣ Gal 4:5–7

20:37
◊ Ex 3:6

20:41–44
//Mk 12:35–37,
Mt 22:41–46

20:42–43
Ⓓ Acts 2:34–35;
◊ Ps 110:1

20:45–47
//Mk 12:38–40

20:46
//Mt 23:6;
Ⓣ Lk 11:43

21:1–4
//Mk 12:41–44

21:5–19
//Mk 13:3–13,
Mt 24:3–14

21:6
Ⓣ Lk 19:44

21:8
//Mary 4:3

20:36 Only Luke's version of this scene uses the title *children* (literally, "sons") *of God*. Except for Luke 6:35, elsewhere in the gospels "son of God" is a title reserved for Jesus, while here it is applied to all who participate in the resurrection.

20:41–44 Jesus gives his enemies a taste of their own medicine, stumping them with a scriptural contradiction.

20:47 The interpretation of *prey on widows* (literally, "de-vour the houses of widows") is difficult. It may refer to the scribes' embezzlement of revenue from estates left to widows in their husbands' wills and entrusted to scribes to manage on their behalf.

21:2 *Quarter* translates *lepton*, the least valuable coin at the time, worth less than 1% of a denarius.

21:7 *These things* refers to the destruction of the temple, not the end of the world (as in Mark 13:4).

Days of distress

*The Human One
comes on clouds*

21:10
◊ 2 Chr 15:6, Is 19:2

21:12–19
// Mt 10:16–23

21:14–15
⊤ Lk 12:11–12

21:18
⊤ Lk 12:7,
Acts 27:34;
◊ 1 Sm 14:45,
2 Sm 14:11,
1 Kgs 1:52

21:20–24
// Mk 13:14–23,
Mt 24:15–28

21:22
◊ Jer 46:10, Hos 9:7

21:23
Cf. Th 79;
⊤ Lk 23:27–31

21:24
◊ Jer 21:7, Dt 28:64

21:25–33
// Mk 13:24–32,
Mt 24:29–36

21:26
◊ Is 34:4

21:27
◊ Dn 7:13

21:32
Cf. Mk 9:1,
Mt 16:28, Lk 9:27

[10]Then he went on to tell them, "Nation will rise up against nation, and empire against empire. [11]There will be powerful earthquakes, and famines and plagues all over the place; there will be dreadful events and spectacular signs from heaven. [12]But before all these things happen, they'll manhandle you, and persecute you, and turn you over to synagogues and deliver you to prisons, and you'll be hauled up before kings and governors on account of my name. [13]This will give you a chance to make your case. [14]So make up your minds not to rehearse your defense in advance, [15]for I will give you the wit and wisdom which none of your adversaries will be able to resist or refute. [16]You'll be turned in, even by parents and brothers and relatives and friends; and they'll put some of you to death. [17]And you'll be universally hated because of me. [18]Yet not a single hair on your head will be harmed. [19]By your perseverance you will secure your lives.

[20]"**When you see Jerusalem** surrounded by armies, know then that its destruction is just around the corner. [21]Then the people in Judea should head for the hills, and those inside the city flee, and those out in the countryside not re-enter. [22]For these are days of vengeance, when everything that was predicted will be fulfilled. [23]It'll be too bad for pregnant women and for nursing mothers in those days! There will be utter misery throughout the land and wrath ⟨will fall⟩ upon this people. [24]They will fall by the edge of the sword, and be hauled off as prisoners to all the foreign countries, and Jerusalem will be overrun by pagans, until the period allotted to the pagans has run its course.

[25]"**And there will be omens** in the sun and moon and stars, and on the earth nations will be anguished in their confusion at the roar of the surging sea. [26]People will faint from terror at the prospect of what is coming over the civilized world, for the heavenly forces will be shaken. [27]And then they will see the Human One coming a cloud with great power and splendor. [28]Now when these things begin to happen, stand tall and hold your heads high, because your deliverance is just around the corner!"

[29]Then he told them a parable: "Observe the fig tree, or any tree, for that matter. [30]Once it puts out foliage, you can see for yourselves that summer is near. [31]So, when you see these things happening, you should realize that the empire of God is near. [32]Let me tell you, this generation certainly won't pass

---

21:11 *Earthquakes* are standard apocalyptic imagery (see Hag 2:6).

spectacular signs: See 2 Macc 5:2–3 for signs in the sky which preceded the invasion of Jerusalem in 169 BCE. Josephus describes two signs at the destruction of the temple in 70 CE: "a star resembling a sword, which stood over the city, and a comet, which lasted a whole year" (*War* 6.5.3).

21:16 *put to death*: This happens to Stephen and James in Acts 7:54–60 and 12:1–2.

21:19 *lives*: The Greek word *psychē* can also mean "soul."

21:22 *days of vengeance*: It is not clear what the vengeance is for.

21:25 These signs are standard apocalyptic imagery (e.g., Joel 2:30–31; Isa 13:10; 34:4) and are possible allusions to Ps 46:2–3 and LXX Isa 24:19.

21:26 *Heavenly forces* are the celestial bodies mentioned in v. 25.

21:28 Note how Luke connects redemption (*deliverance*) to Jesus' second coming instead of to his death.

away before it all happens. ³³The earth will pass away and so will the sky, but my words will never pass away!

³⁴"**So watch yourselves** so your minds won't be dulled by hangovers and drunkenness and the worries of everyday life, and so that day won't spring upon you suddenly like some trap you weren't expecting. ³⁵It will come down for sure on all who inhabit the earth. ³⁶Stay alert! Pray constantly that you may have the strength to escape all these things that are on their way and the strength to stand before the Human One."

³⁷During the day he would teach in the temple area, and in the evening he would go and spend the night on the mountain called Olives. ³⁸And all the people would get up early to come to the temple area to hear him.

22 **The festival** of Unleavened Bread, known as Passover, was approaching. ²The chief priests and the scholars were still looking for some way to get rid of Jesus, but they feared the people.

³Then Satan took possession of Judas, the one called Iscariot, who was a member of the Twelve. ⁴He went off to negotiate with the chief priests and ⟨temple⟩ police how to turn Jesus over to them. ⁵They were delighted and agreed to pay him in silver. ⁶And Judas accepted the deal and began looking for a good opportunity to turn him in when a crowd was not around.

⁷**The festival** of Unleavened Bread arrived, when the Passover ⟨lambs⟩ had to be sacrificed. ⁸So Jesus sent Peter and John, with these instructions: "Go get things ready for us to eat the Passover."

⁹They said to him, "Where do you want us to get things ready?"

¹⁰He said to them, "Look, when you enter the city, a man carrying a water-pot will meet you. Follow him into the house he enters, ¹¹and say to the head of the house, 'The Teacher asks you, "Where is the guest room where I can celebrate Passover with my disciples?"' ¹²And he will show you a large upstairs room that's been arranged; that's the place where you should get things ready."

¹³They set off and found things exactly as he had told them; and they got things ready for Passover.

¹⁴When the time came, he took his place ⟨at the meal⟩, and the apostles joined him. ¹⁵He said to them, "I have looked forward with all my heart to celebrating this Passover with you before my ordeal begins. ¹⁶For I'm telling you, I certainly won't eat it again until everything is fulfilled in God's empire."

¹⁷Then he took a cup, gave thanks, and said, "Take this and share it among yourselves. ¹⁸For I'm telling you, I certainly won't drink any of the fruit of the vine from now on until God's empire is established!"

21:33
Ⓣ Lk 16:17

21:34–36
//Mk 13:33–37,
Mt 24:37–51

21:34
Ⓣ Lk 12:45–46

22:1–2
//Mk 14:1–2,
Mt 26:1–5

22:2
Ⓣ Lk 19:47–48,
20:19; Judas 6:12

22:3–6
//Mk 14:10–11,
Mt 26:14–16;
cf. Acts 1:16–20

22:3
Cf. Jn 13:2

22:7–13
//Mk 14:12–16,
Mt 26:17–19

22:8–9
//GEbi 7:1

22:14–20
//Mk 14:22–25,
Mt 26:26–29;
cf. 1 Cor 11:23–25

22:18
Cf. GHeb 9:2,
GEbi 7:2

22:3 This is the time (*kairos*) the devil has waited for since 4:13.
22:10 This is probably a pre-arranged signal, since carry-ing water was women's work. The Greek *anthrōpos* does not connote a male, but this seems implied since a woman carrying water would not be an unusual sight.

Servant is greatest

Peter takes an oath

Two swords

[19]And he took a loaf, gave thanks, broke it into pieces, offered it to them, and said, "This is my body, which is offered for you. Do this as my memorial."

[20]And, in the same manner, he took the cup after dinner and said, "This cup is the new covenant in my blood, which is poured out for you."

[21]"But look! Right here with me at this very table is the one who is going to turn me in. [22]The Human One goes to meet his destiny; and yet damn the one responsible for turning him in!"

[23]And they began to ask one another which of them could possibly attempt such a thing.

[24]**Then they got into an argument** over which of them should be considered the greatest. [25]He said to them, "Among the foreigners, it's the kings who lord it over everyone, and those in power are addressed as 'benefactors.' [26]But not so with you; rather, the greatest among you must behave as a beginner, and the leader as one who serves. [27]Who is the greater, after all: the one reclining ⟨at a banquet⟩ or the one doing the serving? Isn't it the one who reclines? But here among you I am the one doing the serving.

[28]"You are the ones who have stuck by me in my ordeals. [29]And I confer on you the right to rule, just as surely as my Father conferred that right on me, [30]so you may eat and drink at my table in my empire, and be seated on thrones and sit in judgment on the twelve tribes of Israel.

[31]"**Simon, Simon**, look out: Satan is after all of you, to sift you like wheat. [32]But I have prayed for you that your trust won't give out. And once you've recovered, you are to shore up these brothers of yours."

[33]He said to him, "Master, I'm prepared to follow you not only to prison but all the way to death."

[34]He said, "Let me tell you, Peter, the rooster will not crow tonight until you deny three times that you know me."

[35]**And he said to them**, "When I sent you out with no purse or knapsack or sandals, you weren't short of anything, were you?"

They said, "Not a thing."

[36]He said to them, "But now, if you have a purse, take it along; and the same goes for a knapsack. And if you don't have a sword, sell your coat and buy one. [37]For I'm telling you, this scripture,

And he was considered a criminal,

22:19
Cf. GHeb 9:4;
Ⓣ Lk 9:16, 24:30

22:20
//GSav 14:18;
◊ Ex 24:8, Jer 31:31, Zec 9:11

22:21–23
//Mk 14:18–21, Mt 26:21–25, Jn 13:21–30

22:22
Ⓣ Lk 9:22, 44, 17:25, 18:31, 24:7, 26, 46

22:24–27
//Mk 10:41–45, Mt 20:24–28

22:26
Cf. Mk 9:35, Mt 23:11–12, Lk 9:48

Q22:28–30
//Mt 19:28

22:31–34
//Mk 14:26–31, Mt 26:30–35, Jn 13:36–38

22:33
Ⓣ Acts 21:13

22:35–36
Ⓘ Lk 9:3, 10:4

22:37
◊ Is 53:12

22:19–20 A few mss omit *which is offered for you* and all of v. 20.

22:25 *Benefactor* was an honorific title often bestowed on gods and rulers.

22:28 The reference to *ordeals* is unclear. The only event Luke calls an ordeal is Jesus' temptation, at which the disciples were not present.

22:31 The *you* is plural in Greek. To *sift like wheat* is to separate wheat from chaff.

is destined to be completed in my life; for what is written about me is reaching completion."

³⁸And they said, "Look, Master, here are two swords."

And he said to them, "That's plenty."

³⁹**Then he left** and walked, as usual, over to the Mount of Olives; and the disciples followed him. ⁴⁰When he arrived at his usual place, he said to them, "Pray that you won't be put to the test."

⁴¹And he withdrew from them about a stone's throw away, got down on his knees, and began to pray, ⁴²"Father, if you so choose, take this cup away from me! Yet not my will, but yours, be done."

⁴⁵And when he got up from his prayer and returned to the disciples, he found them asleep, weary from grief. ⁴⁶He said to them, "What are you doing asleep? Get up and pray that you won't be put to the test."

⁴⁷**Suddenly**, while he was still speaking, a crowd appeared with the one called Judas, one of the Twelve, leading the way. He stepped up to Jesus to give him a kiss.

⁴⁸But Jesus said to him, "Judas, would you turn in the Human One with a kiss?"

⁴⁹And when those around him realized what was coming next, they said, "Master, should we use our swords?" ⁵⁰And one of them struck the chief priest's slave and cut off his right ear.

⁵¹But Jesus responded, "Stop! That's enough!" And he touched his ear and healed him.

⁵²Then Jesus addressed the chief priests and temple police and elders who had come out after him: "Have you come with swords and clubs to arrest me as you would an insurgent? ⁵³When I was with you day after day in the temple area, you didn't lay a hand on me. But it's your turn now, and the authority of darkness is on your side."

⁵⁴They arrested him and marched him away to the house of the chief priest.

Peter followed at a distance. ⁵⁵When they had started a fire in the middle of the courtyard and were sitting around it, Peter joined them.

⁵⁶Then a slave woman noticed him sitting there in the glow of the fire. She stared at him, then spoke up, "This guy was with him too."

Jesus in Gethsemane

Judas turns Jesus in

Peter denies Jesus

22:39–46
//Mk 14:32–42, Mt 26:36–46

22:41–42
//GSav 14:14

22:42
Cf. Jn 18:11

22:47–53
Mk 14:43–52, Mt 26:47–56, Jn 18:1–11

22:54–62
//Mk 14:53–54, 66–72; Mt 26:57–58, 69–75; Jn 18:13–18, 25–27

22:42 Many mss add another two verses, traditionally numbered 22:43–44: "⁴³An angel from heaven appeared to him and gave him strength. ⁴⁴In his anxiety he prayed more fervently, and it so happened that his sweat fell to the ground like great drops of blood." (It is very doubtful that these verses were part of the original text.)

22:38 *That's plenty*: Because of its immediate context, this obscure remark probably indicates that two swords are sufficient to fulfill the prophecy quoted in v. 37.
22:39 *as usual*: See 21:37.
22:42 *Cup* is a biblical metaphor for one's destiny (see, e.g.,

Jer 25:15).
22:47–48 A *kiss* was a ritual greeting that signaled respect.
22:51 Only in Luke's gospel does Jesus heal the slave's wound.

Guards humiliate Jesus

Trial before the Council

Trial before Pilate

[57] He denied it. "Lady," he said, "I don't know him."

[58] A little later someone else noticed him and said, "You're one of them too." "Not me, mister," Peter replied.

[59] About an hour went by and someone else insisted, "No question about it; this guy's also one of them; he's even a Galilean!"

[60] But Peter said, "Mister, I don't know what you're talking about."

And all of a sudden, while he was still speaking, a rooster crowed. [61] And the Master turned and looked straight at Peter. And Peter remembered what the Master had told him: "Before the rooster crows tonight, you will disown me three times." [62] And he went outside and wept bitterly.

[63] **Then the men** who were holding Jesus in custody began to make fun of him and rough him up. [64] They blindfolded him and demanded: "Prophesy! Guess who hit you!" [65] And this was only the beginning of their insults.

[66] **When day came**, the elders of the people convened, along with the chief priests and scholars. They had him brought before their Council, where they interrogated him: [67] "If you are the Anointed One, tell us."

But he said to them, "If I tell you, there's no way you'll believe me. [68] If I ask you a question, there's no way you'll answer. [69] But from now on the Human One will be seated at the right hand of the power of God."

[70] And they all said, "So you, are you the son of God?"

He said to them, "You're the ones who say so."

[71] And they said, "Why do we still need witnesses? We have heard it ourselves from his own mouth."

23

At this point the whole assembly got up and took him before Pilate. [2] They introduced their accusations by saying, "We have found this man to be a corrupting influence on our people, opposing the payment of taxes to Caesar and claiming that he himself is an anointed king."

[3] Pilate questioned him, "*You* are 'the King of the Judeans'?"

In response he said to him, "If you say so."

[4] And Pilate said to the chief priests and the crowds, "In my judgment there is no case against this man."

[5] But they persisted, saying, "He foments unrest among the people by going around teaching everywhere in Judea and as far away as Galilee and everywhere between."

[6] When Pilate heard this, he asked whether the man were a Galilean. [7] And once he confirmed that he was from Herod's jurisdiction, he sent him on to Herod, who happened to be in Jerusalem at the time.

22:61
ⓣ Lk 22:34

22:63–65
Mk 14:65,
Mt 26:67–68

22:66–71
Mk 14:55–64,
Mt 26:59–66,
Jn 18:19–24

22:69
ⓣ Lk 21:27,
Acts 7:55–56;
◊ Dn 7:13, Ps 110:1

23:1–5
//Mk 15:1–5;
Mt 27:1–2, 11–14;
Jn 18:28–38

23:2
ⓣ GSav 13:8

23:6–12 Only in Luke's gospel is Jesus brought before Herod.

⁸**Now Herod** was delighted to see Jesus. In fact, he had been eager to see him for quite some time, since he had heard so much about him, and was hoping to see him perform some sign. ⁹So Herod plied him with questions; but Jesus would not answer him at all. ¹⁰All this time the chief priests and the scholars were standing around, hurling accusation after accusation against him. ¹¹Herod and his soldiers treated him with contempt and made fun of him; they put a magnificent robe around him, then sent him back to Pilate. ¹²That very day Herod and Pilate became friends; prior to this they had been constantly at odds.

¹³**Pilate then called** together the chief priests, the rulers, and the people, ¹⁴and addressed them. "You brought this man to me because you claim he's been corrupting the people. Now look, after interrogating him in your presence, I have found in this man no grounds at all for your charges against him. ¹⁵Nor has Herod, since he sent him back to us. In fact, he has done nothing to deserve death. ¹⁶So I will teach him a lesson and set him free."

¹⁸But they all cried out in unison, "Do away with this man, and set Barabbas free." (¹⁹This man had been thrown into prison for murder and for an act of insurrection carried out in the city.)

²⁰But Pilate, who wanted to set Jesus free, addressed them again, ²¹but they shouted out, "Crucify, crucify him!"

²²For the third time he said to them, "Why? What has he done wrong? In my judgment there is no capital case against him. So, I will teach him a lesson and set him free."

²³But they kept up the pressure, shouting their demands that he be crucified. And their shouts were prevailing, ²⁴so Pilate ruled that their demand should be carried out. ²⁵He set free the man they had asked for, who had been thrown into prison for insurrection and murder; but Jesus he handed over to their will.

²⁶**And as they were marching** him away, they grabbed someone named Simon, a Cyrenian, as he was coming in from the country. They loaded the cross on him, to carry behind Jesus. ²⁷A huge crowd of the people followed him, including women who mourned and lamented him. ²⁸Jesus turned to them and said, "Daughters of Jerusalem, do not weep for me. Weep instead for yourselves and for your children. ²⁹Look, the time is coming when they will say, 'Congratulations to those who are infertile, to the wombs that never gave birth, and to the breasts that never nursed!'

23:13–25
//Mk 15:6–15,
Mt 27:15–26,
Jn 18:39–19:16;
① Acts 3:13–15

23:18–19
Cf. GNaz 9

23:26
//Mk 15:21,
Mt 27:32

23:29
Cf. Lk 21:23, Th 79

23:16 Many mss add another verse, traditionally numbered 23:17: "He was required to release one man to them during the festival." A few mss place this verse after verse 19.

23:16, 22 *teach him a lesson:* Pilate's euphemism for flogging. Luke is the only gospel to report that Pilate's plan was to flog Jesus instead of executing him.
23:18–25 Luke does not explain why the crowd called for

Barabbas' release or why Pilate did as they asked. In contrast, see Mark 15:6–15 and Matt 27:15–23.
23:25 In Luke's story Jesus is not flogged, as in the other three gospels (Mark 15:15, Matt 27:26, John 19:1).

³⁰Then they will beg the mountains:
> "Fall on us;"

and the hills:
> "Bury us."

³¹If they behave this way when the wood is green, what will happen when it dries out?"

³²Two others, who were criminals, were also taken away with him to be executed.

³³**And when they reached** the place called "The Skull," they crucified him there along with the criminals, one on his right and the other on his left. ³⁴They divided up his clothes after they cast lots ⟨for them⟩. ³⁵And the people stood around looking on.

And the rulers kept sneering at him, "He saved others; he should save himself if he is God's Anointed One, the Chosen One!"

³⁶The soldiers also made fun of him. They would come up and offer him sour wine, ³⁷and they would say, "If you're the King of the Judeans, why not save yourself?"

³⁸There was also this placard over him: "This is the King of the Judeans."

³⁹One of the criminals hanging there kept taunting him: "Aren't you supposed to be the Anointed One? Save yourself and us!"

⁴⁰But the other ⟨criminal⟩ rebuked the first: "Don't you even fear God, since you're under the same sentence? ⁴¹We are getting justice, since we are getting what we deserve. But this man has done nothing wrong."

⁴²And he implored, "Jesus, remember me when you come into your empire."

⁴³And Jesus said to him, "Let me tell you, today you'll be with me in Paradise."

⁴⁴**It was already about noon**, and darkness blanketed the whole land until mid-afternoon, ⁴⁵during an eclipse of the sun. The curtain of the temple was torn down the middle.

⁴⁶Then Jesus shouted at the top of his voice, "Father, into your hands I entrust my spirit!" Having said this, he breathed his last.

23:30
◊ Hos 10:8

23:33–43
//Mk 15:22–32,
Mt 27:33–44,
Jn 19:17–24,
Pet 4:1–4

23:34a
//Acts 7:60

23:34b
◊ Ps 22:18

23:35–39
Ⓣ GSav 11:1

23:35
◊ Ps 22:7

23:36
//Mk 15:35–36,
Mt 27:47–48,
Jn 19:29, Pet 5:2;
◊ Ps 69:21

23:44–49
//Mk 15:33–41,
56, 30

23:44–45
◊ Am 8:9

23:44
Cf. Pet 5:1, 6:2

23:46
//Acts 7:59
◊ Ps 31:5

23:34 Many mss add "And Jesus said, 'Father, forgive them because they don't know what they're doing'" at the beginning of the verse.
23:38 Many mss add that the notice "was written in Greek, Latin, and Hebrew."
23:42 Many mss read "with" instead of *into*.

23:36 *Sour wine* is not vinegar, but the cheap, dry wine from the soldiers' rations (ordinary wine being sweet).
23:43 *Paradise*: a Greek word meaning a shaded garden, used in LXX for the garden of Eden. The word was used in contemporary Judaism for the abode of the souls of the just.

23:45 This seems to refer to a solar eclipse, which, however, is physically impossible at Passover, which always falls at the time of a full moon. Moreover, eclipses last for a few minutes, not for several hours.

[47]Now when the Roman officer saw what happened, he praised God and said, "This man really was innocent!"

[48]And when the throng of people that had gathered for this spectacle observed what had transpired, they all returned home beating their chests. [49]And all his acquaintances, including the women who had followed him from Galilee, were standing off at a distance watching these events.

[50]**There was a man** named Joseph, a Council member, a decent and upright man, [51]who had not endorsed their decision or gone along with their action. He was from the town of Arimathea in Judea, and he lived in anticipation of the empire of God. [52]This man went to Pilate and requested the body of Jesus. [53]Then he took it down and wrapped it in a shroud, and laid him in a tomb cut from the rock, where no one had ever been buried. [54]It was the day of preparation, and the Sabbath was about to begin. [55]The women who had come with him from Galilee followed. They kept an eye on the tomb, to see how his body was laid to rest. [56]Then they went home to prepare spices and ointments. On the Sabbath they rested in observance of the commandment.

24 **On Sunday**, at daybreak, they made their way to the tomb, bringing the spices they had prepared. [2]They found the stone rolled away from the tomb, [3]but when they went inside they did not find the body of the Master Jesus.

[4]And it came to pass, while they were still uncertain about what to do, that two men in dazzling clothes suddenly appeared and stood beside them. [5]They were terrified and knelt with their faces to the ground. The men said to them, "Why are you looking for the living among the dead? [6]He is not here—he was raised. Remember what he told you while he was still in Galilee: [7]'the Human One is destined to be turned over to sinners, to be crucified, and on the third day to rise.'" [8]Then they recalled what he had said.

[9]And returning from the tomb, they related everything to the Eleven and to everybody else. [10]The group included Mary of Magdala and Joanna and Mary the mother of James, and the rest of the women companions. They related their story to the apostles; [11]but their story seemed nonsense to them, so they refused to believe the women.

[12]But Peter got up and ran to the tomb. He peeked in and saw only the linen wrappings, and returned home, marveling at what had happened.

Joseph buries Jesus

The women discover the empty tomb

23:48
Cf. Pet 7:1;
Ⓣ GSav 11:1
23:49
Ⓘ Lk 8:2–3;
◊ Ps 38:11
23:50–56
//Mk 15:42–47,
Mt 27:57–61,
Jn 19:38–42
23:50–52
//Pet 2:1
23:53
//Pet 6:1–4
23:54
◊ Dt 21:22–23
24:1–12
//Mk 16:1–8,
Mt 28:1–10,
Jn 20:1–18,
Pet 12:1–13:3
24:7
Ⓘ Lk 9:44, 18:32

24:6 A few mss omit *He is not here—he was raised.*
24:12 A few mss omit this verse.

23:54 The *day of preparation* is the day before the Sabbath, which begins at sunset on Friday.

24:12 *returned home*: Not only is this verse textually doubtful, it is implausible, for Peter's home was in Capernaum.

On the road
to Emmaus

In Emmaus

Jesus appears
in Jerusalem

¹³**Now, that same day** a couple of them were traveling to a village named Emmaus, about seven miles from Jerusalem. ¹⁴They were engaged in conversation about all that had taken place. ¹⁵And it came to pass, during the course of their discussion, that Jesus himself approached and began to walk along with them. ¹⁶But they couldn't recognize him.

¹⁷He said to them, "What were you discussing as you walked along?"

Then they paused, looking depressed. ¹⁸One of them, named Kleopas, said to him in reply, "Are you the only visitor to Jerusalem who doesn't know what's happened there these last few days?"

¹⁹And he said to them, "What are you talking about?"

And they said to him, "About Jesus of Nazareth, who was a prophet powerful in word and deed in the eyes of God and all the people, ²⁰and about how our chief priests and rulers turned him in to be sentenced to death, and crucified him. ²¹We were hoping that he would be the one who was going to ransom Israel. And as if this weren't enough, it's been three days now since all this happened. ²²Meanwhile, some women from our group gave us quite a shock. They were at the tomb early this morning ²³and didn't find his body. They came back claiming even to have seen a vision of heavenly messengers, who said that he was alive. ²⁴Some of those with us went to the tomb and found it exactly as the women had described; but nobody saw him."

²⁵And he said to them, "You people are so dim, so reluctant to trust everything the prophets have said! ²⁶Wasn't the Anointed One destined to endure these things and enter into his glory?" ²⁷Then, starting with Moses and all the prophets, he interpreted for them every passage of scripture that referred to himself.

²⁸**They had gotten close** to the village to which they were headed, and he acted as if he were going on. ²⁹But they insisted, "Stay with us; it's almost evening, the day is practically over." So he went in to stay with them.

³⁰And it came to pass, as soon as he took his place at table with them, that he took a loaf, and gave a blessing, broke it, and started passing it out to them. ³¹Then their eyes were opened and they recognized him, but he vanished from their sight. ³²They said to each other, "Weren't our hearts burning within us while he was talking to us on the way, and explaining the scriptures to us?" ³³And they got up at once and returned to Jerusalem.

And when they found the Eleven and those with them gathered together, ³⁴they said, "The Master really has been raised, and has appeared to Simon!"

24:19
Ⓣ Acts 2:22, 10:38

24:21
Ⓣ Lk 1:68, 2:38

24:13 The location of Emmaus is disputed.
24:19 Moses is similarly described in Acts 7:22, 36, 38.
24:21 Moses is similarly described in Acts 7:35.
24:26 No Jewish text earlier than the NT (including the

OT) contains the idea of a suffering messiah and no other NT author explicitly speaks of Jesus in these terms.
24:34 No gospel narrates an appearance to Peter, though Paul reports one (1 Cor 15:5).

35Then they described what had happened on the road, and how they came to recognize him in the breaking of bread.

36While they were talking about this, he himself appeared among them and says to them, "Peace be with you." 37But they were terrified and frightened, and figured that they were seeing a ghost.

38And he said to them, "Why are you upset? Why do such thoughts run through your minds? 39You can see from my hands and my feet that it's really me. Touch me and see—a ghost doesn't have flesh and bones as you can see that I have."

41And while for sheer joy they still didn't know what to believe and were bewildered, he said to them, "Is there anything here to eat?" 42They offered him a piece of grilled fish, 43and he took it and ate it in front of them.

44Then he said to them, "This is the message I gave you while I was still with you: everything written about me in the Law of Moses and the Prophets and the Psalms is destined to be fulfilled."

45Then he prepared their minds to understand the scriptures. 46He said to them, "This is what is written: the Anointed One will suffer and rise from the dead on the third day. 47And all peoples will be called on to change their hearts for the forgiveness of sins, beginning from Jerusalem. 48You are witnesses to this. 49And be prepared: I'm sending down on you what my Father promised. Stay here in the city until you are invested with power from on high."

50**Then he led them** out as far as Bethany, and lifting up his hands he blessed them. 51And while he was blessing them, it came to pass that he departed from them, and was carried up into the sky. 52And they paid homage to him and returned to Jerusalem full of joy, 53and were continually in the temple blessing God.

24:36 A few mss omit *and says to them, "Peace be with you."*
24:39 Many mss add a v. 40, "As he said this, he showed them his hands and his feet," taken from John 20:20.
24:51 Some mss omit *and was carried up into the sky.*
24:52 A few mss omit *paid homage to him and.*

24:36–49
//Jn 20:19–23;
cf. Mt 28:16–20,
Mk 16:14–18

24:38
Cf. Mary 3:2

24:48 A very important theme in Acts (see, e.g., Acts 1:8, 22; 2:32; 3:15; 5:32).
24:49 *what my Father promised*: the holy spirit (Acts 1:4–5).
24:50 *Bethany* is less than two miles from Jerusalem, on the Mount of Olives.

24:51 According to the timeline in Luke's story, Jesus' ascension takes place on Sunday, the same day his empty tomb is discovered. In Acts the ascension takes place forty days later (Acts 1:3–11).
24:53 *in the temple*: The Gospel ends where it began (1:8–9).

Gehenna/Hades/Hell

The Greek (and Hebrew) terms for places under the earth—the underworld or nether world—are especially difficult to distinguish in English since the term Hell is in general use for them all.

Gehenna comes from a Hebrew phrase meaning "valley of Hinnom," a ravine running along the west and south of Jerusalem. In Jeremiah's day it was known as a place of human sacrifice to the gods Baal and Molech. Later it became a trash dump and so was perpetually on fire.

Gehenna came to symbolize the place where the dead were punished because of their sins. It is always used in this symbolic sense in the gospels.

In order to avoid associations with the term Hell, the SV translators have retained the Greek (Hebrew) word in English dress. The English transliteration appears in English for the first time around 1600.

Hades is the Greek equivalent of the Hebrew term *Sheol,* the place or abode of the dead, where wicked and righteous alike go. Hades is the name of the god of the underworld in Greek mythology; the name was later transferred to the place or domain of the god.

Hades is accessible by gates (Matt 16:18) since it is located under the earth, like Sheol. In Hades the dead lead a shadowy existence.

The SV translators have retained Hades in Matt 16:18 and in the parable of the rich man and Lazarus (Luke 16:23), but elsewhere have translated it "Hell" because it occurs in the phrase "go to Hell," which can scarcely be represented in idiomatic English by "go to Hades."

Hades was introduced into English as a word in its own right around 1600 in connection with controversies over the Apostles' Creed.

Hell can be used to represent either Gehenna or Hades in English. The term Hell is derived from Old Teutonic *Hel,* where it is the name for the goddess of the infernal regions. The Book of Revelation ("lake of fire," "the abyss"), Dante, and other authors have contributed to the associations connected with the term. The preaching of fire and brimstone sermons by Puritan divines and others have given the term a graphic life in American English.

Outer darkness. In ancient cosmology, the sky was thought to be held up by mountains at the ends of the earth. Beyond these mountains lay the regions of darkness. The Garden of Eden or Paradise was widely thought to lie in the east, the outer darkness in the extreme west. In rabbinic sources, Gehenna is equated with this darkness. In the New Testament, this particular phrase is used only by Matthew.

The Signs Gospel

Introduction

Hypothetical text

As with the Q Gospel—an early collection of Jesus' sayings taken up by Matthew and Luke—many scholars are convinced that a good deal of the narrative in John comes from a document now lost. If so, this was not a collection of Jesus' words, as in Q, but rather an account of his deeds, principally his miracles, perhaps seven of them. These were meant to be understood as "signs" (that is, demonstrations) that Jesus was the Jewish Messiah, the Anointed One. (This point is elaborated in the note on 2:11.) Like Q, the existence of this document is hypothetical; we have no manuscript copies of it. It survives only embedded within the text of the Gospel of John and must be reconstructed, by trying to read backward from John, just as Q is recovered by working backward from Matthew and Luke.

The Signs Gospel is reconstructed chiefly by looking for points in John where obvious literary seams appear; such seams often indicate inconsistencies and even contradictions in the text of the completed gospel. These rough spots are infrequent in the synoptic gospels, even where Matthew or Luke reproduces material from Mark or Q. But they are common in John and seem to suggest that when using the hypothetical "source," the author of John quoted it practically verbatim; the author simply allowed the rough connections and inconsistencies to stand. Perhaps the document was so familiar and revered by John's audience that it could not be rewritten or even paraphrased, although it had undoubtedly become in some way obsolete. It could be reinterpreted or corrected only by adding brief comments, rearranging it, or interpolating new material.

Both Q and the Signs Gospel have until recently been appreciated chiefly as sources for the later New Testament gospels. But in this volume we explore Q and the Signs Gospel not as sources for the later writings, but rather as documents in their own right. Neither was written in order to be a source for a later writer, but as a distinctive presentation of the Christian claim.

The fact that these documents happened later to be employed as sources led not only to their disappearance but also in a way to their preservation, buried in the later gospels that used them as literary sources. Mark also was used as a source by Matthew and Luke, and it was probably only by chance that Mark survived on its own; it was almost discarded, since virtually all of it is now to be found, somewhat reworded, in either Matthew or Luke, or in both.

A rudimentary gospel

This lost document was a gospel—as perhaps, in an altogether different way, was Q. Though rudimentary, it announces the single message of early Christianity: the good news that at last the Messiah, the Anointed One, has come. It presents Jesus' miracles as self-evident and self-sufficient proofs of this good news, and calls on its readers to believe it—to perceive the miracles as signs—just as the original disciples are shown to have done. Because of this singular focus on Jesus' signs, this "book" (John 20:30) can be called the Signs Gospel.

"Proof" that Jesus was Messiah

The historical Jesus was a faith healer, but he did not heal people in order to make any claim about himself or to convince people to "believe" in him. Yet perhaps twenty years or more before Mark, the earliest extant gospel, stories recounting these characteristic acts of Jesus supplemented with still more impressive feats such as walking on the sea, turning a few loaves into enough to feed a huge crowd, or changing water into wine had been transformed by the Signs Gospel into theological proofs. How did this happen? In what context?

Answering the latter question is easier, and helps us solve the former. The context was evidently a Greek-speaking synagogue whose members believed that Jesus was the Messiah. The religion of these believers was Judaism. They were "Christians" only in the literal sense of the word, that is, believers in Jesus as the Christ, the Messiah (the Anointed One). A more precise name for these Christian Jews would be Messianists. These Messianists collected stories about Jesus' wonders to serve a missionary purpose. As to the first question: the model for reshaping these miracle stories as messianic proofs was the series of "signs" that Moses had worked in Exodus. Over the centuries it had been expected that the future Messiah would be the Prophet that Moses had promised, who would be, like himself, the representative of Israel's God (see Deut 18:15–18). The prophet Elijah also had performed miracles, and his reappearance was another way of imagining the Messiah. (See further the notes on 1:20–21 and 41, [43], 45, below.) So a Signs Gospel would have been, for a time at least, a most effective way of presenting the Christian message to fellow Jews, both as announcement and as claim.

Before long, however, tension arose between Christian Jews and Jews who did not accept that Jesus was the Anointed One, tension that led ultimately to a separation. For some time prior to the schism that was gradually taking place among Jews throughout the Roman empire, the collected sign stories proved to be less and less effective in convincing Jews that Jesus was the Anointed One.

Apology for Jesus' death

A reason for this growing failure, perhaps the chief one, was the question: How could the Anointed One depicted in these miracles stories have come to the shameful death Jesus experienced at the hand of the Roman governor? How, in fact, could the Messiah have died at all? This objection was a serious weakness in the case for believing that Jesus was the Messiah, and it seems to have troubled Christian Jews as well. To answer it, an "apology" (that is, a defense) was developed, one parallel to the account underlying Mark 14–16. It showed that Jesus' suffering, death, and resurrection had been occasioned, indeed foreordained, by God. Evidence for this could be found in the prophecies of scripture, by rereading them in the light of Christian beliefs. Proof-texts were gathered and, together with such memories and suppositions as had circulated in the tradition about Jesus, were worked into a continuous account of Jesus' passion. This was at some point appended to the original Signs Gospel. Such proof-texts appear explicitly in 2:17; 12:38, 40; 12:15; 19:24, (28), 36, 37. Allusions to such proof-texts also occur, for example, at 18:2 (Ps 109:3; also at John 19:1, 3); 19:18 (Isa 53:12); 19:29 (Ps 69:21). Virtually all of these OT references are in the passion account. (See also the note on 2:14–19.) The text says that the events occurred "*in order to fulfill the Scriptures.*"

The earlier form of the Signs Gospel was no haphazard collection of miracle stories. It was a book containing a connected account of how Jesus' activity began with John the Baptizer and of the signs Jesus performed, first in Galilee, then in Jerusalem. In time, as just now noted, the passion and resurrection story were added, probably after a transitional summary of how the account only of Jesus' signs had in the end met with disbelief: the Council's plot to have Jesus killed and a justification for that death from scripture.

The earliest gospel?

From this narrative combining Jesus' signs with his death and resurrection was born what ever since has been thought essential to a book that could be called a "gospel." The Signs Gospel and Mark developed much the same format for telling the good news, and apparently did so independently. Mark differs from this format mainly by the introduction of some of Jesus' teaching—a development meager in Mark compared to Matthew, Luke, and John, but noticeable in comparison with the Signs Gospel's almost total lack of sayings. In the Signs Gospel, then, we have perhaps the earliest, certainly the most rudimentary of gospels.

The recovered text

What follows is an attempt to recreate what a Signs Gospel would have looked like. It is based largely on the work of R. T. Fortna, *The Fourth Gospel and its Predecessor* (1988), which to some degree is overlapped by U. C. von Wahlde's reconstruction, *The Earliest Version of John's Gospel* (1989). Three types of passages are enclosed in square brackets—[ ]: (a) those questionably assigned to the Signs Gospel, (b) those whose placement within it suggests Johannine rearrangement or is not certain, and (c) those involving more hypothetical reconstruction.

The reader comparing this reconstruction with John will notice that the order of individual narrative units in John differs from that evident in the Signs Gospel, as reflected by the (Johannine) chapter and verse numbers. In John the units have been greatly rearranged from their earlier order (see the outline below) and interpolated with later material. A comparison will also show that only some of the parenthetical remarks now dotting that gospel are thought to have been original to the Signs Gospel. Those that translate a Greek term or name back into its Semitic original (for example, 19:13) belong to the source. Those that do the reverse (see the note, for example, on 1:38)—evidently for the benefit of readers who knew only Greek—are attributable to the later Johannine redaction. Creating the Gospel of John involved reinterpreting the Signs Gospel, evidently necessitated by the final and bitter split in the community out of which this source arose. Christian Jews were expelled, late in the first century, from the synagogue.

In a few passages, the Johannine redactor's reinterpretation has been sufficiently extensive that recreation of the pre-Johannine text is more uncertain than usual. This is especially true in the following sections: John the Baptizer's witness to Jesus and to his disciples (1:23–36), the resurrection of Lazarus (11:1–45), and Jesus' trials before the high priest and Pilate (18:13, 19–24 and 18:33–19:16a).

There are several points in John where an older account very likely underlies the Johannine gospel but is not recoverable, namely, other material about John the Baptizer (3:22–30; 10:40–42), Jesus and Nicodemus (3:1–2), and Jesus and the Samaritan woman (4:1–42). To this list belongs above all the Last Supper (chapter 13; 14:30b), including in particular Jesus' prediction (13:38) that Peter will disown him (as in 18:16b–27) and perhaps also that the disciples present at the meal will abandon him (14:35). The latter is not fulfilled in John, unless it is implied by the presence only of women disciples at Jesus' execution and finally at the burial, and by the fact that Mary of Magdala went alone to the tomb on Sunday and was the first to find it empty. Whether any of this material listed above was part of the Signs Gospel is a matter of debate; perhaps in the meantime it was redacted more than once, making the recovery of its earliest written form virtually impossible.

A purely narrative gospel

What is quite clear, however, is that Jesus' lengthy and lofty teaching about himself in relation to his "Father," together with his instruction to (clearly future) followers, had no place in the Signs Gospel. This manner of speech is most distinctive of the Johannine portrayal of Jesus and reaches its fullest expression in the so-called Farewell Discourse during the Last Supper (13:31–17:26). But already in early chapters, besides minor interpolations, a number of the signs stories serve now only as the pretext for extended dialogue between Jesus and "the Judeans" (for example, 5:9b–47).

As noted above, the Signs Gospel, as hypothetically recovered, is no mere compilation of miracle stories or passion episodes. Its components fit together naturally, with logical geographic and temporal transitions. At some points there is clear evidence of the pre-Johannine author's compositional skill. For example, that author plays down the importance of John the Baptizer, reducing his role solely to testifying that Jesus is the Anointed One—unlike in the other gospels where John baptizes Jesus. The author's literary skill is evident also in using the three titles that John the Baptizer denies for himself in 1:21–22 (the Anointed One, Elijah, and the Prophet) as the titles with which the first apostle's discovery of Jesus is spread from one of them to another (1:41–45, as we have reconstructed verse 43b).

Outline of the Signs Gospel

The Opening
John's announcement (1:6–7, 19–34)
John's disciples and the Messiah (1:35–50)

Jesus' Signs in Galilee
Water into wine (2:1–11)
An official's son healed (2:12a; 4:46b–54)
A huge catch of fish (21:1–14)
Loaves and fish for 5,000 (6:1–14)
Jesus walks on the sea (6:16–21)

Jesus' Signs in Jerusalem
Lazarus raised (11:1–45)
A blind man given sight (9:1–8)
A crippled man healed (5:2–9)

The Culmination of Jesus' Signs
The Council's plan (11:47–53)
Jesus in the temple (2:14–19)
The Messiah must die (12:37–40)

The Prelude to Jesus' Passion
Mary anoints Jesus (12:1–8)
Jesus enters Jerusalem (12:12–15)

Jesus' Passion
The Last Supper (13:1–38; 14:31b)
Judas turns Jesus in (18:1–11)
Trial before the high priest & Peter's denials (18:12–27)
Trial before Pilate (18:28–19:16a)
Jesus is crucified (19:16b–37)
Joseph buries Jesus (19:38–42)

Jesus' Resurrection
Mary and Peter at the tomb (20:1–10)
Mary meets Jesus (20:11–18)
Jesus gives the spirit (20:19–22)

The Closing
Conclusion (20:30–31ab)

The Signs Gospel

1 ⁶**There appeared a man** sent from God named John. ^{7ac}He came to make an announcement, so everyone would believe through him.

¹⁹This is what John announced when priests and Levites [came to him] from Jerusalem to ask him, "Who are you?"

²⁰He declared "I'm not the Anointed One."

²¹And they asked him, "Then what are you? Are you Elijah?"

And he replies, "I am not."

"Are you the Prophet?"

He answered, "No."

^{22ac}So they said to him, "What have you got to say for yourself?"

²³He replied, "I am 'the voice of someone shouting in the desert, "Make the way of the Lord straight,"—that's how Isaiah the prophet put it."

²⁵"So," they persisted, "why are you baptizing if you're not the Anointed One, not Elijah, and not the Prophet?"

^{26a}"I baptize, yes, but only with water. Right there with you is ²⁷the one who is coming after me. I don't even deserve to untie his sandal straps. ^{31c}I came so he would be revealed to Israel. ^{32b}I have seen the spirit coming down upon him like a dove out of the sky; ^{33d}that's the one who baptizes with holy spirit. ³⁴I have seen this and I announce: This is the son of God."

³⁵**John was standing** there with two of his disciples. [³⁶When he noticed Jesus walking by, he says, "Look, there's the lamb of God."]

³⁷His two disciples heard him ⟨say this⟩, and they followed Jesus. ³⁸Jesus turned around, saw them following, and says to them, "What are you looking for?"

They said to him, "Rabbi, where do you live?"

³⁹He says to them, "Come and see."

They went and saw where he was staying and spent ⟨the rest of the⟩ the day with him. It was about four in the afternoon.

John's announcement

John's disciples & the Messiah

1:19–34
Cf. Mk 1:2–11;
Mt 3:1–2, 13–17;
Lk 3:1–22

1:21
Ⓣ Mt 11:13–14;
◊ Mal 4:5

1:23
//Mk 1:2–3, Mt 3:3,
Lk 3:4–6;
◊ Is 40:3

1:26b–27
//Q 3:16, Mt 3:11,
Lk 3:16

1:32b
//Mk 1:10, Mt 3:16,
Lk 3:22

1:33d
Ⓣ Acts 1:5, 11:16,
19:1–7

1:6–7, 19–34 As in a few other scenes, here the author of the canonical Gospel of John has considerably altered the Signs Gospel (SG).

1:6–7 The natural beginning of a narrative.

1:7 *everyone:* that is, all of Israel (v. 31).

would believe: namely, that Jesus was the Messiah (vv. 40–49), the major theme of this early gospel.

1:20–21 *the Anointed One . . . Elijah . . . the Prophet:* Three

ways of designating the savior whom many in Israel were awaiting. John denies for himself the three titles that are evidently applied to Jesus in the next section (vv. 41–45).

1:38 *Rabbi:* There is no need to translate the Semitic word into Greek, as in the present gospel; evidently SG's original audience was bilingual. Similarly, *Messiah* in v. 41 and *Kephas* in v. 42.

Water into wine

[40]Andrew, Simon Peter's brother, was one of the two who followed Jesus after hearing John ⟨speak about him⟩. [41ab]First he goes and finds his brother Simon and tells him, "We have found the Messiah," [42ab]and he led him to Jesus.

Jesus looked straight at him and said, "You're Simon, son of John; you're going to be called Kephas."

[43b]⟨Then⟩ he finds Philip and says to him, ["We've found Elijah," and he led him to Jesus and he says to him] "Follow me."

[44]Philip was from Bethsaida, the hometown of Andrew and Peter.

[45]Philip finds Nathanael and tells him, "We've found the one Moses wrote about in the Law, and the prophets mention too: Jesus, son of Joseph, from Nazareth."

[46]"From Nazareth?" Nathanael said to him. "Can anything good come from that place?"

Philip replies to him, "Come and see."

[47]Jesus saw Nathanael coming toward him, and he remarks about him: "There's a genuine Israelite—not a trace of deceit in him."

[48]"Where do you know me from?" Nathanael asks him.

Jesus replied, "I saw you under the fig tree before Philip invited you ⟨to join us⟩."

[49]Nathanael responded to him, "Rabbi, you are the son of God! You are King of Israel!"

[50]Jesus replied, "Do you believe just because I told you I saw you under the fig tree? You're going to see a lot more than that."

2 [1][**On a Tuesday**] there was a wedding in Cana, Galilee. Jesus' mother was there. [2]Jesus was also invited to the wedding along with his disciples. [3a]When the wine had run out, Jesus' mother says [5b]to the servants, "Whatever he tells you, do it."

[6ac]Six stone water jars were standing there, and each could hold twenty or thirty gallons.

1:41
Ⓣ Mk 8:29,
Mt 16:16, Lk 9:20

1:42
Ⓣ Mk 3:16,
Mt 10:2, Lk 6:14

1:49
Ⓣ Mt 16:16

1:43b A hypothetical reconstruction of material that was evidently omitted by the author of John. When *Elijah* is restored here, the balance between the titles denied by John for himself in vv. 20–21 and those now applied to Jesus is established.

Follow me: Only here does Jesus in some sense call the disciples, as in the synoptic gospels.

1:44 This kind of information is common in SG (see the hour of the day in v. 39 and many other instances).

Peter: The original reader or hearer, if bilingual (see the note on v. 38), would recognize that both *Kephas* (v. 42) and its Greek equivalent here refer to Andrew's brother, Simon (v. 41).

1:45 *the one Moses wrote about in the Law:* After *Messiah* in v. 41 and, apparently, *Elijah* in v. 43b, this designation, which refers to Deut 18:15, 18, ascribes to Jesus the last of the three titles John denied for himself, namely *the Prophet* (vv. 20–21).

2:1–11 The site of the preceding sections is unspecified, apart from Isaiah's "desert" (1:23). Beginning with this episode Jesus works only in Galilee until the story of the loaves and fish (6:1–14) is complete.

2:1 *Tuesday* (literally, "the third day ⟨of the week⟩") evidently was a common day for weddings.

2:2 *along with his disciples:* Jesus' newly acquired followers are present at all the "signs" Jesus now begins to perform.

[7]"Fill the jars with water," Jesus tells them.

So they filled them to the brim.

[8]Then he tells them, "Now dip some out and take it to the caterer."

And they did so. [9ac]When the caterer tasted the water, now changed into wine, he calls the groom aside [10]and says to him, "Everyone serves the best wine first; later, when people are drunk, they serve the cheaper wine. But you've held back the good wine till now."

[11]Jesus performed this sign, his first, in Cana, Galilee. [He showed himself], and his disciples believed in him.

[12a]**Then he set out** for Capernaum, he and his mother and brothers and disciples.

4 [46b]In Capernaum there was a government official whose son was sick. [47a]When he heard that Jesus was coming, he approached him and pleaded with him: [49b]"Sir, please come down before my child dies."

[50ac]Jesus says, "Go home, your son will live."

The man went home. [51]While he was still on his way home, his slaves met him and told him that his boy was alive. [52]So he asked them when he had begun to recover, and they told him, "The fever broke yesterday at one o'clock."

[53]Then the father realized that one o'clock was precisely the time Jesus had said to him, "Your son will live." And he believed, as did his whole household. [54a]This ⟨was⟩ the second sign Jesus performed.

21 [1ac]**Jesus showed himself** again to his disciples by the Sea of Tiberias. This is how he did it.

[2]When Simon Peter and Thomas were together, along with Nathanael from Cana, Galilee, the sons of Zebedee, and two other disciples, [3]Simon Peter says to them, "I'm going fishing."

"We're coming with you," they reply.

2:12a
Cf. Mk 1:21,
Mt 4:12–13, Lk 4:31

4:46b–54
Cf. Q 7:1–10,
Mt 8:5–13,
Lk 7:1–10

21:1–8
Cf. Lk 5:4–11

2:11 *this sign, his first:* SG puts the spotlight on its singular focus, the miracles of Jesus.

his disciples believed in him: the immediate effect, and the intended one.

2:12a *Then he set out for Capernaum:* a natural transition to Jesus' second sign (4:46b–54). In John, with the intervention of 2:13–4:46a, the statement is left hanging and continues, lamely, "and they did not stay there many days"—an *aporia* (see the note on 6:1).

4:47 *was coming:* In SG Jesus is on his way from Cana to Capernaum, not—as in the present arrangement of John—returning from Judea.

4:50ac *the man went home:* In SG his belief is not at Jesus' word (as in the Johannine v. 50b) but comes only at the end

of the episode, and as its climax (v. 53b).

4:54 *This ⟨was the⟩ second sign Jesus performed:* that is, in its own right, not simply "after he had returned from Judea to Galilee," as in John's gospel.

21:1–14 The assignment of this story to SG (as well as its placement here) is a bit more hypothetical than is the case for most other episodes.

21:1 *showed himself:* not the risen Lord appearing to them, as later in John, but demonstrating once again by his signs that he is the Anointed. The verb is the same as at 2:11b.

21:2 *Thomas:* SG need not explain to its audience that in Greek this disciple is "known as the Twin"—the Semitic name means just that.

Loaves & fish
for 5,000

They went down and got into the boat, but that night they didn't catch a thing.

[4a]It was already getting light and Jesus was standing on the shore.

[5]"You boys haven't caught any fish, have you?" Jesus asks them.

"No," they replied.

[6]He told them, "Cast your net on the right side of the boat and you'll have better luck."

So they cast the net, but then couldn't haul it in because of the huge number of fish. [7b]Simon Peter tied his cloak around himself, since he was stripped for work, and [leapt] into the water. [8]The rest of the disciples came by boat, dragging the net full of fish. They were not far from land.

[11]Then Simon Peter went ashore and ⟨helped⟩ haul in the net full of large fish—one hundred fifty-three of them. Even though there were so many of them, the net still didn't tear.

[14ac]This was now the third [sign] that Jesus [performed].

6

[1]**After these events**, Jesus crossed the Sea of Tiberias. [3]Jesus climbed up the mountain, and he sat down there with his disciples. [5]Jesus looks up and sees a big crowd approaching him, and he says to Philip, "Where are we going to buy enough bread to feed these people?"

[7]"Two hundred denarii wouldn't buy enough bread for everyone to have a bite," Philip said.

[8]One of his disciples, Andrew, Simon Peter's brother, says to him, [9]"There's a kid here with five loaves of barley bread and two fish; but what does that amount to for so many?"

6:1–14
//Mk 6:30–44,
8:1–10;
Mt 14:13–21,
15:32–39;
Lk 9:10–17;
◊2 Kgs 4:42–44

[10]Jesus said, "Have the people sit down." (They were in a grassy place.) So they sat down. (The men ⟨alone⟩ numbered about five thousand.) [11]Jesus took the loaves, gave thanks, and passed them around to the people sitting there, along with the fish, and all of them had as much as they wanted. [12]And when they had eaten their fill, he says to his disciples, "Gather up the leftovers so that nothing goes to waste."

21:4a *was standing:* This direct translation fits SG better than "appeared."

21:5 This leads solely to the miracle, not also to an Easter appearance by the risen Jesus and a meal with him, as in John.

21:7 *leapt into the water:* Here Peter does not desperately "throw himself," as in John 21 but only hurries to wade ashore to help land the catch.

21:11 The original sign story continues.

he went ashore and ⟨helped⟩ haul in . . .: The word usually taken to mean "went aboard [the boat]" equally can mean "went onto land."

one hundred fifty-three of them: The detail demonstrates the miracle's magnitude and is an instance of SG's interest in verisimilitude; see the note on 1:44.

6:1 *crossed the Sea of Tiberias:* After the first two or three signs in Galilee, this transition is entirely natural; after chapter 5 as in our present John it is one of several "aporias," that is, rough spots in the flow of the story that help us recover the earlier source (SG).

6:7 *Two hundred denarii* was more than half a year's wages, a denarius being the standard pay for a day of labor.

[13]So they gathered them up and filled twelve baskets with scraps from the five barley loaves—from what was left over. [14]When these folks saw the sign he had performed they were saying, "This has to be the Prophet who is to come into the world!"

[16]**As evening approached**, his disciples went down to the sea. [17]They boarded a boat and were trying to cross the sea to Capernaum. It had already gotten dark, and Jesus still had not joined them. [18]A strong wind began to blow and the sea was getting rough. [19]When they had rowed about three or four miles, they catch sight of Jesus walking on the sea and coming toward the boat. They were frightened, [20]but he says to them, "Don't be afraid! It's me." [21]Then they would have taken him on board, but the boat instantly arrived at the shore they had been making for.

11 [1]**Now someone named Lazarus** had fallen ill; he was from Bethany, the village of Mary and her sister Martha. [2](This was the Mary who anointed the Master with perfumed ointment and wiped his feet with her hair; it was her brother Lazarus who was sick.) [3]So the sisters sent for Jesus: "Master, the one you love is sick."

[4a]But when Jesus heard this he said, "Lazarus is dead; [15b]let's go to him." [17]When Jesus arrived, he found out that Lazarus had been buried four days earlier. [32]When Mary got to where Jesus was and saw him, she knelt at his feet. "Master," she said, "if you'd been here, my brother wouldn't have died."

[33]When Jesus saw her crying, he was agitated and deeply disturbed. [34]"Where have you put him?" he asked.

"Master," they say, "come and see."

[35]Then Jesus wept.

[38]Jesus arrives at the tomb; it was a cave, and a stone lay up against the opening. [39a]Jesus says, "Take the stone away." [41a]So they took the stone away, and Jesus [43]shouted at the top of his voice, "Lazarus, come out!" [44]The dead man came out, his hands and feet bound in strips of burying cloth. Jesus says to them, "Free him and let him go."

[45ac]As a result, many came to believe in him.

6:14
◊ Dt 18:15–18

6:16–21
//Mk 6:45–52,
Mt 14:22–33

6:22–25
//Mk 6:53–56,
Mt 14:34–36

11:2
① SG 12:3

11:35
① Lk 19:41

6:14 *saw the sign he had performed:* Unlike the first three signs, from this episode onward the signs are no longer numbered. Perhaps such notices were original to all the signs and were necessarily omitted with their rearrangement in John.

the Prophet: the messianic title used in 1:21.

6:21 *the boat instantly arrived:* another miracle but probably secondary to Jesus' walking on the water.

11:1–45 This story is the most difficult of the original signs to recover since it has been repeatedly interpolated with later material. Further, it is only tentatively assigned this place in SG, because it occasions Jesus' going to Jerusalem (see the note on 11:17).

11:17 *buried four days earlier:* Presumably it took at least two days for Mary's message to reach Jesus in Galilee, sent when Lazarus was still alive, and so two or more for his journey to Bethany, a village just outside Jerusalem.

11:35 *Then Jesus wept:* perhaps one of the details often used in SG to lend a sense of factuality.

*A blind man given
sight*

*A crippled man
healed*

The Council's plan

9 ¹**As Jesus was leaving** he saw a man who had been blind from birth. ⁶He spat on the ground, made mud with his saliva, and smeared the mud on the man's eyes. ⁷Then Jesus said to him, "Go, rinse off in the pool of Siloam." So he went, rinsed off ⟨his eyes⟩, and came back with his sight restored.

⁸Then his neighbors, who recognized him as the one who had been a beggar before, were saying, "Isn't this the guy who used to sit and beg?"

5 ²**In Jerusalem**, by the Sheep ⟨Gate⟩, there is a pool, called *Bethzatha* in Hebrew. It has five colonnades, ³among which numerous invalids—blind, lame, paralyzed—were usually lying around. ⁵One man had been crippled for thirty-eight years. ⁶Jesus observed him lying there and realized he had been there a long time.

"Do you want to get well?" he asks him.

⁷The crippled man replied, "Sir, I don't have anyone to put me in the pool when the water is agitated; while I'm trying to get in someone else beats me to it."

⁸"Get up, pick up your mat, and start walking," Jesus tells him.

⁹And at once the man recovered; he picked up his mat and started walking.

11 ⁴⁷**So the chief priests** called the Council together and posed this question to them: "What are we going to do now that this man performs so many signs? ⁴⁸If we let him go on like this, everybody will come to believe in him. Then the Romans will come and destroy our nation."

5:2–9
Cf. Mk 2:1–12,
Mt 9:1–8,
Lk 5:17–26

9:1–8 This very brief story (of only three or four verses) may no longer contain all of its original material, particularly the transition from v. 1 to v. 6. Its placement in SG, like the episodes before and after it, is based on the natural but unobtrusive itinerary it affords. See the notes on 9:1 and 5:2, below.

9:1 *As Jesus was leaving:* that is, perhaps, leaving Bethany on his way into the city. The pool of Siloam is just outside Jerusalem.

9:8 This verse is possibly part of the original ending; or something has been lost here, too. Otherwise, there is none of the typical reaction to the sign.

5:2 *In Jerusalem, by the Sheep ⟨Gate⟩:* Jesus has now come into the city's center, perhaps to one of the very gates of the temple precinct.

It has five colonnades: The present tense here (taken over into John, which usually retains the wording of the source verbatim) suggests that the source, but not the completed Gospel of John, was written before the destruction of the Jerusalem temple in 70 CE.

5:7 *when the water is agitated:* Apparently it was believed to be curative only then. (This bare notice must have given rise to the vivid and elaborate legend that was much later interpolated into John, as vv. 3b–4.)

5:8 *start walking:* The Greek here is precisely repeated in the man's compliance (v. 9), a common feature in SG.

11:47–53 If, as is probable, SG did not at first contain a passion narrative, it would probably have ended here—that is, after the healing of the blind man—with the concluding words of 20:30–31a. It seems likely, however, that by the time it served (according to the hypothesis) as basis for much of the narrative in John it would already have been joined with, or extended to include, the account of Jesus' arrest, trial, execution, and burial. This so-called Passion Source would have had a distinct origin from a purely Signs Source, each serving a quite different purpose; the latter sought to prove that Jesus' was the Messiah, the former to account for his death.

This episode, interrupting the account of Jesus' public activity, provides the turning point. With Jesus' signs now complete and the people's response to them patent, the authorities react, citing the very danger Jesus' popularity posed.

11:48 *The Romans will come and destroy our nation:* The Council fears that belief in Jesus as the Anointed One will be seen as support for a leader who is challenging Roman rule and thus lead to the loss of such nationhood as Israel was allowed.

[49]One of them, Caiaphas, that year's chief priest, addressed them as follows: [50]"Don't you realize that you're better off having one man die for the people than having the whole nation wiped out?" [[51]He didn't say this on his own authority, but since he was that year's chief priest he could foresee that Jesus would die for the nation.] [53]So from that day on they began plotting how to kill him.

2 [14]**In the temple area** Jesus found people selling oxen and sheep and doves, and others exchanging currency. [15]He made a whip out of rope and drove them all out of the temple area, sheep and oxen; then he knocked over the exchange tables and scattered the coins. [16]And to the dove merchants he said, "Get these birds out of here! How dare you use my Father's house as a public market."

[17b]⟨This was to fulfill⟩ the words of scripture:

> Zeal for your house will eat me alive.

[18]To this ⟨they⟩ responded, "What sign can you show us to justify doing all this?"

[19]Jesus replied, "Destroy this temple and I'll raise it in three days."

12 [37]**Although he had performed** so many signs before their eyes, they did not believe in him, [38]in order that the word the prophet Isaiah spoke would be fulfilled:

> Lord, who has believed our message?
> To whom is God's might revealed?

[39]So they were unable to believe, for Isaiah also said,

Jesus disrupts the temple

Disbelief at the signs

11:53
Cf. Mk 3:6,
Mt 12:14,
Mk 11:18,
Lk 19:47–48,
Mk 14:1–2,
Mt 26:3–5,
Lk 22:1–2

2:14–17
//Mk 11:15–17,
Mt 21:12–13,
Lk 19:45–46

2:17b
◊ Ps 69:9

2:18–19
Cf. Mk 11:27–33,
Mt 21:23–27,
Lk 20:1–8

2:19
//Mk 14:57–58,
15:29; Mt 26:60–61,
27:40;
cf. Th 71

12:37–40
Cf. Mk 4:10–12,
Mt 13:10–17,
Lk 8:9–10

12:38
◊ Is 53:1

11:53 Jesus' fate is sealed, an outcome altogether out of keeping with the expectations his signs have raised. This inconsistency is explained in 12:37–40.

2:14–19 The Passion Source underlying John 18–19 (as well as parts of John 11–13 and including this story, now in John 2) serves the purpose of an *apology*, a "defense" of Jesus' crucifixion. It does this by a single device: showing that the Anointed One's death was foreordained in Scripture and therefore happened by divine necessity. That device appears here for the first time (v. 17), the explicit fulfillment of a specific passage from the Hebrew scriptures. This episode, before it was removed to John 2, furthers the transition to an account of Jesus' end: the unfailing belief that the signs evoked gives way to suspicion of Jesus' right to take decisive steps in the temple.

2:14 *In the temple area:* In resuming Jesus' activity, after the Council's secret decision, the narrative flow from the healing of the lame man—most likely near a gate into the temple area (see the note on 5:2, above)—is smooth.

2:17b ⟨*This was to fulfill*⟩ *the words of scripture:* that is, Jesus did this *because* of the passage in Ps 69:10. See below, on 12:38.

Will eat me alive is perhaps deliberately ambiguous. It accounts for the vehemence of Jesus' act; it also foreshadows the deadly consequence this act will have.

2:19 *Destroy this temple means* "If you kill me."

I'll raise it in three days: Instead of displaying another sign, Jesus promises one—it will be his greatest and will give the best apology imaginable for his death. His assertion that he will accomplish his own resurrection is virtually unique in the NT.

12:37–40 This interpretive comment by SG's author brings the recital of Jesus' public activity formally to a close, admits its failure, and explains how this contradiction was inevitable (see on v. 38, below).

12:38 *in order that the word the prophet Isaiah spoke would be fulfilled:* This is the first instance of this formula, making explicit the divine necessity, and therefore acceptability, of Jesus' death.

who has believed oue message?: In Isa 53:1 the prophet displays the same defeat that the author of SG now expresses.

Marty anoints Jesus

*Jesus enters
Jerusalem*

Jesus washes feet

⁴⁰He has blinded their eyes,

and closed their minds,

to make sure they don't see with their eyes

and understand with their minds,

or else they would turn ⟨their lives⟩ around

and I would heal them.

¹**Six days before Passover** Jesus came to Bethany, where Lazarus lived, the one Jesus had raised from the dead. ²There they gave a dinner for him; Martha did the serving, and Lazarus was one of those who ate with him. ³Mary brought in a pound of expensive aromatic ointment made from pure nard and anointed Jesus' feet and wiped them with her hair. And the house was filled with the ointment's fragrance. ⁴Judas Iscariot, the disciple who was going to turn him in, says, ⁵"Why wasn't this ointment sold? It would bring three hundred denarii, and the money could have been given to the poor." [⁶He didn't say this because he cared about the poor, but because he was a thief. He was in charge of the common purse and now and again would pilfer money put into it.]

⁷"Leave her alone," Jesus said. "Let her keep it for the day of my burial. ⁸There will always be poor around, but I won't always be around."

¹²**The next day** the huge crowd that had come for the festival heard that Jesus was coming into Jerusalem. ¹³They got palm fronds and went out to meet him. They began to shout,

Hosanna! Blessed is the one who comes in the name of the Lord!

⟨Blessed is⟩ the King of Israel!

¹⁴Then Jesus found a young donkey and rode on it, as scripture puts it,

¹⁵Fear not, daughter of Zion.

Look, your king comes riding on a donkey's colt.

13 ¹ᵃ**Before the Festival** of Passover ²ᶜat supper ⁴Jesus got up from the meal, took off his shirt, put it aside, and wrapped a towel around himself. ⁵Then he

12:40
◊Is 6:9–10

12:1–8
//Mk 14:3–9,
Mt 26:6–13;
cf. Lk 7:36–50

12:8
◊Dt 15:11

12:12–15
//Mk 11:1–10,
Mt 21:1–11,
Lk 19:28–40

12:13
◊Ps 118:26

12:15
◊Zec 9:9

12:40 Indeed, as God had once hardened Pharaoh's heart (e.g., Exod 9:12), it is by God's design that the leaders did not, could not, believe. The story of Jesus' passion can now proceed with neither anxiety nor incomprehension.

12:3 *anointed:* Jesus has been the Anointed One from the beginning of SG; this anointing only points forward to his burial (v. 7).

12:4 Judas' fateful role is recognized from his first appearance.

12:6 Unless added to SG in its revision as John, this explanation represents an intermediate stage in the tendency to heighten Judas' blame. Note John 6:70 and 13:10.

12:12–13 *Blessed is the one who comes in the name of the*

Lord: Jesus is given the traditional welcome as for any festal pilgrim, but here it is far more; *the crowd that had come for the festival* acclaims Jesus as *King of Israel*, just as Nathanael had done at the beginning of SG (1:49).

12:14 *as scripture puts it:* Jesus' preordained role continues (see above, on 2:17), as Zech 9:9 requires.

12:15 *your king comes riding on a donkey's colt:* Jesus' humility hints already at his otherwise inconceivable submission to the abasement and execution that lie before him.

13 SG's version of the Last Supper is an entirely different memory or tradition than that found in the synoptic gospels, and one closer to the burden of Jesus' teaching.

13:4 *took off his shirt:* Jesus strips to the waist, like a slave.

poured water into a basin and began to wash the disciples' feet and dry them with the towel around his waist. ¹²When he had washed their feet, he put his shirt back on and returned to his place at the meal. "Do you realize what I've done?" he asked. ¹³ᵃ"You call me Teacher and Master. ¹⁴So if I am your master and teacher and have washed your feet, you should wash each other's feet. [¹⁵In other words, I've set you an example: you are to do as I've done to you.]

³⁷ᵃᶜPeter says to him, "I'd give my life for you."

³⁸Jesus responded, "Let me tell you this: the rooster won't crow before you disown me three times."

14 ³¹ᵇCome on, let's get out of here."

18 ¹ᵇᶜ**Jesus went out** with his disciples across the Kidron valley. There was a garden there where he and his disciples went. ²But because Jesus had often gone there with his disciples, Judas, who was about to turn him in, knew the place too. ³So it wasn't long before Judas arrives, bringing with him some of the police from the chief priests, with their lanterns and torches and weapons.

⁴ᵇJesus went right up to them and says, "Who is it you're looking for?"

⁵"Jesus the Nazarene," was their reply.

"That's me," says Jesus.

¹⁰Simon Peter had brought along a sword, and now he drew it, slashed at the chief priest's slave, who was called Malchus, and cut off his right ear.

¹¹ᵃ"Put the sword back in its scabbard," Jesus told Peter.

¹²**Then the police** arrested Jesus and bound him. ¹³They took him first to Annas. (Annas was the father-in-law of that year's chief priest, Caiaphas.) [²⁴Annas sent him, still bound, to Caiaphas.]

¹⁵Simon Peter and another disciple were trailing along behind Jesus. This other disciple, who was an acquaintance of the chief priest, went in with Jesus to the chief priest's courtyard. ¹⁶Peter was [left] standing outside the gate; so this other disciple, the acquaintance of the chief priest, went out, had a word with the woman who kept watch at the gate, and got Peter in.

¹⁷The slave woman says to Peter, "You're not one of this man's disciples too, are you?"

"No, I'm not," he replies.

¹⁸Meanwhile, since it was cold, the slaves and police had made a charcoal fire and were standing around it, trying to keep warm. Peter was standing there too, warming himself.

¹⁹Now the chief priest interrogated Jesus about his disciples and about his teaching.

Judas turns Jesus in

Trial before the chief priest

18:1–11
//Mk 14:43–52,
Mt 26:47–56,
Lk 22:47–54

18:1
//Mk 14:32,
Mt 26:36

18:11
Ⓣ Mk 14:36,
Mt 26:39, Lk 22:42

18:15–27
//Mk 14:55–72;
Mt 26:55–75;
Lk 22:58–62, 66–71

18:1 *Jesus went out with his disciples:* presumably from the place of the Last Supper.
18:24 John moved this verse, thereby dividing SG's single

hearing before the chief priest (SG 18:12–27) into two, one before Annas (John 18:12–23) and another before Caiaphas (John 18:24–27).

Peter's denials

Trial before Pilate

²⁰"I have spoken openly to anyone and everyone," Jesus replied. "I've always taught in the temple area, in places where all Jewish people gather. I've said nothing in secret. ²¹Why are you asking me? Ask those who heard what I said. You'll see that they know what I said."

²²As soon as he said this, one of the policemen on duty there slapped Jesus. "How dare you talk back to the chief priest!" he said.

²⁵**Meanwhile, Simon Peter** was still standing outside, keeping warm. The others there said to him, "You're not one of his disciples too, are you?"

He denied it. "No, I'm not," he said.

²⁶One of the chief priest's slaves, a relative of the one whose ear Peter had cut off, says, "I saw you in the garden with him, didn't I?"

²⁷Once again Peter denied it.

At that very moment a rooster crowed.

²⁸**They then take Jesus** from Caiaphas' place to the governor's residence. By now it was early morning. Pilate says to them, "What charge are you bringing against this man?"

³⁰"If he hadn't committed a crime," they retorted, "we wouldn't have turned him over to you."

³³Then Pilate summoned Jesus and asked him, "Are you the King of the Judeans?" . . .

³⁸ᶜ⟨Pilate⟩ says to them, "In my judgment there is no case against him. ³⁹But it's your privilege at Passover to have me free one prisoner for you. So, do you want me to free 'the King of the Judeans' for you?"

⁴⁰At this they shouted back, "Not this guy—Barabbas!" (Barabbas was an insurgent.)

19

¹Then Pilate had Jesus taken away and flogged.

²And the soldiers wove a crown out of thorns and put it on his head; they also dressed him up in a purple robe. ³They began marching up to him and saying, "Greetings, 'King of the Judeans,'" as they slapped him in the face.

Jesus came outside, still wearing the crown of thorns and the purple robe.

⁶When the chief priests and the police saw him, they screamed, "Crucify! Crucify!"

¹³Pilate sat on the judge's seat in the place called Stone Pavement (*Gabbatha* in Hebrew). ¹⁴(It was now about twelve noon on the day of preparation for Passover.) He says to them, "Look, here's your king."

18:20b
Cf. Mk 14:49,
Mt 26:55, Lk 22:53

18:28a–40
//Mk 15:1–15;
Mt 27:1–2, 11–26;
Lk 23:1–7, 13–25

18:33–38
Cf. Mk 15:2,
Mt 27:1, Lk 23:2–3

19:1–3
//Mk 15:16–20,
Mt 27:27–31,
Pet 2:36–3:4

19:6–16a
//Mk 15:1–15;
Mt 27:11–26;
Lk 23:1–7, 13–25

18:28–19:16a In John the Roman trial is a drama of seven scenes, but in SG it was probably rather brief; its reconstruction is unclear at several points.

18:29 *"What charge are you bringing against this man?"*: From Pilate's question to Jesus in what follows (v. 33) it is clear enough that Jesus is being charged with insurrection.

19:1–3 The ritual scourging of a condemned man would most naturally come here in the story.

19:14a *the day of preparation*: for Passover, or the Sabbath day, or both; see also 19:31, 42. Passover was not the night before, at the last supper, as it is in the other gospels.

[15]But they screamed, "Get him out of here! Crucify him!"

[16]And so, in the end, Pilate turned him over to be crucified.

So they took Jesus, [17]who carried the cross by himself, out to the place called Skull (known in Hebrew as *Golgotha*). [18]There they crucified him, and with him two others—one on each side, with Jesus in the middle.

[19]Pilate also had a notice written and posted it on the cross; it read: "Jesus the Nazorean, the King of the Judeans." [20]Many of the Judeans read the notice, since Jesus was crucified near the city and it was written in Hebrew, Latin, and Greek. [21]The ranking priests tried protesting to Pilate: "Don't write, 'The King of the Judeans,' but instead, 'This man said, "I am King of the Judeans."'"

[22]Pilate answered them, "What I have written stays written."

[23]When the soldiers had crucified Jesus, they took his clothes and divided them into four shares, one share for each soldier. But his shirt was woven continuously without seam. [24]So they said to each other, "Let's not tear it, but toss to see who gets it."

This happened so that the scripture would be fulfilled that says,

> They divided my garments among them,
> and for my clothes they cast lots.

So that is what the soldiers did. [25]Meanwhile, Jesus' mother, his mother's sister, Mary the wife of Klopas, and Mary of Magdala were standing near his cross. [28]Then Jesus says in order to fulfill the scripture, "I'm thirsty."

[29]A bowl of sour wine was sitting there, and so they filled a sponge with wine, stuck it on some hyssop, and held it to his mouth. [30]When Jesus had taken some wine, he said, "It's all over."

Lowering his head, he gave up the spirit.

[31]Since it was the day of preparation, they asked Pilate to have the legs of the three broken and the bodies taken away. Otherwise their bodies would remain on the cross during the Sabbath.

[32]So the soldiers came and broke the legs of the first man, and then of the other who had been crucified with him. [33]But when they came to Jesus, they could see that he was already dead, so they didn't break his legs. [34]Instead, one of the soldiers jabbed him in the side with his spear, and right away blood and water came pouring out. [36]This happened so the scripture that says,

> No bone of his shall be broken,

would be fulfilled, [37]as well as another scripture that says,

> They shall look at the one they have pierced.

19:16–30
//Mk 15:22–37,
Mt 27:33–50,
Lk 22:32–46,
Pet 4:1–5

19:24
◊ Ps 22:18

19:28–30
Cf. Pet 5:1–5

19:28–29
◊ Ps 69:21

19:31
◊ Dt 21:22–23

19:36
◊ Ps 34:20

19:37
◊ Zec 12:10

19:24 *This happened so that the scripture would be fulfilled:* All this is happening—here in precise detail—by divine necessity.

19:36–37 SG's justification of Jesus' death culminates in a double proof-text, with the usual formula. The first seems to be a combination of Ps 34:20 with passages from Torah about the paschal lamb (Exod 12:46; Num 9:12); the second quotes Zech 12:10.

Joseph buries Jesus

*Mary & Peter at
the tomb*

Mary meets Jesus

*Behind locked
doors*

Conclusion

[38]**After all this**, Joseph of Arimathea, a disciple of Jesus, asked Pilate's permission to take Jesus' body down. Pilate agreed, so Joseph came and took his body down [40b] and wound it up in strips of burial cloth. [41]Now there was a garden in the place where he had been crucified and a new tomb in the garden where no one had ever been laid to rest. [42]Since this tomb was handy and because it was the Jewish day of preparation, it was here that he laid Jesus.

20

[1]**Early on Sunday**, while it was still dark, Mary of Magdala comes to the tomb and sees that the stone has been moved away. [2]So she runs and comes to Simon Peter and tells him, "They've taken the Master from the tomb, and we don't know where they've put him."

[3]So Peter went out and makes his way to the tomb. [6]He goes in and sees the strips of burial cloth there, [7]and also the cloth they had used to cover his head, lying not with the strips of burial cloth but rolled up by itself. [9]But since he did not yet understood the prophecy that he was destined to rise from the dead, [10]he went back home.

[11]**Mary, however, stood crying** outside, and in her tears she stooped to look into the tomb, [12]and she sees two heavenly messengers in white seated where Jesus' body had lain, one at the head and the other at the feet.

[13]"Lady, why are you crying?" they ask her.

"They've taken my master away," she tells them, "and I don't know where they've put him."

[14a]No sooner had she said this than she turned around and sees Jesus standing there.

[15b]Thinking that he was the gardener, she says to him, "Please, mister, if you've moved him, tell me where you've put him so I can take him away."

[16]"Mary," says Jesus.

She turns around and exclaims in Hebrew, "*Rabbuni!*"

[17]Jesus tells her, "Go to my brothers and tell them."

[18]Mary of Magdala goes and reports to the disciples, "I've seen the Master."

[19]**Now that Sunday evening**, the disciples had locked the doors, but Jesus came and stood in front of them and he greets them: "Peace."

[22]And at this he breathed over them and says, "Here's holy spirit. Take it."

[30]**Although Jesus performed** many more signs for his disciples to see than are written down in this book, [31ab]these are written down so you will believe that Jesus is the Anointed One, the son of God.

19:38–42
//Mk 15:42–47;
Mt 27:57–61;
Lk 23:50–56;
Pet 2:1–3a, 6:1–4

20:1–10
//Mk 16:1–6,
Mt 28:1–6,
Lk 24:1–7;
cf. Pet 12:1–13:3

20:11–18
//Mt 28:7–9,
Lk 24:9–10

20:17
Ⓣ SJas 6:13

20:19–22
//Lk 24:33–49;
cf. Mk 16:14–18

20:1 No *stone* was mentioned at Jesus' burial, but it was a common practice to close a tomb in this way (see 11:38–39).

20:2 *tells him:* With the later addition of "the disciple that Jesus loved" to this scene, this would have been changed to "them," as now in John.

20:22 *Here's holy spirit. Take it:* This fulfills the promise the

Baptizer had given at 1:33, having himself just seen Jesus receive the spirit.

20:30–31ab Perhaps this once was the ending of a Signs Source in the narrow sense, without a passion narrative. Here these words—because of Jesus' greatest sign, his own resurrection (2:19)—properly conclude the Signs Gospel.

"Judeans" and "Jews"

The Greek word *Ioudaios* confronts translators with unique challenges. Etymologically, the word denoted someone from the land of Judah/Judea. The translation "Judean" transmits this geographical meaning, as do such words as "Roman" or "Egyptian." But *Ioudaios* also carried cultural and religious connotations, which is why it has traditionally been translated as "Jew."

Translating *Ioudaios* in the gospels is a thorny problem because the word is used to refer to the opponents and enemies of Jesus, often in harsh polemical tones, especially in the Gospel of John. Translations of the gospels have thus contributed to an insidious and disgusting stereotype of "the Jews" as unbelieving, unrepentant, and perversely wicked people who "rejected" and persecuted Jesus. Such terminology has also obscured the historical fact that Jesus and his followers were just as "Jewish" as those with whom they argued.

Appropriate translation of *Ioudaios* must be based on the recognition that the religious tradition known today as Judaism, the religion practiced by Jews, has a long history, which historians typically divide into three major periods:

> The religion of the first temple (c. 950–586 BCE)
> The religion of the second temple (c. 520 BCE–70 CE)
> The religion of rabbis and synagogue (c. 70 CE and continuing)

By convention, scholars refer to the religion of the first temple as "Israelite religion." The first temple was constructed in Jerusalem by King Solomon in the mid-tenth century BCE. After Solomon's death the nation split into northern and southern kingdoms; the northern kingdom became known as "Israel," the southern as "Judah." When the northern kingdom was conquered by the Assyrians in 721 BCE, its citizens were deported by the thousands and the kingdom ceased to exist. The temple in Jerusalem (the capital of Judah) was destroyed by the Babylonians in 586 BCE.

Around 520 BCE a second temple was built in Jerusalem under the protection of the Persian empire. Over the next several centuries, the state of Judah existed as a small unit in the Persian and Hellenistic empires, and for a time was an independent kingdom until it was swallowed up by the Roman empire. The religion of the second temple was centered on the sacrificial cult connected with the temple and supervised by a priestly caste. However, various groups both within and outside the ancient homeland developed diverse expressions of their religion, all of which claimed to be authentic representations of the ancestral traditions of Israel.

The religion of the second temple came to an end when the Romans destroyed the temple in 70 CE. The religion that subsequently evolved has been led by rabbis rather than priests and, since the temple was never rebuilt, remains centered in the synagogue and the family. The religion of this third major period is universally known as "Judaism" and those who practice it as "Jews."

Since the religion of the second temple was significantly different from Rabbinic Judaism, scholars do not agree on what to call the religion and people of this period. Hence the problem in translating this term in the Christian gospels, which were written in the third period but focus on Jesus, who lived in the second.

The word *Ioudaios* emerges out of the concern for social boundaries and group identity during the period of the second temple. It described a person from a specific land of origin (Judea, hence, "Judean"). Those who maintained the traditions of the people of that land practiced *Ioudaismos* (Judaism). *Ioudaios* was not originally a self-descriptive term used by all Israelites, but represents the perspective of foreigners describing those who live in or come from the land of Judea. Only secondarily does the term become useful for followers of Judaism as a self-designation within the ethnic mix of the Greco-Roman world. Those who saw themselves within the tradition of Israel would identify themselves primarily as "Israelite," "descendent of Abraham," "of the tribe of (e.g., Benjamin)," "Hebrew," or "of the nation of Israel." On the other hand, they would use *Ioudaios* when distinguishing between those within the Israelite traditions and outsiders. The term *Ioudaios* is, in effect, a borderland word, a definition useful in negotiating with the Gentile world.

The negative sense of the word that can be found in the gospels comes from inter-Judaic competition. Judaism in the first century was hardly monolithic, for a variety of sects considered themselves the authentic bearers of the Israelite tradition. The negative aspect of "Judean" allowed one group to denigrate another by using a word that carried a "foreign" tone. In the gospels *Ioudaios* is found mainly in the Gospel of John, which uses the word negatively 70 out of 72 times—a strategy by which the Johannine community casts a negative light on fellow Israelites who do not accept Jesus as the messiah. In the Acts of the Apostles the term is also employed largely in this negative fashion, and the same is true in the Gospel of Peter, whose audience supposedly lives "in fear of the *Ioudaioi*" (the plural form of the word).

In this present revision of SV, the translators have determined that *Ioudaios* is used in three ways:

(1) A neutral sense, as when the customs, rites, and particularities of the people of Judea are described or referred to. Here "Judean(s)" is used.

(2) A sense that implies some ethnic interaction and competition. In some instances in which *Ioudaios* has this sense, the word carries hints of what later became the Jewish/Christian separation. Here SV uses the term "Jews" and "Jewish."

(3) *Ioudaios* could be used to slur an opponent because rather than the primary indicator of social identity (such as "Israelite," "descendent of Abraham," "of the tribe of ...") it was a term that foreigners commonly applied to Israelites. In these cases *Ioudaios* is better translated as "Judean" to convey or suggest a demeaning intent. One could put down fellow Israelites using a term that does not convey the richness of identity and social pedigree. One's opponent is thus diminished by being given a foreigner's label.

The Gospel of John

Introduction

John and the synoptic gospels

From early times Christians have recognized that "the Gospel according to John" is dramatically different from the synoptic gospels (Mark, Matthew, Luke). In John there is nothing of Jesus' teaching in parables or his associating with the outcast. He performs no exorcisms and barely gives ethical teaching. He speaks of the empire of God on only one occasion (3:3, 5) but claims an empire of his own (18:36). Virtually nothing is found here of the eschatology found in the synoptics (see the notes on 5:24, 8:51, and 14:3). We hear of chief priests and Pharisees (perhaps reflecting the author's own experience more than Jesus' time), but nothing of Sadducees, Zealots, scholars, elders, toll collectors, prostitutes, rich and poor. Jesus accomplishes miracles but in the Greek they are called "signs"—just what the synoptics' Jesus refuses to give (Mark 8:11–12)—and are done solely to prove that Jesus is the incarnate Son of God. This focus on Jesus' divinity—established not by birth narratives as in Matthew and Luke but by the sonorous theological language of the hymn to the eternal divine word become human (1:1–18)—is both more prominent and at the same time simply taken for granted. Jesus speaks not like the first-century itinerant teacher that he in fact was but as if he were from heaven, revealing the nature of God ("my Father," see especially 5:18). All the gospels paint a Christian, that is, a post-resurrection, portrait of Jesus, but this gospel far more than the others. The later Christian creeds were based on the theological language of John's gospel much more than on that of the synoptic gospels.

This gospel's uniqueness does not stem, apparently, from a deliberate intent to differ from the synoptic gospels, for it was probably independent of them literarily. It overlaps with them in the narratives—of Jesus' miracles and of his "passion" and resurrection—but this overlap is probably due to common sources underlying the various gospels.

Jesus' teaching

It is the discourses of Jesus, his long monologues on truth, life, light, that distinguish this gospel's portrait of him. There is virtually nothing of this teaching in the synoptics, and it seems to be the expression partly of a Jesus tradition unique to this gospel and partly of the interpretation given that tradition within the gospel's Christian Jewish community, in the light of what that community has experienced. This discourse tradition may be rooted in the teaching of the shadowy figure known as "the disciple Jesus loved," perhaps the founder of the distinctive Christian community out of which this gospel arises. But despite what is claimed in the comment inserted in 21:24, there is in this gospel very little of the historical Jesus' actual teaching (see further the notes on that verse). And it is not certain that this Beloved Disciple, as he has usually been known, was in fact a real person.

The words of the Johannine Jesus are often ambiguous, even deliberately confusing his listeners (e.g., 3:3), conveying two levels of meaning at once. Thus, Jesus frequently says "I am," which at face value means only something like "It's me" (e.g., 6:20), but equally expresses the divine I AM of the Hebrew Scriptures. He cryptically refers to his "time" (e.g., 2:4), points out how frequently his hearers do not understand what he is saying, and announces his solemn declarations with the formula, "Let me tell you this," and with its double preface (literally, "Amen Amen") the formula is still more mysterious than in the synoptics. He refers to himself as "the Human One," just as in the other gospels, but here it means something closer to "the true human being," as expressed by Pilate when he presents Jesus to the hostile crowd in 19:5.

A Jewish-Christian gospel

The ideological milieu of this gospel is thoroughly Jewish; even the abstract and dualistic symbolism (such as light/darkness) comes from a world that has very little to do with gentile culture. Nevertheless, this document is ardently anti-Jewish. Only here are the Jewish people spoken of monolithically and from the outside; in the other gospels only Pilate alone uses the phrase "the Judeans." The explanation appears to be that this group of Christian Jews has recently been expelled from the synagogue (9:22, 34; 12:42; 16:2) and therefore has a highly ambivalent, and frequently hostile, attitude toward *Ioudaioi*. Traditionally translated into English as "Jews," the term is indistinguishable in Greek from "Judeans"; at the time, "Jews" were simply those who survived the fall of the Kingdom of Judah and had their spiritual base, and in many cases their actual residence, in what Rome called Judea. This gospel has given rise, still more than Matthew, to savage Christian anti-Semitism down the subsequent centuries. For this, and other reasons (see the cameo essay "Jews and Judeans," pp. 203–204), in almost every case the phrase is here translated by the more neutral term, "the Judeans."

Despite its utter Jewishness, the so-called Fourth Gospel has a mentality quite different from that of Jesus, and from Matthew too, the most Jewish of the synoptics. Instead of portraying the empire of God breaking into human history for the sake of redeeming or judging Israel, this gospel thinks on a cosmic scale.

The very term "world" (*kosmos*) is fundamental in the Johannine vocabulary, and it is used negatively to speak of the nationalistic realms of Roman and Jew alike—7:7 (see the note there) is only one instance of many—as well as positively, affirming all of creation and humanity. This broadened worldview is probably due both to the "wisdom" tradition that has informed the Johannine version of Jesus' teaching and to the fact that the Christians for whom the gospel was written could no longer think of themselves in nationalist terms. The universality that Paul espoused and that of John are arrived at by rather different paths, but both contribute to early Christianity's growing awareness of itself as a religion separate from and more inclusive than Judaism.

Thus, the Jesus of this gospel argues with the Jewish scholars, sometimes about arcane matters of biblical interpretation (e.g., 10:34–36), sometimes about the ultimate issues of salvation and truth and authentic life. As the incarnate son of God, savior of the world, this Jesus both appeals to the authority of the Jewish ancestors Abraham and Moses and presents himself as anterior and superior to them. The interlocking themes of continuity and discontinuity run like tapestry threads through the theological debates that comprise so much of this gospel. Jesus goes so far as to say, "Before there was an Abraham, I am," daring to pronounce the divine I AM, which breaks upon its hearers with shock and rage 8:58–59).

If the synoptics' Jesus appeals to the "trust" of those who hear and would follow him, for our gospel the same term (*pistis*) means "belief"—in Jesus' divine sonship and in the rescue from the world's stranglehold that he offers. Jesus' miracles, along with all that he has said and done, are written "so you will come to believe that Jesus is the Anointed One, the son of God—and by believing this have life in his name" (20:30–31).

Origin

Where and when was this gospel written? It is addressed: to an audience of whom part are (or until recently were) bilingual, thinking in both Greek and "Hebrew"; to a city having a substantial and effective Jewish presence, over against which those "who were born out of God" (1:13) and "have believed in his name" (20:31) understand themselves as a beleaguered but divinely vindicated minority; and to a perspective not far removed from that of Galilee and Judea. A small city in Syria is perhaps the best informed guess. The date would be within the decade or two following the centralized Jewish decision to expel believers in Jesus from the synagogue, that is, during the last fifteen years or so of the first century—roughly contemporary with, but evidently independent of, the writing of Matthew and Luke. The author, like the three other gospel writers, is anonymous and only a century later was identified with John, the son of Zebedee (and he with "the disciple Jesus loved").

The work divides, at the beginning of chapter 13, roughly into two halves: (1) the account of Jesus' public career, with its miracles and the discourses they occasion, and (2) the Last Supper (consisting mostly of Jesus' farewell instructions to "his own"), followed immediately by his arrest, trial, and execution, and finally the resurrection. Chapter 21 appears to be a later appendix to the original gospel.

The Human One

The Greek term *ho huios tou anthrōpou* literally means "the son of the human being," traditionally translated "the Son of Man." That rendering is inexact and misleading because the Greek *anthrōpos* designates our species, *homo sapiens,* both its male and female members.

Ho huios tou anthrōpou is a Greek translation of a Semitic idiom. In the Hebrew Bible, except in cases when a specific parent or ancestor is named, "son of X" conveys the sense that one has the quality or nature of X. For example, when God repeatedly addresses the prophet Ezekiel as a "son of a human being" (*ben adam* in Hebrew), it means "human one" or "mortal." Another clear example is Psalm 8:4, where the Hebrew word for a human being, *adam,* has a collective rather than an individual sense: "What are human beings (*adam*) that you are mindful of them, mortals (*ben adam*) that you care for them?" Two of Jesus' disciples are identified both as sons of Zebedee and "sons of thunder" (Mark 3:17), a nickname presumably reflecting their temperaments. Also reflecting the Semitic idiom are "sons of this world" and "sons of light" (Luke 16:8), "sons of the empire" and "sons of the evil one" (Matt 13:38), and "sons of God" and "sons of the resurrection" (Luke 20:36). In short, the SV rendering "the Human One" does not translate the word "son" literally, but instead renders it according to the matrix of meaning of the original Hebrew idiom.

Because it was a Greek translation of a Semitic idiom, *ho huios tou anthrōpou* would have sounded strange and foreign to Greek speakers. Besides, the grammar of the phrase, with the second "the" before the *anthrōpos,* is unusual in Greek and so would have sounded awkward. Similarly, "the Human One" is meant to sound somewhat awkward and foreign to English speakers.

Finally, the term functions in the gospels as a title, and is heard only on the lips of Jesus; no one else refers to the Human One or addresses Jesus in this way. The gospels presuppose the term to be Jesus' self-designation, even in places where he seems to be referring to someone other than himself. Accordingly, SV's "the Human One" signals that the term is a title by capitalizing it.

The Gospel of John

1 **In the beginning** there was the divine word and wisdom.

*The divine word
& wisdom*

The divine word and wisdom was there with God,

and it was what God was.

²It was there with God from the beginning.

³Everything came to be by means of it;

and without it not one thing that exists came to be.

⁴In it was life,

and this life was the light of humanity.

⁵Light was shining in darkness,

and darkness did not master it.

⁶There appeared a man sent from God named John. ⁷He came to testify—to testify about the light—so everyone would believe through him. ⁸He was not the light; he came only to testify about the light.

⁹Genuine light—the kind that enlightens everyone

—was coming into the world.

¹⁰Although it was in the world,

and the world came to be through it,

the world did not recognize it.

¹¹It came to its own place,

but its own people were not receptive to it.

¹²But to all who did embrace it,

to those who believed in it,

it gave the right to become children of God.

¹³They were born not from blood,

not from physical desire,

nor from male desire;

they were born out of God.

¹⁴The divine word and wisdom became human

1:1
Cf. Gn 1:1
1:9–11
Ⓣ Th 24:3
1:14
Ⓣ Th 28:1,
SJas 6:23, DSav 2

1:1–18 With the exception of vv. 6–8 and 15, which seem to be interruptions, this prologue is in the form of Semitic poetry.
1:1 *the divine word and wisdom:* This double phrase attempts to express for the moment the complex and difficult Greek term *Logos*, whose various meanings include *concept, pattern, reason, speech*, and *revelation*. Its precise function here will become clearer as this prologue unfolds.

there with: or "facing," difficult to express in English.

it: Not until v. 14 will it emerge that "the divine word and wisdom" is to be identified with a person, God's *only son.*
1:5 *did not master:* a deliberate ambiguity, meaning both "did not overcome" and "did not understand."
1:6–8 See the note on vv. 1–18.

A voice in
the desert

and resided among us.
We have seen its glory,
glory appropriate
to a Father's only son,
brimming with generosity and truth.

¹⁵John testifies about him and has called out, "This is the one I was talking about when I said, 'The one who's coming after me ranks ahead of me, because he was before I was.'"

¹⁶From his richness
all of us benefited—
one gift after another.
¹⁷The Law was given through Moses;
mercy and truth came through Jesus the Anointed One.
¹⁸No one has ever seen God;
the only son, close to the Father's heart—he has disclosed ⟨him⟩.

¹⁹**This is John's testimony** when the Judeans sent priests and Levites from Jerusalem to ask him, "Who are you?"

²⁰He made it clear—he wouldn't deny it—"I'm not the Anointed One."

²¹And they asked him, "Then what are you? Are you Elijah?"

And he replies, "I am not."

"Are you the Prophet?"

He answered, "No."

²²So they said to him, "Tell us who you are so we can report to those who sent us. What have you got to say for yourself?"

²³He replied, "I am 'the voice of someone shouting in the desert, "Make the way of the Lord straight"—that's how Isaiah the prophet put it.'"

(²⁴It was the Pharisees who had sent them.)

²⁵"So," they persisted, "why are you baptizing if you're not the Anointed One, not Elijah, and not the Prophet?"

1:15
Cf. Q 7:19,
Mt 11:2–3, Lk 7:19

1:18
◊ Ex 33:20

1:19–28
Cf. Mk 1:2–8,
Mt 3:1–2, Lk 3:1–20

1:21
Ⓣ Mt 11:13–14;
◊ Mal 4:5

1:23
//Mk 1:2–3, Mt 3:3,
Lk 3:4–6;
◊ Is 40:3

1:18 Some mss read "only begotten God" in place of *only son*.

1:14 *generosity:* The same word (*charis* usually rendered "grace") is translated *gift* in v. 16 and *mercy* in v. 17.

1:15 See the note on vv. 1–18.

testifies: Greek narrative alternates between past and present tense, rather like our use in story telling ("When I told her, do you know what she says to me?") but in Greek more acceptably written than in English. Other translations usually render these "historic presents" in the past tense, depriving the Greek narration of its immediacy and freshness. Sometimes, as here and, e.g., 1:29, the present calls attention to a new element in the story.

when I said: This refers to an event still to come, in 1:30.

1:17 There is no conjunction logically connecting the two clauses of this verse. To supply either "but" or "and" would do violence to what is very likely meant to be ambiguous; the gospel affirms both the contrast and the continuity between Judaism and Christianity, represented here respectively by Moses and Christ.

1:21 *the Prophet:* probably the one like himself promised by Moses (Deut 18:15); this was another figure like *the Anointed One*, who as with *Elijah*, was expected by some at the beginning of the Age to Come.

1:24 *who had sent them:* or, *who had been sent.*

²⁶John answered them, "I baptize, yes, but only with water. Right there with you is someone you don't yet recognize; ²⁷he's the one who is coming after me. I don't even deserve to untie his sandal straps."

²⁸All this took place in Bethany on the far side of the Jordan, where John was baptizing.

²⁹**The next day** John sees Jesus approaching and says, "Look, there's the lamb of God, who takes away the sin of the world. ³⁰This is the one I was talking about when I said, 'A man is coming after me who ranks ahead of me, because he was before I was.' ³¹Even I didn't know who he was, although it was my mission to baptize with water so he would be revealed to Israel."

³²And John continued his testimony: "I have seen the spirit coming down like a dove out of the sky, and it hovered over him. ³³I wouldn't have recognized him, but the very one who sent me to baptize with water told me, 'When you see the spirit come down and hover over someone, that's the one who baptizes with holy spirit.' ³⁴I have seen this and I have testified: this is the son of God."

³⁵The next day John was standing there again with two of his disciples. ³⁶When he noticed Jesus walking by, he says, "Look, there's the lamb of God."

³⁷His two disciples heard him ⟨say this⟩, and they followed Jesus. ³⁸Jesus turned around, saw them following, and says to them, "What are you looking for?"

They said to him, "Rabbi" (which means "Teacher"), "where do you live?"

³⁹He says to them, "Come and see."

They went and saw where he was staying and spent ⟨the rest of⟩ the day with him. It was about four in the afternoon.

⁴⁰**Andrew, Simon Peter's brother**, was one of the two who followed Jesus after hearing John ⟨speak about him⟩. ⁴¹First he goes and finds his brother Simon and tells him, "We have found the Messiah" (which is translated "Anointed One"), ⁴²and he led him to Jesus.

Jesus looked straight at him and said, "You're Simon, son of John; you're going to be called Kephas" (which means Peter ⟨or Rock⟩).

⁴³**The next day** Jesus decided to leave for Galilee. He finds Philip and says to him, "Follow me."

⁴⁴Philip was from Bethsaida, the hometown of Andrew and Peter. ⁴⁵Philip finds Nathanael and tells him, "We've found the one Moses wrote about in the Law, and the prophets mention too: Jesus, son of Joseph, from Nazareth."

1:26–27
//Q 3:16, Mt 3:11,
Lk 3:16

1:29–34
Cf. Mk 1:9–11,
Mt 3:13–17,
Lk 3:21–22, GHeb 3

1:30
① Jn 1:15

1:32
//Mk 1:10, Mt 3:16,
Lk 3:22

1:33
Ⓣ Acts 1:5, 11:16,
19:1–7

1:41
Ⓣ Mk 8:29,
Mt 16:16, Lk 9:20

1:42
Ⓣ Mk 3:16,
Mt 10:2, Lk 6:14

1:43
Cf. Mk 1:14,
Mt 4:12, Lk 4:14

1:28 Some mss read "Bethabara" in place of *Bethany*.

1:27 *To untie sandal straps* was a slave's task.

1:28 *Bethany on the far side of the Jordan:* a place otherwise unknown, possibly intended to balance the Bethany of 11:1 (see 10:40).

1:29 *the world:* Possibly this phrase here lacks the negative meaning it often has in this gospel; see the note on 7:7.

1:41 *First:* A sequel to this word is missing.

Messiah: In the NT, only here and at 4:29 is found the Aramaic original behind the Greek word *Christos* (Anointed One).

Kephas: from *kepha*, the Aramaic word for rock.

Peter: from *petra*, the Greek word for rock.

Miracle at Cana

⁴⁶"From Nazareth?" Nathanael said to him. "Can anything good come from that place?"

Philip replies to him, "Come and see."

⁴⁷Jesus saw Nathanael coming toward him, and he remarks about him: "There's a genuine Israelite—not a trace of deceit in him."

⁴⁸"Where do you know me from?" Nathanael asks him.

Jesus replied, "I saw you under the fig tree before Philip invited you ⟨to join us⟩."

⁴⁹Nathanael responded to him, "Rabbi, you are the son of God! You are King of Israel!"

⁵⁰Jesus replied, "Do you believe just because I told you I saw you under the fig tree? You're going to see a lot more than that."

⁵¹Then he adds, "Let me tell you this: you'll see the sky split open and God's messengers ascending and descending on the Human One."

2 **Three days later** there was a wedding in Cana, Galilee. Jesus' mother was there. ²Jesus was also invited to the wedding along with his disciples. ³When the wine had run out, Jesus' mother says to him, "They're out of wine."

⁴Jesus replies to her, "Lady, what do you want with me? It's not my time yet."

⁵His mother says to the servants, "Whatever he tells you, do it."

⁶Six stone water jars were standing there—for use in the Jewish purification ritual—and each could hold twenty or thirty gallons.

⁷"Fill the jars with water," Jesus tells them.

So they filled them to the brim.

⁸Then he tells them, "Now dip some out and take it to the caterer."

And they did so. ⁹When the caterer tasted the water, now changed into wine—he had no idea where it had come from, even though the servants who had taken the water out knew—he calls the groom aside ¹⁰and says to him, "Everyone serves the best wine first; later, when people are drunk, they serve the cheaper wine. But you've held back the good wine till now."

¹¹Jesus performed this sign, his first, in Cana, Galilee; it displayed his glory, and his disciples believed in him.

¹²Then he went down to Capernaum, he and his mother and brothers and disciples; but they stayed there only a few days.

1:49
ⓉMt 16:16

1:51
Cf. Mk 14:62,
Mt 26:64, Lk 22:68

2:4
Cf. Mk 5:7, Lk 8:28

2:12
Cf. Mk 1:21,
Mt 4:12–13, Lk 4:31

1:51 *ascending and descending:* like the angels on the ladder in Jacob's dream (Gen 28:12).

2:4 *Lady, what do you want with me?:* a strangely hostile way for a man to address his mother; *Lady* (literally, "Woman") is abrupt and disrespectful, and the question is the same as that used by demons to address Jesus in Mark 1:24 and Luke 4:34 (see 1 Kgs 17:18).

my time: Jesus' *time* has a special significance in this gospel; see 4:21; 5:25; 13:1. That he seems to object to his mother's implied request and then proceeds to work the miracle is puzzling; evidently there is something improper about wanting a miracle. See 2:18; 20:29, and the note on 6:26.

2:11 *it displayed:* or *he displayed.*

¹³**It was almost time** for the Jewish Passover festival, so Jesus went up to Jerusalem. ¹⁴In the temple area he found people selling oxen and sheep and doves, and others exchanging currency. ¹⁵He made a whip out of rope and drove them all out of the temple area, sheep and oxen; then he knocked over the exchange tables and scattered the coins. ¹⁶And to the dove merchants he said, "Get these birds out of here! How dare you use my Father's house as a public market."

¹⁷His disciples were reminded of the words of scripture:

> Zeal for your house will eat me alive.

¹⁸To this the Judeans responded, "What sign can you show us to justify doing all this?"

¹⁹Jesus replied, "Destroy this temple and I'll raise it in three days."

²⁰"It has taken forty-six years to build this temple," the Judeans said, "and you're going to raise it in three days?"

(²¹However, he was referring to his body as a temple. ²²When he had been raised from the dead his disciples remembered that he had made this claim, and so they came to believe both the word of scripture and the word Jesus had spoken.)

²³When he was in Jerusalem at the Passover festival, many believed in him once they saw with their own eyes the signs he performed. ²⁴But Jesus didn't trust himself to them, because he understood them all too well. ²⁵He didn't need to know more about humanity; he knew what people were really like.

3 **A Pharisee named Nicodemus**, a leader in the Jewish community, ²came to Jesus during the night and said, "Rabbi, we know that you've come as a teacher from God; after all, nobody can perform the signs you do unless God is with him."

³Jesus replied to him, "Let me tell you this: no one can experience the empire of God without being reborn from above."

⁴Nicodemus says to him, "How can an adult be reborn? Can you re-enter your mother's womb and be born a second time?"

⁵Jesus replied, "Let me tell you this: no one can enter the empire of God without being born of water and spirit. ⁶What is born of the human realm is

*Jesus disrupts
the temple*

*Conversation with
Nicodemus*

2:13–17
//Mk 11:15–17,
Mt 21:12–13,
Lk 19:45–46
2:17
◊ Ps 69:9
2:18–22
Cf. Mk 11:27–33,
Mt 21:23–27,
Lk 20:1–8
2:19
//Mk 14:57–58,
15:29; Mt 26:60–61,
27:40;
Cf. Th 71
3:2
Cf. Mk 12:14,
Mt 22:16, Lk 20:21,
EgerG 3:2
3:3–8
Cf. Th 22
3:3–5
SJas 2:6
3:3
Cf. Mk 10:15,
Mt 18:3, Lk 18:17
3:6
Th 112

2:17 *will eat me alive:* There may be a wordplay here, meaning both "will demand all my attention" and "will lead to my destruction."

2:20 *forty-six years:* Herod's reconstruction of the temple was evidently begun in 20/19 BCE, so this datum, if it is accurate, would suggest the year 27/28 CE as the date for such a statement as this, or its origin. Some have suggested consequently that Jesus' age is to be taken as 46 years (see 8:57: "You're not even 50 years old"), but a factual concern such as this does not appear to be any more important in

this gospel than in the others, with the possible exception of Luke (see Luke 3:23).

2:23 *believed in him:* literally, "believed in his name" (as in 1:12 and 3:18), perhaps a formula meaning "became a Christian."

3:2 *during the night:* See the note on 13:30.

3:3 *reborn from above:* an attempt to capture both senses in Jesus' ambiguous phrase (literally meaning either "reborn" or "born from above"), a Johannine wordplay that Nicodemus fails to grasp (v. 4).

human, but what is born of the spiritual realm is spirit. ⁷Don't be surprised that I told you, 'Every one of you must be reborn from above.' ⁸The spirit blows every which way, like wind: you hear the sound it makes but you can't tell where it's coming from or where it's headed. That's how it is with everyone reborn of the spirit."

⁹"How is that possible?" Nicodemus replied.

¹⁰Jesus replied, "You are a teacher of Israel, and you don't understand this? ¹¹Let me tell you this: we tell what we know, and we give evidence about what we've seen, but none of you accepts our evidence. ¹²If I tell you about what's earthly and you don't believe, how will you believe if I tell you about what's heavenly? ¹³No one has gone up to heaven except the one who came down from there: the Human One."

¹⁴In the desert Moses elevated the snake; in the same way the Human One is destined to be elevated, ¹⁵so every one who believes in him can have unending life. ¹⁶This is how God loved the world: God gave up an only son, so that every one who believes in him will not be lost but have unending life. ¹⁷After all, God sent the son into the world not to condemn the world, but to rescue the world through him. ¹⁸Those who believe in him are not condemned. Those who don't believe in him are already condemned: they haven't believed in God's only son. ¹⁹This is the verdict ⟨on them⟩: light came into the world but people loved darkness instead of light. Their actions were evil, weren't they? ²⁰All those who do evil things hate the light and don't come into the light—otherwise their deeds would be exposed. ²¹But those who do what is true come into the light so the nature of their deeds will become evident: their deeds belong to God.

²²**After this** Jesus and his disciples went to Judea, and he extended his stay with them there and began to baptize. ²³John was baptizing too, in Aenon near Salim, since there was plenty of water around; and people kept coming to be baptized. (²⁴Remember, John hadn't yet been thrown in prison.)

²⁵A dispute over purification broke out between John's disciples and one of the Judeans. ²⁶They came to John and reported: "Rabbi, that guy who was with you across the Jordan—you spoke about him earlier—guess what! Now he's baptizing and everyone is flocking to him."

3:14
◊Nm 21:9   **3:13** Some mss add "who is in heaven" after *the Human One*.

3:11 *Let me tell you:* addressed to Nicodemus, but from this point he fades from view and Jesus addresses his audience (presumably the Judeans in general) with the second person plural.

3:13 Under the constraints of modern punctuation, it is usual to end Jesus' words either here or at v. 21. No such problem faced the ancient writer; Jesus' words merge into those of the evangelist—or perhaps no such distinction is to be made.

3:22 *to Judea:* or, *into the Judean countryside*; in Jerusalem, Jesus is of course already in Judea.

²⁷John answered, "No one can take advantage of anything unless it's a gift from heaven. ²⁸You yourselves can confirm this: I told you I was not the Anointed One but had been sent on ahead of him. ²⁹The bride belongs to the groom, and the best man stands with him and is happy enough just to be there next to him. So I couldn't be happier. ³⁰He's destined to grow in importance; I'm destined to diminish."

³¹**The one who comes** from above is superior to everyone. Those who are of the earth have an earthly nature and speak in earthly terms. The one who comes from heaven ³²testifies to what he has seen and heard—little wonder that no one accepts his testimony. ³³Whoever does accept his testimony can guarantee that God is truthful. ³⁴In other words, the one God sent speaks God's language, since God does not portion out the spirit. ³⁵The Father loves the son and has entrusted everything to him. ³⁶Those who entrust themselves to the son have unending life, but those who refuse the son will not see life; no, they remain the object of God's wrath.

4 **Jesus was aware** of the rumor that had reached the Pharisees: that he is recruiting and baptizing more disciples than John. (²Actually, Jesus himself didn't baptize anyone; his disciples did the baptizing.) ³So he left Judea again for Galilee. ⁴His route took him through Samaria.

⁵He came to a Samaritan town called Sychar, near the field Jacob had given to his son Joseph—⁶that's where Jacob's well was. Jesus was exhausted from traveling, so he sat down on the edge of the well. It was about noon. ⁷When a Samaritan woman comes to get water, Jesus asks her, "Give me a drink." (⁸You see, his disciples had already gone off to town to buy food and drink.)

⁹The woman replies to him, "You're Jewish. What are doing asking a Samaritan woman for a drink?" (You see, Jewish people don't associate with Samaritans.)

¹⁰Jesus answered her, "If you knew what God can give you, and who just said to you, 'Give me a drink,' you would ask him and he would give you living, life-giving water."

3:35
Cf. Q 10:22,
Mt 11:27, Lk 10:22,
Th 61:3;
ⓣ Jn 13:3

4:5
◊ Gn 33:18–19

4:10
ⓣ GOxy 840 2:9

4:1 Some mss read "the Lord" in place of *Jesus.*
4:9 A few mss lack the sentence in parentheses.

3:31–36 It is unclear who speaks here. See the note on 3:13.
4:2 *Jesus himself didn't baptize* contradicts the obvious sense of 3:22. Perhaps 4:2 is a late gloss, added to accentuate the difference between Jesus and John the Baptizer.
4:9 The antipathy of Jews/Judeans toward Samaritans was, among other things, based on the fact that Samaritans were considered neither pure nor ritually "clean"; since the fall of the northern kingdom of Israel there had been intermar-

riage in the territory of Samaria, and the Samaritans did not follow the rabbinic interpretation and practical application of Torah that was developing in Judaism.
4:10–11 *Living, life-giving:* There is a wordplay here; "living water" is flowing water, as opposed to water in a cistern, but the term soon gains a metaphoric meaning as well (v. 14). The gospel uses the verb "live" and the noun "life" in many important ways.

¹¹"Mister, you don't have anything to draw water with," she says, "and the well is deep; just where will you get this 'living, life-giving water'? ¹²Can you do better than our patriarch Jacob? He left us this well, which used to quench his thirst and that of his family and his livestock."

¹³Jesus responded to her, "Whoever drinks this water will get thirsty again; ¹⁴but all who drink the water I'll provide them with will never get thirsty again; it will be a source of water within them, a fountain of unending life."

¹⁵The woman says to him, "Sir, give me some of this water, so I'll never be thirsty or have to keep coming back here for water."

¹⁶Jesus says to her, "Get your husband and come back."

¹⁷"I don't have a husband," she answered.

"You're right to say that you don't have a husband," Jesus says. ¹⁸"In fact, you've had five husbands, and the man you are now living with is not your husband; you've told the truth."

¹⁹"Master," she exclaims, "I can tell you're a prophet. ²⁰Our ancestors worshiped on this mountain; you people claim Jerusalem is the only place for worship."

²¹Jesus says to her, "Lady, believe me, the time is coming when you won't worship the Father either on this mountain or in Jerusalem. ²²You people worship God-knows-what; we worship what we know—'the Jewish people are the source of salvation,' and all that. ²³But the time is coming—in fact, it's already here—for true worshipers to worship the Father as he truly is, without regard to place. It's worshipers of this sort that the Father is looking for. ²⁴God is not tied to place, and those who worship God must worship him as he truly is, without regard to place."

²⁵The woman continues, "All I know is that the Messiah, the one called Anointed, is going to come; when he does he'll tell us everything."

²⁶Jesus says to her, "He's been speaking with you the whole time; I am he."

²⁷**But just then** his disciples returned. They were puzzled that he was talking with a woman, but no one said, "What do you think you're doing? Why are you talking with her?" ²⁸At this the woman left her water jar, hurried off to town,

---

4:13–15
Cf. Th 13:5

4:13–14
Ⓣ Th 108:1

4:11 *Mister:* The same word (*kyrios*) is translated *sir* in v. 15 and *master* in v. 19, as the woman gradually gains first respect and then devotion toward Jesus.

the well is deep: The word used here (*phrear*) denotes only a deep shaft, not necessarily an underground spring; but in v. 6 this "well" was referred to as also a water source (*pēgē*), an important distinction in that part of the world. The woman assumes that Jesus speaks of "living" water only at the bottom of such a good, deep well; Jesus, however, as so often in this gospel, is speaking on another level of meaning.

4:20 The Samaritan temple on Mt. Gerizim, the most

prominent sight from Sychar and Jacob's well, was regarded as a direct competitor and even affront to the temple in Jerusalem, for Jews *the only place for worship*.

4:23 *without regard to place*: literally, "in spirit."

4:24 *God is not tied to place*: literally, "God is spirit."

4:26 *I am he*: Greek, simply *I am*, used frequently in the gospel in this everyday sense but often with divine resonance as well, since "I AM" is a version of God's name in the Hebrew Bible (see Exod 3:14–15).

4:27 It was considered indecent in Jewish culture for a man to talk alone with a woman, even in a public place.

and tells everyone, ²⁹"Come and see someone who told me everything I ever did. Could he be the Anointed One?"

³⁰They set out from their town and were on the way to him.

³¹Meanwhile the disciples pleaded with him, "Rabbi, have something to eat."

³²He replied to them, "I have food to eat, food you know nothing about."

³³The disciples said to one another, "Has someone already brought him food?"

³⁴"Doing the will of the one who sent me and completing his work—that's my food," Jesus tells them. ³⁵"You have a saying: 'It's still four months till harvest.' But I'm telling you: look at the fields, they're ripe for harvesting. ³⁶The harvester is already getting paid; he is gathering the crop ⟨that sustains⟩ unending life, so planter and harvester can celebrate together. ³⁷Here too the proverb holds true: 'One plants, another harvests.' ³⁸I sent you to harvest what you haven't labored over; others have labored, and you've benefited from their labor."

³⁹**Many Samaritans** from that town came to believe in him because of the woman's testimony: "He told me everything I ever did." ⁴⁰So when those Samaritans got to him they kept begging him to stay with them. And he stayed there for two days. ⁴¹And many more believed because of what he said. ⁴²They told the woman, "We no longer believe because of what you said. Now we've listened to him ourselves and we realize that he really is the savior of the world."

⁴³Two days later he left there for Galilee. (⁴⁴Remember, Jesus himself had observed, "A prophet gets no respect on his own turf.")

⁴⁵So when he came to Galilee, the Galileans welcomed him because they had seen everything he had done at the festival in Jerusalem. (They had gone to the festival too.) ⁴⁶Then he came back to Cana, Galilee, where he had turned the water into wine.

In Capernaum there was a government official whose son was sick. ⁴⁷When he heard that Jesus had returned to Galilee from Judea, he approached him and pleaded with him to come down and cure his son, who was about to die.

⁴⁸Jesus said to him, "You people refuse to believe unless you see signs and omens."

⁴⁹The official responds, "Sir, please come down before my child dies."

⁵⁰Jesus says, "Go home, your son will live."

The man believed what Jesus told him and went home. ⁵¹While he was still on his way home, his slaves met him and told him that his boy was alive. ⁵²So he asked them when he had begun to recover, and they told him, "The fever broke yesterday at one o'clock."

4:35
Cf. Q 10:2, Mt 9:38,
Lk 10:2, Th 73

4:44
//Mk 6:4, Mt 13:57,
Lk 4:24, Th 31

4:46–54
Cf. Q 7:1–9,
Mt 8:5–13,
Lk 7:1–10

4:48
◊Ex 11:10 (LXX)

4:43 *Two days later:* that is, at the end of his stay (v. 40).
4:44–45 Despite the datum that Jesus is from Nazareth (1:45) or a Nazarene (19:19), in this gospel Jesus' home-

land is evidently to be understood as Judea, not Galilee (see 1:11). This differs from the synoptic gospels.

⁵³Then the father realized that one o'clock was precisely the time Jesus had said to him, "Your son will live." And he believed, as did his whole household. ⁵⁴Jesus performed this second sign after he had returned from Judea to Galilee.

5 **After these events**, on the occasion of a Jewish festival, Jesus went up to Jerusalem. ²In Jerusalem, by the Sheep ⟨Gate⟩, there is a pool, called *Bethzatha* in Hebrew. It has five colonnades, ³among which numerous invalids—blind, lame, paralyzed—were usually lying around. ⁵One man had been crippled for thirty-eight years. ⁶Jesus observed him lying there and realized he had been there a long time.

"Do you want to get well?" he asks him.

⁷The crippled man replied, "Sir, I don't have anyone to put me in the pool when the water is agitated; while I'm trying to get in someone else beats me to it."

⁸"Get up, pick up your mat, and walk around," Jesus tells him.

⁹And at once the man recovered; he picked up his mat and started walking.

Now that was a Sabbath. ¹⁰So the Judeans said to the man who had been cured, "It's the Sabbath; you're not permitted to carry your mat around."

¹¹But he explained, "The man who cured me told me, 'Pick up your mat and walk around.'"

¹²They asked him, "Who is this man who said to you, 'Pick it up and walk'?"

¹³Now the man who'd been cured had no idea who it was, since Jesus had withdrawn because people were crowding around.

¹⁴Later, Jesus finds him in the temple area and said to him, "Look, you're well now. Don't sin anymore, or something worse could happen to you."

¹⁵The man went and told the Judeans it was Jesus who had cured him. ¹⁶And this is the reason the Judeans continued to hound Jesus: he would do things like this on the Sabbath.

¹⁷ Jesus responded, "My Father never stops working, and I work as well."

5:2–9
Cf. Mk 2:1–12,
Mt 9:1–8,
Lk 5:17–26

5:10
◊Jer 17:21,
Neh 13:19

5:14
Cf. EgerG 2:4

5:2 *Bethzatha:* The name varies considerably among mss, *Bethesda* being the most widely attested alternative.

5:3 At the end of this verse, many mss add the following explanatory gloss: "waiting for some movement of the water. (You see, a heavenly messenger would descend into the pool from time to time and agitate the water; when that happened the first one (into the pool) would be cured of whatever disease he or she had.)"

5:2 *the Sheep ⟨Gate⟩:* There is no noun in Greek after the word "sheep." On the basis of archeological evidence this is the best guess.

in Hebrew: The term explained here (as frequently in the gospel) is not actually in Hebrew but in the cognate Aramaic.

5:15 The very person Jesus has cured turns informer, perhaps a common enough occurrence in the late first-century conflict between Christians and "Judeans" that underlies the gospel.

¹⁸So this is the reason the Judeans then tried even harder to kill him: not only did he violate the Sabbath; worse still, he would call God his father, making himself out to be God's equal.

¹⁹**This is how Jesus responded**: "Let me tell you this: the son can't do anything on his own, but only what he sees the Father doing. Whatever the Father does, the son does as well. ²⁰The Father loves the son, and shows him everything he does. He is going to show him even greater works, so that you'll be amazed. ²¹Just as the Father raises the dead and gives them life, the son also gives life to everyone he wants. ²²Not that the Father condemns anyone; rather, he has turned all such decisions over to the son, ²³so that everyone will respect the son, just as they respect the Father. Whoever does not respect the son does not respect the Father who sent him.

²⁴"Let me tell you this: those who hear my word and believe the one who sent me have unending life and do not come up for trial. No, they have passed through death into life. ²⁵Let me tell you this: the time is coming—in fact, it's already here—for the dead to hear the voice of God's son and, because they've heard it, to live. ²⁶Just as the Father is himself the source of life, he has also made the son to be the source of life. ²⁷And he has given him the authority to do the judging, because he is the Human One. ²⁸Don't be surprised; the time is coming when all who are in their graves will hear his voice ²⁹and come out—those who have done good will be raised to life, and those who have done vile deeds raised to stand trial.

³⁰"I can do nothing on my own authority. I base my decision on what I hear; and my decision is the right one, because I'm not seeking to do my own will, but the will of the one who sent me. ³¹If I give evidence on my own behalf, my testimony is not reliable. ³²Someone else testifies on my behalf, and I am certain the evidence he gives about me is reliable. ³³You've sent ⟨messengers⟩ to John, and he has provided reliable testimony. ³⁴I'm not interested in evidence from a human source; rather, I'm saying these things so you will be rescued. ³⁵John was a bright shining light, and you were willing to bask in that light of his for a while. ³⁶But I have given evidence that is even weightier than John's: the tasks the Father gave me to carry out. These very tasks I am performing are

5:19–20
Ⓣ SJas 6:24–26
5:23
Cf. Q 10:16;
Mt 10:40; Lk 10:16;
Jn 12:44, 13:20
5:29
Ⓣ Mt 25:46,
Lk 14:14;
◊ Dn 12:2

5:19 *the son:* Typically of this gospel, Jesus speaks of himself in the language of late first-century Christians.

what he sees the Father doing: because of the intimacy and mutual knowledge between Father and son implied already in 1:1–18.

5:23 *respect the son, just as they respect the Father:* evidently justifying the Judeans' objection in v. 18 that Jesus *was making himself out to be God's equal* (see the Introduction).

5:24 *they have passed through death into life:* Despite some

hints of an eventual last judgment when finally the dead will be raised and the righteous awarded a place in the new age, this gospel mostly declares that as believers Christians have already undergone that transformation. See the combination of both views in the following verse (*the time is coming—in fact, it's already here—for the dead to hear the voice of God's son*) and the statements that Jesus' followers will *never die* (8:51; 11:26).

evidence that the Father has sent me. [37]The one who sent me has himself also given evidence on my behalf. You've never heard his voice, you've never seen his image, [38]and his message doesn't find a home in you, since you don't believe the one he has sent.

[39]"You pore over the scriptures, because you imagine that in them there's unending life to be had. They do indeed give evidence on my behalf, [40]yet you refuse to come to me to have life. [41]I'm not interested in any human praise; [42]but I also know that you have none of God's love in you. [43]I've come in my Father's name, and you don't welcome me; if others come in their own name, you'll welcome them. [44]How can you believe, since you accept praise from each other but don't even consider the praise that comes from the only God? [45]Don't suppose that I'll be your accuser before the Father. You have an accuser, and it's Moses—the one you were relying on. [46]But if you really believed Moses, you'd believe me; after all, I'm the one he wrote about. [47]But since you don't really believe what he wrote, how are you going to believe what I say?"

6 **After these events**, Jesus crossed to the far side of the Sea of Galilee, ⟨also known as the Sea of⟩ Tiberias. [2]A huge crowd was following him, because they wanted to see the signs he was performing for the sick. [3]Jesus climbed up the mountain, and he sat down there with his disciples. [4]It was about time for the Jewish festival of Passover. [5]Jesus looks up and sees a big crowd approaching him, and he says to Philip, "Where are we going to buy enough bread to feed these people?" ([6]He was saying this to test him; you see, Jesus already knew what he was going to do.)

[7]"Two hundred denarii wouldn't buy enough bread for everyone to have a bite," Philip said.

[8]One of his disciples, Andrew, Simon Peter's brother, says to him, [9]"There's a kid here with five loaves of barley bread and two fish; but what does that amount to for so many?"

[10]Jesus said, "Have the people sit down." (They were in a grassy place.) So they sat down. (The men ⟨alone⟩ numbered about five thousand.) [11]Jesus took the loaves, gave thanks, and passed them around to the people sitting there, along with the fish, and all of them had as much as they wanted. [12]And when they had eaten their fill, he says to his disciples, "Gather up the leftovers so that nothing goes to waste."

[13]So they gathered them up and filled twelve baskets with scraps from the five barley loaves—from what was left over. [14]When these folks saw the sign he

5:37
◊Dt 4:12

5:39
//Th 52:1, EgerG 1:2

5:45
//EgerG 1:3

5:46
Cf. EgerG 1:6

6:1–15
//Mk 6:30–44,
8:1–10;
Mt 14:13–21,
15:32–39;
Lk 9:10–17;
◊2 Kgs 4:42–44

6:14
◊Dt 18:15–18

5:45–47 The comparison of Jesus with Moses (1:17) reappears. His writings—the five books of the Law—testify to Jesus (see 1:45) and his actions prefigure what Jesus does (3:14); therefore Moses himself judges those who don't believe in Jesus. The Judeans are pictured as not even believing

their own scriptures.

6:1 *the Sea of Galilee,* ⟨*also known as the Sea of*⟩ *Tiberias:* or, *the Galilean Sea of Tiberias.* In modern terms this body of water is more a lake than, as traditionally rendered, a "sea."

had performed they were saying, "This has to be the Prophet who is to come into the world!" [15]Jesus perceived that they were about to come and force him to be king, so he retreated once again to the mountain by himself.

[16]**As evening approached**, his disciples went down to the sea. [17]They boarded a boat and were trying to cross the sea to Capernaum. It had already gotten dark, and Jesus still had not joined them. [18]A strong wind began to blow and the sea was getting rough. [19]When they had rowed about three or four miles, they catch sight of Jesus walking on the sea and coming toward the boat. They were frightened, [20]but he says to them, "Don't be afraid! It's me." [21]Then they would have taken him on board, but the boat instantly arrived at the shore they had been making for.

[22]**The next day**, the crowd, which was still on the other side of the sea, remembered that there had been only one boat there, and that Jesus had not gotten into that boat with the disciples, but that his disciples had set off alone. [23]Other boats came out from Tiberias, near the place where they had eaten bread. [24]So when the crowd saw that neither Jesus nor his disciples were there, they too got into boats and set out for Capernaum to look for Jesus.

[25]They found him on the other side of the sea and asked him, "Rabbi, when did you get here?"

[26]Jesus replied, "Let me tell you this: you're looking for me only because you ate the bread and had all you wanted, not because you witnessed signs. [27]Don't work for food that spoils, but for food that lasts—food for unending life—which the Human One will give you; on him God the Father has put his stamp of approval."

[28]So they asked him, "What do we have to do to accomplish the work God wants done?"

[29]Jesus answered, "This is the work God wants you to do: to believe in the one whom God has sent."

[30]They asked him, "What sign are you going to perform so we can see it and come to believe in you? What 'work' are you going to do? [31]Our ancestors had manna to eat in the desert. As the scripture puts it,

> He gave them bread from heaven to eat."

6:16–21
//Mk 6:45–52,
Mt 14:22–33

6:22–24
//Mk 6:53–56,
Mt 14:34–36

6:27
◊Is 55:2

6:28–29
Ⓣ DSav 41:4

6:30
Ⓣ Mk 8:11;
Mt 12:38, 16:1;
Lk 11:16

6:31
◊Neh 9:15;
Ps 78:24, 105:40;
Ex 16:14

6:23 At the end of this verse, many mss add "after the Lord had given thanks."

6:14 *the Prophet who is to come into the world:* See the note on 1:21.

6:20 *It's me:* literally, "I am." See the note on 4:26.

6:26 Evidently really to *witness signs* involves more than seeing and even benefitting from them.

6:29 Christian belief is especially important in this gospel: It is presented as fulfilling God's chief wish for humanity.

6:30 *What sign are you going to perform?:* Jesus has just worked a miracle, which provoked this very conversation. The questioners' blindness is obvious.

6:30–31 The crowd, in requesting a miracle—and after a miraculous feeding of a multitude with bread—ironically imply that Moses' miracle of feeding the multitude of their *ancestors* with *manna* is greater than anything Jesus can do, thereby falling into their own argumentative trap.

Eating Jesus' flesh   ³²Jesus responded to them: "Let me tell you this: it was not Moses who gave you bread from heaven; rather, it is my Father who gives you real bread from heaven. ³³That is to say, God's bread comes down from heaven and gives life to the world."

³⁴"Sir," they said to him, "give us this bread every time."

³⁵Jesus explained to them, "I am the bread of life. Anyone who comes to me will never be hungry again, and anyone who believes in me will never again be thirsty. ³⁶But I told you this: you've even seen me, yet you still refuse to believe. ³⁷Every one the Father gives me will come to me, and I would never reject anyone who comes to me. ³⁸Understand, I have come down from heaven, not to do what I want, but to do what the one who sent me wants. ³⁹This is what the one who sent me wants: that I lose nothing put in my care, but that I raise it on the last day. ⁴⁰My Father's intent is that all those who see the son and believe in him will have unending life, and I'll raise them on the last day."

⁴¹**The Judeans then began** to grumble about him because he had said, "I am the bread that came down from heaven." ⁴²They were saying, "Isn't this Jesus, son of Joseph? Don't we know both his father and his mother? How can he now say, 'I've come down from heaven'?"

⁴³Jesus replied, "Don't grumble under your breath. ⁴⁴People cannot come to me unless the Father who sent me takes them in, and I will raise them on the last day. ⁴⁵As the prophets put it:

And they will all be taught by God.

"Everyone who listens to the Father and learns from him comes to me. ⁴⁶Not that anyone has seen the Father; the only one who has seen the Father is the one who is from God. ⁴⁷Let me tell you this: the believer has unending life. ⁴⁸I am the bread of life. ⁴⁹Your ancestors ate the manna in the desert, but they still died. ⁵⁰This is the bread that comes down from heaven: anyone who eats it never dies. ⁵¹I am the life-giving bread that came down from heaven. Anyone who eats this bread will live forever. And the bread that I will give for the world's life is my flesh."

⁵²At this point the Judeans began quarreling among themselves: "How can this guy give us his flesh to eat?"

⁵³So Jesus told them, "Let me tell you this: if you don't eat the Human One's flesh and drink his blood, you won't have life in you. ⁵⁴Everyone who feeds on

6:37
Ⓣ SJas 9:6

6:42
Cf. Mk 6:2–3,
Mt 13:55–57,
Lk 4:22

6:45
◊ Is 54:13

6:48–58
Cf. Mk 14:22–25,
Mt 26:26–29,
Lk 22:17–20,
1 Cor 11:23–25

6:51–57
Cf. GSav 8:3

6:36 A few mss omit *me*.
6:52 Some mss omit *his*.

6:32 Just as Jesus claims that he only executes what the Father in fact does, he robs Moses of any credit in the giving of *bread from heaven* in the wilderness. And he shifts attention from what God did in the past to what God is doing now (*gives you real bread from heaven*).

6:46 See 1:18.
6:49 *but they still died:* Again the comparison of Moses and Jesus only shows the former's inferiority.
6:53–58 Just as this gospel lacks any depiction of Jesus' actual baptism, so also (at the last supper in chapter 13) Jesus

my flesh and drinks my blood has unending life, and I will raise them on the last day. [55]For my flesh is real food, and my blood real drink. [56]Those who feed on my flesh and drink my blood remain in me, and I in them. [57]The living Father sent me, and I live because of the Father. Just so, anyone who feeds on me will live because of me. [58]This is the bread that comes down from heaven. Unlike your ancestors who ate ⟨manna⟩ and then died, anyone who feeds on this bread will live forever."

[59]He said these things while he was teaching in the meeting place at Capernaum.

[60]**When the disciples heard** this, many responded, "This sort of talk is hard to take. Who can take it seriously?"

[61]Jesus knew his disciples were grumbling about it and said to them, "So does this shock you? [62]What if you were to see the Human One going back up to where he was to begin with? [63]The spirit is life-giving; flesh is good for nothing. The words I have used are spirit and life. [64]Yet some of you still don't believe." (Jesus was aware from the start which ones were not believers, and he knew who would turn him in.) [65]And so he was saying, "This is why I told you: people cannot come to me unless the Father has granted it to them."

[66]As a result, many of his disciples dropped out and would no longer travel around with him.

[67]Jesus then said to the Twelve, "Do you want to leave too?"

[68]Simon Peter replied to him, "Master, is there anyone else we can turn to? You have the words of unending life. [69]We have become believers and have realized that you are the holy one of God."

[70]Jesus responded to them, "Isn't this why I chose the twelve of you? Even so, one of you is a devil." ([71]He was of course referring to Judas, son of Simon Iscariot, one of the Twelve, who was going to turn him in.)

7 **After this,** Jesus moved around in Galilee; he decided not to go into Judea, because the Judeans were looking for a chance to kill him. [2]The Jewish festival of Sukkoth was coming, [3]so his brothers said to him, "Get out of here; go to Judea so your disciples can see the works you're doing. [4]No one who wants public

Disciples grumble

To Jerusalem or not?

6:61
Ⓣ Mt 13:57
6:63
Ⓣ SJas 7:7
6:68–69
Cf. Mk 8:29,
Mt 16:16, Lk 9:20;
Ⓣ Mk 1:24,
Lk 4:34
6:70–71
Ⓘ Jn 13:2, 27

6:71 *Iscariot:* Here and elsewhere many mss have variants of this obscure name.

does not "institute" the other great Christian sacrament, the eucharist or Lord's supper. It is debated whether these are deliberate omissions of the traditions firmly embedded in the synoptic gospels. The present passage reflects an elevated understanding of the Christian eucharist, but even here it is not clear that the reader is to think of the communion bread.

6:63 *flesh:* The same Greek word, used so exaltedly in 1:14 (where it is translated "human") and just above (vv. 51–56), here contrasts with that usage, applying only to Jesus, and means what is ordinary, earthly, material, natural.

7:2 *Sukkoth:* also known as the Feast of Booths, or Tabernacles.

recognition does things in secret. If you're going to do these things, let the world see you." (⁵Evidently, even his brothers didn't have any confidence in him.)

⁶Jesus replies, "It's not my time yet. It's always your time. ⁷The world can never hate you, but it hates me because I provide evidence that its actions are evil. ⁸You go ahead to the festival; I'm not going to this one because my time has not yet arrived."

⁹With this piece of advice, he stayed behind in Galilee.

¹⁰After his brothers had left for the festival, he went too; he didn't go openly, but traveled incognito. ¹¹So the Judeans kept an eye out for him at the festival, inquiring repeatedly, "Where is that guy?" ¹²There was a lot of muttering about him in the crowd. Some were saying, "He's a good guy," but others were saying, "No, he's just scamming the crowd." ¹³Yet no one spoke openly about him for fear of the Judeans.

¹⁴**When the festival** was half over, Jesus went up to the temple area and started teaching. ¹⁵The Judeans were taken aback, saying, "This man is uneducated; how come he's so articulate?"

¹⁶To this Jesus responded, "What I'm teaching does not originate with me but with the one who sent me. ¹⁷Anyone who sets out to do what God wants knows well enough whether this teaching originates with God or whether I'm speaking on my own. ¹⁸All who speak on their own are out for their own glory. But as for him who is out for the glory of the one who sent him, he is truthful; there is nothing dishonest about him.

¹⁹"Moses gave you the Law, didn't he? (Not that any of you people observes the Law!) Why are you bent on killing me?"

²⁰The crowd answered, "You're possessed! Who's trying to kill you?"

²¹"I do one miracle," Jesus replied, "and you're stunned. ²²That's why Moses gave you circumcision—not that it really came from Moses, but from our ancestors—and you can circumcise someone on the Sabbath. ²³If someone can be circumcised on the Sabbath without breaking Moses' Law, why are you outraged at me for making an entire person healthy on the Sabbath? ²⁴Don't judge by appearances; judge by what is right."

²⁵Some of the Jerusalemites began to say, "Isn't this the one they're trying to kill? ²⁶Look, here he is, speaking in public, and they say nothing to him. You don't suppose the authorities have now concluded that he is the Anointed One?

7:15
ⓣ Mk 6:2,
Mt 13:54–56

7:20
ⓣ Mk 3:22;
Jn 8:48, 52; 10:20

7:4 *let the world see you:* Either Galilee is not *the world*, but only Jerusalem, or Jesus' brothers express a stereotyped view of rural unsophistication.

7:7 In contrast to his brothers (v. 4), Jesus speaks of *the world* here in a negative sense, expressing all that is organized against God and therefore against Jesus, deliberately or not.

7:13 The risk in speaking about Jesus that evidently prevailed when this gospel was written is read back into Jesus'

lifetime.

7:19 *Not that any of you people observes the Law!:* Jesus' hearers are shown as guilty not only of failing to believe the Law (5:47), but of disobeying its commandments; they are unworthy representatives of Judaism.

7:21 *one miracle:* evidently the healing of the lame man in chapter 5; the debate over this action *on the Sabbath*, last heard of in 5:18, is resumed.

²⁷But wait—we know where this man's from. When the Anointed One comes, no one is supposed to know where he's from."

²⁸And while he was teaching in the temple area, Jesus shouted out, "So you know me and you know where I'm from? I haven't come on my own—the one who sent me, whom you don't know, is truthful. ²⁹I do know him, because I came from him and he is the one who sent me."

³⁰They would have arrested him then and there, but no one laid a hand on him, because his time had not yet come.

³¹Many people in the crowd believed in him and were asking, "When the Anointed One comes, is he likely to perform any more signs than this man?"

³²The Pharisees heard the crowd muttering such things about him; so the chief priests and the Pharisees sent temple police to arrest him.

³³Then Jesus said, "I'll be with you a little longer; then I'll return to the one who sent me. ³⁴You'll look for me, but you won't find me; where I am you can't come."

³⁵So the Judeans said to one another, "Where is this man going to go, that we won't find him? Will he go to the Greek Diaspora, to teach the Greeks? ³⁶What's this line he's giving us: 'You'll look for me, but you won't find me; where I am you can't come'?"

³⁷On the last and most important day of the festival, Jesus stood up and shouted out, "Anyone who's thirsty must come to me and drink. ³⁸The one who believes in me—as scripture puts it—

> will be the source of rivers of life-giving water."

(³⁹He was talking about the spirit that those who believed in him were about to receive. You realize, of course, that there was no spirit as yet, since Jesus hadn't been glorified.)

⁴⁰**When they heard** this declaration, some in the crowd said, "This man has to be the Prophet." ⁴¹Others said, "He's the Anointed One!" Still others objected, "The Anointed One won't come from Galilee, will he? ⁴²Doesn't scripture teach that the Anointed One is to be descended from David and come from the village of Bethlehem, where David lived?" (⁴³As you can see, the crowd was split over who he was.)

7:29
Ⓣ Jn 13:3

7:30–32
Cf . EgerG l:8

7:33–34
Cf. Th 38:2, 59

7:33
Ⓣ SJas 2:4

7:36
Cf. Th 38:2

7:37
Cf. Th 108:1

7:42
Ⓣ Mk 12:35–37,
Mt 22:41–45,
Lk 20:41–44
◊ Mi 5:2

7:43–44
Cf. Lk 19:47–48,
20:19; EgerG 1:9

7:39 A few mss read "the spirit had not yet been given" in place of *there was no spirit as yet.*

7:30 Causality is not in the hands of humans, not even the most powerful Judean leaders; they will only occasion Jesus' death, and not until *his time comes.*

7:32 *The Pharisees heard the crowd muttering such things about him:* This may reflect as much the situation in which the gospel was written as Jesus' lifetime.

7:34 *where I am:* presumably after the resurrection.

7:35 *the Greek Diaspora:* Greek-speaking Jews living outside of Judea.

7:38 It is unknown which *scripture* is quoted (or more likely paraphrased) here.

7:39 *there was no spirit as yet:* See 14:16.

7:40 *the Prophet:* See the note on 1:21.

7:41 *from Galilee:* Despite the implication at 4:43–45 that Jesus' *own turf* (or "homeland") was Judea, it is known that he was *a Nazarene* (18:5), that is, *from Nazareth* in Galilee (1:45).

Jesus' discourse
in Jerusalem

[44] Some were in favor of arresting him, but no one laid a hand on him. [45] Then the temple police came back to the chief priests and the Pharisees, who said to them, "Why haven't you brought him in?"

[46] The police answered, "No one ever talked like that before!"

[47] The Pharisees came back at them, "Don't tell us you've been duped too! [48] None of the authorities or the Pharisees have believed in him, have they? [49] As for this mob, they are ignorant of the Law. To hell with them!"

[50] Then Nicodemus, who was one of their number—he had earlier paid Jesus a visit—challenges them: [51] "Since when does our Law pass judgment on someone without first letting him speak for himself, and without establishing the facts?"

[52] They shot back, "You wouldn't be from Galilee too, now would you? Check for yourself: no prophet has ever arisen from Galilee."

8 [12] **Jesus spoke out again**, saying to them, "I am the light of the world. My followers won't ever have to walk in the dark; no, they'll have the light of life."

[13] The Pharisees came back at him: "You're giving evidence on your own behalf; your evidence is invalid."

[14] Jesus answered them, "Even if I give evidence on my own behalf, my evidence is valid, because I know where I came from and where I'm going. You, on the other hand, don't know where I come from or where I'm going. [15] You judge by human standards; I pass judgment on no one. [16] But if I do render judgment, my decisions are valid because I do not render these judgments by myself; rather, the Father who sent me joins me in them. [17] Your Law stipulates that the testimony of two is valid. [18] I offer evidence on my own behalf and the Father who sent me also offers evidence on my behalf."

[19] So they asked him, "Where is your father?"

Jesus replied, "You don't recognize me or my Father. If you recognized me, you would also recognize my Father."

[20] He made these remarks while he was teaching near the treasury in the temple area. But no one arrested him because his time had not yet come.

[21] He spoke to them again. "I am going away. You'll try to find me, but you'll die in your sin. Where I'm going you can't come."

[22] The Judeans then said, "Does he intend to kill himself—is that what he means when he says, 'Where I'm going you can't come'?"

7:46
Ⓣ Mk 1:22;
Mt 7:28–29;
Lk 4:32, 36

8:12
Cf. Mt 5:14, Th 77a,
GSav 1:4;
Ⓓ Jn 9:5

8:17
◊ Dt 19:15

8:20
Cf. EgerG 1:9

8:21
Cf. Th 59

7:53–8:11 Some mss insert here the story of the woman caught in adultery. See pp. 460–61 in Orphan Sayings and Stories.

7:52 *You wouldn't be from Galilee too, now would you?:* Here to be *from Galilee* seems to mean virtually to "believe in Jesus."

8:20 *But no one arrested him:* See the note on 7:30.

²³So he would respond to them, "You belong down here, I belong up above. You're right at home in this world, I'm not at home in this world. ²⁴I told you that you would die in your sins. If you don't believe that I am ⟨what I say I am⟩, you will die in your sins."

²⁵So they countered, "Who are you?"

"What I told you from the start," Jesus replied. ²⁶"There's a lot I could say about you and judge you for; but the one who sent me is the real authority, so I'll tell the world what I've heard from him."

(²⁷They didn't realize that he was talking to them about the Father.)

²⁸Then Jesus continued, "When you elevate the Human One, then you'll know that I am, and that I don't act on my own. Rather, I say what my Father taught me. ²⁹The one who sent me is with me. He hasn't left me on my own, because I always do what pleases him."

³⁰While he was saying this, many came to believe in him.

³¹Then Jesus began to tell the Judeans who had come to believe in him, "If you adhere to my teaching you really are my disciples ³²and you'll know the truth and the truth will liberate you."

³³They protested: "We're Abraham's descendants, and we've never been slaves to anyone. How can you say, 'You'll be liberated'?"

³⁴Jesus answered them, "Let me tell you this: everyone who commits sin is a slave. ³⁵No slave is ever a permanent member of the family; but a son is. ³⁶So if the son liberates you, you'll really be free.

³⁷"I recognize that you are Abraham's descendants, yet you're trying to kill me because my teaching gets nowhere with you. ³⁸I'm telling you what I saw when I was with the Father, and you do only what you learned from your own father."

³⁹"Our father is Abraham," they repeated.

Jesus says, "If you really are children of Abraham, act as Abraham did. ⁴⁰As it is, you're trying to kill me, even though I've told you the truth I heard from God. Abraham never did that. ⁴¹No, you're doing what your father does."

They replied, "We're not bastards; we have only one father: God."

⁴²Jesus responded, "If in fact God were your father, you'd love me, since I've come from God and am here—not on my own initiative; God sent me. ⁴³Why don't you understand what I'm saying? It's because you can't hear my message. ⁴⁴You are your father's children all right—children of the devil. And you are bent on satisfying your father's cravings. He was a murderer from the start; he is far from truth. In fact, there's no truth in him at all. When he tells his lies, he is

8:32
Ⓣ DSav 41:6

8:35
◊Gn 21:10

8:36
Ⓣ GSav 3:4, 13:15

8:39
Ⓣ Q 3:8, Mt 3:8, Lk 3:8

8:23 *this world:* See the note on 7:7.

8:24 *I am ⟨what I say I am⟩:* The "I am" here is deliberately ambiguous and can also be the divine name, as it is in vv. 28 and 58. See the note to 4:26.

8:41 *We're not bastards:* In Greek "we" is emphasized. The suggestion is that by contrast Jesus' birth was illegitimate; is this because he claims God as his Father?

8:44 *children of the devil:* one of the several extreme expressions of anti-Judaism in this gospel; see also v. 47, for example, and the Introduction.

expressing his nature, because he is a liar and breeds lying. ⁴⁵But since I tell the truth, you don't ⟨want to⟩ believe me. ⁴⁶Who can charge me with sin? If I speak truthfully, why don't you believe me? ⁴⁷Everyone who belongs to God can hear God's words. That's why you don't listen: you don't belong to God."

⁴⁸The Judeans replied, "Aren't we right to say, 'You're a Samaritan and possessed by a demon'?"

⁴⁹"I'm not possessed," Jesus replied. "I am respecting my Father, but you are disrespecting me. (⁵⁰Not that I'm looking for glory; there is one who seeks that for me and who acquits me.) ⁵¹Let me tell you this: whoever follows my teaching will never die."

⁵²To this the Judeans retorted, "Now we're certain you're possessed! ⟨Even⟩ Abraham died, and so did the prophets, and here you are claiming, 'Whoever follows my teaching will never taste death.' ⁵³Are you greater than our father Abraham? He died, and so did the prophets. Just who do you think you are?"

⁵⁴Jesus replied, "If I were to glorify myself, that glory of mine would mean nothing. But in fact my Father glorifies me—the one you call your God, ⁵⁵though you've never known God. But I know him; if I were to say I don't know God I would be a liar like you. I do know God, and I follow God's teaching. ⁵⁶Your father Abraham would have been overjoyed to see my day; in fact, he did see it and it made him happy."

⁵⁷The Judeans said to him, "You aren't even fifty years old and you've seen Abraham?!"

⁵⁸Jesus said to them, "Let me tell you this: before there was an Abraham, I am."

⁵⁹They picked up stones to hurl at him, but Jesus disappeared from the temple area.

9 **As Jesus was leaving** he saw a man who had been blind from birth. ²His disciples asked him, "Rabbi, was it this man's sin or his parents' that caused him to be born blind?"

³Jesus responded, "This man did not sin and neither did his parents. ⟨He was born blind⟩ so God could display his work through him. ⁴We must carry out the work of the one who sent me while the light lasts. Nighttime is coming

---

8:47
Ⓣ SJas 6:33

8:48
Ⓣ Mk 3:22;
Jn 7:20, 10:20

8:51
Cf. Th 1, 111:2

8:52
Ⓣ Mk 3:22;
Jn 7:20, 10:20

8:59
Cf. Lk 4:28–30,
EgerG 1:7

9:2
◊ Ex 20:5

8:53 A few mss omit *our father*.
9:4 Many mss read "I" in place of *we*. Some mss read "us" in place of *me*.

8:48 *a Samaritan:* that is, an enemy of the Judeans.
8:51 *never die:* See the note on 5:24.
9:2 *this man's sin:* It was often believed that all misfortune was deserved, the result of some someone's sin. In the case of a congenital disability there arose the question whether the victim had *caused it* or—perhaps because such sin was hard to attribute to an unborn baby—the victim's parents.
9:3 *so God could display his work:* Jesus cuts through the

disciples' speculation and, as common in this gospel, interprets special events, particularly those done through him, as having an essentially theological purpose, that is, to show what God is like. This purpose overclouds any concern for the victim such as Jesus displays in the synoptic gospels.
9:4–5 The anomalous mixture of plural and singular personal pronouns (but see the text-critical note) is perhaps to be explained as a combination of an affirmation of the

and then no one will be able to do any work. [5]So long as I am in the world I am the light of the world."

[6]With that he spat on the ground, made mud with his saliva, and smeared the mud on the man's eyes. [7]Then Jesus said to him, "Go, rinse off in the pool of Siloam" (the name means "Emissary"). So he went over, rinsed off ⟨his eyes⟩, and came back with his sight restored.

[8]Then his neighbors, and those who recognized him as the one who had been a beggar before, were saying, "Isn't this the guy who used to sit and beg?"

[9]Some were saying, "It's him"; others were saying, "No, it only looks like him."

He kept saying, "It's me."

[10]So they asked him, "How were your eyes opened?"

[11]He answered, "Some guy named Jesus made some mud and smeared it on my eyes; he told me, 'Go to Siloam and rinse it off.' So I went, and when I rinsed it off, I could see."

[12]They said to him, "Where is this guy?"

He says, "I don't know."

[13]They take the man who had been blind to the Pharisees. ([14]It was the Sabbath when Jesus made mud and opened his eyes.) [15]So the Pharisees asked him again how he could see.

"He put mud on my eyes, I washed, and I can see," he told them.

[16]Then some of the Pharisees said, "That man is not from God, because he does not observe the Sabbath." But others said, "How can a sinner perform such signs?" And they were divided among themselves. [17]So they ask the blind man again, "What do you have to say about him, since it was your eyes he opened?"

He said, "He's a prophet."

[18]The Judeans wouldn't believe that he had been blind and got his sight until they called in the parents of the man who had recovered his sight. [19]They asked them, "Is this your son that you claim was born blind? So how come he can see now?"

[20]His parents replied, "We know this is our son; we know he was born blind; [21]but we don't know how he can see now or who opened his eyes. Ask him, he's an adult; he can speak for himself." ([22]His parents said this because they were afraid of the Judeans, for the Judeans had already agreed that anyone who

9:5
Cf. Mt 5:14,
Th 77:1;
Ⓓ Jn 8:12

Johannine community (*we*) with a saying from its tradition of Jesus' teaching (*me, I*).

9:7 *the name means "Emissary"*: probably a fanciful etymology. Either it is meant simply to suggest the aptness of Jesus' sending the blind man to this pool or it subtly reminds the reader that Jesus is himself the emissary of God.

9:8–12 The *neighbors* and others display the inability of many witnesses of Jesus' deeds to see them as "miracles"

(6:26), and perhaps the responses reflect the varying effect of these stories on their hearers at the time the gospel was written. Even those who accept the miracle display mainly curiosity.

9:17 *a prophet*: Like the Samaritan woman in chapter 4, the man healed of his blindness only gradually recognizes what Jesus is. See vv. 33, 38.

acknowledged ⟨Jesus as⟩ the Anointed One would be banned from their congregation. ²³That's why his parents said, "He's an adult, ask him.")

²⁴So for a second time they called in the man who had been blind, and said to him, "Give the credit to God, for we know this man is a sinner."

²⁵He replied, "Whether he's a sinner I don't know; the one thing I do know is that I was blind, and now I can see."

²⁶They asked him, "What did he do to you? How did he open your eyes?"

²⁷He answered them, "I told you already and you wouldn't listen to me. Why do you want to hear it again? You don't want to become his disciples too, do you?"

²⁸They hurled insults at him: "You may be his disciple; we're disciples of Moses. ²⁹We know God spoke to Moses; we don't even know where this man came from."

³⁰"Now isn't that wonderful?" he responded. "You don't know where he's from and yet he opened my eyes! ³¹God doesn't listen to sinners; we know that. But if someone is devout and does God's will, God listens. ³²It's unheard of that anyone ever opened the eyes of someone born blind. ³³If this man were not from God, he couldn't do anything at all."

³⁴"You're a born sinner and you're going to lecture us?" they replied. And they threw him out.

³⁵Jesus heard they had thrown him out; so he found him and said, "Do you believe in the Human One?"

³⁶He replied, "Master, who is he, so I can believe in him?"

³⁷Jesus said to him, "You've already seen him; he's speaking with you right now."

³⁸He said, "Master, I believe," and paid him homage.

³⁹Jesus said, "I came into this world to hand down this verdict: the blind are to see and those with sight are to be blind."

⁴⁰When some of the Pharisees around him heard this, they said to him, "We're not blind, are we?"

⁴¹Jesus said to them, "If you really were blind, you would be free of sin; but now since you say, 'We see,' your sin is confirmed."

10 "**Let me tell you this**: anyone who does not enter the sheep pen through the gate, but climbs in some other way, is nothing but a thief and a bandit. ²But the one who enters through the gate is the shepherd. ³The gatekeeper lets him

9:29
//EgerG 1:4

9:39
Cf. Mk 4:10–12,
8:17–18;
Mt 13:10–17;
Lk 8:9–10;
◊ Is 6:9–10

9:40–41
Ⓣ Mt 15:14, 23:16,
17, 19, 24, 26;
GOxy 840 2:7

9:22 *banned from their congregation:* See the Introduction.
9:34 *they threw him out:* The consequence his parents feared (v. 22) now applies to this new convert, as apparently to Christians generally in the circumstances where the gospel was written.
10:1–38 The extended *figure of speech* (v. 6) of the Good

Shepherd is the closest parallel in this gospel to the parables Jesus so characteristically tells in both the synoptic gospels and Thomas. Like some of them, in their present form, this metaphor becomes allegorical (see the note on v. 8).
10:1 The words of Jesus continue, but they can hardly be taken as addressed simply to the Pharisees of chapter 9.

in. The sheep recognize his voice; he calls his own sheep by name and leads them out. ⁴When he has driven out the last of his own sheep, he walks in front of them, and the sheep follow him because they know his voice. ⁵They would never follow a stranger, but would run away from him, since they don't know the voice of strangers."

⁶Jesus used this figure of speech with them, but they didn't understand what he was talking about.

⁷Jesus went on to say, "Let me tell you this: I am the gate for the sheep. ⁸All who came before me are nothing but thieves and bandits, but the sheep haven't paid any attention to them. ⁹I am the gate; whoever enters through me will be safe and will go in and out and find pasture. ¹⁰The thief comes only to steal and slaughter and destroy. I came so they can have life and have it to the full.

¹¹"I am the good shepherd. The good shepherd gives his life for his sheep. ¹²A hired hand, who isn't a shepherd and doesn't own the sheep, would see the wolf coming and run off, abandoning the sheep; then the wolf could attack the sheep and scatter them. ¹³He would run off because he's a hired hand and the sheep don't matter to him. ¹⁴I am the good shepherd. I know my sheep and my sheep know me, ¹⁵just as the Father knows me and I know the Father, and I give my life for my sheep. ¹⁶Yet I have sheep from another fold, and I must lead them too. They'll recognize my voice, and there'll be one flock, one shepherd.

¹⁷"This is the reason my Father loves me: I am giving up my life so I can take it back again. ¹⁸No one can take it away from me; I give it of my own free will. I have the power to give it up and the power to take it back again. I have been charged with this responsibility by my Father."

¹⁹Once more the Judeans were divided among themselves because he made these claims. ²⁰Many of them were saying, "He's possessed by a demon and out of his mind. Why pay any attention to him?" ²¹Others would say, "These aren't the words of someone who's possessed. A demon can't open the eyes of the blind, can it?"

²²**It was then the Festival** of Lights in Jerusalem, and it was wintertime. ²³Jesus was walking around in the temple area, in Solomon's Colonnade. ²⁴Judeans surrounded him. "How long are you going to keep us in suspense?" they kept asking. "If you are the Anointed One, just say so."

²⁵Jesus answered them, "I did tell you, and you don't believe. The work I do in my Father's name is evidence on my behalf. ²⁶But you don't believe me,

10:6
Ⓣ SJas 6:5

10:8
◊ Ez 34:2

10:11
//GSav 4:8

10:14–15
Ⓣ Q 10:22,
Mt 11:27, Lk 10:22

10:15–18
Ⓣ GSav 4:9

10:15
Ⓣ Jn 15:13,
1 Jn 3:16

10:16
◊ Is 56:8

10:20
Ⓣ Mk 3:22;
Mt 12:24; Lk 11:5;
Jn 7:20; 8:48, 52

10:24–25
Cf. Mk 14:61,
Mt 26:63,
Lk 22:66–68

10:25–26
Ⓣ SJas 6:33

10:8 *All who came before me:* The allegorical meaning of aspects of the Good Shepherd metaphor like this (and, for example, the *hired hand* or the *wolf* in v. 12) was undoubtedly apparent to this gospel's original audience but probably a matter of guesswork for later readers. They may refer either to the Jewish leaders in conflict with the Christians to whom this gospel is addressed or, just possibly, to some conflict among Christian leaders, as in 1 John.

10:16 *one flock:* On the matter of unity among Jesus' followers, see further chapter 17.

10:22 The *Festival of Lights* is Hanukkah, which celebrates the rededication of the temple in 164 BCE.

10:25 *I did tell you, and you don't believe:* perhaps the common experience of Christian evangelists among the Judeans in the author's own time.

because you're not my sheep. ²⁷My sheep recognize my voice; I know them and they follow me, ²⁸and I provide them with unending life; they'll never be lost, nor will anyone grab them out of my hand. ²⁹What my Father has given me is greatest of all, and no one can grab it from the hand of the Father. ³⁰I and the Father are one."

³¹Again the Judeans picked up stones to stone him. ³²Jesus responded, "I showed you many wonderful works that were really the Father's. Which of these works makes you want to stone me?"

³³The Judeans answered him, "We're not stoning you for some 'wonderful work,' but for blasphemy—you, a mere human, make yourself out to be God."

³⁴Jesus answered them, "Isn't it written in your Law: 'I said, You are gods'? ³⁵The scripture can't be wrong: if God has called people gods—those for whom God's word was intended—³⁶do you mean to say to the one the Father set apart and sent to earth, 'You're blaspheming,' just because I said, 'I am God's son'? ³⁷If I don't do my Father's works, don't believe me; ³⁸if I do, even if you can't believe in me, believe in the works, so that you'll fully understand that the Father is in me and I am in the Father."

³⁹Again they tried to arrest him, but he escaped.

⁴⁰**He went away** once more, to the place across the Jordan where John had first baptized, and there he stayed. ⁴¹Many people came to him; they kept repeating, "John didn't perform any sign, but everything John said about this man was true." ⁴²And many came to believe in him there.

11 Now someone named Lazarus had fallen ill; he was from Bethany, the village of Mary and her sister Martha. (²This was the Mary who anointed the Master with perfumed ointment and wiped his feet with her hair; it was her brother Lazarus who was sick.) ³So the sisters sent for Jesus: "Master, the one you love is sick."

⁴But when Jesus heard this he said, "This illness is not fatal; it is to show God's glory, so God's son also will be glorified by it."

10:30
//GSav 4:6;
cf. EgerG 6:1

10:31
Cf. EgerG 1:7

10:33
◊Lv 24:16

10:34
◊Ps 82:6

10:39
//EgerG 1:10;
cf. Lk 4:29–30

11:1
//MysMk 1:1

11:2
① Jn 12:3

10:29 Some mss have one or another variant of "my Father, who has given (them) to me" in place of *what my Father has given me*.
10:38 Some mss read "know and believe" in place of *fully understand*.

10:30 While this can mean that Jesus believes himself to be in perfect harmony with God's will, it can also be taken as Jesus' claim to be divine, which is how the Judeans understand it in v. 33.
10:33 *make yourself out to be God:* See v. 30 and 5:18.
10:40 *the place across the Jordan where John had first bap-*

tized: See 1:28.
11:1 *Bethany:* not the Bethany of 1:28, but the well-known village just outside of Jerusalem (v. 18).
11:2 *the Mary who anointed the Master:* a reference to what will be depicted in 12:1–8.

⁵Jesus loved Martha and her sister and Lazarus. ⁶When he heard that Lazarus was sick, he lingered two more days where he was; ⁷then he says to the disciples, "Let's go back to Judea."

⁸The disciples say to him, "Rabbi, just now the Judeans were looking for the opportunity to stone you; are you really going back there?"

⁹"Aren't there twelve hours in the day?" Jesus responded. "Those who walk during the day won't stumble; they can see by this world's light. ¹⁰But those who walk at night are going to stumble, because they don't have the light within."

¹¹He made these remarks, and then he tells them, "Our friend Lazarus has fallen asleep, but I'm going to wake him up."

¹²"Master, if he's only fallen asleep," said the disciples, "he'll be okay." (¹³Jesus had been speaking of death but they thought that he meant he was only asleep.)

¹⁴Then Jesus told them plainly, "Lazarus is dead; ¹⁵and I'm happy for you that I wasn't there, so you can believe. Now let's go to him."

¹⁶Then Thomas, called "the Twin," said to his fellow disciples, "Let's go along too, so we can die with him."

¹⁷When Jesus arrived, he found out that Lazarus had been buried four days earlier. ¹⁸Bethany was near Jerusalem, about two miles away, ¹⁹and many of the Judeans had come to Martha and Mary to console them about their brother. ²⁰When Martha heard that Jesus was coming, she went to meet him; Mary stayed at home. ²¹"Master," said Martha, "if you'd been here, my brother wouldn't have died. ²²Still, I know that whatever you ask of God, God will grant you."

²³Jesus says to her, "Your brother will be raised."

²⁴Martha responds, "I know he'll be raised—in the resurrection on the last day."

²⁵Jesus said to her, "I am resurrection and life; those who believe in me, even if they die, will live, ²⁶but everyone who is alive and believes in me will never die. Do you believe this?"

²⁷"Yes, Master," she says, "I believe that you are the Anointed One, the son of God, who is to come to earth."

²⁸At this point she went to call her sister Mary, telling her privately, "The Teacher is here and is asking for you." ²⁹When she heard that, she got up quickly and went to him.

11:25 A few mss omit *and life*.

11:9–10
Cf. Jn 12:35

11:6 *where he was:* presumably the place (also named Bethany) of 10:40.

11:16 *called "the Twin":* Or *called Didymus* or *which means Twin.* The name *Thomas* is derived from the Hebrew word for twin; *Didymus,* a Greek personal name, is from the Greek word for twin. The phrase is used at every appearance of Thomas except 14:5 (i.e., 20:24 and 21:2).

die: the first of several allusions in this story—also the tomb covered by a stone, the head cloth, etc.—to the account of Jesus' own death and resurrection (which is, as here, a demonstration that Jesus himself accomplishes; see 2:19).

11:24 *the resurrection on the last day:* Many first-century Jews believed that at the Last Judgment God would raise the just to life in the Age to Come.

11:26 *never die:* See the note on 5:24.

Deliberations of the Council

(³⁰Jesus hadn't yet arrived at the village; he was still where Martha had met him.)

³¹When the Judeans, who were keeping her company in the house to console her, saw Mary get up and go out quickly, they followed her, thinking she was going to the tomb to grieve there. ³²When Mary got to where Jesus was and saw him, she knelt at his feet. "Master," she said, "if you'd been here, my brother wouldn't have died."

³³When Jesus saw her crying, and the Judeans who accompanied her crying too, he was agitated and deeply disturbed. ³⁴"Where have you put him?" he asked.

"Master," they say, "come and see."

³⁵Then Jesus wept.

³⁶So the Judeans observed, "Look how much he loved him." ³⁷But some wondered: "He opened the blind man's eyes; couldn't he have kept this man from dying?"

³⁸Again greatly agitated, Jesus arrives at the tomb; it was a cave, and a stone lay up against the opening. ³⁹Jesus says, "Take the stone away."

Martha, sister of the dead man, replies, "But Master, by this time the body will stink; it's been four days."

⁴⁰Jesus says to her, "Didn't I tell you, if you believe you'll see God's glory?" ⁴¹So they took the stone away, and Jesus looked upwards and said, "Father, thank you for hearing me. ⁴²I know you always hear me, but I say this because of the people standing here, so they'll believe that you sent me." ⁴³Then he shouted at the top of his voice, "Lazarus, come out!" ⁴⁴The dead man came out, his hands and feet bound in strips of burying cloth, and his face covered with a cloth. Jesus says to them, "Free him ⟨from the cloth⟩ and let him go."

⁴⁵**As a result**, many of the Judeans who had come to Mary and observed what Jesus had done came to believe in him. ⁴⁶But some of them went to the Pharisees and reported what Jesus had done.

⁴⁷So the chief priests and Pharisees called the Council together and posed this question to them: "What are we going to do now that this man performs so many signs? ⁴⁸If we let him go on like this, everybody will come to believe in him. Then the Romans will come and destroy our ⟨holy⟩ place and our nation."

⁴⁹Then one of them, Caiaphas, that year's chief priest, addressed them as follows: "Don't you know anything? ⁵⁰Don't you realize that you're better off having one man die for the people than having the whole nation wiped out?"

(⁵¹He didn't say this on his own authority, but since he was that year's chief priest he could foresee that Jesus would die for the nation. ⁵²In fact, he would

11:35
Ⓣ Lk 19:41

11:38
Ⓣ MysMk 1:4

11:39
Cf. MysMk 1:6

11:47 *the Council:* the ruling body of the Judeans.
11:48 ⟨*holy*⟩ *place:* the temple.
11:50 *for the people:* The preposition used here can mean

simply "in place of" or "for the benefit of." The irony that Caiaphas *could foresee* this is made explicit in the following comment by the author (vv. 51–52).

Mary anoints Jesus

die not only for the nation, but to gather together all God's dispersed children and make them one people.)

⁵³So from that day on they began plotting how to kill him. ⁵⁴As a consequence, Jesus no longer moved about among the Judeans publicly, but withdrew to a region bordering the desert, to a town called Ephraim, and there he stayed with the disciples.

⁵⁵It was almost time for the Jewish Passover, and many of the country people went up to Jerusalem before Passover to purify themselves. ⁵⁶They were on the lookout for Jesus, and as they stood around in the temple area, they were saying to one another, "What do you think? He certainly won't come to the festival, will he?" (⁵⁷The chief priests and the Pharisees had given orders that anyone who knew his whereabouts was to report it, so they could arrest him.)

12 **Six days before Passover** Jesus came to Bethany, where Lazarus lived, the one Jesus had raised from the dead. ²There they gave a dinner for him; Martha did the serving, and Lazarus was one of those who ate with him. ³Mary brought in a pound of expensive aromatic ointment made from pure nard and anointed Jesus' feet and wiped them with her hair. And the house was filled with the ointment's fragrance. ⁴Judas Iscariot, the disciple who was going to turn him in, says, ⁵"Why wasn't this ointment sold? It would bring three hundred denarii, and the money could have been given to the poor." (⁶He didn't say this because he cared about the poor, but because he was a thief. He was in charge of the common purse and now and again would pilfer money put into it.)

⁷"Leave her alone," Jesus said. "Let her keep it for the day of my burial. ⁸There will always be poor around, but I won't always be around."

⁹When the huge crowd of Judeans found out he was there, they came not only because of Jesus but also to see Lazarus, the one he had raised from the dead. ¹⁰So the chief priests planned to kill Lazarus too, ¹¹since he was the reason many of the Judeans were defecting and believing in Jesus.

11:53
Cf. Mk 3:6,
Mt 12:14;
Mk 11:18,
Lk 19:47–48;
Mk 14:1–2,
Mt 26:3–5,
Lk 22:1–2

12:1–8
//Mk 14:3–9,
Mt 26:6–13;
cf. Lk 7:36–50

12:8
◊Dt 15:11

12:8 A few mss lack this verse.

11:52 *to gather together all God's dispersed children and make them one people:* what the Messiah would do, according to widespread expectations.
11:53 Before this there have been several official attempts to kill Jesus. Perhaps this represents the first concerted plan to get rid of him.
12:3 Mary's act would ordinarily be considered both brazen and indecent in that cultural context. It will naturally provoke objection, and it does so in all versions of this story. Except for Luke 7:39, the objection takes the form of the disciples' (here only Judas') criticizing the woman's extravagance. Jesus justifies her action as percipiently pointing to his approaching death (v. 7).
12:8 *There will always be poor around:* not an acceptance of poverty's inevitability, as this saying (along with Deut 15:11) is usually understood. Jesus wryly comments, perhaps, on the inaptness of Judas' objection: "It's interesting that you should mention the poor just now."
12:9 *the huge crowd:* apparently the same as in 11:55–56.

¹²**The next day** the huge crowd that had come for the festival heard that Jesus was coming into Jerusalem. ¹³They got palm fronds and went out to meet him. They began to shout,

> Hosanna!
> Blessed is the one who comes
>   in the name of the Lord!
> ⟨Blessed is⟩ the King of Israel!

¹⁴Then Jesus found a young donkey and rode on it, as scripture puts it,

> ¹⁵Fear not, daughter of Zion.
> Look, your king comes
>   riding on a donkey's colt.

(¹⁶His disciples didn't understand what was going on, but when Jesus had been glorified, they then recalled that what had happened to him matched the things written about him.)

¹⁷The people who were with Jesus when he had summoned Lazarus from his tomb and raised him from the dead kept repeating this story. (¹⁸That's why the crowd went out to meet him: they heard that he had performed this sign.)

¹⁹So the Pharisees said to themselves, "You see, you can't win; look, the world has gone over to him."

²⁰**There were some Greeks** among those who had come up to worship at the festival. ²¹These people came to Philip, who was from Bethsaida, Galilee, and requested of him, "Sir, we would like to meet Jesus."

²²Philip goes and tells Andrew, and both Andrew and Philip go and tell Jesus. ²³And Jesus responds: "The time has come for the Human One to be glorified. ²⁴Let me tell you this: unless the kernel of wheat falls to the earth and dies, it remains a single seed, but if it dies, it produces a great harvest. ²⁵If you love your life you'll lose it, but if you hate your life in this world you'll preserve it for unending life. ²⁶Whoever serves me must follow me, for wherever I am, my servant must be there also. Whoever serves me, the Father will honor.

²⁷"Now 'my life is in turmoil,' but should I say, 'Father, rescue me from this moment'? No, it was to face this moment that I came. ²⁸Father, glorify your

12:12–15
//Mk 11:1–10,
Mt 21:1–11,
Lk 19:28–40

12:13
◊ Ps 118:26

12:15
◊ Zec 9:9

12:24
Ⓣ SJas 6:9–11

12:25
//Mk 8:35;
Mt 10:39, 16:25;
Lk 9:24, 17:33

12:26
Cf. Q 12:8,
Mt 10:32, Lk 12:8

12:27
Ⓣ Mk 14:34–36,
Mt 26:38–39,
Lk 22:41–42

12:17 Some mss read "kept repeating that he had summoned Lazarus from his tomb" in place of *when he had summoned Lazarus . . . kept repeating this story.*

12:13 *Hosanna!:* This Hebrew word, once a prayer meaning "Save (us)," has evidently become, as in the other gospels, an expression of praise.

12:20 *Greeks:* See the note on 7:35.

12:23 *The time has come:* Beginning with 2:4 there have been a number of references to Jesus' *time,* until now always in the future. Here at last it begins. See also 13:1.

to be glorified: Jesus' *time* is understood not so much as his death, which nevertheless is central to it, as his vindication and exaltation.

name!" Then a voice spoke out of the sky, "I have glorified it and I will glorify even more."

²⁹The crowd there heard this, and some people remarked that it was thunder, others that a heavenly messenger had spoken to him.

³⁰"That voice did not come for me but for you," Jesus answered. ³¹"Now sentence is passed on this world; now the ruler of this world will be driven out. ³²And if I'm elevated from the earth, I'll take everyone with me." (³³He said this to show what kind of death he was going to die.)

³⁴The crowd replied to him, "We've learned from the Law that the Anointed One will stay forever, so how can you say that the Human One is destined to be 'elevated'? Who is this 'Human One' anyway?"

³⁵So Jesus said to them, "The light is still with you for a while. Walk while you have light, so darkness won't overpower you. Those who walk in the dark don't know where they're going. ³⁶Since you have the light, believe in the light, so you will become children of light." When Jesus had said this, he left and went into hiding.

³⁷**Although he had performed** so many signs before their eyes, they did not believe in him, ³⁸in order that the word the prophet Isaiah spoke would be fulfilled:

> Lord, who has believed our message?
> To whom is God's might revealed?

³⁹So they were unable to believe, for Isaiah also said,

> ⁴⁰He has blinded their eyes,
>   and closed their minds,
>   to make sure they don't see with their eyes
>   and understand with their minds,
>   or else they would turn ⟨their lives⟩ around
>   and I would heal them.

⁴¹Isaiah said these things because he saw his glory and spoke about it.

⁴²Nevertheless, many did believe in him, even many of the ruling class, but because of the Pharisees they did not admit it, so they wouldn't be thrown out of

12:31
ⓣ EgerG 1:5,
Lk 10:18

12:34
◊ Is 9:7

12:35–36
ⓣ SJas 8:5

12:35
Cf. Th 24:3;
ⓣ DSav 8:3

12:37–40
Cf. Mk 4:10–12,
Mt 13:10–17,
Lk 8:9–10

12:38
◊ Is 53:1

12:40
◊ Is 6:9–10

12:32 A few mss read "everything" in place of *everyone*.

12:31 *the ruler of this world:* either Satan (13:27), or a human representative such as the emperor.
12:32–33 Jesus' word about being *elevated from the earth* is taken to refer to his crucifixion.
12:38–40 These passages from Isaiah, and especially the

one quoted in v. 40, helped the Christian movement explain why so few Jews accepted Jesus as the Messiah.
12:41 *his glory:* This could refer either to Jesus' glory or to God's.
12:42 See the Introduction.

their congregations. ([43]You see, they were more concerned with human approval than with God's.)

[44]**Then Jesus proclaimed** aloud, "Those who believe in me believe not only in me, but in the one who sent me. [45]And those who see me see the one who sent me. [46]I am light come into the world, so all who believe in me need not remain in the dark. [47]I won't pass judgment on those who hear my message but don't keep it. You see, I didn't come to pass judgment on the world; I've come to save the world. [48]But those who reject me and don't accept my message have a judge: the message I've spoken will itself be their judge on the last day. [49]For I don't speak on my own authority, but the Father who sent me ordered me to say what I have said and will say, [50]and I know that his commandment is unending life. Therefore, I say just exactly what the Father told to me to say."

13 **Before the Festival** of Passover Jesus knew that the time had come for him to leave this world and return to the Father. He had loved his own in the world and would love them to the end. [2]Now that the devil had planted it in the mind of Judas, son of Simon Iscariot, to turn him in, at supper [3]Jesus could tell that the Father had left everything up to him and that he had come from God and was going back to God. [4]So he got up from the meal, took off his shirt, put it aside, and wrapped a towel around himself. [5]Then he poured water into a basin and began to wash the disciples' feet and dry them with the towel around his waist. [6]He comes to Simon Peter.

Peter says to him, "Master, you're going to wash my feet?"

[7]Jesus replied, "Right now you don't understand what I'm doing, but later you will."

[8]"There's no way you'll wash my feet," Peter says.

Jesus answered him, "Unless I wash you, you won't have anything in common with me."

[9]"In that case, Master," Peter says, "⟨wash⟩ not just my feet but my hands and my head too."

[10]Jesus says, "People who have bathed only have to wash their feet; nevertheless, they're clean all over. And you are clean—but not quite all of you."

([11]He knew, of course, who was going to turn him in; that's why he said, "You're not all clean.")

[12]When he had washed their feet, he put his shirt back on and returned to his place at the meal. "Do you realize what I've done?" he asked. [13]"You call me Teacher and Master, and you're right: that's who I am. [14]So if I am your master and teacher and have washed your feet, you should wash each other's feet. [15]In

12:44–45
Cf. Mk 9:37;
Q 10:16, Mt 10:40,
Lk 10:16, 9:48;
Jn 5:23, 13:20

13:2
Ⓣ Jn 6:70–71,
13:27; Lk 22:3

13:3–4
Cf. Th 61:3

13:3
Ⓣ Jn 3:35,
Q 10:22, Mt 11:27,
Lk 10:22

13:14
Ⓣ Mk 9:35,
Mt 23:11, Lk 9:48;
Mk 10:42–45,
Mt 20:25–28,
Lk 22:25–27

12:47 *the world:* See the note on 7:7.
13:1 *to the end:* This highly ambiguous phrase can mean "until his death," "fully," or "to the end of the age."

13:4 *took off his shirt:* so that he is as scantily dressed as a slave.

other words, I've set you an example: you are to do as I've done to you. [16]Let me tell you this: slaves are never better than their masters; messengers are never superior to those who send them. [17]If you understand this, congratulations if you can do it. [18]I'm not talking about all of you; I know the ones I've chosen. But scripture has to be fulfilled:

> The one who has shared my food has turned on me.

[19]I'm telling you this now, before it happens, so that when it does happen you'll believe that I am. [20]Let me tell you this: if they receive anyone I send, they are receiving me; and if they receive me, they are receiving the one who sent me.

[21]**When he had said all this**, Jesus became agitated. He declared, "Let me tell you this: one of you will turn me in."

[22]The disciples stole glances at each other, at a loss to understand who it was he was talking about. [23]One of them, the disciple Jesus loved, was reclining next to him. [24]So Simon Peter leans over to ask that disciple who it was Jesus was talking about. [25]He, in turn, leans back on Jesus' chest and asks him, "Master, who is it?"

[26]Jesus answers, "I am going to dip this piece of bread, and the one I give it to is the one." So he dips the piece of bread and gives it to Judas, son of Simon Iscariot. [27]The moment ⟨he had given Judas⟩ the piece of bread, Satan took possession of him. Then Jesus says to him, "Go ahead and do what you're going to do."

([28]Of course no one at dinner understood why Jesus had made this remark. [29]Some had the idea that because Judas kept charge of the funds, Jesus was telling him, "Buy whatever we need for the festival," or to give something to the poor.) [30]Judas left as soon as he had eaten the piece of bread. It was nighttime.

[31]**When Judas had gone**, Jesus says, "Now the Human One is glorified, and God is glorified through him. [32]If God is glorified through him, God in turn will glorify him through himself, and will glorify him at once. [33]Little children, I'm going to be with you only a little while longer. You'll look for me, but, as I said to the Judeans, I'm going where you can't come. Now I'm saying this to you. [34]I am giving you a new commandment: love each other. Just as I've loved you, you are to love each other. [35]Then everyone will recognize you as my disciples— if you love each other."

13:32 Several mss omit *if God is glorified through him.*

13:19 *I am:* See the note on 4:26.
13:23 *the disciple Jesus loved:* The identity of this nameless figure, appearing here for the first time, is perhaps the most puzzling element in the gospel. See the Introduction and note on 21:23.
13:30 *It was nighttime:* Undoubtedly this is not intended

as a mere matter of fact but is symbolic, as perhaps at 3:2. See what Jesus has said about the *night* in 9:4 and 11:10.
13:34 *love each other:* The ethic in this gospel has been reduced from the other gospels' ethic of love of neighbor, even of enemy, and is restricted to love within the Christian community.

Judas' betrayal predicted

A new commandment

13:15–17
Ⓣ Mk 10:43–44,
Mt 20:26–27,
Lk 22:26–27

13:16
//Q 6:40,
Mt 10:24–25,
Lk 6:40, DSav 20:1

13:17
Cf. Lk 11:28,
Th 79:2;
Ⓣ Jas 1:25

13:18
◊Ps 41:9

13:20
Cf. Mk 9:37;
Q 10:16; Mt 10:40;
Lk 10:16, 9:48;
Jn 5:23, 12:44–45

13:21–30
//Mk 14:18–21,
Mt 26:21–25,
Lk 22:21–22

13:27
Ⓣ Jn 6:70–71, 13:2

13:31–32
Ⓣ GSav 14:22

13:33
Cf. Th 59

*Peter's denial
predicted*

The way

The advocate

[36] **Simon Peter says** to him, "Master, where are you going?"

Jesus answered, "For now you can't follow me where I'm going; you'll follow later."

[37] Peter says to him, "Master, why can't I follow you now? I'd give my life for you."

[38] Jesus responded, "You'd give your life for me? Let me tell you this: the rooster won't crow before you disown me three times."

14

"**Don't give in** to your distress. You believe in God; believe also in me. [2] There are plenty of places to stay in my Father's house. If it weren't true, I would have told you. I'm on my way to prepare a place for you. [3] And if I go to prepare a place for you, I'll return and embrace you, so where I am you can be too. [4] You know where I'm going and you know the way."

[5] Thomas says to him, "Master, we don't know where you're going. How can we possibly know the way?"

[6] "I am the way, and I am truth, and I am life," replies Jesus. "No one gets to the Father unless it is through me. [7] If you recognize me, you will recognize my Father also. From this moment on you know him and you've even seen him."

[8] "Let us see the Father," Philip says to him, "and we'll be satisfied."

[9] "I've been around you all this time," Jesus replies, "and you still don't know me, do you, Philip? Anyone who has seen me has seen the Father. So how can you say, 'Let us see the Father'? [10] Don't you believe that I'm in the Father and the Father is in me? I don't say what I say on my own. It is the Father living in me who does his work. [11] Believe me: I'm in the Father and the Father is in me. If not, believe because of the works themselves. [12] Let me tell you this: anyone who believes in me will perform the works I perform and will be able to perform even greater feats, because I'm on my way to the Father. [13] In addition, I'll do whatever you request using my name, so the Father can be glorified in the son. [14] If you request anything using my name, I'll do it."

[15] "**If you love me**, you'll obey my commandments. [16] At my request the Father will provide you with yet another advocate, the spirit of truth, who will be

13:36–38
Cf. Mk 14:26–31,
Mt 26:30–35,
Lk 22:31–34

13:36
Ⓣ SJas 2:4

14:1–5
Ⓣ GSav 5:1–2

14:2
Ⓣ SJas 8:7

14:3–5
Ⓣ SJas 2:4

14:3
Ⓣ SJas6:23

14:4–7
Cf. Th 24:1

14:5
Ⓣ DSav28:1

14:7–9
Ⓣ DSav 16:5

14:9
Ⓣ SJas9:2

14:10–11
Ⓣ DSav 41:4

14:13–14
Cf. Mk 11:24;
Mt 21:22;
Q 11:9–10,
Mt 7:7–8,
Lk 11:9–10;
Th 2; 92:1; 94;
Ⓓ Jn 15:7, 16;
16:23

14:16–17
Ⓣ Jn 15:26–27,
16:13

14:15 Some mss read "obey" in place of *you'll obey*.

13:36 *For now you can't follow . . . ; you'll follow later:* This is spoken to Peter alone and perhaps refers to Jesus' death and the possibility that Peter would also be crucified (21:19). Or it is clarified by Jesus' promise to all the disciples in 14:2 that they would eventually join him in his *Father's house*.
14:3 *if I go . . . I'll return:* Usually these two predictions are taken to refer to the synoptic view of Jesus' resurrection and his eventual coming again, but in the context of this Fare-

well Address (chapters 14–17) at the last supper, they probably refer instead to his approaching death and resurrection.
14:6 *No one gets to the Father unless it is through me:* This may state the rhetoric of Jewish/Christian conflict that occasions this gospel—or one side of it—as much as the absolute claim it is usually taken to be. Perhaps Jesus here speaks mainly positively, to reassure his followers, as v. 7 shows.
14:16 *yet another advocate:* that is, beside Jesus himself.

with you forever. [17]The world is unable to accept this spirit because it neither perceives nor recognizes him. You recognize him because he dwells with you and will be within you.

[18]"I won't abandon you as orphans; I'll come to you. [19]In a little while the world won't see me any longer, but you'll see me because I'm alive as you will be alive. [20]At that time you'll come to know that I'm in my Father and that you're in me and I'm in you. [21]Those who accept my commandments and obey them— they love me. And those who love me will be loved by my Father; moreover, I will love them and reveal myself to them."

[22]Judas (not Iscariot) says to him, "Master, what has happened that you are about to reveal yourself to us but not to the world?"

[23]Jesus replied to him, "Those who love me will heed what I tell them, and my Father will love them, and we'll come to them and make our home with them. [24]Those who don't love me won't obey my words. Of course, the things you heard me say are not mine but come from the Father who sent me.

[25]"I have told you these things while I am still here with you. [26]Yet the advocate, the holy spirit the Father will send in my name, will teach you everything and remind you of everything I told you. [27]Peace is what I leave behind for you; my peace is what I give you. What I give you is not a worldly gift. Don't give in to your distress or be overcome by terror. [28]You heard me tell you, 'I'm going away and I'm going to return to you.' If you loved me, you'd be glad that I'm going to the Father, because the Father is greater than I am. [29]I have now told you all this ahead of time so you will believe when it happens.

[30]"Time does not permit me to tell you much more; you see, the ruler of this world is already on the way. [31]However, so the world may know that I love the Father, I act exactly as my Father instructed me. Come on, let's get out of here."

15 "**I am the real vine** and my Father is the farmer. [2]He prunes every branch of mine that does not bear fruit, and every branch that does bear fruit he dresses so it will bear even more fruit. [3]You have already been 'dressed' by the word I've spoken to you. [4]You must stay attached to me, and I to you. Just as a branch cannot bear fruit by itself—if it is detached from the vine—so you can't bear fruit unless you stay attached to me. [5]I am the vine, you are the branches. Those who stay attached to me—and I to them—produce a lot of fruit; without me you can't do anything. [6]Those who don't remain attached to me are thrown away

The real vine

14:18
Ⓣ GSav 5:1–2
14:21–23
Ⓣ SJas 6:7
14:23
Ⓣ SJas 4:4, 6:23
14:25
Ⓣ SJas 9:7
14:26
Ⓣ Mk 13:11,
Mt 10:20, Lk 12:12
14:27
Cf. Mary 3:12, 7:2
14:31
//GSav 4:2;
cf. Mk 14:42,
Mt 26:46
15:2–8
Ⓣ SJas 6:9–11
15:4
Ⓣ SJas 6:23
15:5–6
Cf. Th 40
15:6
Cf. Q 3:9, Mt 3:10,
Lk 3:9

14:17 *The world:* See the note on 7:7.

he dwells with you and will be within you: A major element of the comfort that this gospel seeks to provide the beleaguered community it addresses is the reassurance of permanence and dependability in otherwise unreliable circumstances. The word for *dwell* (or "stay") consequently appears many times (e.g., 6:27, 8:35).

14:30 *the ruler of this world:* See the note on 12:31.

14:31 *Come on . . . :* Jesus' address to the disciples seems to end here, but evidently it has been extended after chapter 14 was completed.

15:1 *I am the real vine:* another metaphor for Jesus' relation to the Father and to his followers.

World's hatred

Jesus departs

like dead branches: they're collected, tossed into the fire, and burned. ⁷If you stay attached to me and my words live in you, ask whatever you want and it will happen to you. ⁸My Father is glorified by the great quantity of fruit you produce in being my disciples.

⁹"I loved you in the same way the Father loved me. Live in my love. ¹⁰If you obey my commandments, you'll live in my love, just as I have obeyed my Father's commandments and live in his love.

¹¹"I have told you all this so my happiness can be in you and your happiness can be complete. ¹²This is my commandment to you: you shall love each other just as I loved you. ¹³There is no greater love than to give up your life for your friends. ¹⁴You are my friends when you do what I command you. ¹⁵I no longer call you slaves, since a slave does not know what his master is up to. I have called you friends, because I let you know everything I learned from my Father. ¹⁶You didn't choose me; I chose you. And I selected you to go out and produce fruit. And your fruit will last because my Father will provide you with whatever you request using my name. ¹⁷This is what I command you: you shall love each other.

¹⁸"**If the world hates you**, don't forget that it hated me first. ¹⁹If you were at home in the world, the world would befriend ⟨you as⟩ its own. But you are not at home in the world. On the contrary, I have chosen you out of the world; that's why the world hates you. ²⁰Recall what I told you: 'slaves are never better than their masters.' If they persecuted me, they'll surely persecute you. If they follow my teaching, they'll also follow yours. ²¹Yet they are going to do all these things to you because of me, since they don't know the one who sent me.

²²"If I hadn't come and spoken to them, they wouldn't be guilty of sin. But as it is, they have no excuse for their sin.

²³"Those who hate me also hate my Father.

²⁴"If I hadn't performed feats among them such as no one else has ever performed, they wouldn't be guilty of sin. But as it is, they have witnessed ⟨these feats⟩ and come to hate both me and my Father. ²⁵This has happened so the saying in their Law would be fulfilled:

> They hated me for no reason.

²⁶"When the advocate comes, the one I'll send you from the Father, the spirit of truth that emerges from the Father, he will testify on my behalf. ²⁷And you are going to testify because you were with me from the beginning."

16

"**I've told you these things** to keep you from being misled. ²They are going to throw you out of their congregations. But the time is coming when those

---

15:7
//Q 11:9–10,
Mt 7:7–8,
Lk 11:9–10;
Cf. Mk 11:24;
Mt 21:22; Th 2,
92:1, 94;
Ⓣ Jn 14:13–14,
16:24

15:13
Ⓣ Jn 10:15,
1 Jn 3:16,
GSav 4:9

15:14
Cf. Mk 3:35,
Mt 12:50, Lk 8:21

15:16
Cf. Jn 14:13–14,
16:24;
Ⓣ Gnaz 11

15:18–19
Cf. GSav 13:12–15

15:18
Cf. Mk 13:13,
Mt 10:22, Lk 21:17

15:20
//Q 6:40,
Mt 10:24–25,
Lk 6:40, DSav 20:1;
Ⓘ Jn 13:16

15:23
Cf. Q 10:16,
Mt 10:40, Lk 10:16

15:25
◊ Ps 35:19, 69:4

15:26–27
Ⓣ Jn 14:16–17,
16:13

16:1–2
//Mk 13:9–13,
Mt 24:9–12,
Lk 21:12–19

16:2
Cf. Mt 10:17,
Lk 21:16;
◊ Is 66:5

15:13 *friends:* See the note on 13:34.   **15:18–19** *the world:* See the note on 7:7.
15:15 *no longer . . . slaves:* Contrast 8:33–34.

who kill you will think they are offering devotion to God. [3]They are going to do these things because they never knew the Father or me. [4]Yet I have told you all this so, when the time comes, you'll recall that I told you about them. I didn't tell you these things at first because I was with you then. [5]Now I am on my way to the one who sent me, and not one of you asks me, 'Where are you going?' [6]Yet because I've told you these things, you are filled with grief. [7]But I'm telling you the truth: you'll be better off if I leave. You see, if I don't leave, the advocate can't come to you. But if I go, I'll send the advocate to you.

[8]"When the advocate comes, he will show the world how wrong it is about sin, righteousness, and judgment: [9]about sin because they don't believe in me; [10]about righteousness because I am going to the Father and you won't see me anymore; [11]about judgment because the ruler of this world stands condemned.

[12]"I still have a lot to tell you, but you can't handle it just now. [13]When the advocate comes, the spirit of truth, he will guide you to the complete truth. He will not speak on his own authority, but will tell only what he hears and will disclose to you what is going to happen. [14]He will glorify me because he will disclose to you what he gets from me. [15]Everything the Father has belongs to me; that's why I told you, 'He will disclose to you what he gets from me.' [16]After a time you won't see me anymore, and then again a little later you will see me."

[17]Some of his disciples remarked to each other, "What does he mean when he tells us, 'After a time you won't see me, and then again a little later you will see me'? And what does he mean by, 'I'm going to return to the Father'?" [18]So they asked, "What does 'a little later' mean? We don't understand what he's talking about."

[19]Jesus realized that they wanted to ask him questions, so he said to them, "Have you been discussing my remark 'After a time you won't see me, and then again a little later you will see me'? [20]Let me tell you this: you will weep and mourn, but the world will celebrate. You will grieve, but your grief will turn to joy. [21]A woman suffers pain when she gives birth because her time has come. When her child is born, in her joy she no longer remembers her labor because a human being has come into the world. [22]And so you are now going to grieve. But I'll see you again, and then you'll rejoice, and no one will be able to take

---

16:4–5
ⓣ Th 92:2,
SJas 9:7–8

16:5
ⓣ SJas 2:4

16:7
ⓣ SJas 6:34

16:13
ⓣ Jn 14:16–17,
15:26–27; DSav7:4

16:16
ⓣ SJas 6:40

16:20
ⓣ Q 6:21;
Mt 5:4, 6;
Lk 6:21,
DSav 8;
SJas 6:31–32

16:4 Many mss read "their time" in place of *the time*.

16:4 The perspective of this Farewell Address, while given as if during Jesus' lifetime, is the future, when Jesus will no longer be present, and he speaks—as he does characteristically throughout this gospel—as if from heaven.

16:5 *not one of you asks me, "Where are you going?"*: The author here forgets, or does not know about, 13:36. See the note on 14:31.

16:8 *the world:* See the note on 7:7.

16:9–11 The logic, and therefore meaning, of these verses

is notoriously difficult to understand.

16:11 *the ruler of this world:* See the note on 12:31.

16:16–19 *After a time . . . a little later:* These two phrases are synonymous; they translate the same Greek expression.

16:20 *the world:* See the note on 7:7.

16:21 *the world:* In contrast to its use in v. 20 and elsewhere, here the phrase has a positive, or at least neutral, meaning.

your joy away from you. ²³When that time comes you'll ask nothing of me. Let me tell you this: if you ask the Father for anything using my name, he will grant it to you. ²⁴Up until now you haven't asked for anything using my name. Ask and you'll receive, so your joy will be complete.

²⁵"I've been talking to you in figures of speech. The time is coming when I'll no longer speak to you in figures but will tell you about the Father in plain language. ²⁶When that time comes, you will ask using my name. Now I'm not saying that I will ask the Father for you, ²⁷since the Father himself loves you because you have befriended me and have believed that I came from God. ²⁸I came from the Father and entered the world. Once again, I'm going to leave the world and return to the Father."

²⁹His disciples respond, "Now you're using plain language rather than talking in riddles. ³⁰Now we see that you know everything and don't need anyone to question you. That's why we believe you have come from God."

³¹"So now you believe?" Jesus answered. ³²"Look, the time is coming—actually it's already here—for each of you to be scattered to your own home. You'll abandon me, but I won't be alone because the Father is with me. ³³I have told you all this so you can enjoy peace in me. In the world you're going to face persecution. But be brave! I have triumphed over the world."

17 **Jesus spoke these words**, then he looked up to heaven and prayed. "Father, the time has come. Glorify your son, so your son may glorify you. ²Just as you have granted him authority over all humanity, so he can grant unending life to everyone you have given him. ³This is unending life: to know you, the one true God, and Jesus Anointed, the one you sent. ⁴I glorified you on earth by finishing the work you gave me to do. ⁵Now, you Father, glorify me in your own presence with the glory I shared with you before the world began.

⁶"I have revealed who you really are to all those you gave me out of the world. They were yours, you gave them to me, and they have kept your word. ⁷They now recognize that everything you gave me is really from you. ⁸I passed on to them the things you gave me to say, and they've accepted them and have come to know truly that I have come from you; they've also come to believe that you sent me. ⁹I plead on their behalf. I'm not pleading for the world but for those you gave me because they are yours. ¹⁰Everything that belongs to me is yours, and everything that belongs to you is mine, so I have been glorified by them.

¹¹"I am no longer in the world, but they are still in the world, while I go you. Holy Father, keep them under your protection—all those you have given me—

16:23–24
Cf. Mk 11:24,
Mt 21:21–22,
Q11:9–10,
Mt 7:7–8,
Lk 11:9–10;
Ⓣ Jn 14:13–14;
15:7, 16

16:23
Ⓣ SJas6:37

16:25
Ⓣ SJas 6:5

16:28
Ⓣ SJas2:4, 9:7

16:32
//GSav 4:4–5;
cf. Mk 14:27,
Mt 26:31;
◊Zec 13:7

16:33
//GSav 13:14

17:4–5
Ⓣ GSav 14:22

17:4
Ⓣ GSav 4:11

17:5
Ⓣ SJas 6:13

17:6
Ⓣ GNaz 11

16:32 *you'll abandon me:* a prediction that is not fulfilled, unlike the synoptics, in this gospel.
16:33 *the world:* See the note on 7:7.
17:6 *who you really are:* literally, "your name."

17:9 *the world:* See the note on 7:7. Similarly in vv. 11, 14, 15 of this chapter, but in v. 5 and possibly vv. 6, 13 the phrase does not have this negative connotation.

so they may be one just as we are. ¹²When I was with them, I kept them under your protection, and I guarded them. Not one of them was lost, except the one destined to be lost, since scripture has to be fulfilled. ¹³Now I'm returning to you, but I'm saying these things while I'm still in the world, so they can fully share my joy. ¹⁴I have passed on your message to them, and the world has hated them because they are aliens in the world, as I am an alien in the world. ¹⁵I'm not asking you to remove them from the world, but to keep them safe from evil. ¹⁶They are aliens in the world, as I am. ¹⁷Consecrate them in truth. 'Your word is truth.' ¹⁸I sent them into the world just as you sent me into the world. ¹⁹And I now consecrate myself for their sakes, so they too may be consecrated in truth.

²⁰"I am not pleading only for them, but also for those who believe in me as a result of their message: ²¹they should all be one, just as you, Father, are with me and I with you. May they be one with us, so the world will believe that you sent me. ²²The glory you granted me I passed on to them, so they may be one, as we are one, ²³I with them and you with me, so they may be perfectly united, so the world will know you sent me and loved them just as you loved me. ²⁴Father, I want those you gave me to be with me wherever I am, so they can see my glory—the glory you have bestowed on me because you loved me before the foundation of the world. ²⁵Honored Father, even though the world did not know you, I knew you, and these ⟨you gave me⟩ knew that you sent me. ²⁶I also revealed to them who you really are and will continue to reveal that, so the love you have for me may be in them, and I in them."

18 **When he had said all this,** Jesus went out with his disciples across the Kidron valley. There was a garden there where he and his disciples went. ²But because Jesus had often gone there with his disciples, Judas, who was about to turn him in, knew the place too. ³So it wasn't long before Judas arrives, bringing with him the battalion ⟨of Roman soldiers⟩ and some of the police from the chief priests and the Pharisees, with their lanterns and torches and weapons.

⁴Jesus, of course, knew just what would happen to him, so he went right up to them and says, "Who is it you're looking for?"

⁵"Jesus the Nazarene," was their reply.

"I am," says Jesus.

(And all the while Judas, who was turning him in, was standing there with them.) ⁶But as soon as he said, "I am," they all retreated and fell to the ground.

17:17
◊ Ps 119:160

17:18
//GSav 13:11

17:20
Ⓣ SJas 6:36

17:21
Cf. GSav 4:6

17:25–26
Cf. Q 10:22,
Mt 11:27, Lk 10:22

18:1–12
//Mk 14:43–52,
Mt 26:47–56,
Lk 22:47–54

18:1
//Mk 14:32,
Mt 26:36

17:21 Many mss read merely "in us" in place of *one in us.*

18:1 *went out:* that is, from the place of the last supper, chapters 13–17.

Kidron valley: separating Jerusalem and the Mount of Olives.

18:3 *battalion:* a modern approximation of the Roman *co-*hort, consisting of six hundred men; certainly an exaggeration.

18:5 *I am:* See the note on 4:26.

18:6 *retreated and fell to the ground:* This unrealistic reaction is to be understood as the consequence of Jesus' words, reiterated from v. 5.

Before Annas

Peter's first denial

Trial before the chief priest

Peter's second denial

⁷So Jesus asked them again, "Who is it you're looking for?"

"Jesus the Nazarene," they said.

⁸"I told you that I am," Jesus answered, "so if it's me you're looking for, let the others go."

(⁹This was so the prediction he had made would be fulfilled: "I haven't lost one—not one of those you gave me.")

¹⁰Simon Peter had brought along a sword, and now he drew it, slashed at the chief priest's slave, who was called Malchus, and cut off his right ear.

¹¹"Put the sword back in its scabbard," Jesus told Peter. "I have to drink from the cup my Father has given me, don't I?"

¹²**Then the battalion** and their captain, with the Judean police, arrested Jesus and bound him. ¹³They took him first to Annas. (Annas was the father-in-law of that year's chief priest, Caiaphas. ¹⁴Remember, it was Caiaphas who had given the Judeans this advice: You're better off having one man die for the people.)

¹⁵**Simon Peter** and another disciple were trailing along behind Jesus. This other disciple, who was an acquaintance of the chief priest, went in with Jesus to the chief priest's courtyard. ¹⁶Peter was standing outside the gate; so this other disciple, the acquaintance of the chief priest, went out, had a word with the woman who kept watch at the gate, and got Peter in.

¹⁷The slave woman who kept watch at the gate says to Peter, "You're not one of this man's disciples too, are you?"

"No, I'm not," he replies.

¹⁸Meanwhile, since it was cold, the slaves and police had made a charcoal fire and were standing around it, trying to keep warm. Peter was standing there too, warming himself.

¹⁹**Now the chief priest** interrogated Jesus about his disciples and about his teaching.

²⁰"I have spoken openly to anyone and everyone," Jesus replied. "I've always taught in meeting places and in the temple area, in places where all Jewish people gather. I've said nothing in secret. ²¹Why are you asking me? Ask those who heard what I said. You'll see that they know what I said."

²²As soon as he said this, one of the policemen on duty there slapped Jesus. "How dare you talk back to the chief priest!" he said.

²³"If I've said something wrong, show what's wrong with it," Jesus said in reply. "But if I'm right, why are you slapping me?"

²⁴At that Annas sent him, still bound, to the chief priest, Caiaphas.

²⁵**Meanwhile**, Simon Peter was still standing outside, keeping warm. The others there said to him, "You're not one of his disciples too, are you?"

He denied it. "No, I'm not," he said.

²⁶One of the chief priest's slaves, a relative of the one whose ear Peter had cut off, says, "I saw you in the garden with him, didn't I?"

18:11
Ⓣ Mk 14:36,
Mt 26:39, Lk 22:42

18:14
Ⓣ Jn 11:50

18:15–18
//Mk 14:66–68,
Mt 26:69–70,
Lk 22:54–57

18:19–24
//Mk 14:55–65,
Mt 26:59–68,
Lk 22:66–71

18:20
Cf. Mk 14:49,
Mt 26:55, Lk 22:53

18:25–27
//Mk 14:69–72,
Mt 26:71–75,
Lk 22:58–62

²⁷Once again Peter denied it. At that very moment a rooster crowed.

²⁸**They then take Jesus** from Caiaphas' place to the governor's residence. By now it was early morning. (They didn't actually go into the governor's residence, or else they would become unclean, and unable to eat the Passover meal.) ²⁹So Pilate came out and says to them, "What charge are you bringing against this man?"

³⁰"If he hadn't committed a crime," they retorted, "we wouldn't have turned him over to you."

³¹"Deal with him yourselves," Pilate said to them. "Judge him by your own law."

"But it's illegal for us to execute anyone," the Judeans said to him.

(³²They said this so Jesus' prediction of how he would die would be fulfilled.)

³³Then Pilate went back into his residence. He summoned Jesus and asked him, "*You* are 'the King of the Judeans'?"

³⁴"Is this what you think," Jesus answered, "or what other people have told you about me?"

³⁵"Am I a Judean?!" countered Pilate. "It's your own people and the chief priests who have turned you over to me. What have you done?"

³⁶To this Jesus responded, "My empire is not part of this world. If it were, my people would be fighting to keep me from being turned over to the Judeans. But the truth is that my empire does not belong here."

³⁷"So you are a king!" said Pilate.

"You're the one saying I'm a king," responded Jesus. "This is what I was born for, and this is why I came into the world: to testify to the truth. Everyone who belongs to the truth listens to my voice."

³⁸"What is the truth?" says Pilate.

When he had said this, he again went out to the Judeans. "In my judgment there is no case against him," he says to them. ³⁹"But it's your privilege at

18:28–40
//Mk 15:1–15;
Mt 27:1–2, 11–26;
Lk 23:1–7, 13–25

18:33–38
Cf. Mk 15:2,
Mt 27:1, Lk 23:2–3

18:36–37
Ⓣ GSav 13:8

18:28 *become unclean, and unable to eat the Passover meal:* Ritual purification before observing a sacred rite precluded associating too closely with any pagan, that is, unclean, person or thing.

18:29 Pilate begins to shuttle back and forth, between Jesus within the residence and the Judeans outside. The narrative evidently wants to show him at the mercy of two powers, each stronger than himself.

18:31 *it's illegal for us:* The accuracy of this claim is doubtful. It also suggests that the Jewish authorities would have executed Jesus if they could (see the note on 19:16).

18:32 *so Jesus' prediction of how he would die would be fulfilled:* The logic here seems to be that since Jesus has predicted he would be "elevated" (3:14; 12:32–33), taken to

refer to a crucifixion, he must be put to death by the Romans, not given a Jewish execution by stoning. The Jewish leaders' excluding themselves inadvertently determines that Jesus will be crucified.

18:36 *people:* The Greek word, elsewhere translated "police" and used of servants to the Judean authorities, can hardly mean that here.

18:38 *What is the truth?:* An expression of Pilate's bewilderment. He does not cynically raise a hopeless philosophical question, as it is often held, but simply despairs of getting to the bottom of the facts.

18:39 Outside the gospels there is no evidence for such a *privilege.*

Trial before Pilate continues

Passover to have me free one prisoner for you. So, do you want me to free 'the King of the Judeans' for you?"

⁴⁰At this they shouted back, "Not this guy—Barabbas!" (Barabbas was an insurgent.)

19 Then Pilate had Jesus taken away and flogged.

²And the soldiers wove a crown out of thorns and put it on his head; they also dressed him up in a purple robe. ³They began marching up to him and saying, "Greetings, 'King of the Judeans,'" as they slapped him in the face.

⁴Pilate went outside once more. "See here," he says, "I'm bringing him out to make it clear to you that in my judgment there is no case against him."

⁵Now Jesus came outside, still wearing the crown of thorns and the purple robe.

Pilate says to them, "Look at the man!"

⁶When the chief priests and the police saw him, they screamed, "Crucify! Crucify!"

"Deal with him yourselves," Pilate tells them. "You crucify him. I've told you already: I don't find him guilty of any crime."

⁷"We have our law," the Judeans answered, "and our law says that he must die because he has made himself out to be God's son."

⁸When Pilate heard this kind of talk he was even more afraid. ⁹He went back into his residence.

"Where are you from?" he asks Jesus.

But Jesus didn't answer him.

¹⁰"You won't speak to me?" says Pilate. "Don't you get it? I have the power to free you, and I have the power to crucify you."

¹¹"You would have no power of any kind over me," said Jesus, "unless it was given to you from above. That is why the one who turned me in to you has committed the greater sin."

¹²At this, Pilate began to look for a way to release him. But the Judeans screamed at him, "If you free this man, you're no Friend of Caesar! Every self-appointed king is in rebellion against Caesar."

¹³Pilate heard all this, but still he brought Jesus out and sat him on the judge's seat in the place called Stone Pavement (*Gabbatha* in Hebrew). ¹⁴(It was

18:40
Cf. GNaz 9

19:1–3
//Mk 15:16–20,
Mt 27:27–31,
Pet 2:3b–3:4

19:4–16
//Mk 15:1–15;
Mt 27:11–26;
Lk 23:1–7, 13–25

19:9
Cf. Lk 23:9

19:1 Roman *flogging* was a brutal torture reserved for those condemned to death. Metal bits on the ends of whips could inflict horrible wounds.

19:5 *the man:* Or, *the ⟨true⟩ human being*, perhaps the author's irony.

19:11 *the one who turned me in to you:* Usually taken to refer to Judas (18:2–3) but possibly referring to the Judeans.

19:13 *sat him:* or, simply, *sat down*.

Hebrew: As in 5:2 and elsewhere the Semitic word, here of uncertain meaning, is actually in Aramaic.

19:14 *the day of preparation for Passover:* See the note on 19:31.

now about twelve noon on the day of preparation for Passover.) He says to the Judeans, "Look, here's your king."

[15]But they screamed, "Get him out of here! Crucify him!"

"Am I supposed to crucify your king?" asks Pilate.

The chief priests answered him, "The only king we have is Caesar!"

[16]And so, in the end, Pilate turned him over to them to be crucified.

So they took Jesus, [17]who carried the cross by himself, out to the place called Skull (known in Hebrew as *Golgotha*). [18]There they crucified him, and with him two others—one on each side, with Jesus in the middle.

[19]Pilate also had a notice written and posted it on the cross; it read: "Jesus the Nazorean, the King of the Judeans." [20]Many of the Judeans read the notice, since Jesus was crucified near the city and it was written in Hebrew, Latin, and Greek. [21]The chief Judean priests tried protesting to Pilate: "Don't write, 'The King of the Judeans,' but instead, 'This man said, "I am King of the Judeans."'"

[22]Pilate answered them, "What I have written stays written."

[23]When the soldiers had crucified Jesus, they took his clothes and divided them into four shares, one share for each soldier. But his shirt was woven continuously without seam. [24]So they said to each other, "Let's not tear it, but toss to see who gets it."

This happened so that the scripture would be fulfilled that says,

> They divided my garments among them,
> and for my clothes they cast lots.

So that is what the soldiers did. [25]Meanwhile, Jesus' mother, his mother's sister, Mary the wife of Klopas, and Mary of Magdala were standing near his cross. [26]When Jesus saw his mother, and the disciple he loved standing nearby, he says to his mother, "Lady, here is your son." [27]Then he says to the disciple, "Here is your mother." And from that moment the disciple made her part of his family.

[28]**Then, since Jesus knew** that everything was now completed, he says (in order to fulfill the scripture), "I'm thirsty."

19:16
Cf. GHeb 1:6

19:17–30
//Mk 15:22–37,
Mt 27:33–50,
Lk 22:32–46,
Pet 4:1–5

19:24
◊Ps 22:18

19:28–30
Cf. Pet 5:1–5,
GSav 13:16

19:28–29
◊Ps 69:21

19:15 *The only king we have is Caesar!:* The Jewish leaders are portrayed as rejecting all expectation of their messiah, a thoroughly unhistorical element in the story.

19:16 *to them to be crucified:* In the narrative as it stands, "them" can hardly mean anyone but "the Judeans" (unless this is a careless mistake and refers to the soldiers—see v. 23). The resulting implication that all the Jews/Judeans, or perhaps only some Jewish officials, crucified Jesus—as Pilate had suggested (v. 6)—is wholly inaccurate. In historical fact, whatever Pilate's view of Jesus' guilt, it was certainly he who saw to the execution (see v. 19). The monstrous unreality of this half-verse, if it reads as intended, must be entirely a function of theological or political polemic. See the essay on "Jews/Judeans," pp. 203–204.

19:17 *Hebrew:* See the note on 5:2.

19:19 *notice:* At a crucifixion this sign (*titulus* in Latin) was customarily posted on the cross and indicated the crime deserving execution.

19:23–24 *But his shirt . . . to see who gets it:* This detail, not found in the other gospels, perhaps reflects the assumption that the passage from scripture would *be fulfilled* precisely as it is worded.

Joseph buries Jesus

²⁹A bowl of sour wine was sitting there, and so they filled a sponge with wine, stuck it on some hyssop, and held it to his mouth. ³⁰When Jesus had taken some wine, he said, "Now it's complete."

Lowering his head, he handed over the spirit.

³¹Since it was the day of preparation, the Judeans asked Pilate to have the legs of the three broken and the bodies taken away. Otherwise their bodies would remain on the cross during the Sabbath. (You see, that Sabbath was a high holy day.)

³²So the soldiers came and broke the legs of the first man, and then of the other who had been crucified with him. ³³But when they came to Jesus, they could see that he was already dead, so they didn't break his legs. ³⁴Instead, one of the soldiers jabbed him in the side with his spear, and right away blood and water came pouring out. (³⁵The one who observed this has given this testimony and his testimony is true. He knows he is telling the truth, so you too will believe.) ³⁶This happened so the scripture that says,

No bone of his shall be broken,

would be fulfilled, ³⁷as well as another scripture that says,

They shall look at the one they have pierced.

³⁸**After all this**, Joseph of Arimathea—a disciple of Jesus, but a secret one because he was afraid of the Judeans—asked Pilate's permission to take Jesus' body down. Pilate agreed, so Joseph came and took his body down. ³⁹Nicodemus, the one who had first gone to him at night, came too, bringing a mixture of myrrh and aloes weighing about seventy-five pounds. ⁴⁰So they took Jesus' body, and wound it up in strips of burial cloth along with the spices, as the Jews customarily do to bury their dead. ⁴¹Now there was a garden in the place where

19:29
◊ Ps 69:21

19:31
◊ Dt 21:22–23

19:34
Cf. GSav 13:17

19:35
//GSav 13:18

19:36
◊ Ps 34:20

19:37
◊ Zec 12:10

19:38–42
//Mk 15:42–47;
Mt 27:57–61;
Lk 23:50–56;
Pet 2:1–3a, 6:1–4

19:35 Some mss read "continue to believe" in place of *believe*.

19:29 *hyssop:* Possibly an allusion to one of the uses of this plant in Jewish ceremonial, but here the word has often been regarded as an error and variously adapted. The precise species of plant must be uncertain, but the plant usually called hyssop is too delicate to support a sponge full of wine.

The offering of *sour wine* may be either a humane act (the soldiers sharing some of their ordinary wine) or—in view of Jesus' remark—a form of mistreatment like that described in Psalm 69:21.

19:31 *to have the legs of the three broken:* Perhaps a formality declaring the victim dead, or a practice designed to hasten death.

Otherwise their bodies would remain on the cross during the Sabbath: According to Jewish practice the dead must if

possible be buried before sundown; otherwise no later than the next day. But no such work could be done on the Sabbath. This notice seems unaware of the requirement in Deut 21:22–23 that a hanged (including crucified) man must in any case be buried on the same day.

a high holy day: Being also Passover; *the day of preparation* (here and in v. 14) can mean either the day before Passover or simply Friday; in this case it is both.

19:35 This parenthetical remark, with its emphatic validation of the details in v. 34 and its insistence of historical accuracy, is puzzling. Some believe that it has been inserted by a later hand than the author's; if so, the puzzle remains.

19:39 *seventy-five pounds:* a wildly extravagant amount.

he had been crucified, and a new tomb in the garden where no one had ever been laid to rest. ⁴²Since this tomb was handy and because it was the Jewish day of preparation, it was here that they laid Jesus.

20 Early on Sunday, while it was still dark, Mary of Magdala comes to the tomb and sees that the stone has been moved away. ²So she runs and comes to Simon Peter and the other disciple, the one that Jesus loved, and tells them, "They've taken the Master from the tomb, and we don't know where they've put him."

³**So Peter and the other disciple** went out and they make their way to the tomb. ⁴The two of them were running along together, but the other disciple ran faster than Peter and was the first to reach the tomb. ⁵Stooping down, he could see the strips of burial cloth lying there; but he didn't go in. ⁶Then Simon Peter comes along behind him and went in. He too sees the strips of burial cloth there, ⁷and also the cloth they had used to cover his head, lying not with the strips of burial cloth but rolled up by itself. ⁸Then the other disciple, who had been the first to reach the tomb, came in. He saw all this, and he believed. ⁹But since neither of them yet understood the prophecy that he was destined to rise from the dead, ¹⁰these disciples went back home.

¹¹**Mary, however**, stood crying outside, and in her tears she stooped to look into the tomb, ¹²and she sees two heavenly messengers in white seated where Jesus' body had lain, one at the head and the other at the feet.

¹³"Lady, why are you crying?" they ask her.

"They've taken my master away," she tells them, "and I don't know where they've put him."

¹⁴No sooner had she said this than she turned around and sees Jesus standing there—but she didn't realize that it was Jesus.

¹⁵"Lady," Jesus says to her, "why are you crying? Who is it you're looking for?"

Thinking that he was the gardener, she says to him, "Please, mister, if you've moved him, tell me where you've put him so I can take him away."

¹⁶"Mary," says Jesus.

She turns around and exclaims in Hebrew, "*Rabbuni!*" (which means "Teacher").

¹⁷"Let go of me," Jesus tells her, "because I have not yet ascended to the Father. But go to my brothers and tell them this: 'I'm ascending to my Father and your Father—to my God and your God.'"

20:1–18
//Mk 16:1–8,
Mt 28:1–15,
Lk 24:1–11;
cf. Pet 9:1–13:3

20:14–18
Cf. Mary 7:1–2

20:17
//GSav 12:6;
Ⓣ SJas 6:13

20:16 *in Hebrew:* See the note on 5:2.
20:17 *Let go of me:* The meaning of these words is much debated; see the next note.

   because I have not yet ascended to the Father: It is not clear what this, together with the injunction that it seeks

to explain, means: that Jesus must not be deterred from his destination? that he is in an intermediate or unclean state and must not be touched? that Mary's attempt is somehow, in her love for him, to try to draw him back into her world? or what?

¹⁸Mary of Magdala goes and reports to the disciples, "I've seen the Master," and relates everything he had told her.

¹⁹**Now that Sunday evening**, the disciples had locked the doors out of fear of the Judeans, but Jesus came and stood in front of them and he greets them: "Peace."

²⁰Then he showed them his hands and his side. The disciples were delighted to see the Master. ²¹Jesus greets them again: "Peace," he says. "Just as the Father sent me, so now I'm sending you."

²²And at this he breathed over them and says, "Here's some holy spirit. Take it. ²³If you cancel anyone's sins, they are cancelled; if you retain them, they are retained."

²⁴**Now Thomas**, the one known as "the Twin," one of the Twelve, hadn't been with them when Jesus showed up. ²⁵So the other disciples tried to tell him, "We've seen the Master."

But he responded, "Unless I see the holes the nails made, and put my finger in them and my hand in his side, I'll never believe."

²⁶A week later the disciples were again indoors, and this time Thomas was with them. The doors were locked, but Jesus comes and stood in front of them, and said, "Peace." ²⁷Then he says to Thomas, "Put your finger here, and look at my hands; take your hand and put it in my side. Stop doubting and start believing."

²⁸Thomas responded, "My Master! My God!"

²⁹"Do you believe because you've seen me?" asks Jesus. "Congratulations to those who believe without seeing."

³⁰Although Jesus performed many more signs for his disciples to see than could be written down in this book, ³¹these are written down so you will come to believe that Jesus is the Anointed One, the son of God—and by believing this have life in his name.

21 **Some time after** these events, Jesus again appeared to his disciples by the Sea of Tiberias. This is how he did it.

²When Simon Peter and Thomas, the one known as "the Twin," were together, along with Nathanael from Cana, Galilee, the sons of Zebedee, and two other disciples, ³Simon Peter says to them, "I'm going fishing."

"We're coming with you," they reply.

20:18
//Mary 6:4

20:19–23
//Lk 24:33–49;
cf. Mk 16:14–18

20:21
//GSav 13:11

20:23
Cf. Mt 16:19, 18:18

20:29
Cf. SJas 3:6–7;
Ⓣ SJas 8:6,
GSav 12:5

21:1–8
Cf. Lk 5:4–11

20:31 Some mss read "continue to believe" in place of *come to believe*.

20:24 *Twin:* See the note on 11:16.
20:30–31 These verses conclude the original gospel, in the view of most scholars, chapter 21 being a later addition, whether by the same author or (more likely) another.
21:2 *Twin:* See the note on 11:16.

They went down and got into the boat, but that night they didn't catch a thing. ⁴It was already getting light when Jesus appeared on the shore, but his disciples didn't recognize that it was Jesus.

⁵"You boys haven't caught any fish, have you?" Jesus asks them.

"No," they replied.

⁶He told them, "Cast your net on the right side of the boat and you'll have better luck."

So they cast the net, but then couldn't haul it in because of the huge number of fish. ⁷That disciple whom Jesus loved exclaims to Peter, "It's the Master!"

When Simon Peter heard, "It's the Master," he tied his cloak around himself, since he was stripped for work, and threw himself into the water. ⁸The rest of the disciples came by boat, dragging the net full of fish. (Actually, they were not far from land, only about a hundred yards.)

⁹**When they got to shore**, they see a charcoal fire burning, with fish cooking on it, and some bread. ¹⁰Jesus says to them, "Bring some of the fish you've just caught."

¹¹Then Simon Peter went aboard and ⟨helped⟩ haul in the net full of large fish ashore—one hundred fifty-three of them. Even though there were so many of them, the net still didn't tear.

¹²Jesus says to them, "Come on, eat."

None of the disciples dared ask, "Who are you?" They knew it was the Master. ¹³Jesus comes, takes the bread, and gives it to them, and passes the fish around as well.

¹⁴This was now the third time after he had been raised from the dead that Jesus appeared to his disciples.

¹⁵**When they had eaten**, Jesus asks Simon Peter, "Simon, son of John, do you love me more than they do?"

"Of course, Master; you know I love you," he replies.

"Then feed my lambs," Jesus tells him.

¹⁶Jesus asks him again, for the second time, "Simon, son of John, do you love me?"

"Yes, Master; you know I love you," he replies.

"Tend my sheep."

¹⁷Jesus says to him a third time, "Simon, son of John, do you love me?"

21:7 *tied his cloak around himself, since he was stripped for work:* This sentence is usually rendered "put on his (outer) garment, for he was naked" or similarly; so understood it is highly anomalous in view of Peter's jumping into the water that follows. Peter's action means literally "girded himself" and the word for "naked" need mean only "not fully clad." As translated here the difficulty disappears. Peter was stripped to the waist for heavy work in the boat and so girded up the garments tied about his waist, so as to swim and wade ashore.

21:11 *aboard:* or, *ashore,* the Greek word meaning either.

Peter was hurt that he had asked him for the third time, "Do you love me?" and he says to him, "Master, you know everything; you know I love you."

Jesus says to him, "Feed my sheep. ¹⁸Let me tell you this: when you were young you used to gather your cloak about you and go where you wanted to go. But when you've grown old, you'll stretch out your arms, and someone else will get you ready and take you where you don't want to go."

(¹⁹He said this to indicate the kind of death by which Peter would glorify God.)

And after saying this, he adds, "Keep following me."

²⁰**Peter turns** and sees the disciple Jesus loved following them, the one who had leaned back on Jesus' chest at supper and asked, "Master, who's going to turn you in?" ²¹When Peter saw this disciple ⟨following⟩, he asks Jesus, "Master, what about this one?"

²²Jesus replies to him, "What's it to you if I want him to stay around till I come? You keep on following me."

(²³Because of this the rumor spread among the family of believers that this disciple wouldn't die. But Jesus had not said to him, "He won't die"; he said, "What's it to you if I want him to stay around till I come?")

²⁴**This is the disciple** who is testifying to all this and has written it down, and we know that his testimony is truthful.

²⁵Jesus of course did many other things. If they were all to be recorded in detail, I doubt that the entire world would hold the books that would have to be written.

21:24
Cf. GSav 13:18   **21:23** Some mss omit *What's it to you?*

21:18 *you'll stretch out your arms:* Apparently a prediction that Peter is to be crucified (see the note on v. 19).

get you ready: or, *gird you,* that is, perhaps, "tie you (to a cross)?"

21:23 Evidently it had been believed at one time in the Johannine community that "the disciple Jesus loved" (13:23) would not die. (Was this disciple—mentioned first only in chapter 13—identified with Lazarus of chapters 11–12, "whom Jesus loved" and who had already died? Or does this disciple exemplify Jesus' promise in 8:51?) Presumably this figure, if a real person, had in fact died by the time this chapter was written, and the saying that would have given rise to the belief is shown to have been misunderstood.

21:24 *This is the disciple who is testifying to all this:* Possibly "the disciple Jesus loved" had functioned as an authority standing at the beginning of the Johannine tradition. On the other hand, this assertion, together with the confidence that the evidence is *true,* may be either inadvertently inac-

curate or even (some would claim) deliberately invented. It is widely thought unlikely that very much of the information in this gospel has historical accuracy (since that is what "true" here seems to mean).

and has written it down: This cannot be true. In its completed form this gospel, like the other three, was hardly written by an eyewitness to the events it records. And perhaps still less than the synoptic gospels does it contain tradition that would have stemmed from one of Jesus' disciples. It is interesting, nevertheless, that this gospel alone contains, as a brief epilogue to the appended chapter 21, a claim as to its authorship. The title at the work's beginning, "[The Gospel] according to John," as with the other gospels, was prefixed to the text only in the latter half of the second century. There is no suggestion in the text that "the disciple Jesus loved" was named John.

21:25 This exaggerated observation seems to have been modeled on the earlier conclusion, 20:30–31.

Sayings and Dialogue Gospels

The final page of the Coptic Gospel of Thomas with the subscript title "The Gospel according to Thomas." Below the title is the beginning of the Gospel of Philip. *Photograph courtesy of the Institute for Antiquity and Christianity, Claremont, CA. Used by permission.*

The Q Gospel

Introduction

A hypothetical text

"Q" is an abbreviation of the German word *Quelle*, meaning "source." It is used to designate a document that most scholars believe the authors of Matthew and Luke used in writing their gospels. These gospel writers, it is believed, also used the Gospel of Mark. While Mark is an extant text, Q is a hypothetical construct. No independent copy of it exists. But it is widely believed that the passages in Matthew and Luke that are almost the same, often in the same sequence, and that did not come from Mark, must have come from this lost source, Q. The non-Markan passages common to Matthew and Luke agree word-for-word so often that most scholars believe Q must have been a written document and not simply oral tradition, though oral tradition also probably played a role. The theory that Q and Mark were literary sources for the Gospels of Matthew and Luke is called the Two Document Theory. This theory was first proposed about 150 years ago. In recent years, there has been renewed interest in Q, and significant progress has been made in isolating and understanding it.

One convention of scholarship has to do with how to refer to passages in Q. Since Q scholars believe that the sequence of sayings and often their wording are best preserved in Luke's gospel, references to Q adopt the chapter and verse numbers of Luke. Accordingly, Q 3:7–9 refers to the Q material behind Luke 3:7–9 (and its Matthean parallel).

A sayings gospel

Q is a collection of the sayings of Jesus, similar in form to the Gospel of Thomas. Unlike the sayings in Thomas, however, most of the sayings in Q are gathered into discourses. One of these is the Sermon on the Mount (Matthew) or Plain (Luke)—see the different settings for this discourse in Matt 5:1 and Luke 6:12. Other discourses focus on John the Baptist (Q 7:18–35), mission instructions to the disciples (10:2–16), prayer (11:9–13), exorcism (11:14–26), condemnation of Pharisees (11:39–52), and other subjects. Not all of Q consists of sayings, however. Q also included at least two bits of narrative: the story of the temptation of Jesus in 4:1–13 and a miracle story in 7:1–10.

To call Q a "gospel" is not to ignore the fact that it belongs to a different genre than the canonical gospels, namely a sayings collection. The word "gospel" is used because Q, like the canonical gospels, presents a version of Jesus' message.

The language of Q

Q is not simply a transcript of the words of Jesus. One sign of this is the language in which Q was probably written. Most scholars believe that the first language of Jesus and his followers was Aramaic, though they may also have known some Greek. In any case, Q was written in Greek. The frequent word-for-word agreements between Matthew and Luke make highly unlikely older speculation about Q being originally in Aramaic. Furthermore, most of Q's quotations or allusions to the Old Testament depend upon the Septuagint, the Greek version of the Hebrew Bible.

An early gospel

Since Q was, by definition, earlier than Matthew or Luke, it represents a very early version of the gospel. Q has generated much interest because it lacks many things one might expect in an early document dealing with Jesus, especially stories about Jesus' death and resurrection. It also lacks the title "Anointed"(Christ or messiah). No disciples are named. There are no birth stories, and all but one of the many miracle stories found elsewhere in the canonical gospels are missing. Because of all this, earlier scholars thought Q was not a gospel in itself, but only a teaching document that assumed its audience was familiar with the stories told in the canonical gospels. The discovery of the Gospel of Thomas, however, demonstrated that a sayings collection could stand by itself as a gospel.

Jesus and his message

Jesus appears in Q as a wise teacher and prophet. In fact, Jesus implicitly links himself to the prophets of Israel's past, who were, Q says, consistently rejected, even killed (Q 6:23; 11:47–49; 13:34–35). This is a perspective on Israel's history that is found in the Hebrew Bible itself (e.g., Neh 9; Jer 7:25–29; 25:3–7; 2 Chr 30:6–9; Zech 7:4–14).

Like the rejected prophets of the past, Jesus called God's people to live according to God's will. Jesus' death is presumed in Q (13:34–35), but not described. It is seen as evidence of the unbelief of the people, not as an act that brings salvation. Jesus' disappearance is hinted at in 13:35, which some scholars see as a reference to Jesus assumption into heaven. If so, then in Q Jesus is not raised from the dead but "taken up" in somewhat the same way as Enoch (Gen 5:24) and Elijah (2 Kgs 2:1,11). From there, Jesus is to return, at some unpredictable time, as the "Human One" (e.g., Q 12:40 and 17:24).

Prophets play a significant role in Q (6:23; 7:24–28; 10:24; 11:47, 49–51; 13:34). Q 6:23 likens the troubles of the Q audience to those of the prophets, indicating that the people who used Q also saw themselves in the prophetic tradition.

The message of the Jesus in Q is that God's empire is at hand and that it is time to embrace this empire by adopting a radical lifestyle. Although no direct reference is made to the inescapable reality of the Roman Empire, the contrast between God's empire and that of Rome would have been obvious. Deep confidence in God's gracious, fatherly rule lies at the basis of Jesus' teachings about non-violence (6:22–23), love of enemies (6: 27–30), and unlimited forgiveness (17:4; see 11:4), as well as his confidence in God's care (11:2b–4, 9–13) and freedom from anxiety about food or clothing (12:22b–31, 33–34). At the same time, the Jesus of Q warns about the hypocrisy of reputed leaders (11:39–44, 46b, 52, 47–48) as well as the temptations of emulating elites.

Wisdom in Q

As a collection of sayings, Q already belongs to a tradition with roots in ancient Israel and the Middle East, namely the wisdom tradition. In addition, in Q we meet the figure of personified Wisdom as a divine feminine figure who sends prophets and sages (Q 11:49; see 7:35; 11:31). This is a figure known from Jewish tradition (e.g., Prov 9:1–6; Sir 24; WisSol 6:12–16; 7:22–30). A double movement is associated with this figure: she both seeks to draw associates to her, and she is sought by them as the source of understanding. Jesus functions that way too in Q. Thus, while Jesus is not specifically identified with Wisdom in Q, the influence of that tradition is clear.

According to Q 11:49, Wisdom sent prophets to Israel. This means that in Q we have a combination of the wisdom and prophetic traditions, though this was not really new (see, e.g., Prov 1:20–33). But as a way of identifying Jesus' role, it does make Q different from the canonical gospels.

The people behind Q

Q seems to be a gospel that is rooted in the rural peasantry of Galilee. It mentions only a few place-names: a town on the north shore of the Sea of Galilee (Capernaum in 7:1 and 10:15, and nearby Chorazin and Bethsaida in 10:13), as well as the Syrian towns of Tyre and Sidon (10:13, 14). Jerusalem (13:34) is a place that rejects prophets. The imagery in Q is also rural, not urban, and when references are made to urban settings, these have a negative tone. Q, thus, is not only a very early gospel, but seems closer to the Jesus of ancient Galilee than the Jesus of the canonical gospels.

One gets the impression from Jesus' Sermon (6:20–49) that the Q people thought of themselves as an oppressed group—poor, hungry, and weeping (6:20–23). This situation required them to reflect on how to respond to their enemies (6:27–38). But they also had a need to maintain internal cohesion and commitment, something demanded in Q 6:39–49 (see also 11:34–36 and 12:2–12). The marginal situation of these people is reflected in the concern about food and clothing in Q 12:22–31.

The mission charge in Q 10:2–16 provides another glimpse into the life of the people who composed and used Q. Their mission was exceedingly demand-ing—and apparently unsuccessful, as we can gather from Q 10:13–15 (see also 7:31–35; 11:29–32, 39–52; 13:34–35). The theme of being rejected occurs over and over again in Q. The Q people seem to have accepted splitting up families as the expected result of following Jesus (9:59–60; 12:53; 14:26).

Most scholars date Q from about 50 to 70 CE because of its use by Matthew and Luke, and because of the unique and rather distinctive nature of its view of Jesus. One may speculate that this early group of followers died out, and that their message survived only by being re-contextualized by its insertion into the different story of Jesus that Matthew and Luke knew from Mark.

It is difficult to know how many of the sayings ascribed to Jesus were uttered by him. We are probably safe in assuming that the selection of the sayings, their composition into discourses, and much of the wording reflect the Q people more than Jesus himself. But even if this is so, it is no loss. For the people who wrote and used Q were an extraordinarily interesting group. And careful readers will be able to read between the lines and recreate in their imaginations some of the very earliest followers of Jesus—and perhaps a more provocative view of Jesus himself.

The reconstructed text of Q

Since the proposal of the Q hypothesis in the mid nineteenth century, scholars have carefully compared Matthew and Luke in order to reconstruct the word-ing of Q. Naturally, the results of such attempts differed in many particulars. Scholars gradually refined the methods for reconstructing Q (see "Establishing the Text of Q" on pp. 261–62) and the differences began to narrow.

In 1989 the International Q Project (IQP) was launched by the Institute for Antiquity and Christianity at Claremont Graduate University in California. For nearly two decades an international team of over forty Q specialists pored over a century and a half of scholarship on Q and collaborated on a meticulous word-by-word analysis of the Greek texts of Matthew and Luke. The result of this erudition was published in 2000 as *The Critical Edition of Q* (edited by James M. Robinson, John S. Kloppenborg, and Paul Hoffmann). The present edition of *The Complete Gospels* incorporates the text of Q produced by the IQP. (The few places where the Scholars Version differs from the IQP text are indicated in the notes.)

In keeping with the high standards of intellectual integrity demanded by critical scholarship, the IQP presents its reconstruction of Q not as a sure thing, but with varying degrees of certainty in different passages. For example, in some places there is so little agreement between Matthew and Luke that the wording of Q cannot be recovered with any acceptable probability. In a few other cases there are good reasons to think that a passage that occurs only in Matthew or Luke nevertheless comes from Q. Such passages can be "admitted" into Q, but with caution. Accordingly, *The Complete Gospels* uses three kinds of markers to identify the more problematic passages in the reconstruction of Q:

> Verses in ***italics*** indicate passages attested only in Luke or Matthew. (Verses attested only in Matthew are identified by their chapter and verse numbers from that gospel, preceded by "QMt." For example, QMt 5:41 designates Q material found in Matt 5:41 but not in Luke.)

> **? ?** Verse numbers enclosed by question marks indicate passages about which there is a very low degree of certainty as to whether the text belongs to Q.

> . . . Three dots mean that there must have been some text in Q, but it cannot be reconstructed at all.

Establishing the text of Q

Q no longer exists as a separate text so it must be reconstructed from Matthew and Luke. Three kinds of reconstruction are necessary: assembling the *contents* of Q, determining the *sequence* of its segments, and establishing its *wording* where Matthew and Luke diverge.

The *contents* of Q are, by definition, those passages that Matthew and Luke have in common but that do not come from Mark. In addition, however, there are a few passages for which Mark, Matthew, and Luke all have similar content, but in which there are sufficient common divergences from Mark by Matthew and Luke that scholars suspect that we have two documents—Q and Mark—being combined by Matthew and Luke. An example is the Parable of the Mustard Seed (Mark 4:30–32, Matt 13:31–32, and Luke 13:18–19). Matthew and Luke agree on "the empire . . . is like," the phrase "that a man took," and the birds nesting "in its branches." These agreements over against Mark suggest that there was a Q version of the parable that differed slightly from Mark's.

The *sequence* of Q is established by comparing the sequence of the material in Matthew and Luke, and then asking how one can account for differences between them. The main tool for doing this is knowledge of the editorial tendencies of Matthew and Luke. For example, consider this sequence:

Matthew	Luke	
5:1–7:27	6:20–49	Jesus' Inaugural Sermon
8:5–13	7:1–10	Healing story
11:2–19	7:18–35	John and Jesus
8:19–22	9:57–60	Following Jesus

The location of the "John and Jesus" discourse varies in Matthew and Luke. The other items occur in the same relative order. Matthew has probably shifted the pericope to a later point in his gospel so that the miracles mentioned in 11:4–5 ("Go report to John what you have heard and seen") can first be described. In fact, Matt 8:5–13 becomes the first of a whole series of miracles reported in Matthew 8–9. By moving the "John and Jesus" segment, Matthew has narrated ample evidence for John's disciples to report to him.

Luke sensed the same problem. He solved it, however, by having Jesus perform many miracles on the spot (7:20–21), just before he has Jesus tell John's disciples to go and report to their master what they have seen and heard.

The *wording* of Q is established in a number of ways: simple logic, the study of the editorial tendencies of Matthew and Luke, comparison with Mark and with other independent traditions, and coherence with other Q materials.

In Q 7:35, for example, Matthew (11:19) reads, "Wisdom is vindicated by her deeds," while Luke 7:35 reads, "Wisdom is vindicated by all her children." While the word "children" in Luke could derive from the preceding parable (Luke 7:31–32), it is difficult to explain why Luke would have substituted the unusual "children" for "deeds," since "deeds" goes logically with "vindicated." It is more likely that Q had "children" both in 7:31–32 and 7:35. Moreover, Matthew introduced the whole discourse by referring to the deeds of the Anointed One (11:2); he concludes the discourse by changing "children" to "deeds" to make the final reference agree with the first.

The process of establishing the text of Q, although highly conjectural at many points, can produce fairly reliable results in recreating the contours of what was probably the first gospel.

The Q Gospel

3 ²John . . . ³the whole region around the Jordan

⁷John would say to the crowds that came out to get baptized, "You spawn of Satan! Who warned you to flee from the impending doom? ⁸Well then, start producing fruit suitable for a change of heart, ⁹and don't even think of saying to yourselves, 'We have Abraham for our father.' Let me tell you, God can raise up children for Abraham right out of these rocks! ¹⁰Even now the axe is aimed at the root of the trees. So every tree not producing choice fruit gets cut down and tossed into the fire.

¹⁶"**I baptize you** with water, but someone more powerful than I will succeed me. I'm not fit to take off his sandals. He'll baptize you with holy spirit and fire. ¹⁷His pitchfork is in his hand, and he'll make a clean sweep of his threshing floor, and gather the wheat into his granary, but the chaff he'll burn in a fire that can't be put out."

²¹**Jesus . . . baptized,** the sky opened up ²²and the spirit . . . on him . . . son

4 ¹**Jesus was guided** into the desert by the spirit ²to be put to the test by the devil. He ate nothing for forty days and forty nights . . . he was famished.

³The devil said to him, "To prove you're God's son, order these stones to turn into bread."

⁴Jesus responded, "It is written,

> Human beings shall not live on bread alone."

⁹Then the devil took him to Jerusalem, set him on the high point of the temple, and said to him, "To prove you're God's son, jump off; ¹⁰remember, it is written,

> To his heavenly messengers he will give orders about you,

3:7
//Mt 23:33;
cf. Mt 12:34;
Ⓣ SJas 6:28–29

3:8
Ⓣ Mt 7:16–20,
12:33–35;
Lk 13:6–9;
Ⓘ Acts 13:24;
◊ Is 51:1–2

3:9
//Mt 7:19;
cf. Jn 15:6, Th 40;
◊ Is 10:33–34,
Jer 22:7

3:16
//Mk 1:7–8,
Jn 1:26–27;
cf. Acts 13:25;
Ⓣ Acts 1:5, 11:16,
19:1–7

3:21–22
Cf. Mk 1:9–11,
Mt 3:13–17,
Lk 3:21–22,
Jn 1:29–34,
GHeb 3, GEbi 4

4:1–13
◊ Wis 1:1–5,
2:12–18

4:1–2
//Mk 1:12–13;
◊ Ex 34:28, Dt 9:9

4:4
◊ Dt 8:3

4:10–11
◊ Ps 91:11–12

3:2–3 These are the only words that can be reconstructed with any confidence.
3:21–22 These are the only words that can be reconstructed with any confidence.

3:7 *The impending doom* is the day of the Lord (Yahweh) spoken of by the prophets, e.g., Isa 13:6–13; Mal 3:2; also Rom 2:5.
3:8 *Children for Abraham* is a self-designation for Israel; see John 8:39; Acts 13:26; Rom 4:11–12.
3:16 The Greek word for *spirit* (*pneuma*) also means "wind."
4:1–13 Jesus' responses are quotations from Deuteronomy. The devil quotes from the psalms in vv. 10–11.

4:1–2 Evil spirits were believed to lurk in the desert; see Lev 16:10; Isa 13:21; 34:14; Q 12:43.
4:3 *God's son:* The Greek lacks the article, and may also be translated "a son of God."
4:9 Where on the temple this *high point* (literally, "wing") was supposed to be is unknown. Early tradition says James, the brother of Jesus, was killed by being pushed off this "high point."

¹¹and

with their hands they will catch you, so you won't even stub your toe on a stone."

¹²And in response Jesus said to him, "It is written,

You shall not put the Lord your God to the test."

⁵Then the devil takes him to a very high mountain and shows him all the empires of the world and their splendor, ⁶and says to him, "I'll give you all these, ⁷if you will kneel down and pay homage to me."

⁸Jesus responded, "It is written,

You shall pay homage to the Lord your God, and him alone shall you revere."

¹³And the devil left him.

6 ²⁰**Then he looked** squarely at his disciples and said,

> Congratulations, you poor!
> > God's empire belongs to you.
> ²¹Congratulations, you hungry!
> > You will have a feast.
> Congratulations, you who grieve!
> > You will be consoled.

²²"Congratulations to you when they denounce you and persecute you and spread malicious gossip about you because of the Human One. ²³Rejoice and be glad! In heaven you'll be more than rewarded. Remember, this is how they persecuted the prophets who preceded you.

> ^{?24?}*Damn you rich!*
> > *You already have your consolation.*
> ^{?25?}*Damn you who are well-fed now!*
> > You will know hunger.
> Damn you who laugh now!
> > *You will learn to weep and grieve.*

^{?26?}*"Damn you when everybody speaks well of you! Bear in mind that their ancestors treated the phony prophets the same way.*

²⁷"**Love your enemies** ²⁸and pray for your persecutors. ³⁵You'll then become children of your Father, for God makes the sun rise on both the bad and the good, and sends rain on both the just and the unjust.

4:12
◊ Dt 6:16

4:8
◊ Dt 6:13

6:20
// Th 54;
cf. Lk 6:24, Jas 2:5

6:21a
// Th 69:2;
cf. Lk 6:25a

6:21b
Cf. Lk 6:25b,
Jn 16:20–22

6:22–23
Cf. Lk 6:26

6:22
// Th 68, 1 Pet 4:14;
cf. Th 69:1,
1 Pet 3:14;
◊ Is 66:5

6:23
Cf. Q 11:47–51,
13:34–35;
1 Pet 4:13;
Ⓣ Acts 7:52

6:28b
// GOxy 1224 6:1,
Rom 12:14;
cf. 1 Pet 3:9

6:24–26 IQP does not include this passage. It is doubtful whether it was part of Q.
6:35c–d SV and IQP follow Matthew's sequence for these sayings.

²⁹"When someone slaps you on the cheek, turn the other as well. If someone is determined to sue you for your shirt, let him have your coat along with it. ^{QMt 5:41}*Further, when anyone conscripts you for one mile, go along an extra mile.* ³⁰Give to those who beg from you; and when someone borrows your things, don't ask for them back.

³¹"**Treat people** the way you want them to treat you.

³²"If you love those who love you, why should you be rewarded for that? Even the toll collectors do as much, don't they? ³⁴And if you lend to those from whom you hope to gain, why should you be rewarded for that? Even the pagans do as much, don't they?

³⁶"Be as compassionate as your Father is.

³⁷"**Don't pass judgment**, so you won't be judged. *Don't forget, the judgment you hand out will be the judgment you get back.* ³⁸And the standard you apply will be the standard applied to you.

³⁹"Can one blind person guide another? Won't they both end up in some ditch?

⁴⁰"Students are not above their teachers. It's enough for students to become like their teachers.

⁴¹"Why do you notice the sliver in your friend's eye, but overlook the timber in your own? ⁴²How can you say to your friend, 'Let me get the sliver out of your eye,' when there is that timber in your own? You phony, first take the timber out of your own eye and then you'll see well enough to remove the sliver from your friend's eye.

⁴³"**A choice tree** does not produce rotten fruit, any more than a rotten tree produces choice fruit; ⁴⁴for each tree is known by its fruit. Since when are figs picked from thorns, or grapes from thistles? ⁴⁵The good person produces good things out of a fund of good; and the evil person produces evil things out of a fund of evil. As you know, the mouth gives voice to what the heart is full of.

⁴⁶"**Why do you call me** 'Master, master,' and not do what I tell you? ⁴⁷Everyone who listens to my words and acts on them ⁴⁸is like a person who built a house on bedrock. Later the rain fell, and the floods came, and the winds blew and pounded that house, yet it did not collapse, since its foundation rested on bedrock. ⁴⁹Everyone who listens ⟨to my words⟩ and doesn't act ⟨on them⟩ is like a person who built a house on sand. When the rain fell, and the floods came, and the winds blew and pounded that house, it collapsed—it totally collapsed."

6:29 *cheek*: It is possible that Q read "right cheek" as in Matt 5:39.

6:31 The "Golden Rule" is based on, but reverses, the ancient principle of retaliation. The Golden Rule antedates Jesus, and is found in various forms in Chinese, Indian, Greek, Persian, Jewish, and Arabic sources.
6:32 Toll collectors were a despised group.
6:38b A common Jewish saying; the metaphor is from measuring grain in the market, suggesting exactness in measuring.
6:47–49 Like some other Jewish sayings collections, the Q Sermon concludes with a comparison with a ruined house. See also Job 3–27; Prov 1–9; 22:17–24:22.

The Golden Rule

On judging

By their fruit

Foundations

6:29a
◊Prv 19:11, 20:22, 24:29; Lam 3:30
6:30
Cf. Lk 6:34, Th 95; ◊Prv 25:21
6:31
Cf. Th 6:3, Rom 13:10, Tob 4:15
6:35c
◊Sir 4:10
6:36
◊Dt 18:13(LXX), Lv 19:2
6:37
//Mary 9:12
6:38b
//Mk 4:24; ◊Sir 35:10
6:39
//Th 34
6:40
Cf. Jn 13:16a, 15:20; DSav 20:1c
6:41–42
//Th 26
6:43–45
//Th 45; ⊤ Mt 3:7–10, 12:33–35, 21:33–43
6:44a
◊Sir 27:6
6:44b
//Jas 3:12
6:45
Cf. Mt 12:37, 1 Sm 24:14, Prv 12:14
6:46
//EgerG 3:5
6:47–49
◊Ps 1; Jer 17:5–8; Sir 22:16, 27:3

7 ¹**And so it happened** that, when he had completed this discourse, he went into Capernaum. ³A Roman officer approached him and pleaded with him, "My servant boy is sick."

And Jesus said to him, "I'll come and cure him."

⁶And the officer replied, "Sir, I don't deserve to have you in my house, ⁷but only say the word and my boy will be cured. ⁸After all, I myself am under orders, and I have soldiers under me. I order one to go, and he goes; I order another to come, and he comes; and I order my slave to do something, and he does it."

⁹As Jesus listened he was amazed and said to those who followed, "I'm telling you, not even in Israel have I found such trust."

¹⁸**When John heard** about all these things, he sent his disciples ¹⁹to ask him, "Are you the one who is to come or do we have to wait for another?"

²²And so he answered them, "Go report to John what you have heard and seen:

> The blind see again
>> and the lame walk;
> lepers are cleansed
>> and the deaf hear;
> the dead are raised,
>> and the poor have the good news preached to them.

²³Congratulations to those who don't take offense at me."

²⁴**After they had left,** Jesus began to talk to the crowds about John. "What did you go out to the desert to gawk at? A reed shaking in the wind? ²⁵What did you really go out to see? A man dressed in fancy clothes? But wait! Those who dress fashionably are found in royal houses. ²⁶Come on, what did you go out to see? A prophet? Yes, that's what you went out to see, and even more than a prophet. ²⁷This is the one about whom it was written:

> Here is my messenger,
>> whom I send on ahead of you
>>> to prepare your way before you.

²⁸I'm telling you, among those born of women no one has arisen who is greater than John; yet the least ⟨important⟩ in the empire of God is greater than he is."

Officer's slave healed

John's inquiry

Jesus praises John

7:1–10
//Jn 4:46–53

7:19
① Q 3:16, 13:35;
Mt 21:9; Lk 19:38;
◊ Mal 3:1, 4:5

7:22
① Q 6:20b,
10:23–24;
Mt 15:30–31;
Lk 4:18–19;
◊ Is 29:18–19,
35:5–6, 61:1

7:24–25
//Th 78;
① Q 3:7

7:27
Cf. Mk 1:2;
① Mt 3:3, Lk 1:17;
◊ Ex 23:20, Mal 3:1

7:28
//Th 46

7:1–10 Though this is a narrative, its emphasis lies on the word of Jesus, and thus does not seem out of place in a sayings collection.

7:1 *Capernaum* was a village on the north shore of the Sea of Galilee; it was where Jesus lived (see Matt 4:13).

7:3 Roman soldiers were not stationed in Galilee in Jesus' day.

7:18 John the Baptizer also had disciples; see Mark 6:29; Luke 5:33; John 4:1.

7:19 The *one who is to come* cannot be identified with any particular messianic figure.

7:26 The "more than" comparison occurs several times in Q; see also Q 11:31, 32; 12:23.

(^{29}*After all, John came to you . . .* toll collectors and . . . ^{30}but *the Pharisees and the legal experts* didn't believe him.)

^{31}"**What does this generation** remind me of? What is it like? ^{32}It is like children sitting in marketplaces who call out to others:

> We played the flute for you,
>> but you wouldn't dance;
> we sang a dirge,
>> but you wouldn't weep.

^{33}"Just remember, John appeared on the scene, eating no bread and drinking no wine, and you say, 'He's possessed.' ^{34}The Human One appeared on the scene both eating and drinking, and you say, 'There's a glutton and a drunk, a crony of toll collectors and sinners!' ^{35}Indeed, Wisdom is vindicated by her children."

9

^{57}**Someone said to him,** "I'll follow you wherever you go."

^{58}And Jesus said to him, "Foxes have dens, and birds of the sky have nests, but the Human One has nowhere to rest his head."

^{59}Another said to him, "Master, first let me go and bury my father."

^{60}But he said to him, "Follow me, and leave it to the dead to bury their own dead."

^{61}*Another said, "I'll follow you, sir; but let me first say good-bye to my people at home."*

^{62}*Jesus said to him, "No one who puts his hand to the plow and looks back is qualified for the empire of God."*

10

^{2}**He would say to his disciples,** "The crop is good, but there are few to harvest it. So beg the harvest boss to dispatch workers to the fields. ^{3}Get going; look, I'm sending you out like sheep into a pack of wolves. ^{4}Carry no purse, no knapsack, no sandals, no staff. Don't greet anyone on the road. ^{5}Whenever you enter a house, first say, 'Peace to this house.' ^{6}If peaceful people live there, your peace will rest on them. But if not, withdraw your peace blessing. ^{7}*Stay at that one house, eating and drinking whatever they provide,* for workers deserve their

---

7:31
◊Nm 32:13;
Ps 78:8, 95:8–11

7:33–34
Cf. Mk 1:6;
① Mt 3:4, Lk 1:15;
Ⓣ Mt 9:10–11,
Lk 5:30

7:34
◊Dt 21:20

9:58
//Th 86

9:61–62
◊1 Kgs 19:19–21

10:2–12
//Mk 6:6b–13,
Lk 9:1–6

10:2
//Th 73;
cf. Jn 4:35

10:4
① Lk 22:35–36;
◊2 Kgs 4:29

10:6
Cf. 1 Pet 4:14

10:7–9
//Th 14:4

10:7
//1 Tm 5:17,
DSav 20:1b;
cf. 1 Cor 9:14

7:29 The words describing what the toll collectors did cannot be reconstructed, but probably had the sense of "responded positively."
9:61–62 SV includes these verses in Q; IQP does not.

7:31 The epithet, *this generation,* is used in Q as a derisive designation for those Jews with whom the Q group was in conflict; see Q 11:29, 31, 32, 51.
7:34 *Toll collectors* are lumped with "sinners" because both were especially despised, both socially and religiously. *Sinners* was a generic terms for people who disregarded Jewish laws.

7:35 *Wisdom* (*Sophia* in Greek) is personified as a female divine figure in Jewish tradition; see Prov 1:20–33; 8:131; Wis 6:12–16; Sir 24:1–22; Bar 3:9–4:4.

Wisdom is shown to be in the right by the *children* who respond affirmatively to her messengers, John and Jesus.
9:59 The burial of one's parents was a duty taking precedence over all other duties, including commands of the Law.

10:9
//Mk 1:14; Mt 3:2,
4:17; Lk 17:21
10:11
① Acts 13:51, 18:6
10:12
//Mt 11:24
10:15
◊ Is 14:11–15,
Ez 28:1–8
10:16
Cf. Mk 9:37;
Mt 18:5; Lk 9:48;
Jn 5:23, 13:20,
12:44–45, 15:23
10:21
① Lk 9:45, 18:34,
19:42;
◊ Is 29:14
(1 Cor 1:19),
Wis 10:21
10:22
Cf. Mt 28:18;
Jn 3:35; 13:3;
17:16–2, 25;
Th 61:3; Eph 1:22
① Q 4:6,
SJas 6:24–26
10:23
Cf. Sir 48:11
11:2b
◊ Is 29:23, Ez 36:23
11:3
//GNaz 3
11:4a
//Mk l 1:25;
Mt 6:14–15, 18:35;
◊ Sir 28:2
11:4b
//SJas 4:2;
cf. Mk 14:38

wages. *Do not move from house to house.* ⁸Whenever you enter a town and they welcome you, eat whatever they offer you. ⁹Cure the sick there and tell them, 'For you, God's empire has arrived.' ¹⁰But whenever you enter a town and they don't welcome you, as you are going out of that town, shake the dust off your feet. ¹²I'm telling you, on that day Sodom will be better off than that town.

¹³"**Damn you, Chorazin!** Damn you, Bethsaida! If the miracles done in you had been done in Tyre and Sidon, they would have ⟨sat⟩ in sackcloth and ashes and changed their ways long ago. ¹⁴But Tyre and Sidon will be better off at the judgment than you. ¹⁵And you, Capernaum, you don't think you'll be exalted to heaven, do you? No, you'll go to hell. ^(QMt 11:23)*Because if the miracles done within your boundaries had been done in Sodom, Sodom would still be around.* ^(QMt 11:24)*I'm telling you, the land of Sodom will be better off on judgment day than you!*

¹⁶"**The one who welcomes** you is welcoming me, and the one who welcomes me is welcoming the one who sent me."

²¹**At that point** he said, "I praise you, Father, master of earth and sky, because you have hidden these things from the wise and the learned but revealed them to the unsophisticated; yes indeed, Father, because that is the way you want it. ²²My Father has turned everything over to me. No one knows the son except the Father, and no one knows the Father except the son—and anyone to whom the son wishes to reveal him.

²³"**How privileged** are the eyes that see what you see! ²⁴I'm telling you, many prophets and kings wanted to see what you see, and never saw it, and to hear what you hear, and never heard it."

11 ²"**When you pray,** you should say:

Father, your name be revered.

Your empire be established.

³Provide us with the bread we need for the day.

⁴Forgive our sins, since we too forgive everyone in debt to us.

And don't make us face the test.

10:13–15 + Matt 11:23b–24: SV includes these verses from Matthew in Q; IQP does not.

10:8 The command to *eat whatever they offer you* may imply that food laws could be suspended; see 1 Cor 10:27.
10:12 *Sodom* and Gomorrah were destroyed by God because of their wickedness (Genesis 18–19), and became proverbial (see Rom 9:29 [Isa 1:9]; 2 Pet 2:6; Jude 7).
10:13 *Chorazin and Bethsaida* were villages on the north shore of the Sea of Galilee, near Capernaum. *Tyre and Sidon* were cities in Syria (now Lebanon), to the northwest of Galilee (see Matt 15:21). Wearing *sackcloth and ashes* was a sign of repentance and grief; see Isa 58:5; 1 Macc 3:47.

10:15 *Hell* here translates the Greek word *Hades*, which refers to the abode of the dead, not to a place of punishment. *Heaven* is simply where God was thought to live.
11:2 It is unclear whether God is to see to it that God's name is *revered*, or whether people are to do this.

Your empire be established is a common petition in Jewish prayers, though the date of these prayers is uncertain.
11:4 *Debts* usually means simply financial debts or social obligations, but can also have the religious meaning, "sins."

⁹"**I'm telling you**: ask—it'll be given to you; seek—you'll find; knock—it'll be opened for you. ¹⁰Everyone who asks receives; everyone who seeks finds; and for the one who knocks it is opened. ¹¹Who among you would hand a son a stone when he's asking for bread? ¹²Again, who would hand him a snake when he's asking for fish? ¹³So if you, worthless as you are, know how to give your children good gifts, isn't it much more likely that your Father in the heavens will give good things to those who ask him?"

¹⁴**Jesus was driving out a demon** that was mute, and when the demon had departed the mute man spoke. And the crowds were amazed. ¹⁵But some of them said, "He drives out demons with the power of Beelzebul, the head demon."

¹⁷But he knew what they were thinking, and said to them, "Every empire divided against itself is devastated, and no household divided against itself can survive. ¹⁸If Satan is divided against himself, how will his empire survive? ¹⁹Suppose I do drive out demons with the power of Beelzebul, then with whose power do your own people drive ⟨them⟩ out? That's why they will be your judges. ²⁰But if I drive out demons with the finger of God, then the empire of God has come for you.

²¹ . . . ²² . . .

²³"Those who aren't with me are against me, and those who don't gather with me scatter.

²⁴"**When an unclean spirit** leaves a person, it wanders through waterless places in search of a place to rest. When it doesn't find one, it says, 'I will go back to the home I left.' ²⁵It then returns, and finds the place swept and put in order. ²⁶Next, it goes out and brings back seven other spirits more vile than itself, who enter and settle in there. So that person ends up worse off than when he or she started."

¹⁶**Some were demanding** a sign from him. ²⁹But he said, "This generation is an evil generation. It demands a sign, but it will be given no sign—except the

11:9–10
//Jn 15:7, 16:23–24; Th 2:1–2; 92:1; 94; cf. Mk 11:24; Mt 18:19, 21:22; Jn 15:16; 1 Jn 3:22; ◊ Prv 8:17

11:10
//Mary 4:7; GHeb 6b; cf. DSav 7:2, 11:5

11:14–23
//Mk 3:22–27

11:14–15
//Mt 9:32–34

11:20
◊ Ex 8:12–15

11:23a
//Mk 9:40, GOxy 1224 6:2

11:24–26
Ⓣ 2 Esd 7:78–80

11:26b
Ⓣ 2 Pet 2:20

11:29
Cf. Mk 8:11–12; Mt 16:1, 4

11:21–22 Q probably had some text here, but it cannot be reconstructed with any confidence. The sense of this passage was probably something like: "A strong man's home cannot be looted. But if a stronger man overpowers him, he does get looted."

11:11–12 *Bread* and *fish* were staples of the Mediterranean diet.

11:15 *Beelzebul* is a title whose exact meaning is unknown. "Beel-" is "Baal," meaning "lord" or "master," and used in the OT for various Canaanite deities. It was not uncommon to use the name of an opponent's deity as a term for a demon or, as here, the prince of demons.

As a supernatural spirit, a demon could be evicted from its human host only at the command of a higher ranking

spirit, whether good (God) or evil (Satan).

11:18 Jesus treats *Satan* as the equivalent of Beelzebul.

11:19 *Your own people* are other Jewish exorcists; see Acts 19:13–16.

11:24 The *home* is the person from whom the demon was exorcised.

11:29 *This generation:* See note to Q 7:31.

The *sign of Jonah* is probably the call by John and Jesus for Israel to repent.

On light

*Damn you
Pharisees*

*Damn you legal
experts*

*Blood of the
prophets*

11:31
◊1 Kgs 10:1–13

11:33
//Mk 4:21, Lk 8:16,
Th 33:2–3

11:34
//Th 24:3, 61:5;
DSav 6:1–2;
Mary 7:4

11:35
Cf. Jn 11:10,
Th 70:2

11:42
◊Mi 6:8

11:39–40
//Th 89

11:39
Cf. GOxy 840 2:8

11:43
//Mk 12:38–40

11:52
//Th 39:1–2;
cf. Th 102;
Ⓣ Mt 21:31–32

11:47–48
Cf. Acts 7:51–53;
Ⓣ Q 6:23

11:49–52
Cf. 1 Thes 2:14–16

11:49–51
Ⓣ Q 13:34–35,
Mk 12:1–12

sign of Jonah! ³⁰You see, just as Jonah became a sign for the Ninevites, so the Human One will be a sign for this generation.

³¹"On judgment day, the queen of the south will be brought back to life along with members of this generation, and she will condemn them, because she came from the ends of the earth to listen to Solomon's wisdom. Yet take note: what is right here is greater than Solomon. ³²On judgment day, the citizens of Nineveh will come back to life along with this generation and condemn it, because they had a change of heart in response to Jonah's message. Yet take note: what is right here is greater than Jonah.

³³"**No one lights a lamp** and then puts it in a cellar, but instead on a lampstand so that those who come in can see the light.

³⁴"The eye is the body's lamp. If your eye is clear, your whole body will be flooded with light. If your eye is clouded, your whole body is shrouded in darkness. ³⁵If, then, the light within you is darkness, how dark that can be!

⁴²"**Damn you, Pharisees!** You pay tithes on mint and dill and cumin too, but ignore justice and mercy and trust. It's these you should have practiced without ignoring the others.

³⁹ᵇ"Damn you, Pharisees! You wash the outside of cups and plates, but inside they are full of greed and self-indulgence. ⁴¹Clean the inside of the cup and the outside will be clean too.

⁴³"Damn you, Pharisees! You love the best couches at banquets and the prominent seats in synagogues and respectful greetings in marketplaces.

⁴⁴"Damn you, Pharisees! You're like unmarked graves that people walk on without realizing it.

⁴⁶"**Damn you legal experts** too! You load people down with crushing burdens, but you yourselves don't lift a finger to help carry them. ⁵²Damn you legal experts! You slam the door of God's empire in people's faces. You yourselves don't go in, and you block the way of those trying to go in.

⁴⁷"**Damn you!** You build the tombs of the prophets whom your ancestors murdered. ⁴⁸So, you witness against yourselves: you are descendants of your ancestors. ⁴⁹That's why Wisdom has said, 'I will send them prophets and sages, and

---

11:30 *Jonah* was sent to Nineveh, the capital of Israel's enemy, the Assyrians, to call for repentance; much to Jonah's consternation, they repented (Jonah 3).

11:31 The *queen of the south* is the queen of Sheba, a kingdom in southern Arabia.

11:34 The condition of the *eye* is described by a word (*haplous*) whose meaning is unclear; it can be "single," "simple," "sincere," "generous," or "sound."

11:42 *Pharisees* were laymen dedicated to the application of the OT Law, including rules of purity, to the details of daily life.

The *tithe* was a tax (10%) for the support of the temple,

but tithing was also part of dietary law; produce needed to be tithed before it could be consumed.

11:44 Contact with the dead rendered one ritually unclean; see Num 19:11–13, 16.

11:47–51 The OT portrays God as having sent prophets to Israel who refused to heed them (Jer 7:25–26; 44:4–5; Zech 1:4; 7:12; Bar 1:21–22), even killing the prophets (Neh 9:26; 1 Kgs 19:10, 14). This persistent refusal to hear the prophets leaves Israel under the continuing threat of God's wrath (Bar 1:15–22).

11:49 *Wisdom:* See note to Q 7:35.

some of them they are always going to kill and persecute.' [50]So, this generation will have to answer for the blood of all the prophets that has been shed since the world was founded, [51]from the blood of Abel to the blood of Zechariah, who perished between the altar and the sanctuary. Yes, I'm telling you, this generation will have to answer for it."

12 [2]"**There is nothing** covered up that won't be exposed, or hidden that won't be made known. [3]What I say to you in the dark, say in the light, and what you hear whispered in your ear, announce from the rooftops.

[4]"**And don't fear** those who kill the body but cannot kill the soul; [5]instead, fear the one who can destroy both the soul and the body in Gehenna. [6]What do five sparrows cost? Five bucks? Yet not one of them will fall to the ground without your Father's consent. [7]As for you, even the hairs on your head have all been counted. So, don't be so timid; you're worth more than a flock of sparrows.

[8]"**Everyone who acknowledges** me in public, the Human One will acknowledge in front of God's messengers. [9]But whoever disowns me in public will be disowned in front of God's messengers.

[10]"And the one who speaks a word against the Human One will be forgiven; but the one who speaks a word against the holy spirit won't be forgiven.

[11]"And when they make you appear in front of synagogues, don't worry about how or what you should say. [12]The holy spirit will teach you at that moment what you ought to say.

[22]"**That's why I tell you:** don't fret about your life—what you're going to eat—or about your body—what you're going to wear. [23]There's more to living than food and clothing, isn't there? [24]Think about the crows: they don't plant or harvest or gather into barns. Yet God feeds them. You're worth more than the birds, aren't you? [25]Can any of you add one hour to life by fretting about it? [26]Why worry about clothes? [27]Notice how the wild lilies grow: they don't toil and they never spin. But let me tell you: even Solomon at the height of his glory was never decked out like one of them. [28]If God dresses up the grass in the field, which is here today and is thrown into an oven tomorrow, won't ⟨God care for⟩ you even more, you with your meager trust? [29]So don't fret. Don't say, 'What

Announce what is whispered

Have no fear

Acknowledgement and defense

Don't fret

12:2
//Mk 4:22; Lk 8:17;
Th 5:2, 6:5–6;
cf. 1 Cor 4:5;
◊2 Kgs 6:12;
2 Mc 12:41

12:3
//Th 33:1

12:5
◊Ps 119:120

12:7a
//Lk 21:18,
Acts 27:34b;
cf. 1 Sm 14:45,
2 Sm 14:11,
1 Kgs 1:52

12:7b
ⓣ Mt 12:12

12:8–9
Cf. 1 Jn 2:23;
ⓣ 1 Sm 2:30

12:8
Cf. Jn 12:26, Rv 3:5

12:9
//Mk 8:38, Lk 9:26,
2 Tm 2:12b

12:10
//Mk 3:28–29,
Th 44;
cf. 1 Sm 2:25;
ⓣ Wis 1:6

12:11–12
//Mk 13:9, 11;
cf. Lk 21:14–15

12:22
//Th 36

12:24a
ⓣ Job 12:7–8;
◊Ps 147:9, Job 38:41

12:24b
ⓣ Q 12:6–7

12:29
ⓣ Q 10:4

12:11–12 Some scholars include Luke 12:13–14 and 12:16–21 in Q; SV and IQP do not.
12:22b–31 IQP inserts Q 12:33–34 after Q 12:11–12; SV follows Luke's sequence.

11:51 The *blood of Abel,* the first person in the OT to be killed, cried out to God from the ground for vengeance (Gen 4:10). The *Zechariah* referred to here is probably the Zechariah in 2 Chr 24:17–22, who was murdered and, in death, called on God to avenge his death. Neither Abel nor Zechariah was a prophet.

12:5 A warning to fear God, who has power to cast one into *Gehenna,* the valley of fire (see Matt 5:22; Jas 3:6). Gehenna is Greek for Valley of Hinnom, south of Jerusalem; probably because of Jer 19:1–10, it became a metaphor for the place God would punish the wicked.

12:30
Ⓣ Q 11:13

12:31
Cf. Rom 14:17;
Ⓣ Mt 19:29,
Lk 18:29b–30

12:33
//Th 76:3;
cf. Mk 10:21,
Mt 19:21, Jas 5:2–3;
Ⓣ Lk 12:16–21,
18:22; Tob 4:9,
12:8–9

12:39
//Th 21:5; 103

12:44
Ⓣ Q 19:17, 22:28–
30; Mt 25:21, 23

12:45–46
Cf. Mk 13:35;
Ⓣ Lk 21:34

12:49
//Th 10;
cf. Th 82;
Ⓣ Q 3:16;
Lk 9:54–55,
17:28–30

12:51–53
//Th 16;
cf. GNaz 11

12:53
//Mk 13:12;
Ⓣ Q 14:26;
◊Mi 7:6

12:56
//Th 91:2

13:18–19
//Mk 4:30–32,
Th 20;
cf. Mt 13:24;
Ⓣ DSav 36:1

13:19c
◊Ez 17:23, 31:6

are we going to eat?' or 'What are we going to drink?' or 'What are we going to wear?' [30]These are all things pagans seek. After all, your heavenly Father is aware that you need them all. [31]Seek God's empire and all these things will come to you as a bonus.

[33]"***Don't pile up possessions*** *here on earth, where moths and insects eat away and where burglars break in and steal.* Instead, gather your nest egg in heaven, where neither moths nor insects eat away and where no burglars break in or steal. [34]As you know, what you treasure is your heart's true measure.

[39]"**Mark this well:** if the homeowner had known what time the burglar was coming, he would not have let anyone break into his house. [40]You too should be prepared. Remember, the Human One is coming when you least expect it.

[42]"Who then is the trustworthy and prudent slave to whom the master assigns responsibility for his household, to provide them with food at the right time? [43]Congratulations to the slave who's on the job when his master arrives. [44]Let me tell you, he'll put him in charge of all his property. [45]But suppose that slave says to himself, 'My master is taking his time,' and begins to beat his fellow slaves, and starts eating and drinking with drunks, [46]that slave's master will show up on the day he least expects and at an hour he doesn't suspect. He'll cut him to pieces, and assign him a fate among the disloyal.

[49]"*I came to set the earth on fire, and how I wish it were already ablaze!* [51]Do you think I came here to bring peace on earth? I didn't come to bring peace, but a sword! [53]After all, I've come to pit a man against his father, a daughter against her mother, and a daughter-in-law against her mother-in-law."

[54]**He said to them,** "When it's evening, you say, 'It'll be fair weather because the sky looks red.' [55]Early in the morning you say, 'The day will bring winter weather because the sky looks red and dark.' [56]You know how to read the face of the sky, but you can't interpret the present time.

[58]"**When you're on your way** ⟨to court⟩ with your accuser, do your best to settle with him on the way, or else your accuser will hand you over to the judge, and the judge to the bailiff, and the bailiff will throw you in jail. [59]I'm telling you, you'll never get out of there until you've paid the last dime."

13 [18]**What is the empire of God like?** What does it remind me of? [19]It is like a mustard seed that a man took and tossed into his garden. It grew and became a tree, and the birds of the sky roosted in its branches.

12:39 The arrival (*parousia* in Greek) of the *Human One* is frequently compared to the arrival of a thief, for example, in 1 Thess 5:2 and Rev 3:3.

12:45–46 Many horror stories were told in Antiquity about the misbehavior of slaves when their master was gone.

12:58 The *accuser* is a creditor demanding payment of a debt (see Matt 18:23–34).

13:19 There is deliberate exaggeration: the *mustard seed* does not grow into a tree.

²⁰And again: what does the empire of God remind me of? ²¹It is like leaven that a woman took and concealed in fifty pounds of flour until it was all leavened.

²⁴"**Get in through the narrow door;** many will try to get in, but only a few will succeed. ²⁵Once the master of the house gets up and bars the door, you'll be left standing outside and knocking at the door: 'Master, open up for us.' But he'll answer you, 'I don't know you.' ²⁶Then you'll start saying, 'We ate and drank with you, and you taught in our streets.' ²⁷But he'll reply, 'I don't know you; get away from me, you subverters of the Law!'

²⁹"**Many will come** from east and west and dine ²⁸with Abraham and Isaac and Jacob in the empire of God, but you'll be thrown out into the utter darkness. There'll be weeping and grinding of teeth out there. ³⁰The last will be first and the first last.

³⁴"**Jerusalem, Jerusalem,** you murder the prophets and stone those sent to you! How often I wanted to gather your children as a hen gathers her chicks under her wings, but you wouldn't let me. ³⁵Can't you see, your house is being abandoned? I'm telling you, you certainly won't see me until the time comes when you say, 'Blessed is the one who comes in the name of the Lord.'"

The narrow door

Dining with the patriarchs

Jerusalem indicted

13:20–21
//Th 96

13:21
Cf. 1 Cor 5:6

13:24
Ⓣ 2 Esd 7:6–8

13:25–26
Ⓣ Q 6:46

13:25
//Mt 25:12

13:27
◊ Ps 6:9

13:28–29
Ⓣ Q 14:16–24

13:28
Ⓣ Mt 13:42, 22:13, 24:51, 25:30;
◊ Hos 9:17

13:29
Ⓣ 2 Esd 1:38–40, GSav 1:3;
◊ Ps 107:3; Is 25:6–8, 43:5–6; Mal 1:11; Bar 4:36–37

13:30
//Mk 10:31;
Mt 19:30, 20:16;
Th 4:2;
cf. Mk 9:35

13:34–35
Cf. 2 Esd 1:28–34;
Ⓣ Q 6:23, 11:47–51, 14:16–24, 20:9–18; Mt 21:33–43;
◊ 1 Kgs 9:6–9, Jer 26:4–6

13:34a
◊ Dt 32:11, Ps 91:4, Is 31:5

13:35a
◊ Tob 14:4, Is 49:14

13:35b
//Mk 11:9, Mt 21:9, Lk 19:38;
◊ Ps 118:26

13:21 The *leaven* here is sourdough.
13:34–35 The speaker here is probably Wisdom. See also 2 Bar 1:28–33.
13:34 On prophets sent and killed, see the note to Q 11:47–51.
13:35a The *house* is probably the temple, the dwelling place of God. The statement "*you won't see me*" may refer to Jesus' "assumption" into heaven, like Enoch (Gen. 5:24) or Elijah (2 Kgs 2:1,11). If that is the case, it would mean that Q understood that God's vindication of the crucified Jesus happened through assumption rather than resurrection.

14

[11] **"Those who promote themselves** will be demoted, and those who demote themselves will be promoted.

[16] **Someone was giving a big dinner** and invited many guests. [17] At the dinner hour the host sent his slave to tell the guests, "Come, it's ready now." [18] One excused himself because of his farm, ?[19]? . . . ?[20]? . . . [21] So the slave ⟨came back and reported⟩ these ⟨excuses⟩ to his master. Then the master of the house was outraged and instructed his slave, [23] "Go out into the streets and invite anybody you find so my house will be filled."

[26] **"Unless you hate** your father and mother, you cannot be my disciple; and unless you hate your son and daughter, you cannot be my disciple . [27] Unless you carry your own cross and follow after me, you cannot be my disciple.

17

[33] **"By finding your life,** you'll lose it, but by losing your life for my sake, you'll find it.

14

[34] **"Salt is good,** but if it loses its zing, how will it be renewed? [35] It's no good for either earth or manure. It just gets thrown away."

16

[13] **"No one can** be a slave to two masters. That slave will either hate one and love the other, or be devoted to one and disdain the other. You can't be enslaved to both God and Mammon.

14:11
//Lk 18:14;
Cf. Mt 18:4;
Phil 2:8–9;
1 Pet 5:6; Jas 4:10;
Prv 29:23; Sir 10:14;
Ez 17:24, 21:31;
2 Esd 8:48–49

14:16–24
//Th 64;
Ⓣ Prv 9:1–6

14:17
Ⓣ Q 13:34

14:21–23
Ⓣ Q 13:28–29

14:21
Ⓣ Lk 14:13

14:26–27
//Th 55

14:26
//Th 101;
cf. Mk 10:29–30,
Mt 19:29,
Lk 18:29b–30;
◊ Dt 33:8–9

14:27
//Mk 8:34,
Mt 16:24, Lk 9:23

17:33
//Mk 8:35,
Mt 16:25, Lk 9:24,
Jn 12:25

14:34
//Mk 9:50

14:35
Ⓣ Q 3:9

16:13
//Th 47:1–2;
cf. Jas 4:4;
Ⓣ Q 12:34

14:19–20 Q must have had some text here, but it cannot be reconstructed. The sense of the missing verses apparently was something like: "Another excused himself because of his business. A third excused himself . . ."

16:13 *Mammon,* an Aramaic word meaning "wealth," is best understood here as "resources" for living, and thus security.

[16]"**The Law and the Prophets** were until John; since then the empire of God has been breaking in violently, and violent men are trying to seize it. [17]But it's easier for earth and sky to pass away than for one iota or one serif of the Law to drop out.

[18]"**Everyone who divorces** his wife and marries another commits adultery; and the one who marries a divorced woman commits adultery."

17 [1]"**It's inevitable that traps** will be set; but still, damn those who set them! [2]You'd be better off if you had a millstone tied around your neck and were dumped into the sea than to entrap and exploit one of these little ones.

15 [4]"**Is there any one of you** who owns a hundred sheep and one of them gets lost, who wouldn't leave the ninety-nine in the hills and go look for the one that got lost? [5]And if he should find it, [7]I'm telling you, he'll rejoice over it more than over the ninety-nine that didn't wander off.

> [8]*Or is there any woman with ten drachmas, who if she loses one, wouldn't light a lamp and sweep the house and search high and low until she finds it? [9]When she finds it, she invites her friends and neighbors over and says, "Celebrate with me, because I've found the drachma I lost."*

[10]"I'm telling you, it's just like that among God's messengers: they celebrate when one sinner has a change of heart.

17 [3]"**If your companion** wrongs you, scold that person; if there is a change of heart, forgive the person. [4]If someone wrongs you seven times a day, you must forgive that person seven times.

[6]"**If you had trust** no bigger than a mustard seed, you could tell this mulberry tree, 'Uproot yourself and plant yourself in the sea,' and it would obey you."

[20]*When asked when* the empire of God would come, he answered them, "You won't be able to observe the coming of the empire of God. [21]People won't be able to say, 'Look, here it is!' or 'Over there!' On the contrary, the empire of God is among you.*

Marginal notes

God's empire and violence

On divorce

Millstone around your neck

Lost and found

Forgiveness

The power of trust

God's empire among you

16:16
Ⓣ SJas 6:2–4
16:17
Cf. Mk 13:31,
Mt 24:35, Lk 21:33,
Th 11:1
16:18
//Mk 10:11–12;
Ⓓ Mt 19:9;
◊ Dt 24:1–4
17:1–2
Cf. Mk 9:42, 14:21;
Mt 18:6, 26:24;
Lk 22:22
15:4–7
//Th 107
15:4
◊ Ez 34:11–12,
15–16; Ps 119:176
15:7
Ⓣ Mk 2:17,
Mt 9:13,
Lk 5:32, 19:10,
2 Esd 7:59–60
17:3b
Ⓣ Gal 6:1,
Jas 5:19–20
17:4
//GNaz 5:1;
Ⓣ Q 11:4
17:6
//Mk 11:23,
Mt 21:21;
cf. Th 48;
Ⓣ Mk 9:23,
1 Cor 13:2
17:20–21
//Th 3:1–3; 113;
cf. DSav 9:13,
Mary 4:4–5

16:16 The *Law* is the first five books of the Hebrew Bible; the *Prophets* are the prophetic writings.
16:18 Here *divorce* itself is not prohibited, but remarriage is stigmatized as *adultery*.

15:8 The woman's coins are called *drachmas*, a Greek term probably used for the common Roman silver *denarius* which apparently was what a day-laborer could earn in a day (Matt 20:9).

²³**"If they should say** to you, 'Look, he's in the desert,' don't go out there; or, 'Look, he's in one of the inner rooms,' don't pursue it. ²⁴For just as lightning comes out of the east and is visible all the way to the west, that's what the Human One will be like in his day. ³⁷For wherever there's a corpse, that's where vultures gather.

²⁶"And just as it was in the days of Noah, that's how it will be in the day of the Human One. ²⁷That's how people behaved then: they ate and drank, married and were given in marriage, until the day Noah boarded the ark, and the flood came and swept them all away. ^{?28?}*That's also the way it was in the days of Lot. Everyone ate, drank, bought, sold, planted, and built.* ^{?29?}*But on the day Lot left Sodom, fire and sulfur rained down from the sky and destroyed them all.* ³⁰It will be like that on the day the Human One is revealed. ³⁴I'm telling you, there will be two men in the field; one will be taken and one will be left. ³⁵Two women will be grinding at the mill; one will be taken and one left."

19 ¹²**A man was going** on a trip. ¹³He called ten of his slaves, gave them ten minas, and told them, "Do business with this while I'm away."

¹⁵After a long absence, the master of those slaves returned to settle accounts with them. ¹⁶The first came in and reported, "Master, your mina has increased ten times over."

¹⁷He said to him, "Well done, you competent slave! You've been trustworthy in a little so I'll put you in charge of a lot."

¹⁸The second came in and reported, "Master, your mina has increased five times over."

¹⁹And he said to him, "Well done, you competent and trustworthy slave. You've been trustworthy in a little so I'll put you in charge of a lot."

²⁰Then the other ⟨slave⟩ came in and said, "Master, ²¹I know that you're a ruthless man, reaping where you didn't sow and gathering where you didn't scatter. Since I was afraid, I went out and buried your money in the ground. Look, here it is!"

²²He said to him, "You incompetent slave! So you knew that I reap where I didn't sow and gather where I didn't scatter, did you? ²³Then you should have taken my money to the bankers. Then when I returned I would have recovered what's mine, plus interest. ²⁴So take the mina away and give it to the one who has ten."

17:23
//Mk 13:21,
Mt 24:23, Th 113:2
17:24
◊Ps 77:18, 97:4
17:37
◊Job 39:30b
17:34–35
//Th 61:1

17:28–29 IQP does not include these verses. It is doubtful whether they were part of Q.

17:23 The *desert* (Matt 24:26) could be seen as the place of salvation; see Isa 40:3.
17:37 The Greek word *aetos* usually means "eagle," but since eagles do not eat carrion, translators often prefer "vul-

ture." This obscure saying may allude to the eagle as the standard of the Roman legions, and thus by extension to the legions themselves.

²⁶"In fact, to everyone who has, more will be given; and from those who don't have, even what they do have will be taken away.

22 ²⁸**You who have followed me** ³⁰will be seated on thrones and sit in judgment on the twelve tribes of Israel."

Judging Israel

19:26
//Mk 4:25,
Mt 13:12, Lk 8:18,
Th 41

22:30
Cf. 1 Cor 4:8;
Rv 2:26, 3:21;
Ⓣ Mt 20:21;
◊Wis 3:8, Sir 4:15

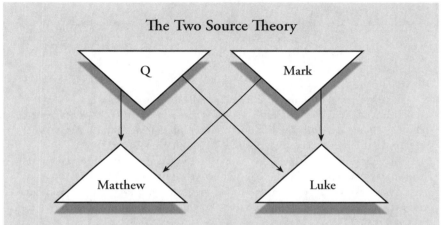

The Two Source Theory is the view that Matthew and Luke made use of two written sources—Mark and the Sayings Gospel Q—in composing their gospels.

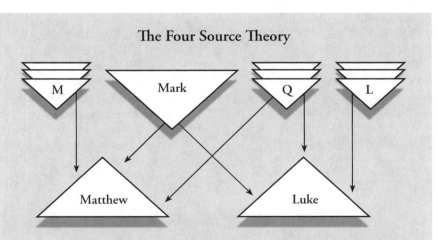

The Four Source Theory is a common explanation of the relationships found in the Synoptic Gospels. Matthew used Mark, Q, and his own special source called M. Luke also used Mark and Q, but had another source called L, that Matthew did not have. The material in M and L probably comes from oral tradition.

The mystery of the double tradition

In addition to the verbal agreements Matthew and Luke share with Mark, they also have striking verbal agreements in passages where Mark offers nothing comparable. There are about 200 verses that fall into this category. Virtually all of the material in the double tradition, as it is known, consists of sayings or parables. Verbal agreement is sometimes very high; at other times it is difficult to determine whether Matthew and Luke are copying from a common source because the agreement is so minimal.

The material Matthew and Luke take from this hypothetical common source is not arranged in their own gospels in the same way. It appears that Matthew and Luke have inserted material from the sayings source into the outline they have borrowed from Mark, but they have distributed that sayings material in very different ways.

A sample of the double tradition is laid out in matching lines below. In this segment, Matt 3:7–10//Luke 3:7–9, verbal agreement is 99%: only in the choice of one verb and whether one noun is singular or plural do they differ, except for the transitional remarks in v. 7 in both gospels.

The German scholar who first proposed a written document to explain the striking agreements of the double tradition simply referred to that document as a *Quelle*, which means "source" in German. The abbreviation "Q" was later adopted as its name. Scholars now refer to this hypothetical document as the Q Gospel.

Matt 3:7–10	Luke 3:7–9
⁷When he saw that many of the Pharisees and Sadducees were coming for baptism, John said to them,	⁷So (John) would say to the crowds that came out to get baptized by him,
"You spawn of Satan! Who warned you to flee from the impending doom? ⁸Well then, start producing *fruit* suitable for a change of heart, ⁹and don't even *think of* saying to yourselves, 'We have Abraham for our father.' Let me tell you, God can raise up children for Abraham right out of these rocks! ¹⁰Even now the axe is aimed at the root of the trees. So every tree not producing choice fruit gets cut down and tossed into the fire."	"You spawn of Satan! Who warned you to flee from the impending doom? ⁸Well then, start producing *fruits* suitable for a change of heart, and don't even *start* saying to yourselves, 'We have Abraham for our father.' Let me tell you, God can raise up children for Abraham right out of these rocks. ⁹Even now the axe is aimed at the root of the trees. So every tree not producing choice fruit gets cut down and tossed into the fire."

The Gospel of Thomas

Introduction

The Gospel of Thomas is a sayings gospel. It consists, for the most part, of sayings attributed to Jesus, listed serially and presented using simple stock phrases such as "Jesus said." It thus has virtually no narrative element, a characteristic which distinguishes it from the better known canonical examples of early Christian gospel literature, Matthew, Mark, Luke, and John. As such, it does not purport to give an account or interpretation of Jesus' life, but focuses instead on Jesus' words, his preaching.

Discovery

Though scholars had known for years of the existence of a certain Gospel of Thomas in the early Christian period, it was thought that no copy of it had survived Antiquity. This changed in 1945, when a copy of the lost gospel was discovered as part of a large collection of ancient religious texts known as the Nag Hammadi Library, so called after the Egyptian city near which the collection was found. The copy of Thomas discovered at Nag Hammadi is actually a Coptic (the common language of Egypt during the Christian period) translation of the original, which was probably written in Greek. Although fragments of the Greek text of Thomas were actually discovered some forty-five years before the sensational find at Nag Hammadi, until scholars had the Coptic text of Thomas in hand, the identity of those fragments could not be ascertained with any certainty.

The Greek fragments consist of three pieces of papyrus excavated from the Roman-era city of Oxyrhynchus in Egypt and are known to scholars as Papyrus Oxyrhynchus (POxy) 1, 654, and 655. These three fragments are not all from the same manuscript, but in fact from three different copies of Thomas. They contain the complete or partial text of twenty-two sayings. In several sayings the Greek version differs considerably from its Coptic counterpart; these differences are discussed in the text-critical notes to the relevant sayings. In the case of at least one saying (Thom 30) the Oxyrhynchus version is closer to the original wording than is the Coptic translation.

The Gospel of Thomas as a sayings collection

The Gospel of Thomas is a collection of sayings presented serially and organized primarily around the principle of catchword association. Such collections were common in Antiquity. The students of famous philosophers, such as Epicurus or Epictetus, often collected the wise and witty sayings of their tradition into *gnomologia*, or "words of insight," which they might then use as they evangelized the public in the marketplaces and streets of the ancient world. Jews and other ethnic groups of the eastern Roman empire also gathered the aphoristic wisdom of their sages into collections of *logoi sophōn*, or "sayings of the wise," such as one finds, for example, in the Book of Proverbs. The gathering of Jesus' sayings into such a collection places him among the sages of the past, the prophets of Sophia (the feminine personification of wisdom in Jewish lore) sent into every generation with her saving words of wisdom (see Wis 7:27).

Authorship and provenance

As with all early Christian gospels, the ascription of the Gospel of Thomas to an apostolic figure probably derives from an urge to guarantee the reliability of the tradition rather than from accurate historical memory. Thus, we simply do not know who originally assembled this collection.

It is noteworthy, however, that the opening line of the gospel reads: "These are the secret sayings that the living Jesus spoke and Didymos Judas Thomas recorded." Didymos Judas Thomas seems to have been a popular legendary figure from apostolic times, especially in Syria. In fact, it is only in eastern Syria that we find precisely this form of the name, where it occurs in the Acts of Thomas. In early Christianity the names of particular apostles often acquired special significance within specific geographical areas. For example, Peter is associated with Rome, John with Asia Minor, and James with Jerusalem. We cannot be certain whether such associations are grounded in historical memories of the evangelization of these areas, or are purely legendary. Thomas, or Didymos Judas Thomas, was apparently the patron apostle for Syria. As such, most scholars now assume that the Gospel of Thomas, in more or less its present form, came originally out of Syria. It is certainly possible, however, that an earlier version might have originated in Palestine. Saying 12 in this gospel, after all, appeals not to the authority of Thomas, but to that of James, who was associated in early Christianity with the Jerusalem church (see Gal 1:19).

Date

The date for the compilation of a sayings collection such as Thomas may be given only in rough approximation. One must assume that as a sayings collection, this text would have enjoyed much greater flexibility of content than is generally true of narrative texts. In each new appropriation of the collection, new sayings could easily be added, even as older, outmoded sayings were sloughed away. Still, several factors point to a date sometime in the latter decades of the first century CE. First, the collection belongs to a time when individual Christian communities were still appealing to the authority of particular apostles (not to "the Twelve" as a whole) as the guarantor of their traditions. In this respect Thomas is comparable to Mark, which dates to around 70 CE. Second, the genre of Thomas, the sayings collection, seems to have fallen into disuse among Christians by the end of the first century. Later church fathers revived the form, but always took care to cite the sources for their material, usually the canonical gospels. This is quite different from Thomas, which derives its material not from the canonical gospels, but from the same oral traditions on which these gospels themselves rely. This in turn suggests a third factor: Thomas was assembled before Matthew, Mark, Luke, and John had attained the ascendency that the later church codified in the form of a "canon," a process that began in the second century. All of these factors place Thomas approximately in the same period as the canonical gospels (about 70–100 CE).

Theology

The theology of the Gospel of Thomas is as distinctive as its form. As a sayings collection, Thomas belongs generally to the theological tradition that produced such collections as Proverbs, Ecclesiastes, and the Wisdom of Solomon. It is a wisdom gospel. As such it places a premium on the words of the sage: "Whoever discovers the interpretation of these sayings will not taste death" (Thom 1). The point of such a collection is to draw the reader/hearer into sustained reflection on the meaning of the wisdom disclosed through the words of the sage: "Those who seek should not stop seeking until they find" (2:1). Within this framework Thomas includes dozens of aphorisms and parables of Jesus, many of them familiar: "Love your friends like your own soul" (25:1); "When you take the timber out of your own eye, then you will see well enough to remove the sliver from your friend's eye" (26:2); "Don't fret . . . about what you're going to wear" (36); "Grapes are not harvested from thorn trees" (45:1). Such aphorisms and proverbs are well-suited to the genre, for they invite reflection. So do the parables: a fisherman who releases his entire catch only to apprehend a single large and beautiful fish (8); a sower who sows carelessly and yet still reaps an abundant harvest (9); a rich farmer who dies before he can enjoy his wealth (63)—the parables are stories designed to goad the imagination and encourage deeper thought.

But the theology of the Gospel of Thomas involves considerably more than the simple sayings collection form would suggest. Saying 3 says: "The ⟨Father's⟩ empire is inside you and outside you. When you know yourselves, then you will be known and you will understand that you are children of the living Father." The admonition to "know yourself" is a significant clue to Thomas' intellectual milieu. In the period of Christian origins this idea was associated with a broad revival of interest in the ideas of Plato. After many years of skepticism about the ability of philosophers to speak of unseen things, like the soul or the heavenly realms, students of the great Athenian master began mining his works once again for insights into the nature of the cosmos and of human existence, as well as our origin and destiny in the great eternal scheme of things. The result was a popular Hellenistic philosophical movement known as Middle Platonism. Many Hellenized Jews, like Philo of Alexandria, began to read with Plato in one hand and the Bible in the other. Many of Thomas' more speculative insights seem at home in this movement. For example, when Thomas Christians read in Genesis that God created the human being, "male and female God created him," they might well have assumed, like Philo did, that Genesis was referring to the same divine image that Plato spoke of, a perfect androgynous form to which all will someday return (see Thom 22). Or in Genesis 2:7, the second creation story, they might have heard—again, like Philo did—echoes of Plato's complex tripartite anthropology, in which a person consists of a body and a soul, conjoined in a mix that could produce trouble (see Thom 87 and 112), but that each person also possessed a spirit, a piece of God breathed into the human being at creation, and dwelling now as an alien within the human body (see Thom 29). This spirit, they believed, was the image of God, the true self concealed within the earthly self (84). The goal of this philosophical-religious tradition was to attend to the spirit, recover the lost image of God, and join the ranks of the chosen who, as "children of the living Father," will someday return to the heavenly realms (49). The chosen are "people of light" (24:3); they have "come from the light" and will return to the "place where the light came into being" (50:1), their heavenly home.

The world, for the Middle Platonists, was not evil, but simply material—a nuance that distinguishes this movement from what is commonly called "Gnosticism." The Gospel of Thomas speaks of the world as something dead (56, 80), and as such, a distraction (21, 28) unworthy of attention and effort (110–111). The enlightened are expected to "fast from the world" (27). It is, no doubt, in this vein that the Thomas Christians found guidance and inspiration in many of the strongly counter-cultural sayings of Jesus, well-known from the synoptic gospels, and now appearing here: "No prophet is welcome in his home town" (31:1); "Whoever does not hate father and mother cannot be my disciple" (55:1); "If you have money . . . give it to someone from whom you won't get it back" (95); "seek his treasure that is unfailing and enduring, where no moth comes to eat and no worm destroys" (76:3). In this way, the Platonizing worldview of the Gospel of Thomas provided a home for the counter-cultural sayings of Jesus that placed him so much at odds with many who heard him in the early days of the Jesus movement.

Earlier interpreters were inclined to see in the Gospel of Thomas the beginnings of Christian Gnosticism, but this is less the case today. The reasons for this are multiple. First, Gnosticism itself has become a category in need of revision. As a catch-all term for any text whose theology is somewhat speculative it has ceased to have much heuristic value. Second, when Gnosticism is defined more precisely, one of its central tenets is the conviction that the material world exists as a kind of cosmic mistake, created by a subordinate and rebellious creator god in a colossal lapse of judgment. Thomas does not reflect this view. Finally, much of what passed for the speculative strains of Gnosticism in early Christian and Jewish texts can now be seen as part of a resurging interest in Plato during this period. The speculative theology of the Gospel of Thomas, it seems, is best explained in this way.

Interpretation

The interpretation of the Gospel of Thomas is still in an early phase. This gospel, unlike those of the New Testament, has only been available for study for a few decades. Its interpretation is complicated by the fact that the only surviving complete text of Thomas is in Coptic, a language which few scholars have mastered. Finally, there is the troubling issue of esotericism in Thomas. Even a cursory reading of Thomas will reveal that many of its sayings are quite obscure, some perhaps intentionally so, often using paradox or opaque metaphors to make their point. Some of the more difficult problems are addressed in the notes to the text, but the reader should be aware that such explanations are tentative at best. There is still much work to be done before this text is fully understood.

The Gospel of Thomas

Prologue These are the secret sayings that the living Jesus spoke and Didymos Judas Thomas recorded.

1 And he said, "Whoever discovers the interpretation of these sayings will not taste death."

2 Jesus said, "Those who seek should not stop seeking until they find. ²When they find, they will be disturbed. ³When they are disturbed, they will marvel ⁴and will rule the universe."

3 Jesus said, "If your leaders say to you, 'Look, the ⟨Father's⟩ empire is in the sky,' then the birds of the sky will precede you. ²If they say to you, 'It's in the sea,' then the fish will precede you. ³Rather, the ⟨Father's⟩ empire is inside you and outside you. ⁴When you know yourselves, then you will be known, and you will understand that you are children of the living Father. ⁵But if you don't know yourselves, then you live in poverty, and you are the poverty."

Prologue
Cf. GHeb 5
Ⓣ Th 37:3; 59;
111:2

1
Cf. Jn 8:51;
Ⓣ Th 18:3, 19:4,
85:2, 111:2; Mk 9:1;
Mt 16:28; Lk 9:27

2:1
Ⓓ Th 92:1; 94;
//Mt 7:8, Lk 11:10,
Mary 4:7, GHeb 6b

3
Ⓣ Th 113, 51

3:1–2
Cf. Mk 13:21–23,
Mt 24:23–28,
Lk 17:20–25;
◊Job 28:12–14,
20–22 (LXX);
Bar 3:29–32, 35–37;
Dt 30:11–14 (LXX);
Sir 1:1–3

3:3a
//Lk 17:21b;
cf. DSav 9:2–4,
Mary 4:5

2:3–4 The Greek version of this saying is worded differently in these verses: "[When they are] disturbed, they will rule, and [when they rule], they will [rest]."

Prologue *Didymos Judas Thomas:* This name appears in this form elsewhere only in the Syrian *Acts of Thomas* (ch. 1), although the name Judas Thomas occurs in some Syrian manuscripts of John 14:22 and in the prologue of *Thomas the Contender*, also of Syrian origin. Of the three names only Judas is a bona fide name; Didymos and Thomas are the Greek and Semitic words for "Twin," respectively, although Thomas does function as a given name elsewhere. In the colophon title, which occurs at the end of the gospel and was probably added late, one finds the simple name "Thomas." In the Acts of Thomas, Judas Didymos Thomas is sometimes referred to simply as Thomas, but one should not confuse this figure with the apostle Thomas who appears in John 20. In Syrian tradition, Thomas and Judas Didymos Thomas were known as two distinct apostles, as the apostolic list at the beginning of the Acts of Thomas indicates. There Judas Thomas is also called Judas, the brother of James, a name that also appears in Luke's lists of the apostles (Luke 6:16, Acts 1:13), but nowhere else. In Greek manuscripts of John 14:22 he is referred to as "Judas (not Iscariot)" to distinguish him from the Judas who betrayed Jesus. Perhaps it was this potential confusion that led to the

use of the nickname Thomas and the gradual dropping of the name Judas.

2:4 (Greek) *rest:* This term is quite common in Thomas. Its soteriological significance is clear: to find rest is tantamount to salvation. Here its association with the quest for insight reflects its roots in the wisdom tradition (see Sir 51:26–27 and 6:23–31). In Thomas, one achieves rest through insight in the present, not in a future existence (Thom 51). By contrast, later Gnostic groups spoke of the hoped for reunion of the Gnostic soul with the God of heavenly remove as achieving "rest." In the New Testament "rest" is also associated with a future hope (e.g., Rev 14:13).

3:1 *the ⟨Father's⟩ empire:* The Coptic word *tmntero* is conventionally rendered "kingdom," but as elsewhere in Scholars Version translations, here also this archaism has been abandoned. Often in the Gospel of Thomas the term is used without predication, that is, without specifying "of God," "of Heaven," "of the Father," etc. To render these technical uses of *tmntero* more clearly for the modern reader, SV supplies ⟨Father's⟩, the most common predication for this term found in Thomas.

4 Jesus said, "The person old in days won't hesitate to ask a little child seven days old about the place of life, and that person will live. ²For many of the first will be last, ³and will become a single one."

5 Jesus said, "Know what's in front of your face, and what's hidden from you will be disclosed to you. ²For there's nothing hidden that won't be revealed."

6 His disciples asked him, "Do you want us to fast? How should we pray? Should we give to charity? What diet should we observe?"

²Jesus said, "Don't lie, ³and don't do what you hate, ⁴because all things are disclosed before heaven. ⁵After all, there's nothing hidden that won't be revealed, ⁶and there's nothing covered up that will remain undisclosed."

7 Jesus said, "Happy is the lion that the human will eat, and the lion becomes human. ²And cursed is the human that the lion will eat, and the lion will become human."

8 And he said,

The human being is like a wise fisherman who cast his net into the sea and drew it up from the sea full of little fish. ²Among them the wise fisherman discovered a fine large fish. ³He threw all the little fish back into the sea, and easily chose the large fish.

⁴ "Whoever has ears to hear should listen."

4:1
Cf. Q 10:21,
Mt 11:25, Lk 10:21;
Ⓣ Th 22:1–3, 46:2;
DSav 14:1

4:2
//Mk 10:31;
Mt 19:30, 20:16;
Lk 13:30

4:3
Ⓣ Th 22:5, 23:2

5:2
//Mk 4:22; Lk 8:17,
12:2; Mt 10:26;
Ⓓ Th 6:5–6

6:1
Ⓣ Th 14:1–3

6:3
◊Tob 4:15

6:5–6
//Mk 4:22; Lk 8:17,
12:2; Mt 10:26;
Ⓓ Th 5:2

8
//Mt 13:47–50

---

5 The Greek version of this saying adds a third verse: "and ⟨nothing⟩ buried that [will not be raised]."

4:3 *and will become a single one:* This phrase is opaque, but also occurs in Thomas 22:5 and 23:2. Here, as in 23:2, it designates a kind of soteriological status without further explanation. In 22:5, however, it is associated with the notion of androgyny. Some Hellenistic Jewish theologians speculated on the basis of Genesis 1–2 that the original human being was created both male and female—a perfect androgyne, but that the differentiation of male from female led to humankind's fall from grace. Thus, the ultimate human destiny is to return to a primordial state of androgyny, the state of divine perfection before the fall.

5:3 (Greek) The text breaks off, leaving the completion of the final phrase in doubt. The present text is a reconstruction based upon a similar saying from a fifth- or sixth-century burial shroud from Oxyrhynchus. Since Thomas does not directly speak of the resurrection anywhere else, this may well represent a later addition to the text, a probability

reinforced by the absence of this verse in the Coptic version.
7 The meaning of this saying is obscure. In Antiquity the lion often symbolizes feelings of passion and pathos. To eat the lion may be to overcome such feelings. Likewise, to be consumed by the lion (7:2a) is to be overcome by them. 7:2b, however, may hold out hope. One interpretation of this clause is that though the passions may temporarily dominate a person, ultimately he/she will overcome them. But the phrase is very obscure.
7:1 *Happy:* The Greek, *makarios,* is conventionally rendered "blessed." SV has replaced this archaism with a number of alternatives, which better reflect the versatility of this word. Here the lion's fate is viewed as good fortune, for in being consumed it has become part of the human.
8:1 *The human being:* literally, "The person" (Coptic: *prome*). The referent is unclear.

9 Jesus said,

> Look, the sower went out, took a handful ⟨of seeds⟩, and scattered ⟨them⟩. ²Some fell on the road, and the birds came and gathered them. ³Others fell on rock, and they didn't take root in the soil and didn't produce heads of grain. ⁴Others fell on thorns, and they choked the seeds and worms ate them. ⁵And others fell on good soil, and it produced a good crop: it yielded sixty per measure and one hundred twenty per measure.

10 Jesus said, "I have cast fire upon the world, and look, I'm guarding it until it blazes."

11 Jesus said, "This heaven will pass away and the one above it will pass away. ²The dead are not alive and the living will not die. ³During the days when you ate what is dead, you made it come alive. When you are in the light, what will you do? ⁴On the day when you were one, you became two. But when you become two, what will you do?"

12 The disciples said to Jesus, "We know that you are going to leave us. Who will be our leader?"

²Jesus said to them, "No matter where you have come from, you are to go to James the Just, for whose sake heaven and earth came into being."

13 Jesus said to his disciples, "Compare me to something and tell me what I'm like."

²Simon Peter said to him, "You are like a just angel."

³Matthew said to him, "You are like a wise philosopher."

⁴Thomas said to him, "Teacher, my mouth is utterly unable to say what you're like."

9
//Mk 4:2–9,
Mt 13:3–9, Lk 8:4–8
10
//Lk 12:49;
cf. Th 16:1–2,
Mt 10:34;
Ⓣ GSav 12:9
11:1
Cf. Mk 13:31;
Mt 5:18, 24:34–35;
Lk 16:17, 21:33;
Th 111:1–2;
◊Ps 102:25–27,
Is 34:4
11:4
Ⓣ Th 22:4–7
13
Cf. Mk 8:27–30,
Mt 16:13–20,
Lk 9:18–22

9:5 It is not clear what the double *it* refers to. This might be a grammatical error.

Scholars often assert that the yields of *sixty* and *one hundred twenty per measure* are extraordinarily large. But if the reports of contemporary historians (Pliny, Herodotus) are any indication, they are quite average.

10 *fire:* The image of fire is chosen here for its provocative and threatening effect. Fire was a constant menace in Antiquity. Though apocalyptic visions often involve fiery conflagration, this need not be the sense in which it is used here.

11:1 *This heaven . . . and the one above it:* Ancient cosmology presupposed the existence of a number of heavenly spheres suspended above the earth's surface, enclosing it like thick layers of ethereal paint. Paul presupposes this no-

tion in 2 Cor 12:2–4, where he refers to the esoteric Jewish mystical tradition of ascending through these heavenly realms, eventually to come into the presence of God. These multiple heavenly spheres were considered to be part of the created order. Hence, their transitory nature here is used to emphasize the transitory nature of the entire created order.

11:4 *when you were one, you became two:* The phrase, though obscure, may refer to the fall from primordial undifferentiated unity, an original perfection to which the enlightened anticipates returning. For this concept, see the note on Thom 4:3.

12:2 *James the Just:* James the brother of Jesus (Mark 6:3; Matt 13:55; Gal 1:19) was known as James the Just in Antiquity (Eusebius, *Ecclesiastical History* 11, xxiii, 4–7).

⁵Jesus said, "I'm not your teacher. Because you have drunk, you have become intoxicated from the bubbling spring that I have dug."

⁶And he took him, and withdrew, and spoke three sayings to him.

⁷When Thomas came back to his friends, they asked him, "What did Jesus say to you?"

⁸Thomas said to them, "If I tell you one of the sayings he spoke to me, you will pick up rocks and stone me, and fire will come from the rocks and devour you."

14 Jesus said to them, "If you fast, you'll bring sin upon yourselves, ²and if you pray, you'll be condemned, ³and if you give to charity, you'll harm your spirits. ⁴When you go into any region and walk about in the countryside, when people take you in, eat what they serve you and care for the sick among them. ⁵After all, what goes into your mouth won't defile you; what comes out of your mouth will."

15 Jesus said, "When you see one who was not born of woman, prostrate yourselves and worship. That one is your Father."

16 Jesus said, "Perhaps people think that I've come to cast peace upon the world. ²They don't know that I've come to sow conflict upon the earth: fire, sword, war. ³For there'll be five in a house: there'll be three against two and two against three, father against son and son against father, ⁴and they will stand alone."

17 Jesus said, "I will give you what no eye has seen, what no ear has heard, what no hand has touched, what has not arisen in the human heart."

18 The disciples said to Jesus, "Tell us, how will our end come?"

13:5
Ⓣ Th 28:2;
cf. Jn 4:13–15, 7:38

14:1–3
Ⓣ Th 6:1

14:4
//Q 10:8–9,
Lk 10:8–9,
Mt 10:5–8;
cf. Mk 6:8–13;
Mt 10:5–15;
Lk 9:2–6, 10:1–12;
Ⓣ 1 Cor 10:27

14:5
//Mk 7:15,
Mt 15:11

15
Cf. DSav 23:2

16
//Q 12:51–53,
Mt 10:34–39,
Lk 12:51–53;
cf. GNaz 11

16:2
Cf. Th 10, Lk 12:49;
Ⓣ GSav 12:9

16:3
◊Mi 7:5–6

16:4
Ⓣ Th 49:1; 75

17
//1 Cor 2:9;
cf. Q 10:23–24,
Mt 13:16–17,
Lk 10:23–24,
DSav 22:2–4;
◊Is 64:3

13:5 *dug:* The Coptic translator may have confused two very similar verbs here, writing *shite* ("measure") for *shit* ("dig"). SV assumes *shit* was original.

13:5 *I'm not your teacher. Because you have drunk, you have become intoxicated:* Or, "I am not your teacher, for you have drunk and have become intoxicated."

14:4 *care for:* or, "heal."

countryside: The Greek word here translated as countryside is ambiguous. Literally it means "places," but the places in question could be either the rural areas in between small towns or the towns themselves.

16:4 *alone:* In other texts this Greek loan word (*monachos*) may indicate a unique, solitary, or lonely one, an unmarried one, or (later, as a technical term) a monk. It may have similar connotations here. Though this is far too early in history to think of Christian "monks" per se, discipleship of this order in Thomas probably involves the solitary life of the wandering ascetic. This type of apostle became common in later Syrian Christianity.

²Jesus said, "Have you found the beginning, then, that you are looking for the end? You see, the end will be where the beginning is. ³Congratulations to the one who stands at the beginning: that one will know the end and will not taste death."

19 Jesus said, "Happy is the one who existed before coming into being. ²If you become my disciples and pay attention to my sayings, these stones will serve you. ³For there are five trees in Paradise for you; they do not change, summer or winter, and their leaves do not fall. ⁴Whoever comes to know them will not taste death."

20 The disciples said to Jesus, "Tell us what Heaven's empire is like."
²He said to them,

> It's like a mustard seed. ³⟨It's⟩ the smallest of all seeds, ⁴but when it falls on prepared soil, it produces a large branch and becomes a shelter for birds of the sky.

21 Mary said to Jesus, "What are your disciples like?"
²He said, "They are like servants who are entrusted with a field that is not theirs. ³When the owners of the field come, they will say, 'Give us back our field.' ⁴They strip ⟨it⟩ bare in front of them so as to give it back to them and return their field to them.

⁵For this reason I say, if the owners of a house know that a thief is coming, they will be on guard before the thief arrives, and won't let the thief break into their house and steal their possessions. ⁶As for you, then, be on guard against the world. ⁷Prepare yourselves with great strength, so the robbers can't find a way to get to you, for the privation you expect will come.

⁸Let there be among you a person who understands. ⁹When the crop ripened, he came quickly carrying a sickle and harvested it.

¹⁰Whoever has ears to hear should listen."

22 Jesus saw some babies nursing. ²He said to his disciples, "These nursing babies are like those who enter the ⟨Father's⟩ empire."

18:3
Ⓣ Th 1, 19:4, 85:2, 111:2

19:4
Ⓣ Th 1, 18:3, 85:2, 111:2

20
//Mk 4:30–32, Mt 13:31–32, Lk 13:18–19

20:4
◊Dn 4:20–21 (LXX), Ez 17:23 (LXX)

21:5
//Q 12:39–40, Mt 24:42–44, Lk 12:35–40; Ⓣ Th 103

21:9
//Mk 4:29 ◊Joel 3:13 (LXX)

22:2
Cf. Mk 10:14–15, Mt 18:3, Lk 18:16–17; Ⓣ Th 46

18:2 *the end will be where the beginning is:* In Hellenistic Judaism there a common idea that the world will someday be restored to perfection, and human beings will also be restored to the original Adamic perfection they enjoyed, before the fall. In the *end* it will all be as it was in the *beginning.*

21:2–4 The parable is a simple harvest scene. In previous translations this has been overlooked, creating the rather implausible image of "children" in a field who "strip bare"

when the owners of the field arrive.

21:2 *servants:* The Coptic means literally "little children," but this is probably the translation of a Greek word (*pais*) that can mean either "child" or "servant." The context suggests the latter.

21:4 *strip ⟨it⟩ bare:* The Coptic literally says that the servants "strip naked," but the verb can also be used to refer to the way harvesters take the grain of a field, wool off a sheep, etc. SV assumes this more figurative meaning.

³They said to him, "So do we have to enter the ⟨Father's⟩ empire as babies?"

⁴Jesus said to them, "When you make the two into one, and when you make the inside like the outside and the outside like the inside, and the upper like the lower, ⁵and when you make male and female into a single one, so that the male will not be male nor the female be female; ⁶when you make eyes in place of an eye, a hand in place of a hand, a foot in place of a foot, an image in place of an image, ⁷then you will enter [the ⟨Father's⟩ empire]."

23 Jesus said, "I shall choose you, one from a thousand and two from ten thousand, ²and they will stand as a single one."

24 His disciples said, "Show us the place where you are, for we must seek it."

²He said to them, "Whoever has ears to hear should listen. ³There is light within a person of light, and it shines on the whole world. If it does not shine, it is dark."

25 Jesus said, "Love your friends like your own soul, ²protect them like the pupil of your eye."

26 Jesus said, "You see the sliver in your friend's eye, but you don't see the timber in your own eye. ²When you take the timber out of your own eye, then you will see well enough to remove the sliver from your friend's eye."

27 "If you don't fast from the world, you won't find the ⟨Father's⟩ empire. ²If you don't observe the Sabbath as a Sabbath, you won't see the Father."

28 Jesus said, "I took my stand in the midst of the world, and in flesh I appeared to them. ²I found them all drunk and I did not find any of them thirsty. ³My soul ached for the human race, because they are blind in their hearts and do not see, for they came into the world empty and they also seek to depart from the world empty. ⁴But meanwhile they are drunk. When they shake off their wine, then they will change their ways."

29 Jesus said, "If the flesh came into being because of spirit, that is a marvel, ²but if spirit came into being because of the body, that is a marvel of marvels. ³Yet I marvel at how this great wealth has come to dwell in this poverty."

22:5b
Cf. Gal 3:27–28;
Ⓣ Th 114
22:6
◊Dt 19:21(LXX)
23:2
Ⓣ Th 4:3, 22:5
24:1
Ⓣ Jn 14:1–6,
DSav 30
24:3
//Q 11:34–35,
Mt 6:22–23,
Lk 11:34–35;
cf. Mt 5:14–16;
DSav 6, 8;
Ⓣ 2 Cor 4:6
25:1
//Mk 12:31;
Mt 22:39, 19:19;
Lk 10:27;
Ⓣ Rom 13:8,
Jas 2:8;
◊Lv 19:18 (LXX)
26
//Q 6:41–42,
Mt 7:3–5,
Lk 6:41–42
27:1a
Ⓣ Th 14:1; 110
28:1a
Ⓣ Jn 1:14
28:1b
◊Prv 1:20–33,
Bar 3:37
29
Ⓣ Th 87, 112;
Gal 5:16–18

22:4–5 For the notion of primordial unity, especially androgyny, see the note on 4:3.

22:5 *and when you make:* or, "in order that you may make."

23:2 On the term *single one* see the note on 4:3.

24:3 *it:* or, "he."

27:2 *observe the Sabbath as a Sabbath:* The Coptic phrase is difficult. It probably intends observing the Sabbath with integrity. Criticism of contemporary Sabbath observance is, of course, not unknown in the Jesus tradition (see Mark 2:27–28).

30 Jesus said, "Where there are three deities, they are divine. ²Where there are two or one, I am with that one."

31 Jesus said, "No prophet is welcome in his home town; ²doctors don't cure those who know them."

32 Jesus said, "A city fortified and built on a high hill cannot fall, nor can it be hidden."

33 Jesus said, "What you will hear in your ear, proclaim from your rooftops. ²After all, no one lights a lamp and puts it under a basket, nor does one put it in a hidden place. ³Rather, one puts it on a lampstand so that all who come and go will see its light."

34 Jesus said, "If a blind person leads a blind person, both of them will fall into a hole."

35 Jesus said, "You can't enter a strong man's house and take it by force without tying his hands. ²Then you can loot his house."

36 Jesus said, "Don't fret, from morning to evening and from evening to morning, about what you're going to wear."

30
//Mt 18:20

31
//Mk 6:4–6a,
Mt 13:57–58,
Lk 4:23–24, Jn 4:44

32
//Mt 5:14;
◊ Is 2:2–3, Mi 4:1–2

33:1
//Q 12:3, Mt 10:27,
Lk 12:3

33:2–3
//Mk 4:21; Lk 8:16,
11:33; Mt 5:15

34
//Q 6:39, Mt 15:14,
Lk 6:39

35
//Mk 3:27,
Mt 12:29,
Lk 11:21–22

36
//Q 12:22, Mt 6:25,
Lk 12:22

---

30 The Coptic version of this saying is deficient, based perhaps on a scribal error. The Greek version is closer to the original: "Where there are [three, they are without] God, and where there is only [one,] I say, I am with that one." Also, the Greek version continues with the words: "Lift up the stone, and you'll find me there. Split a piece of wood, and I'm there." The additional verses are found in the Coptic version at Thom 77:2–3.

33:1 *in the other ear:* This difficult phrase may well represent an instance of dittography—that is, a scribe's inadvertent duplication of words already transcribed. Otherwise, it may indicate the ear of another, or perhaps one's own inner ear.

36 The Greek version of this saying is longer. After the second *morning* it adds: "[about] your [food], what [you're going to] eat, or about [your clothing]." At the end of the saying it adds: ²"[You're much] better than the lilies, which don't card and never [spin]. ³As for you, when you have no garment, what [are you going to put] on? ⁴Who could add to your life span? That same one will give you your garment."

---

36 In the longer Greek version of this saying (see above), vv. 3–4 at first appear obscure. The *garment* in question may refer to a baptismal garment, a simple linen overlay given to the initiate for use in the ceremony. In Thomas it may also have more abstract theological connotations. Some early Christian groups believed that at death the soul flees the body only to be clothed in a new, heavenly body suitable for the transcendent world (see 1 Cor 15:35–50). This idea was common in Jewish theology as it developed in the Greek world during the period of Christian origins. Sometimes the metaphor of clothing is used to describe this mystery: the old garments are shed, the new garments of immortality are put on. This is probably the concept behind vv. 3–4.

37 His disciples said, "When will you appear to us, and when will we see you?"

²Jesus said, "When you strip without being ashamed, and you take your clothes and put them under your feet like little children and trample them, ³then [you] will see the son of the Living One and you won't be afraid."

38 Jesus said, "You've often wanted to hear these sayings that I am speaking to you, and you have no one else from whom to hear them. ²There will be days when you'll seek me and you won't find me."

39 Jesus said, "The Pharisees and the scholars have taken the keys of knowledge and hidden them. ²They have not entered, nor have they allowed those who want to enter to do so. ³As for you, be as sly as snakes and as simple as pigeons."

40 Jesus said, "A grapevine has been planted apart from the Father. ²Since it's not strong, it will be pulled up by its root and will perish."

41 Jesus said, "Those who have something in hand will be given more, ²and those who have nothing will be deprived of even the little they have."

42 Jesus said, "Be passersby."

43 His disciples said to him, "Who are you to say these things to us?"

²"Don't you understand who I am from what I say to you? ³Instead, you've become like the Jews, for they love the tree but hate its fruit, or they love the fruit but hate the tree."

44 Jesus said, "Whoever blasphemes against the Father will be forgiven, ²and whoever blasphemes against the son will be forgiven, ³but whoever blasphemes against the holy spirit will not be forgiven, either on earth or in heaven."

37:2
Ⓣ DSav 34;
◊Gn 2:25 (3:1 LXX)

38:2
//Jn 7:33–36

39:1–2
//Q 11:52,
Mt 23:13, Lk 11:52;
Ⓣ Th 102

39:3
//Mt 10:16

40
Cf. Mt 15:13,
Jn 15:5–6

41
//Mk 4:24–25;
Mt 13:10–13, 25:29;
Lk 8:18, 19:26

43:3
Cf. Mt 12:33

44
//Mk 3:28–30,
Mt 12:31–32,
Lk 12:10

37:2 *When you strip without being ashamed:* The phrase is obscure. Clues from later literature suggest several alternatives for understanding the concept. 1) Removal of one's clothing may indicate one's sexual indifference, sexual desire having been overcome through asceticism. 2) The phrase could refer to a baptismal ritual, wherein the participants disrobe. Early Christian initiates were usually baptized in the nude. 3) It could refer symbolically to the Platonic and later Gnostic notion that upon death, the soul sheds the body (metaphorically referred to as one's "clothing") and proceeds upward to the heavenly realm from whence it came (see Thom 29, 87, and 112).

42 The saying may be taken literally, as a call to take up the itinerant life of the disciple. Some, however, have seen in it a call to the enlightened to pass through this world without becoming mired in it.
43:2 The sentence may be read as a statement as well: "You don't understand who I am."
43:3 The critical treatment of "the Jews" here is typical of early Christian writing, which reflects the point of view of a small, sectarian group securing its identity over against the majority culture. Since there is no reason to think that Thomas Christians were themselves not Jewish (see Thom 27), it is inaccurate to see any anti-Judaism in this saying.

45 Jesus said, "Grapes are not harvested from thorn trees, nor are figs gathered from thistles, for they yield no fruit. ²Good persons produce good from what they've stored up; ³bad persons produce evil from the wickedness they've stored up in their hearts, and say evil things. For from the overflow of the heart comes evil."

46 Jesus said, "From Adam to John the Baptizer, among those born of women, no one is so much greater than John the Baptizer, so his eyes should not be downcast. ²But I have said that whoever among you becomes a child will recognize the ⟨Father's⟩ empire and will become greater than John."

47 Jesus said, "No one can mount two horses or bend two bows. ²And a slave cannot serve two masters, otherwise that slave will honor the one and offend the other.

³"Nobody drinks aged wine and immediately wants to drink new wine. ⁴New wine is not poured into old wineskins, or they might break, and aged wine is not poured into a new wineskin, or it might spoil. ⁵An old patch is not sewn onto a new garment, since it would create a tear."

48 Jesus said, "If two make peace with each other in a single house, they will say to the mountain, 'Move from here!' and it will move."

49 Jesus said, "Congratulations to those who are solitary, the chosen ones, for you will find the ⟨Father's⟩ empire. For you have come from it, and you will return there again."

50 Jesus said, "If they say to you, 'Where have you come from?' say to them, 'We have come from the light, from the place where the light came into being by itself, established [itself], and appeared in their image.' ²If they say to you, 'Is it you?' say, 'We are its children, and we are the chosen of the living Father.' ³If they ask you, 'What is the evidence of your Father in you?' say to them, 'It is motion and rest.'"

45
//Mt 7:15–20,
12:33–35;
Lk 6:43–45;
Ⓣ Jas 3:12

46
//Q 7:28, Mt 11:11,
Lk 7:28

46:2
//Mk 10:15,
Mt 18:3, Lk 18:17;
Ⓣ Th 22:2

47:2
//Q 16:13, Mt 6:24,
Lk 16:13

47:3–5
//Mk 2:21–22,
Mt 9:16–17,
Lk 5:36–39

48a
Cf. Mt 18:19

48b
Ⓓ Th 106;
cf. Mk 11:22–23;
Mt 21:21, 17:20b;
Lk 17:5–6;
Ⓣ 1 Cor 13:2

49
Ⓣ Th 16:4; 75;
DSav 1–2

50:1
Ⓣ Th 83, 84

50:3
Ⓣ Th 51:1; 60:6;
90; Mt 11:28–29;
DSav25;
◊ Sir 51:26–27,
6:23–31

46:1 *downcast:* literally, "broken." The Coptic idiom is obscure, but it seems to mean that John has no reason to be ashamed.

49–50 Together these sayings form a kind of primitive catechism for the spirit's journey to heaven. The interlocutors of whom Jesus warns the disciples are no doubt guardians of the way heavenward; the precisely communicated responses of the disciples are intended to placate those who guard the way. The context is probably the Platonic notion of the spirit's return to heaven upon death, but it might also refer to mystical ascent, a kind of dress rehearsal for the final journey home.

49 *solitary:* For the significance of this term in Thomas see the note on "alone" in Thom 16:4.

50:3 *motion and rest:* This odd phrase probably comes from the realm of Platonic anthropological speculation, in which the mind, or spirit, is said to reach a kind of steady state in the body after a period of tumult and unrest.

51 His disciples said to him, "When will the rest for the dead take place and when will the new world come?"

²He said to them, "What you are looking forward to has come, but you don't know it."

52 His disciples said to him, "Twenty-four prophets have spoken in Israel, and they all spoke of you."

²He said to them, "You have disregarded the living one who is in your presence, and have spoken of the dead."

53 His disciples said to him, "Is circumcision useful or not?"

²He said to them, "If it were useful, their father would produce ⟨children⟩ already circumcised from their mother. ³Rather, the true circumcision in spirit has become profitable in every way."

54 Jesus said, "Congratulations to the poor, for the empire of Heaven belongs to you."

55 Jesus said, "Whoever does not hate father and mother cannot be my disciple, ²and whoever does not hate brothers and sisters, and carry the cross as I do, will not be worthy of me."

56 Jesus said, "Whoever has come to know the world has discovered a corpse, ²and whoever has discovered a corpse, of that person the world is not worthy."

57 Jesus said,

The Father's empire is like someone who had [good] seed. ²His enemy came during the night and sowed weeds among the good seed. ³The man did not let the ⟨workers⟩ pull up the weeds, but said to them, "Don't, or else you might go to pull up the weeds and pull up the wheat along with them." ⁴For on the day of the harvest the weeds will be conspicuous, and will be pulled up and burned.

51:1 Ⓣ Th 50:3; 60:6; 90; Mt 11:28–29; DSav 25; ◊ Sir 51:26–27, 6:23–31

51:2 Ⓣ Th 3, 113; Lk 17:20–21; Mk 9:12–13; Mt 17:11; 2 Tm 2:17–18

52 Ⓣ EgerG 1:2–6, 3:2; Jn 5:39–40

53 Ⓣ Rom 2:29, Phil 3:3, 1 Cor 7:19, Gal 6:15, Col 2:11–12

54 //Q 6:20b, Mt 5:3, Lk 6:20b

55 //Q 14:26–27, Mt 10:37–38, Lk 14:26–27; Ⓓ Th 101

56 Ⓓ Th 80

57 //Mt 13:24–30

51:1 *rest*: Since "rest" is not a state achieved in death but in life (see Thom 2 and 50), it is possible that a mistake has occurred here, and a scribe has written "rest" instead of "resurrection," perhaps because "rest" is mentioned in Thom 50. SV retains the Coptic text as it stands, but the original might have asked about the "resurrection of the dead."

51:1 *rest*: On this term see the note on 2:4.

52:1 *twenty-four*: The number twenty-four is intriguing. It is the number of books in the Hebrew scriptures (see 2 Esd 14:45). See also Rev 4:4, as well as ancient magical texts, where twenty-four elders appear.

of you: literally, "in you."

53:2 *Their father* is ambiguous; it could refer either to God or to human males.

children: The Coptic text reads simply "them;" SV supplies the noun object ⟨children⟩ for clarity's sake.

57:3 *workers:* The Coptic text simply reads "them"; SV supplies the noun object ⟨workers⟩ for clarity's sake.

58 Jesus said, "Congratulations to those who have struggled and found life."

59 Jesus said, "Look to the Living One as long as you live, or else you might die and then try to see the Living One, and you won't be able to see."

60 ⟨He saw⟩ a Samaritan carrying a lamb and going to Judea. ²He said to his disciples, "That person is holding tight to the lamb."

³They said to him, "So that he can kill it and eat it."

⁴He said to them, "He will not eat it while it is alive, but only after he has killed it and it has become a carcass."

⁵They said, "Otherwise he can't do it."

⁶He said to them, "So also with you: seek for yourselves a place for rest, or you might become a carcass and be eaten."

61 Jesus said, "Two will recline on a couch; one will die, one will live."

²Salome said, "Who are you, mister? You have climbed onto my couch and eaten from my table as a stranger."

³Jesus said to her, "I am the one who comes from the one who is unwavering. I have been given some of the things of my Father."

⁴"I am your disciple."

⁵"For this reason I say, if anyone becomes unwavering, they will be filled with light, but if anyone becomes divided, they will be filled with darkness."

62 Jesus said, "I disclose my mysteries to those [who are worthy] of [my] mysteries. ²Don't let your left hand know what your right hand is doing."

63 Jesus said,

> There was a rich man who had a great deal of money. ²He said, "I shall invest my money so that I may sow, reap, plant, and fill my storehouses with produce, that

58
Cf. Q 6:22–23,
Mt 5:10–13,
Lk 6:22–23,
Mt 11:28–30;
Ⓣ Jas 1:12;
1 Pet 3:14a,
4:13–14;
◊ Sir 51:26–27

59
Cf. Th 38:2,
Jn 7:33–36

60
Ⓣ Th 7, 11:3

60:6
Ⓣ Th 50:3; 51:1;
90; Mt 11:28–29;
DSav25;
◊ Sir 51:26–27,
6:23–31

61:1
//Q 17:34–35,
Mt 24:40–41,
Lk 17:34–35

61:3b
//Q 10:22,
Mt 11:27, Lk 10:22;
cf. Jn 3:35, 13:3–4

62:1
Ⓣ Mk 4:10–11,
Mt 13:10–11,
Lk 8:9–10

62:2
//Mt 6:3

63
//Lk 12:16–21;
◊ Sir 11:18–19

60:1 ⟨He saw⟩: Or, "They saw." Neither phrase occurs in the manuscript. SV has emended the text on the assumption that the ancient scribe erred in omitting it.

60:2 Scribal error has created a defective text here. Perhaps it once read: "⟨Why does⟩ that person ⟨carry⟩ around the lamb?" It may also be read literally: "That person is around the lamb," but it is unclear what such a statement would mean.

61:5 *if anyone becomes unwavering:* SV has emended the text here. Without the emendation the text reads: "if one is desolate."

---

59 *Living One:* Perhaps Jesus (see the Prologue).

60:6 *rest:* On this term see the note on 2:4.

61:2 *Salome:* In the NT Salome appears only in Mark (15:40; 16:1). Elsewhere in early Christian literature she is to be found in the Infancy Gospel of James, the Mystical Gospel of Mark, the Gospel of the Egyptians, as well as several Gnostic works (*Pistis Sophia, First Apocalypse of James, Manichaean Psalm Book*).

as a stranger: The meaning of the Coptic is unclear. It could also mean "as someone special."

I may lack nothing." ³These were the things he was thinking in his heart, but that very night he died.

⁴"Whoever has ears to hear should listen."

64 Jesus said,

A man was receiving guests. When he had prepared the dinner, he sent his slave to invite the guests. ²The slave went to the first and said, "My master invites you."

³ He replied, "Some merchants owe me money; they're coming to me tonight. I have to go and give them instructions. Please excuse me from dinner."

⁴The slave went to another and said, "My master has invited you."

⁵He said to him, "I've bought a house and I've been called away for a day. I won't have any time."

⁶He went to another and said, "My master invites you."

⁷He said to him, "My friend is to be married and I have to arrange the banquet. I won't be able to come. Please excuse me from dinner."

⁸He went to another and said, "My master invites you."

⁹He said to him, "I've bought an estate and I'm going to collect the rent. I won't be able to come. Please excuse me."

¹⁰The slave returned and said to his master, "Those whom you invited to dinner have asked to be excused."

¹¹The master said to his slave, "Go out on the roads and bring back whomever you find to have dinner."

¹²"Buyers and merchants [will] not enter the places of my Father."

65 He said,

A [greedy] man owned a vineyard and rented it to some farmers, so they could work it and he could collect its crop from them.

²He sent his slave so the farmers would give him the vineyard's crop. ³They grabbed him, beat him, and almost killed him, and the slave returned and told his master.

⁴His master said, "Perhaps he didn't know them."

⁵He sent another slave, and the farmers beat that one as well.

⁶Then the master sent his son and said, "Perhaps they'll show my son some respect."

⁷Because the farmers knew that he was the heir to the vineyard, they grabbed him and killed him.

64
//Q 14:16–23,
Mt 22:1–10,
Lk 14:16–24;
◊ Dt 20:5–7

64:7
◊ Dt 24:5

64:12
◊ Sir 26:29–27:2,
Zec 14:13

65
//Mk 12:1–9,
Mt 21:33–41,
Lk 20:9–16

65:1 A lacuna in the papyrus makes the Coptic here uncertain; the hole can be filled in to read either "good man" or "greedy man."
65:4 *Perhaps he didn't know them*: Some scholars believe that the text should be emended here to read: "Perhaps they didn't know him."

[8]"Whoever has ears to hear should listen."

66 Jesus said, "Show me the stone that the builders rejected: that is the keystone."

67 Jesus said, "Those who understand the universe, but are lacking in themselves, are utterly lacking."

68 Jesus said, "Congratulations to you when you are hated and persecuted; [2]and no place will be found, wherever you've been persecuted."

69 Jesus said, "Congratulations to those who've been persecuted in their hearts: they are the ones who have truly come to know the Father. [2]Congratulations to those who go hungry, so the stomach of the needy may be filled."

70 Jesus said, "If you bring forth what is within you, what you have will save you. [2]If you do not have that within you, what you don't have within you [will] kill you."

71 Jesus said, "I will destroy [this] house, and no one will be able to build it [. . .]."

72 A [person said] to him, "Tell my brothers to divide my father's possessions with me."

[2]He said to the person, "Mister, who made me a divider?"

[3]He turned to his disciples and said to them, "I'm not a divider, am I?"

73 Jesus said, "The crop is huge but the workers are few, so beg the boss to send workers to the fields."

66
//Mk 12:10–11,
Mt 21:42–43,
Lk 20:17–18;
Ⓣ Acts 4:11–12,
1 Pet 2:4–8;
◊Ps 118:22

67
Cf. Mk 8:36–37,
Mt 16:26, Lk 9:25

68
//Q 6:22–23,
Mt 5:11–12,
Lk 6:22–23;
Ⓣ Jas 1:12

69:1
//Q 6:22–23,
Mt 5:11–12,
Lk 6:22–23;
Ⓣ Jas 1:12

69:2
//Q 6:21a,
Mt 5:6, Lk 6:21a

71
//Mk 14:58, 15:29;
Mt 26:61, 27:40;
Jn 2:19;
cf. Mk 13:2,
Acts 6:14

72
//Lk 12:13–14

73
//Mt 9:37–38,
Lk 10:2

---

74 *drinking trough:* Some scholars think that the Coptic here has been misspelled, and should read "well." The present translation assumes that the word is spelled correctly.

   well: The Coptic here makes no sense; most scholars assume that the word has been misspelled by a scribe and emend the text to read "well."

68:2 The second half of this saying is obscure. *Place* may refer to that seat of knowledge in the heart of the enlightened. Thus, no such place is found where the Thomas Christians have been persecuted. Alternatively, the text could be corrupt (a displaced negative) such that the original text would have read: "a place will be found in which you will not be persecuted."

69:1 *in their hearts:* The phrase probably refers to the inner struggle for insight in which the Thomas Christian is invited to engage (see Thom 2).

69:2 *so that the stomach of the needy may be filled:* or, "for the stomach of the one who desires will be filled."

71 *house:* It is noteworthy that Thomas' "temple" saying makes no direct reference to the temple. Of course, *house* could here refer obliquely to the temple. It could also invite a number of other referents: the ruling (Herodian) house; a family household; or metaphorically, the body as the house of the soul.

74 He said, "Master, there are many around the drinking trough, but there is nothing in the well."

75 Jesus said, "There are many standing at the door, but those who are solitary will enter the wedding hall."

76 Jesus said,

> The Father's empire is like a merchant who had a supply of merchandise and then found a pearl. ²That merchant was prudent; he sold the merchandise and bought the single pearl for himself.

³"So also with you: seek his treasure that is unfailing and enduring, where no moth comes to eat and no worm destroys."

77 Jesus said, "I am the light that is over all things. I am all: from me all came forth, and to me all attained. ²Split a piece of wood; I'm there. ³Lift up the stone, and you'll find me there."

78 Jesus said, "Why have you come out to the countryside? To see a reed shaken by the wind? ²And to see a person dressed in soft clothes, [like your] rulers and your powerful ones? ³They are dressed in soft clothes and they cannot understand truth."

79 A woman in the crowd said to him, "Congratulations to the womb that carried you and the breasts that fed you."

²He said to [her], "Congratulations to those who've heard the word of the Father and have truly kept it. ³For there will be days when you will say, 'Congratulations to the womb that has not conceived and the breasts that have not given milk.'"

80 Jesus said, "Whoever has come to know the world has discovered the body, ²and whoever has discovered the body, of that one the world is not worthy."

75
Ⓣ Th 16:4, 49:1;
DSav 19:7

76:1–2
//Mt 13:44–46

76:3
//Q 12:33–34,
Mt 6:19–21,
Lk 12:33–34

77:1a
Cf. Jn 8:12;
◊Wis 7:24–30

77:1b
Ⓣ Rom 11:36,
1 Cor 8:6

78
//Q 7:24–26,
Mt 11:7–9,
Lk 7:24–26

79:1–2
//Lk 11:27–28;
cf. Jn 13:17

79:3
//Lk 23:28–29

80
Ⓓ Th 56

77:2–3 The Greek version of this saying is preceded by the words: [Jesus says], "Where there are [three, they are without] God, and where there is only [one], I say, I am with that one." In the Coptic version these words are found in Thom 30:1–2.

---

74 *He:* Curiously, the saying is not explicitly attributed to Jesus. It may be that Saying 74 forms a dialogue together with Saying 73 and/or 75.

75 *solitary:* For the significance of this term in Thomas see the note on "alone" in Thom 16:4.

78:3 *They:* The Coptic here is ambiguous. This could also be the relative pronoun "who," the antecedent for which would be "rulers and your powerful ones."

80 In the ancient world the body was first of all part of the body politic. The connection between one's body and the world means that to withdraw from the world one must first understand one's body. See Thom 56.

81 Jesus said, "Whoever has become wealthy should rule, ²and whoever has power should renounce ⟨it⟩."

82 Jesus said, "Whoever is near me is near the fire, ²and whoever is far from me is far from the ⟨Father's⟩ empire."

83 Jesus said, "Images are visible to people, but the light within them is hidden in the image. ²The Father's light will be revealed, but his image is hidden by his light."

84 Jesus said, "When you see your likeness, you're happy. ²But when you see your images that came into being before you and that neither die nor become visible, how much you will have to bear!"

85 Jesus said, "Adam came from great power and great wealth, but he was not worthy of you. ²For had he been worthy, [he would] not [have tasted] death."

86 Jesus said, "[Foxes have] their dens and birds have their nests, ²but the human being has no place to lie down and rest."

81
//Th 110;
Ⓣ Mk 10:23,
Mt 19:23, Lk 18:24,
1 Cor 4:8

81:2
Cf. DSav 11

82
//GSav 12:9

86
//Q 9:58, Mt 8:20,
Lk 9:58

83:1–2 As in most ancient manuscripts, the Coptic Gospel of Thomas lacks punctuation. In this saying "the Father's light" might be attached as a modifier to the word "image" in 83:1 (so, "the image of the Father's light"), or be used in 83:2 as the subject (assuming a slight error in transcription). SV assumes the latter.

---

82 This saying, known also from Origen, among others, may be based loosely upon a proverb of Aesop: "Whoever is near to Zeus is near the thunderbolt." The gist of the saying is the risk that comes with enjoying the god's favor. Likewise, in our saying the risks of discipleship are explored. Fire is also an image associated with the beatific vision in Jewish mysticism.

83 Our understanding of the saying is hampered by textual problems. The original SV had: "the light within them is hidden within the Father's light. He will be disclosed, but . . ." But now it seems more likely that a small error in transcription has obscured the original, which the current translation now reflects.

The term *image* is probably used here in its Platonic sense, referring to material things (as opposed to ideas). Thus, the saying speaks on the one hand of the light dwelling undetected within each person (83:1), their light hidden within their image. But with the Father it is different. His image is overwhelmed by his light, so that all one sees

is his light. This may be a comment on mystical experiences, in which the beatific vision is often experienced as overwhelming light.

84 Like Thom 83, the saying features the term *image*. But here, it is set in contrast to *likeness*, which seems to refer to the material nature, the substance of a person. *Image* here then has a different meaning than in 83. It seems to derive from the notion in Hellenistic Judaism and contemporary Platonism that each person is endowed with a piece of the divine, the "image of God" imparted at creation. To discover this image of God is apparently an overwhelming experience.

86:2 *human being:* The Coptic here reads literally "son of man." Elsewhere in SV where this term is a title for Jesus it is translated as "the Human One." But here the term is not intended as a title for Jesus, but is rather the Semitic idiom meaning simply "human being." Occasionally, however, the phrase may be used self-referentially as a circumlocution for "I."

87 Jesus said, "How miserable is the body that depends on a body, [2]and how miserable is the soul that depends on these two."

88 Jesus said, "The messengers and the prophets will come to you and give you what belongs to you. [2]You in turn, give them what you have, and say to yourselves, 'When will they come and take what belongs to them?'"

89 Jesus said, "Why do you wash the outside of the cup? [2]Don't you understand that the one who made the inside is also the one who made the outside?"

90 Jesus said, "Come to me, for my yoke is comfortable and my authority is gentle, [2]and you will find rest for yourselves."

91 They said to him, "Tell us who you are so that we can believe in you."

[2]He said to them, "You examine the face of heaven and earth, but you have not come to know the one who is in your presence, and you don't know how to examine the present moment."

92 Jesus said, "Seek and you will find. [2]In the past, however, I didn't tell you the things about which you asked me then. Now I'm willing to tell them, but you're not seeking them."

93 "Don't give what is sacred to dogs, or else they might throw them on the manure pile. [2]Don't throw pearls [to] pigs, or they might . . . it [. . .]."

94 Jesus [said], "One who seeks will find, [2]and for [one who knocks] it will be opened."

95 [Jesus said], "If you have money, don't lend it at interest. [2]Instead, give [it] to someone from whom you won't get it back."

87
ⓘ Th 112;
Ⓣ Th 29,
Gal 5:16–18

89
//Q 11:39–40,
Mt 23:25–26,
Lk 11:39–40;
Ⓣ GOxy 840 2:8

90
//Mt 11:28–30;
◊ Sir 51:26–27,
6:23–31

91:2
//Mt 16:1–3,
Lk 12:54–56

92:1
ⓘ Th 2:1; 94;
//Q 11:9–10;
Mt 7:7–8;
Lk 11:9–10;
DSav 7:2, 11:5;
Mary 4:7;
cf. GHeb 6b

92:2
Ⓣ Th 38, Jn 16:4–5

93
//Mt 7:6

94
ⓘ Th 2:1, 92:1;
//Q 11:9–10;
Mt 7:7–8;
Lk 11:9–10;
DSav 7:2, 11:5;
Mary 4:7;
cf. GHeb 6b

95
//Q 6:30, 34–35;
Mt 5:42;
Lk 6:30, 34–35

93:2 The text is deficient here. Among proposals for its restoration are the following: "bring it [to naught]" and "grind it [to bits]."

---

87 This obscure saying seems to comment on two levels of depravity, one in which one becomes mired in corporeal existence, and yet another in which even the soul fails to realize its freedom over against the body. In contemporary Platonic thinking, the human being contained body, soul, and mind (or spirit). Body and soul were both mortal, the mind (or spirit) immortal. Still, in some early Christian theologians the soul could rise above the body, if properly oriented to wisdom. This saying may warn against the soul's demise when dragged down by the body.

88:1 *messengers:* The Coptic here could also mean "angels" in the sense of heavenly messengers (see Mark 8:38). But as in Greek, it may simply mean messengers in the ordinary sense as well (see Luke 9:51–52). Here it has been rendered in the latter sense because it is paired with *prophets*, an early Christian title for its itinerant preachers (see Didache 11:36).

90 *rest:* On this term see the note on 2:4.

96 Jesus [said],

The Father's empire is like [a] woman ²who took a little leaven, [hid] it in dough, and made it into large loaves of bread.

³"Whoever has ears to hear should listen."

97 Jesus said,

The [Father's] empire is like a woman who was carrying a [jar] full of meal. ²While she was walking along [a] distant road, the handle of the jar broke and the meal spilled behind her [along] the road. ³She didn't know it; she hadn't noticed a problem. ⁴When she reached her house, she put the jar down and discovered that it was empty.

98 Jesus said,

The Father's empire is like someone who wanted to kill a strong man. ²While still at home he drew his sword and thrust it into the wall to find out whether his hand would be strong enough. ³Then he killed the strong man.

99 The disciples said to him, "Your brothers and your mother are standing outside."

²He said to them, "Those here who do what my Father wants are my brothers and my mother. ³They're the ones who will enter my Father's empire."

100 They showed Jesus a gold coin and said to him, "Caesar's people demand taxes from us."

²He said to them, "Give Caesar what belongs to Caesar, ³give God what belongs to God, ⁴and give me what is mine."

101 "Whoever does not hate [father] and mother as I do cannot be my [disciple], ²and whoever does [not] love [father and] mother as I do cannot be my [disciple]. ³For my mother [. . .], but my true [mother] gave me life."

96:1–2
//Q 13:20–21,
Mt 13:33,
Lk 13:20–21

96:2
Ⓣ Th 8:2, 20:4

99
//Mk 3:31–35,
Mt 12:46–50,
Lk 8:19–21, GEbi 5

99:2
//GHeb 4a

100
//Mk 12:13–17,
Mt 22:15–22,
Lk 20:20–26,
EgerG 3:1–6

101
//Q 14:26–27,
Mt 10:37–38,
Lk 14:26–27;
Ⓓ Th 55

97:2 *While she was walking along [a] distant road:* The text is deficient here; an alternative rendering is: "While she was walking on [the] road, still far off."
101:3 The lacuna cannot be filled in with certainty. One proposal: "For my mother [gave me falsehood]."

97:3 *she hadn't noticed a problem:* or, "she had not understood how to toil."
98:2 The parable probably envisions a modest peasant home of mud brick, whose walls would serve well as a surface on which to practice one's thrust.

102 Jesus said, "Damn the Pharisees! They are like a dog sleeping in the cattle's feeding trough: the dog neither eats nor [lets] the cattle eat."

103 Jesus said, "Congratulations to the one who knows where the brigands are going to attack. [He] can take action, mobilize his kingdom, and be prepared before the brigands invade."

104 They said to Jesus, "Come on, let's pray today, and let's fast."

²Jesus said, "What sin have I committed, or how have I been undone? ³Rather, when the groom leaves the wedding hall, then let people fast and pray."

105 Jesus said, "Whoever knows the father and the mother will be called the child of a whore."

106 Jesus said, "When you make the two into one, you will become children of Adam, ²and when you say, 'Mountain, move from here!' it will move."

107 Jesus said,

The ⟨Father's⟩ empire is like a shepherd who had a hundred sheep. ²One of them, the largest, went astray. He left the ninety-nine and looked for the one until he found it. ³After he had struggled, he said to the sheep, "I love you more than the ninety-nine."

108 Jesus said, "Whoever drinks from my mouth will become like me; ²I myself shall become that person, ³and the hidden things will be revealed to him."

109 Jesus said,

The ⟨Father's⟩ empire is like a man who had a treasure in his field but didn't know it. ²And [when] he died he left it to his [son]. The son [did] not know

---

102
Cf. Th 39:1–2,
Q 11:52, Mt 23:13,
Lk 11:52

103
Ⓣ Th 21:5–7,
Q 12:39–40,
Mt 24:42–44,
Lk 12:39–40

104:3
//Mk 2:19–20,
Mt 9:15,
Lk 5:34–35;
Ⓣ Th 6:1; 14:1; 27

106
Ⓓ Th 48

106:1a
Ⓣ Th 22:4

106:2
//Mk 11:22–23;
Mt 17:19–20, 21:21;
cf. Lk 17:5–6;
Ⓣ 1 Cor 13:2

107
//Q 15:4–7,
Mt 18:12–14,
Lk 15:4–7

108:1
Ⓣ Th 13:5;
Jn 4:13–14,
7:37–39;
◊ Sir 24:21

109
//Mt 13:44

---

105 *child of a whore:* The saying is obscure. Of possible relevance may be the charge, common in early Jewish-Christian debate, that Jesus was the illegitimate child of Mary and a certain Roman soldier.

106:1 *children of Adam:* The Coptic reads literally "sons of men." If *make the two one* has to do with the return to some primordial state of non-differentiated perfection (androgyny), the expression may have originally read "sons of the Anthropos," meaning the original human being, Adam. Some early Christians believed that Adam was androgynous before the fall; a return to the perfection of the created order

would then involve a return to androgyny, hence "sons of Adam." As it is, the expression is difficult.

108:1 Comparing revelation to water, from which the recipient drinks to satisfaction is common in wisdom and Gnostic texts. The reference here to Jesus' *mouth* as the source of this satisfying drink is no doubt related to Thomas' presentation of Jesus as one who speaks words of revelation. In principle, the concept is the same as that presupposed in John 4:13–14.

109:1 Wisdom is sometimes likened to hidden *treasure* (Prov 2:1–5; Sir 20:30–31).

⟨about it either⟩. He took over the field and sold it. ³The buyer went plowing, [discovered] the treasure, and began to lend money at interest to whomever he wished.

110 Jesus said, "Whoever has found the world, and has become wealthy, should renounce the world."

111 Jesus said, "The heavens and the earth will roll up in your presence, ²and whoever is living from the Living One will not see death."

³Does not Jesus say, "Those who have found themselves, of them the world is not worthy"?

112 Jesus said, "Damn the flesh that depends on the soul! ²Damn the soul that depends on the flesh!"

113 His disciples said to him, "When will the ⟨Father's⟩ empire come?"

²"It won't come by watching for it. ³It won't be said, 'Look, here!' or 'Look, there!' ⁴Rather, the Father's empire is spread out upon the earth, and people don't see it."

114 Simon Peter said to them, "Make Mary leave us, for females are not worthy of life."

²Jesus said, "Look, I will guide her to make her male, so that she too may become a living male spirit, like you. ³For every female who makes herself male will enter the empire of Heaven."

110
//Th 81;
Ⓣ Mk 10:23,
Mt 19:23, Lk 18:24,
DSav 11:4

111
Ⓣ Th 11:1–2

111:1
Ⓣ Mk 13:30–31;
Mt 5:18, 24:34–35;
Lk 16:17, 21:32–33;
◊ Is 34:4,
Ps 102:25–27

111:3
Ⓣ Th 56, 80

112
Ⓓ Th 87;
Ⓣ Th 29, Jn 3:6,
Gal 5:16–18

113
//Lk 17:20–21;
cf. Th 3:1–3,
Mary 4:4–5;
Ⓣ Th 51,
Mk 13:21,
Mt 24:23, Lk 17:23

114:2–3
Ⓣ Th 22:5,
Mary 5:8

113:3 *It won't be said:* or, "They will not say."

114:1 The Petrine tradition is not notably kind to women. In the NT the Petrine epistles place women in a subordinate role (1 Pet 3:1–6). In the extra-canonical tradition Peter is portrayed as critical of Mary in particular (e.g., in the Gospel of Mary and the *Pistis Sophia*). While some Gnostic groups were egalitarian with respect to gender, many were somewhat misogynist, identifying the origin of evil and sin in the world with the feminine.

114:2–3 The theological rationale for Jesus' reply is similar, but not identical to the notion elsewhere in Thomas that salvation consists in returning to the state of primordial, androgynous perfection (Thom 4:3; 22:5). Here, of course, the ideal is not to become androgynous, but to "become male." In other texts dealing with ideas from Gnosticism or speculative wisdom the transition from male to female is used as a metaphor for translation from earthly to heavenly existence, from mortality to immortality. There may also be a practical side to the saying, as women philosophers often disguised themselves as men.

Sayings of Jesus in dialogues

Early followers of Jesus remembered and recorded sayings attributed to him in a variety of ways. Some sayings, especially parables, were retold as separate stories or teachings without any fixed introduction or conclusion. Other sayings, especially "one-liners" or aphorisms, were showcased in short dialogues—conversations between Jesus and other characters. At least three types of dialogues are found in the early gospels.

1. Sometimes Jesus is confronted by opponents—typically scholars and/or Pharisees—whose questions or objections are answered by a saying that the early Christian community considered authoritative. An example is Mark 2:15–17, which concludes with the pronouncement, "Since when do the able-bodied need a doctor? It's the sick who do."

2. Some dialogues feature a question concerning belief or conduct in the Christian community—what should we believe? what should we do?—that is given an authoritative answer by quoting Jesus' words. Such is the case in Mark 9:38–41, which spotlights the saying in 9:40: "Whoever is not against us is on our side."

3. In other dialogues aphorisms are presented with short biographical introductions that provide a situation in which the sayings would make sense. An example is Mark 6:1–6, in which Jesus' saying in 6:4 ("No prophet is disrespected, except on his home turf and among his relatives and at home") is given the appropriate context of a visit by Jesus to his hometown (6:1).

Dialogues were also created to make Jesus' sayings palatable to fresh converts and to an increasingly settled Christian community that included affluent members. In this process some of Jesus' strictest demands were explained or expanded so as to soften or entirely remove their harshness. In Mark 10:23–27, for example, Jesus' exclusion of the rich from the empire of God (10:25) is followed by a popular proverb, "Everything's possible for God!" (10:27), which in effect declares that God can overrule even Jesus' saying in verse 25!

Gradually it became the fashion to place Jesus' sayings in newly created conversations with his disciples. By the middle of the second century, or perhaps even earlier, Christian authors began to create dialogues between the resurrected Jesus and his apostles, and thereby establish the authority of what "Jesus said" for new and different situations.

The Secret Book of James

Introduction

The Secret Book of James relates that 550 days after his resurrection and immediately prior to his ascension, Jesus imparted a private revelation to James and Peter. The account of this revelation is a "secret book" (*apocryphon*, 1:2, 5), which James introduces within the framework of a letter.

Even though Secret James makes no claim to be a gospel, it still deserves to be included in a collection of early Christian gospels. It makes use of various sayings traditions, some of which appear in the New Testament gospels, while others are preserved only in Secret James. In addition, the figures of James and Peter lend authority to the "revealed" (1:2, 5) status of Jesus' teaching, a device also used in the composition of the New Testament gospels (see, e.g., Peter in Matt 16:15–9; the eleven in Luke 24:48). Finally, the term "remembering" (2:1) was widely used to preface the quotation of oral sayings material (e.g., Acts 20:35). The dialogue and discourse are essentially a collection of sayings, some relatively primitive in form (e.g., 8:3), others substantially reworked (e.g., 6:9–11), and still others clearly late formulations (e.g., 6:17).

Character and origins of the papyrus text

There is but a single extant manuscript of Secret James; it has survived in the collection of bound documents (codices) discovered near Nag Hammadi, Egypt, in 1945. The text, inscribed on papyrus, is a Coptic translation of a lost Greek original. Though the manuscript is untitled, the text derives its modern name from its introductory material, in which an unknown author appropriates and speaks through the person of James, the brother of the Lord. Writing under a pseudonym of this manner was conventional in Antiquity, and is well represented within the Nag Hammadi library itself.

It is difficult to date Secret James. Since it deals with martyrdom (5:3–5) it probably was not written after 313 CE, when the emperor Constantine officially ended the persecution of Christians. Indeed, several factors point to a much earlier date. Its witness to the compiling or "remembering" of sayings traditions, the conspicuous deference to James and Peter, and the primitiveness of much of its content suggest that it may well have been written in the first half of the second century.

Message to an ancient audience

The document's enthusiasm for martyrdom (5:3–5) is part of a vigorous exhortation to earnestness (4:3–5:6; 9:1) and is likely meant to challenge complacency within the community to which it is addressed (4:5–7). The Savior dwells with the believer (6:23) and urges him or her to participate in the realization of salvation (e.g., 6:7, 39; 7:3). Salvation consists of the knowledge or "fullness" (8:3–4) of the empire of heaven (8:4, 11) or the spirit (3:18).

James himself assures his readers of their connection with and superiority to the broader church. It is James who transmits the private revelation (and, ostensibly, a previous one, 1:5) and narrates it in the first person. During the dialogue, Peter speaks twice (3:12; 9:1) but misunderstands Jesus; James alone is addressed directly by name (6:20), and he maintains the more dominant voice. It is significant that as James and Peter return to the other disciples after Jesus' ascension, it is James who sends "each one" on his way (10:9), travels to Jerusalem (10:9), and prays for inclusion among those for whose sake James has received the promise of salvation (10:7, 9).

A wedding of religious ideas

In Secret James, traces of Gnosticism blend with concepts that are more expressly Christian. Entrance into the empire of heaven, for example, presupposes not childlikeness (e.g., Mark 10:15) but being "full," a term associated in gnostic sources with knowledge and salvation ("fill" or "full" occurs fifteen times in Secret James; see, e.g., 2:6–7; 3:13–18). Similarly, the empire of heaven is discovered through knowledge (6:18), the means of salvation in Gnosticism. The gnostic elements in Secret James, however, do not constitute a special system or doctrine; they are expressed through particular vocabulary and by association with other Christian notions (e.g., 9:4).

The structure

Although the document contains a minimum of narrative detail, it has a discernible literary pattern:

1. Introductory letter (1:1–7).
2. Secret book (2:1–10:9).
   a. Post-resurrection appearance (2:1–3:1).
   b. Dialogue and Discourse (3:2–9:13).
   c. Ascension (10:1–9).
3. Postscript (11:1–4).

The revelatory portion (2:1–10:9), which occupies most of the work, concludes with not only Jesus' ascension but also with the attempt of his companions, James and Peter, to follow. They are thwarted by the inquisitiveness of their fellow disciples (10:6).

Literary unity of the text

There are abrupt changes and inconsistencies between major sections of Secret James. Three theories, all of them plausible, have been advanced to explain this feature of the book. The first regards the letter (1:17) and the secret book as originally separate. The unity of the two sections, therefore, would be the work of a redactor, who in the process of editing embellished the material by enhancing the position of James. Another proposal considers the passages on martyrdom (4:1–5:6) and prophecy (6:1–4) as secondary additions; their omission leaves a conceivably earlier document consisting of shorter sayings. A third theory views the document as the work of one author, for both the letter segment and the secret book use a rare grammatical feature, the beatitude with the verb in the future tense (1:4; 7:3; 8:3, 9). However, this could also be the work of a redactor attempting to harmonize the two sections.

Jesus through the community of Secret James

Secret James is an important witness to the diversity of forms in which sayings of Jesus were preserved in the early church. Parables (e.g., 6:10, 17; 8:3), prophecies (e.g., 6:28–30), and wisdom sayings (e.g., 2:4, 6; 8:5) are easily identifiable within the discourse and dialogue. In Secret James, therefore, we can see how traditional sayings of Jesus were handed down and transposed in response to communal requirements, a process that continued until the widespread adoption of the "Fourfold Gospel." The most ancient of the sayings absorbed into Secret James may well belong to the earliest period of collected sayings traditions.

The cross as a symbol of Jesus' suffering is present in Secret James, though the brief account of Jesus' condemnation, imprisonment, death, and burial (4:6) has no direct literary relationship to the New Testament passion narratives. The treatise affirms the redemptive value of the crucifixion: belief in Jesus' "cross and death" leads to life and God's empire (4:11–5:2). Still, the death of Jesus is not a major concern of the document. Its interest, rather, lies in Jesus' teaching and in the furnishing of a foundational revelation for a community of gnostic Christians. In order to accomplish this, Secret James assembles and transforms sayings of Jesus, selectively preserving fragments of the Savior's salvific teaching "in parables" (6:5; see Mark 4:2).

The Secret Book of James

1 [James, writing] to [—]thos. Peace [to you from] peace, [love from] love, [grace from] grace, [faith] from faith, life from holy life!

²Since you asked me to send you a secret book that was revealed to Peter and me by the Master, I could neither refuse you nor dissuade you; so [I have written] it in Hebraic letters and have sent it to you—and to you alone. ³Nevertheless, you should do your best, as a minister of the salvation of the saints, to take care not to disclose this book to many—the things the Savior did not wish [to] disclose to all of us, his twelve disciples. ⁴Still, congratulations to those who will be saved through the trustworthiness of this text.

⁵Ten months ago I sent you another secret book that the Savior revealed to me. ⁶However, that one you are to regard in this way, as revealed to me, James. ⁷And this one [. . . revealed . . .] those who [. . .], therefore, and seek [. . .] so it is [. . .] salvation [. . .].

2 Now the twelve disciples [used to] sit all together at the [same time], remembering what the Savior had said to each one of them, whether secretly or openly, and setting it down in books. ²I was writing what went in [my book]—suddenly, the Savior appeared, [after] he had departed from [us, and while we were watching] for him. ³And so, five hundred fifty days after he rose from the dead, we said to him, "You went away and left us!"

⁴"No," Jesus said, "but I shall go to the place from which I have come. If you wish to come with me, come on!"

⁵They all replied, "If you bid us, we'll come."

⁶He said, "Let me tell you, no one will ever enter the empire of heaven at my bidding, but rather because you yourselves are full. ⁷Let me have James and Peter, so that I may fill them."

2:1
ⓣ Th Prologue

2:3
ⓣ Acts 1:3

2:4
ⓣ Jn 7:33; 13:36; 14:3–5; 16:5, 16–20, 28; Pet 13:2

2:6–3:1
ⓣ Jn 3:3–5

2:6
ⓣ Mk 10:15, Mt 18:3, Lk 18:17

1:1–7 Along with 10:8–11:1, this is probably the final major addition in the composition of Secret James. (See the Introduction.)

1:1 Lists of virtues are frequent in early Christian literature. See Gal 5:22–23; Eph 6:23–24; 2 John 3.

1:3 The title *Savior* is applied to Jesus only in the later phases of the document's composition (see also 1:5; 2:1, 2; 11:3). *Master* is the preferred address in the secret revelation itself (2:1–10:7). Also, it appears that the disciples as *twelve* (see 2:1) is a standard formula.

2:1 The Gospel of John associates the notion of *remembering* with the departure of Jesus (John 14:25–26; 15:20, 27; 16:4).

2:3–4 Other writings of the period provide differing accounts of the length of time between Jesus' resurrection and his ascension. In Acts 1:3, he remains for 40 days; in the Ascension of Isaiah 9:16, for 545 days; in Irenaeus *Against Heresies* 1.3.2, for 18 aeons; *Against Heresies* 1.30.14, for 18 months.

2:6 The term *full* (and its related forms) is common in gnostic writings, where it usually indicates the attainment of knowledge or the virtue gained by knowledge. In both gnostic and apostolic literature, it also represents present or eventual salvation, the possession of grace, or the indwelling of the Spirit. For the sense here, see the note to 9:4.

3 And when he called these two, he took them aside, and commanded the rest to carry on with what they had been doing.

²The Savior said, "You have received mercy [. . .] become [. . .] they wrote [. . .] book, as [. . .] to you [. . .] and just as [. . .] they [. . .] hear and [. . .] they [. . .] understand. ³Don't you want to be filled? And is your heart drunk? Don't you want to be sober? ⁴You should be ashamed of yourselves! ⁵And now, waking or sleeping, remember that you have seen the Human One, and with him have you spoken, and to him have you listened. ⁶Damn those who've seen the Human One. ⁷Congratulations to those who haven't seen that man, and who haven't associated with him, and who haven't spoken with him, and who haven't listened to a thing he said. Yours is life! ⁸Know, therefore, that he treated you when you were sick, so that you might reign. ⁹Damn those who've been relieved of their sickness, for they will relapse again into sickness. ¹⁰Congratulations to those who haven't been sick, and have experienced relief before they got sick. The empire of God belongs to you! ¹¹Therefore, I say to you, become full and leave no place within you empty, or else the one who is coming will be able to mock you."

¹²Then Peter responded, "Look, three times you've told us, 'Become [full;' but] we are full."

¹³The [Master replied], "This [is why I told] you, ['Become full,' so] that [you] might not [be lacking; those who are lacking] will not [be saved]. ¹⁴For fullness is good [and lacking] is bad. ¹⁵Therefore, inasmuch as it's good for you to lack but bad for you to be filled, whoever is full tends to be lacking. ¹⁶One who lacks is not filled in the same way that someone else who lacks is filled; but whoever is full receives what he deserves. ¹⁷Therefore, it's fitting to lack while it's possible to fill yourselves, and to be filled while it's possible to lack, so that you may be able [to fill] yourselves the more. ¹⁸Therefore, [become] full of the spirit but lacking in reason. For reason is of the soul; indeed, it is soul."

4 And I responded, "Master, we can obey you if you wish, for we have forsaken our fathers and our mothers and our villages and have followed you. ²Give us the means, [then], not to be tempted by the evil devil."

3:3–5
Ⓣ 1 Thes 5:4–8,
Th 28

3:5–7
Cf. SJas 8:5–6,
Jn 20:29

4:1
Cf. Mk 10:28,
Mt 19:27, Lk 18:28

4:2
Cf. Q 11:4, Mt 6:13,
Lk 11:4

3:6–7 The curse in v. 6 would be most unusual in the NT gospels, but here serves a polemical function for its intended audience of gnostic Christians. In v. 5 being an eyewitness is positive and desirable. Verse 7, on the other hand, denigrates the belief among mainstream apostolic Christians as compared to the faith transmitted (ostensibly by James) to gnostic Christians via a secret revelation.

3:14–15 The seeming conflict between the statements about being *filled* with those about *lacking* is explained by 3:18. See further the note to 7:6–8.

3:18 In Secret James, *spirit* is prized above both *reason* and *soul*. See the note at 7:6–8.

[3]The Master replied, "If you do the Father's will, what credit is that to you—unless he gives you, as part of his gift, your being tempted by Satan? [4]But if you are oppressed by Satan, and are persecuted, and you do his will, I [say] that he will love you, and will make you equal with me, and will regard [you] as having become [beloved] through his providence according to your own choice. [5]So won't you cease being lovers of the flesh and afraid of suffering? [6]Or don't you realize that you haven't yet been abused and haven't yet been accused unjustly, nor have you yet been locked up in prison, nor have you yet been condemned unlawfully, nor have you yet been crucified ⟨without⟩ reason, nor have you yet been buried in the sand, as I myself was, by the evil one? [7]Do you dare to spare the flesh, you for whom the spirit acts as an encircling wall? [8]If you think about the world, about how long it existed ⟨before⟩ you and how long it will exist after you, you will discover that your life is but a single day, and your sufferings but a single hour. [9]Accordingly, since what is good will not enter this world, [10]you should scorn death and be concerned about life. [11]Remember my cross and my death, and you will live!"

5 And I answered him, "Master, don't proclaim the cross and death to us, for they are far from you."

[2]The Master replied, "Let me tell you, no one will be saved without believing in my cross; [for] the empire of God belongs to those who have believed in my cross. [3]Become seekers of death, therefore, like the dead who are seeking life, for what they seek is manifest to them. So what do they have to worry about? [4]When you inquire into the subject of death, it will teach you about being chosen. [5]Let me tell you, those who fear death will not be saved; for the empire of ⟨God⟩ belongs to those who are dead. [6]Become better than I; be like the son of the holy spirit!"

6 Then I asked him, "Master, how will we be able to prophesy to those who ask us to prophesy to them? For there are many who inquire of us, and who hope to hear an oracle from us."

[2]The Master replied, "Don't you realize that the head of prophecy was severed with John?"

4:4
ⓣ Jn 14:23

4:10–5:3
ⓣ Mk 8:34–35; Mt 10:38–39, 16:24–25; Lk 9:23–24

6:2
Cf. Mk 6:14–29, Mt 14:1–12

6:2–4
ⓣ Q 16:16, Mt 11:12–13, Lk 16:16, Eph 4:15–16

4:4 *Providence according to your own choice* refers to the tension between predestination and the exercise of one's free will. Other hints of predestination are in 6:38 and 9:13.

4:6 This is the closest Secret James comes to describing the suffering and death of Jesus. *Buried in the sand* differs from the general tradition about the death of Jesus. The author was probably ignorant of first-century Judean burial practices and familiar with specific local interment methods, in Egypt for example.

4:9 *what is good will not enter this world*: Put another way,

suffering is inevitable for all those who enter the world. Similar ideas are stated in 7:8 and 8:8.

5:5 *Belongs to those who are dead* can be translated "those who put themselves to death," i.e., offer themselves for martyrdom.

5:6 *Become better than I* is mediated by the second half of the verse, *be like the son of the holy spirit*, i.e., like Jesus himself, or at least like another man filled with the spirit. The emphasis is on facing death fearlessly, not on the goal of surpassing Jesus.

6:5–6
Cf. Mk 4:10–13,
4:33–34;
Mt 13:10–17,
13:34–35; Lk 8:9–
10; Jn 10:6, 16:25;
◊ Ps 78:2, Is 6:9–10

6:7
Ⓣ Jn 14:21–23

6:9–11
Ⓣ Jn 12:24,
15:2–8; Jas 5:7

6:13
Ⓣ Jn 17:5, 20:17

6:15a
//Q 15:4–7,
Mt 18:12–14,
Lk 15:3–7, Th 107,
Jn 10:11–17

6:15b
//Mk 4:3–9, 26–29,
Mt 13:1–13,
Lk 8:4–10, Th 9

6:15c
//Q 6:47–49,
Mt 7:24–27,
Lk 6:47–49

6:15d
//Mt 25:1–13

6:15e
//Mt 20:1–16

6:15f
//Lk 15:8–10

6:15g
//Q 13:20–21,
Mt 13:33,
Lk 13:20–21

6:16
Ⓣ 1 Cor 13:13

6:17
Cf. Mk 4:13–20,
Mt 13:18–23,
Lk 8:11–15

6:19
Ⓣ Mt 24:4,
Gal 6:7, 1 Thes 5:8,
Jas 1:16

³But I said, "Master, it's not possible to cut off the head of prophecy, is it?"

⁴The Master said to me, "When you comprehend what 'head' means, and that prophecy issues from the head, understand what 'Its head was cut off' means. ⁵At first I spoke with you in parables and you did not understand. Now I am speaking with you plainly and you still don't understand. ⁶Still, for me you were a parable among parables, and the disclosure of openness.

⁷"Be eager to be saved without being urged. Instead, become zealous on your own and, if possible, surpass even me. For that is how the Father will love you.

⁸"Become haters of hypocrisy and evil intent. For intent is what produces hypocrisy, and hypocrisy is far from the truth.

⁹"Don't let the empire of heaven wither away. ¹⁰For it is like a date palm shoot whose fruit fell down around it. It put forth buds, and when they blossomed, something made its productivity dry up. ¹¹So it also is with the fruit that came from this singular root: when it was picked, fruit was gathered by many. Truly, that was good. ¹²Isn't it possible to produce new growth now? Can't you discover how?

¹³"Since I was glorified in this way before now, why do you detain me when I am eager to go? ¹⁴For after my [labors] you have constrained me to stay with you eighteen more days for the sake of parables. ¹⁵It was enough for some people to pay attention to the teaching and understand 'the shepherds,' and 'the seed,' and 'the building,' and 'the lamps of the maidens,' and 'the wage of the workers,' and 'the drachmas,' and 'the woman.'

¹⁶"Become eager for instruction. For the first prerequisite for instruction is faith, the second is love, the third is works; now from these come life. ¹⁷For instruction is like a grain of wheat. When they sowed it they had faith in it; and when it sprouted they loved it, because they envisioned many grains in place of one; and when they worked they were sustained, because they prepared it for food, then kept the rest in reserve to be sown. ¹⁸So it's possible for you, too, to receive for yourselves the empire of heaven: unless you receive it through knowledge, you will not be able to discover it.

¹⁹"Therefore, I'm telling you, be sober; don't go astray. ²⁰Moreover, I've often said to you all together—and also to you alone, James, have I said—be saved. ²¹I've commanded you to follow me, and I've taught you how to respond in

---

6:10 The parable of the date palm shoot is unique to Secret James, occurring nowhere else in the early gospel traditions. The basic comparison between the shoot and the empire of heaven could be quite early, but the remainder of the saying is a second-century expansion.

6:11 *This singular root* refers to *the empire of heaven* in v. 9. The *fruit* in question may represent the gnostic Christian believer or the knowledge which she or he possesses.

6:15 This parable list would seem to prove that the NT gospels were familiar to the audience of Secret James, but it is the only such instance. As the list does not relate to the parables which precede and follow it, it is probably a later insertion into the text.

6:21 The Coptic word for *rulers*, borrowed from Greek, refers either to heavenly rulers or to earthly ones. Most scholars tend toward the latter, though hostile heavenly rulers or powers are hinted at in 10:3.

the presence of the rulers. [22]Observe that I've descended, and have spoken, and have expended myself, and have won my crown, in order to save you. [23]For I descended to dwell with you so that you might also dwell with me. And when I found your houses to be without roofs, I dwelt instead in houses that could receive me at the time of my descent.

[24]"Therefore, rely on me, my brothers; understand what the great light is. [25]The Father does not need me. For a father does not need a son; it's the son who needs the father. [26]To him do I go, for the Father of the Son is not in need of you.

[27]"Pay attention to instruction, understand knowledge, love life. And no one will persecute you, nor will any one oppress you, other than you yourselves.

[28]"You wretches! You unfortunates! You pretenders to the truth! You falsifiers of knowledge! You sinners against the spirit! [29]Do you even now dare to listen, when you should have spoken from the beginning? Do you even now dare to sleep, when you should have been awake from the beginning, so that the empire of heaven might receive you? [30]Let me tell you, it's easier for a holy one to descend into defilement, and for an enlightened person to descend into darkness, than for you to reign—or even not to!

[31]"I have remembered your tears and your grief and your sorrow; they are far from us. [32]Now, then, you who are outside the Father's inheritance, weep where it's called for, and grieve, and proclaim what is good: how the Son is ascending, as he should. [33]Let me tell you, were I sent to those who would listen to me, and were I to have spoken with them, I would never have come down to earth. From now on, then, be ashamed for them.

[34]"Look, I'm going to leave you and go away; I don't want to stay with you any more—just as you haven't wanted it either. Now, then, follow me eagerly. [35]Therefore, I say to you, for your sake I descended. [36]You are the beloved; it is you who will become the cause of life for many. [37]Call on the Father, pray to God frequently, and he will give to you. [38]Congratulations to whoever has envisioned you along with him when he is proclaimed among the angels and glorified among the saints.

"Yours is life! [39]Rejoice and exult as children of God. Keep [his] will, so that you may be saved. Accept reproof from me and save yourselves. [40]I am pleading for you with the Father, and he will forgive you much."

7 When we heard these things, we became elated, for we had despaired over what we recounted earlier. [2]But when he saw us rejoicing, he said, "Damn you

6:23
Ⓣ Jn 1:11, 14a; 14:3, 23; 15:4

6:24–26
Ⓣ Q 10:22, Mt 11:27, Lk 10:22, Jn 5:19–20

6:28–30
Ⓣ Q 3:7–9, Mt 3:7–10, Lk 3:7–9

6:31–32
Ⓣ Jn 16:20

6:33
Ⓣ Jn 8:47, 10:25–26

6:34–40
Cf. Jn 14:3–28

6:34
Ⓣ Jn 16:7

6:36
Ⓣ Jn 17:20

6:37
Ⓣ Jn 16:23

6:38
Ⓣ 1 Tm 3:16

6:40
Ⓣ Jn 14:16

6:22 *Crown* is often used to denote salvation after martyrdom.
6:23 *Without roofs* could be translated "unable to hold [me]," which would suggest the disciples' inability to receive

the revealed word.
6:25–26 Rejection of the Son is not the point; v. 25 broadly illustrates the declaration of v. 26.

who require an intercessor! Damn you who stand in need of grace! ³Congratulations to those who've spoken out fearlessly and have obtained grace for themselves. ⁴Compare yourselves to foreigners: how are they regarded by your city? Why abandon your home on your own, making it available for those who want to live in it? You outcasts and runaways! Damn you, for you will be caught. ⁵Or perhaps you think that the Father is a lover of humanity? Or that he is persuaded by prayers? Or that he grants favors to one on behalf of another? Or that he puts up with someone who seeks? ⁶For he knows about desire, as well as what the flesh needs: does it not long for the soul? ⁷For without the soul the body does not sin, just as the soul is not saved without the spirit. But if the soul could be saved from evil, and the spirit were also saved, then the body would become sinless. For the spirit is what animates the soul, but the body is what kills it—in other words, it is the soul which kills itself. ⁸Let me tell you, he will never forgive the sin of the soul, nor the guilt of the flesh; for none of those who have worn the flesh will be saved. ⁹Do you think, then, that many have found the empire of heaven? Congratulations to those who have envisioned themselves as the fourth one in heaven."

8 When we heard these things, we became distressed. ²But when he saw that we were distressed, he said, "This is why I'm telling you this, that you may know yourselves. ³For the empire of heaven is like a head of grain that sprouted in a field. When it ripened, it scattered its fruit and, in turn, filled the field with heads of grain for another year. ⁴You also: be eager to reap for yourselves a head of the grain of life, so that you may be filled with the empire.

⁵"As long as I am with you, pay attention to me and obey me; but when I take leave of you, remember me. Remember me because I was with you, though you didn't know me. Congratulations to those who have known me. ⁶Damn those who've heard and haven't believed! Congratulations to those who haven't seen [but] have [had faith].

⁷"Once again I [appeal] to you. For I am revealed to you building for you a house of great value, since you take shelter in it; likewise, it can support your neighbors' house when theirs is in danger [of] collapsing. ⁸Let me tell you,

---

7:7
Ⓣ Jn 6:63

8:3
Cf. Mk 4: 3–9, 4:26–29; Mt 13:3–9; Lk 8:4–8; Th 9

8:5–6
Ⓣ SJas 3:5; Jn 12:35–36, 20:29

8:7
Ⓣ Mt 7:27, Jn 14:2

7:5 The precise intention of these rhetorical questions is difficult to gauge. But see the note to 6:25–26.

7:6–8 The conceptual division of the person into *body*, *soul*, and *spirit* was common in Antiquity. *Spirit* is the highest nature of the three, governing the *soul* and the *body* (or *flesh*) that the *soul* inhabits. The *soul* encompasses the non-physical capacities of a person (e.g., reason), and can be oriented toward good or toward evil; the *spirit*, which is from faith in the divine, guides the *soul* in its choices (see the note to 3:18).

7:9 *fourth one in heaven*: There is no consensus among

scholars as to the meaning, identification, or status of such a figure.

8:7 The author's rendering of the parable of the building (6:15; see Matt 7:24–27) uses the term *house* as an image of the spiritual constitution of the believer. How it can function to *support your neighbors' house* is unclear, though the spread of knowledge or faith may be envisioned here.

8:8 For a fuller account, see 6:33–34. Consider the Epistle of the Apostles 39: "Whoever has kept my commandments shall be a son of light. But because of them that corrupt my words do I come down from heaven."

damn those for whose sake I was sent down here! ⁹Congratulations to those who are on the way to the Father. ¹⁰Again I admonish you. You who exist, be like those who don't exist, so that you may dwell with those who don't exist.

¹¹"Don't let the empire of heaven become desolate among you. ¹²Don't be arrogant about the light that enlightens. ¹³Rather, behave toward yourselves in the way that I have toward you: I placed myself under a curse for you, so that you could be saved."

9 To this Peter responded, "Sometimes, Master, you urge us on toward the empire of heaven, yet at other times you turn us away. Sometimes you make appeals, draw us toward faith, and promise us life, yet at other times you drive us away from the empire of heaven."

²The Master replied to us, "I've offered you faith many times; moreover, I've revealed myself to you, James, and you have not understood me. ³On the other hand, now I see you rejoicing again and again. And even though you are elated over [the] promise of life, you still despair and become distressed when you are taught about the empire of ⟨heaven⟩. ⁴But you, through faith [and] knowledge, have received life. ⁵So disregard rejection when you hear [it]; but when you hear about the promise, exult all the more. ⁶Let me tell you, whoever receives life and believes in the empire will never leave it—not even if the Father wishes to banish him!

⁷"This is all I'm going to tell you at this time. Now I'm going to ascend to the place from which I've come. ⁸But you, when I was eager to go, have rebuffed me; and instead of accompanying me, you've chased me away. ⁹Still, pay attention to the glory that awaits me and, having opened your hearts, listen to the hymns that await me up in heaven. ¹⁰For today I must take my place at the right hand of my Father. I have spoken my last word to you; I shall part from you. ¹¹For a chariot of spirit has lifted me up, and from now on I shall strip myself so that I may clothe myself. ¹²So pay attention: congratulations to those who proclaimed the Son before he descended, so that, having come, I might ascend. ¹³Congratulations three times over to those who [were] proclaimed by the Son before they existed, so that you could have a share with them."

9:2
Ⓣ Jn 14:9
9:6
Ⓣ Jn 6:37
9:7–8
Ⓣ Jn 16:4–5
9:7
Ⓣ Jn 14:25, 16:28; Pet 13:2
9:11
Ⓣ Th 37

8:10 In gnostic and Christian writings, a tension is often established between true and false or illusory being. Those *who exist* are identified with the former. However, to not exist is a positive value in this verse, and the implication is that *those who don't exist* really do, but on another level—they *dwell*. Perhaps they are believers who have reached a fullness of knowledge. Notice as well the stylistic resemblance to 3:13–18.

8:13 *Under a curse* refers either to Christ becoming human, or to the fulfillment of OT law (Deut 21:23; quoted in Gal 3:13).

9:1–2 Peter asks the question, but Jesus answers James.

9:4 *Faith* and *knowledge* are virtually equated. Knowledge (*gnosis*) was highly valued in Gnosticism.

9:11 *I shall strip myself so that I may clothe myself:* i.e., in glory. The notion of stripping off to be clothed anew can be baptismal, but *from now* on precludes that once-for-all-time possibility.

9:13 *Those who [were] proclaimed by the Son before they existed* are those chosen for salvation even before their earthly existence. Alternately, the phrase could indicate that those same chosen individuals existed before their own human births (see 6:38; 11:4).

10 When he said this, he went away. ²So Peter and I knelt down, gave thanks, and sent our hearts up to heaven. ³We heard with our ears and saw with our eyes the sound of battles and a trumpet's blast and utter turmoil.

⁴And when we passed beyond that place, we sent our minds up further. We saw with our eyes and heard with our ears hymns and angelic praises and angelic rejoicing. Heavenly majesties were singing hymns, and we ourselves were rejoicing.

⁵After this, we also desired to send our spirits heavenward to the Majesty. ⁶And when we went up, we were not permitted to see or hear a thing. For the rest of the disciples called to us and asked us, "What did you hear from the Teacher?" and, "What did he tell you?" and, "Where has he gone?"

⁷We answered them, "He has ascended. He has given us a pledge, and promised all of us life, and disclosed to us children who are to come after us, having bid [us to] love them, since we will [be saved] for their sake."

⁸And when they heard, they believed the revelation, yet were angry about those who would be born. ⁹So, not wishing to give them an occasion to take offense, I sent each one to a different place. And I myself went up to Jerusalem, praying that I might obtain a share with the beloved who are to appear.

11 Now I pray that a beginning may take place with you. For this is how I can be saved—since they will be enlightened through me, through my faith and through another's that is better than mine, for I wish for mine to be more lowly. ²So do your best to be like them, and pray that you may obtain a share with them. ³For the Savior did not disclose revelation to us, other than what I have reported. ⁴For their sake do we proclaim a share with those for whom this has been proclaimed, those whom the Master has made his children.

10:1–3
//Lk 24:51,
Acts 1:9–11
10:4
Cf. Rv 14:2–3
10:7
Ⓣ Mt 28:16–20
10:8–9
Ⓣ Th 12

10:7 *We will [be saved] for their sake* refers to Jesus' declaration in 9:13, and later, to James' advice in 11:2. Each of these verses likely has gnostic Christians in mind.
10:8–9 The disciples' anger is not fully explained in the narrative, but it probably points to the historical conflict between the main apostolic church and the gnostic Christians.

With the dispersal of the twelve apostles and the decisive action by James, the gnostic Christian community for whom the document was originally written understands its origins through James' association with the twelve. By virtue of his privileged relationship with the Lord, the community believes its foundation to be rooted in Jesus.

The Dialogue of the Savior

Introduction

A gospel about baptism

The Dialogue of the Savior is a dialogue between "the Lord" and several disciples composed in its final form probably around 150 CE. It was originally written in Greek, but now survives only in one fragmentary Coptic manuscript from Nag Hammadi. The central theme of the Dialogue is a process of salvation described in the Gospel of Thomas: "Those who [seek] should not stop [seeking until] they find. When they find, [they will be disturbed. When they are] disturbed, they will rule, and [when they rule], they will [rest]" (Thomas 2, Greek version). This theme supports the Dialogue of the Savior's invitation to baptism (1–3). It is even likely that the author intended the writing as a discussion of baptism, and in particular of the question: do baptized persons belong in heaven, or should they continue their struggle in the flesh, i.e., on earth?

The author answers the question as follows. First, the writing looks backwards; it describes a moment in the past, when Jesus and his disciples were together. But the reader sees the disciples not only as historical people; he or she finds that they stand for the community's catechumens (converts in training) being instructed by their teacher (34:1). In this way, the instructions to the disciples in the Dialogue are probably addressed to those in the author's community who are preparing for baptism.

Baptism and the destiny of the soul

The disciples are invited to witness the journey of a soul. What they see is also the journey of their own souls, for which this "single soul" stands as an example: along with its "consort" (5:3), the soul is transported to the height and given garments of light. The critical stage of the journey is described in 1:5: "the passage by which the chosen and the solitary will pass." This process is probably the same as the "little" becoming one with the "great" (5:1; 17:18; 25:3). The disciples are amazed by what they see, and accept the vision and its interpretation "in faith" (17:11; cf. 29:2).

According to the Dialogue of the Savior, the purpose of baptism is not to make this heavenly journey unnecessary, for example by bringing about a spiritual "rebirth." In fact, discussion of any type of birth other than that from a woman is ruled out (37:4). The believer's soul, which is "from the truth" (23:2), needs no second birth. Instead baptism stands for the journey that the believer's soul will make in the future, at the time of death. Therefore baptism does not involve receiving future rewards ahead of time, but the instruction, by word and by ritual, about the nature of the world. The baptized do not yet see the All, but only know their true selves (14:1–4); they do not yet rule over the archons (or heavenly rulers), but at "the time of dissolution" (3:1) they will (19:1–6).

Therefore in the Dialogue three "eras" are described. The first is the pictured, fleeting history of a believer's soul being redeemed. The second is the climax in the history of the Lord and his disciples, mentioned in the Dialogue's opening and long in the past by the time of the reader. The third is the future of the author's community, whom the author hopes to convince that death, and life, may now be faced without fear.

Sources and composition

Several things about this document make it almost certain that the final author combined various written sources to produce the present Dialogue of the Savior. First, a series of long speeches of the Lord seem to belong together, in terms of subject matter and style (see especially 1–3; 8:2–8; 12:2–11; 15:4–16:8; 38; 41:3–7). Second, several of the speeches have transitions that interrupt the flow of the dialogue (see especially in 12:12; 17:1–12, 14–21). Third, there are some abrupt changes of subject matter, as if the author switched from one source to another and back again.

Because of these features, it is now widely held that the author of the Dialogue made use of four sources: (1) a dialogue between the Lord and his disciples; (2) a creation myth; (3) a wisdom list (or catalog of elementary substances); and (4) an apocalyptic vision (or heavenly revelation). To these the author added an introduction (1–3), concluding instructions (41:6), and various other sentences that enable the Dialogue of the Savior to be read as a continuous whole.

The dialogue (4–8; 11; 13:1–15:10; 18:4–41:7) consists of short speeches; in each of these a traditional saying of Jesus is quoted, or reflections on a traditional saying. Although numerous similar sayings are found in the synoptic gospels and in the Gospel of Thomas, it is unlikely that the author ever quotes the New Testament gospels. A wide range of topics is covered, and individual questions and answers are frequently linked by catchwords (words or phrases in two or more adjacent lines); but the dialogue does not follow a particular pattern of questions and answers. The author does not even state whether the Lord is speaking before or after the resurrection.

The chapters that include the creation myth (9–10; 12) do not give a complete "myth." They are pieces of a mythic drama, based on ideas in Genesis 1–2, presumably known to the readers in a fuller form.

In quoting from a wisdom list (15:11–16:8), the author quotes a pattern of negative conditions ("If not . . .") and their consequences ("then . . .") built on a well known list of cosmic elements: earth, air, fire, and water. This list is made specifically Christian; it is also expanded with a statement of belief concerning the Son and the Father.

Finally, the apocalyptic vision (17) is unique in the Dialogue of the Savior, because it includes a lengthy descriptive narrative and someone identified as "the Human One." This "Human One," distinct from "the Lord" conversing with the disciples, directs and describes the journey of "a single soul" (17:16) from the abyss to the heights of heaven. Meanwhile the author tells us that the disciples see this drama in a vision, which they witness from "the edge of heaven and earth" (17:1).

Title

The final author or editor is probably responsible for the work's title, because after his first speech the Lord is identified simply as "the Savior" in the introductions to only two speeches (4:2; 6). Everywhere else the revealer is called "the Master" or simply identified as "he/him." His conversation partners, in order of appearance, are (1) Matthew (10 speeches); (2) Judas (18 speeches, including three addressed not to the Lord but to Matthew [17:4; 34:1; 37:7]); (3) "(all) his disciples" (7 speeches, including "his disciples, twelve in number" [32:1]); and (4) Mary (13 speeches). In addition, (5) the Human One has two speeches (17:8–10, 17).

Similarity to other gospels

The Dialogue of the Savior is obviously different in style and tone from the New Testament gospels and the Gospel of Thomas. But the differences are more in degree than in kind. For example, the combination of several older sources is similar to the composition of Matthew or Luke, each of which draws on Q, Mark, and other materials. Similarly, the concern of the Dialogue with baptism, and more generally with the support of young believers, is not so unlike what we find in Matthew, a gospel often thought of as catechetical. Again, the lack of narrative (stories about what Jesus did) shows that the Dialogue continues the tradition of sayings gospels, like Q and Thomas.

Above all, what the Dialogue of the Savior shares with all the other gospels is an interest not only in what Jesus said, but in what he meant. And for the Dialogue, as for the other gospels, the meaning of Jesus' sayings was to be applied to the community's actual experience and concerns. The distinctive feature of the Dialogue of the Savior, its dialogue form, recognizes how such meaning might be sought and presented: by the written imitation of conversation between the Lord and his disciples.

The Dialogue of the Savior

1 The Savior said to his disciples, "The time has now come, ⟨my⟩ brothers, for us to leave our labor and rest, for the one who rests will rest forever. ²And I say to you, be always in heaven [. . .] time [. . .] you [. . .] afraid [. . .] to you. ³I [say to you] anger [is] to be feared [. . .] who stirs up anger [. . .]. ⁴But when you had [. . .] they received these words concerning it in fear and trembling, and it set them among archons, for nothing came from it. ⁵But when I came, I opened the way and taught them, the chosen and the solitary, the passage by which they will pass—those who know the Father, since they have believed the truth, and all the praises with which you ⟨are to⟩ give praise."

2 "So when you give praise, do it in this way: ²'Hear us, Father, as you heard your only begotten Son and received him to yourself, ⟨and⟩ gave him rest from many [labors. ³You] it is whose power [. . .] your armor [. . .] light [. . .] living [. . . who] cannot be touched [. . .] the word of [. . .] repentance of life [. . . fr]om you. ⁴You are the solitary's purpose and freedom from all care.' ⁵Again: 'Hear us, as you heard your chosen ones, those ⟨who⟩ through your sacrifi[ce] are to enter by their good works, whose souls have been saved from these blind limbs so that they might remain forever. Amen.'"

3 "I will teach you: When the time of dissolution comes, the first power of darkness will come upon you. ²Do not fear and say, 'Look, the time has come!' ³But when you see a single staff [which . .] this [. . .] [. . .]you [. . .] understand that [. . .] from the work [. . .] and the archons [. . .] come upon you [. . .] ⁴Now, fear is the pow[er . . .] ⁵If then you fear what is to come upon you, it will swallow you up, since there is not one among them who will spare you or have mercy on you. ⁶But in this way look at [the . . .] in it, for you have been victorious over every word that is upon earth. ⁷It [will] take you up to the pl[ace . . .] in which

1:1
Ⓣ Heb 4, 10–11; Rv 14:13
1:5
Ⓣ 2 Thes 2:12, Th 49:1
2:2
Ⓣ Jn 1:14; 3:16, 18
2:3
Ⓣ Eph 6:11–17
2:5
Ⓣ Eph 5:2; Heb 10:10, 14; 1 Pet 1:9; Jas 1:21
3:1
Ⓣ 2 Tm 4:6, Col 1:13

1:1 *Savior*: In the NT gospels this title is used of Jesus only in Luke 2:11 and John 4:42.

rest: a term for reaching heaven.

1:4 *concerning it*: the pronoun *it* refers back to *anger*; so too the subject of the next verb.

archons: literally, "rulers," i.e., hostile heavenly forces.

1:5 *chosen and solitary*: These terms, used also in Thom 37:2, describe those considered to be among God's elect.

2:1 Probably a liturgical rubric; see the late first- or early second-century Didache 9:1–2 and 10:1–2: "Give thanks in this way: 'We give thanks to you, Holy Father . . .'"

2:2 With this prayer compare another prayer from the Nag Hammadi writings, in the *Epistle of Peter to Philip* 133:121–26: "Father . . . hear us just as [. . .] in thy holy child Jesus Christ."

2:5 *by their good works*: The Coptic can also be translated "into their good things" (i.e., their heavenly reward). A comparable statement is found in Clement of Alexandria, *Excerpts from Theodotus* 86.3: "who . . . did not enter into the good things which have been prepared."

3:1–4 This fragmentary chapter appears to summarize the soul's journey after death.

3:5 *not one among them*: i.e., among the archons (see 1:4).

there is no rule [. . . ty]rant. [8]When you [. . .] you will see the things that [. . .] and also [. . .] tell you that [. . .], the design [. . .] design which is [. . . pla]ce of truth [. . .] but [. . .] [9]But you [. . .] of the truth, this [. . .] living [mind] because of [. . .] your joy [. . .] [10]So then, [. . .] so that [. . .] your souls [. . .] lest it [. . .] the word [. . .] lift up [. . .] they did not [. . .] your [in]side [and your outside] [. . .] [11]For the crossing place is to be feared be[fore . . .] [12]But as for you, [with a] single mind pass it by, for its depth is great ⟨and⟩ [its] height very great [. . .] a single mind [. . .] and the fire wh[ich . . .] is [. . .] [. . .] all the powers [. . .] you, they will [. . .] and the pow[ers . . .] they [. . .] [13]I te[ll you . . .] this soul [. . .] become a [. . .] in everyone [. . .] you are t[he . . .] and that [. . .] forgetfulness [. . .] children of [. . .] and you [. . .] you [. . .]."

4 [Mat]thew said, "How [. . .] [. . .]?"

[2]The Savior said, "[. . .] the things that are in you [. . .] will remain, [but] you [. . .]."

5 Judas [said], "Master, [. . .] the works [. . . th]ese souls, these [. . .] these little ones, when [. . .] where will they be? [. . .] the spirit [. . .]."

[2]The Master [said], "[. . .] [. . .] recei[ve th]em. [3]These do not die [. . .] they do not perish, for they have known [their] consorts and the one who will re[cei]ve them. [4]For the truth seeks [after] the wise and the righteous."

6 The Savior s[aid], "The lamp [of the b]ody is the mind. [2]As long as [the things that are] in you are rightly ordered, that is, [. . .] your bodies are [light]. As long as your heart is da[rk], your light which you await [. . .] [3]I have call[ed. . .] that I shall go [. . .] my word [. . .] I send to [. . .]."

7 His discipl[es said, "Master,] who is the one who seeks and [. . .] reveals?"

[2][The Master] sai[d to them,] "The one who seeks [is also the one who] reveals [. . .]."

[3]Matt[hew said to him, "Master, wh]en I [hear . . .] and [when] I speak, who is the one who [speaks, and who] the one who hears?"

[4]The [Master] said, "The one who speaks is also the one who h[ears], and the one who sees is also [the one who] reveals."

8 M[ar]y said, "Master, tell me, from where [do I] carry the body [when I] weep, and from where ⟨do I carry it⟩ when I [laugh]?"

3:12
Ⓣ Th 42

6:1
//Q 11:34,
Mt 6:22–23,
Lk 11:34

7:2
Cf. Q 11:10; Mt 7:8;
Lk 11:10; Th 92:1,
94:1

7:4
Ⓓ DSav 31:2;
Ⓣ Jn 16:13

8:1
Ⓣ DSav 16:4,
Lk 6:21, Jn 16:20

5:3 *consort*: The Greek word *syzygos*, literally "yoke-part-ner," occurs only once in the NT (Phil 4:3). In Gnostic theology it often stands for the pairing of aeons (heavenly beings or realms).

7:3 The same question is found in another Nag Hammadi writing, the *Testimony of Truth* 42:3–4: "Who is the one who speaks? And who is the one who hears?"

8:1 To *carry the body* means to live a mortal human life.

²The Master said, "[. . .] weep because of its works [. . .] remain and the mind laughs [. . .] [. . .] spirit. ³If you do not [. . . the] darkness, you will [not] be able to see [the light]. ⁴So then, I tell you [. . . of the] light is the darkness. ⁵[And if you do not] stand in [the darkness, you will] not [be able] to see the light. ⁶[. . .] the lie [. . .] were brought by [. . .] ⁷You will give [. . . lig]ht and [. . .b]e forever. [. . .] in the [. . .] one [. . .] forever. ⁸Then [all] the powers will [. . .] you, those that are above and those [that] are below, in the place where [there will] be weeping and grinding of teeth concerning the end of a[ll] these things."

9 Judas said, "Tell [us, M]aster, what [there was] before heaven and earth came into being."

²The Master said, "There was darkness and water and a spirit upon ⟨the⟩ wa[ter.] ³And I say to [you, . . .] what you seek [and] search for, lo[ok, it is wi]thin you, and [. . .] the power and the mys[tery . .] spirit, because from [. . .] wickedness comes [. . .] the mind and [. . .]. ⁴Look, [. . .][. . .]."

10 [. . .] said, "Master, tell us where [the soul st]ands, and where the true m[ind] is."

²The Master said, "The fire of [the] spirit came into being in [. . .] both of them. ³Because of this the [. . .] came into being, ⟨and⟩ the true mind came into being wi[thin] them [. . .] ⁴If you se[t your so]ul on high, the[n you will be] exalted."

11 And Matthew asked him, "[. . .] took it, namely [. . .] those who [. . .]."

²The Master said, "[. . .] stronger than him who [. . .] you [. . .] him to follow [yo]u and all the works [. . .] your heart. ³For just as your hearts [. . .], [. . . in this] way you shall be victorious over the powers that are [abo]ve and those that are below [. . .]. ⁴I say to you, those [who have] power should deny [it and] change their ways. ⁵And those who [. . .] seek and find and rejo[ice]."

8:3
ⓉJn 12:35

8:8
ⓉMt 8:12; 13:42, 50; Q 13:28; Mt 8:12; Lk 13:28; ◊Ps 112:10

9:1–4
◊Gn 1:1

9:2
◊Gn 1:2

9:3
Cf. Lk 7:21, Th 3:3

11:4
//Th 81:1–2; ⓉMk 8:34

11:5
Cf. Q 11:10; Mt 7:8; Lk 11:10; Jn 16:24; Th 2, 92:1, 94:1; GHeb 6

8:5 The saying is reconstructed from DialSav 15:11.

8:5 The same topic is discussed in the Nag Hammadi *Teachings of Silvanus* 102:23–26: "Understand . . . that those who are in darkness will not be able to see anything unless they receive the light and recover ⟨their⟩ sight by means of it."

8:8 *concerning the end*: or "until the end" (see 1 Cor 1:8).

10:1 *The true mind* may indicate composure or "rest" (see 1:1) or the higher part of human existence.

11:3 The *powers* above and below are supernatural forces (e.g., archons) and earthly authorities.

11:5 This saying, in various forms, is widespread in early Christian literature; in addition to the references above see, e.g., *The Book of Thomas the Contender* 140:40–141:2: [Blessed are] the wise who [sought after the truth, and] when they found it, they rested upon it forever and were unafraid of those who wanted to disturb them"; 145:10–16: "As you pray, you will find rest, for you have left behind the suffering and the disgrace. For when you have come forth from the sufferings and passions of the body, you will receive rest from the good one, and you will reign with the king."

12 Judas said, "Look! See that everything is [. . .] just like these signs that are over [the earth]. Because of this they came to be so."

²The Master [said], "When the Fa[ther establi]shed the world, he [gathered] water from it, [and the] Word came forth from it. ³He appeared in many [. . .], and was higher than the pa[th of the stars which surround] the whole earth. ⁴They [. . .], for the water that was gather[ed . . .] was beyond them [. . .] of the water, a great fire [surr]ounding them like a wall. ⁵And [. . .] time, when many things were separated from [what] was inside. ⁶When the [Word] was set in place he looked at [. . .] and said to it, 'Go and [. . .] from you, so that [. . .] in want from generation to gene[ration an]d from age to age.' ⁷Th[en it] cast forth from itself [spr]ings of milk and spri[ngs of] honey and oil and w[ine] and go[od] fruit and sweet taste and good roots, s[o that] it might lack nothing from generation [to] generation and from age to age.

⁸"And it is above [. . .] [. . .]set, namely [. . .] its beauty [. . .] ⁹And beyond [. . .] was a great light, [more] powerful [than] the one like it, for this is [the one which] rules over the aeons that are [abo]ve and that are below. ¹⁰[The light was] taken from the fire and was scattered over the [Pleni]tude that is above and that is [be]low. ¹¹On them all things depend."

¹²When Judas heard these things he bowed down and [worshi]ped, and praised the Master.

13 [Ma]ry asked her brothers, "Where will you set down [the things] about which you ask the Human [One]?"

²The Master [said] to her, "Sister, [no one] will be able to inquire about these things ex[cept one] who has a place to set them down in the heart. ³[. . .] to come forth [. . .] and enter [. . .] so that they might not be bound [to] this miserable world."

14 [Matt]hew said, "Master, I wish [to see] that place of life [. . .] where there is no wickedness [but only] pure [li]ght."

²The Master said, "Brother Matthew, you will not be able to see it as l[ong as you] bear flesh."

³[Mat]thew said, "Master, ev[en if I will not be able to] see it, let me [know it]."

12:1
◊ Gn 1:14

12:6 *Word:* All that is certain is that this word is masculine.

12:2 *from it*: The pronoun *it* refers back to *water*, or *cosmos*, or *him*.

12:3 *He appeared*: or "it appeared."

12:10 *Plenitude* translates *Pleroma*, literally "fullness," referring to the heavenly realm.

12:12 *Judas*: Probably Judas (the same name as "Jude," literally "Jew") the apostle (see Luke 6:16); much less likely he is the brother of Jesus (see Mark 6:3 and Matt 13:55).

13:2 *Sister*: i.e., sister in the faith (see "brothers" in 13:1).

⁴The Master said, "Those who have known themselves have seen [it in] everything that is given them to do [for them]selves, and they have come to be [. . .] it in their goodn[ess]."

15 Judas responded, "Tell me, Master, as for the shak[ing] that moves the earth—how does it move?"

²The Master took a sto[ne and] held it in his hand, [saying, "What] is this that I am holding in my hand?"

³He said, "[It is] a stone."

⁴He said to them, "That which supports the ear[th] is that which supports the heaven.

⁵"When a word comes forth from the Majesty, it will come upon that which supports the heaven and the earth. ⁶For the earth ⟨itself⟩ does not move—if it moved it would fall—but ⟨it does not fall⟩ so that the first word might not be nullified. ⁷For that is the one who established the world and came to be in it and received ⟨sweet⟩ fragrance from it. ⁸For [. . .] thing that does not move I [. . .] you, all of humankind, for you are from that place: you are in the heart of those who speak from jo[y] and truth. ⁹Even if it comes forth among humankind from the body of the Father and is not received, it returns again to its place. ¹⁰The one who knows [. . . thi]ng⟨s⟩ of perfection kno[ws] nothing. ¹¹If you do not stand in the darkness, you will not be able to see the light."

16 "If you do not [understand] how fire came to be, you will burn in it, because you do not know its root. ²If you do not first understand water, you know nothing; for what ⟨then⟩ is the use of your receiving baptism in it? ³If you do not understand how the wind that blows came to be, you will fly away with it. ⁴If you do not understand how the body which you bear came to be, you will perish with it. ⁵And if you do not know [the S]on, how will you know the [Father]? ⁶And you will not know the root of all things; they are hidden from you. ⁷Those who will not know the root of wickedness are not strangers to it.

14:4
Cf. Th 3:4

15:8
Ⓣ Th 50:1

16:4
Ⓣ DSav 8:1

16:5
Ⓣ Mt 11:27,
Jn 14:7–9

16:7
Ⓣ 1 Tm 6:10

15:4 *That which*: or "The one who."

15:6 This verse affirms the truth of God's creative word ("and God said . . .") in Genesis 1.

15:9 *it comes forth*: probably a reference back to the "word" in 15:5.

   the body of the Father. A curious expression, not found in other early Christian literature. The early fourth-century heretic Arius suggested the orthodox Nicene Creed implied that God had a body.

16:7 *root of wickedness*: This phrase, also found in 1 Tim

6:10, appears twice in a short treatise on hidden things in the Nag Hammadi *Gospel of Philip* 82:30–84:13, where the author states: "[Most things] in the world, as long as their [inner parts] are hidden, stand upright and live. . . . So with the tree: while its root is hidden it sprouts and grows. If its root is exposed, the tree dries up. So it is with every birth that is in the world, not only with the revealed but with the hidden. For so long as the root of wickedness is hidden, it is strong. But when it is recognized, it is dissolved. When it is revealed, it perishes."

⁸Those who will not understand how they came will not understand how they will go; and they are no strangers to this world which will [. . . and] which will be humbled."

17 Then he [took] Judas and Matthew and Mary [. . .] the end of heaven [and] earth. ²[An]d when he placed his [hand] upon them, they hoped that they might [see] it. ³Judas lifted his eyes and saw a place of great height, and he saw the place of the abyss below. ⁴Judas said to Matthew, "Brother, who will be able to go up to this height, or down below to the abyss? For there is a great fire there, and great terror."

⁵At that instant a word came forth from it. ⁶As he stood there he saw how it came [do]wn.

⁷Then he said to it, "Why have you come down?"

⁸And the Human One greeted them and said to them, "A seed from a power was deficient, and went down below to the earth's abyss. ⁹And the Majesty remembered [it], and sent the wo[rd to] it. ¹⁰It brought it up into [his pre]sence, so that the first word might not fail."

¹¹T[hen] hi[s dis]ciples marveled at [ever]ything that he had told them, and received them in [tr]ust. ¹²And they understood that there is no need to endure the sight of wickedness.

¹³Then he said to his disciples, "Did I not tell you that just like a visible flash of thunder and lightning, so will the good be taken up to the light?"

¹⁴Then all his disciples praised him and said, "Master, before you appeared here, who was there to give you praise—for from you all praises come to be? ¹⁵Or who was there to bless [you]—for from you comes all blessing?"

¹⁶As they stood there, he saw two spirits bearing a single soul with them in a great flash of lightning. ¹⁷And a word came forth from the Human One, saying, "Give them their garments."

17:11
Ⓣ DSav 29:2

16:8 Clement of Alexandria quotes the classic Gnostic formula, part of which seems to be reflected here: "It is not the bath alone that makes us free, but also the knowledge of who we were and what we have become; where we were, into what we have been cast; to what we are hastening, from where we are redeemed; what is birth, what rebirth" (*Excerpts from Theodotus* 78).

17:5 *from it*: i.e., from the great height (see 17:3 and 17:6).

17:6 *he stood*: i.e., Judas (see 17:3, 4).

17:8 *the Human One*: This figure acts as an *angelus interpres,* a heavenly being who interprets a vision (see Rev 7:13–17). The title "Human One" is commonly used of Jesus in the NT gospels, but it is also used to refer to a heavenly agent of God (see Dan 7:13–14).

deficient: Gnostic theology commonly referred to a defective or sinful element in the heavenly realm that "fell" to earth.

17:10 *so that . . . fail*: or "because the first word was abrogated"; but see 15:6.

17:14–15 These verses show early Christian reflection on the "double presence" of the Lord (in earth and on heaven); see, e.g., Melito, *Passover Homily* frag. 14: "He was seen as a lamb, but remained a shepherd; . . . treading the earth, and filling heaven"; Hippolytus, *Against Noetus* 4:11: "Who, then, was he in heaven but the fleshless Word—he who was sent for the purpose of showing that he who is on earth is in heaven too?"; and esp. Gospel of Bartholomew 31–32: "Bartholomew asked: 'Lord, when you lived among us, did you receive the sacrifices in paradise?' Jesus answered: 'I swear to you, I sat at the right hand of the Father and received the sacrifices in paradise.'"

¹⁸[And] the small one became just like the great one. ¹⁹They were [. . .] those who received them. ²⁰[. . .] each other. ²¹Then [. . .] disciples, those whom he [. . .]

18 Mary [said, ". . .] see the evil [. . .] them from the beginning [. . .] each other."

²The Master said [to her], "When you see them [. . .] become great, they will [. . .]. ³But when you see the One who is forever, that is the great vision."

⁴Then they all said to him, "Make it known to us."

⁵He said to them, "How do you wish to see it: [in] a vision that will pass or in an eternal vision?" ⁶Again he said, "Strive to save the one who is able to follow [you], and seek him and speak with him, so that as you seek him everything may be in harmony with you. ⁷For I say to you, truly, the living God [is] in you [. . .] in him."

19 Judas [said], "Truly I wish [. . .]."

²The M[aster] said to him, "[. . .] living [. . .] is [. . .] whole [. . .] of the deficiency."

³Judas [said], "Who is it [. . .]?"

⁴The Master said, "[. . .] all the works which are [. . .] the remainder, it is they over which you [shall rule]."

⁵Judas said, "Look, the archons are above us; so, then, it is they who will rule over us!"

⁶The Master said, "It is you who will rule over them. ⁷But when you remove envy from you, then you will clothe yourselves with light and enter the wedding hall."

⁸Judas said, "How will our garments be brought to us?"

⁹The Master said, "There are some who will bring ⟨them⟩ to you, and others who will receive [them], for it is they [who will give] you your garments. ¹⁰For who [will] be able to reach that place [which is th]e reward? ¹¹But the garments of life were given to such people because they know the way by which they will go. ¹²Indeed, for me too it is a burden to reach it."

20 Mary said, "Just so: 'The wickedness of each day ⟨is sufficient⟩,' and 'Laborers are worthy of their food,' and 'Disciples resemble their teachers.'" ²She spoke this word as a woman who fully understood.

19:6
Ⓣ 1 Cor 6:3
19:7
Ⓣ 1 Pet 2:1, Th 75
20:1a
//Mt 6:34
20:1b
//Q 10:7, Mt 10:10, Lk 10:7
20:1c
//Q 6:40, Mt 10:24, Lk 6:40, Jn 13:16

18:6 This *striving* probably includes missionary work, however understood (see DialSav 24:1–2).
19:11 Unless *such people* are examples of the *single soul* in 17:16, this statement may be proverbial: "The garments of life are given to humankind . . . ."
19:12 The Savior too must bear the burden of the journey (see 1:5) to the place of reward; the importance of this as-sertion is suggested by its repetition in 38:8 (and see 38:7).
20:1 Three abbreviated aphorisms are given, as if the full form of each is familiar to the reader.
20:2 That Mary *fully understood* (see DialSav 26) may indicate that Mary can supply the missing (and essential) elements in the aphorisms in 20:1.

21 The disciples said to him, "What is the Plenitude and what is the deficiency?"

²He said to them, "You are from the Plenitude and you are in the place where the deficiency is. ³And look, his light has ⟨been⟩ poured out upon me."

22 Matthew said, "Tell me, Master, how the dead die and how the living live."

²The Master said, "[You have] asked me about a saying [. . . that] which eye has not seen, nor have I heard it, except from you. ³But I say to you that when that which moves a person is drained out, that person will be called dead; ⁴and when what is living leaves what is dead, ⟨it⟩ will be called alive."

23 Judas said, "Why then, in truth, do ⟨the living⟩ die and ⟨the dead⟩ live?"

²The Master said, "Whatever is from the truth does not die; whatever is from woman dies."

24 Mary said, "Tell me, Master, why have I come to this place—to gain or to lose?"

²The Master said, "⟨You have come⟩ to reveal the greatness of the revealer."

³Mary said to him, "Master, is there then a place that [. . .] or lacks the truth?"

⁴The Master said, "The place where I am not."

⁵Mary said, "Master, you inspire fear and wonder, and [. . .] those who do not know you."

25 Matthew said, "Why do we not together take ⟨our⟩ rest?"

²The Master said, "When you leave behind these burdens."

³Matthew said, "How does the small unite with the great?"

⁴The Master said, "When you leave behind the things that cannot follow you, then you will rest."

26 Mary said, "I wish to understand everything—[just how] it comes into being."

24:3–4
Ⓣ Th 24:1

25:2
Ⓣ Mt 11:28;
Th 37:2, 90:1–2

21:1 *Plenitude*: the "fullness" of the heavenly realm.
21:3 *And*: perhaps with the sense "yet": the paradox of the disciples' condition.
22:4 *leaves*: or "sets free"; the Coptic verb can also mean: appoint, make, esteem, admit.

24:1 *this place*: i.e., earth.
25:1 *together*: literally, "at once." The translation *together* suggests the meaning: "Why do we ⟨disciples⟩ not rest ⟨now⟩ together ⟨with you, the Master⟩?" The question is not fully answered until 25:4.

²The Master said, "Those who seek life—this indeed is their wealth. ³For this world's [re]st is [false] and its gold and its silver are error."

27 His disciples said to him, "What shall we do, that our work may be perfect?"

²The Master [said] to them, "Be [re]ady before the whole ⟨creation⟩. ³Congratulations to those who have found [. . .] the struggle with their eyes [. . .]. ⁴They have not killed, nor have [they] been killed, but they came forth victorious."

28 Judas said, "Tell me, Master, what is the beginning of the way."

²He said, "Love and goodness. ³For if one of these had been among the archons, wickedness would never have come to be."

29 Matthew said, "Master, without wearying you have spoken about the end of the whole ⟨creation⟩."

²The Master said, "Everything that I have said to you you have understood and received in faith. ³If you know them, then they are yours; if not, then they are not yours."

30 They said to him, "What is the place to which we shall go?"

²The Master said, "[Stand in] the place that you can reach."

31 Mary said, "Everything that endures in this way is seen."

²The Master said, "I have told you [that] the one who sees is the one who reveals."

32 His disciples, twelve in number, asked him, "Teacher, [. . .] freedom from ca[re . . .] teach us [. . .]."

²The Master said, "[. . .] everything that I have [told you], you will [. . .] you [. . .] everything."

33 Mary said, "There is but one word that I shall [sp]eak to the Master concerning the mystery of truth, this one in which we stand and ⟨in which⟩ we appear to the worldly."

34 Judas said to Matthew, "We wish to understand what kind of garments we are to be clothed with when we come forth from the corruption of the [fle]sh."

26:3
Ⓣ Jas 5:3
28:1
Ⓣ Jn 14:5
29:2
Ⓣ DSav 17:11
31:2
Ⓓ DSav 7:4

26:3 *[re]st*: This word (*a[nap]ausis*) may also be reconstructed *a[pol]ausis*, "enjoyment."

27:2 *Be ready*: Readiness, i.e., preparedness and eager expectation, was highly valued in early Christianity.

²The Master said, "The archons and the administrators have garments that are given ⟨only⟩ for a while and that are impermanent. ³[But] you, as children of truth, are not to clothe yourselves with these garments that are impermanent. ⁴Rather, I say to you that you will be blessed when you strip yourselves. ⁵For it is not a great thing [. . .] beyond."

35 [. . .] said [. . . , ". . ."] speak, I am [. . .]."
²The Master said, "[. . .] your Father [. . .]."

36 Mary said, "[Of wha]t kind is this mustard seed? ²Is it from heaven or from earth?"

³The Master said, "When the Father established the world for himself, he left many things with the Mother of All. ⁴Because of this he speaks and acts."

37 Judas said, "You have told us this from the mind of truth. When we pray, how are we to pray?"

²The Master said, "Pray in a place where there is no woman."

³Matthew said, "He tells us, 'Pray in the place where there is no woman,' that is, 'Destroy the works of the female'; ⁴not because there is another birth but because they will cease [giving birth]."

⁵Mary said, "They will never be destroyed."

⁶The Master said, "Who is it that knows that they will [not] dissolve and [the works] of [the female] be [destroyed in this pl]ace [too]?"

⁷Judas said [to Matt]hew, "The works of the [female] will dissolve [. . .] the archons will [. . . ⁸. . .] shall we become ready for them in this way?"

38 The Master said, "Certainly not. They see yo[u and they] see those who receive [yo]u. ²But look, a true word is coming forth from the Father [to the] abyss in silence, with a flash of lightning. ³Do they see it or over[power] it? ⁴⟨No, they do not,⟩ but you know better [the wa]y, that which neither [ang]el nor [authority . . .]. ⁵Rather it is the Father's and the So[n's, be]cause [the]y are both a single [. . .]. ⁶A[nd] you will travel the [wa]y that you have come to know. ⁷Even if the archons become great they will not be able to reach it. ⁸Bu[t lo]ok! For me too it is a burden to reach it."

34:4
Cf. Th 37

36:1
Ⓣ Mk 4:30–32,
Mt 17:20,
Q 13:18–19,
Mt 13:31–32,
Lk 13:18–19, Th 20

36:2
Cf. Mk 11: 30,
Mt 11:25, Lk 20:4

37:1–2
Cf. Th 6:1

34:2 *administrators*: another class of heavenly powers.

34:3 *not*: The Coptic word *an* (or emended to *on*) is either a negative ("not") or an adverb ("also," "too"; see 7:4; 19:12).

36:3 *Father* and *Mother*: a basic pairing of heavenly beings.

37:3–4 Clement of Alexandria (*Miscellanies* 3:63) quotes from the Gospel of the Egyptians: "The Savior himself said, 'I am come to undo the works of the female,' by the female meaning lust, and by the works meaning birth and decay";

and (*Miscellanies* 3:45): "When Salome asked, 'How long will death have power?' the Lord answered, 'So long as you women bear children'—not as if life was something bad and creation evil, but as teaching the sequence of nature."

37:4 The concept of rebirth is rejected; see John 3:6.

38:1–8 The Savior assures the disciples that they know the way they will travel, and cautions them to avoid the false way of the archons.

39 [Mary] said to the Master, "When the works [. . . which] dissolves a w[ork]."

²[The Lo]rd [said], "Now you know [. . .] if I dissolve [. . .] will go to his pla[ce]."

40 Judas said, "In what does the sp[irit] appear?"

²The Master said, "In what does the sword [appear]?"

³Judas said, "In what does the light appear?"

⁴The Master said, "[. . .] in it forever."

41 Judas said, "Who is it who forgives whose works? ²As for the works which [. . .] the world, [. . . wh]o forgives the works."

³The Master [said], "Who is it [. . .? ⁴. . .] who have understood the works, it is for them to do the [wi]ll of the Father. ⁵But as for you, [st]rive to remove an[ger] and [en]vy from yourselves, and strip yourselves of your [. . .], and not to [. . . *approximately 13 lines missing or incapable of restoration*].

⁶"For I say to you, [. . .] you take the [. . .] you [. . .] who have inquired [. . .] this, will [. . .] they will live for[ever. ⁷But] I say to you, [. . .] that you not lead astray [your] spirits and your souls."

41:4
Cf. Mk 3:35,
Mt 12:50, Lk 8:21;
Ⓣ Jn 6:28–29,
14:10–11

41:6
Ⓣ Jn 8:32; Th 1, 2

41:7
Ⓣ Wis 17:1

Emendation and restoration

Not one ancient text survives in the original copy, or "autograph," written by its author. The texts that have come down to us are the result of several centuries of copying and editing by hand, and the destructive forces of history and climate. Most ancient documents have not survived exactly as they were first written, but only in (a) diverse copies that are often riddled with mistakes of grammar or spelling (in addition to scribes' attempts to "improve" the text), or (b) copies that clearly show the signs of aging and decay, with letters, words, sentences, or whole sections missing.

Modern scholars, as a consequence, are faced with the task of correcting the mistakes or changes made by the scribes who copied or recopied the ancient manuscripts, and/or of filling in the lacunae (literally, "gaps") left by the wear and tear of heavy use or natural disintegration. These two tasks are known as *emendation* and *restoration*.

In the case of scribal error (the surviving text is nonsense because a scribe has misunderstood or wrongly transcribed a previous copy of the text), the modern scholar is forced to *emend* the spelling or wording of the surviving text, by changing, adding, or deleting letters or words. In some places this emendation is virtually certain, as when a word or phrase is accidentally repeated (dittography), for example in Thom 33:1 (see the note to this verse). In other places a word or phrase has been accidentally left out because nearby words end with the same or similar letters (haplography). For example, in Thom 60:1 "He saw" (Coptic *afnau*) or "They saw" (Coptic *aunau*) is missing from the text, probably because a scribe's eye skipped ahead from the last word in Thom 59, "to see" (Coptic *enau*). In still other places the scribe has simply written the wrong letter. For example, the Coptic text of Thom 74 ends with the word *shōne, a* masculine noun meaning "disease." This cannot be correct. Not only does it make no sense, it is grammatically wrong, for the manuscript has the feminine article preceding this masculine noun. Since the first line of the saying ends with *jōte* ("drinking trough"), the best guess is that *shōne* should be changed to the feminine noun *shōte* ("well"). With this emendation the second line is grammatically correct and both lines end in words that are closely related in meaning, and which sound nearly identical.

In the case of a lacuna (gap), either the context (the sense of the surrounding words) or the presence of distinct letters on either side of the gap is usually enough to permit the specialist to suggest some *restoration* of the text: the original letters or words most likely to have been in the manuscript before its corruption. In such cases, restoration is indicated in modem editions and translations by the use of square brackets—[and]—around the restored text. For example, in DialSav 4:1 it is obvious that the speaker's name is "Matthew," even though only the second half of his name is actually preserved in the manuscript.

Needless to say, in many places scholars have been unable to emend or restore a satisfactory or readable text—passages where even the specialists have not worked out what was probably in the original text. In such cases, modern editions and translations either print a question mark (?) after an attempted emendation, or print square brackets with periods—[. . .]—to show that a gap cannot be filled with any confidence.

These instances are a sober reminder that when we read ancient documents we are always at the mercy of scribal mistakes, historical accidents, and geographical fortune or misfortune. This is especially so when dealing with documents not included in the New Testament. The fact that the New Testament writings themselves require relatively little emendation or restoration is due to the victory that Christianity won over the Roman empire: in the fourth and later centuries many copies of the Greek Bible were made by imperial decree, thus ensuring that at least some of the best manuscripts from the fourth and later centuries would be widely used, repeatedly copied, and protected as the official text of these "canonical" writings.

The Gospel of Mary

Introduction

To those familiar with the New Testament stories of Jesus, much will seem familiar in the Gospel of Mary. Some of the words and most of the characters evoke memories of Matthew, Mark, Luke, and John. In other matters, the reader may well agree with Andrew's complaint that Mary's teachings are strange (10:1–2). Strange to us, perhaps. But in the first and second centuries, they were firmly embedded in Christian debates about the meaning of Jesus' teaching, the roles of women, and how to attain salvation. The Gospel of Mary reproduces the contours of those debates, most especially in the contention among the disciples themselves over the authority and teachings of Mary of Magdala. Moreover, the Gospel of Mary's interpretation of early traditions about Jesus show some of the fluidity and some of the passion with which such matters were engaged.

Story

As the text opens, the Savior is engaged in dialogue with his disciples, answering questions they have about the end of the world and the nature of sin. The Savior teaches them that salvation is achieved by seeking the true spiritual nature of humanity within oneself and overcoming the entrapping material nature of the body and the world. He warns them against those who would lead them astray by telling them to follow some heroic leader or a set of rules and laws. After commissioning them to go forth and preach the gospel, he departs.

At the Savior's departure, a controversy erupts. All the disciples except Mary Magdalene and Levi have failed to comprehend the Savior's teaching. Rather than seek peace within, they are distressed at their leader's absence and worried about their own deaths. When Mary tries to comfort them and give them further instruction, Andrew and Peter turn on her. Mary has recounted to them special teaching the Savior gave her about how to win the battle against the wicked, illegitimate Powers of the world that seek to keep the soul imprisoned in the fleshly body and ignorant of its truly spiritual nature. But their false pride, offended over the fact that Jesus seems to have preferred a woman to them, makes it impossible for Andrew and Peter to comprehend the truth of her teaching. When the gospel concludes, the controversy is far from resolved. Although Levi has defended Mary, it is not clear whether Peter, Andrew, and the others have understood the Savior's teaching. The reader must wonder what kind of gospel such proud and ignorant men will preach.

A debate over who can preach the gospel

Many early Christian writings affirm that Jesus gave superior teaching to his disciples in private or in visions and appearances after the resurrection (for example, Mark 4:10–11; 1 Cor 2:7; 3:1–3; 15:3–8). Indeed, Mary Magdalene's vision of the Savior in the Gospel of Mary probably reflects the same tradition known to John 20:16–18. Yet Andrew's objection to Mary's teaching in the Gospel of Mary raises a core problem much debated in early Christian circles: how can the validity of such teaching be determined? Given that Christians understood Jesus' teachings in very different ways, who could be trusted? Later Christians would appeal to a common creed, canon, or a succession of apostolic authority, but the Gospel of Mary was written before any of these had become firmly established. For Andrew, Mary's words did not seem to conform to the Savior's teaching that he knew and that he was using as a standard for the truth. But Mary's stability of character and advanced teaching present her as the model disciple. When the other disciples are afraid and jealous, Mary remains steadfast and is able to turn their hearts toward God and give them higher instruction. In this way, the Gospel of Mary clearly affirms the truth and authority of Mary's teaching.

Many early Christian writings also portray the disciples as often misunderstanding the import of Jesus' teaching. One of his disciples even betrays him. Sometimes Peter is singled out for rebuke, as when Jesus accuses him of being in league with Satan (Mark 8:33), or when Peter denies Jesus three times during the trial. It comes as no surprise, then, that some Christians might question the reliability of such disciples' teaching. By portraying Andrew and especially Peter as jealous hot-heads, the Gospel of Mary clearly is questioning whether apostolic witness is sufficient to ensure the gospel is preached in truth. The true apostolic witness is identified with Mary of Magdala.

The role of women

The preeminence of Mary of Magdala offers the strongest argument for the legitimacy of women's leadership in any early Christian writing. The Coptic version of this gospel in particular raises this issue in a forceful way. Peter was willing to admit that the Savior loved Mary Magdalene "more than all other women," but he balks at the idea that the Savior may have preferred her, a woman, to the male disciples (10:3–4). Yet Levi states explicitly that this is the case (10:9–10). The issue is not simply one of sentimentality, however. At the Savior's departure, Mary takes over his role. She comforts the distressed disciples and gives them teaching that will allow them to overcome the sin of the world (5:4–9). In every way, the text affirms that her leadership of the other disciples is based upon a superior spiritual understanding. Peter, however, cannot see past the superficial sexual differentiation of the flesh to Mary's true spiritual power.

He fails to grasp that because the true self is spiritual, any distinctions written on the body are bound to pass away when the body is dissolved at death. He again shows his ignorance of the Savior's true teaching, while the Gospel of Mary unreservedly supports the leadership of spiritually advanced women.

The story is a simple one. Yet in this astonishingly short narrative—fewer than eight pages survive—the Gospel of Mary gives a radical interpretation of Jesus' teachings as a path to inner spiritual knowledge; it rejects his suffering and death as a way to gain eternal life; it exposes the erroneous view that Mary Magdalene was a prostitute for what it is—a piece of theological fiction; it presents the most straightforward and convincing argument for the legitimacy of women's leadership to be found in any ancient writing; it offers a sharp critique of illegitimate power and a utopian vision of spiritual perfection; it challenges our rather romantic views about the harmony and unanimity of the first Christians; and it asks us to rethink the basis for church authority. And all of this was written in the name of a woman.

Theological outlook

In the end, the Gospel of Mary communicates a vision that the world is passing away, not toward a new creation or a new world order, but toward the dissolution of an illusory chaos of suffering, death, and illegitimate domination. The Savior has come so that each soul might discover its own true spiritual nature, its "root" in the Good, and return to the place of eternal rest beyond the constraints of time and matter and false morality.

Toward the end of the second century, many of the views found in the Gospel of Mary came under sharp attack. Other Christians particularly opposed its belief in the eternal salvation of the soul, not the resurrection of the body; its rejection of a savior who atones for sin or comes at the end of time in favor of affirming that Jesus' teaching brings salvation; and finally its support for the legitimacy of women's leadership. Condemned by later Christians as heresy, these strands of early Christian theology receded from view. The rediscovery of the Gospel of Mary restores a fragment of this heritage to early Christian history.

The rediscovery of the Gospel of Mary

Unlike the canonical gospels, each of which is attested by hundreds of manuscripts, no complete copy of the Gospel of Mary exists. Indeed, for centuries, the Gospel of Mary remained completely unknown. Only three fragmentary manuscripts are known to have survived into the modern period: two third-century Greek fragments (P. Oxyrhynchus 3525 and P. Rylands 463), published in 1938 and 1983 and a longer fifth-century Coptic translation (Berolinensis Gnosticus 8052,1), first published in 1955.

State of the texts

The two earlier and shorter fragments are written in the original language of the Gospel of Mary, Greek. The most complete manuscript of the text, however, is the translation into Coptic. But even this more complete text is but a fragment. Six pages of the manuscript are missing at the beginning, and four more are lacking from Mary's narrative of the Savior's special teaching to her. In all, perhaps half of the total text is still lost.

Moreover, there are some important variations between the Greek and Coptic manuscripts. Although the translation here primarily follows the Coptic text, when there are significant variations between the Greek fragments and the longer Coptic text, the SV gives preference to the Greek fragments and makes the Coptic variants available in the notes. Preference is given to the Greek fragments because they are earlier and are written in the original language of the text, but the Coptic variants reflect important theological tendencies. For example, the Coptic version stresses that Mary's teaching had been hidden from the disciples, whereas the Greek implies merely that the other disciples simply didn't know these matters (6:3). Or again, the Coptic version more pointedly associates Peter with the adversarial, cosmic Power of Wrath, rather than just portraying him as an adversary of Mary, as in the Greek version (10:7–8). Such differences tend to intensify the opposition between Mary and the other disciples, possibly representing increasing tensions among Christians as the debates heated up.

Date and place of composition

Nothing is known about who first wrote down the Gospel of Mary or where it was composed, although both Egypt and Syria have been suggested. Dating is also highly tentative, but the Gospel of Mary may arguably have been written sometime in the early to mid-second century.

The Gospel of Mary

1 *(Six manuscript pages are missing.)*

2 "...**Will m[a]tter** then be utterly [destr]oyed or not?"

²The Savior replied, "Every nature, every modeled form, every creature, exists in and with each other. ³They will dissolve again into their own proper root. ⁴For the nature of matter is dissolved into what belongs to its nature.

⁵"Anyone with two ears able to hear should listen!"

3 **Then Peter said** to him, "You have been explaining every topic to us; tell us one other thing. ²What is the sin of the world?"

³The Savior replied, "There is no such thing as sin; ⁴rather you yourselves are what produces sin when you act in accordance with the nature of adultery, which is called 'sin.' ⁵For this reason, the Good came among you, pursuing ⟨the good⟩ which belongs to every nature. ⁶It will set it within its root."

⁷Then he continued. He said, "This is why you get si[c]k and die: ⁸because [you love] what de[c]ei[ve]s [you. ⁹Anyone who] thinks should consider ⟨these matters⟩!

¹⁰"[Ma]tter gav[e bi]rth to a passion that has no Image because it derives from what is contrary to nature. ¹¹A disturbing confusion then occurred in the

*The nature
of matter*

*The nature of sin
& the Good*

2:2–4
Cf. 1 Cor 7:31;
2 Pet 3:10–12
2:5
//Mk 4:23 par;
ⓓ Mary 3:14
3:2
Cf. Jn 1:29
3:3
Cf. Rom 4:15
3:10–13
Cf. 2 Pet 1:4

2:1–5 While everything material is interconnected, in the end all things will dissolve back into their constituent natures. Anyone with two ears should realize that the material world is temporary and therefore has no ultimate spiritual value. Compare Gospel of Philip 53:14–23: "Light and darkness, life and death, right and left, are brothers of one another. It is not possible to separate them from each other. For this reason, neither are the good good, nor the evil evil, nor is life life, nor death death. This is why each one will dissolve into its original source. But those who are exalted above the world will not be dissolved, for they are eternal." Or compare the description of the end of the world in *Origin of the World* 127:3–5: "And the deficiency will be pulled by its root down into the darkness. And the light will go back up to its root."

2:1 Whether matter is pre-existent (and therefore eternal) or created (and therefore subject to destruction) was an issue debated among philosophers.

3:3–4 Because God is completely good and the author of everything which exists, sin does not really exist. Rather spiritual human beings *produce sin* when they turn away from God by adulterously consorting with material nature.

3:5–6 People overcome sin when God (the *Good*) establishes people in their proper *root* (the true spiritual nature of all human beings).

3:7–8 Illness and death arise because people wrongly orient themselves toward the deceptive needs and desires of mortal flesh and fleeting material concerns.

3:9 To *think* is to understand that one's nature is spiritual and to live accordingly, and so overcome one's ignorant love of perishable things.

3:10–11 Everything which is true and good is an Image of the divine reality above. *Matter has no Image* means that matter does not have a heavenly origin and is contrary to the true nature of spiritual Reality. *Matter* is the formless, chaotic "stuff," devoid of all qualities such as life and mind, out of which all things have been formed. Matter is thus the cause of passion, suffering, and confusion of the whole body. The body is a false image of the human self, one that leads people away from the truth of their own spiritual natures by keeping them absorbed with thinking falsely that their bodies are their true selves.

The commission

*Mary comforts the
other disciples*

whole body. [12]That is why I told you, 'Become content at heart, [13]while also remaining discontent; indeed, become contented ⟨only⟩ in the presence of every ⟨true⟩ Image of nature.'

[14]"Anyone with two ears able to hear should listen!"

4 **When the Blessed One** had said these things, he greeted them all. "Peace be with you!" he said. [2]"Acquire my peace within yourselves!

[3]"Be on your guard [4]so that no one deceives you by saying, 'Look over here' or 'Look over there.' [5]For the Human One exists within you. [6]Follow it. [7]Those who search for it will find it.

[8]"Go then, preac[h] the good news about the kingdom. [9][Do] not lay down any rule beyond what I determined for you, [10]nor promulgate law like the lawgiver, or else you might be dominated by it."

[11]After he said these things, he left them.

5 **But they were** distressed and wept greatly. [2]"How are we going to go out to the rest of the world to announce the good news about the kingdom of the Human One?" they said. [3]"If they didn't spare him, how will they spare us?"

[4]Then Mary stood up. She greeted them all, addressing her brothers and sisters, [5]"Do not weep and be distressed nor let your hearts be irresolute. [6]For his grace will be with you all and will shelter you. [7]Rather we should praise his greatness, [8]for he has united us and made us ⟨true⟩ human beings."

[9]When Mary said these things, she turned their mind [to]ward the Good, [10]and they began to deba[t]e the wor[d]s of [the Savior].

3:12
Cf. Jn 14:1

3:14
//Mk 4:23 par;
Ⓓ Mary 2:5

4:1
//Jn 20:19, 21, 26

4:2
Cf. Jn 14:27

4:3
//Mk 13:5, Mt 24:4,
Lk 21:8

4:4
//Mk 13:21;
Mt 24:23;
Lk 17:21, 23;
Th 113:3

4:5
Cf. Lk 17:21;
Th 3:3, 113:4

4:7
//Q 11:10; Mt 7:8;
Lk 11:10; Th 2:1,
92:1, 94:1; GHeb 6b

4:8
Ⓣ Mk 13:10,
16:15; Mt 4:23,
9:35, 24:14

4:9–10
Cf. Rom 7:5–11

5:5
Cf. Jn 14:27

5:8
Cf. Jn 17:11

5:8 *united*: The Coptic has "prepared."

5:9 *mind*: The Coptic has "heart."

3:12–13 True contentment comes from conforming not to the demands of the material world, but to the spiritual Image of the true heavenly nature, the Good.

4:3–7 Because every human being is created in the divine Image of the perfect Human, people need to seek within to find the Human One. They must guard against those who try to lead them astray by requiring that a person conform to what is outside by following a leader who is *over here* or *over there*.

4:5 *the Human One*: Traditionally translated "Son of Man," in the Gospel of Mary this term refers to the archetypal Image of humanity within each person.

4:6–7 *it*: The Human One within is neither male nor female, but transcends sexual difference.

4:9–10 The Savior cautions his disciples against laws they themselves set because spiritual advancement cannot be achieved through external regulations based on the desire to dominate, for example excluding women from leadership roles.

5:1–3 The assumption that evangelizing will lead to suffering may indicate a general situation in which Christians who openly proclaim the gospel are at risk of persecution. The disciples' fear and grief show that they have not understood the Savior's teaching to focus on their spiritual natures.

5:3 *If they didn't spare him*: a reference to the death of Jesus.

6 **Peter said to Mary**, "Sister, we know that the Savior loved you more than all other women. [2]Tell us the words of the Savior that you remember, the things which you know that we don't because we haven't heard them."

[3]Mary responded, "I will report to you [as much as] I remember that you don't know." [4]And she began to speak these words to them.

7 **She said**, "I saw the Master in a vision [2]and I said to him, 'Master, I saw you today in a vision.'

[3]"He answered me, 'Congratulations to you for not wavering at seeing me! [4]For where the mind is, there is the treasure.'

[5]"I said to him, 'So now, Master, does a person who sees a vision see it ⟨with⟩ the soul ⟨or⟩ with the spirit?'

[6]"The Savior answered, 'A person does not see with the soul or with the spirit. [7]Rather the mind, which exists between these two, sees the vision an[d] that is w[hat . . .]

8 *(Four manuscript pages are missing.)*

9 "'. . . it.'

[2]"And Desire said, 'I did not see you go down, yet now I see you go up. [3]So why do you lie since you belong to me?'

6:4
//Jn 20:18

7:1–2
Cf. Jn 20:14–18

7:4
//Q 12:34, Mt 6:21,
Lk 12:34

*Peter asks Mary
to teach*

*Mary's teaching on
vision & mind*

*On the ascent of
the soul*

6:3 In Coptic Mary's response reads: "I will teach you about what is hidden from you."

6:1–4 John 20:14–18 also preserves a tradition that Mary was the first disciple to see the resurrected Jesus, and that she subsequently reported his words to the disciples.

7:1–2 Mary has a vision of Jesus' exalted nature already during his earthly ministry, similar perhaps to the transfiguration story of Mark 9:2 or GSav 14:2–16.

7:3 The term *wavering* carries important connotations in ancient thought, where it is contrasted with stability. Mary's stability illustrates her conformity to the spiritual state of God who is eternal and unchanging. It is one more indication of her spiritual superiority.

7:4 Compare Clement of Alexandria: "For where a person's mind is, his treasure is there too" (*Who is the Rich Man that shall be saved?* 17:1).

7:6–7 The true nature of all humans is made up of *soul*, *mind*, and *spirit*. The soul is living nature, the spirit is higher divine nature. The mind mediates between the two, allowing souls living in the world to perceive a vision of the higher spiritual Reality.

8 Four pages are missing from the Coptic manuscript of the Gospel of Mary at this point. There are no parallel Greek fragments so we can only speculate about the contents.

9:1 The manuscript continues in the middle of Mary's account of the ascent of the soul out of its bondage to the material realm, represented symbolically by four Powers. The soul overcomes their domination by understanding its true spiritual nature, rejecting false judgment and condemnation, and renouncing all violence. The soul has just successfully overcome the first Power, whose name probably was Darkness, and is now moving on to the second Power, *Desire*.

9:2–3 *Desire* did not see the soul descend from the heavens above, so it assumes that the soul belongs to the world below and is falsely trying to escape.

4"The soul answered, 'I saw you. You did not see me nor did you know me. 5You ⟨mis⟩took the garment ⟨I wore⟩ for my ⟨true⟩ self. 6And you did not recognize me.'

7"After it had said these things, it left rejoicing greatly.

8"Again, it came to the third Power, which is called 'Ignorance.' 9[It] examined the soul closely, saying, 'Where are you going? 10You are bound by wickedness. 11Indeed you are bound! 12Do not judge!'

13"And the soul said, 'Why do you judge me, since I have not passed judgment? 14I have been bound, but I have not bound ⟨anything⟩. 15They did not recognize me, but I have recognized that the universe is to be dissolved, both the things of earth and those of heaven.'

16"When the soul had overcome the third Power, it went upward and saw the fourth Power. 17It had seven forms. 18The first form is darkness; 19the second is desire; 20the third is ignorance; 21the fourth is zeal for death; 22the fifth is the realm of the flesh; 23the sixth is the foolish wisdom of the flesh; 24the seventh is the wisdom of the wrathful person. 25These are the seven Powers of Wrath.

26"They interrogated the soul, 'Where are you coming from, human-killer, and where are you going, space-conqueror?'

27"The soul replied, saying, 'What binds me has been slain, and what surrounds me has been destroyed, and my desire has been brought to an end, and

9:12
//Q 6:37, Mt 7:1,
Lk 6:37

9:15
Cf. Mk 13:31;
2 Pet 3:10–12

9:23
Ⓣ 1 Cor 3:18–19,
2 Cor 1:12

9:24
Ⓣ Rom 4:15

9:4–7 The soul unmasks the blindness of Desire and shows its own superior knowledge. The Power did not see it (9:2), but it sees the Power. To *see* is a metaphor for understanding the true nature of a thing. The Power was able to perceive only the material, bodily husk that the soul wore like a *garment,* obscuring its own spiritual nature from view.

The text exploits the double meaning of the word "see" to ridicule the ignorant Power. It sees but does not understand. The soul both sees and understands the Power's true nature as well as its own. The joke is on the sinister but weak Power; the soul moves on in glee.

9:8–12 Again the soul's insight into its own true identity allows it the discernment to overcome the illegitimate domination of the third Power, Ignorance. *Ignorance* challenges the soul's ascent. It judges the soul, pointing out its fornication (adulterous union with the flesh). Because of this sin, in the Power's view, the soul has no power of discernment: *Do not judge!*

9:13–15 The soul rejects the Power's judgment, knowing it to be ignorant. The soul proclaims the injustice committed against it (that it has been *judged* and *bound* to the material world) and it proclaims its own innocence (that it has not *passed judgment* or *bound* another). The soul recognizes

that the material universe, both the earth and the planetary heavens along with its Powers, will come to an end. Again, the conversation of the soul shows considerable wit in pointing out that the Power itself has acknowledged that the soul's knowledge is true: sin is due to the domination of the flesh. Without the flesh, there is no sin, judgment, or condemnation; this insight frees the soul.

9:16–25 The fourth Power, *Wrath,* is not righteous anger, but unthinking rage and lust for violence. The seven names of Wrath (vv. 18–24) indicate that the world below is opposed to the world above. The upper world is light, peace, knowledge, love, and life; the lower world is ruled by darkness, desire, ignorance, and death (vv. 18–21). The lower domain of the flesh is opposed to the heavenly domain of the Human One (vv. 22–23; see the note to 4:5). The foolish wisdom of the flesh and wrath below is opposed to the true wisdom above (v. 24).

9:26 Again the Powers challenge the right of the soul to pass. *Human-killer* refers to the soul having cast off the flesh. *Space-conqueror* refers to the spheres of the Powers that it has overcome.

9:27 *What binds me*: the material elements and the passions of the flesh.

ignorance has died. ²⁸In a [wor]ld, I was set loose from a world [an]d in a type, from a type which is above, and ⟨from⟩ the chain of forgetfulness which exists in time. ²⁹From this hour on, for the time of the due season of the age, I will receive rest i[n] silence.'"

³⁰After Mary said these things, she was silent, ³¹since it was up to this point that the Savior had spoken to her.

10 **Andrew sai[d**, "B]rothers and sisters, what is your opinion of what was just said? ²I for one do not believe that the S[a]vior said these things, for what she said appears to give views that are [dif]ferent from h[is th]ought."

³After examining these ma[tt]ers, ⟨Peter said⟩, "Has the Sa[vior] spoken secretly to a wo[m]an and ⟨not⟩ openly so that [we] would all hear? ⁴[Surely] he did[n't want to show] that [she] is more worthy than we are?"

⁵Then [M]ary wept and said to Peter, "My brother Peter, what are you imagining? ⁶Do you think that I have made all this up by myself or that I am telling lies about the Savior?"

⁷Levi said to Peter, "Peter, you are al[ways] rea[dy] to give in to you[r] perpetual inclination to anger. ⁸And even now you're doing exactly that by questioning the woman as if you're her adversary. ⁹For if the Savior made her worthy,

---

10:1–2 The Coptic reads: "Andrew responded, addressing the brothers and sisters, 'Say what you will about the things she has said, but I do not believe that the S[a]vior said these things, f[or] indeed these teachings are strange ideas.'"

10:3–4 The Coptic reads: "Peter responded, bringing up similar concerns. He questioned them about the Savior, 'Did he, then, speak with a woman in private without our knowing about it? Are we to turn around and listen to her? Did he choose her over us?'"

10:7–8 The Coptic reads: "Levi answered, speaking to Peter, 'Peter, you have always been a wrathful person. Now I see you contending against the woman like the Adversaries.'"

10:2
Cf. Lk 24:10–11

10:3
Cf. Jn 4:27

10:6
Cf. Lk 24:10–11

10:7
Cf. Jn 18:10–11

9:28–29 The soul contrasts the world from which it was freed with that to which it goes. It distinguishes the deceitful image (*type*) below from the true Image of Reality above, and mortality (the chain of time) from immortality (*rest in silence*).

9:30 Mary's *silence* symbolizes the perfect rest of the soul set free.

10:7–8 In the Coptic version, Levi calls Peter a *wrathful person* and then accuses him of acting like one of the Adversaries (Powers) by opposing Mary. *Wrathful person* is also the name of the seventh form of the Powers of Wrath (9:24). The Coptic version clearly aligns Peter with the Powers that

try to entrap the soul, much as Jesus in the Gospel of Mark calls Peter "Satan" (Mark 8:33).

10:9 *made her worthy*: Compare Thomas 114: "Simon Peter said to them, 'Make Mary leave us, for females are not worthy of life.' Jesus said, 'Look, I will guide her to make her male, so that she too may become a living male spirit like you. For every female who makes herself male will enter the empire of Heaven.'" In both Thom 114 and this gospel, Mary's worthiness is based on her having achieved a supreme spiritual state, metaphorically expressed in Thom 114 as "being male" or in the Gospel of Mary as "truly human" (5:8).

just who do you think you are to reject her? ¹⁰For he knew her completely ⟨and⟩ loved her stea[df]ast[ly].

¹¹"Rath[e]r [we] should be ashamed and, once we have clothed [ou]rselves with the p[erfec]t Human, we should do what [w]e were commanded ¹²and announce the good news, ¹³and not be la[y]ing down any rules or maki[n]g laws."

¹⁴After he said [the]se things, Le[vi] le[ft] (and) began to anno[unce the good ne]ws.

¹⁵[The Gos]pel according to Mary.

10:10 The Coptic reads: "Assuredly the Savior's knowledge of her is completely reliable. That is why he loved her more than us."

10:11 The Coptic reads: "Rather we should be ashamed. We should clothe ourselves with the perfect Human, acquire it for ourselves as he commanded us,"

10:13 The Coptic adds: "that differ from what the Savior said."

10:11
Cf. Gal 3:27;
Eph 4:13; Col 1:28

10:14 The Coptic reads: "After [he said these] things, they started going out [to] teach and to preach."

10:10 Compare Gospel of Philip 63:34–64:5: "And the companion of the S[avior . . .] Mary Magdalene [. . . loved] her more than [all] the disciples [and used to] kiss her [often] on her [. . .]. The rest of [the disciples . . .]. They said to him, 'Why do you love her more than all of us?' The Savior answered them, 'Why do I not love you like her?'"

10:11 The passage may have a baptismal reference. Compare Gospel of Philip 75:21–24: "The living water is a body. It is necessary that we put on the living human being. For this reason, when people are about to go down into the water, they unclothe themselves, so that they might put on (the living human being)."

The Gospel of Judas

Introduction

Despite Judas Iscariot's pivotal role in the New Testament gospels, little information is given about him or his motivations. The Gospel of Judas purports to tell the inside story of the events leading up to his betrayal of Jesus. As it was written much later than the New Testament gospels, the Gospel of Judas offers no new information about the circumstances of Jesus' death, but rather reflects the concerns and controversies of some second-century Christians. The fragmentary and obscure nature of the text has led to much scholarly disagreement about the message of this gospel, particularly about whether it aims to rehabilitate the character of Judas or to demonize him even more than the canonical gospels. Ultimately, however, attempts to show that the gospel presents a purely good or evil Judas fail to do justice to the subtlety and complexity of the narrative.

Genre and structure

The Gospel of Judas assumes familiarity with the canonical gospels, but in terms of genre and content, it is quite different. Rather than providing a narrative overview of Jesus' life and death, it focuses on one episode—the events leading up to Jesus' death—and explores its implications. The gospel consists of two main parts: a series of conversations between Jesus and his disciples—including Judas Iscariot—and, embedded within those conversations, a long mythological narrative that recounts the creation of the universe and of humankind.

The gospel's introduction (1:1–5) depicts Jesus' appearance on earth for the salvation of humanity and relates his choice of twelve disciples. In the very first scene, however, we learn that the disciples have gone astray: Jesus laughs at their celebration of the Eucharist and tells them they are worshiping the wrong god. He then singles out Judas and, recognizing that he has greater understanding than the others, promises him special revelation.

In the next scene (2:1–8), Jesus appears to the disciples again and tells them about "a great and holy race" that no mortal can join. The disciples are completely confused and do not know how to respond.

At Jesus' third appearance (2:9–3:10), the disciples relate troubling dreams about a temple where wicked priests sacrifice animals, and even human beings—their own wives and children, no less. Jesus interprets their dreams, revealing that the disciples themselves are these wicked priests who are misleading their "crowd" and thereby, as it were, "sacrificing" them like animals upon an altar.

In the next, and longest, section (3:11–6:10) Judas tells Jesus of his own dream, in which the other disciples pursue him and stone him until he follows Jesus to a place of refuge. In response, Jesus reveals to him the "mysteries of the kingdom," including a long mythological narrative about the creation of the universe and humanity, the brevity of life that the malicious world-ruler placed upon Adam and his descendents, and predictions about the end of time. Finally, in this gospel's climactic prophecy, Jesus predicts that Judas will sacrifice "the man who bears" him—that is, Judas will sacrifice Jesus' body, but not his true self. The good news in all this is that the wicked world-ruler "will be wiped out," and the fruit of Adam's great race will be exalted.

The brief final scene (6:11–16) brings the narrative back to the familiar territory of the canonical gospels with the chief priests and scholars approaching Judas to give him money in return for his betrayal of Jesus.

Date and discovery

The earliest reference to the Gospel of Judas is in a book written around 180 CE by Irenaeus, bishop of Lyons, called *Against the Heresies*. However, it is impossible to be sure whether Irenaeus knew the text presented here, since in Antiquity different writings often circulated under the same name. Probably written in the second century CE, the gospel now survives in a single papyrus codex from the third or fourth century, known as Codex Tchacos. The document is in Coptic, although scholars believe that the gospel was originally written in Greek. Because like all Coptic texts it borrows a number of words from Greek, the notes to this gospel sometimes refer to Greek words (for example at 1:7 and 3:12).

Little is known of the history of Codex Tchacos before it came on the antiquities market in Egypt in the 1980s. A series of antiquities dealers took possession of the manuscript and attempted several times to sell it to different scholarly institutions, none of which could raise the huge prices demanded. Eventually a cultural conservation organization bought the document and had it restored, after which a team of scholars finally edited it and published it in 2006. By this time, however, the papyrus had become so badly damaged by improper handling on the part of those attempting to sell it that much of the text could not be reconstructed, and the narrative suffers from frustratingly large gaps.

The holy race and the mortal races

Jesus repeatedly refers to a "holy race" in the Gospel of Judas, and contrasts it to the "human races." This language echoes many ancient texts in which Christians defined themselves in ethnic or racial terms, either calling themselves a "new race," the "true Israel" or the "third race," or making extensive arguments that connected them genealogically to particular ancestors or cultural traditions.

In the Gospel of Judas, Jesus states that "no one born of mortals" can join the holy race (2:6), but this assertion should probably not be taken to mean that all humans are excluded. Rather, the Gospel of Judas seems to suggest that humans must be spiritually reborn (perhaps through baptism, or some other ritual practice) in order to claim their spiritual identity and membership in the immortal race.

Criticism of the apostolic church

Jesus' disciples receive a good deal of criticism from their master in the Gospel of Judas. To be sure, the New Testament gospels also frequently portray the disciples in unflattering ways: misunderstanding parables, falling asleep in the Garden of Gethsemane, and disowning Jesus as he faces execution. Yet, in those gospels Jesus ultimately bestows authority on the disciples and they become faithful missionaries of his message. By the second century, ecclesiastical writers and authorities supported the belief in apostolic succession, i.e., the doctrine that religious authority had been passed on from the apostles through an unbroken succession of bishops. The extremely negative depiction of the disciples in the Gospel of Judas may therefore have been intended as an attack on the bishops themselves. If indeed the bishops' authority was inherited from a group of people who, as the Gospel of Judas claims, had worshiped the wrong god and had never learned Jesus' secret teachings, then it was surely illegitimate. Conflicts over authority among early Christian groups often revolved around claims to have inherited secret teachings given to only one disciple (as in the Gospel of Mary). This gospel is unique, however, in assigning this special eminence to Judas—whom the canonical gospels excluded from the community of the Twelve—in order to undermine the authority of all the other apostles, and thereby of all who claimed authority from them.

Sacrifice and martyrdom

Jesus' most serious charge against the disciples in the Gospel of Judas occurs in his interpretation of their vision about twelve wicked priests performing sacrifices in a temple. Jesus identifies the disciples with these priests who offer up their congregations like sacrificial animals. What could this accusation mean? It is likely that the Gospel of Judas is criticizing the bishops' endorsement of martyrdom. While most people are familiar with Christian glorification of martyrs, it is less well known that some early Christians opposed martyrdom, denying that God wanted such "human sacrifice," and denouncing church leaders who encouraged Christians to choose death over a denial of faith. Such a view probably lies behind the accusation in this gospel that "some [of the priests] sacrifice their very own children, some their wives" (2:15), and that they are "leading ⟨the crowd⟩ astray on the altar" (2:23).

Relationship to other early Christian texts

Many of the mythological references in the gospel resonate with second- and third-century texts that scholars characterize as "Sethian," because they frequently appeal to Seth, the third son of Adam and Eve (Gen 4:25), as the spiritual ancestor of a holy race, known as "the seed of Seth."

Sethian writings exhibit a keen interest in the origins of evil and human suffering, often interpreting and embellishing the early chapters of Genesis (the narratives of the creation, the lives of Adam and Eve, and the flood) to account for their conviction that most of humanity lives in unconscious enslavement to a false god and his army of wicked angels. Sethian texts characteristically demote the creator god of Israel to the status of a lower and malicious demi-god, while introducing a pantheon of higher heavenly powers far above him (for example, an Invisible Spirit, his consort Barbelo, and their son, "Self-Generated") who collectively represent true, benevolent divinity in the universe. Divine providence—appearing variously in the form of the Spirit, Seth, or Jesus—brings salvation to humanity by enlightening them about their spiritual origins in the heavenly race of Seth, and conferring upon them the transformative power of ritual baptism. We know very little about the people behind these "Sethian" writings. That each text narrates its own story or variation of a mythological drama tells us that their authors and readers had a complex relationship both with each other and with various other religious groups in Antiquity.

Scholarly study of the Gospel of Judas is still in its preliminary phases, and even specialists still have much to understand. Still, it is clear that the Christians who cherished this gospel held significantly different beliefs and values from those forms of Christianity that eventually prevailed. Those Christians who used the Gospel of Judas appreciated distinctive mythologies and cosmologies, believed that the god of the Hebrew Bible was a malevolent being inferior to the true God, felt a sense of alienation from the hierarchies and teachings of the established church, and held a harshly critical view of those who encouraged martyrdom. The Gospel of Judas is valuable not because it provides any new information on the life or teachings of the historical Jesus, but because it helps to deepen and broaden our understanding of the diversity of early Christianity.

The Gospel of Judas

1 **The secret account** of the judgment that Jesus pronounced to Judas Iscariot over eight days, leading up to the three days before he observed Passover.

Prologue

²**When he appeared on earth,** he performed signs and great wonders for the salvation of humanity. ³While some people were walking in the path of righteousness and others in the path of their wrongdoing, the twelve disciples were called. ⁴He began to speak with them about the mysteries above the world and what's going to happen at the end. ⁵Sometimes he didn't reveal himself to his disciples, but instead [they] would find him among themselves as a child.

Jesus' miracles and teaching

Jesus laughs at their thanksgiving

⁶**One day in Judea** he came to his disciples and found them sitting together, training in godliness. ⁷When he met his disciples sitting together, giving thanks over the bread, he laughed.

⁸But his disciples said to him, "Teacher, why are you laughing at our thanksgiving? Haven't we done what's right?"

⁹He replied, "I'm not laughing at you. You're not doing this of your own free will, but because your god will be praised by it."

¹⁰They said, "But teacher, you're the son of our god."

¹¹Jesus said to them, "How do you know me? I'm telling you, no race of your people will know me."

¹²When his disciples heard this, they began to get angry, cursing and blaspheming him in their hearts.

1:5 *child:* The form of this Coptic word is otherwise unknown, but seems to be a variant spelling of a similar word that means "child." Jesus appears as a child in the Secret Book of John, and in the Gospel of the Savior, Jesus tells his disciples, "I am among you as a child" (GSav 13:2).

1:5
Ⓣ GSav 13:2

1:6 *training:* The Greek word here is *gymnaze*, which usually referred to physical exercise or training (hence the English word "gymnasium"). A close parallel to this phrase occurs in 1 Tim 4:7 (see also 2 Tim 2:5). In 1 Cor 9:24–27, Paul compares the spiritual life to an athletic contest.

godliness: The word translated "godliness" can also mean "divinity," "divine nature," and "piety." Here, the idea may mean that the disciples are exercising their own divine natures in the ritual context of the Eucharist, or that they are simply acting piously by offering Eucharist prayer over their bread (1:7).

1:7 *giving thanks:* The Greek word here is *eucharisti.* While the word literally means "giving thanks," it had already by the second century become a technical term for the Christian ritual of sharing bread and wine (Eucharist). Already

in the New Testament, the Eucharist was associated with the sacrifice of Christ (1 Cor 11:23–26); sacrifice is an important recurring theme of the Gospel of Judas (2:9–31; 6:1–3).

1:8 *thanksgiving:* or "Eucharist."

1:9 Jesus' statement refers to the idea that the god whom the disciples worship is in fact a false god. As we find out later, he is nothing more than a rebellious angel (5:1–4).

1:11 Words meaning *race* occur frequently in the Gospel of Judas, in line with many other early Christian texts that describe Christians as a race or people. The Gospel of Judas implies a division between the holy race of people who recognize the true god, and the mortal races who worship the inferior creator god.

Jesus chooses Judas

The holy race

¹³But when Jesus saw their foolishness, he said, "Why has confusion led to anger? Your god who is among you and his [. . .] have become angry with your souls. ¹⁴Whoever of you is powerful should bring forth the perfect human, and stand and face me."

¹⁵**And they all said,** "We are strong," but their spirits could not dare to stand in his presence, except for Judas Iscariot. ¹⁶He could stand in front of him, but couldn't look him in the eye. Instead, he turned his face away.

¹⁷Judas said to him, "I know who you are and where you came from. You came from the immortal realm of Barbelo. ¹⁸And I'm not worthy even to name the one who sent you."

¹⁹Now since Jesus knew that ⟨Judas⟩ was thinking about different, higher things, he said to him, "Separate yourself from them and I will tell you the mysteries of the kingdom; not so that you'll go there, but so that you'll mourn deeply. ²⁰In fact, there's someone else who will take your place, so that the twelve disciples will again be complete in their god."

²¹And Judas said to him, "On what day will you tell me these things and when will the great day of light dawn for [that] race?"

²²But after he said this, Jesus left him.

2 Now when morning came, ⟨Jesus⟩ appeared to his disciples and they said to him, "Teacher, where did you go and what did you do after you left us?"

²Jesus replied, "I went to another great and holy race."

³His disciples said to him, "Master, what is the great and holy race that's exalted above us and isn't in these realms?"

⁴Now when Jesus heard this, he laughed and said to them, "Why are you wondering in your hearts about the strong and holy race? ⁵I'm telling you, no one born of this realm will see [that race]. ⁶No angelic army of the stars will rule

1:20
ⓣ Acts 1:16–26

2:5
ⓣ Jn 3:5;
1Cor 15:50;
Cf. 2 Cor 5:1–8;
Judas 3:20

1:14 In ancient philosophical thought, the *perfect human* was a sage who achieved the highest degree of virtue, living in serenity while controlling all bodily passions like anger and appetite. Sethian mythology associates this state of perfection with heavenly Adamas, the pre-incarnate ideal of humanity whom the creator god and his angels use as a model to mold the earthly Adam (see 4:14–17 and 5:11–12). Thus Jesus commands his disciples to show their true, heavenly nature and moral perfection.

1:17 In Sethian mythology, *Barbelo* appears as the divine mother of all, second only to the Father, or highest god.

1:19 It is unclear what *the kingdom* means in the this gospel, since the text seems to use it inconsistently to refer to various dominions. In some cases it could refer to the upper, celestial realms, where the divine luminaries are said to "rule" (4:7–12), but in others to the lower realms ruled

by the wicked angels (cf. 3:5; 3:22, 3:24). The Gospel of Judas also refers to the kingdom that Adam received on earth (5:17), which is apparently different from that of the wicked angels (5:21).

As in other gospels, such as the Gospel of Thomas and the Gospel of Mary, Jesus chooses one of the disciples to receive special revelations. Compare with the Gospel of John, in which Jesus also has a favorite, the "disciple Jesus loved" (see, for example, John 13:23 and 19:26).

mourn deeply: Jesus probably means that Judas will mourn over the fact that someone else will take his place among the Twelve, and that he will not join the holy race (1:20, 3:25–27).

2:6 *angelic army:* Ancient Jews and Christians frequently associated angels with the stars, and imagined them to be a heavenly army organized like a human one, with chiefs

over that race, nor will anyone born of mortals be able to join it, because [that race] does not come from [. . .] which became [. . .] the race of people among [them]. ⁷But it is from the race of the great people [. . .] powerful authorities who [. . .] nor any power [of the realms in which] you are kings."

⁸When his disciples heard this, each of them was disturbed in his spirit, and they found nothing to say.

⁹**When Jesus came to them** another day, they said to him, "Teacher, we saw you in a dream, for we had powerful [dreams last] night."

¹⁰[He said], "Why did you [. . .] and hide yourselves?"

¹¹And they [said, "We] saw a great house [with a] great altar in it, and twelve people—we think they're priests—and a name. ¹²And there was a crowd devoted to that altar, until the priests [came out] and [took in] the offerings. ¹³And we ourselves were devoted to it."

¹⁴[Jesus] said, "What are [the . . .] like?"

¹⁵And they said, "Some fast for two weeks; some sacrifice their very own children, others their wives, all the while praising and acting humbly toward each other. ¹⁶Some sleep with men, some murder, some commit many sins and crimes. ¹⁷The people standing over the altar are invoking your name. And that [altar] is filled through all their empty sacrifices."

¹⁸After they said this they stopped talking because they were confused.

¹⁹**And Jesus said to them,** "Why are you confused? I'm telling you, all the priests standing over that altar are invoking my name. ²⁰And I'm also telling you, my name was written on this house of the races of the stars by the human races, and [they] shamefully planted some fruitless trees in my name."

²¹And Jesus said to them, "It's you taking the offerings to the altar that you saw; that ⟨altar⟩ is the god you worship. ²²And the twelve men you saw, they're you! ²³The animals you saw brought as sacrifices, they're the crowd you're lead-

---

2:14 *[the . . .]:* The lacuna could be restored with "priests" or "people."

2:20
Ⓣ Mt 3:10,
7:16–20, 12:33;
Lk 3:9, 6:43–44

---

over ranks of thousands, hundreds, fifties, and tens (see, for example, Dan 8:10, the Books of Enoch, and Luke 2:13). The idea that no angelic army will "rule" over the holy race relates to the ancient Jewish notion that God had appointed "angels of the nations" to rule over the various kingdoms of the earth (cf. Deut 32:8; Sir 17:17; Dan 10:13, 12:1). Drawing on this tradition, Judas depicts the stars as hostile powers in service of the wicked world ruler.

The ancient world commonly associated angels with *stars.*

2:7 *you are kings:* Compare Matt 19:28. Though this passage is fragmentary, the idea that the twelve disciples are "kings" may reflect the early church tradition of the "mo-narchical episcopate," that is, that the bishops, as successors of the apostles, have sole authority over their churches. One also finds in early Christian literature references to the "thrones of the apostles" (e.g., Tertullian, *Prescription Against the Heretics* 36).

2:10 This verse is too fragmentary to understand.

2:11 The *great house* presumably refers to the Jewish temple in Jerusalem; however, it may also have been intended to evoke pagan temples.

2:20 *my name was written on this house of the races of the stars by the human races:* This ambiguous statement may mean that the human races dedicated the temple of the stars to Jesus.

ing astray on that altar. ²⁴ [Your minister] will stand, and this is the way he will use my name, and the pious races will be devoted to it. ²⁵After this someone else will offer up those who are [sexually immoral]. And another will offer up those who murder children; and another ⟨will offer up⟩ men who sleep with men and with those who abstain; ²⁶and ⟨another will offer up those who commit⟩ the rest of the impurities and crimes and errors. ²⁷And those who say, 'We are equal to angels,' indeed they are the stars who bring all things to fulfillment.' ²⁸For they said to the human races, 'Look, god received your sacrifice through the hands of priests,' —that is, the minister of error. ²⁹But the Lord—he who is the Lord of the universe—commands that on the final day they will be disgraced."

³⁰And Jesus said [to them], "Stop [sacrificing the animals] that you [offered up] on the altar. They are with your stars and angels, having already been completed there. ³¹So regard them as [vanities], and let them [be] visible [to you]."

³²His disciples [said, "Master,] purify us from the [wickedness] we committed in the error of the angels."

³³Jesus said to them, "It's impossible [. . .] kings [. . .] Nor is it [possible for] a fountain to extinguish the [fire] of the entire inhabited world. ³⁴[Nor] is it possible for a [city] spring to water all the races, except for the great, stable race. ³⁵And no single lamp will shine on all the realms, except on the second race. ³⁶Nor can a baker feed the whole creation under [heaven]."

³⁷And [when his disciples] heard this, they said to him, "Master, help us, and save us."

2:25
Ⓣ Judas 5:27

2:24 *[Your minister]:* Another possible restoration is "The great minister." Compare with the "minister of error" in 2:28.

2:35 *second race:* The text is uncertain and may be corrupt.

2:24 *[Your minister]:* The Greek word here, *diakonos* (which could also be translated "deacon"), probably refers generally to a church official. In the ancient world, temple officials were often called "ministers" or "servants" of the temple. This figure is probably to be identified with the "minister of error" mentioned in 2:28.

devoted to it: that is devoted to Jesus' name; or *devoted to him*, the "minister."

2:25–27 *offer up:* This obscure word can also mean "stand up from," "stand up for," and "take the side of." However, in ritual contexts like the present passage, it also means "to present" or "offer" as sacrifice (as in Romans 12:1). In Judas 5:26, the word is used more clearly to explain how the races (presumably of humanity) are "presented" or "offered" to the false god Saklas.

The whole sense of the current passage could be understood as a criticism of those who sacrifice various sorts of sinners: sexually immoral people, child-killers, and crimi-

nals. This gospel obviously also considers homosexuals to be sinners. In the previous verses (2:14–23), Jesus criticized the twelve disciples for being immoral priests, and especially for offering human sacrifice; now he criticizes the sacrifices themselves for their blemished character. Jesus' criticism is in line with ancient ideas about sacrifice that maintained that both the one who sacrifices and the sacrifice itself had to be pure in order for the ritual to be effective.

2:25 *sleep with . . . those who abstain:* Although the Coptic syntax is ambiguous, the criticism seems to be of people who "sleep with" would-be abstainers, that is, those who seduce or corrupt people attempting to abstain from sexual activity.

2:28 *they:* the people who claim equality with angels.

The minister of error could refer to "god" (i.e., the false god Saklas). But it could also refer to the "priests."

2:30–31 This passage is partially reconstructed and remains obscure.

³⁸Jesus said to them, "Stop arguing with me. Each of you has his own star [and] [. . .] of the stars will [. . .] what belongs to him. [. . .] ³⁹I was not sent to the corruptible race, but to the mighty and incorruptible race. ⁴⁰For no enemy has ruled [over] that race, nor one among the stars. ⁴¹I'm telling you, the pillar of fire will fall quickly, and that race shall not be moved [. . .] stars."

⁴²After Jesus said this, he left, [taking] Judas Iscariot with him.

3 He said to ⟨Judas⟩, "The water [. . .] the high mountain is from [. . .] in [. . .] he did not come to [. . .] [the spring] of the tree [. . . *1 line missing* . . .] of this realm [. . .] after a time [. . .]. ²Instead, he came to water the garden of god and the [fruit] that will endure, because [he will] not corrupt the path of that race, but [it will exist] for all eternity."

³Judas said to him, "[Tell] me, what's the fruit of this race?"

⁴Jesus said, "The souls of each human race will die. ⁵But these, when they have completed the time of the kingdom, and the spirit leaves them, their bodies will die, but their souls will live on and they will be taken up."

⁶Judas said, "So what will the rest do—⟨I mean⟩, the human races?"

⁷Jesus said, "It's impossible to sow on rock so that they'll receive their [fruit]. ⁸And in the same way, it's [impossible for] the souls of the [defiled] race, along with perishable wisdom [and] the hand that created mortals, to ascend to the realms on high. ⁹I'm telling you, neither [ruler] nor angel nor power will be able to see those ⟨realms⟩ that [this great] holy race [will see]."

2:41 *moved [. . .] stars*: This could be restored as "moved [by the] stars."
3:1 *The water [. . .] the high mountain*: This could be restored as "The water [from] the high mountain".
3:2 *[fruit]*: This could also be restored as "race."

3:3–5
Ⓣ Judas 5:19
3:7
Ⓣ Mk 4:5,
Mt 13:5, Lk 8:6

2:38 This could reflect the common idea in ancient astrology that each individual has a personal star. Alternately, it may be that only the twelve disciples have their own stars, perhaps corresponding to the twelve angels who serve the false gods Nebro and Saklas (5:5–6).

2:41 *The pillar of fire* might symbolize the false god Saklas, since in the Bible the God of Israel led his people in the desert by appearing as a pillar of fire (see Exod 13:21–22). That the pillar will *fall* could refer to Saklas' future destruction (compare 5:24 and 6:5). It could also echo the fall of Satan "like lightning from heaven" in Luke 10:18.

3:1–2 The three occurrences of *he* can also be translated "it," referring to "the water."

3:2 *water the garden of god:* This obscure reference could be to the past salvation activity of Seth, since according to the ancient Jewish philosopher Philo, Seth's name means "irrigation." The Sethian writing entitled *The Holy Book of the*

Great Invisible Spirit describes the heavenly Seth's descent into the world as a savior at various times in history. In his final appearance, Seth comes in the form of Jesus.

3:5 Here *the kingdom* clearly refers to life on earth; but see 1:19.

This gospel distinguishes between the *spirit* and *soul* here and in 5:19. The *spirit* may be understood as an animating life-force, possessed by everyone, which leaves the person at the time of death. The *soul*, on the other hand, appears to be the true "self" which, if one belongs to the holy race, will *live on* and *be taken up* after death (perhaps an allusion to resurrection).

3:8 Because of the breaks in the manuscript, it is unclear whether *wisdom* (Greek *sophia*) is personified in this passage, or whether *perishable wisdom* simply refers to the human races' inferior capacity of understanding.

Judas's vision ¹⁰After Jesus said this, he left.

Jesus interprets
Judas's vision ¹¹**Judas said, "Teacher,** now listen to me like you listened to all of them. For I've seen a great vision."

¹²But when Jesus heard this, he laughed and said to him, "What are you getting worked up about, thirteenth spirit? Now speak, and I'll bear with you."

¹³Judas said to him, "I saw myself in the vision. The twelve disciples are stoning me—they're really hounding me. ¹⁴Then I came to the place [. . .] after you. ¹⁵I saw [a house in that place], and my eyes couldn't measure how big it was. ¹⁶There were some eminent people surrounding it, and that house had a roof of lightning. ¹⁷And in the middle of the house there was a crowd [. . . *2 lines missing* . . .] ¹⁸Teacher, receive me along with these people."

¹⁹**And Jesus replied,** "Your star has led you astray, Judas. ²⁰No one born of mortals is worthy to enter the house you saw. ²¹That's the place kept for the holy ones, the place where neither the sun nor moon nor day will rule, but they will always stand in the realm with the holy angels. ²²So, I've told you the mysteries of the kingdom, and I've taught you about the straying of the stars. And [. . .] sent [. . . *1 line missing* . . .] over the twelve realms."

²³Judas said, "Teacher, surely my seed doesn't dominate the rulers?"

²⁴And Jesus replied to him, "Come here so I can speak [with you] [. . . *1.5 lines missing* . . .], but so you will mourn deeply when you see the kingdom with its whole race."

3:20
Cf. Judas 2:5

3:16 *roof of lightning:* "Roof of greenery" or "a single room" are other possible readings. The idea that God's heavenly house has a roof of lightning appears in the famous Jewish apocalyptic writing 1 Enoch (ch. 14).

3:10–11 That Jesus leaves, but Judas speaks to him is an odd turn in the narrative and could indicate a redactional seam, where the author pasted together two different sources. Or, perhaps, a later scribe accidentally omitted a line about Judas leaving with Jesus (compare 2:42).

3:12 *spirit:* This word (Greek *daimon*) could also be rendered "god," or "demon." The translation "spirit" is preferable because it conveys the neutral meaning of the word, since in ancient Greek and Jewish thought *daimons* were considered lower-order divinities, like angels, who were responsible for the administration of the universe's lower regions, and could be swayed toward good or evil. Hence they occupy an intermediate place in the universe, both spatially and morally. That Judas is called the "thirteenth *daimon*" signifies that he will transcend the twelve disciples and the twelve realms of the lower universe (3:22, 5:1, 5:5–7). His fate is to rule over the human races, while his star rules over the "thirteenth realm" (3:26, 5:27). Some Sethian literature identifies the false god, often named Saklas as in the Gospel of Judas, with the "god of the thirteen realms." It remains an open question whether this gospel demonizes Judas by making him the ruler of the thirteenth realm, or if it rehabili-

tates Judas by appointing him to the "middle-management" position formerly occupied by the false god.

3:22 *straying of the stars:* The straying or "wandering" of the stars is a popular theme in Jewish and Christian apocalyptic literature. In the Books of Enoch, the fallen angels are described as stars who strayed from their appointed heavenly courses, and who led humanity astray through evil teaching. Compare with the Epistle of Jude 1:13–14. A similar idea appears in the Gospel of Judas (see 2:6, 27, 32, 40–41; 3:19; 5:23–25).

3:23 Judas's question is apparently prompted by what Jesus told him in the previous verse (22), which, though now heavily damaged, appears to involve Judas being "sent [. . .] over the twelve realms." It is not clear who the seed of Judas is, but the sense seems to be that Judas will be exalted to a position of authority over the twelve lower realms of the universe currently controlled by the false god and his twelve angelic rulers (5:1, 6). The Gospel of Judas expresses the same idea elsewhere, when Jesus tells Judas that he will "become the thirteenth" and "rule" over the other races, while his "star will [rule] over the thirteenth realm" (3:26–27; 5:27).

²⁵When Judas heard this, he said to him, "What good has it done me that you've set me apart from that race?"

²⁶Jesus replied, "You will become the thirteenth and you will be cursed by the rest of the races and you will rule over them. ²⁷In the last days they ⟨will . . .⟩ to you. And you won't go up to the holy race."

4 Jesus said, "[Come,] and I will teach you about [the mysteries] that no human will see. ²For there is a great and limitless realm whose size no angelic race has seen. ³There's [a great Invisible Spirit in it],

> whom no angelic eye has seen,
> nor inner thought received,
> nor has he been called by any name.

⁴"In that place a luminous cloud appeared, and ⟨the Invisible Spirit⟩ said, 'Let an angel come into being to attend me.' ⁵And a great angel, Self-Generated, the god of light, came out of the cloud. ⁶Then four other angels came out of another cloud for him, and they came into being to attend the angelic Self-Generated.

⁷"And Self-Generated said, 'Let a [realm] come into being,' and it happened [just as he said]. ⁸And he [established] the first light to rule over it. ⁹He said, 'Let some angels come into being to serve it,' and a countless myriad came into being. ¹⁰Then he said, 'Let a luminous realm come into being,' and it came into being. ¹¹He established the second light to rule over it, with countless myriads of serving angels. ¹²In this way, he created the rest of the realms of light, and he caused them to be ruled over. ¹³And he created countless myriads of angels to serve them.

3:27 The text here seems to be corrupt due to a scribal error. About one line or so may have been omitted.
4:7 Some scholars reconstruct this verse as "And Self-Generated said, 'Let A[damas] come into being,' and [the emanation] occurred."

4:3 This hymn-like passage offers a variation on a popular formula that some ancient Christians used to legitimize the teaching of revelations and hidden mysteries. Compare with 1 Cor 2:9 (perhaps based on Isa 64:4) and Thomas 17. Here, Jesus uses the formula to refer to the great Invisible Spirit, who in Sethian mythology is the Father and most transcendent divinity.
4:5 *Self-Generated* (or *Autogenes* in Greek) is the Son in the traditional Sethian trinity (Father/Invisible Spirit, Mother/Barbelo, and Son/Autogenes). Judas does not elaborate on the relationship between Self-Generated and Jesus, although some relationship may be implied since Jesus came from the realm of Barbelo, probably at the behest of the Invisible Spirit who is attended by Self-Generated (see 1:17–18).
4:8, 11 *first light* and *second light:* This creation narrative may be inspired by the first chapter of Genesis (especially Gen 1:16), where God creates a first and second light—the sun and moon—then the stars. However, Judas is not simply recounting the creation story of Genesis 1. Instead, it is offering its own version of how the Invisible Spirit and his angelic assistant, Self-Generated, created the transcendent heavenly realms prior to the creation described in Genesis. Here, the *first light* and *second light* are not the sun and moon, but the first two lights in a series of twelve heavenly luminaries ruled by twelve heavenly realms (these are referred to explicitly in 4:19). For more on Judas' cosmology, see the note for 4:18–22.
4:12 *he caused them to be ruled over:* that is, Self-Generated caused the twelve lights to rule over the twelve realms (4:19).

¹⁴"**Adamas was** in the first cloud of light that not a single angel called 'god' has seen. ¹⁵And he [. . . *2 lines missing* . . .] [after] the image [. . .] and likeness of this angel. ¹⁶And he revealed the imperishable race of Seth [to] the twelve androgynous [lights. ¹⁷Afterward], he revealed the seventy-two lights in the imperishable race by the will of the Spirit.

¹⁸"**Now the seventy-two lights** themselves revealed three hundred and sixty lights in the incorruptible race by the will of the Spirit, so that their number is five for each. ¹⁹And their father is the twelve realms of the twelve lights. ²⁰And for each realm there are six heavens, so that there are seventy-two heavens for the seventy-two lights. ²¹And for each of ⟨the seventy-two heavens⟩ there are five skies, so that they have three hundred and sixty skies. ²²And [they] were given authority with a great, countless angelic army giving praise and [worship], and also some virginal [spirits] giving praise and worship to all the realms and the heavens and their skies.

²³"Now the crowd of those immortals is called 'cosmos,' that is, 'perishability,' by the Father and by the seventy-two lights that are with Self-Generated and his seventy-two realms, ²⁴the [place] where the first human appeared with his imperishable powers. ²⁵And this is the realm that appeared with its race, this one in which the cloud of knowledge resides with the angel named El[eleth]. [. . . *3 lines missing* . . .]

4:16 Some scholars render this fragmentary passage as "he made the incorruptible [generation] of Seth appear [. . .] the twelve [. . .] twenty-four [. . .]." However, *androgynous* is more likely than "twenty-four."

4:14 *called 'god'*: or, "called 'divine'."

4:15–16 In Sethian mythology, *Adamas* is the divine archetype of humanity (see "first human" in 4:24), and father of the heavenly Seth and his imperishable race. Although this passage is broken, it could relate how heavenly Adamas was created in the image and likeness of "this angel," perhaps referring to Self-Generated (who is called an angel at 4:5). Or, it could relate how Adamas created Seth after his own "image and likeness," projecting Gen 5:3 onto the heavenly plane. Later in this gospel the heavenly Adamas is probably "the likeness and the image" after which the wicked angels fashion the earthly Adam (see 5:11 and Gen 1:26–27).

4:18–22 If *the twelve realms of the twelve lights* (4:19) constitute the father of the seventy two lights (see 4:12), then there would be six lights for each of the twelve realms. This sequence creates an alternating pattern of multiplication (×6 / ×5 / ×6 / ×5) in the present creation myth: (i) 6 lights × 12 realms = 72 lights; (ii) 5 lights × 72 lights = 360 lights;

(iii) 6 heavens × 12 realms = 72 heavens; (iv) 5 skies × 72 heavens = 360 skies. This constellation comprises a three-tiered hierarchy of 12 realms with 12 lights, followed by 72 lights with 72 heavens, followed by 360 lights with 360 skies. The point of the scheme is probably to illustrate that the universe is numerically well-ordered and harmonious.

4:22 *virginal [spirits]*: "pure spirits" who populate the transcendent realms.

4:23 *'cosmos,' that is, 'perishability'*: This immortal *cosmos*, or "universe," probably refers to all the lights, heavens, and skies enumerated in 4:18–22. Many ancient philosophers believed that while the universe is itself eternal, it is also perishable, or "corruptible," because its various elements undergo change and periodic dissolution.

4:24 *The first human* probably refers to Adamas (4:14; see also the "perfect human" in 1:14).

4:25 In Sethian mythology, *Eleleth* is one of the four angels, or luminaries, who attend Self-Generated (see 4:6).

5 "**After this [Eleleth] said**, 'Let twelve angels come into being to rule over chaos and the underworld.' [2]And indeed, an angel appeared from out of the cloud, his face spewing forth fire. [3]Now his likeness was [defiled] with blood, and his [name] was Nebro, which translates as 'apostate.' Others say 'Yalda-baoth.' [4]And another angel too, Saklas, came out of the cloud.

[5]"Then Nebro created six angels—and ⟨so did⟩ Saklas—to be in attendance. [6]These produced twelve angels in the heavens, and each of them received a share in the heavens.

[7]"And the twelve rulers said to the twelve angels, 'Let each one of you [. . .]' and they [. . .] race [. . .] angel.

> [8]The first [is . . .]th, he who is called the Lord.
> The [second] is Harmathoth, who [. . .].
> [9]The [third] is Galila.
> The fourth [is] Yobel.
> The fifth is Adonaios.

[10]"These are the five who rule over the underworld and are the first over chaos.

[11]"**Then Saklas said** to his angels, 'Let's create a human being after the likeness and the image.' [12]And they formed Adam and his wife Eve. [13]Now in the cloud she is called Zoe, for in this name all the races seek him, and each one of them calls her by their names. [14]But Sakla[s] did not [command] [. . .] create, except [. . .] among the races [. . .], which is [. . .]. [15]And [the angel] said to him, 'The lives of you and your children will last for a ⟨fixed⟩ time.'"

[16]And Judas said to Jesus, "[What's] the longest that a person will live?"

[17]Jesus answered, "Why are you surprised that Adam, along with his race, received his time in a limited way, in the place where he received his kingdom in a limited way, along with his ruler?"

5:8 *[. . .]th, he who is called the Lord:* Some scholars reconstruct this phrase as "[Se]th who is called Christ." However, the name of the ruler in question is too fragmentary to reconstruct with confidence, and could be any name of three or four letters ending in *-th.*

5:11
◊ Gen 1:26–27;
Cf. Judas 4:14–15

5:3–4 *Nebro, Yaldabaoth,* and *Saklas* also appear in other Sethian writings as the names of wicked creator gods.

5:3 *Others say Yaldabaoth:* that is, others call Nebro "Yalda-baoth."

5:7 The reference to *twelve rulers* comes abruptly because the gospel does not explicitly mention them in the preceding narrative. One explanation may be a redactional seam, indicating that the author began drawing from a source which he or she did not seamlessly incorporate into the narrative. However, one could also explain the sudden appearance of the twelve rulers through a nuanced reading of 5:5–6: Nebro and Saklas each create six angels, for a total

of twelve; then "these," that is the twelve angels, produce yet another twelve angels, which in 5:7 are called rulers. In Judas, the terms "angel," "ruler," "star," even "god" are often interchangeable.

5:8–10 In Sethian mythology twelve malicious rulers serve under the lower creator gods (Judas 5:1, 5:6–7). However, Judas has shortened the list to five.

5:13 *Zoe* is the Greek word for "life," which translates the Hebrew "Eve" in Gen 3:20.

5:17 *Received his kingdom* refers to God's giving humans authority over the rest of creation in Gen 1:28.

¹⁸And Judas said to Jesus, "Does the human spirit die?"

Jesus said, "This is the way God commanded Michael to give the spirits of humans to them while they serve: as a loan. ¹⁹But the Great One commanded Gabriel to give the spirits to the great kingless race, the spirit and the soul. ²⁰Because of this, the [other] souls [. . .] [. . . *1 line missing* . . .] light [. . .] the chaos [. . . *1 line missing* . . .] seek [after] the spirit within you that you've made to inhabit this flesh in the angelic races. ²¹But God [had] knowledge given to Adam and those with him so that the rulers of chaos and the underworld would not rule over them."

²²But Judas said to Jesus, "So what will those races do?"

²³**And Jesus said,** "Really, I'm telling you, the stars are coming to fulfillment over all of them. ²⁴And when Saklas completes the time allotted to him, their first star will come with the races and the things mentioned will be fulfilled. ²⁵Then they'll commit sexual immorality in my name, and they'll kill their children, and [they'll] [. . .] wickedness, and [. . . *3 lines missing* . . .] the realms, bringing their races and offering them to Sakla[s. ²⁶And] afterward, [. . .]rael will come, bringing the twelve tribes of [Israel] from [. . .]. And all the [races] will serve Saklas while sinning [in] my name. ²⁷And your star will [rule] over the thirteenth realm."

²⁸Now after this Jesus [laughed. ²⁹And Judas] said, "Teacher, [why are you] laughing at us?"

³⁰Jesus] replied, "I'm not laughing [at you, but] at [the straying] of the stars, because these six stars are going astray with these five warriors, and all of them will perish with their creations."

³¹And Judas said to Jesus, "Well, what will those who have been baptized in your name do?"

³²Jesus said, "Really, I'm telling you, this baptism [. . . in] my name [. . . *3 lines missing* . . .] he will wipe out the entire race of earthly Adam. ³³Tomorrow they will torture him who bears me. ³⁴Indeed I say to you, no hand of mortal human [will] sin against me."

5:19 Calling the holy people a *kingless race* signifies their freedom from external domination.

the spirit and the soul: See the note to 3:5.

5:23–27 *the stars are coming to fulfillment over all of them:* The stars are influencing the fate of the human races, apparently leading them into sin and error, and together with the twelve tribes of Israel, into the service of the false god Saklas (5:24–26; cf. 2:32; 3:19). According to this prophecy, all this will transpire when Saklas "completes the time allotted to him" (perhaps when he comes to the end of his reign over humanity), while Judas usurps Saklas' position with his star coming to "rule over the thirteenth realm."

5:24 The *things mentioned* which *will be fulfilled* refers to

Jesus' earlier description of a future outbreak of wickedness, first introduced in his interpretation of the disciples' dream (2:15–16), and continued in his prophecy about sinful offerings (2:24–27). There, Jesus also refers to the "stars who bring all things to fulfillment" (2:27).

5:30 *these six stars are going astray with these five warriors:* This highly obscure phrase cannot easily be understood on the basis of the extant text. The six stars may refer to some of the angels created by Nebro and Saklas (5:5), and the five warriors to the five rulers of the underworld (5:8–10). The total of eleven figures may symbolically refer to the other eleven disciples, whom Judas elsewhere associates with stars and going "astray" (2:21–23, 38).

6 "Really, I'm telling you, Judas,** that those who offer sacrifice to Saklas [. . .] [2]them all [. . .] over [. . .] all [. . .] every [wicked] thing. [3]But you yourself will do more than all of them, for you will sacrifice the man who bears me. [4]Already your horn is raised up, your anger is full, your star has passed, and your heart has [prevailed]. [5]Really, I'm telling you, your final [. . . *3 lines missing* . . .] of the realm [. . .] [and] the kings have become weak, and the races of the angels have mourned, and wickedness [. . . *1 line missing* . . .] the [ruler], who will be wiped out. [6]And then the [fruit] of Adam's great race will be raised up, because before heaven and earth and the angels that race exists in the realms.

[7]**"So, you've been told everything.** [8]Look up and see the cloud and the light within it, and the stars surrounding it. And the leading star—that's your star."

[9]Then Judas looked up, he saw the luminous cloud, and he entered it. [10]Those standing on the ground heard a voice coming out of the cloud, saying "[. . .] great race [. . .] image [. . . *2 lines missing* . . .]."

[11]**Then Judas stopped** looking at Jesus. And immediately, there was a commotion among the Jews, greater than [. . .] [12]Their chief priests were angry because ⟨Jesus⟩ went into the guest room to pray. [13]And some scholars were there watching carefully to seize him in prayer, for they were afraid of the people because they all saw him as a prophet. [14]And they went up to Judas and said to him, "What are you doing here? You are Jesus' disciple."

[15]And Judas responded the way they wanted.

[16]He accepted some money, and handed him over to them.

6:10
Ⓣ Mk 9:7,
Mt 17:5, Lk 9:34–35

6:12
Ⓣ Mk 14:1;
Mt 21:46, 26:4–5;
Lk 20:19, 22:2

6:6 *[fruit]:* This restoration is tentative. Other possibilities are "image" and "place."

6:3 The *man who bears* Jesus refers to Jesus' body, following a common ancient metaphor. Judas will sacrifice the body of Jesus, thereby will be *doing more* than those who offer sacrifice to Saklas (the twelve disciples and their devoted crowd in 2:9–30). This "doing more" is difficult to interpret, partly because of the breaks in the text. Does Judas "do more" evil than the others by sacrificing Jesus, that is, by betraying, even murdering, him? Or does Judas "do more" good than the others, because his sacrifice of Jesus is understood as an act of redemption and salvation that leads to the obliteration of the wicked ruler and the exaltation of the great race (6:5–6)?

6:4 In the biblical tradition, an exalted *horn* symbolizes power, victory, kingship, and even arrogance (for example, 1 Sam 2:1; Ps 75:4–10, 89:17–27). Its meaning here is ambiguous. Does the gospel intend to demonize Judas by portraying him as a defiant and angry disciple who "sacrifices" Jesus? Or does Judas' raised horn and anger symbolize his victory over the wicked ruler "who will be wiped out" (6:5)?

6:6 *The [fruit] of Adam's great race* probably refers to mortals who have converted to the holy race. See 3:3–9.

6:9 *And he entered it: he* could refer to Judas or Jesus.

6:12 The *guest room* refers to the room where Jesus and disciples celebrated Passover (Mark 14:14, Luke 22:11).

Heavenly messenger

The Greek word *angelos* means "messenger," which is how it is translated when it refers to human who carry messages (as in Luke 7:24). When the word refers to a supernatural being, the traditional translation is "angel," which is actually an English version of the Greek term. An angel is a messenger or envoy dispatched by God or the gods to carry messages to humankind. Angels are therefore intermediaries between the divine and human realms. In order to avoid popular associations with the standard word and to refurbish the concept in English, the SV translators decided to employ the phrase, *heavenly messenger.*

Infancy Gospels

Codex Atheniensis 355, a fifteenth-century MS that includes the Infancy Gospel of Thomas, was first published in 1907. Shown here is folio 64 recto which contains part of the sixth chapter in which Jesus confront the teacher Zacchaeus. *Photograph courtesy of the Department of Manuscripts, The National Library of Greece, Athens.*

The Infancy Gospel of James

Introduction

Contents

The earliest Christian traditions (say, the creed of 1 Corinthians 15:35 or the hymn of Philippians 2:6–11) focus attention on the end of Jesus' life, on his death and resurrection. By the end of the first century, Christians show interest in the beginning of Jesus' life, in the circumstances of his birth, as is evident from the birth stories that open the gospels of Matthew and Luke. This interest continues into the second and later centuries and in fact prompts a new genre of Christian writing, the infancy gospel, or narratives that focus exclusively on the birth or on the childhood of Jesus.

One such gospel is the Infancy Gospel of James. This gospel ends with the birth of Jesus and its immediate aftermath in Herod's murder of the infants, but the ending is not the culmination or goal of the narrative. For the birth story comprises at most one-third of the narrative. The real narrative interest is in Mary; it is her story—the circumstances of her birth, the years of her infancy and childhood, the announcement of her conception—that is central to the narrative as a whole.

The story of the Infancy Gospel of James falls into three roughly equal parts. The first eight chapters narrate the miraculous circumstances of Mary's birth and the unusual circumstances of her childhood. The story opens with the plight of the wealthy, righteous, but childless couple, Joachim and Anna. Their childlessness is particularly grievous, but their laments and prayers to God are eventually heard, so that Anna becomes pregnant. Their gratitude is so great that they promise their offspring to the Lord, and so at age three, Mary is sent to serve the Lord in the temple in Jerusalem.

The second eight chapters begin with the crisis posed by Mary's becoming a woman and thus her imminent pollution of the temple. The priests resolve the crisis by turning her over to a divinely chosen widower, the carpenter Joseph, who agrees to be her guardian, but refuses to marry her. While he is out of town plying his trade, Mary is visited by an angel and told of her favor with the Lord. By the time Joseph returns she is visibly pregnant. A priest suspects that Joseph is responsible and accuses them both. The two are put to a test, but pass and are publicly exonerated.

The last eight chapters begin with Caesar's edict of enrollment that requires Joseph to register in Bethlehem. Here the story has reached the point where it begins to follow the accounts in the opening chapters of Matthew and Luke. But the infancy gospel, while recalling the canonical stories, does not hesitate to go its separate way. Thus Joseph and Mary go to Bethlehem (see Luke 2:1), but are now accompanied by his grown sons from his previous marriage (17:5). Mary gives birth to Jesus (see Luke 2:7) but is visited, though not helped, by local midwives (19:1–20:12), who testify to the miraculous nature of the birth: Mary, though she has given birth, is still a virgin (19:18). The astrologers trick Herod, who responds by murdering the infants (see Matt 2:16), but now Jesus is saved by being hidden in a feeding trough (22:4) and even the infant John is threatened by Herod but saved by his father Zechariah's martyrdom and by Elizabeth's hiding in the hills with him (22:5–23:8).

The infancy gospel ends with the author, James, claiming that he has written his account shortly after the death of Herod (25:1).

Authorship and dating

The claim that a certain James wrote this infancy gospel and did so shortly after the death of Herod in 4 BCE would, if true, imply that the narrative was composed by the James known in the New Testament as "James the Lord's brother" (Gal 1:19; see Mark 6:3), but here as only one of the sons of Joseph from a previous marriage. But, whatever the relation, James is thereby an eyewitness of the birth of Jesus and of Mary's life, at least from the time she became Joseph's ward. Thus the claim to authorship by James functions to establish the credibility and truth of the account.

But is the claim true? The answer is no. The claim falls on the following argument. The gospels of Matthew and Luke both narrate the birth of Jesus, but they do so quite differently. One difference is that only Matthew's account includes the visit of the astrologers and the subsequent murder of the infants by Herod (see Matt 2:1–12, 16–18), and only Luke's account includes the parallel story of the birth of John the Baptizer to Zechariah and Elizabeth (see Luke 1:5–25, 39–80). An observant reader of both gospels, however, might ask: How did John, born only months apart from Jesus, escape Herod's soldiers?

The Infancy Gospel of James answered this question by having Zechariah choose death rather than tell of John's whereabouts and by having Elizabeth flee to the hills with John. The author thereby shows that he knew of the canonical accounts, and since Matthew and Luke were written toward the end of the first century, well after James's death in 62 CE, the author of the infancy gospel could not have been James.

Just who wrote the infancy gospel can no longer be determined, but whoever did write it wrote after Matthew and Luke and probably around the middle of the second century, when evidence of this document begins to show up in other Christian writings.

Origins and thematic focus

The origins of the Infancy Gospel of James probably lie in a trajectory that begins with the Gospel of Mark, written about 70 CE. This gospel opens with the simple claim that Jesus is the son of God (Mark 1:1). This claim may then have prompted Matthew and Luke, writing independently of each other a decade or two later, to explain how it was that Jesus came to be the literal son of God (Matthew 1–2; Luke 1–2).

In many ways, the Infancy Gospel of James is dependent on the traditions preserved in the Matthean and Lukan accounts, as evidenced by the numerous quotations, phrases, and echoes in the infancy gospel from these accounts, not to mention other portions of the New Testament and the Septuagint (see the cross references). In fact, the infancy gospel expands on the canonical traditions, developing their logic, for example, by solving the problem of John's fate during the murder of the infants.

And yet, in other ways, the Infancy Gospel of James is not simply a development of the New Testament birth stories. For, despite all the bits and pieces taken from these stories and other Christian literature, the infancy gospel also shows an independence from this literature and a unity of its own. This independence is evident in the various narrative deviations from the stories in Matthew and Luke. But more important are the changes in characterization. Thus Joseph, who in the Matthean and Lukan accounts was betrothed to Mary and later married to her (Matt 1:18, 24–25; Luke 2:5), is now turned into an old man, a widower with grown sons who is embarrassed to accept Mary even as a ward (9:11) and becomes at most only her protector (13:1; 14:1; 16:7). Similarly, Mary, the central character, is no longer a virgin in the ordinary sense of a young woman of marriageable age, but a virgin of extraordinary purity and unending duration.

Indeed, Mary's purity is so emphasized that it becomes thematic and thus answers the fundamental question which guides the narrative: why Mary, of all the virgins in Israel, was chosen to be the mother of the son of God. The answer: no one could have been any purer. Thus Anna transforms Mary's bedroom into a sanctuary where she receives no impure food and is amused by the undefiled daughters of the Hebrews (6:5). When she turns three years of age, these young women escort her to the temple in Jerusalem where she spends the next nine years in absolute purity and is even fed by the hand of an angel (7:4–8:2). When, at age twelve, she is made the ward of Joseph, she spends her time spinning thread for the temple with the other virgins from Israel (10:1–12:1). When she is later suspected of impurity, she passes a test and has her innocence proclaimed by the high priest (15:1–6:7). Finally, when she gives birth to Jesus, two midwives certify that she remains a virgin (19:18–20:11). In short, it is through her purity that Mary fulfills the blessing which the priests made when she was only one year old: that she might be blessed with a blessing that could not be surpassed (6:9).

Purity and virginity

Why was Mary allegedly chosen by God to be the mother of Jesus? The Infancy Gospel of James was written to provide an answer. Mary remained pure throughout her childhood, both at home and in the temple. She maintained her virginity after becoming a woman, and even after giving birth to Jesus.

The emphasis on purity and virginity clearly develops in part out of the characterization of Mary in the canonical gospels. There it is her obedience that qualifies her to bear Jesus (so Luke 1:30), and Joseph marries her even if he does not sleep with her until after Jesus is born (Matt 1:24–25).

The increased focus on purity and virginity derives from one of the cultural trends of the period. In both philosophical and more popular literary sources there is an increasing value placed on the cardinal virtue *of sōphrosyne,* self-control of the tongue, the belly, and, to use the euphemism of the day, the things below the belly. It was clearly control of what is below the belly that was most admired.

Mary is very like the heroines of the romance, the most popular literature of that day. The romance featured characters who preserved their chastity against all odds. But even in the romances the heroines remain chaste only outside of marriage. In this respect Mary exceeds them and remains always a virgin, and thus perfectly pure.

The Infancy Gospel of James

1 **According to the records** of the twelve tribes of Israel, there once was a very rich man named Joachim. [2]He always doubled the gifts he offered to the Lord, [3]and would say to himself, "One gift, representing my prosperity, will be for all the people; the other, offered for forgiveness, will be my sin offering to the Lord God."

[4]Now the great day of the Lord was approaching and the people of Israel were offering their gifts. [5]Reubel confronted Joachim and said, "You're not allowed to offer your gifts first because you haven't fathered an Israelite child."

[6]Joachim got very upset and went to the book of the twelve tribes of the people, saying to himself, "I'm going to check the book of the twelve tribes of Israel to see whether I'm the only one in Israel who hasn't fathered a child." [7]He searched ⟨the records⟩ and found that all the righteous people in Israel did indeed have children. [8]He he remembered the patriarch Abraham because in his last days the Lord God had given him a son, Isaac.

[9]So he continued to be very upset. He did not see his wife, but banished himself to the desert and pitched his tent there. [10]Joachim fasted forty days and forty nights. He would say to himself, "I will not go back for food or drink until the Lord my God visits me. Prayer will be my food and drink."

2 **Now his wife Anna** was mourning and lamenting on two counts: "I lament my widowhood and I lament my childlessness."

[2]The great day of the Lord approached, however, [3]and her slave Juthine said to her, "How long are you going to humble yourself? Look, the great day of the Lord has arrived, and you're not supposed to mourn. [4]What you should do instead is take this headband. The mistress of the workshop gave it to me, but I'm not allowed to wear it because I'm your slave and because it bears a royal insignia."

[5]But Anna said, "Get away from me! I won't take it. The Lord God has greatly shamed me. Maybe a trickster has given you this, and you've come to involve me in your sin."

Childless Joachim

Childless Anna

1:1
◊ Sus 4
1:8
◊ Gn 21:1–7
1:10
Ⓣ Q 4:2, Mt 4:2, Lk 4:2;
◊ Ex 24:18, 1 Kgs 19:8
2:1
Ⓢ 1 Sm 1:2
2:5
◊ Is 64:12

1:4 In the OT and NT *the great day of the Lord* usually refers to the day of judgment, but here (and in 2:2) a festival seems more likely. The Festival of Sukkoth might be in view, but the vagueness of the reference precludes any more precise determination.

2:4 The words *headband* and *mistress of the workshop* are obscure, and no solution has been achieved.
2:5 The word translated *trickster* is obscure, but may refer to a clever young man with whom Juthine has had an affair.

[6]Juthine the slave replied, "Should I curse you just because you haven't paid any attention to me? The Lord God has made your womb infertile so you won't bear any children for Israel."

[7]Anna, too, became very upset. She took off her mourning clothes, washed her face, and put on her wedding dress. [8]Then, in the middle of the afternoon, she went down to her garden to take a walk. She spied a laurel tree and sat down under it. [9]She took a rest and then prayed to the Lord: [10]"God of my ancestors, bless me and hear my prayer, just as you blessed our mother Sarah and gave her a son, Isaac."

3 **Anna looked up** toward the sky and saw a nest of sparrows in the laurel tree. [2]She immediately began to lament, saying to herself: "Poor me! Who gave birth to me? What sort of womb bore me? [3]For I was born under a curse in the eyes of the people of Israel and I've been reviled and mocked and banished from the temple of the Lord my God.

[4]"Poor me! What am I like? I'm not like the birds of the sky, because even the birds of the sky reproduce in your presence, O Lord.

[5]"Poor me! What am I like? I'm not like domestic animals, because even domestic animals bear young in your presence, O Lord.

[6]"Poor me! What am I like? I'm not like the wild animals of the earth, because even the animals of the earth reproduce in your presence, O Lord.

[7]"Poor me! What am I like? I'm not like these waters, because even these waters are productive in your presence, O Lord.

[8]"Poor me! What am I like? I'm not like this earth, because even the earth produces its crops in season and blesses you, O Lord."

4 **Suddenly a messenger** of the Lord appeared to her and said, "Anna, Anna, the Lord God has heard your prayer. You will conceive and give birth, and your child will be talked about all over the world."

[2]Anna said, "As the Lord God lives, whether I give birth to a boy or a girl, I'll offer it as a gift to the Lord my God, and it will serve him its whole life."

[3]Right then two messengers reported to her: "Look, your husband Joachim is coming with his flocks." ([4]You see, a messenger of the Lord had come down to Joachim and said, "Joachim, Joachim, the Lord God has heard your prayer. Get down from there. Look, your wife Anna is pregnant.")

[5]Joachim went down right away and summoned his shepherds with these instructions: "Bring me ten lambs without spot or blemish; they'll be for the

4:5–7
◊Jgs 13:15–20

2:6 Childlessness was understood, not as having a natural cause, but as a sign of divine punishment (see Gen 16:2; 20:18; and especially 1 Sam 1:5–6).
2:7 Putting on her *wedding dress* suggests that Anna is an-

ticipating the outcome of her plea to God for a blessing similar to that which God gave Sarah, that is, for the blessing of offspring.

Lord God. ⁶Also, bring me twelve tender calves; they'll be for the priests and the council of elders. ⁷Also, one hundred goats; they'll be for the whole people."

⁸So Joachim came with his flocks, while Anna stood at the gate. ⁹When she spotted Joachim approaching with his flocks, she rushed out and threw her arms around his neck. "Now I know that the Lord God has blessed me greatly. This widow is no longer a widow, and I, once childless, am now pregnant!"

¹⁰And Joachim rested the first day at home.

5 **The next day**, as he was presenting his gifts, he thought to himself, "If the Lord God has really been merciful to me, the polished disc on the priest's headband will make it clear to me." ²And so Joachim was presenting his gifts and paying attention to the priest's headband until he went up to the altar of the Lord. And he saw no sin in it. ³Joachim said, "Now I know that the Lord God has been merciful to me and has forgiven all my sins." ⁴He came down from the temple of the Lord vindicated and went back home.

⁵And so Anna's pregnancy came to term, and in the ninth month she gave birth. ⁶She asked the midwife, "Is it a boy or a girl?"

⁷And her midwife said, "A girl."

⁸And Anna said, "I have been greatly honored this day." Then the midwife put the child to bed.

⁹Now when the prescribed days were completed, Anna cleansed herself of the flow of blood. ¹⁰And she offered her breast to the infant and gave her the name Mary.

6 **Day by day** the infant grew stronger. ²When she was six months old, her mother put her on the ground to see if she could stand. She walked seven steps and went to her mother's arms. ³Then her mother picked her up and said, "As the Lord my God lives, you will never walk on this ground again until I take you into the temple of the Lord."

⁴And so she turned her bedroom into a sanctuary and did not permit anything profane or unclean to pass the child's lips. ⁵She sent for the undefiled daughters of the Hebrews and they kept her amused.

Birth of Mary

Mary's first birthday

5:1
◊ Ex 28:36–38

5:4
Ⓢ Lk 18:14

5:8
Ⓢ Lk 1:46

5:9
◊ Lv 12:1–8

6:1
Ⓢ Lk 2:40

4:9 The mss differ over whether Anna is *pregnant* or will be pregnant. The future tense would be more likely if the word *rested* in the next sentence were a euphemism for sexual intercourse, but since this word is used of Joseph in much the same circumstances (see 15:2) and no such euphemism is intended there, it is probably better to prefer the literal meaning and so the present tense (*is pregnant*). Thus, Anna's conceiving a child becomes as much a miracle as Mary's will be later.

5:1–2 A metal *disc* was part of the high priest's garb and was attached to his headband (Exod 28:36), but its use here, to reveal sin, is otherwise unattested. The disc may have been a mirror, and mirrors were used to obtain revelations.

5:9 Childbirth rendered a woman ritually unclean, unable to touch anything holy or enter the temple. For the regulations on how and when a woman *cleansed herself* after childbirth, see Lev 12:1–8.

Mary at the temple

⁶Now the child had her first birthday, and Joachim gave a great banquet and invited the chief priests, priests, scholars, council of elders, and all the people of Israel. ⁷Joachim presented the child to the priests, and they blessed her: "God of our fathers, bless this child and give her a name that will be on the lips of future generations forever."

⁸And everyone said, "So be it. Amen."

⁹He presented her to the chief priests, and they blessed her: "Most high God, look on this child and bless her with the ultimate blessing, one which cannot be surpassed."

¹⁰Her mother then took her up to the sanctuary (the bedroom) and gave her breast to the child. ¹¹And Anna composed a song for the Lord God:

> I will sing a sacred song to the Lord my God
>> because he has visited me
>> and taken away the disgrace
>>> attributed to me by my enemies.
> ¹²The Lord my God has given me
>> the fruit of his righteousness,
>> single yet manifold before him.
> ¹³Who will announce to the sons of Reubel
>> that Anna has a child at her breast?
> "Listen, listen, you twelve tribes of Israel:
>> Anna has a child at her breast!"

¹⁴Anna made her rest in the bedroom (the sanctuary) and then went out and began serving her guests. ¹⁵When the banquet was over, they left in good spirits and praised the God of Israel.

7 **Many months went by.** When the child reached two years of age, Joachim said, "Let's take her up to the temple of the Lord, so that we can keep the promise we made, or else the Lord will be angry with us and our gift will be unacceptable."

²Anna said, "Let's wait until she's three, so she won't miss her father or mother."

³Joachim agreed: "Let's wait."

⁴When the child turned three years of age, Joachim said, "Let's send for the undefiled daughters of the Hebrews. ⁵Have them each take a lamp and light it, so the child won't turn back and have her heart captivated by things outside the temple of the Lord." ⁶And this is what they did until the time they ascended to the Lord's temple.

6:6
◊ Gn 21:8

6:11
Ⓢ Lk 1:25;
◊ Gn 21:1, 30:23

6:13
◊ Gn 21:7

7:1
◊ 1 Sm 1:22;
① InJas 4:2

6:12 The meaning of *single yet manifold before him* is obscure.

[7]The priest welcomed her, kissed her, and blessed her: "The Lord God has extolled your name among all generations. [8]In you the Lord will reveal his redemption to the people of Israel during the last days."

[9]He sat her down on the third step of the altar, and the Lord showered favor on her. [10]And she danced, and the whole house of Israel loved her.

8 **Her parents left** for home, marveling and praising and glorifying the Lord God because the child did not look back at them. [2]And Mary lived in the temple of the Lord. She was fed there like a dove, receiving her food from the hand of a heavenly messenger.

[3]When she turned twelve, however, there was a meeting of the priests. "Look," they said, "Mary has turned twelve in the temple of the Lord. [4]What should we do with her so she won't pollute the sanctuary of the Lord our God?" [5]And they said to the chief priest, "You stand at the altar of the Lord. Enter and pray about her, and we'll do whatever the Lord God reveals to you."

[6]So the chief priest took the vestment with the twelve bells, entered the Holy of Holies, and began to pray about her. [7]And suddenly a messenger of the Lord appeared. "Zechariah, Zechariah, go out and assemble the widowers of the people and have them each bring a staff. [8]She will become the wife of the one to whom the Lord God shows a sign." [9]And so heralds covered the surrounding territory of Judea. The trumpet of the Lord sounded and all the widowers came running.

9 **And Joseph, too,** threw down his carpenter's axe and left for the meeting. [2]When they had all gathered, they went to the chief priest with their staffs. [3]After the chief priest had collected everyone's staff, he entered the temple and began to pray. [4]When he had finished his prayer, he took the staffs and went out and began to give them back to each man. [5]But there was no sign on any of them. Joseph got the last staff. [6]Suddenly a dove came out of this staff and perched on Joseph's head. [7]"Joseph, Joseph," the chief priest said, "you've been chosen by lot to take the virgin of the Lord into your care and protection."

[8]But Joseph objected, "I already have sons and I'm an old man; she's only a young woman. I'm afraid that I'll become the butt of jokes among the people of Israel."

[9]The chief priest answered, "Joseph, fear the Lord your God and remember what God did to Dathan, Abiron, and Kore: the earth was split open and they

7:7
Ⓢ Lk 1:48
7:8
◊ 1 Sm 18:16
8:1
Ⓢ Lk 2:39–40
8:7
Ⓢ Lk 1:11;
◊ Nm 17:1–11
9:9
◊ Nm 16:25–33

8:4 Mary would *pollute the sanctuary* when she began to menstruate. The Law considered a woman ritually unclean during her period. See Lev 15:19–24.

9:7 This is the first occurrence of the word *virgin*, which plays a prominent role in Mary's characterization for the

remainder of the story.

9:8 That Joseph has *sons* and is an *old man* marks a significant change in the portrayal of Joseph from that in the canonical accounts.

were all swallowed up because of their objection. [10]So now, Joseph, you need to be careful so the same thing won't happen to your family."

[11]And so out of fear Joseph took her into his care and protection. [12]He said to her, "Mary, I've gotten you from the temple of the Lord, but now I'm leaving you at home. I'm going away to build houses, but I'll come back to you. The Lord will protect you."

10 **Meanwhile, there** was a council of the priests, who agreed, "Let's make a curtain for the temple of the Lord."

[2]And the chief priest said, "Summon the undefiled virgins from the tribe of David." [3]So the temple assistants left and searched everywhere and found seven. [4]And the chief priest then remembered the girl Mary, that she, too, was from the tribe of David and was undefiled in God's eyes. [5]And so the temple assistants went out and got her.

[6]They took the girls into the temple of the Lord. [7]The chief priest said, "Cast lots for me to decide who'll spin ⟨which threads for the curtain:⟩ the gold, the white, the linen, the silk, the violet, the scarlet, and the true purple."

[8]And the true purple and scarlet threads fell to Mary. She took them and returned home. [9]Now it was at this time that Zechariah became mute, and Samuel took his place until Zechariah regained his speech. [10]Meanwhile, Mary had taken up the scarlet thread and was spinning it.

11 **Mary took** her water jar and went out to fill it with water. [2]Suddenly there was a voice saying to her, "Greetings, highly favored one! The Lord is with you. Blessed are you among women." [3]Mary began looking around, both right and left, to see where the voice was coming from. [4]She became terrified and went home. After putting the water jar down and taking up the purple thread, she sat down on her chair and began to spin the thread.

[5]Suddenly a heavenly messenger stood in front of her and said, "Don't be afraid, Mary. You see, you have found favor in the sight of the Master of all. You will conceive by his word."

9:11
Ⓢ Mt 1:24

10:7
◊ Ex 26:31, 36;
35:25; 2 Chr 3:14

10:9
Ⓢ Lk 1:20–22, 64

11:2
//InThom 19:4;
Ⓢ Lk 1:28

11:5
Ⓢ Lk 1:30–33

9:11 That *Joseph took her* recalls Matt 1:24, but with this significant difference: there it is as his wife, here merely as his ward.

10:1 The story assumes that the *curtain* in the temple, presumably the one in front of the Holy of Holies, was a recent innovation. However, according to the OT (2 Chr 3:14), the curtain was part of the original design of Solomon's temple.

10:2 Strictly speaking, there was no *tribe of David*. Accord-

ing to Luke, Mary is related to Elizabeth, who belongs to the tribe of Aaron (Luke 1:5, 36).

10:9 The *time that Zechariah became mute* reflects an attempt on the part of the author to place his narrative in the context of the canonical account (see Luke 1:20–22, 64).

10:10 It is ironic that Mary spins thread for the temple curtain that will be destroyed when Jesus dies (see Mark 15:38).

Mary & Elizabeth

Joseph accuses Mary

[6]But as she listened, Mary was puzzled and said, "Am I going to conceive by the Lord, the living God, the way every woman does who gives birth?"

[7]And the messenger of the Lord replied, "No, Mary. The power of God will cast its shadow on you. And so the child to be born will be called holy, son of the Most High. [8]You will name him Jesus because he will save his people from their sins."

[9]And Mary said, "In the presence of the Lord, here I am, his slave. I pray that everything you've told me comes true."

12 **She finished spinning** the purple and the scarlet thread and took her work up to the chief priest. [2]The chief priest accepted it and blessed her and said, "Mary, the Lord God has extolled your name and so you will be blessed by all the generations of the earth."

[3]Mary rejoiced and left to visit her relative Elizabeth. [4]She knocked at the door. Elizabeth heard her, tossed aside the scarlet thread, ran to the door, and opened it for her. [5]And she blessed her and said, "Who am I that the mother of my Lord should visit me? Look, the baby inside me has jumped for joy and blessed you."

[6]But Mary forgot the mysteries which the heavenly messenger Gabriel had spoken, and she looked up to the sky and said, "Who am I, Lord, that every generation on earth should congratulate me?"

[7]She spent three months with Elizabeth. [8]Day by day Mary's womb kept swelling. She became frightened and returned home, where she hid from the people of Israel. [9]She was just sixteen years old when these mysterious things happened to her.

13 **She was in her sixth month** when one day Joseph came home from his building projects, entered his house, and saw that she was pregnant. [2]He struck himself in the face, threw himself to the ground on sackcloth, and began to cry bitterly: "How can I show my face to the Lord God? [3]What prayer can I say for her since I took her in as a virgin from the temple of the Lord God and didn't protect her? [4]Who has set this trap for me? Who has done this evil thing in my house? Who has lured this virgin away from me and violated her? [5]I'm reliving

11:6
Ⓢ Lk 1: 34
11:8
Ⓢ Lk 1:35, Mt 1:21
11:9
Ⓢ Lk 1:38
12:2
Ⓢ Lk 1:42, 48
12:3–6
Ⓢ Lk 1:39–44
12:6
Ⓢ Lk 1:48
12:7
Ⓢ Lk 1:56
12:8
Ⓢ Lk 1:24

11:6 Some mss read "If I am going to conceive by the Lord, the living God, will I also give birth the way every woman does?" in place of *Am I going to conceive by the Lord, the living God, the way every woman does who gives birth?* The latter reading, in which Mary asks if she will conceive naturally (*the way every woman does*), is more likely to be original because it is less congruent with later Christian orthodoxy.

12:3 The author assumes that readers will know who *Elizabeth* is. She is the wife of Zechariah and mother of the future John the Baptizer (see 22:5; Luke 1:5).

12:9 *She was just sixteen years old*: The gospel emphasizes Mary's youth and continues to refer to her as a *child* (Greek: *pais*) even after she is pregnant (14:5, 15:8, 16:4, 17:2).

the story of Adam, aren't I? Adam was off by himself praying when the serpent came and found Eve. He deceived and corrupted her. Now the same thing has happened to me."

⁶So Joseph got up from the sackcloth and summoned Mary and said to her, "God has taken special care of you—how could you have done this? ⁷Have you forgotten the Lord your God? You were raised in the Holy of Holies and fed by a heavenly messenger. Why have you brought shame on yourself?"

⁸But she began to cry bitter tears: "I'm innocent. I'm still a virgin."

⁹So Joseph said to her, "Then where did the child you're carrying come from?"

¹⁰She replied, "As the Lord my God lives, I don't know."

14 **Now Joseph became** very frightened. He no longer spoke with her as he pondered what he was going to do with her. ²He said to himself, "If I try to cover up her sin, I'll end up going against the Law of the Lord. ³But if I disclose her condition to the people of Israel, I'm afraid that her pregnancy might be heaven-sent and I'll end up handing over innocent blood to a death sentence. ⁴So what should I do with her? I guess I should divorce her quietly."

⁵But that night a messenger of the Lord suddenly appeared to him in a dream and said: "Don't be afraid of this child, because a holy spirit is responsible for her pregnancy. ⁶She will give birth to a son and you will name him Jesus because he will save his people from their sins." ⁷Joseph got up from his sleep and praised the God of Israel, who had done him this favor. ⁸And so he began to protect the child.

15 **Then Annas** the scholar came to him and said to him, "Joseph, why haven't you attended our assembly?"

²And he replied, "I was worn out from my trip and I rested my first day home."

³Then Annas turned and saw that Mary was pregnant.

⁴He left in a hurry to see the chief priest and said to him, "You remember Joseph, don't you—the man you yourself vouched for? Well, he has committed a serious offense."

⁵The chief priest asked, "In what way?"

13:5
◊ Gn 3:1–13

13:6
◊ Gn 3:13

13:7
① InJas 8:2

13:8
Ⓢ Lk 1:34;
Ⓓ InJas 15:13

14:1–6
Ⓢ Mt 1:19–24

14:2
◊ Dt 22:23–24

14:3
Ⓢ Mt 27:3–4

13:9–10 That Mary is unable to say where her child came from is surprising, given the explicit announcement (see 11:7). Incredibly, Mary apparently forgot what the angel had told her, as also in her conversation with Elizabeth (see 12:6).

14:3 That there could be a *death sentence* derives from Deut 22:23–24.

14:4 That Joseph should *divorce her quietly* makes little

sense here because they are neither betrothed nor married. The author is clearly dependent on Matt 1:19.

14:5 The command here, *Don't be afraid of this child*, differs significantly from the parallel account in Matt 1:20 ("Don't be afraid to take Mary as your wife"). This difference is deliberate, reflecting the very different relationship between Joseph and Mary in this gospel.

6"Joseph has violated the virgin he received from the temple of the Lord," he replied. "He has stolen her wedding and hasn't disclosed this to the people of Israel."

7The chief priest asked him, "Has Joseph really done this?"

8Annas replied, "Send temple assistants and you'll find the girl pregnant."

9And so the temple assistants went and found her just as Annas had reported. So they brought her, along with Joseph, to the court.

10"Mary, why have you done this?" the chief priest asked her. "Why have you humiliated yourself? 11Have you forgotten the Lord your God? You were raised in the Holy of the Holies and were fed by heavenly messengers. 12You heard their hymns and danced for them; you of all people—why have you done this?"

13And she wept bitterly: "As the Lord God lives, I stand innocent before him. I'm still a virgin."

14The chief priest said, "Joseph, why have you done this?"

15And Joseph said, "As the Lord lives, I am innocent. I had nothing to do with this."

16And the chief priest said, "Don't perjure yourself; tell the truth. You've stolen her wedding and haven't disclosed this to the people of Israel. 17And you haven't humbled yourself under God's mighty hand, so that your offspring might be blessed."

18But Joseph was silent.

16 Then the chief priest said, "Return the girl you received from the temple of the Lord."

2And Joseph, bursting into tears . . .

3The chief priest said, "I'm going to give you the Lord's drink test. It will disclose your sin clearly to both of you."

4The chief priest took the water and made Joseph drink it and sent him into the desert, but he returned unharmed. 5And he made the child drink it, too, and sent her into the desert. She also came back unharmed. 6And everybody was surprised because their sin had not been revealed. 7And so the chief priest said, "If the Lord God has not exposed your sin, then neither do I condemn you." So he let them go. 8Joseph took Mary and returned home, celebrating and praising the God of Israel.

The drink test

15:11
① InJas 8:2
15:13
① InJas 13:8
15:17
Ⓢ 1 Pet 5:6
16:3
◊ Nm 5:11–31
16:7
Ⓢ Jn 8:11
16:8
Ⓢ Lk 5:25

16:2 There is probably a lacuna here, for no finite verb accompanies the participle *bursting*. How much has dropped out is difficult to tell, but perhaps nothing more than "said nothing" is missing.

15:6 That Joseph should be held responsible for having *violated* Mary and made her pregnant is odd because, when he had left to work on his building projects, she was twelve years old (see 8:3) but now she is sixteen (see 12:9).

16:3 *The Lord's drink test* reflects a similar, yet far from identical, test described in Num 5:11–31. For another such test, outside the biblical tradition, see Achilles Tatius, *Cleitophon and Leucippe*, 8.3.3; 6.115; 13.1–14.2.

On the way to
Bethlehem

Time stands still

17 **Now an order came** down from Augustus the Emperor that everybody in Bethlehem of Judea be counted in a census.

²And Joseph wondered, "I'll register my sons, but what am I going to do with this child? How will I register her? ³As my wife? I'm ashamed to do that. As my daughter? The people of Israel know she's not my daughter. ⁴This is the day of the Lord; he will do whatever he decides."

⁵So he saddled his donkey and had her get on it. His son led it and Samuel brought up the rear. ⁶As they neared the three-mile marker, Joseph turned around and saw that she was gloomy. ⁷He said to himself, "Perhaps the baby she is carrying is causing her discomfort." ⁸Joseph turned around again and saw her laughing and said to her, "Mary, what's going on with you? One minute I see you laughing and the next minute you're gloomy."

⁹She replied, "Joseph, it's because I imagine two peoples in front of me, one weeping and mourning and the other rejoicing and celebrating."

¹⁰Halfway through the trip Mary said to him, "Joseph, help me down from the donkey—the child inside me is ready to be born."

¹¹And he helped her down and said to her, "Where will I take you to give you some privacy, since this place is out in the open?"

18 **He found a cave** nearby and took her inside. He stationed his sons to guard her ²and went to look for a Hebrew midwife in the countryside around Bethlehem.

³Now I, Joseph, was walking along and yet not going anywhere. ⁴I looked up at the dome of the sky and saw it standing still, and then at the clouds and saw them stopped in amazement, and at the birds of the sky suspended in midair. ⁵As I looked down on the ground, I saw a bowl lying there and workers reclining around it with their hands in the bowl; ⁶some were chewing and yet did not

---

17:1–11
Ⓢ Lk 2:1–7

17:9
Ⓢ Gn 25:23,
Lk 2:34

18:3 From here on the earliest ms differs sharply from later mss in that it omits the vision of Joseph (18:3–11) and has shorter accounts of the incidents that follow.

17:1 With the *order from Augustus the Emperor* the gospel begins to follow the sequence of events narrated in Luke 2:1–20, with some attention to Matt 2:1–16. Note, however, that Augustus' order here extends only to *Bethlehem of Judea*, not to the whole world, as in Luke 2:1.

17:4 *the day of the Lord*: an expression that implies a time of judgment or decision. "Day" might refer to some particular day, but, if so, it is not clear which one. Or it might refer simply to that day that Joseph travels, since every day belongs to the Lord. Or it might refer to the series of events culminating in the census, which is how it is taken here.

17:5 No *Samuel* is mentioned among the brothers of Jesus in Mark 6:3.

18:1 That Jesus is born in a *cave* outside Bethlehem differs from Luke's stable at an inn there (Luke 2:7).

18:3–11 Joseph's vision, which begins with his claim to be *walking along and yet not going anywhere*, seems to describe an experience in which everything—the winds, birds, workers, herds, herders, and himself—are momentarily frozen in whatever activity they were engaged in. This moment would seem to be the time when, back at the cave, Jesus was born.

chew; some were picking up something to eat and yet did not pick it up; and some were putting food in their mouths and yet did not do so. ⁷Instead, they were all looking upward.

A child is born

⁸I saw sheep being herded along and yet the sheep stood still; ⁹the shepherd was lifting his hand to strike them, and yet his hand remained raised. ¹⁰And I observed the current of the river and saw goats with their mouths in the water and yet they were not drinking. ¹¹Then all of a sudden everything and everybody went on with what they had been doing.

19 "Then I saw a woman coming down from the hill country. She asked, 'Where are you going, sir?'

²"I replied, 'I'm looking for a Hebrew midwife.'

³"She inquired, 'Are you an Israelite?'

⁴"I told her that I was.

⁵"'And who's the one having a baby in the cave?' she asked.

⁶"'My betrothed,' I replied.

⁷"She asked me, 'You mean she isn't your wife?'

⁸"I told her, 'She is Mary, who was raised in the temple of the Lord; I obtained her by lot as my wife. ⁹But she's not really my wife; she's pregnant by a holy spirit.'"

¹⁰"Really?" the midwife said.

¹¹"Come and see," Joseph responded.

¹²So the midwife went with him. ¹³As they stood in front of the cave, a dark cloud overshadowed it. ¹⁴The midwife said, "I've really been privileged, because today my eyes have seen a mystery: salvation has come to Israel."

¹⁵Suddenly the cloud withdrew from the cave and a light appeared inside it that was so intense their eyes could not bear to look. ¹⁶And a little later that light receded until an infant became visible. He came and took the breast of his mother Mary.

¹⁷Then the midwife shouted: "What a great day this is for me! I've seen this new miracle!"

¹⁸And the midwife left the cave and met Salome and said to her, "Salome, Salome, let me tell you about a new marvel: a virgin has given birth, something we all know is impossible!"

¹⁹And Salome replied, "As the Lord my God lives, unless I insert my finger and examine her, I will never believe that a virgin has given birth."

19:13
◊ Ex 16:10
19:14
Ⓢ Lk 2:30
19:19
Ⓢ Jn 20:25

19:6 That Joseph should refer here to Mary as his *betrothed* is odd, given the author's deliberate attempt elsewhere to depict their relationship as that of merely guardian and ward.
19:15–16 The dark *cloud* and bright *light* obscure the ac-

tual manner of the birth. The author can thus have Jesus born in a miraculous manner without narrating what actually happened.
19:19 Salome inserting her *finger* recalls the language and story of doubting Thomas in John 20:24–25.

20

The midwife entered and said, "Mary, position yourself for an examination. You are facing a serious test."

²And so Mary, when she heard these instructions, positioned herself, and Salome inserted her finger into Mary. ³And then Salome cried aloud and said, "I'll be damned because of my transgression and my disbelief; I have put the living God on trial. ⁴Look! My hand is disappearing! It's being consumed by flames!"

⁵Then Salome fell on her knees in the presence of the Master, with these words: "God of my ancestors, remember me because I am a descendant of Abraham, Isaac, and Jacob. ⁶Do not make an example out of me for the people of Israel, but give me a place among the poor again. ⁷You yourself know, Master, that I've been healing people in your name and have been receiving my payment from you."

⁸And suddenly a messenger of the Lord appeared and said, "Salome, Salome, the Master of all has heard your prayer. ⁹Hold out your hand to the child and pick him up, and then you'll have salvation and joy."

¹⁰Salome approached the child and picked him up and said, "I'll worship him because he's been born to be king of Israel." ¹¹And Salome was instantly healed and left the cave acquitted.

¹²Then a voice said abruptly, "Salome, Salome, don't report the mysteries you've seen here until the child goes to Jerusalem."

21

Joseph was about ready to depart for Judea when a great uproar broke out in Bethlehem in Judea. ²It all started when astrologers came inquiring, "Where is the one born to be king of the Judeans? We have observed his star at its rising and have come to pay him homage."

³When the news reached Herod, he was visibly shaken and sent his assistants to the astrologers. ⁴He also sent for the chief priests and questioned them in his palace: "What has been written about the Anointed One? Where is he supposed to be born?"

⁵They said to him, "In Bethlehem, Judea, that's what the scriptures say." ⁶And he dismissed them.

⁷Then he questioned the astrologers: "What sign have you seen regarding the one who has been born king?"

⁸The astrologers said, "We saw a star in the sky that was so brilliant that it dimmed the other stars to the point where they were no longer visible. That

20:11
Ⓢ Lk 18:14

21:1–12
Ⓢ Mt 2:1–12

21:5
◊ Mi 5:1

20:12 The author seemingly refers to Joseph's and Mary's last trip *to Jerusalem*, which is narrated in Luke 2:22–39.
21:1 *Judea*: Here and in v. 12 "Judea" must refer to the city of Jerusalem.

21:5 It is remarkable that after the words *what the scriptures say* the quotation from Micah 5:1, 3, which follows these very words in Matt 2:6, is omitted here.

is how we know that a king was born for Israel. We have come to pay him homage."

⁹Herod instructed them: "Go and begin your search, and if you find him, report back to me, so I can also go and pay him homage."

¹⁰The astrologers departed. And there it was: the star they had seen in the East showed them the way until they arrived at the cave; then the star stopped directly above the head of the child. ¹¹After the astrologers saw him with his mother Mary, they took gifts out of their pouches: gold, pure incense, and myrrh.

¹²Since they had been advised by the heavenly messenger not to go into Judea, they returned to their country by another route.

22 **When Herod realized** he had been duped by the astrologers, he flew into a rage ²and dispatched his executioners with instructions to kill all the infants two years old and younger.

³When Mary heard that the infants were being killed, she was frightened ⁴and took her child, wrapped him in strips of cloth, and put him in a feeding trough used by cattle.

⁵As for Elizabeth, when she heard that they were looking for John, she took him and went up into the hill country. ⁶She kept searching for a place to hide him, but there was none to be had. ⁷Then she groaned and said out loud, "Mountain of God, please take in a mother with her child." (You see, Elizabeth was unable to go on climbing.) ⁸But suddenly the mountain was split open and let them in. This mountain allowed the light to shine through to her, ⁹since a messenger of the Lord was with them for protection.

23 **Herod, though,** kept looking for John ²and sent his agents to Zechariah, who was serving at the altar. They asked him, "Where have you hidden your son?"

³But he answered them, "I am a minister of God, attending to his temple. How should I know where my son is?"

⁴So the agents left and reported all this to Herod, who got angry and said, "Is his son going to rule over Israel?"

Slaughter of the infants

Murder of Zechariah

21:11
◊ Is 60:6
22:1–2
Ⓢ Mt 2:16–18
22:4
Ⓢ Lk 2:7
23:1–9
Ⓢ Mt 23:35,
Lk 1:5–25

22:4 The *strips of cloth* and *feeding trough* recall Luke 2:12, but here these items are used in the Matthean context of Herod's threat to Jesus' life. By having Mary wrap Jesus up and hide him in a trough, the author can dispense with the escape of Joseph, Mary, and Jesus to Egypt, which is Matthew's solution to the threat (Matt 2:3–15).
22:5 For the significance of why Elizabeth took John and *went up into the hill country,* see the Introduction.

22:8 The translation of the phrase *This mountain allowed the light to shine through to her* is very tentative, for the Greek is opaque and probably corrupt.
23:2 Zechariah's presence at the *altar,* where he will be killed, shows that the author has apparently identified this Zechariah, the father of John, with another Zechariah, mentioned in Matt 23:35, who did die at the altar.

[5]He sent his agents back with this message: "Tell me the truth. Where is your son? Don't you know that your life is in my hands?"

[6]The agents went and reported this message to him.

[7]Zechariah answered, "I am a martyr for God. Take my life. [8]The Master, though, will receive my spirit because you are shedding innocent blood at the entrance to the Lord's temple."

[9]And so at daybreak Zechariah was murdered, but the people of Israel did not know that.

24 **At the hour of formal** greetings the priests departed, but Zechariah did not meet and bless them as was customary. [2]And so the priests waited around for Zechariah, to greet him in prayer and to praise the Most High God.

[3]But when he did not show up, they all became fearful. [4]One of them, however, summoned up his courage, entered the sanctuary, and saw dried blood next to the altar of the Lord. [5]And a voice said, "Zechariah has been murdered! His blood will not be cleaned up until his avenger appears."

[6]When he heard this utterance he was afraid and went out and reported to the priests what he had seen and heard. [7]And they summoned up their courage, entered, and saw what had happened. [8]The panels of the temple cried out and the priests ripped their robes from top to bottom. [9]They didn't find Zechariah's body, but they did find his blood, which had turned to stone. [10]They were afraid and went out and reported to the people that Zechariah had been murdered. [11]When all the tribes of the people heard this, they began to mourn; and they beat their breasts for three days and three nights.

[12]After three days, however, the priests deliberated about whom they should appoint to Zechariah's post. [13]The lot fell to Simeon. ([14]This man, you see, is the one who was informed by the holy spirit that he would not see death until he had seen the Anointed one in the flesh.)

25 **Now I, James,** am the one who wrote this account at the time when the uproar over the death of Herod broke out in Jerusalem. [2]I withdrew to the desert until the uproar in Jerusalem died down. [3]There I praised the Lord God, who gave me the wisdom to write this account.

[4]Grace will be with all those who fear the Lord. Amen.

Birth of Mary

Revelation of James

Peace to the writer and the reader.

23:7–8
Ⓢ Mt 23:35,
Acts 7:59

24:1
Ⓣ Lk 1:21

24:8
Ⓣ Mk 15:38,
Mt 27:51

24:14
Ⓢ Lk 2:25–26

24:9 *They didn't find Zechariah's body* presumably because the murderers carried the body away and buried it without a name.

25:1 For the historical problems raised by having *James* compose this gospel after the *death of Herod,* see the Introduction.

The Infancy Gospel of Thomas

Introduction

Story and structure

The Infancy Gospel of Thomas belongs to the popular genre of legends about the youthful years of Jesus. Such legends developed in the early centuries of the Christian movement and were constantly elaborated and expanded from late Antiquity through the Middle Ages for purposes of edification and instruction.

The Infancy Gospel of Thomas attempts to fill the gap between Jesus' birth and his visit to Jerusalem recorded in Luke 2:41–52. It consists of a series of loosely connected episodes recording events at various intervals of Jesus' youth. The text notes certain stages in Jesus' development, his actions at age five (2:1), six (11:1), eight (12:4), and twelve (19:1). Apart from these temporal markers there are no other overt indications of structure.

The initial episodes portray a petulant Jesus at play, a sometimes hot-tempered lad ready to use his remarkable abilities in destructive or self-serving ways, and a prodigy at school, impatient with the limitations of his merely human teachers. As time progresses, he becomes a child devoted to his parents and siblings, finally eager to use his powers to help and to heal those in need.

Origins of the gospel

The Infancy Gospel of Thomas survives in various forms in a number of languages, including Syriac, Greek, Latin, and Slavonic. The earliest extant is a Syriac manuscript dating to the sixth century. The variations among these versions make it difficult to reconstruct the earliest form of the work. The earliest clear attestation of an episode from the gospel is in the work of the church father Irenaeus, bishop of Lyons in the late second century. In his treatise *Against Heresies*, written around 185 CE, he mentions "spurious and apocryphal writings" that include a "tale which tells that when the Lord was a child learning the alphabet, the teacher, as is customary, said to him 'Say Alpha,' and he replied, 'Alpha.' When the teacher next told him to say Beta, the Lord answered, 'Tell me first what Alpha is, and then I shall tell you what Beta is.'" This is obviously an allusion to the episode found in chapters 6–8 and 14–15.

Patristic testimonies continue in the late second early third century with Hippolytus (*Refutation of all Heresies* 5.7) and Origen (*Homily I on Luke*), who mention the existence of a Gospel of Thomas of uncertain contents. Some of these testimonies may refer not to a narrative of Jesus' childhood but to the Gospel of Thomas, the collection of sayings of Jesus found in Nag Hammadi in Egypt in 1945.

The evidence provided by Irenaeus indicates that a version of Infancy Thomas was in circulation in the second century. Nothing certain, however, can be said about the place or circumstances of its composition.

Aims and themes

The orthodox Christian writers of the late second century associated this infancy gospel with circles that they considered heretical, particularly with groups of Gnostic Christians. Scattered evidence confirms that such Christians did know the work. This evidence takes the form of allusions to stories reminiscent of Infancy Thomas in certain Gnostic works such as the Gospel of Truth (19:19–20). While Gnostics may have been able to interpret stories in Infancy Thomas for their own ends, it is unlikely that they originally composed the work with the aim of propagating their theological positions.

Some scholars have argued that certain features of the work, especially its christology, are heterodox. All versions of the work obviously consider Jesus to be endowed from his earliest years with remarkable power, and some explicitly affirm that he is the incarnation of a divine being. These christological beliefs were hardly confined to Gnostics. They were present from the earliest generations of the Christian movement and were widespread in the second century. Hints have also been found of a "docetic" christology, tendencies, that is, to suggest that the humanity of Jesus is merely a matter of appearance. Yet these elements too have been overemphasized. Although endowed with supernatural power, Jesus is, in many episodes, all too human.

There may be a certain naivete in the portrait of Jesus in the work, but its understanding of Christ is what one would expect to find in the popular traditions of the Christian movement in the late first or second century. This gospel affords us a view of how Jesus was regarded in the unsophisticated religious imaginations of ordinary early Christians, rather than in the more abstract theological affirmations of Christian intellectuals.

The translation

The present translation is based on a new critical Greek text prepared especially for the Scholars Version.

The Infancy Gospel of Thomas

1 **I, Thomas** the Israelite, am reporting to you, all my non-Jewish brothers and sisters, to tell you about the extraordinary childhood of our Lord Jesus Christ—what he did after his birth in my part of the world. This is how it all started.

Prologue

Jesus & the sparrows

The curse on Annas' son

2 **When this boy, Jesus,** was five years old, he was playing at the ford of a rushing stream. [2]He was collecting the flowing water into ponds and with a single command he made the water instantly pure. [3]He then made soft clay and shaped it into twelve sparrows. He did this on the Sabbath, and a lot of other boys were playing with him.

[4]But when a Jew saw what Jesus was doing while playing on the Sabbath, he immediately went off and told Joseph, Jesus' father: "See here, your boy is at the ford and has violated the Sabbath by taking mud and making twelve birds with it."

[5]So Joseph went there, and as soon as he spotted him he shouted, "Why are you doing what's not permitted on the Sabbath?"

[6]But Jesus simply clapped his hands and shouted to the sparrows, "Go on, fly away, and remember me, you who are now alive!" And the sparrows took off and flew away noisily.

[7]The Jews watched with amazement, then left the scene to report to their leaders what they had seen Jesus doing.

3 **The son of Annas** the scholar was standing there with Jesus. He took a willow branch and drained the water Jesus had collected. [2]Jesus saw what had

---

3:1 Some versions of this gospel place the curse on Annas's son (chapter 3) before the scene of Jesus and the sparrows (chapter 2).

---

1 In the synoptic gospels Thomas is regularly linked with Matthew (Mark 3:18; Matt 10:3; Luke 6:15). In the Gospel of John (11:16, 14:5; 20:24–28; 21:2) Thomas is known as Didymus, "the twin." This is presumably the same apostle as the Didymus Judas Thomas who figures in the Gospel of Thomas and the Judas Thomas, the twin of Jesus, who is the hero of the *Acts of Thomas*.

2:2 For the power of Jesus' command over the elements, see Mark 4:41, Matt 8:27, and Luke 8:25.

2:3, 6 This miracle is also attested in the Quran: "Jesus will say, 'I bring you a sign from your Lord. From clay I will

make for you a likeness of a bird. I shall breathe into it and, by God's leave, it shall become a living bird'" (3:49, also 5:113, Dawood translation).

2:4 Profaning the Sabbath, usually by an act of healing, frequently occasions controversy in the gospel tradition. See Mark 2:23–28; 3:1–6; Matt 12:1–12; Luke 6:1–11; 13:10–17; 14:2–6; John 5.

3:1 *Annas the scholar* also appears in the Infancy Gospel of James 15. In the New Testament, Annas is a chief priest (Luke 3:2; John 18:13, 24; Acts 4:6).

Curse on a clumsy child

Joseph disciplines Jesus

Jesus teaches his teacher

happened and got angry and said to him, "Damn you, you ungodly ignoramus! What harm were the ponds of water doing you? From now on you, too, will dry up like a tree, and you'll never produce leaves or roots or bear fruit."

³In an instant the boy had completely withered away. Then Jesus departed and left for the house of Joseph. ⁴The parents of the boy who had withered away picked him up and were carrying him out, in grief because he was so young. And they came to Joseph and accused him: "It's your fault—your boy did all this."

4 **Later on he was going** through the village when a boy ran by and bumped him on the shoulder. Jesus got angry and said to him, "Your trip is over!" ²And all of a sudden he fell down and died.

³Some people saw what had happened and said, "Where has this boy come from? Everything he says happens instantly!"

⁴The parents of the dead boy came to Joseph and blamed him, saying, "Teach your boy to bless and not curse, or else you can't live with us in the village. He's killing our children!"

5 **So Joseph summoned** his child and scolded him in private, "Why are you doing all this? These people hate and harass us because they are suffering."

²Jesus said, "I know that the words I spoke are not my own. Still, I'll keep quiet for your sake. But those people must take their punishment." At that very moment his accusers were struck blind.

³Those who saw this were very frightened and didn't know what to do. All they could say was, "Every word he says, whether good or bad, turns into a fact—a miracle, even!"

⁴When Joseph saw that Jesus had done such a thing, he got angry and grabbed his ear and pulled very hard. ⁵The boy became infuriated with him and replied, "It's one thing for you to seek but not find; it's quite another for you to act this unwisely. ⁶Don't you know that I don't really belong to you? Don't get me angry."

6 **A teacher** by the name of Zacchaeus was listening to everything Jesus was saying to Joseph, and was astonished. He said to himself, "He is just a child, and

3:2–3
Cf. Mk 11:12–14, Mt 21:18–19

4:3
◊ Ps 33:9; 148:5

5:5
Cf. Q 11:9–10;
Mt 7:7–8;
Lk 11:9–10;
Th 38:2, 92, 94;
Jn 7:33–34

6:1–7:11
Cf. Jn 3:1–14

3:2–3 The withering of the child may recall the episode of the withered fig tree (Mark 11:12–14; Matt 21:18–19).
4:1–2 The punishment meted out to a clumsy child might have been remotely inspired by the punishment of the malicious children who abused a prophet. See 2 Kgs 2:23–35.
5:5–6 The response by Jesus to Joseph's rebuke is obscure. The command to seek and find (or receive) is common in gospel sources. See Matt 7:7; Luke 11:9–13; John 16:24;

Gospel of Thomas 1, 92, 94. The remark to Joseph that he can *seek but not find* might reflect the critical remarks about Jesus' earthly family at Mark 3:31–35 and Matt 12:47–50. Joseph can seek to discipline Jesus but won't be able to find the means to do so.
6:1 *Zacchaeus* is also the name of the tax collector in Luke 19.

he's saying this!" ²And so he summoned Joseph and said to him, "You have a bright child, and he has a good mind. Hand him over to me so he can learn his letters. I'll teach him everything he needs to know so he won't be out of control."

³Joseph replied, "No one can control this child except God alone. Don't consider him to be a small cross, brother."

⁴When Jesus heard Joseph saying this he laughed and said to Zacchaeus, "Believe me, teacher, what my father told you is true. ⁵I am the Lord of these people and I'm present with you and have been born among you and am with you. ⁶I know where you've come from and how long you'll live. Let me tell you, teacher, I existed when you were born. If you wish to be a perfect teacher, listen to me and I'll teach you a wisdom that no one else knows except for me and the One who sent me to you. ⁷It's you who happen to be my student. I know how old you are and how long you have to live. ⁸When you see the cross that my father mentioned, then you'll believe that everything I've told you is true."

⁹The Jews who were standing by and heard Jesus marveled and said, "How strange and paradoxical! This child is barely five years old and yet he says such things. In fact, we've never heard anyone say the kinds of things this child does."

¹⁰Jesus said to them in reply, "Are you really so amazed? Think about what I've said to you. The truth is that I also know when you were born, and your parents, and I announce this paradox to you: when the world was created, I existed along with the One who sent me to you."

¹¹The Jews, once they heard the child speaking like this, got angry but were unable to say anything back. ¹²But the child skipped forward and said to them, "I've made fun of you because I know that your tiny minds marvel at trifles."

¹³When, therefore, they thought that they were being comforted by the child's exhortation, the teacher said to Joseph, "Bring him to the classroom and I'll teach him the alphabet."

¹⁴Joseph took him by the hand and led him to the classroom. ¹⁵The teacher wrote the alphabet for him and began the instruction by repeating the letter Alpha over and over again. But the child clammed up and did not answer him for a long time. ¹⁶No wonder, then, that the teacher got angry and struck him on the head. The child took the blow calmly and replied to him, "I'm teaching you instead of being taught by you: I already know the letters you're teaching me, and your condemnation is great. To you these letters are like a bronze pitcher or a clashing cymbal, which can't produce glory or wisdom because it's all just noise. ¹⁷No one can understand the extent of my wisdom." ¹⁸When he got over being angry he rapidly recited the letters from Alpha to Omega.

¹⁹Then he looked at the teacher and told him, "Since you don't know the real nature of the letter Alpha, how are you going to teach the letter Beta? ²⁰You

6:6
Cf. Jn 8:58,
Q 10:21–22,
Mt 11:25–27,
Lk 10:21–22

6:8
Cf. Jn 8:28

6:10
Cf. Jn 1:1–2

6:16
Cf. 1 Cor 13:1

6:19
Cf. Q 6:42, Mt 7:5,
Lk 6:42

6:18 *Alpha* and *Omega* are the names of the first and last letters of the Greek alphabet. Other versions of this gospel use the names of the letters of the native alphabets.

*The teacher's
lament*

*Jesus revokes his
curse*

phony, if you know, teach me first the letter Alpha and then I'll trust you with the letter Beta." [21]He began to quiz the teacher about the first letter, but he was unable to say anything.

[22]Then while many were listening, he said to Zacchaeus, "Listen, teacher, and observe the arrangement of the first letter: [23]How it has two straight lines or strokes proceeding to a point in the middle, gathered together, elevated, dancing, three-cornered, two-cornered, not antagonistic, of the same family, providing the alpha has lines of equal measure."

7 **After Zacchaeus the teacher** had heard the child expressing such intricate allegories regarding the first letter, he gave up trying to defend his teaching. [2]He spoke to those who were present: "Poor me, I'm completely at a loss, wretch that I am. I've heaped shame on myself because I took on this child. [3]I beg you, brother Joseph, take him away. I can't bear his harsh stare or his brilliant speech. [4]This child is no ordinary mortal; he can even tame fire! Perhaps he was born before the creation of the world. [5]What sort of womb bore him, what sort of mother nourished him? I don't know. [6]Poor me, friend, I've lost my mind. [7]I've deceived myself, I'm totally miserable. I struggled to get a student, and it turns out I have a teacher. [8]Friends, think of the shame: I'm an old man, but I've been defeated by a mere child. [9]Now I can only despair and die because of this boy; I can't look him in the face. [10]When they say that I've been defeated by a small child, what can I say back? And what can I report about the lines of the first letter which he told me about? I just don't know, friends. For I don't know its beginning or its end. [11]So I have to ask you, brother Joseph, to take him back to your house. What great thing he is—God or angel or whatever else I might call him—I don't know."

8 **While the Jews** were advising Zacchaeus, the child laughed loudly and said, "Now let the infertile bear fruit and the blind see and the deaf hear in the un-

7:5
Cf. InJas 3:2

6:22–23 The point of the story in all of its forms is that Jesus finds a deep symbolic significance in the shape of the first letter of the alphabet. The Greek version suggests that the letter A is symbolic of the Trinity.

6:23 *How it has two straight lines*: These are the only words of this most difficult and undoubtedly corrupt sentence that make sense. The rest of the translation is guesswork or simply a translation of words, if they are known at all. Some words are not even listed in Greek dictionaries. No wonder Zacchaeus despairs of taking on Jesus as a student.

7:4 The remark that Jesus *can even tame fire* perhaps alludes to a lost episode. Zacchaeus unwittingly makes a christological confession when he speculates that Jesus might have been begotten before the creation of the world. See John

1:1–3; Heb 1:2–3.

8:1–3 The combination of cursing and saving is awkward. As the text stands it suggests that Jesus would ascend into heaven where he could curse his enemies, but then call them upward. When he ceases speaking, those who had been afflicted by his potent words are healed. Yet the crowds remain fearful that they might be cursed. This sequence may reflect the fact that people who transmitted the story were uncomfortable with the notion that Jesus would curse and maim.

8:1 For the blind to receive sight is characteristic of the activity of Jesus. See Mark 10:46; Matt 11:5, 21:14; Luke 7:21–22; John 9.

derstanding of their heart. ²"I've come from above to rescue those below and call them to higher things, just as the One who sent me to you commanded me."

³When the child stopped speaking, all those who had fallen under the curse were instantly saved. ⁴And from then on no one dared to anger him for fear of being cursed and maimed for life.

9 **A few days later** Jesus was playing on the roof of a house when one of the children playing with him fell off the roof and died. When the other children saw what had happened, they ran away and left Jesus all by himself.

²The parents of the dead child came and accused Jesus, "You troublemaker you, you're the one who threw him down."

³Jesus responded, "I didn't throw him down; he threw himself down. He just wasn't being careful; he jumped down from the roof and died."

⁴Then Jesus himself jumped down from the roof and stood over the body of the child and shouted in a loud voice: "Zeno!"—that was his name—"Get up and tell me: Did I push you down?"

⁵He got up immediately and said, "No, Lord, you didn't push me down; you raised me up."

⁶Those who saw this were astonished. The child's parents worshiped Jesus and praised God for the miracle that had happened.

10 **A few days later** a young man in the neighborhood was splitting wood when his axe slipped and cut off the bottom of his foot. He was dying from the loss of blood.

²The crowd rushed there in an uproar, and the boy Jesus ran up, too. He forced his way through the crowd and grabbed hold of the young man's wounded foot. It was instantly healed.

³He said to the young man, "Get up now, split your wood, and remember me."

⁴The crowd saw what had happened and worshiped the child, saying, "Truly the spirit of God dwells in this child."

11 **When he was six years old,** his mother sent him to draw water and bring it back to the house. ²But he lost his grip on the pitcher in the jostling of the

A fallen child raised

Jesus heals a cut foot

Jesus fetches water

9:3 Jesus' denial that he pushed the boy off the roof is not found in this Greek version, but has been supplied from the Syriac and Slavonic versions.

8:2 Cf. Jn 16:28, 17:2

9:4 The name *Zeno*, well attested in Greek culture, is not found in the canonical gospels.

10:2–3 The episode perhaps echoes the saying preserved in the Gospel of Thomas 77: "Split a piece of wood: I am there."

11:1–4 A single story about Jesus at age six. Jesus' mother plays a relatively minor role in this gospel, appearing only here and at 14:5 and 19:1–12.

*A miraculous
harvest*

*Miraculous
woodworking*

Jesus fells a teacher

crowd, and it fell and broke. ³So Jesus spread out the cloak he was wearing and filled it with water and carried it back to his mother.

⁴His mother, once she saw the miracle that had occurred, kissed him; but she kept to herself the mysteries that she had seen him do.

12 **Again, during the sowing season,** the child went out with his father to sow their field with grain. While his father was sowing, the child Jesus sowed one measure of grain. ²When he had harvested and threshed it, it yielded one hundred measures. ³Then he summoned all the poor in the village to the threshing floor and gave them grain. Joseph carried back what was left of the grain. ⁴Jesus was eight years old when he did this miracle.

13 **Now Jesus' father** was a carpenter, making plows and yokes at that time. He took an order from a rich man to make a bed for him. ²When one board of what is called the crossbeam turned out shorter than the other, and Joseph didn't know what to do, the child Jesus said to his father Joseph, "Put the two boards down and line them up at one end."

³Joseph did as the child told him. Jesus stood at the other end, grabbed hold of the shorter board, and, by stretching it, made it the same length as the other.

⁴His father Joseph looked on and marveled, and he hugged and kissed the child, saying, "How lucky I am that God has given me this child."

14 **When Joseph saw** how earnest the child was, and how intelligent he was for his age, he again resolved that it was high time for Jesus to learn to read. So he took him and handed him over to another teacher. ²The teacher said to Joseph, "First I'll teach him Greek, then Hebrew." This teacher, of course, knew of the child's previous experience at school and was afraid of him. Still, he wrote out the alphabet and instructed him for quite a while, though Jesus was unresponsive.

³Then Jesus spoke: "If you're really a teacher, and if you know the letters well, tell me the meaning of the letter Alpha, and I'll tell you the meaning of Beta."

11:4
ⓣ Lk 2:19, 51; InThom 19:11

13:4 One Greek ms ends here with the comment: "When they had returned to town, Joseph told Mary. When she had heard and seen the wondrous deeds of her son, she rejoiced, glorifying him along with the Father and the Holy Spirit now and forever and ever. Amen."

12–17 A series of stories about Jesus at age eight (12:4; cf. 18:1).
12:2 The yield of *one hundred measures* is perhaps inspired by Mark 4:8, Matt 13:8, Luke 8:8.
13:1 For Joseph's trade, see Mark 6:3 and Matt 13:55. In

Acts of Thomas 3, Jesus' "twin," Judas Thomas, indicates that he knows how to make such implements as plows and yokes.
14–15 The stories in these chapters are doublets of the account in chapters 6–7.

[4]The teacher became exasperated and hit him on the head. Jesus got angry and cursed him, and the teacher immediately passed out and fell facedown on the ground.

[5]The child returned to Joseph's house. But Joseph was upset and instructed his mother, "Don't let him go outside, because those who annoy him end up dead."

15

Some time later another teacher, a close friend of Joseph, said to him, "Send the child to my schoolroom. Perhaps with some flattery I can teach him his letters."

[2]Joseph replied, "If you can muster the courage, brother, take him with you." And so he took him along with much fear and trepidation, but the child was happy to go.

[3]Jesus strode confidently into the schoolroom and found a book lying on the desk. He picked up the book but did not read the letters in it. Rather, he opened his mouth and spoke by the power of the holy spirit and taught the Law to those standing there.

[4]A large crowd gathered and stood listening to him, and they marveled at the maturity of his teaching and his readiness of speech—a mere child able to say such things.

[5]When Joseph heard about this he feared the worst and ran to the schoolroom, imagining that this teacher was having trouble with Jesus.

[6]But the teacher said to Joseph, "Brother, please know that I accepted this child as a student, but already he's full of grace and wisdom. So I'm asking you, brother, to take him back home."

[7]When the child heard this, he immediately smiled at him and said, "Because you have spoken and testified rightly, that other teacher who was struck down will be healed." And right away he was. Joseph took his child and went home.

16

Joseph sent his son James to bundle up some wood and carry it back to the house, and the child Jesus followed. While James was gathering the firewood, a viper bit his hand. [2]And as he lay sprawled out on the ground, dying, Jesus came and blew on the bite. Immediately the pain stopped, the animal burst open, and James got better on the spot.

17

After this incident a baby in Joseph's neighborhood became sick and died, and his mother grieved terribly. Jesus heard the loud wailing and the uproar that was going on and quickly ran there.

15:3–4
ⓘ InThom 19:4–5;
Ⓣ Lk 2:46–47

16:1–2
Cf. Acts 28:1–6

17:1–4
Cf. Mk 5:21–24,
35–43;
Mt 9:18–19, 23–26;
Lk 8:40–42, 49–56

16:2 For another split serpent, see *Acts of Thomas* 33.

²When he found the child dead, he touched her chest and said, "I say to you, infant, don't die; live, and be with your mother."

³And immediately the infant looked up and laughed. Jesus then said to the woman, "Take your child, offer her your breast, and remember me."

⁴The crowd of onlookers marveled at this: "Truly this child was God or a heavenly messenger of God—whatever he says instantly happens." But Jesus left and went on playing with the other children.

18 **A year later,** while a building was under construction, a man fell from the top of it and died. There was quite a commotion, so Jesus got up and walked over. ²When he saw the man lying dead, he took his hand and said, "I say to you, sir, get up and go back to work." And he immediately got up and worshiped him.

³The crowd saw this and marveled: "This child's from heaven—he must be, because he has saved many souls from death, and he can go on saving all his life."

19 **When he was twelve years old** his parents went to Jerusalem, as usual, for the Passover festival, along with their fellow travelers. ²After Passover they began the journey home. But while on their way, the child Jesus went back up to Jerusalem. His parents, of course, assumed that he was in the traveling party. ³After they had traveled one day, they began to look for him among their relatives. When they did not find him, they were worried and returned again to the city to search for him.

⁴After three days they found him in the temple area, sitting among the teachers, listening to the Law and asking them questions. ⁵All eyes were on him, and everyone was astounded that he, a mere child, could interrogate the elders and teachers of the people and explain the main points of the Law and the parables of the prophets.

⁶His mother Mary came up and said to him, "Child, why have you done this to us? Don't you see that we've been worried sick looking for you."

⁷"Why are you looking for me?" Jesus said to them. "Don't you know that it's my destiny to be in my father's house?"

⁸Then the scholars and the Pharisees said, "Are you the mother of this child?" ⁹She said, "I am."

19:1–11
//Lk 2:41–52

19:4–5
Ⓘ InThom 15:3–4

19:5
Ⓣ Mk 1:22,
Mt 7:28–29

17:3 The concern to feed the resuscitated child resembles Mark 5:43.

18:2 For the command to arise, see Mark 5:41 and Luke 7:14.

19:1 *twelve years old*: Twelve years of age meant one thing for a girl, quite another for a boy. The former was consid-ered ready for marriage and motherhood, the latter was still regarded as a child for two more years. Jesus at twelve engaging the teachers in the temple area further underscores how precocious he was. He is referred to as *a mere child* in v. 5.

¹⁰And they said to her, "You more than any woman are to be congratulated, for God has blessed the fruit of your womb! For we've never seen nor heard such glory and such virtue and wisdom."

¹¹Jesus got up and went with his mother, and was obedient to his parents. His mother took careful note of all that had happened. ¹²And Jesus continued to excel in learning and gain respect.

¹³To him be glory for ever and ever. Amen.

19:10
//Lk 1:42;
Cf. InJas 11:1,
Lk 11:27, Th 79:1
19:11
//Lk 2:40;
Ⓣ InThom 11:4
19:12
Ⓣ Lk 2:19, 51

Lost Gospels and "Non-Gospels"

Lost Gospels

There are at least eleven lost early Christian works that were called gospels. No trace of them remains and we have no evidence that any ancient writer quoted from them. We know these lost gospels existed only because they are mentioned by early Christian authors. These lost works are thus known only by their names.

The Gospel of the Four Heavenly Regions
The Gospel of Perfection
The Gospel of Eve
The Gospel of the Twelve
The Gospel of Matthias
The Gospel of Bartholomew
The Gospel of Cerinthus
The Gospel of Basilides
The Gospel of Marcion
The Gospel of Appelles
The Gospel of Bardesanes

Perhaps some of these lost gospels will be one day be recovered. The Gospels of Peter and Thomas were known only by name until manuscripts were discovered, in 1886 and 1945 respectively. The Gospel of Judas was until recently known solely by name. It was published only in 2006.

Four gospels in *The Complete Gospels* were totally unknown until their discoveries in the twentieth century. The fragments from which we know the Gospel of Mary were published between 1938 and 1983. The Dialogue of the Savior and the Secret Book of James were discovered at Nag Hammadi in 1945. And the Gospel of the Savior lay unrecognized in a German museum until two scholars stumbled across it in the 1990s.

The Q Gospel and the Gospel of Signs are, paradoxically, "lost" gospels that we can read. Though no manuscripts of these gospels have been found, scholars have reconstructed most of the texts of these two works by painstaking analysis of the other gospels that copied from them. In addition, the three Jewish-Christian gospels (the Gospels of the Hebrews, Ebionites, and Nazoreans) and the Mystical Gospel of Mark are lost in the sense that no copies of them survive.

The little we know about them is based on excerpts from them quoted by early Christian writers.

Three other gospels in this volume, the Egerton Gospel and the Gospels Oxyrhynchus 840 and 1224, are known to us only in small fragments—even their ancient names are unknown. Finally, the "orphan" story about Jesus and the woman arrested for adultery, which was inserted by ancient copyists into different places in the Gospels of John and Luke (see pp. 460–61), might possibly have originally belonged to some other lost gospel.

Who knows what other ancient gospels might be lost under the sand, hidden in caves, or unnoticed in museums?

"Non-Gospels"

Among the religious texts in the Nag Hammadi library there are three that are called "gospels" but do not deserve the name because they do not meet the standard literary definition of a gospel: a writing consisting of stories about Jesus and/or sayings or teachings attributed to him.

The *Gospel of Truth* is a homily discussing esoteric interpretations of some gospel passages and a theological treatise on the nature of the relationship between the Father and the Son.

The *Gospel of Philip* is an anthology of various Gnostic teachings. Although it contains a number of statements attributed to Jesus, this work is primarily given to theological reflections about human nature and the sacraments, especially the sacrament of marriage.

The Coptic *Gospel of the Egyptians*, which also calls itself the *Holy Book of the Great Invisible Spirit*, is a Gnostic treatise about the origin of the supernatural world, the heavenly Seth who came to earth in the form of Jesus, and the process of salvation. It is not be confused with another early Christian writing also known as the Gospel of the Egyptians, written in Greek. Unfortunately, no copy of that Greek gospel survives. All that remains of it are brief excerpts quoted by Clement of Alexandria that came from a dialogue between Jesus and a Salome, a disciple, about the value of celibacy.

It is possible, even probable, that some of the eleven lost gospels listed above were actually "non-gospels." However, lacking any information about their contents, we cannot even speculate on this matter.

Fragmentary Gospels

Papyrus Köln, discovered and published in 1987, has been identified as a piece of the Egerton Gospel. *Used by permission of the Institut für Altertumskunde der Universität zu Köln.*

The Gospel of Peter

Introduction

In 1886 French archaeologists discovered a small papyrus codex in a monk's grave at Akhmim in Upper Egypt. The contents of this codex include a fragmentary gospel narrative containing significant portions of a passion story, a miraculous epiphany, an empty tomb story, and an introduction to what is probably a resurrection story. Small crosses and ornamentation in the codex at the beginning and end of the narrative indicate that the writer was copying an already fragmented text. The cursive handwriting in the manuscript dates from the eighth or ninth century. This gospel fragment became known as the Gospel of Peter due to the fact that Simon Peter is presented as its author (14:3, 7:2).

Relationship to the canonical gospels

The first phase of the scholarly study of the Gospel of Peter centered on the question of whether or not it is dependent on the canonical gospels. A consensus emerged in the early twentieth century that Peter was dependent on the canonical gospels and composed no earlier than the first half of the second century. This view prevailed until the last quarter of the twentieth century, when two developments led scholars to reconsider the position and significance of the Gospel of Peter in the development of early Christianity.

First, a small fragment of papyrus (Oxyrhynchus Papyrus 2949) from the late second or the early third century was published in 1972. On this papyrus is the story of Joseph of Arimathea's request to Pilate for the body of Jesus. This request appears to occur before Jesus' execution, a sequence that contradicts the order of events in the canonical gospels, but closely resembles the story in Peter 2:1–3a. This Oxyrhynchus fragment comes either from an earlier version of the Gospel of Peter than the one we have or from another, independent passion narrative with this peculiar sequence of events.

Second, New Testament scholarship has long since undermined the basic assumption of the early interpreters of Peter: that the early gospels are based on historically accurate memories. The initial consensus that Peter was later than and dependent on the canonical gospels, therefore, defended the traditional belief that the canonical gospels are historical while the extracanonical gospels are fictional. However, twentieth-century scholarship gradually established that because the canonical gospels are witnesses to a very complex interpretive enterprise, both oral and literary, and were subject to the various formats and patterns of ancient communication, they cannot be simple historical reports. This means that the extracanonical gospels, such as Peter, must also be reevaluated.

This rethinking has been based on the discovery that almost every sentence of the passion narrative of Peter appears to be composed out of references and allusions to the psalms and the writings of the prophets. In effect, "scriptural memory" may well have been a major influence in the formation of this early passion narrative. Furthermore, more recent studies of Peter that are not interested in searching for some historical core have tentatively identified an original compositional layer within this gospel whose form and content was shaped by the Jewish tradition of the suffering righteous one.

The origins of the passion traditions

The most important result established by this research is that the original stage of Peter (found in 2:3c–6:1, 8:1b) may well be the earliest passion story in the gospel tradition and, as such, may contain the seeds of subsequent passion narratives. In contrast to those early interpreters of Peter who assumed some sort of factual account at the core, more recent scholarship argues that the passion tradition began not as a simple historical description but as a creative response to the trauma of Jesus' fate, expressed in the stock form of the Jewish tale of the righteous one who is unjustly persecuted and subsequently vindicated. The story pattern of this tale (see Wisdom 2–5) is as follows. The actions and claims of a righteous person provoke his opponents to conspire against him. This leads to an accusation (Pet 3:2?; 4:2?), trial (1:1), condemnation (2:3), and ordeal (3:1–4; 4:1; 5:2). In some instances this results in his shameful death (5:5). The hero of the story reacts characteristically (4:1), with prayers expressing his innocence, frustration, or trust in God (5:5), while there are also various reactions to his fate by characters in the tale (4:3–5). Either at the brink of death or in death itself the innocent one is rescued (5:5) and vindicated (5:6–6:1). This vindication entails the exaltation (5:5) and acclamation (8:1) of the hero as well as the reaction (8:1) and punishment (5:1, 3–4) of his opponents.

Building on this basic narrative, the composer(s) of the Gospel of Peter added a miraculous epiphany story (chapters 8–11), detailing a divine breakthrough and intensifying the vindication of the righteous sufferer. After an introduction (8:1–9:1), we find a visit by heavenly beings (9:2–3), the miraculous opening of the tomb (9:4), a supernatural appearance (10:2–3), and reaction by witnesses (11:3). One can also note further additions: an empty tomb story (chapters 12–13) and the probable beginning of a resurrection appearance story (chapter 14). On this analysis, the figure of Simon Peter (7:2; 14:3) appears only at the final stage of the gospel's composition. These findings not only move the date of the earliest stage of Peter to the middle of the first century, but also challenge basic assumptions about the historical development of early Christian literature.

The Gospel of Peter

1 . . . **but of the Judeans** no one washed his hands, neither Herod nor any one of his judges. Since they were [un]willing to wash, Pilate stood up. ²Then Herod the king orders the Master to be [taken away], saying to them "Do to him what I commanded you."

2 **Joseph, the friend of Pilate** and the Master, stood there. When he realized that they were about to crucify him, he went to Pilate and asked for the Master's body for burial. ²And Pilate sent to Herod and asked for his body. ³And Herod replied, "Brother Pilate, even if no one had asked for him, we would have buried him, since the Sabbath is drawing near. ⁴For it is written in the Law, 'The sun must not set upon one who has been executed.'"

⁵And he turned him over to the people on the day before their festival, known as Unleavened Bread, began.

3 **They took the Master** and kept pushing him along as they ran; and they were saying, "Let's drag the son of God along, since we have him in our power." ²And they threw a purple robe around him and sat him upon the judgment seat

Hand washing

Request for the body

Paying their respects

2:1
//Mk 15:43–45,
Mt 27:57–58,
Lk 23:50–52,
Jn 19:38–42

2:4
◊ Dt 21:22–23

2:5
//Mk 15:15,
Mt 27:26,
Lk 23:24–25,
Jn 19:16

3:1
◊ Ps 117:13 (LXX)

3:2–3
◊ Zec 3:1–5, Is 58:2;
//Mk 15:17,
Mt 27:28–29,
Lk 23:11,
Jn 19:2, 13

1:1 The text begins in the middle of a scene. The ornamentation at the beginning of the material indicates that the writer copied an already fragmented text.
1:2 *[taken away]*: Another possible restoration is "escorted."

1:1 The text begins abruptly in a scene from the passion narrative. Evidently the Judean officials have refused to join Pilate in a washing ritual in which he declared his innocence. In the Gospel of Matthew this declaration occurs with the washing (Matt 27:24) whereas in Peter it comes later (11:4).

Judeans (see also 6:3, 7:1, 11:6, 12:1, 3): This term does not appear in the earliest layer of Peter (2:3c–6:1, 8:1b). It belongs to the later edition of Peter, which was composed after the fall of Jerusalem (7:1), when different groups within the traditions of Israel were trying to establish themselves (at the expense of others) in the aftermath of the destruction of the second temple. The use of the term *Judean* does not necessarily imply an outright rejection of Judaism, but rather reflects a mixed social situation within the Greco-Roman world, probably somewhere in Syria, where group distinctions were important in defining social identity. See the cameo essay on "Judeans" and "Jews" (pp. **000–000**).
1:2 In contrast to the canonical gospels, Herod assumes control of the trial of Jesus. See Luke 13:31–33.

Master is the principal title in Peter for Jesus. Others are *son of God* and *savior of humanity*.
2:1 In contrast to the canonical versions, Joseph asks for the body of the Master before his crucifixion.
2:3–4 This quotation (see Deut 21:22–23) refers originally to the hanging of an executed criminal upon a tree. The law was apparently interpreted to include cases of crucifixion, which carried the stigma of social disgrace. The onset of the Sabbath demanded the removal of such defilement.
2:5 The *festival of Unleavened Bread* is the Passover.
3:1 *They* refers to *the people* in 2:5. Unlike the canonical gospels, the people are in control of the fate of Jesus. Herod's control ends in 2:3.
3:1–4 Crucifixion was often preceded by torture and flogging. Since this was an act of public humiliation, a royal mockery, involving a throne, crown, robe, scepter, and title, was not uncommon. This may have had the important social function of diverting hatred for the dominating class onto scapegoats.

Crucifixion

On the cross

and said, "Judge justly, king of Israel." ³And one of them brought a crown of thorns and set it on the head of the Master. ⁴And others standing about would spit in his eyes, and others slapped his face, while others poked him with a rod. Some kept flogging him as they said, "Let's pay proper respect to the son of God."

4 **And they brought** two criminals and crucified the Master between them. But he himself remained silent, as if in no pain.

²And when they set up the cross, they put an inscription on it, "This is the king of Israel." ³And they piled his clothes in front of him; then they divided them among themselves and gambled for them.

⁴But one of those criminals reproached them and said, "We're suffering for the evil that we've done, but this man, who has become a savior of humanity, what wrong has he done to you?"

⁵And they got angry at him and ordered that his legs not be broken so he would die in agony.

5 **It was midday** and darkness covered the whole of Judea. They were confused and anxious for fear that the sun had set while he was still alive. ⟨For⟩ it is written,

> The sun must not set upon one who has been executed.

²And one of them said, "Give him vinegar mixed with something bitter to drink." And they mixed it and gave it to him to drink.

³And they fulfilled all things and brought to completion the sins on their head. ⁴Now many went around with lamps, and, thinking that it was night, they lay down.

3:4
◊ Is 50:6;
//Mk 14:65, 15:15, 19; Mt 26:67–68; 27:26, 30; Jn 19:1, 3

4:1
◊ Is 53:7;
//Mk 15:27,
Mt 27:38,
Lk 23:32–33,
Jn 19:18;
cf. Mk 14:61; 15:5;
Mt 26:63

4:2
//Mk 15:26,
Mt 27:37, Lk 23:38,
Jn 19:19

4:3
◊ Ps 22:18;
//Mk 15:24,
Mt 27:35, Lk 23:34,
Jn 19:23–24

4:4
//Lk 23:39–41

4:5
Cf. Jn 19:31–37

5:1
◊ Dt 21:22–23,
Am 8:9;
//Mk 15:33,
Mt 27:45, Lk 23:44,
Jn 19:31

5:2
◊ Ps 69:21;
//Mk 15:23, 36;
Mt 27:34, 48;
Lk 23:36;
Jn 19:28–29

5:3
Ⓣ 1 Thes 2:16

5:1 ⟨For⟩ is added to clarify the cause of the confusion and anxiety.
5:4 *lay down*: Another possible restoration is "fell down."

4:1 *As if in no pain* is modeled on Isa 53:7 and so does not imply Docetism.
4:2 This *inscription* is worded somewhat differently than in the canonical gospels.
4:3 This is modeled on Ps 22:18.
4:5 Breaking the legs of the crucified was done in order to hasten death. See John 19:32–33.
5:1 Untimely *darkness* is a feature of apocalyptic narratives.

5:2 The *bitter* substance is probably myrrh (see Mark 15:23), which may have been given to crucified victims to dull the pain. This is likely an allusion to Ps 69:21.
5:3 The language here suggests Jewish prophetic tradition where the actions of the people are criticized and understood to bring down divine wrath. See 1 Thess 2:16 and Matt 23:32.

⁵And the Master cried out, saying, "My power, ⟨my⟩ power, you have abandoned me." When he said this, he was taken up. ⁶And at that moment, the curtain of the Jerusalem temple was torn in two.

6 **And then they pulled** the nails from the Master's hands and set him on the ground. And the whole earth shook and there was great fear. ²Then the sun came out and it turned out to be three o'clock in the afternoon. ³Now the Judeans rejoiced and gave his body to Joseph so that he might bury it, since ⟨Joseph⟩ had observed how much good he had done.

⁴⟨Joseph⟩ took the Master, washed ⟨his body⟩ and wound a linen ⟨shroud⟩ around him, and brought him to his own tomb, called "Joseph's Garden."

7 **Then the Judeans** and the elders and the priests perceived what evil they had done to themselves, and began to beat their breasts and cry out "Our sins have brought disasters down on us! The judgment and the end of Jerusalem are at hand!"

²But I began weeping with my friends. And quivering with fear in our hearts, we hid ourselves. (You see we were being sought by them as criminals and as people who wanted to burn down the temple.) ³As a result of all these things, we fasted and sat mourning and weeping night and day until the Sabbath.

8 **When the scholars** and the Pharisees and the priests had gathered together, and when they heard that all the people were moaning and beating their breasts, and saying, "If his death has produced these overwhelming signs, he must have been completely innocent!" ²They became frightened and went to Pilate and begged him, ³"Give us soldiers so that ⟨we⟩ can guard his tomb for three [days], in case his disciples come and steal his body and the people assume that he is risen from the dead and do us harm."

Burial

Regrets

Sealing the tomb

5:5
◊Ps 22:1;
//Mk 15:34, 37;
Mt 27:46, 50;
Lk 23:46; Jn 19:30;
cf. Acts 1:2

5:6
//Mk 15:38,
Mt 27:51, Lk 23:45

6:1
//Mt 27:51

6:2
//Mk 15:33,
Mt 27:45, Lk 23:44

6:3–4
//Mk 15:43–47,
Mt 27:57–60,
Lk 23:50–53,
Jn 19:42

7:1
◊Is 3:96,
Zec 12:10–12;
cf. Lk 23:48

7:3
Cf. Mk 16:10

8:1
Cf. Mk 15:39;
Mt 27:19, 54;
Lk 23:47

8:2–6
//Mt 27:62–66

5:5 *Taken up* might be a euphemism for death or it might refer to an ascension into heaven. The latter meaning would suggest a rescue combined with an exaltation of a suffering son of God.

5:6 Along with the apocalyptic darkness in 5:1, this event is part of a series of cataclysmic events (see 6:1). The *curtain* separated the precincts of the temple from the inner sanctuary (see Exod 26:31–35, 40:21).

6:1 This implies that the feet were not nailed. The procedure of crucifixion allowed for tying one set of the victim's extremities while nailing the other.

The *shaking* of the ground is a further apocalyptic feature.

6:4 Joseph prepares the corpse of Jesus in the usual Jewish manner. 12:3–4 suggests that the burial ritual is incomplete.

7:1 The Judean officials are portrayed as repenting and as

understanding that their deeds call for divine condemnation. This may well be an allusion to the fall of Jerusalem in 70 CE. Notice the apparent contradiction to their reaction in 11:6.

7:2 While this might reflect the tradition found in Mark 14:58, Matt 26:61, John 2:19, and Acts 6:13, it also might refer to the horrors of the burning of the temple (see Josephus, *The Jewish War* 6.250–280).

7:3 *Night and day* suggests that some time has passed (see 2:3). Yet 9:1–2 points to the Sabbath mentioned in 2:3.

8:1 *Beating their breasts* indicates the people's repentance over their role in the death of a righteous one. This may have originally followed 6:1. The gospel seems to play the *people* off against the official leaders by contrasting their different reactions to the sign in 6:1. It also may be that 7:1 comes from a later version of Peter.

Two from the sky

*Three men &
a cross*

Report to Pilate

[4]So Pilate gave them the officer Petronius with soldiers to guard the tomb. And elders and scholars went with them to the tomb. [5]And all who were there ⟨with⟩ the officer and the soldiers helped roll a large stone against the entrance to the tomb. [6]And they put seven seals on it. Then they pitched a tent there and kept watch.

9 **Early, at first light** on the Sabbath, a crowd came from Jerusalem and the surrounding countryside to see the sealed tomb. [2]But during the night before the Lord's day dawned, while the soldiers were on guard, in pairs during each watch, a loud noise came from the sky, [3]and they saw the skies open up and two men come down from there in a burst of light and approach the tomb. [4]The stone that had been pushed against the entrance began to roll by itself and moved away to one side; then the tomb opened up and both young men went inside.

10 **Now when these soldiers** saw this, they roused the officer from his sleep, along with the elders. (Remember, they were also there keeping watch.) [2]While they were explaining what they had seen, again they see three men leaving the tomb, two supporting the third. And a cross was following them.

[3]The heads of the two men reached up to the sky, while the head of the third, whom they led by the hand, reached beyond the skies. [4]And they heard a voice from the skies that said, "Have you preached to those who sleep?"

[5]And an answer was heard from the cross: "Yes!"

11 **These men then consulted** with one another about going and reporting these things to Pilate. [2]While they were still thinking about it, again the skies appeared to open and some sort of human being came down and entered the tomb. [3]When those in the officer's unit saw this, they rushed out into the night to Pilate, leaving the tomb that they were supposed to be guarding. And as they were recounting everything they had seen, they became deeply disturbed and cried, "He really was God's son!"

9:3–4
//Mk 16:5,
Mt 28:2–4, Lk 24:4;
cf. Mk 9:4, Acts 1:10

10:4
Ⓣ 1 Pet 3:18–20

11:3
//Mt 27:54;
cf. Mk 15:39

8:4 *Petronius:* Although the Roman officer is named here, he is not named again when he is mentioned later in this gospel (8:5; 10:1; 11:3, 5, 7). The name may indicate that 8:4 comes from a later version.

8:5 The fact that the soldiers complete the burial of Jesus by *rolling a large stone* against the tomb may be evidence of a tradition about the burial of Jesus that differs from the canonical story.

8:6 *seven seals:* the highest level of security.

9:2 *The night before the Lord's day dawned* is ambiguous. It can refer to the time either before sunrise on Sunday or after sunset on Saturday.

The *noise from the sky* indicates a divine communication.

9:4 In contrast to *both young men* 13:1 mentions only one. The movement of the stone *by itself* indicates divine agency.

10:2–3 *The third* presumably refers to the Lord. The size of the figures symbolizes their supernatural status.

10:4–5 *A voice from the skies* indicates a divine communication.

Preaching *to those who sleep* suggests the mythical descent into the underworld.

The speaking cross is unique in early Christian literature.

11:2 *some sort of human being*: a heavenly figure, the "young man" of 13:1.

[4]Pilate responded by saying, "I am clean of the blood of the son of God; this was all your doing."

[5]Then they all crowded around ⟨Pilate⟩ and began to beg and urge him to order the officer and his soldiers to tell no one what they had seen. [6]"You see," they said, "it's better for us to be guilty of the greatest sin before God than to fall into the hands of the Judean people and be stoned."

[7]Pilate then ordered the officer and the soldiers to say nothing.

12 **Early on the Lord's day**, Mary of Magdala, a disciple of the Master, was fearful on account of the Judeans and, since they were inflamed with rage, she did not do at the Master's tomb what women usually do for their loved ones who die. [2]Nevertheless, she took her friends with her and went to the tomb where he had been laid. [3]And they were afraid that the Judeans might see them and were saying, "Although on the day he was crucified we could not weep and beat our breasts, we should now perform these rites at his tomb. [4]But who will roll away the stone for us, the one placed at the entrance of the tomb, so that we can enter and sit beside him and do what ought to be done?" [5](Remember, it was a huge stone.) "We fear that someone might see us. And if we are unable ⟨to roll the stone away⟩ we should, at least, place at the entrance the memorial we brought for him, and we should weep and beat our breasts until we go home."

13 **And they went** and found the tomb open. They went up to it, stooped down, and saw a young man sitting there ⟨in⟩ the middle of the tomb; he was handsome and wore a splendid robe. He said to them, [2]"Why have you come? Who are you looking for? Surely not the one who was crucified? He is risen and gone. If you don't believe it, stoop down and take a look at the place where he lay—he's not there. You see, he is risen and has gone back to the place he was sent from."

[3]Then the women fled in fear.

14 **Now it was the last day** of Unleavened Bread, and many began to return to their homes because the festival was over. [2]But we, the twelve disciples of the

Mary at the tomb

Empty tomb

Departure

11:4
① Pet 1:1;
cf. Mt 27:24,
Lk 23:4

11:7
//Mt 28:11–15

12:1–2
//Mk 16:1–2,
Mt 28:1, Lk 24:1,
Jn 20:1

12:4
//Mk 16:3

13:1–2
//Mk 16:4–7,
Mt 28:2–7,
Lk 24:2–5,
Jn 20:11–13

13:3
//Mk 16:8, Mt 28:8,
Lk 24:9

12:1 *Disciple of the Master* may reflect the early tradition that women were equal to men in terms of the mission and message of Jesus.

fearful on account of the Judeans: See 7:2 and 12:3.

12:3 The women are probably bringing burial spices for a final anointing. They intend to perform the customary rites of mourning (*weep and beat our breasts*).

13:1 The *young man* is an angelic interpreter whose function is to shed light on the situation.

13:2 The words of the heavenly interpreter are probably drawn from the standard preaching of the early Jesus movement.

13:3 The reaction of the women is typical of people experiencing a divine epiphany.

14:1 This indicates that seven days have passed since the beginning of the festival of Passover. See Exod 12:18.

14:2 This is the only mention of *twelve disciples* in Peter.

Master, continued to weep and mourn, and each one, still grieving because of what had happened, left for his own home. ³But I, Simon Peter, and Andrew, my brother, took our fishing nets and went away to the sea. And with us was Levi, the son of Alphaeus, whom the Master . . .

14:3
Cf. Mk 2:14,
Lk 5:2–11,
Jn 21:1–14

14:3 The text breaks off abruptly. The ms has ornamentation immediately following these words, which suggests that it was copied from an already fragmented text.

14:3 This may reflect early traditions about a post-Easter vision to Peter (see John 21:1–14; Luke 5:2–11; 1 Cor 15:5). *The sea* most likely refers to the Sea of Galilee.

The use of *I* with *Simon Peter* is the basis for the title "Gospel of Peter."

The Gospel of the Savior

Introduction

Set shortly before the crucifixion, this highly fragmentary gospel offers the reader a different view of events leading up to the death of Jesus. The narrative is at once both familiar and strange, since it incorporates elements of the traditional story in new ways. In addition to dialogues between the Savior and his apostles (Andrew, John, and either Jude or Judas are mentioned), it features short collections of loosely connected sayings by the Savior, a vision or heavenly journey of the apostles in which they are transformed into "spiritual bodies," and a retelling of the passion of the Savior. Many of the sayings of the Savior closely parallel sayings of Jesus known from the canonical gospels (principally Matthew and John) and the Gospel of Thomas.

Discovery

Where and by whom this ancient text was originally discovered in modern times is unknown. It was acquired by the Egyptian Museum in West Berlin as a collection of parchment fragments in 1967 from a Dutch antiquities dealer. It lay about in the storeroom of the museum until "rediscovered" by Paul A. Mirecki (1991) and Charles W. Hedrick (1995) independently of each other. Its character as an early Christian gospel went unnoticed until 1996.

A fragmentary gospel

So much of this ancient gospel is missing—including both the beginning and ending of the text, where we would expect to find a title—that we do not know its original designation. The present title of the gospel is a modern convention based on the appellation given to the major character in the gospel (the same term "savior" is also used to identify the protagonist of Gospel Oxyrhynchus 840). The title "Christ" and the personal name "Jesus" do not appear among the fragments, although the Christian honorific "Master" does. Nevertheless, it is clear that the Savior is meant to be the Jesus of the canonical gospels. This gospel originally consisted of thirty-four fragments in all, some rather large but most very small. Several of the fragments are large enough to be considered fragmentary pages. What remains of this gospel, estimated to be about thirty pages if complete, are only ten fragmentary pages and twenty-nine smaller fragments. Fortunately, several page numbers were preserved among the fragments and three of the larger pieces of parchment were fragmentary sheets (a sheet being a large piece of parchment which, when folded in the center, becomes the backs and fronts of four separate pages). Although these data made it possible to establish a certain sequence for most of the fragmentary pages, there remain several fragments whose original location in the gospel cannot be determined.

A very close linguistic relationship exists between the Gospel of the Savior and the highly fragmentary Strasbourg Coptic Papyrus, which was identified in 1899 as an "apocryphal" gospel. The Strasbourg Papyrus and the Berlin parchment might be two different copies of the Gospel of the Savior, one written on papyrus and the other on parchment. If so, the multiple copies published using two different materials (papyrus and parchment) and the excellent quality of the parchment suggest that it was a popular text in Antiquity.

Date

The text is written in Coptic, but is likely a translation of a Greek original. A comparison of the scribe's handwriting with other datable Coptic texts suggests that this copy of the Gospel of the Savior was made in the fifth or sixth century. But the gospel itself was originally composed no later than the latter half of the second century, when the oral Jesus tradition still competed with written texts, and the canonical gospels had not yet achieved sufficient prominence to marginalize other early gospels.

Sayings traditions and written gospels

Only about one-third of this text survives, but this remaining portion suggests that the work in its entirety would be a rich source for those interested in the evolution of the sayings tradition. The close parallels with sayings known from the canonical gospels, particularly John and Matthew, suggest that the author of the Gospel of the Savior knew those works in some form, although they are not cited by name. When sayings attributed to the Savior are compared to those known from the canonical tradition, we find both verbal agreement and unique features. One example of a verbal agreement is the parallel between GSav 4:7 and the Coptic version of Matt 26:31, both of which reproduce exactly a quotation of Zech 13:7 that appears in a different form in the Coptic version of Mark 14:27. Other close parallels show variety. For example, GSav 4:2 performs a saying known in part from John 14:31 and in full from Matt 26:46. GSav 13:14 expands a saying known in John 16:33. GSav 14:14 adds an exclamatory intensifier not found in Matt 26:39. Most striking, however, is a single saying of two parallel members (GSav 1:4): "You are the salt of the earth and the lamp that lights the world." This saying appears in Matt 5:13–15 as two independent sayings, each of which is followed by clarifying commentary: "You are the salt of the earth" (Matt 5:13a) . . . "You are the light of the world" (Matt 5:14a). . . . For other close parallels see GSav 4:6 (John 10:30); 4:8–9 (John 10:11); 12:6 (John 20:17); and 13:18 (John 19:35).

Except for one citation from the Old Testament, the author does not quote religious texts as authority because for the author of the Gospel of the Savior authority resides in the person of the Savior, who is the sanction standing behind both written texts and oral tradition. It is also significant that the author attributes to the savior a saying appearing in the Gospel of Thomas (82): "Who is near to me is near to the fire; who is far from me is far from life" (GSav 12:9). This parallel shows that the author drew from sources outside the New Testament canon.

The Gospel of the Savior was composed in the early competitive period before what later became Orthodoxy had established canon and creed as the norms for determining the nature of what was Christian. At this early period all writers drew from an undifferentiated Jesus tradition, using what was useful to them for telling their version of the story. Matthew and Luke, for example, reworked material in Mark and added sayings from the Q Gospel to present unique versions of the story about Jesus. In like manner the author of the Gospel of the Savior used and reworked both written and oral material to develop yet another version of the story about Jesus. The authors of both the Gospel of John and the Gospel of the Savior were able to create remarkably new and different stories from materials available in whatever source seemed appropriate. For example, GSav 19:3 is a poetic section, perhaps a hymn addressed to the cross, that reflects concerns marginalized (though not eliminated) from the canonical texts, but celebrated in early radical Christian texts, such as The Treatise on the Resurrection: "Strong is the system of the Plenitude; small is that which broke loose and became the world" (46:35–38). The Gospel of the Savior describes the Savior's mission as the perfection of the Plenitude (19:3). The author, however, has a decided preference for traditions and sayings that are closely identified with the orthodox understanding of Jesus: note for example the descent into Hell (GSav 2:1, see 1 Pet 3:19), the Eucharist (GSav 8:3), the Passion traditions (GSav 13:16–18; 14:14–16), and the sayings tradition.

Belief system

Although the fragmentary nature of the Gospel of the Savior renders observations about its belief system necessarily tentative, some ideas seem fairly clear. Inasmuch as the gospel focuses its retelling of the story about Jesus on the crucifixion, and dedicates considerable effort to the re-performing of Jesus' sayings, it is obvious that Jesus plays a pivotal role in this gospel's belief system. Jesus is called the savior who suffers because of the sins of the world (13:5), but he is not a martyr sacrificed to appease a righteous God. He seems more of a precursor in faith, one who goes before as guide for those who follow. For example, he has become free from the world and challenges his followers to do the same (4:1; 3:3; 13:10–11, 14–15). He lays down his life as an example for his followers and in return they should to lay down their lives for their friends, for this is what pleases the Father (4:9–11). The Savior is confident that they will be able to follow the path he charted (13:7; 3:3).

Although the Savior claims to be divine (4:12) and to have a close relationship with the Father ("I and my Father are a single one," 4:6), he is not a spiritual being from outside the natural world, but a human being whose death was real (8:3; 1:6). His crucifixion does have cosmic significance, however, for his death will correct a deficiency in the heavenly world (19:3), an idea met particularly in speculative Christian thought associated with Valentinianism. The author has also been influenced by Platonic thought, which held that the soul was eternal and originated in the heavenly world before it came to be housed in a material body (see 4:1). In the Gospel of the Savior salvation seems to consist partly in overcoming of the urges of the material body (13:2–15) and partly in managing to escape from the world (5:1–2; 18). Sharing a view widespread among Mediterranean religions, the author represents the ultimate heavenly realm as separated from the present world by a series of intermediary stages that must be negotiated by means of spiritual transformation or visionary insight (7:1–6; 14:2–12).

The author seems to be situated on the periphery of an orthodox Hellenistic Christian community that treasured the tradition of Jesus' sayings and that stressed such traditional theological concepts as the Eucharist (1:6; 8:3), the crucifixion of Jesus, and the descent into Hades (2:1). On the other hand, Christianity's Jewish roots are marginalized in this gospel, for the author is unsure how Jews fit into God's plan and questions whether they will even be acceptable to God on the day of judgment (14:9).

The Gospel of the Savior

1 [. . .] the empire [. . . *3 lines lost* . . .²] heaven's empire at your right hand.
³Congratulations to whoever dines with me in heaven's empire. ⁴You are the salt of the earth and the lamp that lights the world. ⁵Do not sleep or slumber [. . . *2 lines lost* . . .⁶] in the garment of the empire, which I bought with the blood of the grape.

Andrew replied, "Master [. . . *23 lines lost* . . .]

2 If I have cared for the things of the world, it is also fitting that I go down to Hades because of the souls bound there. ²Now, therefore, what is fitting [. . . *23 lines lost* . . .]

3 [. . .] everything with assurance. ²I myself will joyously reveal to you. ³For I know that you are able to do everything joyously. ⁴For the human being is unconditionally free [. . . *9 lines lost* . . .]

4 [. . .] Now, therefore, while you are in the body, do not let matter rule over you. ²Get up, let's leave this place because the one who will hand me over is near. ³And all of you will flee. ⁴And you will be offended by me. ⁵All of you will flee and leave me alone, but I do not remain alone because my Father is with me. ⁶I and my Father are a single one. ⁷For it is written,

> I will strike the shepherd and the sheep of the flock will be scattered.

⁸Yet I am the good shepherd. ⁹I will lay down my life for you. You also lay down your lives for your friends so that you might be pleasing to my Father. ¹⁰For no

1:2
ⓣ Mk 10:37, 40; Mt 20:21, 23
1:3
//Lk 14:15;
ⓣ Q 13:29, Mt 8:11; Lk 13:29
1:4
//Mt 5:13, 14; cf. Jn 8:12
1:6
◊Gen 49:11;
ⓣ Mk 14:23–25, Mt 26:27–29, Lk 22:18–20
ⓘ GSav 8:3
2:1
//1 Pet 3:19;
Pet 10:4–5
3:4
ⓣ Jn 8:36
4:1
ⓣ Mk 14:38, Gal 5:16–17
4:2
//Mk 14:42, Mt 26:46, Jn 14:31
4:4–5
//Jn 16:32
4:6
//Jn 10:30; cf. Jn 17:21
4:7
◊Zec 13:7;
//Mk 14:27, Mt 26:31
4:8–12
Cf. GSav 14:18
4:8
//Jn 10:11
4:9
ⓣ Jn 10:15–18, 15:13

1:1–2 *Heaven's empire* is equivalent to the more usual "God's empire." Matthew's gospel also prefers this terminology.

1:2 *Your* (plural) *right hand*: At whose right hand is unclear, but in this context it is likely that the expression refers to the apostles.

1:6 *garment of the empire*: In 14:8–9 robes are distributed in the throne room of the Father.

The *blood of the grape* is wine. It is a poetic reference to the blood of the Savior (see 8:3) and the Eucharist.

3:4 Being *unconditionally free* likely refers to liberation from the powerful urges of the flesh (see 4:1 and 13:15).

4:1 The saying affirms a body and spirit/soul dualism. It envisions an inner soul/spirit, which is the real person, inhabiting a material body. The apostles are urged to master the passions of their fleshly bodies (see 13:15).

4:2 Following the testing of the disciples in Gethsemane in Mark 14:42 and Matt 26:46, this command to the disciples *to leave this place* signals the commencement of the Passion of Jesus. In John 14:31, however, it is followed by a series of discourses (John 15–17). Like the Gospel of John, in the Gospel of the Savior the command is followed by a discourse. *This place* may be the Mount of Olives (Matt 26:30–46; Mark 14:26–42).

commandment is greater than this: that I lay down my life for humanity. ¹¹Because of this my Father loves me, for I completed his will. ¹²For I am divine; I became human because [. . . *12 lines lost* . . .]

5 [. . .] after how much time? ²Or if not, will you remember us, summon us, and take us out of the world, so that we may come to you? [. . . *25 lines lost* . . .]

6 [. . .] by sight. ²The Savior said to us, "O my holy members, my blessed seeds, [. . . *3 lines lost* . . .] pray [. . . *23 lines lost* . . .]

7 [. . .] upon the mountain and we too became like spiritual bodies. ²Our eyes opened up to every side, and the entire place was revealed before us. ³We approached the heavens, and they rose up against each other. ⁴Those who watch the gates were disturbed. ⁵The angels were afraid, and they fled to the [. . .] They thought that they would all be destroyed. ⁶We saw our Savior after he broke through all the heavens. [⁷. . .] foot [. . .] of the [. . . *11 lines lost* . . .]

8 [. . . *4 pages lost* . . .] the one who will [. . .] I will [. . .] him myself. Amen. ²he one who [. . .] to me [. . .] I [. . .] will cause him [. . .] with me. Amen. [. . .] ³The one who does not receive my body and my blood is a stranger to me. Amen. [⁴. . .] to him complete [. . . *23 lines lost* . . .]

9 You are the [. . .] since [. . .] cross [. . .] Amen. [². . .] cast a shadow over [. . .] namely, those on the right apart from those on the left [. . .] cross [. . .] will release [. . .] for [. . . *15 lines lost* . . .]

4:11
ⓣ Jn 17:4

4:12
ⓣ Jn 1:1–18, Phil 2:5–11

5:1–2
ⓣ Jn 14:1–5, 18

6:2
ⓣ GSav 12:10; cf. 1 Cor 6:15, 12:12–31; Rom 12:4–5; Eph 5:30

7:1–7
ⓣ 2 Cor 12:1–4

7:1
ⓣ 1 Cor 15:35–50

7:4
ⓣ Dn 4:10–20

8:3
Cf. Jn 6:51–57; ⓘ GSav 1:6

9:2 Perhaps 20:2–4 is meant to follow immediately after 9:2, after a lapse of several lines.

6:2 *My holy members* and *blessed seeds* are the Savior's designations for the apostles. In Matthew's explanation of the allegory of the Good Seed and Weeds (Matt 13:24–30), the Human One sows the good seed, the field is the world, and the good seed are the sons of the empire of Heaven (Matt 13:37–38).

7:1–7 Heavenly journeys are common in ancient religious texts. Paul, for example, describes such a journey to the third heaven (2 Cor 12:2) "whether in the body or out of the body I do not know; God knows." In GSav 7:1–7 the apostles are transformed and take such a journey through the heavens. It is not clear whether this is "in the body or out of the body" (i.e., a vision). Their presence caused a great tumult (7:3–5). The Savior apparently prepared the way through the heavens, disturbing those who guard the gates of each heaven.

7:1 The *mountain* might be the Mount of Transfiguration, where Jesus was transformed and Moses and Elijah appeared with him (Mark 9:2–8; Matt 17:1–8; Luke 9:28–36). However, it could also be the Mount of Olives (see note to GSav 4:2).

8:1–3 Each saying concludes with *Amen*, as a solemn affirmation. It is unclear whether it is spoken by the Savior or by the apostles.

8:3 Only those who participate in the Eucharist are members of the Savior (cf. 6:2).

9:2 Perhaps this is an eschatological sorting of humanity (as in Matt 25:31–33) as a result of the efficacy of the cross (i.e., the crucifixion), which is modeled on the two thieves between whom Jesus was crucified (Luke 23:32–43, cf., Mark 15:27–32; Matt 27:38–44; John 19:18).

10 [. . .] Do not weep, O [. . .] but rather rejoice, and understand [. . .] Lord, since he [. . .] ²For [. . .] and he will [. . .] Amen. [³. . .] the second [. . . *22 lines lost* . . .]

11 [. . .] they looked toward you, one mocking and deriding; another weeping, mourning, and wailing. ²You were eager for me, O cross; I also will be eager for you. [. . . *17 lines lost* . . .]

12 [. . .] see them. ²Therefore, do not be disturbed if you see me. ³We said to him, "Master, in what form will you reveal yourself to us, or in what kind of body will you come? Tell us."

⁴John replied, saying: "Master, when you come to reveal yourself to us, do not reveal yourself in all your glory, but change your glory into another glory so that we can bear it, lest we see you and despair from fear" [. . .]

⁵And the Savior replied [. . .] to you this [. . .] before which you are afraid, in order that you might see and believe. ⁶But, indeed, do not touch me until I go up to my Father, who is your Father, and my God, who is your God, and my Lord, who is your Lord. ⁷And whoever is near me will burn. ⁸I am the fire that blazes; ⁹whoever is near me is near the fire; whoever is far from me is far from life. ¹⁰Now then, gather to me, O my holy members, for [. . .] you [. . . *1 line lost* . . .]

13 [. . .] namely the Savior, before he [. . . *1 line lost* . . .] to him. ²He said to us, "As for me, I am among you as a child." ³He said "Amen. A little longer am I among you." ⁴He replied, "Amen [. . .] the plan against me [. . . *2 lines lost* . . .] after me, for I am a stranger to him. ⁵Therefore, now listen up, I suffer because of the sins of the world. ⁶But I rejoice over you, for you have continued well in

10:1
//GSav 13:13
11:1
Ⓣ Mk 15:18–20, 29–31;
Mt 27:29–31, 39–41;
Lk 23:27, 35–39, 48
12:4
Ⓣ Phil 3:21
12:5
Ⓣ Jn 20:29
12:6
//Jn 20:17
12:9
//Th 82;
Ⓣ Lk 12:49;
Th 10, 16:1–2
12:10
Ⓣ GSav 6:2
13:2
Ⓣ Judas 1:5
13:3
//Jn 16:6
13:5
Ⓣ 1 Pet 3:18

10:3 Perhaps 19:1–3 is meant to follow immediately after 10:3, after a lapse of several lines.

11:1 This might be the reaction of those who witnessed the suffering of Jesus.

11:2 In contrast to the reluctant Jesus of Gethsemane when faced with the cross, the Savior in this text is eager for the cross.

12:1–4 The apostles are disturbed that the Savior's appearance in all his glory might be harmful to them (see Exod 33:18–23).

12:7–8 In the Old Testament, *fire* is associated with both the presence and protection of God (Exod 3:2–4, 13:21–22; Zech 2:4–5), as well as with God's judgment (Gen 19:24, Deut 4:24).

13:2 The Savior is again speaking to the apostles. Several ancient texts present Jesus as a child.

13:3–4 Both times *Amen* seems to be uttered by the Savior in solemn affirmation of his imminent death.

13:4 The Savior did not originate in the natural world and hence is a *stranger* to it (see John 1:1–2, 10).

13:5 *sins of the world*: perhaps the control of the inner person through human passions, which the Savior makes possible to break by his own Passion; see 4:1 and 13:14.

the world. [⁷. . .] therefore, in order that you may be useful to me, and I will rejoice over your work. ⁸I am the king. Amen. I am the son of the king. Amen. I am [. . . *4 lines lost* . . .] ⁹And you did not have [. . .] Amen. ¹⁰I contend for you; you too take up the fight. Amen. ¹¹I am sent; I also wish to send you. Amen. [¹². . .] O [. . .] to you [. . .] I wish to announce to you joy for the world, but [. . .] concerning the world, since, indeed, you have not entered it. Amen. ¹³Do not weep from now on but rejoice instead. Amen. ¹⁴I have overcome the world; do not then let the world overcome you. Amen. ¹⁵I have become free from the world; you become free from it too. Amen. [¹⁶. . .] will give me to drink [. . . *1 line lost* . . .] and [. . .] life and rest. Amen. ¹⁷I will be pierced with a lance in my side. ¹⁸Let him who saw bear witness. And his witness is true. Amen. [. . . *4 pages lost* . . .]

14 [. . .] from all the heavens. ²Then as for us apostles this world became as darkness before us. ³We became like those among the glorious Aeons. ⁴Our [. . .] of all the heavens as [. . .] commissioned us as apostles. ⁵And we saw our Savior after he attained to the fourth heaven. [. . . *6 lines lost* . . .] disturbance. ⁶The angels and the archangels fled. They are over the [. . .⁷. . .] the Cherubim [. . .] under the [. . . *1 line lost* . . .] even though they do not descend [. . . *6 lines lost* . . .⁸] they cast their crowns down before the throne of the Father. ⁹All the holy ones received their robes. [. . .¹⁰. . .] after [. . .] son [. . . *7 lines lost* ¹¹. . .] why are you weeping and distressed so that the entire angelic (army) is

---

13:8
ⓉJn 18:36–37;
Mk 15:2–3, 12,
18, 26;
Mt 27:11, 29, 42;
Lk 23:2, 3, 37;
Mt 25:34, 40

13:10
ⓉEph 6:10–17

13:11
//Jn 17:18, 20:21

13:12–15
Cf. Jn 15:18–19

13:12
//Lk 2:10

13:13
//GSav 10:1

13:14
//Jn 16:33

13:15
ⓉJn 8:36

13:16
Cf. Jn 19:28–30;
ⓉMk 15:36,
Mt 27:48,
Lk 23:36, Pet 5:2

13:17
Cf. Jn 19:34

13:18
//Jn 19:35;
cf. Jn 21:24

14:6
ⓉEz 10:1–22

14:8
//Rev 4:10

14:9
//Rev 6:11;
ⓘ GSav 1:5

13:16 The words *life and rest* also appear on a small fragment of this gospel: "[as for you] rest yourselves [by] the ⟨spring⟩ of [the water] of life." The original location of this fragment within the gospel cannot be determined.

13:8–18 A series of statements followed by *Amen*, which appears to be spoken by the apostles indicating their solemn agreement. However, it is also possible that the Amens are spoken by the Savior to add emphasis to his pronouncements, as in 13:3–4.

13:12–15 *the world*: In its first occurrence in v. 12 *the world* appears to mean its inhabitants to whom joy is announced (cf. Luke 2:10). In its second occurrence in v. 12, as well as in vv. 14–15, *the world* is used in a negative ethical sense to refer to the values opposed to the Savior.

13:12 *you have not entered it*: The *it* can refer to either *joy* or *world*.

13:16 *Will give me to drink* is likely a prediction of the drink the Savior would be offered on the cross (see Mark 15:36 and parallels).

13:17 In the Gospel of John this statement (John 19:34) is

made by the narrator in the description of the crucifixion, but here it is made by the Savior as a prediction.

13:18 In the Gospel of John this statement is a narrator's aside (John 19:35), but here it is made by the Savior.

14:2–12 This narrates a visionary journey by the apostles, as in 7:1–7.

14:3 *Aeons* refer to different things in texts influenced by Gnostic thought. Here the Aeons seem to be glorious ethereal angelic beings, or sanctified and transformed heroes like Moses and Elijah (see Mark 9:2–4).

14:4 *commissioned us as apostles*: This commissioning is similar to Paul's in that it involves a visionary experience (see Gal 1:15–16 and Acts 9:3–9).

14:11 The missing lines make it impossible to tell who is *weeping* or why it disturbs the angels.

disturbed?" ¹²He replied in this manner that [. . . *5 lines lost* ¹³. . .] to this [. . .]
"I am greatly distressed [. . .] kill [. . .] upon the people of Israel. ¹⁴O my Father,
if it is possible, let this cup pass by me. ¹⁵Let them [. . .] by another [. . .] those
who do [. . .] if they [. . .] Israel [. . . *7 lines lost* . . .] [¹⁶. . .] salvation [. . .] come
to the entire world. ¹⁷Then again the son knelt before his Father, saying "O my
Father [. . . *4 lines lost* . . .] ¹⁸I am ready to die with joy and pour out my blood
upon the human race. ¹⁹Yet I weep only for my beloved, Abraham, Isaac, and
Jacob, that they may be able to stand in the day of judgment. ²⁰I will sit upon
my throne and judge the world. ²¹They will say to me that [. . . *4 lines lost* . . .]
[. . . ²². . .] to me [. . . *1 line lost* . . .] shall [. . .] because of the glory that was
given to me upon the earth. ²³O my Father, if it is possible, let this cup pass by
me." [²⁴. . .] for the second time [. . .] son, and you [. . .]

*The sequence of the following fragments in the text is uncertain. Each fragment
is separated by extensive lost text.*

15 [. . .] the son [. . .] the third time, "O my Father, if [. . .]

16 [. . .] He [. . .] complete the service until [. . .] go to them [. . .]

17 [. . .] all [. . . *25 lines lost* . . .] prophet [. . .] he said to us, namely [. . .]
that no portion surpasses your own and there is no glory more exalted than your
own [. . . *28 lines lost* ². . .] the wood of [. . .]

18 [. . .] the strength [. . . *1 line lost* . . .] empire [. . . *28 lines lost* ². . .] shadow
[. . .] O Entirety of [. . .] good [. . .] O cross [. . . *18 lines lost* . . .] cross [. . . *5
lines lost* . . .] in three days, and I will take you to heaven with me, and teach
you. Since your desire [. . .]

14:14
//Mk 14:35–36, 39;
Mt 26:39, 42, 44;
Lk 22:41–42;
Ⓣ GSav 14:17, 23

14:17
Ⓣ GSav 14:14, 23

14:18
//Mk 14:24, Mt
26:28, Lk 22:20;
cf. GSav 4:8–12

14:19
Ⓣ Rom 9:1–5,
10:1–4

14:20
Ⓣ Mt 25:31–33,
Rev 20:11–12

14:22
Ⓣ Jn 13:31–32,
17:4–5

14:23
Ⓣ GSav 14:14, 17

15:1
Cf. Mk 14:41,
Mt 26:44

18:2
Ⓣ Mk 8:31

14:13–24 A description of the Savior's struggle in Gethsemane; see Matt 26:36–46.

14:14 In GSav the Savior prays three times that the *cup pass him by* (14:14, probably 14:17, and 14:23). This matches Matthew, where Jesus prays three times that the cup pass him by (Matt 26:39, 42, 44). In Mark Jesus is represented as praying the prayer twice (Mark 14:36, 39). Between Mark 14:40 and 41 Mark does not refer to a third prayer, but does have Jesus return to the sleeping disciples a third time. Luke represents Jesus as praying the prayer once (Luke 22:41).

14:19 The son *weeps* for Abraham, Isaac, and Jacob that they will be able "to stand" before the Lord on the day of Judgment; that is, that they will be accepted by God (see for example Ps 24:3–6).

15–18 The vocabulary and subject matter of 15–18 are consistent with the text of the larger fragments, but lack of context makes commentary speculative.

19 [². . .] but I am rich. I will fill you with my wealth. ³A little longer, O cross, and that which is lacking is perfected, and that which is diminished is full. A little longer, O cross, and that which fell arises. A little longer, O cross, and all the Plenitude is perfected. [. . .]

20 [. . . *22 lines lost* . . .] to you [. . .] Amen [. . . *26 lines lost* . . .] [². . .] first [. . .] rise up [. . .] O cross, [. . .] to you [. . .] exalted among [. . .] for this is your desire, O cross. ³Do not be afraid; I am rich. I will fill you with my wealth. I will get up on you, O cross.

⁴They will be more numerous than you [. . .].

Twelve additional fragments have a few words legible; seven others have no certain words legible.

19:3 *Plenitude* translates the Greek word *Pleroma,* which appears regularly in texts associated with Gnosticism to designate the heavenly realm. In Gnostic mythology a breach occurs in the Plenitude and particles of the divine world are captured in the material realm. The Gnostic myth describes the recovery of those particles by various means to bring the heavenly realm to its original fullness or completeness. In the New Testament, Plenitude describes divinity (John 1:16; Eph 3:19; Col 1:19, 2:9).

20:3 In GSav, the Savior's death on the cross fills up the lack in the world and restores the Fullness (see 19:1–3).

The Mystical Gospel of Mark

Introduction

The Mystical Gospel of Mark is a version of the Gospel of Mark that was in use in Alexandria at least by the first quarter of the second century. It differs from the standard version of Mark in that it has additional passages, which were intended only for those who had attained a higher degree of initiation into the church than the common crowd. It was, apparently, a version of Mark intended only for insiders.

Discovery

Until 1958 the Mystical Gospel of Mark was unknown to the modern world. In that year, while cataloguing manuscripts at the famous Mar Saba monastery near Jerusalem, Morton Smith discovered a fragment of a previously unknown letter of Clement of Alexandria (ca. 150–215 CE). This letter fragment mentions the Mystical Gospel and contains two excerpts from the mysterious text. Were it not for this meager evidence, the Mystical Gospel of Mark would have remained lost.

The title

Morton Smith named this gospel the "Secret Gospel of Mark," the title by which it has been most widely known. Clement called the gospel *mystikon*, the Greek word that Smith translated as "secret," but "mystical" is more accurate. In Clement's usage, *mystikon* refers to the hidden ("mystical") meanings of scripture that can be revealed through allegorical interpretation. In referring to this text as Mark's *mystikon* gospel, therefore, Clement did not mean that it needed to be kept secret, but that it contained more teachings with allegorical meaning than did Mark's "other" gospel. The new name, the "Mystical Gospel of Mark," restores Clement's meaning.

Authenticity

From the time Smith published Clement's letter in 1973 some scholars have doubted its authenticity, with a few accusing Smith of fraud and forgery, no doubt because some of the contents of the letter can be interpreted erotically. However, the weight of evidence for forgery is weak. In 2009 the Jesus Seminar voted by a strong majority that the Mystical Gospel was not forged by Smith.

The scholarly controversy continues, however, and might never be decisively resolved.

The Clementine fragment

The Clementine letter fragment was found in the back of an edition of the letters of Ignatius of Antioch published in 1646, copied hastily onto the final page and the inside back cover of the book. Learned monks traveling to distant monasteries and libraries commonly took notes in this manner, quickly recording unexpected discoveries on the unused pages of a book to be transported home, where they might be studied more carefully. The handwriting can be dated to around 1750.

The letter is addressed to a certain Theodore, unknown to us outside the letter. Apparently Theodore has come into contact with a group of Carpocratians from whom he has learned of a Mystical Gospel of Mark containing teachings not found in the more public version known to Theodore. It seems that Theodore has even been shown a copy of this mysterious book, for Clement's letter intends to answer his inquiries about the veracity of some of its stories.

Clement's response is most interesting. He begins with an account of how, after migrating from Rome to Alexandria following the death of Peter, Mark revised his gospel to include "whatever would be appropriate for those who are advancing with respect to knowledge (*gnosis*)," and "of which he knew that the interpretation would initiate the hearers into the shrine of the truth that is hidden by seven veils." This account is dependent partly on the legends about Mark communicated by Papias, and partly on local traditions about the origins of the Mystical Gospel itself. However, it is important insofar as it indicates that the Alexandrian church did in fact have two versions of Mark in Clement's day, a "public Mark," thought to have been written in Rome with a more general audience in mind, and a revised version, a "Mystical Mark," allegedly written in Alexandria for a narrow circle of initiates.

Clement goes on to say that not all of what Theodore has related to him concerning the book shown to him by the Carpocratians actually comes from the Mystical Mark used in Clement's church. He therefore charges that Carpocrates must have added unauthorized material of his own, as Clement himself puts it: "mixing the immaculate and sacred words with most shameless lies." This is where the letter becomes most intriguing, for in order to prove his point to Theodore, Clement cites two of the added passages from the "real" Mystical Gospel of Mark so that Theodore can compare them to the passages he has seen in the Carpocratian version and see the difference for himself.

The Mystical Gospel fragments

The first passage is a story of how Jesus miraculously raises a young man (*neaniskos*) who has recently died, at the behest of his bereaved sister. According to Clement, the story was added to Mark between verses 10:34 and 10:35. The story bears a striking resemblance to the raising of Lazarus in the Gospel of John (John 11:1–44). However, since it shows none of the typical marks of Johannine redaction which so strongly color the story about Lazarus, it is unlikely that the Mystical Mark story is directly dependent upon its Johannine parallel. For its part, the version of the story from Mystical Mark has its own peculiarities not found in John, such as the initiation of the young man into the "mystery of the empire of God." The basic story, however, probably derives from the common stock of miracle stories available to both Mark and John, or their sources.

The second fragment is extremely brief, but nonetheless interesting. First, it mentions Salome, who appears in the New Testament elsewhere only in Mark (see 15:40 and 16:1). Secondly, when placed in the slot where Clement indicates it occurs in Mystical Mark (between 10:46a: "Then they came to Jericho," and 10:46b: "As he was leaving Jericho . . ."), it fills a well-known hole in the Markan narrative. The stop in Jericho now seems, in light of the Mystical Gospel, at least a little less futile.

These two fragments do not tell us much about the overall character of the Mystical Gospel of Mark. Whether Mystical Mark contained additional material not mentioned in Clement's letter is not known. If there was more to this gospel, for the present it is lost. Still, we may know more about the Mystical Gospel of Mark that one would initially assume.

Mystical Mark and canonical Mark

One question in the ongoing debate about the Mystical Gospel of Mark is the relationship between what we have come to know as canonical Mark and the version of Mark known to Clement as the Mystical Gospel of Mark. It is clear that what we have come to know as canonical Mark did not reach its final form until relatively late, probably sometime in the second century. This may be deduced from the fact that although both Matthew and Luke made use of a version of Mark as a source in the composition of their respective versions of the gospel, occasionally one encounters an episode, or simply details, in the canonical Markan narrative which neither Matthew nor Luke have included. Rather than assume that by coincidence both Matthew and Luke, independently of one another, chose to alter Mark's story in precisely the same way, scholars have tended to argue that such differences arose when later editors changed the Gospel of Mark after Matthew and Luke had already made use of it. That is to say, Matthew and Luke did not use what we have come to know as the canonical Gospel of Mark, but rather an earlier version of it. Clement's account, which speaks of various versions of Mark known in the second century, generally confirms this view. But more than this, it raises the question of the possible relationship between our canonical Mark and Clement's Mystical Gospel of Mark, for there are a number of affinities between later editorial developments in canonical Mark and the fragments of Mystical Mark quoted by Clement. The most striking similarity concerns the mysterious figure of a young man (*neaniskos*) who appears in canonical Mark in the scene of Jesus' arrest in the Garden of Gethsemane, dressed only in a linen cloth draped about his naked body (14:51–52). (Neither Matthew nor Luke preserve any reference to this young man.) Since the role of this young man in the narrative of canonical Mark is utterly baffling, it is all the more significant that he is dressed in exactly the same way as the young man prepared for initiation in the first Mystical Mark fragment. This and other similarities between canonical Mark and the Mystical Mark fragments have led many to conclude that canonical Mark is not the direct descendent of that early version of Mark used by Matthew and Luke, but rather of the Mystical Gospel of Mark. In other words, what moderns have come to know as the Gospel of Mark is in fact a version of Mystical Mark from which some, but not all, of the esoteric passages have been removed. If this is true, then the Mystical Gospel of Mark will have provided us with some rather striking new information about the early transmission history of the Gospel of Mark.

The Mystical Gospel of Mark

Fragment 1: *To be located between Mark 10:34 and 10:35.* Clement to Theodore, *Folio 1, verso, line 23—Folio 2, recto, line 11.*

1 And they come into Bethany, and this woman was there whose brother had died. ²She knelt down in front of Jesus and says to him, "Son of David, have mercy on me." ³But the disciples rebuked her. ⁴And Jesus got angry and went with her into the garden where the tomb was. ⁵Just then a loud voice was heard from inside the tomb. ⁶Then Jesus went up and rolled the stone away from the entrance to the tomb. ⁷He went right in where the young man was, stuck out his hand, grabbed him by the hand, and raised him up. ⁸The young man looked at Jesus, loved him, and began to beg him to be with him. ⁹Then they left the tomb and went into the young man's house. (Incidentally, he was rich.)

¹⁰Six days later Jesus gave him an order; ¹¹and when evening had come, the young man went to him, dressed only in a linen cloth. ¹²He spent that night with him, because Jesus taught him the mystery of the empire of God. ¹³From there ⟨Jesus⟩ got up and returned to the other side of the Jordan.

Fragment 2: *To be located between Mark 10:46a ("Then they came to Jericho") and 10:46b ("As he was leaving Jericho . . ."). *Clement to Theodore, *Folio 2, recto, lines 14–16*

2 The sister of the young man whom Jesus loved was there, along with his mother and Salome, ²but Jesus refused to see them.

1:1
//Jn 11:1
1:4
Ⓣ Jn 11:38
1:6
Cf. Jn 11:39
1:7a
Ⓣ Mk 14:51, 16:5
1:12
Ⓣ Mk 4:11
2:1b
Ⓣ Mk 15:40, 16:1;
Th 61

1:7a This *young man* seems to play a rather important role in Mark. Most notably, his reappearance in the empty tomb announcing Jesus' resurrection suggests that this story of his own resurrection serves to foreshadow Jesus'.

1:7b The action is comparable to that found in Mark 5:41 and 9:27.

1:7c *Grabbed him by the hand* could be linked with what follows in v. 8, rather than with what precedes: "Grabbing him by the hand, the young man . . ."

1:10 *gave him an order:* The meaning of the Greek is obscure; it may imply that Jesus gave the young man instructions.

1:11 *dressed only in a linen cloth:* The text reads literally: "a linen cloth having been draped over the naked body." The Markan "young man" appears so dressed also in Mark 14:51. The significance of the linen cloth worn over a naked body is a longstanding riddle in Markan scholarship. It may be some sort of early Christian baptismal garb. Hippolytus, *Apostolic Tradition* 21.11, specifies that in the ceremony of baptism both the catechumen and the presbyter are to stand in the water naked.

2:1 The *young man* is the same one as in the first fragment.

Congratulations/Damn

The beatitudes take their name from the Latin term *beati*, used to translate the Greek word, *makarios*. The corresponding Hebrew word *is ashre*. What do these terms mean?

Congratulations. The traditional translation "blessed" lives on primarily in its connection with the Bible, apart from sayings like "bless you" when someone sneezes. In that context, "bless you" invokes God's care for the person coming down with a cold. In colloquial English, "bless" does not mean a declaration of God's favor.

The language of the beatitudes is performative: performative language means that the words accomplish what they say. When the minister says, "I now pronounce you husband and wife," that declaration makes it so. When the judge says, "I sentence you to six months in jail," that statement is the fact. Analogously, when Jesus says, "I declare you poor to be in God's special favor," that is a performative statement. In English we can achieve that sense by translating,

> Congratulations, you poor!/God's empire belongs to you.

"Blessed" is archaic language and now nearly empty of meaning. To translate "happy" or "fortunate" is to introduce connotations that are not present: the poor and the hungry are not "happy" or "fortunate." Further, "happy" or "fortunate" misses the performative character of the language.

Damn. The traditional translation of the Greek interjection *ouai* is "woe." As a noun, a woe refers to a state of intense hardship or suffering of the dimensions of calamities or catastrophes. In the Book of Revelation, woes are cataclysmic events that bring wholesale destruction and condemnation. Woes are more like curses than the mild distress suggested by the English word "woe."

When Jesus says, "Woe to you, Chorazin! Woe to you, Bethsaida!" he is condemning them to a state of intense hardship or suffering (Matt 11:21). The parallel pronouncement in the same passage addresses Capernaum: "And you, Capernaum, you don't think you'll be exalted to heaven, do you? No, you'll go to Hell." The translators of SV concluded that "woe" ought, in contexts like this, to be given its due weight in English by using the English word, "damn." SV reads: "Damn you, Chorazin! Damn you, Bethsaida!" to make it parallel to the assignment of Capernaum to Hell

Traditional translations have avoided the word "damn" probably because it was unacceptable for liturgical use in the churches.

In Luke's version of the beatitudes, there follows a list of curses (Luke 6:24–25). In SV they read:

> Damn you rich! / You already have your consolation.
> Damn you who are well-fed now! / You will know hunger.
> Damn you who laugh now! / You will learn to weep and grieve.

Like the term "congratulations!," damn is performative language: it is like pronouncing sentence on a convicted criminal.

The Egerton Gospel

Introduction

The remains of the Egerton Gospel, named after the Englishman who funded the purchase of the papyrus fragments on which it is preserved, were first published in 1935; one more small portion, Papyrus Köln 255, was discovered and published in 1987. The extant text includes miracle stories, controversy dialogues, and incidents of violence toward Jesus, none of which is wholly preserved. A story in which Jesus miraculously causes vegetative growth and some sayings are unparalleled in other early Christian texts.

Relationship with other gospels

The Egerton Gospel bears some resemblance to the Gospel of Peter and to the story of the adulteress found in late manuscripts of John and Luke, but its closest counterparts are the canonical gospels. The relationship of Egerton to the canonical gospels has long posed a problem for biblical scholars. On the one hand, some scholars have maintained that Egerton's unknown author composed by borrowing from the canonical gospels. This solution has not proved satisfactory for several reasons. The most important reason is that Egerton Gospel's parallels to the synoptic gospels lack editorial language peculiar to the synoptic authors, Matthew, Mark, and Luke. In addition, Egerton's parallels lack features that are common to the synoptic gospels, a difficult fact to explain if those gospels were Egerton's source.

The Egerton Gospel does have very close parallels to John, but because Egerton's versions of these parallels show less development than John's, Egerton may preserve earlier forms of the tradition.

On the other hand, suggestions that the Egerton Gospel served as a source for the authors of Mark and/or John also lack conclusive evidence. The most likely explanation for the Egerton Gospel's similarities to and differences from the canonical gospels is that Egerton's author made independent use of traditional sayings and stories of Jesus that also were used by the other gospel writers. The author combined these elements with other stories and speech material to compose an independent narrative gospel.

Egerton and the formation of the gospels

Although the document's fragmentary state does not permit scholars to determine its exact connection to similar texts, the Egerton Gospel can offer insight

417

into ways the narrative gospels emerged. It provides significant evidence about early variations in the formulation and transmission of written or oral traditions about Jesus. As an analogue to the canonical gospels, Egerton offers independent documentation for the long-held scholarly view that evangelists preserved fairly fixed units of traditional material but freely arranged them into independent literary frameworks. Egerton's contents also suggest that there was early contact between Christian groups that preserved synoptic sources and those that preserved Johannine sources, conceivably before the divergence of these two branches in early Christianity.

Date and provenance

The lone papyrus manuscript of the Egerton Gospel comes from Egypt and probably was copied in the second half of the second century, making it one of the earliest extant Christian manuscripts. The original document perhaps was composed near Palestine/Syria in the second half of the first century, approximately at the same time that the related narrative gospels were being drafted. Like the Gospel of John, the Egerton Gospel probably circulated among Jewish followers of Jesus experiencing strong opposition from fellow Jews who rejected their claims about Jesus.

The Egerton Gospel

Because of the fragmentary condition of the Egerton papyrus, many of its Greek letters and words are not completely visible. However in the translation below, for the sake of readability, missing material is enclosed in square brackets only in those instances where scholars are in significant doubt about how the text should be restored.

1 [. . .] **to the legal experts** [. . .] everyone who acts unjustly [. . .] and not me [. . .] he does, how does he?

Jesus & the scriptures

²Turning to the rulers of the people, ⟨Jesus⟩ made this statement: "Pore over the scriptures. You imagine that in them there is life to be had. They do indeed give evidence on my behalf. ³Don't suppose that I've come to be your accuser before my Father. The one accusing you is Moses, the one you were relying on."

⁴They say, "We know God spoke to Moses. But you—we don't know [where you come from."]

⁵Jesus replied: "Now you stand accused for not trusting those who are [commended by ⟨Moses⟩.] ⁶If you had believed Moses, you would've believed me; after all, he [wrote] about me to your ancestors."

[. . .⁷. . .] stones together [. . .] him [. . .]

1:4 *[where you come from]:* The Greek letters are completely lost, so the restoration is based on the parallel to John 9:29.

1:5 *Those who are [commended]* translates one possible restoration; "those who are [written about]" is another possible restoration.

1:6 *[wrote]* is a restoration based on the parallel to John 5:46; "spoke" is another possible restoration.

1:2
//Jn 5:39
1:3
//Jn 5:45
1:4
//Jn 9:29
1:5
Ⓣ Jn 12:31
1:6
//Jn 5:46
1:7
Cf. Jn 8:59, 10:31

1:1 Although several words can be made out in these lines, the manuscript lacks sufficient legible material to connect them with much confidence. The lines seem to have contained a statement made by Jesus to legal experts.

1:3 Jesus ironically denies a role as accuser here just before he raises an accusation against his opponents. He attributes the accusation to Moses, who was understood by some Jews to play the role of a heavenly advocate for them before God. Jesus contends that Moses' role is more like that of a prosecutor than that of a defense attorney.

my Father: The parallel verse in John has "the Father," which is more characteristic of John (and Thomas) than Egerton's term. "My Father" is found elsewhere in John, also in Q 10:22, Thom 99, and several times in Matthew and Luke. Matthew often embellishes the phrase as "my heavenly Father" or the like. Mark has no instances of "my Father."

1:5 The identity of *those commended by Moses* is uncertain. The phrase could refer to prophetic successors of Moses who are mentioned in Deut 18:15–22.

1:6 *he [wrote] about me to your ancestors:* Moses was thought to be the author of the Pentateuch, which Christians believed to contain predictive prophecies fulfilled in Jesus.

1:7 An indefinite number of lines is missing in the manuscript between 1:6 and 1:7. It is not certain that the threatened violence of 1:7–8 follows immediately upon the heated exchange of 1:2–6, but it is likely because Jesus' opponents are mentioned as rulers in both sections. Although several words can be made out in these lines, the manuscript lacks sufficient legible material to connect them with much confidence. They probably contained a narrative description of an attempt to stone Jesus.

[8][The rulers] laid their hands on him to arrest him and [turn him] over to the crowd. [9]But they couldn't arrest him because the time for him to be turned over hadn't yet arrived. [10]So the Master himself slipped through their hands and got away.

2 Just then a leper comes up to him and says, "Teacher Jesus, in wandering around with lepers and eating with them in the inn, I became a leper myself. [2]If you want to, I'll be made clean."

[3]The Master said to him, "Okay—you're clean!" And immediately his leprosy vanished from him. [4]Jesus says to him, "Go and have the priests examine ⟨your skin⟩. Then offer for your purification what Moses commanded—and no more sinning." [. . .]

3 They come to him and interrogate him as a way of putting him to the test. [2]They ask, "Teacher, Jesus, we know that you are [from God], since the things you do put you above all the prophets. [3]Tell us, then, is it permissible to pay to rulers what is due them? Should we pay them or not?"

[4]Jesus knew what they were up to, and became indignant. [5]Then he said to them, "Why do you pay me lip service as a teacher, but not [do] what I say? [6]How accurately Isaiah prophesied about you when he said,

---

1:8 *[turn him] over:* The number of missing letters is uncertain and another suggested restoration is "throw him to."
3:2 *[from God]:* The letters are completely lost, so the restoration is based on the loose parallel to John 3:2.
3:5 *[do]:* Another possible restoration is "hear."

1:9 Jesus' *time* is a highly developed theme in John, referring to the decisive moment of history when the Son of God's crucifixion becomes his exaltation. But Egerton's use of the term "time" shows no such development and so does not suggest that a divine plan for salvation is at work. Popular notions about a proper time for a person's destiny may underlie Egerton's understanding of the time of Jesus' arrest here.
2:1 The man's social contact with lepers and indeed his approach to Jesus violate Jewish customs. According to Lev 13:45–46 lepers were supposed to be isolated for fear that their impurity was contagious. Unlike the accounts in Mark, Matthew, and Luke, in Egerton the leper makes no gesture of submission to Jesus when he approaches him.
Teacher Jesus: This term of address for Jesus is unique to the Egerton Gospel.
2:2 *If you want to, I'll be made clean:* Egerton's wording of the request is different from that found in Mark, Matthew, and Luke all of whom have: "If you want to, you can make me clean."

2:4 Jesus' series of instructions to the leper in Egerton are completely coherent with Jewish law. Rules for priestly examinations of lepers are found in Lev 13:1–59. Ritual offerings for purification are specified in Lev 14:1–32.

Jesus' command for the man not to sin again implies that his offense consists in not abiding by the Jewish custom of avoiding contact with unclean people such as lepers.

Egerton's account lacks the first command given in Mark, Matthew, and Luke in which Jesus tells the leper to speak to no one.
3:1 *They:* The identity of those who approach Jesus is completely lost. They are no doubt Jewish and could be rulers, like those who argued with Jesus and tried to arrest him in the earlier episodes. Their way of engaging Jesus suggests that they are learned authorities with special interest in the Law.
3:2 In the context of the Egerton fragments it is a reasonable guess that *the things you do* refer to Jesus' miracles. The two that are mentioned are the healing of a leper and a miracle of growth at the Jordan.

This people honors me with their lips,

> but their heart stays far away from me.

Their worship of me is empty,

> [because they insist on teachings that are human] regulations.

[. . .]

4 [. . .] **confined** [. . .] has been subjected uncertainly [. . .] its weight unweighed [. . .] ²As they were perplexed at this strange question, Jesus walked over and stood at the bank of the Jordan River. ³He extended his right hand, [took water,] and scattered it over the [. . .] ⁴And then [. . .] [scattered] water [. . .] the [. . .] and it [became full] before their eyes and produced fruit [. . .] [much] [. . .] into [. . .] [them]

4:3–4 The text of the story about miraculous fruit has been restored in various ways, none of which is entirely convincing. Some reconstructions are translated here.

Milne: ". . . and stretching out his right hand, he took grain and sowed it on the river and then, taking water that had been sown, he cast it down on the ground and it was filled before them and brought forth fruit."

Dodd: ". . . and stretching out his right hand, he filled it with water and sprinkled it upon the shore; and thereupon the sprinkled water made the ground moist, and it was watered before them and brought forth fruit."

Lagrange: ". . . stretching out his right hand he filled it with soil and sowed wheat on the soil. And then he poured over it flowing water. The seed penetrated the ground and was raised up before them and it produced fruit."

Daniels: ". . . and after stretching out his right hand, he took water and sprinkled it upon the tree. And then accordingly he anointed the dry fig tree with the water that had been sprinkled, and it became full before them and he brought forth a fruit."

4:3 *[took water]* is an uncertain restoration. Another possible restoration of the verb is "filled." What Jesus took or filled is lost but the most common suggestion besides water is "seed."

4:4 *[scattered] water* is an uncertain restoration.

[became full]: Other possible restorations are "was watered" and "rose up."

[. . .] [much] [. . .] into [. . .] [them] [. . .]: The fragmentary condition of these lines permits no satisfactory restoration.

4:2
◊2 Kgs 2:13
4:4
◊Nm 17:1–11

4:1 Although several words can be made out in these lines, the manuscript lacks sufficient legible material even to guess at how they should be connected. They probably contained the *strange question* which perplexes unidentifiable people in the next verse.

4:3–4 The verbs in the story are fairly well preserved; what is missing are nouns that would permit one to see what is taking place. It is clear that Jesus approached the Jordan, stood at the water's edge, stretched out his hand, took something, and scattered something. What he took and what he scattered must be guessed at. One more action of Jesus is unclear, but in the end something, probably one or more plants, became full and produced fruit. Whatever he has done in the story, Jesus appears to have produced instantaneous growth.

4:3 *Scattered* could be translated more literally as "sowed."

5 if [. . .] him [. . .] knowing [. . .]

6 [. . .] we are one [. . .] I stay [. . .] stones into [. . .] they kill [. . .] says [. . .]

6
Cf. Jn 10:30

5 The fragmentary condition of these lines permits no satisfactory restoration.
6 The fragmentary condition of these lines permits no satisfactory restoration.

---

6 It is possible that Jesus makes a controversial statement parallel to John 10:30 that is followed by threatened violence, perhaps an attempt to stone him, as above in 1:7–8.

Scholar

In the ancient world a *scholar* was someone who could read and write. Since that ability was uncommon, scholars functioned as secretaries in writing letters, framing petitions, and copying documents for ordinary people who could not read or write.

The term was also frequently used to refer to those who were learned in other respects. Scholars served as high government officials, royal viceroys, or assistants to sages and prophets, as in the case of Baruch's relationship to Jeremiah (Jer 36:32). The traditional translation, "scribe," seems archaic to users of English today, so the SV translators decided to employ a more contemporary word.

In the gospels, the scholars are usually represented as opposing Jesus. They are sometimes associated with the high priest and elders, sometimes with Pharisees. They were probably versed in the Law and rhetoric, so they knew how to conduct an argument over fine points in the Law in public debate. Jesus is pictured as sparring with them on numerous occasions. Once Jesus says, "Damn you, scholars," and calls them impostors and phonies (Matt 23:13).

Since scholars are responsible for the Scholars Version and are versed in the language and interpretation of the gospels, it seems appropriate that they should bear part of the brunt of Jesus' criticism. After all, those exempt from criticism have risked nothing and so have gained nothing.

Gospel Oxyrhynchus 840

Introduction

Nature of the fragment

Gospel Oxyrhynchus 840 is an excerpt from an otherwise unknown narrative gospel that is quite similar to the New Testament gospels in its style and tone. Jesus is shown in Jerusalem with his disciples, arguing over issues of ritual purity in a manner familiar to readers of Matthew 15 or Mark 7, though there the case centers on rituals connected with eating, rather than the need for purification before approaching the temple. There is very little in the fragment to help us place it historically or to label it theologically. It is a bit unusual that Jesus is called "savior" instead of "master" or "teacher" (the Samaritan converts of John 4:42 call Jesus "savior of the world"). An educated guess for the date of composition is sometime before 200 CE; a more precise dating may be impossible unless the fragment could be identified with another known text.

Contents of the fragment

Most of the fragment involves a dispute over true purity held in the temple precincts of Jerusalem between Jesus and a chief priest. The top of the first page of the fragment, however, begins with the conclusion of a preceding episode, where Jesus is exhorting his followers to avoid doing evil and thus escape divine judgment. Then he takes his disciples somewhere within the temple area, into a place called the "purification," provoking a rebuke from a priest, since his followers have not purified themselves before entering this sacred court. Jesus' partner in the dispute is both a Pharisee and a chief priest—an historically unusual combination, to be sure, but not unlike the typical sort of generic opponent of Jesus found in the New Testament stories. Jesus counters by questioning whether the priest has himself really been purified by ritual bathing—after all, thoroughly unclean people (called dogs and swine, prostitutes and entertainers) do this same sort of external washing. Only the "life-giving water" can truly purify.

Circumstance of discovery

British archaeologists uncovered this fragment over a century ago at Oxyrhynchus in Upper Egypt, the same place that the famous "Sayings of the Lord" were found, now known to be part of the Gospel of Thomas. The fragment consists of a single small leaf of vellum, measuring just 8.8 by 7.4 cm., with a writing surface barely two inches wide. A total of forty-five lines survives more or less complete on the two sides of the page. The script used dates most likely to the fourth century CE. The writing was decorated with red ink, used to outline the first letters of sentences, punctuation marks, and strokes used to mark the abbreviation of sacred names. The book itself likely served as an amulet for some ancient Egyptian Christian before this single page became detached. A few other books of similar size have been found from late Antiquity that are thought to have been intended for some such magical use.

Gospel Oxyrhynchus 840

1 [. . .] **before he commits** a crime, he plans carefully. ²But you should be on guard so that you don't suffer a similar fate. ³After all, those who commit crimes against humanity not only get ⟨their due⟩ in this life, they also will have to endure punishment and repeated torture ⟨in the next life⟩.

Planning ahead

Dispute over defilement

2 And taking ⟨the disciples⟩ along, he led them into the inner sanctuary itself, and began walking around in the temple area.

²This Pharisee, a chief priest, Levi by name, also entered, ran into them, and said to the Savior, "Who gave you permission to wander around in this inner sanctuary and lay eyes on these sacred vessels, when you haven't performed your ritual bath, and your disciples haven't even washed their feet? ³You're in an unclean condition and yet you've invaded this sacred place, which is ritually clean. No one walks around in here, or dares lay eyes on these sacred vessels, unless they've taken a bath and changed their clothes."

⁴And right away the Savior stood up, with his disciples, and replied, "Since you're here in the temple, I take it you're clean."

1:3 The phrase *in this life* is a slight but significant correction of the ms, which reads literally "among the animals."

2:2 The name *Levi* is only partially preserved and may not be original.

1:1 The fragment begins toward the end of a passage about an evildoer who plans ahead but will nonetheless be caught up in divine judgment. Presumably the point of the story lay somewhere between Jesus' parables of poor planning (such as the Two Builders in Q 6:48–49 or the Rich Farmer in Luke 12 and Thom 63) and those of the King Going to War and the Tower Builder (Luke 14) or the Assassin (Thom 98), where individuals are shown planning ahead to good effect.

2:1 The phrase used for the *inner sanctuary* (*hagneuterion*, "purification") is otherwise unattested and thus suggests that the gospel writer was unfamiliar with the details of the temple's design. In any case, what is meant is a large open court rather than any particular inner room, and more specifically a place that can be entered only in a state of ritual purity. The most likely candidate is the area usually called the "Court of the Men of Israel." On the need for ritual purity see John 11:55; Josephus *War* 5.5 (227); *Apion* 2.8 (104).

2:2 The temple had a *chief priest* on duty charged with making sure that those who entered were ritually clean. The priest's further identity as *a Pharisee* connects him with other opponents of Jesus in the gospel tradition who dispute with him over questions of ritual.

The *sacred vessels* are the precious items used for libations in the temple service and kept in small rooms opening off of the Court of the Men of Israel.

The *ritual bath* was required to achieve a state of levitical purity. *Washing the feet* seems to have been the minimal cleansing required if a Jewish male was otherwise in a state of levitical purity. See John 13:10: "People who have bathed only have to wash their feet."

2:3 Priests on duty in the temple are known to have *changed their clothes* after bathing. This fragment is our only evidence that putting on new clothes was required of laymen too. This probably indicates that the author is not well informed about temple regulations.

2:4 As is characteristic throughout the gospel tradition, Jesus answers a challenge with a challenge of his own.

⁵He replies to ⟨the Savior⟩, "I am clean. I bathed in the pool of David, you know, by descending into it by one set of steps and coming up out of it by another. ⁶I also changed to white and ritually clean clothes. Only then did I come here and lay eyes on these sacred vessels."

⁷In response the Savior said to him: "Damn the blind who won't see. You bathe in these stagnant waters where dogs and pigs wallow day and night. ⁸And you wash and scrub the outer layer of skin, just like prostitutes and flute girls, who wash and scrub and perfume and paint themselves to entice men, while inside they are crawling with scorpions and filled with all sorts of corruption. ⁹But my disciples and I—you say we are unbathed—have bathed in living, life-giving water that comes down from [. . .] But damn those [. . .]"

2:7
ⓉMt 7:6,
Jn 9:40–41,
2 Pet 2:22, Rv 22:15

2:8
ⓉMk 7:1–23,
Q 11:39–40,
Mt 23:25–26,
Lk 11:39–40, Th 89

2:9
ⓉJn 4:10

2:9 Half a line is missing after the words *water that comes down from.*

2:5–6 The priest details the steps of his purification process. A large double pool found nearby the temple may have been used for this purpose (see "the pool of Bethesda" in John 5). The term *pool of David* is otherwise unattested.

2:7 *stagnant waters*: Because the Greek says literally that the water is "poured out," some scholars argue for the translation "running waters." However, in this context the water has been poured into a ritual bathing pool, so it is not flowing. The standing water in such artificial pools needs replenishment, unlike flowing or "living" streams. Jesus' reference to *dogs and pigs* is not meant literally, as though these animals were actually wallowing in the priests' ritual baths! Instead Jesus is pointing to thoroughly unclean sorts of people, as in Matt 7:6; see further 2 Pet 2:22 and Rev 22:15.
2:8 Jesus dismisses *washing and scrubbing* as mere external adornment, often covering up the evil inside. The sentiment

is similar to that found in Mark 7:1–23, Q 11:39–40, and Thom 89.

Flute girls were slaves who provided musical entertainment at male drinking parties (symposia). As slaves, these young women were sexually available to the guests, and so, like prostitutes (who were also slaves), were considered unclean.

Picturing moral corruption with *scorpions crawling inside* is reminiscent of invective addressed by Jesus elsewhere against the Pharisees (Matt 23:25). More commonly in biblical tradition, the presence or threat of scorpions suggests danger or unusually severe punishment (Deut 8:15; 1 Kgs 12:11, 14; Ezek 2:6; Luke 10:19; Rev 9:3, 5, 10).
2:9 Jesus contrasts ritual bathing with Christian baptism, called *living, life-giving water* from heaven. See also the note to John 4:10–11, to which this verse alludes.

Gospel Oxyrhynchus 1224

Introduction

Gospel Oxyrhynchus 1224 contains fragments of Jesus sayings. It was discovered in 1903 and published in 1914. It consists of two fragments from a Greek papyrus book whose handwriting dates to the early fourth or late third century.

Fragment 1 is very small, 3.5 x 4.3 cm., so that only three partial lines and three full words are visible on the front and two partial lines and one full word on the back. Fragment 2 is much larger, 6.3 x 13.1 cm., and has two columns on both sides. Judging from the page numbers on the two fragments, there are over thirty pages in between them. We cannot be certain, however, that both fragments are from the same work even though both were copied by the same scribe and we cannot presume that other works were not included before or even between those represented by the fragments.

The papyrus is badly mutilated with not even a single complete line anywhere extant. Restorations are therefore highly conjectural. The text does not seem to be dependent on the New Testament gospels since none of their redactional elements are discernible in its few verses. Furthermore, where New Testament parallels exist, it is hard to discern a reason for the papyrus' changes, if indeed those were its sources. As an independent gospel, it belongs, insofar as its fragmentary state allows us to see, not with discourse gospels involving the risen Jesus (e.g., the Secret Book of James and the Gospel of Mary), but with sayings gospels involving the earthly Jesus (e.g., Q and the Gospel of Thomas). The vision in 3:2 and the debates in 4:1–2 and 5:1–2 point to a format closer to Q than to Thomas. No opponents, for example, ever challenge Jesus in the few narrative situations in Thomas as they do here and in Q.

The date when the manuscript was copied tells little about the date of this gospel's composition. It could be as early as the 50s when Christians first began to create books about what Jesus had said and done.

Gospel Oxyrhynchus 1224

1 [. . .] in every [. . .] To you let me tell [. . .]

2 [. . .] you [. . .]

3 [. . .] weighed me down. ²And [standing] there Jesus [i]n a visio[n says,] "Why are you d[iscouraged]? For it is not [y]ou but the [. . .] gave [. . .]"

4 [. . . you s]aid not answer[ing.] ²["What then do you re]nounce? What is the ne[w] teach[ing that they say] you te[ach] or new [proclama]tion [you proclaim? Answ]er and [. . .]"

5 When the scholars an[d Pharise]es and priests observ[ed hi]m, they were indignant [because he reclined ⟨at table⟩ in the com]pany of sin[ners]. ²But Jesus overheard [them and said,] "Those who are he[althy don't need a doctor."]

3:2b The restoration of *discouraged* is little more than guesswork. The word is found in the NT only in Col 3:21.

4:2b The restoration is highly conjectural; *ne[w] teach[ing]* is suggested especially by the parallel in Mark 1:27.

4:2c The line can be restored with either *baptism* or *proclamation*. SV adopts *proclamation* because it continues the redundancy of *teaching/teach* of the previous clause into the parallel *proclamation/proclaim*.

5:1 The word *[Pharise]es* is restored on analogy with Mark 2:16, which has *the scholars of the Pharisees* criticizing Jesus in a similar situation. An alternative word, "[elder]s," is also possible.

5:2 This verse is restored to match Luke 5:31 which has *healthy* rather than *able-bodied* as in Mark 2:17 = Matt 9:12. But since only eight Greek letters remain on the page, very different restorations are possible, for instance, "hearing [that] the ph[onies were an]gry."

5:1–2
//Mk 2:15–17,
Mt 9:10–13,
Lk 5:29–32

1a The phrase *in every . . .* is found in the NT on the lips of Jesus only in Luke 21:36.

1b The phrase *To you let me tell* is never found on the lips of Jesus in the NT in that form, but always as "Let me tell you" (sixty times in the four gospels).

3:1 The verb *weighed down* is found in the NT in Matt 26:43; Luke 9:32; 21:34; 2 Cor 1:8; 5:4; 1 Tim 5:16. The first two cases involve being weighed down by sleep. The subject here is what: sleep? sorrow? fear?

3:2a Matt 17:9 describes the Transfiguration as a *vision*. The only other NT occurrences of the term are in Acts, three times in the phrase *in a vision*. Note that here the vision is given to the individual narrating the story.

4:2a *Renounce* occurs in the NT only in 2 Cor 4:2.

4:2c *proclamation*: The line can also be restored with "baptism" (see textual note above). In that case, on the analogy of Mark 1:4 = Luke 3:3 where John "proclaims a baptism," this excerpt would refer to the Baptizer. If it referred to Jesus, it would be an independent witness to Jesus himself as a baptizer.

5:1 The triple designation *scholars and Pharisees and priests* does not occur in the NT. If the alternative restoration "[elder]s" is adopted (see the textual note above), this phrase might have originally been an attempt to designate the three groups in the Sanhedrin: priests, elders, and scholars.

6 "[A]nd p[r]ay for your [ene]mies. For whoever is not [against y]ou is on your side. ²[Whoever today i]s at a distance, tomorrow will [b]e [near you] and in [. . .] of the advers[ary]"

6:1a
//Q 6:27–28,
Mt 5:44, Lk 6:27–28

6:1b
//Mk 9:40, Lk 9:50

6:2
Cf. Q 11:23,
Mt 12:30,
Lk 11:23

6:2 The restoration of this verse is highly conjectural.

6:1a This aphorism appears as *love your enemies* in Q 6:27–28, 35. However, in versions of the saying that depend on the NT gospels (Did 1:3 and Polycarp's Letter to the Philippians 12:3), it was changed to *pray for your enemies,* as here. The present form might be taken as a softening of a too difficult injunction, but it probably is at least its equivalent, if not its more specific and practical intensification.

6:1b This aphorism appears, opening with a Greek participle, as *not with me = against me* in Q 11:23. It appears, opening with a Greek relative pronoun, as *not against you = on your side* in Mark 9:40 = Luke 9:50. The GOxy 1224 version, however, has the participial opening, as in Q, and the *not against you = on your side* as in Mark. This is an indication that GOxy 1224 did not use any of the NT gospels as a written source.

6:2 The aphorism in 6:1 has a two-verse formulation with *not with me = against me* and *not gather = scatters* in Q 11:23. In Q the verses are parallel in form and content, and the second verse might have been created on the analogy of the first one. In GOxy 1224, however, this next verse is less equivalent. It speaks not of the simultaneity of *not against* and *on your side,* thereby excluding any neutral middle position, but of a future change to *at a distance/near* from a present posture of *against you/on your side.*

Jewish-Christian Gospels

A gold coin from Rome honoring the
Emperor Constantine, under whose
patronage the Council of Nicea was
convened in 325 CE. *Courtesy of Numismatic
Fine Arts International, Inc., Los Angeles.*

The Gospel of the Hebrews

Introduction

"Gospel of the Hebrews" is the title given most frequently by early Christian authors to what they took to be a single Jewish-Christian gospel. It is impossible, however, to reconcile all of the extant fragments into a single gospel and there is broad scholarly agreement that they derive from three gospels, though there is not always consensus on which fragment should be assigned to which gospel. Even when our Christian authors clearly state that a certain quotation comes from the Gospel of the Hebrews, this information cannot be trusted in every case. This gospel is the most widely attested of the three Jewish-Christian gospels. Direct citations are preserved by five authors and three more mention it without quoting from it.

Genre

The surviving fragments of the Gospel of the Hebrews (GHeb) do not give a clear indication of its genre, except that it contained narrative. We cannot tell whether GHeb 1 is a quotation or a summary, but if it is a quotation, it shows that its author worked extensive theological commentary into the narratives, which would make the Gospel of the Hebrews more like the Gospel of John than the synoptics. GHeb 4 takes the form of a first-person report by Jesus himself, giving the reader a privileged insight into Jesus in much the same way as John does in presenting Jesus' final discourse (John 17).

Contents

The contents and structure of the gospel are impossible to determine. GHeb 1 deals with Jesus' pre-existence and birth, 2–3 with his baptism, and 4 probably with his temptation. The call of Levi-Matthias (5) presumably fell near the beginning of the gospel. It is impossible to tell where GHeb 6–8 could have been found, or even whether they were simple sayings or parts of narratives. The appearance of the risen Lord to James (9) came near the end. GHeb 9 presupposes three earlier stories that are nowhere recorded, but of which we can recover something: a last supper scene at which James vowed to fast until he saw the risen Jesus, a resurrection scene in which Jesus gave his shroud to the priest's slave, and, by inference, some sort of burial scene.

The existing pieces of this gospel are enough to indicate that it must have been quite different from other gospels. In a few places, it seems to have been influenced by the wording of passages in the canonical gospels, but for the most part it goes its own way. There is no reason to think that the Gospel of the Hebrews drew from the canonical gospels deliberately or directly, nor that it represents a development of synoptic or Johannine traditions.

Theology

The Gospel of the Hebrews has a distinctive christology. Christ and his mother both existed before their appearance on earth in human form (GHeb 1). At his baptism, Jesus is addressed as son, not by God, but by the holy spirit, which turns out to be his mother (3, 4). Jesus is not merely led by the holy spirit (as in Luke's gospel); he is completely united with her: "the whole fountain of the holy spirit came down and rested on him" (3).

This gospel's depiction of the holy spirit as female is striking. GHeb 4c, 4d, and 4e explain that the Semitic word for "spirit" is feminine in gender, but this way of portraying the spirit is due to more than a peculiarity of Hebrew grammar. This distinctive depiction of the spirit is rooted in Jewish speculation about divine Wisdom, a female personification of one of God's attributes who was believed to dwell with "holy souls" (see the note to 3).

The "seek-find" and "rule-rest" language of GHeb 6 also comes from the wisdom tradition. This saying describes the stages on the way to salvation ("rest") and encourages the believer to imitate heavenly Wisdom and thus to share in her qualities.

The Gospel of the Hebrews gives prominence to James the Just by making him the first believer to see the risen Lord (9). This James was not an apostle, but was known as the brother of the Lord in GHeb 9 and in the New Testament (Mark 6:3, Gal 1:19). Christian tradition remembered him as the leader of the Christian community in Jerusalem and a formidable advocate of Law-observant Christianity. However, the remains of the Gospel of the Hebrews give no indication that it advocated strict Torah observance.

Language

Jerome claims to have translated this gospel from Hebrew (GHeb 4c, 9), but there are good reasons to doubt this, the most important being the fact that his quotation in 4c corresponds so closely (even in word order) to that of Origen's in 4a that it seems certain that Jerome got his quotation from Origen, who wrote in Greek, not from any Semitic document. There is no compelling reason to doubt that the Gospel of the Hebrews was composed in Greek.

The early Christian quotations of the Gospel of the Hebrews are preserved in Coptic (1), Greek (4a, 4b, 5, 6), and Latin (2, 3, 4c, 4d, 4e, 7, 8, 9).

Date and place of origin

Since this gospel seems to know the canonical gospels and since it was used by Christian authors in the mid-second century, it must have been written in the early second century.

We have no direct information as to where the Gospel of the Hebrews was written. Most of its citations come from, or can be traced to, Christians who lived in Egypt. Parallels to some of its teachings are found in Egyptian Christianity, so it may well have been written there, though this is only an educated guess.

Jewish-Christian gospels

Christian authors from the mid-second to the early fifth century refer to gospels that were used by Christians who understood themselves to be deeply rooted in Judaism. No copies of those gospels exist today, not even in independent manuscript fragments. Our sole source of information about the existence and contents of those gospels is the references to and quotations from them in the works of Christian authors.

The lack of any actual copies of these gospels makes our knowledge of them tentative and partial. The authors who transmit quotations from them seem to assume that all their quotations come from the same gospel. However, the literary characteristics and theological tendencies of the different quotations are so inconsistent that it is virtually certain that they derive from more than one gospel. After analyzing all the quotations and piecing together all the clues from all the sources, scholars have reached a consensus that there were three distinct Jewish-Christian gospels: (1) the Gospel of the Hebrews (GHeb), a gospel with gnostic tendencies and little relationship to the canonical gospels; (2) the Gospel of the Ebionites (GEbi), a gospel based on the synoptics; (3) the Gospel of the Nazoreans (GNaz), a gospel quite similar to Matthew.

Three problems further complicate our attempt to understand the Jewish-Christian gospels. First, it is sometimes difficult to ascertain which gospel a given author is referring to. Second, the quotations from these gospels are quite fragmentary—some are extremely brief, a mere line or two. Third, these later authors are sometimes hostile witnesses, since they regard some of the ideas in these gospels as heretical. Information derived from opponents is not always reliable.

These quoted fragments are fraught with difficulties for our understanding of the lost gospels they represent. Still, were it not for these citations, we would know little or nothing about these interesting communities who continued for centuries to consider themselves both Jewish and Christian.

The Gospel of the Hebrews

1 *Paraphrased by Cyril of Jerusalem (4th century),* Discourse on Mary the Mother of God

It is written in the Gospel of the Hebrews that

> [1]when Christ wanted to come to earth, the Good Father summoned a mighty power in the heavens who was called Michael, and entrusted Christ to his care. [2]The power came down into the world, and it was called Mary, and Christ was in her womb for seven months. [3]She gave birth to him and he grew up and he chose the apostles who preached about him everywhere. [4]He fulfilled the appointed time that was decreed for him. [5]The Jews grew envious of him and came to hate him. They changed the custom of their law and they rose up against him and laid a trap and caught him. [6]They turned him over to the governor, who gave him back to them to crucify. [7]And after they had raised him on the cross, the Father took him up into heaven to himself.

2 *Quoted by Jerome (4th–5th century),* Against the Pelagians 3

In the Gospel of the Hebrews . . . the following story is told:

> [1]The mother of the Lord and his brothers said to him, "John the Baptizer baptized for the forgiveness of sins. Let's go and get baptized by him."
>
> [2]But he said to them, "How have I sinned? So why should I go and get baptized by him? Only if I don't know what I'm talking about."

1:6 Cf. Mt 27:2, Jn 19:16
1:7 (T) Phil 2:8–9
2 //GNaz 2
2:1 (T) Mk 1:4, Lk 3:3
2:2 Cf. Mt 3:14; (T) Heb 4:15

1:1–2 According to the Gospel of the Hebrews, both Christ and his mother existed in heaven before coming to earth. Apparently, *Michael* is the name of a *mighty power in the heavens* that came to earth in the form of Mary. In GHeb 4 Michael/Mary is identified with the holy spirit.

1:2 *in her womb for seven months:* According to some Jewish, Greek, and Roman traditions, a number of ancient heroes were born after only seven months. Among them were Isaac, Moses, Samuel, Dionysus, Apollo, and Julius Caesar.

1:3 The Coptic for *he grew up* may reflect the Greek of Luke 2:52.

1:6 *They turned him over to the governor* may reflect the wording of Matt 27:2.

That the governor *gave him back to them to crucify* recalls John 19:16 and makes the Jews, rather than the Romans, responsible for killing Jesus.

2 It cannot be determined with certainty whether this fragment belongs to the Gospel of the Nazoreans or to the Gospel of the Hebrews. Jerome mistakenly believes that all his quotations originate from one Jewish-Christian gospel, which in some cases makes it difficult to distinguish fragments of the Gospel of the Hebrews from those of Nazoreans.

2:2 Jesus' statements do not mean that he refused baptism. If they did, Jerome would have mentioned that this gospel lacked a baptism scene. The purpose of this passage is to avoid any implication that Jesus got baptized because he was seeking forgiveness of his sins. Matthew also deals with this problem, though in a different way (see Matt 3:13–15). This fragment also seems to assume that Jesus' family was baptized along with him.

3   *Quoted by Jerome,* Commentary on Isaiah 4 *(commenting on Isa 11:2)*

In the Hebrew gospel that the Nazarenes read it says,

> [1]The whole fountain of the holy spirit comes down on him. For the Lord is the spirit and where the spirit is, there is freedom.

Later on, in the same gospel, we find the following:

> [2]And it happened that when the Lord came up out of the water, the whole fountain of the holy spirit came down on him and rested on him. [3]It said to him, "My son, I was waiting for you in all the prophets, waiting for you to come so I could rest in you. [4]For you are my rest; you are my first-begotten son who rules forever."

4a   *Quoted and explained by Origen (3rd century),* Commentary on John 2

Those who give credence to the Gospel of the Hebrews, in which the Savior says,

> "Just now my mother, the holy spirit, took me by one of my hairs and brought me to Tabor, the great mountain,"

have to face the problem of explaining how it is possible for the "mother" of Christ to be the holy spirit that came into existence through the Logos. But those things are not difficult to explain. For if "whoever does the will of the heavenly father is his brother and sister and mother," and if the name "brother of Christ" applies not only to humans, but also to beings of a more divine rank, there is nothing absurd in the holy spirit being his mother, when anyone who does the will of the heavenly father is called "mother of Christ."

4b   *Quoted by Origen,* Homily on Jeremiah 15

If someone can accept this

> "Just now my mother, the holy spirit, took me by one of my hairs and brought me to Tabor, the great mountain"

—one can see that she is his mother.

3
//Mk 1:9–11,
Mt 3:13–17,
Lk 3:21–22,
Jn 1:29–34, GEbi 4

3:1–2
◊Is 11:2

3:1
//2 Cor 3:17

3:3
Cf. Wis 7:27,
Sir 24:7

3:4
◊Ps 132:14, 2:7;
Ⓣ Heb 1:6,
Col 1:15, Lk 1:33

4
Cf. Mk 1:12–13;
Lk 4:1–2; Mt 4:1–2,
8–10;
◊Ez 8:3

4a
//Mk 3:35,
Mt 12:50, Lk 8:21,
Th 99:2, GEbi 5:3–4

3 In this version of the baptism scene, the voice is that of the holy spirit, not of God as in the rest of the gospel tradition. Contrary to GEbi 4, Jesus' baptism here does not transform his status; he already was the divine son of the spirit.

3:3 *I was waiting for you in all the prophets:* Wisdom is similarly described in Wis 7:27: "In every generation she enters holy souls and makes them prophets and friends of God."

so I could rest: The holy spirit speaks like divine Wisdom: "I have acquired something among every people and nation. Among all of them I sought rest. I sought to make my home in someone's land" (Sir 24:6–7).

4 This seems to be an excerpt from a unique version of the story of Jesus' temptation, with the holy spirit taking Jesus up to the mountain, a role played by the devil in Matt 4:8. The event is here reported by Jesus himself, which may be the way the Gospel of the Hebrews explains how this private event came to be known publicly.

As in GHeb 1, the holy spirit is understood to be Jesus' mother. GHeb 4c, 4d, and 4e attribute this unusual concept to the gender of the Hebrew word for "spirit." In SecJas 5:6 Jesus calls himself a "son of the holy spirit." Thom 101 may be referring to the holy spirit when Jesus says, "My true mother gave me life."

4c *Quoted and explained by Jerome,* Commentary on Micah 2 *(commenting on Mic 7:6)*

Whoever has read the Song of Songs will understand that the word of God is also the bridegroom of the soul. And whoever gives credence to the gospel circulating under the title "Gospel of the Hebrews," which we recently translated, in which it is said by the Savior himself,

> "Just now my mother, the holy spirit, took me by one of my hairs,"

will not hesitate to say that the word of God proceeds from the spirit, and that the soul, which is the bride of the word, has the holy spirit (which in Hebrew is feminine in gender, *rua*) as a mother-in-law.

4d *Quoted and explained by Jerome,* Commentary on Isaiah 11 *(commentary on Isa 40:9)*

In the Gospel of the Hebrews that the Nazarenes read it says,

> "Just now my mother, the holy spirit, took me."

Now no one should be offended by this, because ⟨the word⟩ "spirit" in Hebrew is feminine, while in our ⟨Latin⟩ language it is masculine and in Greek it is neuter. In divinity, however, there is no gender.

4e *Quoted and explained by Jerome,* Commentary on Ezekiel 4 *(commenting on Ezek 16:13)*

In the Book of Judges we read "Deborah," which means "bee." Her prophecies are the sweetest honey and refer to the holy spirit, who is called in Hebrew by a feminine noun. In the Gospel of the Hebrews that the Nazarenes read, the Savior indicates this by saying,

> "Just now my mother, the holy spirit, whisked me away."

5 *Reported by Didymus (4th century),* Commentary on the Psalms 184 *(commenting on Psalm 33)*

Thomas is also called Didymus, and there are many other people with two names. Scripture seems to call Matthew "Levi" in the Gospel of Luke, but they are not the same person. Rather, Matthias, who replaced Judas, and Levi are the same person with a double name. This is apparent in the Gospel of the Hebrews.

5
Cf. Th Prologue,
Lk 5:27,
Mk 2:14, Mt 9:9,
Acts 1:15–26

---

5 Matt 9:9 identifies Levi the toll collector of Mark 2:14 with Matthew. The Gospel of the Hebrews is unique in identifying Levi with Matthias, the apostle chosen after Jesus' death (Acts 1:15–26). The names "Matthew" and "Matthias" are nearly identical in Greek (*Matthaios* and *Matthias*).

6a *Quoted by Clement of Alexandria (2nd–3rd century),* Miscellanies 2

In the Gospel of the Hebrews it is written,

"Whoever marvels will rule and whoever rules will rest."

6b *Quoted by Clement of Alexandria,* Miscellanies 5

"Those who seek should not stop until they find; when they find, they will marvel. When they marvel, they will rule, and when they rule, they will rest."

7 *Quoted by Jerome (4th–5th century),* Commentary on Ephesians 3 *(commenting on Eph 5:4)*

We can read in the Hebrew gospel that the Lord, speaking to his disciples, said,

"Never be glad except when you look at your brother or sister with love."

8 *Quoted by Jerome,* Commentary on Ezekiel 6 *(commenting on Ezek 18:7)*

The Gospel of the Hebrews that the Nazarenes are used to reading listed this among the most serious crimes:

Those who have saddened their brother's or sister's spirit.

9 *Quoted by Jerome,* On Famous Men 2

I recently translated into Greek and Latin the gospel called the "Gospel of the Hebrews," the one that Origen also frequently uses. After the resurrection of the Savior, it says,

[1]The Lord, after he had given the linen cloth to the priest's slave, went to James and appeared to him. [2](Now James had sworn not to eat bread from the time that he drank from the Lord's cup until he would see him raised from among those who sleep.)

6
Ⓣ Th 50:3, 51:1, 60:6, 90;
Mt 11:28–29;
DSav 11:5;
◊ Sir 51:26–27, 6:23–31

6b
//Th 2:1, 92:1, 94;
Q 11:10; Mt 7:8;
Lk 11:10; Mary 4:7

9:1
Cf. 1 Cor 15:7

9:2
Cf. Mk 14:25,
Mt 26:29, Lk 22:18

6b This is the fullest form of this saying, found in different wordings in the Coptic and Greek versions of Thom 2.

Whoever marvels will rule is a concept from the Jewish wisdom tradition: "The desire for wisdom leads to ruling" (Wis 6:20).

Rest is salvation, the final attainment in the search for wisdom, as in Matt 11:28–29 and Thom 90 (see also Sir 51:26–27 and 6:26–28).

7–8 *Brother or sister* probably refers to a fellow believer, as in GNaz 5 and Matt 18:21–22. In GNaz 6 "brothers and sisters" refers to fellow Jews.

9:1 This account of the resurrection is unique in that James is the first believer to see the risen Jesus (see 1 Cor 15:7),

not Peter or Mary of Magdala, as in the other gospels. It also presupposes that the tomb was guarded by the high priest's personnel rather than by Roman soldiers. Peter 8:1–4 has Pharisees, elders, scholars, and Roman soldiers at the tomb.

9:2–4 That James vowed to fast until the resurrection (see Luke 22:16, where Jesus makes this vow) lets him share sympathetically in Jesus' fate and makes James overcome the disciples' misunderstanding of Jesus' death, an important theme in the synoptic passion predictions and meal scenes. The transformation of James into a hero in this gospel is echoed in Thom 12, where Jesus pronounces James to be the chief authority among the disciples.

³Shortly after this the Lord said,

> "Bring a table and some bread."

⁴And immediately it is added:

> He took the bread, blessed it, broke it, and gave it to James the Just and said
> to him, "My brother, eat your bread, for the Human One has been raised from
> among those who sleep."

9:4
Cf. Mk 14:22,
Mt 26:26, Lk12:19,
1 Cor 11:23–24

"Holy Spirit" or "holy spirit"?

English Bibles typically refer to "the Holy Spirit," while SV features either "the
holy spirit" or "holy spirit," depending on whether the underlying Greek has
the definite article. Like all ancient Greek writings, the gospels were originally
written entirely in capital letters, and it was centuries before copyists developed
lower case cursive letters to make their work easier. Therefore, whether or not
to capitalize terms in an English translation is always an interpretive decision.

Contemporary readers are likely to understand the capitalized "Holy Spirit"
as the third divine person of the Holy Trinity. But since the doctrine of the
Trinity was defined centuries after the gospels were written, it is anachronistic
to read this later theology into the gospels. Furthermore, it is doubtful that the
gospel writers regarded the holy spirit as a personal, conscious being. They use
this term the way "spirit of God" is used in the Hebrew Bible, where it refers to
God's creative and inspiring power.

The same Hebrew word can be translated "spirit," "wind," or "breath," with
the latter representing the life force itself.

- The creation story begins with the spirit/wind of God sweeping/blowing
  over the waters of Chaos:

  > The earth was a formless void and darkness covered the face of the Abyss,
  > while a wind from God swept over the surface of the waters. (Gen 1:2)

- The first human being is given life when God breathes the breath/spirit of
  life into it:

  > Yahweh God formed the human being from the dust of the ground and
  > breathed into his nostrils the breath of life. And the human became a living
  > being. (Gen 2:7)

- God's spirit is identified as the creative force in all earthly life:

  > When you send out your spirit/breath, they [all living things] are created;
  > and you renew the face of the ground. (Ps 104:30)

That the gospel writers employ this Old Testament idiom is especially clear
in the way Luke uses the term in 1:35, where he sets the angel's words to Mary
in two parallel phrases:

> The *holy spirit* will hover over you,
> and the *power of the Most High* will cast its shadow on you.

Called synonymous parallelism, this is a literary device common in biblical poetry; its two lines express the same thought in different words. This example shows that Luke understands "holy spirit" to be the same thing as "power of the Most High."

- In the Hebrew Bible, God's spirit is also the power through which God inspires prophets. The following examples illustrate the point:

> The spirit of God possessed Saul. (1 Sam 10:10)
> The spirit of Yahweh fell upon me and said to me . . . (Ezek 11:5)
> The spirit of the Lord God is upon me. (Isa 61:1)

That the gospels reflect this sense of spirit is evident in Mark 13:11:

> And when they take you away to turn you in, don't be worried about what you should say. Instead, whatever occurs to you at the moment, say that. For it's not you who are speaking but the holy spirit.

The gospels use the term sometimes with and sometimes without the definite article—hence SV's alternation between "the holy spirit" and "holy spirit." This variable syntax further indicates that the gospels are describing an extension of God's power rather than an independent personal entity. (The single exception is when the Gospel of John equates the holy spirit with "the advocate" in John 14:26.)

In short, SV's lower case presentation of "holy spirit" reflects the Old Testament meanings that inform the way the gospels use the term.

The Gospel of the Ebionites

Introduction

All of our quotations from the Gospel of the Ebionites (GEbi) come from the church father Epiphanius of Salamis (ca. 315–403). If this gospel had a title, we do not know what it was. "Gospel of the Ebionites" is a modern title that reflects the fact that all of its citations come from Epiphanius' discussion of the Jewish-Christian group called the Ebionites and that some (though not all) of this gospel's fragments have theological traits that match what we know of the Ebionites from other sources.

Ebionites is a narrative gospel. It is closest to Matthew, but has clear connections also to Mark and Luke. Judging from the way Ebionites combines elements from all three of these gospels, it can best be characterized as a harmony of the synoptics, with various expansions and abridgements.

We possess only seven fragments of this gospel, so we cannot ascertain much about its contents or structure. The fragments have to do with John the Baptizer, Jesus' baptism, his choice of the twelve apostles, and the Last Supper. Two more quotations preserve sayings of Jesus. Epiphanius informs us that Ebionites omitted the birth stories and genealogy of Jesus. This gospel therefore began, like Mark, with the appearance of John.

Christology

This gospel seems to have a distinctive christology. The account of Jesus' baptism (GEbi 4) emphasizes that it changed Jesus' spiritual status in two ways. First, the Spirit not only comes down on Jesus, it "enters him." Jesus is thus "possessed" by the holy spirit (which the Ebionites called "Christ," according to Irenaeus). Second, Jesus becomes God's son at his baptism (see the "today" in 4:4), a belief known as "adoptionism," which held that Jesus was not divine by birth or nature, but that God chose him to become his son, i.e., adopted him. Thus the Ebionites made a distinction between the human Jesus and the divine Spirit ("Christ") that possessed him.

The two reports in GEbi 5 and 6 probably refer to the "Christ" as the divine Spirit possessing Jesus: "they deny that he was human" (5) and "they say that ⟨Christ⟩ was not born of God the Father, but created like one of the archangels" (6). Other writers prior to Epiphanius confirm that the Ebionites believed Jesus to be merely human. The Ebionites seem to have had a unique blend of Jewish monotheism (Jesus was only human, not some "second god") and Christian devotion to Jesus, as the one possessed by divinity.

Language

Epiphanius twice tells us that Ebionites was known as "the Hebrew gospel." Nevertheless, the quotations that he provides show that Ebionites closely followed the Greek text of the synoptic gospels, so there is little doubt that this gospel was originally composed in Greek.

Date and place of origin

Since the only quotations of Ebionites come from a work by Epiphanius in 375, this gospel had to be earlier than this, though how much earlier cannot be determined with certainty. However, there are several indications that give scholars confidence that Ebionites was composed in the first half of the second century.

Irenaeus (ca. 140–200) probably provides the earliest evidence of the existence of the Gospel of the Ebionites. He reports that the Ebionites used only Matthew's gospel, but also that they deny the virgin birth. This means that they must have been using their own gospel and not canonical Matthew, which attests to this belief. Irenaeus' remarks, then, presuppose that by about 175 the Ebionites had a gospel that could be confused with Matthew but that lacked the story of the virgin birth. This gospel was almost certainly the Gospel of the Ebionites, which Epiphanius himself confused with Matthew and which does not contain an infancy narrative.

Ebionites' character as a harmony of the synoptic gospels makes it fit well into the early to mid-second century, since several other synoptic harmonies were composed in this period.

We cannot be sure where this gospel was written. A few early Christian writers indicate that the Ebionites lived in the area east of the Jordan, which is where Epiphanius found the gospel, though this does not mean it was composed there.

The Gospel of the Ebionites

All fragments are quoted by Epiphanius (4th century), Heresies 30

1a Now the beginning of their gospel goes like this:

> ¹In the days of Herod, king of Judea, John appeared in the Jordan river baptizing with a baptism that changed people's hearts. ²He was said to be a descendant of Aaron the priest, a son of Zechariah and Elizabeth. ³And everybody went out to him.

1b By mutilating Matthew's genealogy, they make the beginning say, as we have already stated:

> In the days of Herod, king of Judea, during the high-priesthood of Caiaphas,

they say,

> this man named John appeared in the Jordan river baptizing with a baptism that changed people's hearts,

and so on.

2 At any rate, in the gospel that they call "According to Matthew," which is not complete but adulterated and mutilated—they call it the "Hebrew" gospel—is found the following:

> ¹There was this man named Jesus, who was about thirty years old, who chose us. ²And when he came to Capernaum, he entered the house of Simon, who was nicknamed Peter. He then began to speak as follows:
> ³"As I was walking along by the lake of Tiberias, I chose John and James, sons of Zebedee, and Simon and Andrew and Thaddeus and Simon the Zealot and Judas the Iscariot. ⁴Then I summoned you, Matthew, while you were sitting at the toll booth, and you followed me. ⁵Therefore, I want you to be twelve apostles, to symbolize Israel."

1
Cf. Mk 1:4–5;
Mt 3:5–6;
Lk 3:1–3, 1:5

2:1
Cf. Lk 3:23

2:2
Cf. Mk 1:29,
Mt 8:14, Lk 4:38

2:3
Cf. Mk 1:16–18,
3:16–19;
Mt 4:18–20, 10:2–4;
Lk 5:1–11, 6:14–16

2:4
Cf. Mk 2:14,
Mt 9:9, Lk 5:27–28

---

1 Epiphanius makes it clear in both citations that Ebionites opens with this announcement of John's baptizing. Ebionites has no genealogy or infancy narrative, probably because the ones in Matthew and Luke attest to Jesus' virgin birth, a belief denied by the Ebionites.

1a:2 *descendant of Aaron, son of Zechariah and Elizabeth:* Even though Ebionites has no story of Jesus' birth, this phrase, copied from Luke 1:5, shows that the author knew at least Luke's infancy narrative.

2:1 *chose us:* The first-person plural narration is unusual in a gospel.

2:4 *Matthew:* Mark lists Matthew among the Twelve, but names the toll collector "Levi" (Mark 2:14). Matthew changes "Levi" to "Matthew" (Matt 9:9) and adds "the toll collector" to his name in the list of the Twelve (Matt 10:3). Ebionites' version thus sides with Matthew.

2:5 It is odd that Ebionites specifies twelve apostles, while Epiphanius' quotation names only eight. Perhaps Epipha-

3 And

¹It so happened that John was baptizing, and Pharisees and all Jerusalem went out to him and got baptized. ²And John wore clothes made of camel hair and had a leather belt around his waist. ³His food,

it says,

consisted of raw honey that tasted like manna, like a pancake cooked with oil.

Thus they change the word of truth into a lie and instead of "locusts" they put "pancake cooked with honey."

4 After saying many things, it adds:

¹When the people were baptized, Jesus also came and got baptized by John. ²As he came up out of the water, the skies opened and he saw the holy spirit in the form of a dove coming down and entering him. ³And there was a voice from the sky that said, "You are my son, the one I love—I fully approve of you." ⁴And again, "Today I have fathered you."

⁵And right away a bright light illuminated the place. When John saw this,

it says,

he said to him, "Who are you?" ⁶And again a voice from the sky said to him, "This is my son, the one I love—I fully approve of him."

⁷And then,

it says,

John knelt down in front of him and said, "Please, Master, you baptize me." ⁸But he stopped him and said, "It's all right. This is the way everything is supposed to be fulfilled."

3
//Mk 1:4–6,
Mt 3:4–7

3:2
◊2 Kgs 1:8

3:3
◊Num 11:8,
Ex 16:31

4
//Mk 1:9–11,
Mt 3:13–17,
Lk 3:21–22, GHeb3

4:3–4
//Lk 3:22

4:3
//Mk 1:11;
◊Is 42:1

4:4
◊Ps 2:7

4:6
//Mt 3:17

4:7–8
//Mt 3:14–15

---

nius inadvertently skipped over four names, an easy enough mistake when copying a long list. The four missing apostles, according to Mark 3:8, Matt 10:3, and Luke 6:14–15 are Philip, Bartholomew, James the son of Alphaeus, and Thomas.

3:1–2 combines phrases from Matthew and Mark.

3:3 The omission of locusts from John's diet may indicate, along with GEbi 7, that the Ebionites were vegetarians.

The unusual description of the honey depends on Num 11:8 and Exod 16:31 and is unique to Ebionites. It confirms that this gospel was composed in Greek, for the connection between locusts (*akris*) and pancakes (*egkris*) could be made only in Greek.

4 This story combines phrases mostly from Matthew and Luke. The voice from heaven speaks three times, each time

in words taken from a different gospel (Mark, Luke, then Matthew).

4:2 This report goes beyond the canonical versions of the baptism: the holy spirit not only *comes down* on Jesus, it *enters* him (see the Introduction).

4:4 *Today I have fathered you* could well reflect adoptionist christology, in which Jesus becomes son of God at his baptism.

4:7–8 These verses are derived from Matthew. They subordinate John to Jesus, even though it is John who does the baptizing, and therefore avoid any hint of rivalry between them. This may reflect a controversy between early Christians and the followers of John, who could claim that the Baptizer was greater than the one he had baptized.

5 They deny that he was human, I suppose because of what the Savior said when it was reported to him:

> [1]"Look, your mother and your brothers are outside."
>
> [2]"My mother and brothers—who can they be?"
>
> [3]And he pointed to his disciples and said, "These are my brothers and mother and sisters, [4]those who do the will of my Father."

6 They say that ⟨Christ⟩ was not born of God the Father, but created like one of the archangels, and even more, that he rules over the angels and over everything that was made by the Almighty, and that he came and announced, as it says in the gospel, the one called "According to the Hebrews,"

> "I came to do away with sacrifices, and if you don't stop sacrificing, you won't stop experiencing wrath."

7 They take it on themselves to obscure the logic of the truth and to alter the saying, as is evident to everyone from the context, and make the disciples say:

> [1]"Where do you want us to get things ready for you to eat the Passover meal?"

And apparently they make him answer:

> [2]"I have certainly not looked forward with all my heart to eating meat with you at this Passover, have I?"

Anyone can detect their deceit because the sequence makes it obvious that the *mu* and the *ēta* have been added. Instead of saying, "I have looked forward with all my heart" they add the additional word *mē* ("not"). Now in fact he said, "I

5
//Mk 3:31–35,
Mt12:46–50,
Lk 8:19–21, Th 99

6
Cf. Mt 5:17, 9:13,
12:7;
◊Hos 6:6

7:1
//Mk 14:12,
Mt 26:17, Lk 22:8–9

7:2
Cf. Lk 22:15

---

5 Epiphanius links the Ebionite belief that Jesus was not human to the saying in which he disowns his natural family. This probably presupposes the belief that, prior to his baptism, Jesus was merely human, whereas after it he was God's son and so no longer belonged to his earthly family. This would fit with the adoptionist character of GEbi 4 and the christology implicit in GEbi 6.

6 That ⟨*Christ*⟩ *was created like one of the archangels* and that *he rules over the angels and over everything,* that is, that he is the highest of all creatures (*not born of God the Father*), most probably refers to the divine Spirit that "possessed" Jesus after his baptism (see the Introduction).

I came to do away with sacrifices: This saying seems odd in a Jewish-Christian gospel, even though animal sacrifice ceased to be an option after the destruction of the temple in 70 CE. This saying has no parallel in the gospel tradition. It may be loosely based on Jesus' quotation of Hos 6:6 in Matt 9:13 and 12:7 ("It's mercy I desire instead of sacrifice"), although it directly contradicts Jesus' declaration in Matt 5:17–18. In what might be a reference to GEbi 6, a fourth-century Jewish-Christian text makes the following comment: "In saying, 'I did not come to do away with the Law,' and yet doing away with something, he indicated that what he did away with had not originally been part of the Law" (Pseudo-Clement, *Homilies* 3.51.2).

7:2 *Mu* and *ēta* are Greek letters that spell the word *mē* ("not").

As Epiphanius points out, Ebionites adds the word *meat* to Jesus' statement. Apparently, Jesus objects to eating the Passover meal, not out of any objection to the festival itself, but because the meal includes meat (lamb). Other than GEbi 7 (and possibly GEbi 3), no other source reports that the Ebionites were vegetarians.

have looked forward with all my heart to eating the Passover meal with you." However, they deceive themselves by adding the word "meat," and they do evil by saying, "I'm not looking forward to eating meat with you at this Passover."

The Gospel of the Nazoreans

Introduction

The Gospel of the Nazoreans (GNaz) is a narrative gospel closely related to the Gospel of Matthew. Like the other Jewish-Christian gospels, it is preserved only in a few quotations and citations in the writings of early Christian authors. All the quoted passages show interesting differences between Nazoreans and Matthew. It seems that early Christian authors quote from Nazoreans only when they want to draw attention to passages in which this gospel is peculiar in some way or another. This characteristic of the quotations is an important clue to the overall character of this gospel, because it makes it likely that the rest of Nazoreans (the lost, unquoted material) was basically the same as Matthew. This is the reasoning that leads scholars to the conclusion that its contents were more or less identical to those of Matthew. Nazoreans seems to have diverged from Matthew only in minor ways, usually by slightly expanding Matthew's version and clarifying a few of its details. For example, GNaz 3 explains the meaning of a difficult word in the Lord's prayer, a word whose exact meaning still eludes us; GNaz 7 corrects a reference to a figure in the Hebrew Bible that Matthew seems to have gotten wrong; and GNaz 4 fills out the story of Jesus' healing of the man with the crippled hand by making it clear that the man's condition prevented him from making a living.

Nazoreans can be aptly characterized as a slightly reworked version of Matthew. The existing fragments show no familiarity with any other gospel, nor any contact with the gospel traditions prior to Matthew. Nazoreans does in a modest way to Matthew what Matthew had done in a more sweeping way to Mark and Q. Nazoreans is evidence that the process of clarifying, correcting, and expanding the written accounts of the words and deeds of Jesus continued beyond the writing of the canonical gospels. Since Nazoreans is a rewriting of a gospel rather than a new gospel altogether, it shows us that at least one community of Christians considered Matthew to be authoritative, but not beyond correction or alteration.

Language

The Christian authors who are our sources for information about the Gospel of the Nazoreans (Hegesippus, Origen, Eusebius, Epiphanius, and Jerome) report that it was written in the Hebrew alphabet (GNaz 8, 10) and that it was known as the "Gospel of the Hebrews" (a title Christian authors apparently gave to

449

any gospel they thought had been written in a Semitic language). Scholars are convinced that the original language of Nazoreans was Aramaic, which uses the same alphabet as Hebrew.

Because Nazoreans is based on Matthew and was written in Aramaic, some scholars have speculated that an Aramaic version of Matthew must have once been in circulation. This theory parallels a widespread rumor among early Christian writers that Matthew had originally been composed in Aramaic. However, close analysis of the quoted fragments of Nazoreans shows that this gospel is based on the Greek text of Matthew. Hence, Nazoreans is an Aramaic "translation" of Matthew, though of course not a literal or even necessarily an accurate translation.

The chain of translation between Nazoreans and the modern reader is a complex one. Early Christian authors translated its Aramaic (which was based on Matthew's Greek) into their own languages. GNaz 8 is preserved in Greek, GNaz 11 in Syriac, and the rest of the fragments in Latin. These excerpts are the basis for the Scholars Version of Nazoreans. Since every translation loses some of the original meaning, our English version of these fragments may in some places only approximate the original sense of this gospel.

Date and place of origin

Nazoreans had to have been written after Matthew and before the Christian writer Hegesippus first referred to it in 180. This means that it was probably written in the first half of the second century. In the fourth century, Jerome informs us that the Nazorean community was living in Beroea, a city in Syria. The gospel may have been composed there.

The Gospel of the Nazoreans

1 *Quoted by Jerome (4th–5th century),* On Famous Men 3

Here are two of these ⟨citations from the gospel used by the Nazoreans, in which Matthew quotes the ancient scriptures, not following the Septuagint, but the original Hebrew text⟩:

> I have called my son out of Egypt

and

> for he will be called a Nazorean.

2 *Quoted by Jerome,* Against the Pelagians 3

In the Gospel of the Hebrews . . . the following story is told:

> ¹The mother of the Lord and his brothers said to him, "John the Baptizer baptized for the forgiveness of sins. Let's go and get baptized by him."
>
> ²But he said to them, "How have I sinned? So why should I go and get baptized by him? Only if I don't know what I'm talking about."

3a *Reported by Jerome,* Commentary on Matthew 1 *(commenting on Matt 6:11)*

In the so-called Gospel of the Hebrews (in the Lord's Prayer), instead of "the bread we need for the day" I found *"mahar,"* which means "for tomorrow," so

1
//Mt 2:15, 23;
◊ Hos11:1, Jgs13:5

2
//GHeb 2

2:1
Ⓣ Mk 1:4, Lk 3:3

2:2
Cf. Mk 3:14;
Ⓣ Heb 4:15

3
//Q11:3, Mt 6:11,
Lk 11:3

---

1 *He will be called a Nazorean* presupposes the Greek version of Judg 13:5 (LXX) as the basis for Matt 2:23; Jerome uses "Nazorean" in both places in his translation of the Bible. It is not, despite Jerome's assertion, a quotation from any passage in the Hebrew Bible. This, and several other of Jerome's misleading claims, makes him an unreliable source of information about the Jewish-Christian gospels. While it would be overly skeptical to dismiss everything he reports, the information he provides must be evaluated with great care.

2 It cannot be determined with certainty whether this fragment belongs to the Gospel of the Hebrews or to Nazoreans. Jerome mistakenly believes that all his quotations originate from one Jewish-Christian gospel, which in some cases makes it difficult for us to distinguish fragments of the Gospel of the Hebrews from those of Nazoreans.

2:2 Jesus' statements do not mean that he refused baptism.

If they did, Jerome would have mentioned that this gospel lacked a baptism scene. The purpose of this passage is to avoid any implication that Jesus got baptized because he was seeking forgiveness of his sins. Matthew also deals with this problem, though in a different way (see Matt 3:13–15). This fragment also seems to assume that Jesus' family was baptized along with him.

3 *Mahar* is an Aramaic translation of the Greek *epiousios,* the meaning of which is disputed. Its only certain occurrence in the Greek language is in the Lord's Prayer (Matt 6:11//Luke 11:3). Origen, a Greek author of the third century and one of the greatest early Christian scholars, thought that the word had been coined by the evangelists. Possible translations of *epiousios* are "daily," "for subsistence," and "for the future." GNaz 3 is the earliest example of a Christian attempt to explain this difficult term.

that the sense is "Provide us today with the bread we need for tomorrow"—that is, for the future.

3b *Quoted by Jerome,* Tractate on Psalm 13 5

In the Hebrew Gospel of Matthew it reads thus:

> "Provide us today with the bread we need for tomorrow,"

that is, give us today the bread that you will give us in your empire.

4 *Quoted by Jerome,* Commentary on Matthew 2 *(commenting on Matt 12:13)*

In the gospel that the Nazoreans and Ebionites use ⟨in the story of the healing of the man with the crippled hand⟩, this man who had a crippled hand is described as a stonemason who called for help with words like this:

> "I was a stonemason making a living with my hands. I plead with you, Jesus, give me back my health so that I won't have to beg for my food in shame."

5 *Quoted by Jerome,* Against the Pelagians 3

In the same book ⟨Jesus⟩ said,

> [1]"If your brother or sister has wronged you verbally and has made amends, welcome him or her seven times a day." His disciple Simon said to him, "Seven times a day?" The Master answered him, "That's right; in fact, up to seventy times seven times. [2]The prophets themselves were capable of sinful talk, even after they were anointed with the holy spirit."

6 *Quoted by Origen (3rd century),* On Matthew 15 *(commenting on Matt 19:16–30)*

It is written in a certain gospel called the "Gospel of the Hebrews"—if anyone will accept it, not as authoritative, but to shed light on the question at hand:

> [1]The second rich man said to him, "Teacher, what good do I have to do to live?"
>
> [2]He said to him, "Mister, follow the Law and the Prophets."
>
> He answered, "I've done that."
>
> He said to him, "Go sell everything you own and give it away to the poor and then come follow me."
>
> [3]But the rich man didn't want to hear this and began to scratch his head. And the Master said to him, "How can you say that you follow the Law and the Prophets? In the Law it says: 'Love your neighbor as yourself.' [4]Look around you:

4
Cf. Mk 3:1–6,
Mt 12:9–14,
Lk 6:6–11

5:1
//Q 17:4,
Mt 18:21–22,
Lk 17:4

6
//Mk 10:17–25,
Mt 19:16–24,
Lk 18:18–25

6:3
◊Lv 19:18

---

4 In Matthew, Jesus heals this man in order to make a point about the Sabbath law that provokes his opponents (Matt 12:9–14). By adding the man's request, Nazoreans trans-forms this healing into an act of compassion.
6 Three minor additions to Matthew's version of this scene (Matt 19:16–24) enhance its Jewish coloring: *sons*

many of your brothers and sisters, sons and daughters of Abraham, are living in filth and dying of hunger. Your house is full of good things and not a thing of yours manages to get out to them."

⁵Turning to his disciple Simon, who was sitting with him, he said, "Simon, son of Jonah, it's easier for a camel to squeeze through a needle's eye than for a wealthy person to get into the empire of Heaven."

7 *Reported by Jerome,* Commentary on Matthew 4 *(commenting on Matt 23:35)*

In the gospel that the Nazoreans use, we found "son of Joiada" written instead of "son of Baruch."

8 *Paraphrased by Eusebius (4th century),* Theophany 4 *(discussing Matt 25:19–30)*

The gospel written in the Hebrew alphabet that we have obtained has the threat being made not against the man who had hidden the money, but against the one who had behaved dissolutely. He (the master) had three slaves. One squandered his master's resources with prostitutes and flute girls, one multiplied his earnings, and one hid the money. One was later commended, one was merely criticized, and one was thrown into prison. This makes me wonder whether in Matthew the threat that is made after the statement against the man who did nothing might refer not to him, but rather, by the literary device of echoing, to the first man who had been eating and drinking with the drunks.

9 *Reported by Jerome,* Commentary on Matthew 4 *(commenting on Matt 27:16)*

In the so-called Gospel of the Hebrews the name of the man who was to be condemned for sedition and murder is interpreted as "son of their teacher."

7
Cf. Mt 23:35

8
Cf. Mt 24:45–51,
25:14–30

9
Cf. Mk 15:7,
Mt 27:16,
Lk 23:18–19,
Jn 18:40

---

and daughters of Abraham (v 4) reinforces the meaning of *brothers and sisters* as fellow Israelites, and Jesus and Simon (Peter) are sitting (v 5), i.e., in the posture of Jewish teachers. Nazoreans also embellishes Matthew's version by adding that giving away one's goods should be motivated by compassion for the poor.

7 Matt 23:35 refers to "Zechariah, son of Baruch," who was "murdered between the temple and the altar." According to the OT this prophet was not the son of Baruch but of Jehoiada (2 Chr 24:20). Matthew probably confused that Zechariah with the one mentioned in Zech 1:1. Nazoreans corrects Matthew on this point. Jerome's *Joiada* seems to be a Latin variant spelling of "Jehoiada" in 2 Chronicles.

8 Nazoreans is apparently dissatisfied with the harsh ending of the parable of the Entrusted Money in Matt 25:14–30.

Nazoreans alters the parable so that it includes the opportunistic and abusive slave featured in a nearby parable (Matt 24:45–51). The master punishes him, not (as in Matthew) the slave who merely hid the master's money.

flute girls: See note to GOxy 840 2:8.

9 The man referred to is Barabbas (Matt 27:16). This interpretation of this Aramaic name is extremely puzzling. The name was common and its meaning ("son of the father") was obvious to Aramaic speakers. Why a gospel composed in Aramaic would need to "interpret" it is a mystery. Why it would give an erroneous explanation of it is even more mysterious. Perhaps Jerome mistook it for "Barrabban," which, if it were a name, would mean "son of the teacher." Perhaps also Jerome himself (or one of his sources) supplied *their* to make it clear that "the teacher" was not Jesus.

10a *Reported by Jerome,* Epistle 120

In the gospel that is written in the Hebrew alphabet we read not that the curtain of the temple was torn, but that the lintel of the temple, which was huge, collapsed.

10b *Reported by Jerome,* Commentary on Matthew 4 *(commenting on Matt 27:51)*

In the gospel that we have often mentioned we read that the lintel of the temple, which was immense, was fractured and broken up.

11 *Quoted by Eusebius,* Theophany 4 *(discussing Matt 10:34–36)*

⟨Christ⟩ himself taught the reason for the separation of souls that takes place in households, as we have found somewhere in the gospel that is spread abroad among the Jews in the Hebrew language, in which it is said:

> "I choose for myself the most worthy—the most worthy are those whom my Father in heaven has given me."

10a
Cf. Mk 15:38,
Mt 27:51

11
Cf. Q 12:51–53,
Mt 10:34–36,
Lk 12:51–53, Th 16;
Ⓣ Jn 15:16, 17:6

---

10 In a writing earlier than the one in which he discusses this passage, Jerome had attributed the report that the lintel of the temple collapsed to "some interpreters." Also, a few lines before his discussion of this passage, Jerome mentions an event reported to have happened in the temple at the time of its destruction in 70 CE, but he mistakenly places it at the time of the crucifixion. All this raises a doubt as to whether Jerome personally found this report about the collapse of the lintel in Nazoreans.

11 There is no parallel to this saying in the gospels, though *whom my Father has given me* echoes a phrase in John (6:37, 39; 17:2, 6, 24).

This passage is extant only in a Syriac translation of an early Christian text composed in Greek. This quotation from Nazoreans, therefore, has gone from Aramaic to Greek to Syriac before being translated here into English. We can only hope it is close to the original.

Orphan Sayings and Stories

The Freer Logion, a fifth-century CE Greek manuscript. The box shows the location of the logion in the manuscript. *Courtesy of the Freer Gallery of Art, Smithsonian Institution, Washington, DC.*

Orphan Sayings and Stories

Introduction

The sayings and anecdotes presented below are all fragments, which, over the course of the transmission and production of early gospel manuscripts, were introduced by various scribes into particular known copies of the canonical gospels. Their poor attestation in the broader manuscript tradition indicates that they do not belong to the original text of the gospels in which they are found in the odd manuscript. They are often found in only one or two manuscripts, or are missing from the earliest or best witnesses. For this reason, most scholars disregard them in the study of the canonical gospels, and they have been excluded from most modern editions and translations. The exceptions would be the story of the woman caught in adultery in John 7:53–8:11, and the traditional Longer Ending of Mark (16:9–20), which, for traditional or sentimental reasons, are often retained.

These stray fragments fall into the category of *agrapha*, that is, isolated sayings and stories of Jesus not written in the canonical tradition. Many known agrapha have survived Antiquity. Most are found in the early church Fathers as brief quotations, sometimes taken from a gospel now lost, such as the Gospel of the Hebrews or the Gospel of the Nazoreans, sometimes given without reference to any source at all. Occasionally one finds an agraphon tucked into a later rabbinic story, there placed on the lips of a hapless Christian interlocutor engaged in debate with the rabbis. What follows is a not a complete list of the agrapha, but a selective sample. The texts associated with lost Jewish-Christian gospels are available elsewhere in this volume. As for the anonymous agrapha, their provenance is too uncertain to warrant inclusion here. They might just as well derive from an apocryphal acts tradition (see Acts 20:35) or a lost epistolary tradition (see 1 Thess 4:15–17) as from the early Christian gospel tradition. In any event, a complete catalogue of all the known agrapha could easily occupy an entire volume in its own right. The small collection in this volume is limited to those agrapha that are found within the gospel tradition itself. They thus supply an episode to the overall history of the gospel tradition and contribute to its understanding.

The agrapha must be considered secondary with respect to the larger texts in which they are found and nothing certain is known about their age, provenance, or authorship. Nonetheless, they deserve consideration in the study of the gospel tradition. Their chief value lies in the tale they can tell of the later transmission history of the gospels. They remind us how fluid the situation was with these texts well into the second and third centuries, a point often washed over in the quest for a single canonical text to which one might confidently appeal as authoritative. The problem of the New Testament canon involves not just the question of which books belong, but also in what form certain books were considered to bear authority for the early church. The fact that the ancient record is so "messy" suggests that interest in such a quest belongs more to the modern period than to the ancient.

But apart from what these vagabond sayings and stories tell us of the later transmission history of the gospels, we should not rule out the possibility that they might eventually tell us something about the earlier period as well, the early Jesus movement, perhaps even Jesus himself. Their origins, after all, are unknown, shrouded deeply in the folds of early Christian tradition. These sayings and stories are introduced here without judgments about where they might ultimately fit into the history of the gospel tradition.

Orphan Sayings and Stories

1 *A continuation of Matthew 6:13 (the end of the Lord's Prayer) found in several manuscripts and in Didache 8:2:*

. . . for the empire and the power and the glory are yours forever. Amen.

2 *A continuation of Mark 9:49 in several manuscripts:*

. . . and every sacrifice will be salted with salt.

3 *A saying found replacing Luke 6:5 in one important manuscript, Codex Bezae Cantabrigiensis:*

That day he saw someone working on the Sabbath and said to him, "Mister, if you know what you're doing, congratulations to you, but if you don't, to hell with you; you are ⟨nothing but⟩ a lawbreaker."

4 *A saying found after Luke 9:55 in several manuscripts:*

And he said, "You don't know of what spirit you are. [For] the Human One did not come to destroy human life, but to save it."

5 *A saying found after John 6:56 in one important manuscript, Codex Bezae Cantabrigiensis:*

. . . just as the Father is in me and I am in the Father. Let me tell you this: if you do not receive the body of the Human One as the bread of life, you don't have life in him.

6 *A continuation of Matt 20:25–28 found in a few manuscripts.*

But you ⟨should⟩ seek to grow out of smallness, and from greatness to become less. For example, when you go in some place and are invited to eat, don't recline on one of the places of honor, in case someone more important than you comes in and the host has to come over and tell you, "Move further down," and embarrass you. Rather, it will work to your advantage if you sit down in a lesser

---

1 The text is preserved very irregularly; *empire, power, glory,* and *Amen* are each missing in at least one of the mss.
4 Most mss read *destroy* here, but a few read "kill."
4 Codex Bezae Cantabriensis omits the second sentence.
6 In the Syriac version there is a negation in the second clause of the first sentence: "and *not* from greatness to become less."

6
//Lk 14:8–10

---

3 *to hell with you:* The Greek is a curse (literally, "you are accursed").   **5** *in him:* or, "in it."

place, so that in case someone less important than you comes in, the host will say to you, "Move further up."

7 *A story found following John 17:26 in the obscure Codex evangelii Johannei Parisii in sacro Templariorum tabulario asservatus.*

¹Then, lifting up his hands, Jesus said to his disciples, "Look, the time has come for me to drink from the cup that my Father has given me to drink. ²I am going up to my Father who sent me. ³So I'll tell you once more: I am sending you; obey my instructions, teach ⟨others⟩ what I have taught you, so the whole world might learn it. ⁴For this reason, receive the holy spirit; the sins of anyone you forgive are forgiven, and those of anyone you refuse to forgive are not forgiven.

⁵"Listen to what I have told you: I am not from this world. ⁶The advocate is among you; teach with the help of the advocate. ⁷Just as the Father sent me, so also I am sending you. ⁸Let me tell you this: I am not from this world. ⁹But your father will be John, until he comes with me to Paradise."

¹⁰Then he consecrated them with the holy spirit.

8 *A variant version of John 19:26–30 in the obscure Codex evangelii Johannei Templariorum:*

He says to his mother, "Don't cry. I am returning to my Father, and to eternal life. Here is your son! This man will take my place." Then he says to his disciple, "Here is your mother!" Then, lowering his head, he handed over his spirit.

9 *A story found at various places in the manuscript tradition. In several manuscripts it is found after John 7:52. Many modern editions of the New Testament include it here, assigning it the versification John 7:53–8:11. Another important group of manuscripts includes it after Luke 21:38. In the Georgian tradition it was sometimes located after John 7:44, and in another group it is found after John 21:25.*

7 ⁵³**Then everybody returned** home, **8** ¹but Jesus went to the Mount of Olives. ²Early in the morning he showed up again in the temple area and everybody gathered around him. He sat down and began to teach them.

³The scholars and Pharisees bring him a woman who was caught committing adultery. They make her stand there in front of everybody, ⁴ and they address

7:1 v, 1
//Jn 13:1, 17:1, 18:11

7:1 v, 2
//Jn 16:5, 7, 10

7:1 v, 3
//Jn 14:15

7:1 v, 4
//Jn 20:22–23

7:1 v, 5
//Jn 17:14, 16

7:1 v, 6
//Jn 14:26

7:1 v, 7
//Jn 20:21

7:1 v, 8
//Jn 17:14, 16

7:1 v, 9
//Jn 20:22

Jn 8:1–2
//Lk 21:37–38

Jn 8:3
Ⓣ Mk 4:1, 9:35; Mt 5:1; Lk 4:20

7:6 *advocate:* This Greek word carries a number of related meanings, including witness, spokesperson (terminology associated with the courtroom setting), or one who encourages.

John 8:3 *Scholars* are mentioned nowhere else in John. What happened to the woman's lover?

him, "Teacher, this woman was caught in the act of adultery. [5]In the Law Moses commanded us to stone women like this. What do you say?" ([6]They said this to trap him, so they would have something to accuse him of.)

Jesus stooped down and began drawing on the ground with his finger. [7]When they insisted on an answer, he stood up and replied, "Whoever is sinless in this crowd should go ahead and throw the first stone at her." [8]Once again he squatted down and continued writing on the ground.

[9]His audience began to drift away, one by one—the elders were the first to go—until Jesus was the only one left, with the woman there in front of him.

[10]Jesus stood up and said to her, "Woman, where is everybody? Hasn't anyone condemned you?"

[11]She replied, "No one, sir."

"I don't condemn you either," Jesus said. "You're free to go; but from now on, no more sinning."

The endings of the Gospel of Mark

The ending of the Gospel of Mark is a classic problem in New Testament textual criticism. The scholarly consensus is that Mark originally ended with the abrupt stop at 16:8. The earliest Patristic evidence (Clement of Rome, Origen, Eusebius, and Jerome) gives no indication of any text beyond 16:8. In most manuscripts, however, Mark comes with endings that extend beyond 16:8. These alternative endings are attempts to smooth out the abruptness of 16:8 and to harmonize Mark with the ending of the other gospels.

10 *A story appended to the end of Mark (16:8) in many manuscripts and versions. It is often referred to as the* Longer Ending of Mark, *and assigned the versification Mark 16:9–20.*

16 [9]**Now after he arose** at daybreak on Sunday, he appeared first to Mary of Magdala, from whom he had driven out seven demons. [10]She went and told those who were close to him, who were mourning and weeping. [11]But when those folks heard that he was alive and had been seen by her, they did not believe it.

[12]A little later he appeared to two of them in a different guise as they were walking along, on their way to the country. [13]And these two returned and told the others. They did not believe them either.

Jn 8:5
◊Lv 20:10,
Dt 22:22–24

Jn 8:6
Ⓣ Lk 6:7

Jn 8:7
Ⓣ Rom 2:1

Jn 8:11
Ⓣ Jn 5:14,
EgerG 2:4

Mk 16:9
//Jn 20:11–18,
Lk 8:2;
cf. Pet 12:1

Mk 16:11
//Lk 24:11

Mk 16:13a
//Lk 24:13–35

Mk 16:13b
//Lk 24:11

Jn 8:9 A few mss add "convicted by their conscience" to *his audience.*

John 8:6 The text provides no clue as to what Jesus was supposed to be writing, although a tenth-century manuscript fills in the detail by having Jesus writing the sins of the accusers. The text may simply picture Jesus doodling, thereby showing his contempt for the whole situation.

[14]Later he appeared to the Eleven as they were reclining ⟨at a meal⟩. He reproached them for their close-mindedness and lack of trust, because they did not believe those who had seen him after he had been raised. [15]And he said to them: "Go out into the whole world and announce the good news to every creature. [16]Whoever trusts and is baptized will be saved, but whoever lacks trust will be condemned. [17]These are the signs that will accompany those who have trust: they'll drive out demons in my name; they'll speak in new tongues; [18]they'll pick up snakes with their hands; and even if they swallow poison, it'll never harm them; they'll lay their hands on the sick, and they'll get well."

[19]The Lord Jesus, after he said these things, was taken up into the sky and sat down at the right hand of God. [20]Those ⟨to whom he had spoken⟩ went out and made their announcement everywhere, and the Lord worked with them and certified what they said by means of accompanying signs.

11 *An episode offering a conclusion to the Gospel of Mark, usually found appended to the Longer Ending of Mark, and in at least one instance appended directly to Mark 16:8, without the Longer Ending. It is often referred to as the* Shorter Ending of Mark, *and sometimes assigned the versification 16:21.*

[21]**They promptly reported** to Peter and his companions all the instructions they had been given. Afterwards Jesus himself, using them as agents, broadcast the sacred and imperishable message of eternal salvation from one end of the earth to the other.

12 *An episode to the story found in the Longer Ending of Mark, which is inserted directly after Mark 16:14 in a single known manuscript, Codex Washingtonianus. It is sometimes known as the* Freer Logion, *after the codices' discoverer, Charles L. Freer:*

And they would apologize and say, "This lawless and faithless age is under the control of Satan, who by using filthy spirits doesn't allow the real power of God to be appreciated. So," they would say to the Anointed One, "let your justice become evident now."

And the Anointed One would respond to them, "The time when Satan is in power has run its course, but other terrible things are just around the corner. I was put to death for the sake of those who sinned, so they might return to the truth and stop sinning, and thus inherit the spiritual and indestructible righteous glory that is in heaven."

Mk 16:14
//Lk 24:36–43;
Jn 20:19–23, 26–29

Mk 16:15
//Mt 28:18–20;
Ⓣ Mary 4:8

Mk 16:18a
Cf. Lk 10:19

Mk 16:18c
Cf. Mt 9:18

Mk 16:19
//Lk 24:51;
cf. Mt 26:64

Mk 16:21
//Jn 20:2,
Mt 28:18–20

Glossary

Acts of Thomas: The legendary accounts of the deeds of the apostle Judas Thomas (probably the Judas Didymos Thomas of the Gospel of Thomas), telling of Thomas' missionary journeys east to Parthia and eventually to India. In these adventuresome tales, Thomas preaches the values of asceticism and gnosis as the path to salvation.

Androgyny: The state of being in which an individual possesses both male and female characteristics.

Aphorism: Aphorisms and proverbs are striking one-liners. An aphorism is a short, provocative saying that challenges the accepted view of things. A proverb embodies common sense. A proverb: "Early to bed, early to rise, makes one healthy, wealthy, and wise." An aphorism: "What goes into you can't defile you; what comes out of you can" (Mark 7:15).

Apocalyptic: A type of religious thinking characterized by the notion that through an act of divine intervention the present evil world is about to be destroyed and replaced with a new and better world in which God's justice prevails.

Aramaic: A Semitic language related to Hebrew that was spoken in Palestine at the time of Jesus.

Beatitudes: Literary or oral formulations that confer good fortune on the recipient. They usually begin with the expression "Congratulations to" (more traditionally translated as "blessed is"). The most famous beatitudes are said by Jesus at the opening of the Sermon on the Mount/Plain in Q 6:20–23.

Canon: An authoritative list or collection of books accepted as holy scripture. The canon was determined for Catholics at the Council of Trent (1546), which formally ratified the list of books in use since the fourth century. The canon has never been determined for Protestants, except by common consent.

Carpocratians: Followers of Carpocrates, a Gnostic Christian teacher from Alexandria from the first half of the second century, whose teachings later came to be regarded as heretical.

Catchword: A word repeated in consecutive sayings that serves to link them together in the mind of the audience and so facilitate their memorization.

Catechesis: Religious instruction given to Christian initiates (catechumens) either as preparation for baptism or as a follow-up to it.

Christology: Teaching concerning the role or identity of Jesus.

Chronicler: A name designating the writer or writers responsible for the Old Testament books of 1 and 2 Chronicles, Ezra, and Nehemiah.

Clement of Alexandria: The head of an important Christian school for catechumens in Alexandria. Among his many works is the *Stromateis,* which deals extensively with the question of the relationship between Christian faith and Greek philosophy. It is a letter from Clement that contains the excerpts from the Mystical Gospel of Mark.

Codex: An ancient manuscript in book form, as distinguished from a scroll, which is a book in roll form.

Coptic: The form of the Egyptian language in use at the time of the introduction of Christianity in Egypt.

Council: A Jewish high commission, presided over by the chief priest, which met regularly in the temple to deliberate and rule on religious matters. Under the Roman occupation it had limited political jurisdiction. In Greek it was called the *Sanhedrin,* which means simply to "sit together."

Deuteronomic history: The Old Testament writings that tell of the history of Israel from the theological perspective of the book of Deuteronomy: obedience to God produces prosperity, disobedience trails disaster in its wake, to put it simplistically. The Deuteronomic history includes Joshua, Judges, 1 and 2 Samuel, and 1 and 2 Kings.

Didache: An early Christian compendium of instruction, an incipient catechism, also known as the *Teachings of the Twelve Apostles.* The final form of the Didache, which was discovered in 1875, dates from the early second century, but its main sections go back to the first century.

Docetism: The belief that Christ was not truly human, but only seemed to be so (from *dokeō,* "seem").

Epiphany: An English cognate term for the Greek *epiphaneia* meaning "manifestation," usually of a supernatural being.

Eschatology: Religious teaching about those events supposed to happen at the end of time.

Gehenna, see the cameo essay, p. 184.

Gnosticism: Gnosticism gets its name from the Greek word *gnosis,* meaning "knowledge" or "insight." It was a widespread religious movement in Antiquity, which in general terms focused on the world as a place of fallenness and evil, the illegitimate creation of a rebellious demi-god. Gnostics believed that their origin is not this world of evil, but in a higher realm in which dwells the one true God, who, through a messenger or redeemer, has seen fit to communicate to them the knowledge *(gnosis)* of their true heavenly home. Armed with this *gnosis,* the Gnostic seeks to break free from this world and its rebellious creator, to be reunited with the Godhead in the heavenly realm above. Gnosticism was very adaptable and manifested itself in numerous forms, attaching to and transforming older traditional religious systems, such as Judaism or Christianity.

Human One, see the cameo essay, p. 208.

Josephus: A Jewish historian from the late first century. His two principal works, the *Jewish War* and the *Jewish Antiquities,* are the most important ancient historical sources for Jewish history during the period 200 BCE–100 CE.

Judas (the brother of Jesus): Judas is named as a brother of Jesus in Mark 6:3 and Matt 13:55, along with James, Joses, and Simon. Judas (=Jude), "a servant of Jesus and brother of James," is named as the author of the Letter of Jude. These two figures may be the same person, even though the author of the Letter of Jude demurs from claiming the status of "brother" of Jesus.

Judean, see the cameo essay, pp. 203–204.

Kerygma: A technical term of New Testament scholarship deriving from the Greek word for "preaching." It is used to refer to the earliest Christian proclamation about Jesus. Most scholars agree that the gospels were profoundly influenced by the early Christian kerygma, and thus are more a product of early Christian preaching than a desire to preserve history.

Lacuna: A gap in a manuscript caused by damage or deterioration.

Levites: Descendents of the tribe of Levi who had sacred duties in the Jerusalem temple, but who did not offer sacrifice or conduct worship, duties reserved for priests.

Middle Platonism: Platonic thought as it was revived in the late Hellenistic era. The Middle Platonists rediscovered Plato's more speculative metaphysical writings, such as the *Timaeus,* and used them to speak about the nature of the universe, the nature of human being, and the fate of souls in the world beyond.

Nag Hammadi: The town in Egypt near which a collection of Christian and Gnostic documents, known as the Nag Hammadi library, was discovered in 1945.

Oxyrhynchus: An ancient village in Egypt where numerous papyri have been discovered. Among its most important treasures are Oxyrhynchus Gospels 840 and 1224, fragments of otherwise unknown gospels, and the Greek fragments of the Gospel of Thomas.

Paleography: The study of ancient handwriting. Paleography can often determine the age of a manuscript by the style of its handwriting.

Papyrus: The predecessor to modern paper. Ancient works were written on animal skins, called parchment or vellum, or on papyrus, made from Egyptian reeds.

Parable: A brief narrative or picture. It is also a metaphor or simile drawn from nature or common life, arresting the hearer by its vividness or strangeness, and leaving the mind in sufficient doubt about its precise application to tease it into active thought.

Parousia: Literally "presence"; in the New Testament it refers to the arrival or coming of the Human One, or the messiah (The Anointed One), who will sit in cosmic judgment at the end of history. "Parousia" is thus commonly understood to mean Jesus' "second coming," as distinguished from the first coming or advent of the messiah.

Pericope: A Greek term literally meaning "something cut out." A discrete unit of discourse, such as a paragraph in an essay or a segment of a well-ordered story.

Pharisees: Jewish laymen dedicated to the exacting observance of religion, the rigorous application of the Law to everyday life, and the cultivation of a tradition of teaching not found in the Torah, sometimes called the "oral torah." The Pharisees are routinely parodied and condemned in the gospels. That polemic more accurately reflects conflicts between the synagogue and the Christian communities that produced the gospels in the last quarter of the first century than it does the situation of the historical Jesus.

Redaction: The process of producing a new text by reworking an existing text with a particular purpose in mind. Redaction can include adding or deleting material, rearranging, and rewriting. Redaction criticism is a scholarly method of investigation that seeks to isolate an evangelist's purpose and perspective by analyzing the way he handles material derived from sources. A less technical name for redaction is editing.

Sanhedrin, see Council.

Sophia: Greek for "wisdom." Wisdom is often personified in early Jewish literature as a supernatural female figure. See, for example, Proverbs 8 and Sirach 1.

Synoptic: A term from the Greek *synoptikos,* "seeing together," meaning "having a common view of," referring to the Gospels of Mark, Matthew, and Luke, which are similar in form, outline, and contents.

Torah: The first five books of the Bible, often called simply "the Law."